FREEDOM FROM FEAR

Freedom from Fear

AN INCOMPLETE HISTORY
OF LIBERALISM

ALAN S. KAHAN

PRINCETON UNIVERSITY PRESS

PRINCETON & OXFORD

Published by Princeton University Press
41 William Street, Princeton, New Jersey 08540
99 Banbury Road, Oxford OX2 6JX

press.princeton.edu

Library of Congress Cataloging-in-Publication Data

Names: Kahan, Alan S., author.
Title: Freedom from fear : an incomplete history of liberalism / Alan S. Kahan.
Description: Princeton: Princeton University Press, 2023 | Includes bibliographical
    references and index.
Identifiers: LCCN 2022051043 (print) | LCCN 2022051044 (ebook) |
    ISBN 9780691191287 (hardback) | ISBN 9780691250687 (ebook)
Subjects: LCSH: Liberalism—History | State, The. | BISAC: POLITICAL SCIENCE /
    Political Ideologies / Conservatism & Liberalism | PHILOSOPHY / Ethics &
    Moral Philosophy
Classification: LCC JC574 .K344 2023 (print) | LCC JC574 (ebook) |
    DDC 320.5109—dc23/eng/20230111
LC record available at https://lccn.loc.gov/2022051043
LC ebook record available at https://lccn.loc.gov/2022051044

British Library Cataloging-in-Publication Data is available

Editorial: Ben Tate and Josh Drake
Production Editorial: Theresa Liu
Jacket/Cover Design: Katie Osborne
Production: Danielle Amatucci
Publicity: William Pagdatoon
Copyeditor: Karen Verde

This book has been composed in Classic Arno

Printed on acid-free paper. ∞

Printed in the United States of America

10 9 8 7 6 5 4 3 2 1

For Sarah Bentley, patient reader and editor extraordinaire

CONTENTS

ACKNOWLEDGMENTS

IN WRITING THIS BOOK I have benefited from conversations with innumerable people at many institutions. To all of them, my thanks for the intellectual stimulation they provided, not least to the anonymous British graduate student who first suggested that Mary Wollestonecraft's *Maria* would be a perfect fit for my themes.

Some generous institutions have provided financial support and housing during this very long project, above all the Institut Universitaire de France, as well as the Université de Paris-Saclay, the Université de Versailles / St. Quentin, King's College (University of London), Clare Hall (Cambridge University), the Instituto Bruno Leoni, and the Benson Center at the University of Colorado, Boulder. To all of them, my gratitude.

Various people have been kind enough to read all or part of the manuscript and provide feedback, or sponsored talks at which I could present stages of my work. These include (but I'm sure I have shamefully forgotten someone) Ewa Atanassow, Richard Avramenko, Giandomenica Becchio, Richard Bourke, Richard Boyd, Emmanuelle de Champs, Henry C. Clark, Aurelian Craiutu, George Crowder, Maria Dimova-Cookson, Robin Douglass, Michael Drolet, Steven Grosby, Ryan Hanley, Eugene Heath, Christine Henderson, Jeremy Jennings, Stefan Kolev, Catherine Larrère, Alan Levine, Paul Lewis, Catherine Marshall, Alberto Mingardi, Karen Offen, Helena Rosenblatt, Paul Sagar, Timothy Stanton, Ben Tate, Helga Varden, Bernard Yack, and Michael Zucker.

PART I
Prologue

1

Liberalism

The Four Fears of Liberalism

Liberalism is the search for a society in which no one need be afraid. Freedom from fear is the most basic freedom: if we are afraid, we are not free. This insight is the foundation of liberalism. To proclaim our inalienable right to life, liberty, and the pursuit of happiness is simply an eloquent way of stating the not-so-exalted wish to live without fear.[1]

That no one should be afraid begs the question, "afraid of what?" Of course, some people will always fear spiders, and most people will fear death. Liberalism is powerless against these kinds of fear, which will always trouble our sense of security and limit our freedom. What liberals fear is arbitrary power, and liberalism is about building a society in which we need not fear other people, whether singly, in groups, or, perhaps most of all, in uniform—that of the police officer, the soldier, the priest. At its most basic, liberalism derives from the fear of an all-powerful individual, a despot. The spirit of tyranny hovers over the cradle of liberalism and is never absent from liberal concerns. In any society, the greatest potential enemy of freedom is the sovereign, whether sovereignty is exercised in the name of God, a monarch, or the people, because the sovereign has the greatest opportunities for despotism. Whoever is sovereign

---

1. To contextualists who might object that this definition is not actually used by most people who call themselves liberals, I would reply that it meets Quentin Skinner's criterion that "no agent can eventually be said to have meant or done something which he could never be brought to accept as a correct description of what he had meant or done." Liberals would acknowledge warding off fear as a description of what they were doing. See Skinner, "Meaning and Understanding in the History of Ideas," 48.

is the greatest source of fear. Hence liberal attempts to limit the powers of the sovereign and its agents.

While from a liberal perspective, no one ought to be afraid, from illiberal perspectives, there *are* people who ought to be afraid: those who belong to the wrong religion, the wrong class, the wrong gender, the wrong ethnicity. This is not the case for liberals, or at least, eventually not for liberals. Recognizing that freedom from fear ought to apply to atheists, or Black people, or women is something that takes place over time, and the progression is not linear. Nonetheless, securing the social and political conditions necessary to give people a feeling of security—the feeling that their person and their community are free—is the historical core of liberalism.

Recognition of the crucial role of fear in whether or not we are free goes back at least to Montesquieu, who argued that "political liberty . . . comes from the opinion each one has of his security."[2] Modern historians and political theorists largely ignored this insight until Judith Shklar's brilliant 1989 essay "The Liberalism of Fear" stressed the fundamental role of fear in the creation and development of liberalism.[3] Human beings have been afraid of each other since before civilization began, and the Bible transmits humanity's longing for a time when "every man shall sit under his vine and under his fig tree, and none shall make them afraid."[4] But while despotism is as old as time, and the dream of escaping from it at least as old as the Bible, liberalism is not. People never wanted to be subject to cruelty, but for millennia they had no strategies for ending it. The choices available were fleeing from power, seizing it, or submitting to it. Most people chose submission. Despotism, the reign of fear, as Montesquieu notes, is the worst form of government, yet historically the most common.

It is our equal capacity to be afraid, and our equal need for liberalism to ward off our fears, that is at the root of liberalism's historical relationship with equality. Many people have incorrectly identified liberalism with equality, and it is true that we have less reason to fear our equals than our superiors. But equality can also be a source of fear: a plebiscitary dictatorship is no less a despotism for being the will of the people, and fear of majority tyranny has a long history in liberalism: "unbridled majorities are as tyrannical and cruel as

2. Montesquieu, *The Spirit of the Laws*, 157.

3. Shklar, "The Liberalism of Fear." See also Alan Ryan's development of this point in *The Making of Modern Liberalism*, 9.

4. Micah 4:4, *Bible*.

unlimited despots," wrote John Adams in the eighteenth century.[5] Equality is not constitutive of liberalism the way fear is.

Another, even more common error is to identify liberalism with some list of "rights," whether human, natural, contractual, or constitutional. Claims that people had rights began long before liberalism and have been used by many people who were not liberals. Of course, liberals, too, have often talked about rights. The French Declaration of the Rights of Man and the Citizen of 1789, even if written a few years before the word "liberalism" was invented, is a landmark of liberalism, as is the American Declaration of Independence. As liberals have always recognized, rights can be important bulwarks against fear and enablers of hope. They can be instruments of equality. They can even serve as a substitute for religion.[6] But like equality, rights are not necessarily a panacea for liberals, and their relationship to liberalism has varied. As Robert Nozick put it, liberals have more often adopted a "utilitarianism of rights" than a theory based on rights.[7] The history of rights sometimes parallels, sometimes diverges from the history of liberalism. While "natural rights" or rights based on a social contract have served some liberals as the foundation of liberalism, other liberals rarely or never used "rights talk."[8] Mainstream liberals did not talk much about the social contract before World War II, and when they did talk about rights, these did not necessarily take priority over other claims. Isaiah Berlin grasped this well: "The philosophical foundations of . . . liberal beliefs in the mid-nineteenth century were somewhat obscure. Rights described as 'natural' or 'inherent,' absolute standards of truth and justice, were not compatible with tentative empiricism and utilitarianism; yet liberals believed in both."[9]

Understanding the history of liberalism must begin with studying the *problem* it addresses: the problem of fear. What liberals feared, or feared most, has

5. John Adams to John Stockdale, May 12, 1793. https://founders.archives.gov/documents/Adams/99-02-02-1461.

6. On rights as a substitute for religion, see Tocqueville, *Democracy in America*, henceforth *Democracy*, 1: 391.

7. Nozick, *Anarchy, State and Utopia*, ch. 3.

8. Tocqueville himself is a good example. Despite his remark about rights and religion, there is little discussion of abstract rights in *Democracy in America* or *The Old Regime*. Natural rights and rights in a legal sense play their strongest role in liberal thought in the United States. This has often persuaded Americans that such is the case everywhere. Even in the American case, however, the link is not as strong as sometimes assumed. See Greenstone, *The Lincoln Persuasion*.

9. Berlin, "Political Ideas in the Twentieth Century," in *Liberty*, 65.

changed over time. A history of liberalism must relate the development of liberalism to particular historical fears and name the powers liberals sought to limit at a particular time. Each new form of liberalism is the result of a new fear that has called for a new response. Understanding this is essential to understanding why and how liberalism changes over time. People in the twenty-first century are not liberals for the same reasons Locke or Kant might have been.[10] "Fear" is too abstract in the singular, and "despotism" is too broad a term to tell us much about the source of fear. We need to know just what it is that liberals in a given time and place fear most.

For some observers the fear of a despotic state and a despotic religion is really all that there is to liberalism.[11] For Shklar herself, the liberalism of fear responded to a single, historically undifferentiated fear, the fear of cruelty. In reality, liberals have responded to many different fears. While liberalism originated with a primordial liberal fear of despotism, it evolved historically as the result of four fears which have had particular resonance in Western thought.

These four fears were the fear of religious fanaticism; the fear of revolution and reaction; the fear of poverty; and the fear of totalitarianism. These fears were in turn responsible for proto-liberalism; liberalism proper; modern liberalism and its classical liberal opponents; and anti-totalitarian liberalism. This historical succession led to the complex and layered nature of liberalism today. New forms of liberalism did not necessarily make old forms disappear. The development of modern liberalisms at the end of the nineteenth century, when some liberals began to see the struggle against poverty as central to the liberal project of fighting fear, did not mean the disappearance of the fear of revolution and reaction. Liberalism is like an oyster, and grows by accretion, one layer deposited on top of another, never covering it entirely.[12] Multiple forms of liberalism persist to this day, as they will until the fears that inspired them in the first place no longer exist. As John Dewey put it, we should be "suspicious of all attempts to erect a hierarchy of values: their results generally prove

10. A point made by Joseph Raz, *Ethics in the Public Domain*, 171.

11. Thus Charles Larmore: "since the sixteenth century there have been two basic problems to which liberal thought has sought a solution. The first has been to fix some moral limits to the powers of government. . . . The second problem has stemmed from the increasing awareness that reasonable people tend to differ and disagree about the nature of the good life." Disagreements over the good life are originally religious, according to Larmore. Larmore, "Political Liberalism," 339–340.

12. Michael Freeden makes a similar point in discussing the "layers" of liberalism, although he identifies those layers differently. See *Liberalism*, 37–54.

to be inapplicable and abstract. But there is at every time a hierarchy of problems."[13] The hierarchy of problems liberals face at any given time is the hierarchy of their fears.

The history of liberalism presented here is a history of how certain fears have shaped and dominated liberalism over time. By understanding liberalism in this way, much that has previously perplexed historians and political theorists about the liberal past becomes clear, and liberals will be better positioned to respond to many of the challenges they face today. By paying close attention to their fears, new ways of reading well-known liberal texts become possible. As Iris Murdoch noted, "it is always a significant question to ask of any philosopher: what is he afraid of." This is all the more true when the writer concerned is a liberal. Broadening the concept of the liberalism of fear to all liberalisms clarifies many aspects of liberalism hitherto unclear, and puts into context a whole series of continuities and changes that frequently have been misunderstood or overlooked. It solves a problem remarked by Eric Voegelin and many others, for whom liberalism's "field of optimal clarity is the nineteenth century, which is preceded and followed by fields of decreasing clarity in which it becomes increasingly difficult to establish its identity." Seeing the history of liberalism through the lens of liberal fears restores clarity to liberal identities by making visible how different layers of liberal thought were laid down one atop the other, and how they evolved over time and place.[14]

Summarizing this process makes its benefits for understanding the history of liberalism apparent. In Shklar's view, Western / European history did not deviate from the common pattern of universal despotism and fruitless fear until after the Protestant Reformation. The decades of warfare, torture, and cruelty in God's name during the Wars of Religion that followed led many people to the revolutionary conclusion that religious toleration was a form of "Christian charity," and made religious skeptics like Montaigne decide that fanaticism and cruelty were the greatest vices. "It is out of that tradition that the political liberalism of fear arose and continues amid the terror of our time."[15] This historical judgment might be questioned (Shklar herself is not consistent), but the Protestant Reformation marked a turning point in that it inaugurated a continuing series of political developments in a liberal direction, much as the isolated

13. Dewey, *Individualism Old and New*, 68.

14. Iris Murdoch, *The Sovereignty of Good* (London, 1970), 72; Eric Voegelin, "Liberalism and Its History," *Review of Politics* 36, no. (1974), 504–520: 506.

15. Shklar, "The Liberalism of Fear," 23.

scientific achievements of previous times gave way to the ongoing development that characterized the Scientific Revolution. For Tocqueville, the Reformation also marked a significant moment in the transition from an aristocratic to a democratic society, based on equal status. The proto-liberalism of this period was a response to the new problem of how to preserve people from fear in a democratizing society where theoretically everyone's fears should count equally. It was also a response to the new hopes that democratic society engendered. Liberalism has always been a compound of fear and hope.[16]

After the Reformation the proto-liberals of the seventeenth and eighteenth centuries were focused on the fear of religious fanaticism and the fear of despotism in the form of absolute monarchy. In the aftermath of, or perhaps even during, the American and French Revolutions, "liberal" finally became a noun and "liberalism" a word, and it becomes possible to speak of "liberalism" without anachronism. Sometime shortly before 1800, the new fears and hopes provoked by the revolutions created the new usage. Perhaps the first use of liberal as a noun came in a letter advocating the abolition of slavery signed "A Liberal," written to the *Pennsylvania Packet* in 1780. The usage was nevertheless a little unclear, as the older adjectival meaning of liberal as "generous" or "charitable" might be the implied meaning of the signature, rather than a political position. By the late 1790s, "liberal" was being used in France by authors such as Mme. de Staël and Benjamin Constant to describe particular political positions and institutions, such as representative government, a free press, etc., although the older moral usage did not disappear. The use of "liberalism" came a little later, and only really became common after the revolutions of 1848. In the short nineteenth century (1800–1873), liberals feared despotism and religious fanaticism as their proto-liberal predecessors had, but in addition, and above all, they feared revolution and reaction, fears born with the American and French Revolutions. All these fears were embodied in the state, and thus liberals directed much of their attention during this period to limiting the state's powers. They wrote constitutions and bills of rights to prevent the sovereign of the day from practicing revolutionary or reactionary despotism, al-

---

16. This fulfills Bernard Williams's requirement that any theory of liberalism provide an account of why liberalism has not existed in all times and places. Williams, *In the Beginning*, 9, and in the same work, Hawthorn's "Introduction," xii–xiii. One might add that because the Reformation endured, unlike earlier heresies, there was no longer any prospect of an end to religious pluralism in Europe, and that liberalism was a novel solution to a novel problem. Tocqueville, *Democracy in America*, 1:9.

though the earlier fears of religious or personal despotism were never entirely out of mind.[17]

Thus Liberalism 1.0 took shape, with liberals demanding a variety of changes to address their fears, while opposing those they thought would make people less safe. The particular issues they addressed varied—for example in the short nineteenth century, suffrage questions, for White males at least, were of relatively little importance in the United States, unlike in Europe, and nationalism was not a problem anywhere at the beginning of the period—but the fears to which liberals responded remained essentially the same until the end of the short nineteenth century. During the short nineteenth century, liberalism became a global political discourse, the first.[18] But ubiquity is not a synonym for success. If liberalism has progressed in certain times and places, overall it has failed, or more optimistically it has not yet succeeded. There has never been a time in human history when the majority of humanity has lived in liberal societies. Being in a minority, at least on a global scale, has always been one reason for liberal fear.

In the fin de siècle (1873–1919) many liberals began to fear poverty. The importance of this change as part of the history of liberalism has not been properly recognized. Like cruelty, poverty has been part of human history since at least the end of the hunter / gatherer period, and was no stranger to the nineteenth century. Objectively speaking, in most places in Europe and the United States a smaller percentage of the population went to bed hungry in 1900 than in 1815. But attitudes toward poverty among liberal thinkers underwent a dramatic change around the end of the nineteenth century, on both sides of the Atlantic. Instead of the poor being a threat to freedom, natural supporters of revolution or reaction, "modern liberals" began to see poverty as a threat to the freedom of the poor. It therefore became the business of liberalism to address poverty as a source of fear. This resulted in the creation of a second wave of liberalism, Liberalism 2.0. The majority of fin de siècle liberals were modern liberals, subject to the new fear, who hoped to end poverty once and for all. They turned to the state to help find a remedy for poverty, and thus supported an expansion of its role.[19]

17. Rosenblatt, *Lost History*, 64; Rosenblatt, "The Rise and Fall of 'Liberalism' in France," 168–169.

18. See Atanassow and Kahan, "Introduction," in *Liberal Moments*.

19. Edmund Fawcett used "new liberals" to describe those who called "on the power of the state to tame the power of the market." The problem that concerned the new / modern liberals,

Other fin de siècle liberals, who often described themselves as "classical liberals," did not share the new fear or the new hope, and thought the modern liberals were pursuing a mirage. Worse, the desire to use the government to make war on poverty would create an expensive and terrifying bureaucratic monster. Classical liberals saw in these new government personnel, even without uniforms, new incarnations of the soldier and priest exercising arbitrary powers. They saw the war on poverty, funded by government-enforced redistribution of wealth, put into practice by government bureaucrats, as inherently illiberal because it could only be carried out by a state that made some people afraid. Like the modern liberals, the classical liberals had a new fear: the state—or rather they feared the state for a new reason. Whereas the first wave of liberals had feared the state primarily as an agent of revolutionary or reactionary despotism, classical liberals feared the state primarily because of the new uses modern liberals wished to make of it. In response they adopted a far broader and more rigid adherence to the doctrine of laissez faire than typically found during the short nineteenth century. The classical liberalism of the fin de siècle was not the liberalism of the short nineteenth century, despite what many classical liberals liked to think, and is properly part of second-wave liberalism.[20]

The great cleavage between modern and classical liberals, which in some respects continues to this day, thus began in the fin de siècle. The older fears held in common by modern and classical liberals only served to deepen the split between them, since for classical liberals, the modern liberals were encouraging or even making a revolution, and for modern liberals, classical liberal obstinacy and blindness would lead to one. All continued to hold on to the old liberal fear of revolution / reaction, as well as the old fears of religious fanaticism and despotism, but the question of poverty divided them. The main stream of liberalism divided into two.

After World War I, new revolutions, fascist and communist, created a new kind of fear, the fear of totalitarianism. The fear of totalitarianism dominated

---

however, was usually not the market *per se*, but poverty and its effects. See Fawcett, *Liberalism*, 186. The newness of the idea, at least among liberals, that poverty could be eliminated, was noted by Aron, *Essai sur les libertés*, 64–65.

20. The term "classical liberal" may have been coined in 1883 by the French economist Charles Gide, a modern liberal who used it to describe strict laissez-faire economists, like Bastiat and Say. Gide did not think doctrinaire laissez-faire was a characteristic liberal trait, and considered saying these people should not be viewed as liberals at all before inventing the term classical liberals for them. See Rosenblatt, *Lost History*, 224–225.

twentieth-century liberalism and was the main focus of the third wave of liberalism, Liberalism 3.0. Liberal responses to totalitarianism took a number of forms, sometimes deepening previous liberal divisions, sometimes attempting to overcome them. During the first two generations of anti-totalitarian liberalism, roughly 1920–1950 and 1950–1968, many liberals made enormous efforts to reconcile classical and modern liberalism. Thereafter, liberal differences once again widened. In the third generation of anti-totalitarian liberalism (1968–1992 or 2000), the poverty question was transformed into a question of socioeconomic equality. The fear of poverty became a fear of the consequences of inequality in general, construed not only in economic but also in racial and gender terms. This was not altogether an innovation. Equality of legal status, at least for White men, had been a liberal concern from the beginning. But in the latter part of the twentieth century the concern with equality broadened and deepened. This culminated in the egalitarian liberalism associated with John Rawls. It was rejected by libertarians and neoliberals who, even if they usually accepted the modern liberal fear of poverty, resolutely opposed egalitarianism as a form of totalitarian tyranny. In the late twentieth century, liberals were increasingly divided between egalitarians and their libertarian and neoliberal opponents. A very few dissented altogether from the dueling utopias they embodied, and developed a liberalism of fear that took pains to avoid the utopianism of its rivals.

In the early twenty-first century, liberalism was thrown into flux by the arrival on the scene of a new source of fear incarnated in a new set of opponents, the populists. The rise of populism and the weak and ineffective liberal responses to it challenged liberals to develop a fourth wave of liberalism, Liberalism 4.0. The challenge of populism, however, has not at time of writing found a definitive liberal response. What is clear is the profound threat populism poses to liberal democracy worldwide since 2000. This has imperiled the marriage between liberalism and democracy described in the phrase "liberal democracy." Both the marriage and liberalism are still looking for an effective counselor.

There is another aspect of liberal fear that has changed over time. What matters is not only *what* people are afraid of, but *who* is afraid. Is it as individuals that we are frightened of being dragged out of bed in the middle of the night to be taken to the torture chamber because of what we personally said about the government? Or are we terrified, not because of anything we did, but because of the group or community to which we belong, because we are Jews living under Nazi rule? Or because we are women with no legal recourse when a husband mistreats us? Or Black Americans stopped by the police when walking down a street in a White neighborhood? The question of "who" fears can matter as much as the question of "what" one fears. Over the course of the history of liberalism those whose fears receive priority in liberal thought and practice has varied, just as what liberals have been most afraid of has varied. Contrary to what many have assumed, liberals have not historically focused on the fears of individuals, rather than groups. Class oppression and class expression have very much been traditional liberal concerns. Whether liberalism is individualist or not in philosophical terms is historically a matter of circumstance, not a constitutive characteristic of liberal thought or practice. But the individual or group orientation of liberal fears is not unrelated to the history of those fears. In the fin de siècle modern liberals were more likely to be concerned with the oppression of groups, for example with the pressure on immigrants to conform to someone else's culture and values, or with the oppression of the poor as a class. By contrast, classical liberals tended to think more in terms of individuals, although this usually did not apply to their thinking about women.[21]

Many different groups and individuals have supported liberalism, for many different reasons, motivated by many different fears. Potentially everyone has something to fear from the arbitrary exercise of power, so everyone is a potential liberal. Nevertheless, observers have long recognized that the middle classes are the social group most likely to be liberals, and within the middle classes, the professional classes—those who earn their living from their intellectual capital and expertise—are often the most liberal. The question why this is so is no sooner asked than answered in the context of liberalism as the search for a society in which none need be afraid: the middle classes are historically the most frightened. This explanation works *a fortiori* for those whom Max Weber called "pariah peoples," notably the Jews. However, in some times and places elements of the middle classes and ethnic / religious minorities have been frightened *by* liberalism, and become illiberal in response.[22] Sources of both support and opposition to liberalism have varied over time, as will be seen in many of the chapters below.

Liberals have not cared about all groups, classes, or individuals at all times. As Tocqueville noted, "the same man who is full of humanity for his fellows when the latter are at the same time his equals, becomes insensitive to their

21. See the discussion of Jane Addams in chapter 7.
22. See the discussion of liberalism and populism in chapter 11.

sufferings from the moment when equality ceases." Hence liberals have not taken into account the fears of women, colonized peoples, and other groups and classes because they were not considered equals. The story of the expansion—and contraction—over time of whose fear liberals took into account is one of the subjects of this history. It was by no means a one-way street: many German liberals rejected anti-semitism in the 1840s only to become anti-semites in the 1870s; there were liberals like Herbert Spencer who started out as advocates for women's suffrage and then changed their minds. Liberals were never united in their attitudes toward imperialism and colonialism. But in what must be considered progress, on the whole twenty-first century liberals take into account the fears of more people, both as individuals and groups, as well as more of their fears, than did liberals in the nineteenth.[23]

The Three Pillars of Liberalism

During the short nineteenth century, the great majority of liberal thinkers relied on three pillars to ward off their fears. These three pillars of liberal thought and action were freedom, markets, and morals, or, to put it another way, politics, economics, and religion or morality. Freedom is a notoriously slippery concept. It is used here, as it has been used by liberals, in two ways: very broadly, to designate the sum total of liberal aspirations with regard to markets, morals, and religion as well as politics; and more narrowly, in political terms, to mean the opportunity for political expression and participation, and placing political limits on the arbitrary exercise of power.

Although political freedom is essential to liberalism, liberals have rarely adopted exclusively political means to oppose fear. In order to be safe, more than a parliament and a bill of rights is necessary.[24] Liberals therefore have talked about markets and morals as equally essential means for keeping wolves, human and otherwise, from the door. They have relied on private property, market economies, and religious and moral incentives, as well as constitutions and political institutions, to achieve the dispersion of power necessary to keep people safe.

23. Tocqueville, *Democracy in America*, 4:994. For those who find the idea that liberalism could be about anything but individuals shocking, see Gaus, *Modern Liberal Theory*, and Levy, "From Liberal Constitutionalism to Pluralism," 21–39, 26ff.; Levy sees liberal individualism and group pluralism as in tension. See Levy, *Rationalism, Pluralism, and Freedom.*

24. A point made by Jeremy Waldron, cited in Bell, "What Is Liberalism?," 682–715, 684.

More often than not, liberals have founded freedom in the broad sense on all three pillars; a foundation liable to crack if one of its supports is missing. All three pillars are needed for the construction of a legitimate liberal order, to build a shelter against fear and to create a space in which human aspirations can flourish. Unfortunately, over time there has been an increasing tendency for liberals to rely on only one pillar, and in particular to reject any moral / religious basis for liberalism's struggle against fear.

While most liberal thinkers have always emphasized one or two pillars more than another (there are also national and chronological variations), it was typical of liberalism until around 1873 to rely on all three, although there were always minority voices who excluded one or two of the pillars from their intellectual edifices. This increased from the fin de siècle onward, when many liberals produced competing histories of liberalism designed to prove their own genealogical authenticity and delegitimize their enemies.[25] In order to accomplish this goal they separated what previous liberalisms had joined, whether positive and negative freedom; utilitarianism and perfectionism; laissez-faire and government intervention; and many other views that were more typically found together in historical context.

The most important of the reunifications that this work will urge is a return to the three-pillared arguments that liberals usually relied on during the short nineteenth century, a combination of political, economic; and moral / religious justifications of liberalism that post–WWII liberals too often abandoned in favor of narrower views. Although true of all of them, this is especially the case with regard to one pillar: from the mid-twentieth century, liberal historians and political theorists have tended to ignore the moral pillar of liberalism, or to narrow it down or hollow it out so much as to leave it unable to support anything. For some, notably Isaiah Berlin and many of his successors, liberalism had and ought to have no moral pillar, and liberals ought to hold no "particular positive doctrines about how people are to conduct their lives or what personal choices they are to make." This view was expressed by Berlin in a highly influential essay, "Two Concepts of Liberty," which distinguished between negative freedom, freedom from coercion; and positive freedom, the capacity to become one's own master with concomitant ideas about what sort of life one should lead in order to attain self-mastery, freedom as autonomy.

25. The prime examples will be found in the works of L. T. Hobhouse, A. V. Dicey discussed in chapter 7, but similar efforts can be found in Friedrich Hayek, Isaiah Berlin, and Judith Shklar.

Liberalism, in his view, was exclusively about freedom from coercion. It was not based on any particular way of life or morality, and any attempt to base liberalism on a moral / religious pillar was therefore illiberal.[26]

Historically, the moral pillar has been central to most liberalisms, and most liberals have endorsed a "comprehensive" liberalism, meaning that their notions of freedom relied on "conceptions of what is of value in human life, as well as ideals of personal virtue and character, that are to inform much of our non-political conduct."[27] Most liberals have held strong positions about the kinds of lives people should and should not lead, precisely because they thought such doctrines necessary to avoid societies in which cruelty would flourish. "A republic cannot exist, wrote Benjamin Constant, "without certain kinds of morality."[28] Tocqueville stressed that no American thought that a people could be free if they were not religious, and he agreed.[29] To the question of whether liberalism could survive without the support of religious principles, the answer was typically no, at least through WWI. Most liberals did not imagine that either free markets or free governments could endure without some level of agreement about how people should conduct their lives or what kinds of personal choices they should make. Perfectionism, the view that people ought to strive for what is best, not merely for whatever they want, or for whatever might be useful to the community, usually shared space within liberalism with utilitarian attitudes about non-coercion / negative freedom. Liberals sought both the material progress and happiness characteristic of utilitarianism, and the intrinsically desirable life of perfectionism.[30]

26. Isaiah Berlin, "Two Concepts of Liberty," in *Liberty*, 169, 178. The origins of this view as a reaction against fascism and communism are discussed in chapter 8. Berlin later claimed that he had been misunderstood, in part because of careless writing, and that he had always recognized that negative and positive freedom both had good and bad, liberal and illiberal forms. See chapter 8, and Berlin and Lukes, "Isaiah Berlin: In Conversation with Steven Lukes," 93. The quotation is from Shklar, who endorsed the strong distinction the later Berlin rejected. Shklar, "The Liberalism of Fear," 21.

27. John Rawls, *Political Liberalism*, 175.

28. Benjamin Constant, *Observations on the Strength of the Present Government of France*, tr. James Losh, Google ebook, 79.

29. Tocqueville, *Democracy*, 1:475.

30. This will surprise those who think liberal perfectionism an anomaly. See Weinstein, *Utilitarianism*, 10n27; Damico, "What's Wrong with Liberal Perfectionism?," 397–420; Thomas Hurka, *Perfectionism* (Oxford: Oxford University Press, 1993), 3. The presence of both utilitarianism and perfectionism overlaps with the distinction between pluralist and rationalist traditions of liberalism made by Jacob T. Levy, with pluralist toleration associated with utilitarian

Regarding a moral / religious pillar as necessary to a liberal society, a crucial component in making a world without fear, did not mean that liberals endorsed any form of religious or other fanaticism. Liberals were pluralists—another of Berlin's terms—about how people ought to live their lives. They always accepted that views would diverge, and turned divergence, and even limited conflict, into means of limiting power and encouraging progress. Instead of seeing eternal conflicts among different value systems as tragic, as Berlin did, many liberals recognized them as a means of freeing people by limiting power: the existence of prominent conflicts over values might discourage governments or social groups from enforcing one side. However, liberals usually did not think the content of those diverging views unimportant or irrelevant. They expressed strong views about what was acceptable. The results mattered, not just the process. Stamping out fear required something more than just rules of procedure, whether in politics, economics, or morality. The relationship of liberal views of the good life to illiberal views that required some to be afraid so that others might flourish and realize their salvation has been the subject of much debate within liberalism.[31]

The moral and political pillars of liberalism have generally exerted a considerable influence on the economic pillar of liberalism (and vice versa). This has contributed to the economic pillar being only occasionally a laissez-faire one before liberal argumentation thinned out in the late twentieth century. Great supporter though he was of commercial society, whose development in his view was the greatest check on cruelty in human history, Adam Smith was no doctrinaire advocate of laissez-faire policies—he made exceptions precisely when it came to fostering political community and morality and religion. This was why the majority of proto-liberal and liberal thinkers from Smith through the mid-twentieth century did not endorse a doctrinaire version of laissez-faire, and why laissez-faire economics itself was generally not described as liberal until the late nineteenth century, as will be discussed in chapter 7. Liberals defended the existence of private property and relied on markets, to be sure, but it was not until late in the twentieth century that a reliance on markets and private property to keep people secure was identified

---

views and rationalist autonomy associated with perfectionism. See Levy, "Liberalism's Divide.". For a similar distinction, see Dunn, *Western Political Theory*, 34.

31. See Rosenblatt, *Lost History*, 69, 78, 151; On pluralism see Berlin, "Two Concepts of Liberty" in Berlin, *Liberty*, 212–217.

with laissez-faire policies by many or most liberals. At the same time, until the late twentieth century laissez-faire itself was usually justified on moral grounds by its advocates.[32]

The three pillars were not used just to build liberal castles in the sky. They not only defended people from cruelty in abstract theory but in practical political battles. Liberal parties and politicians used them as much as liberal theorists. A good example is Jonathan Parry's characterization of the political language of the Liberal parliamentary party in Britain in 1830–86 as falling into three main categories: "constitutional themes," that is political freedom; arguments for low taxes and free trade, i.e., markets; and "arguments about moral improvement and the development of the moral conscience." The same was true of liberal parties elsewhere in Europe and America. This will be seen in the chapters devoted to liberal responses to such issues as the suffrage, nationalism, and feminism.[33]

The four waves of liberalism correspond broadly, albeit not perfectly, to the cultivation or neglect of three-pillared arguments for liberalism (see appendix). It is the contention of this book that liberalism has been most convincing as program, language, and social analysis when it has relied on all three pillars, and that the relative weakness of liberalism at the end of the twentieth century and the beginning of the twenty-first has much to do with neglect of the moral pillar of liberalism.

Hope versus Fear

The history of liberal fears is necessary to understand liberalism, but it is not sufficient. Any definition of liberalism, and any history of liberalism, must recognize that liberalism is not just a party of fears, but a party of hopes. Surely nothing could be more utopian than the biblical aspiration for a society in which all could sit under their vine and their fig tree undisturbed. The three pillars of liberalism, freedom, markets, and morals, have supported liberal hope as much as they have been ramparts against liberal fear. Liberals promised more than just progressive liberation from fear. They promised continued, unprecedented improvement in freedom; continued, unprecedented material improvement; and continued, unprecedented opportunities for self-perfection

---

32. Rosenblatt, *Lost History*, 81.
33. Parry, *Politics of Patriotism*, 35.

and moral development.[34] Freedom, markets, and morals supported both the positive and the negative sides of liberalism. Fear was to freedom from coercion as hope was to freedom as autonomy—always recognizing that there was some overlap between the two.[35]

It is a commonplace that nineteenth-century liberalism was characterized by faith in progress. At all times, for every liberal fear, whether of religious fanaticism, revolution, poverty, or totalitarianism, there has been a corresponding liberal hope or set of hopes. Their more or less utopian hopes distinguished liberals from more pessimistic conservative or republican traditions of political thought which focused on ultimately losing battles (in this world at least) with sin and secular forms of corruption.

Many, perhaps all, of the contradictions typical of liberalism derived from efforts to encompass both hopes and fears. The oft-remarked tensions in liberalism between optimism and pessimism, between liberals as the confident heirs of Voltaire or the frightened successors of Robespierre and Napoleon, were based on the concurrent fears and hopes liberals typically harbored. A good example is the liberal cult of education. It was sometimes propelled by fear, as in Robert Lowe's famous statement that "we must at least educate our masters," but it was more often motivated by hope. Such faith and hope (and for that matter charity) could hardly have been generated by fear alone. Even if, in the case of conflict, fear often trumped hope (loss aversion applies in politics as much as in economics), and utopia was subject to indefinite postponement, faith in progress has always been at the heart of liberalism. Liberals have based their hopes on the same three pillars of freedom, markets, and morals that they have used to ward off their fears.

The extent of liberal hope has waxed and waned over time, but liberalism has always been utopian, in the sense that the world liberals strove for, a world without fear, was without historical precedent. The liberalism of the short nineteenth century identified itself with faith in progress and was strongly utopian.

---

34. The list is derived from Kristol, *Two Cheers for Capitalism*, 241. It is characteristic of his period that Kristol ascribes these three promises to "capitalism," rather than "liberalism," partly to avoid the confusion over the word in contemporary American culture, and partly because, although Kristol opposed it, the tendency of liberalism at the time was toward economic reductionism and exclusive reliance on the market pillar.

35. Even if not always. See Alan S. Kahan, "Jacob Burckhardt's Dystopic Liberalism," in *Liberal Moments*, ed. Atanassow and Kahan, 113–119.

In the fin de siècle, modern liberals added the hope of ending poverty to the liberal mix. By contrast, the "end of ideology" movement of the 1950s regarded any whiff of overt utopianism as dangerous because it was identified in their minds with revolution and reaction, or rather totalitarian communism and fascism.[36] They relied on purely technocratic and bureaucratic solutions to what made people afraid as the only safe means of proceeding. In response, the liberalisms of the late twentieth century, whether egalitarian, libertarian, or neoliberal, were almost all utopian. In very different ways, they all stressed how their various paradises could be achieved, and fear finally put to rest. A contrasting reaction, albeit much less influential, was the invention of what its first formulator, Judith Shklar, called "the liberalism of fear." In a sense her liberalism of fear, which in her view was distinct from liberalisms that sought autonomy, prolonged the end of ideology movement. But instead of claiming that ideology was dead in the face of clearly contravening facts, Shklar saw the end of ideology as something to hope for and aspire to. Bernard Williams, however, developed Shklar's liberalism of fear in a perfectionist direction while maintaining an emphasis on realism and a strong sense of the historically possible.[37]

Liberal hopes, varied as they might be, have always had one thing in common: they are based on civil society. For liberals civil society, not the state, is the common source of a free politics, a free market, and of morals / religion. Benjamin Constant distinguished between ancient liberty, exclusively concerned with political participation, and modern liberty, essentially private in nature. The two might be combined to some extent, but the distinctively modern part of freedom was that which was located outside the state. Despite all the liberal emphases on constitutions, theories of representative government, and even the educational role of political participation, it was never solely or even primarily politics that made human beings happy in the liberal view, or made them better people. Liberal hopes for making people happier or more perfect came from civil society. Achieving this was beyond the capacity of the

36. A world without ideology was also unprecedented, and thus radically utopian in its own way.

37. Shklar argued that her liberalism of fear and the liberalism of personal autonomy were entirely separate, in her own way repeating Isaiah Berlin's sometime mistake about negative and positive freedom. There is no justification for this until the late twentieth century, when Shklar and Ryan wrote. The view that the liberalism of fear can be distinguished from liberalism based on personal development or natural rights does not hold up historically, nor in the view of Bernard Williams philosophically. Cf. "The Liberalism of Fear," 26–27; Ryan, *Making of Modern Liberalism*, 8.

state. Liberals always feared the state, they sometimes hoped for its help, but they never expected it to be the source of salvation. Liberal faith lay in civil society.

Understanding liberalism as a blend of fear and hope gives us insight into a phenomenon that has frequently vexed historians: liberal contradictions.[38] This has been clear since liberalism was invented. In the nineteenth century, Mill observed that in France "the *libéraux* comprise every shade of political opinion, from moderate to radical." Critics of liberalism spoke contemptuously of a "liberal cocktail."[39] Some of the contradictions in liberalism arose from the fact that liberals responded to different fears in different proportions. But many derived from the fundamental contrast at the heart of liberalism, and perhaps of human nature, between fear and hope.

If fear and hope are contrasting, even conflicting attitudes, they are not always contradictory. One can be both fearful and hopeful at the same time, and liberals often have been. Indeed, simultaneously holding contrasting or even contradictory attitudes has often been characteristic of liberals and of liberalisms. This has been the case, for example, with regard to utilitarianism and perfectionism; democracy and elitism; spontaneity and design; and historical and eternal truths, contrasting attitudes often found in the same liberal thinker or strand of liberalism. Perhaps the most common contradiction was a situation in which some liberals responded by supporting reforms— they joined what in the nineteenth century was called "the party of movement"—while others wanted to reject or limit reforms and joined the "party of resistance." Many liberals shifted from one to the other depending on circumstances, a phenomenon seen in England after 1832 and France after 1830, or again during the American Civil Rights movement in the 1960s. What is worth stressing is that liberals have often preferred to try to hold both positions simultaneously. Thomas Macaulay alternately adopted perfectionist and utilitarian views; John Stuart Mill argued that all sides in any enduring dispute had an element of the truth in their possession and tried to take all into account; Friedrich Hayek insisted on spontaneity in economics but designed a legal framework for it; all without any anxiety about con-

38. See, among others, Bell, "What Is Liberalism?," 683; Kahan, *Liberalism in Nineteenth-Century Europe*, 1–5.

39. Mill, *Essays on French History and Historians; Collected Works of John Stuart Mill*, 109; cited in Rosenblatt, *Lost History*, 76.

sistency. The history of liberalism is a matter for lumpers more than for splitters.[40]

Definitions of liberalism may express at least four different kinds of illocutionary force: what it *is / was*; what it *ought* to be; how the definition helps *explain* the history of liberalism; and how it *contradicts* previous definitions and improves upon them.[41] The definition of liberalism proposed here, that liberalism is the search for a society in which no one need be afraid, and that it has historically been based on four fears, three pillars, and hope, is an attempt to describe liberalism as it was, is, and ought to be, while explaining its evolution over time, and naturally improving upon previous efforts. It has been structured in such a way that the different illocutionary elements of the definition may be evaluated independently.

For the most part, however, definitions and histories of liberalism express one of two illocutionary intentions: they define or describe what liberalism *is*; and / or state what liberalism *ought* to be. Definitions based on what liberalism *is* usually aim to be comprehensive: what are all the ways in which people use the word? An example defines liberalism as "the sum of the arguments that have been classified as liberal, and recognized as such by other self-proclaimed liberals, across time and space." This definition is useful to the political theorist, crossing "time and space" so that a thinker or text not considered liberal in their own time may still be considered liberal if 200 years later many liberals call them so, allowing political theorists to leap across historical contexts.[42] By contrast, a more purely historical example of a comprehensive definition of what liberalism *is* would be: to "clarify what the terms 'liberal' and 'liberalism'

---

40. Darwin popularized the distinction between "lumpers" and "splitters." Splitters like to see many separate species in nature, where lumpers see only a few. The origin of the distinction may lie with Plato, who in the *Phaedrus* (265c-e) wrote that when we think we engage in both *synagoge* and *diairesis*—"collection" and "division," that is, lumping and splitting (I owe this point to Timothy Stanton). Isaiah Berlin preferred another ancient Greek distinction, that between the hedgehog, who knows one thing, and the fox, who knows many. Many liberals are foxes, but not all.

41. The illocutionary force of a phrase is what it is primarily intended to do by its author. The concept, developed by the English philosopher J. L. Austin, has been fruitfully applied to the history of political thought by Quentin Skinner. See Skinner, "'Social Meaning' and Social Action," in Tully, ed., *Meaning & Context*, 83–84.

42. The intention of this clause is likely to save Locke and Hobbes for liberalism. See Bell, "What Is Liberalism?," 686–687.

have meant to the people who used them."[43] In both cases what is "liberal" is whatever has passed for liberal, at a given moment for the historian, or at any moment for the political theorist or philosopher.

Definitions based on what "liberalism" *ought* to be give a specific content to liberalism that may or may not accord with the actual use of the word. They always exclude some people who call themselves liberals but who, in the eyes of the beholder, are not. These are prescriptive rather than comprehensive definitions of liberalism. They describe the ways people *ought* to use "liberal" even if they fail to do so in practice. Prescriptive definitions involve identifying some core issues or arguments that serve to define liberalism, and then stipulating what liberals ought to say. Frequently, prescriptive definitions create a canon of liberal texts, on the basis of which other texts may be confirmed or rejected as liberal, but when they do so they eliminate rather than illuminate the contradictions characteristic of liberalism in practice.[44]

Beyond defining liberalism as what it is / was and what it ought to be, explanation is a third intention behind definitions of liberalism, one that may motivate definitions of what liberalism is and what it ought to be. A definition of liberalism may be intended to help explain the historical development of liberalism, whether in the comprehensive sense (all uses) or the prescriptive sense (the "correct" uses). Finally, whether the definition of liberalism be intended as an "is" or an "ought," whether it has explanatory ambitions or not, all definitions of liberalism share one particular intention: they suggest that some other definition(s) is wrong.

The story told in this book describes the development of liberalism in the Western world and elaborates on the definition given in the first sentence, that liberalism is the search for a society in which no one need be afraid. It is also an argument for why liberalism needs all three of its pillars to stand up against its enemies, as well as against liberals who pretend that liberalism can or should do without one or more of them. In including all liberalisms, three-pillared and single-pillared, modern and classical, nineteenth and twentieth century, egalitarian and libertarian, fearful and full of hope, the history recounted here is meant to be a liberal history. But this by no means makes it all-inclusive. Some things that would have improved the storytelling have no

43. Bell, "What Is Liberalism?," 685, 689–690, 708n.32; Rosenblatt, *Lost History*, 2.

44. Bell, "What Is Liberalism?," 685. A good example is Jeremy Waldron, who admits that "many liberals may not recognize" themselves in his definition. Waldron, "Theoretical Foundations of Liberalism," 128, 134–44, cited in Bell, "What Is Liberalism?," 687.

doubt been left out by accident. Others have been left out on purpose. One prominent omission, important for deciding where the story should start, is John Locke.

Should We Start at the Very Beginning?
Or, Why Not Locke?

Histories of liberalism today usually start with John Locke (1632–1704). He was certainly a very prominent proto-liberal in the seventeenth century, inspired by the fear of religious fanaticism as well as of arbitrary despotism. Nevertheless, seeing Locke as a foundational figure whose place is at the head of any genealogy of liberalism is a mistake. Starting histories of liberalism with Locke has led historians to misconstrue both Locke and liberalism, based largely on a view of liberalism that was a product of the mid-twentieth century. For the first hundred years of liberalism, liberals simply did not consider Locke a liberal. After the French Revolution, the first generations of liberals to call themselves such thought of Locke as a figure from a different world, full of archaic assumptions.[45] Nineteenth-century European liberals, deeply imbued with historical consciousness, thought Locke a primitive. In America, Locke's political works rapidly fell into obscurity or contempt after the 1770s.

Even in his homeland Britain, Locke's political works were generally dismissed in the nineteenth century. Typical was Mill's discussion of Locke's political theory. Recognizing the proto-liberal in Locke, he praised him for wanting to limit the power of government, but dismissed his discussion of social contracts and inalienable rights. Mill's opponent James Fitzjames Stephen agreed that Locke's political theory was "altogether superannuated and bygone." A 1913 British history of liberalism, by a Liberal party politician, attributed liberalism's origins to the industrial revolution of the 1760s and the American and French Revolutions, not to the Glorious Revolution or the seventeenth century. Locke was simply not part of the story of liberalism as told by English liberals in the nineteenth century.[46]

45. As had already been the case for Adam Smith. Montesquieu did not discuss Locke, but took very different positions on the origins of property, social contracts, religion, etc. See Barrera, *Les lois du monde*, 292–293; Binoche, *Introduction*, 59, 326; Bibby, *Montesquieu's Political Economy*, 114, 193n.10.

46. Blease, *Short History*; Bell, "What Is Liberalism?," 694–697. Among German liberals, Locke's reputation varied. Wilhelm Traugott Krug's 1823 *Geschichtliche Darstellung des Liberal-*

In America Locke played a bigger role, but not for long. During the American Revolution he was at first a central figure, his influence figuring prominently in the Declaration of Independence, but his star rapidly waned, to the point that by the 1780s he was hardly cited in American political writings. Between 1773 and 1917, there was no American edition of Locke's *Two Treatises on Government*. In the early twentieth century, American commentators often saw Locke as a classic example of a failed Enlightenment political theorist. In 1905, the author of the standard American political theory textbook, William Dunning, described Locke as having an "illogical, incoherent system of political philosophy." After WWI, Harold Stearn's *Liberalism in America* did not even mention him, and the 1937 edition of George Sabine's standard political theory textbook described liberalism as a tradition invented in nineteenth-century Britain, and did not classify Locke as a liberal. On the other hand, Vernon Parrington's *Main Currents in American Thought*, written mostly in the 1910s, did call Locke a liberal and gave him prominent if somewhat hostile treatment from a left-wing perspective, and in 1935, John Dewey gave an account of Locke as the founder of natural rights liberalism similar to those often found in late twentieth-century textbooks. Despite this, in Sabine's third edition in 1960, Locke was still considered to have exercised little influence on the "Whig liberalism" of the eighteenth century, and "the actual complexity of Locke's thought . . . makes difficult an estimate of its relations to later theories." Sabine considered Locke's ideas to be more medieval than modern.[47]

---

ismus: alter und neuer Zeit, perhaps the first historical discussion of liberalism, acknowledges the importance of England's Glorious Revolution of 1688 but does not mention Locke. See https://ia800500.us.archive.org/30/items/geschichtlicheda00krug/geschichtlicheda00krug .pdf, 71–73. Bluntschli's *Allgemeines Staatsrecht*, published in three volumes between 1852 and 1881, whose first volume was translated and used as a textbook at Oxford, gave Locke only a footnote in its dismissive discussion of the idea of a social contract in volume one, and did not refer to him in its discussion of religious freedom in the same volume. Its discussion of the "liberal party" in the third volume included Martin Luther and Alexander Hamilton, but not Locke. By contrast, in the early and mid-nineteenth century the *Staatslexikon*, often described as the "Bible of German liberalism," devoted a laudatory article to Locke's political theory. But the *Staatslexikon* did not describe him as a liberal, criticized his over-emphasis on the ahistorical individual, and suggested his work was too purely English in orientation.

47. Lutz, "Relative Influence," 189–197, 193; Arcenas, *America's Philosopher*, 2, 55–56, 59, 70; 84; Bell, "What Is Liberalism?," 697n.69, 700–701; Sabine, *History*, 536, 538–539; Dewey, *Liberalism*, 6–16. On Locke in pre–Civil War America, it is still useful to consult Curti, "Great Mr. Locke," 107–151. On Locke in late nineteenth and early twentieth-century century America, see Gunnell, "Archaeology of American Liberalism," as well as Arcenas, *America's Philosopher*.

Thus, even in America and Britain, Locke's status as a liberal and his importance for liberals were at best unclear before WWII. In 1932, Michael Oakeshott
could write that "it is at least remarkable that at the present time the gospel of
Locke is less able to secure adherents than any other whatever. . . ." Oakeshott
went on to suggest that Locke was not merely dead, but buried.[48]

Yet beginning a little before WWII and gathering steam afterward, there
occurred on both sides of the Atlantic one of the more curious intellectual
phenomena of the twentieth century, the resurrection of John Locke as the
preeminent political philosopher of liberalism. The causes of Locke's resurrection were many, but they essentially boiled down to the fact that in the
second half of the twentieth century, Locke and Lockean arguments were
widely perceived as useful. First, many continental European emigrés to Britain and the United States were desperate to identify liberalism with their new
"Anglo-Saxon" homeland, in opposition to the continent they had fled.[49] The
very English Locke was a suitable mascot for Anglo-Saxon liberalism. Second, many liberals *and* many opponents of liberalism wanted to sharply distinguish liberalism from socialism, or else classical from modern liberalism,
and identified Locke with liberalism or classical liberalism as a means of
doing this. As part of this project, Locke became an important figure in ge-
nealogies of liberalism.

Identified with individualism, Locke was also useful when twentieth-
century writers wanted to see liberalism as an essentially individualist philosophy, whether for good or ill. Harold Laski, a socialist writing a history of
liberalism in 1936, wished to identify the rise of liberalism with the rise of the
bourgeoisie, the better to do away with both; he found identifying Locke as
defining "the essential outlines of the liberal doctrine for nearly two centuries"
a useful tool in this endeavor, as Charles A. Beard and Parrington had already
done in the Unites States, where Merle Curti's 1937 essay on "The Great
Mr. Locke: America's Philosopher, 1783–1861," firmly established Locke as a
supposedly perennial presence in American political thought. After WWII the
opponents of liberalism continued to find it useful to emphasize Locke's importance in order to give point and relevance to their attack on him as a "possessive individualist," the enemy of community and the defender of capitalist
exploitation, colonialism, and even slavery. This was a way to attack liberalism's

48. Oakeshott, cited in Dunn, "Measuring Locke's Shadow," 260.

49. Hayek went so far as to declare Tocqueville and some of his other continental favorites
part of this "Anglo-Saxon" tradition. Hayek, *The Constitution of Liberty*, 110–111.

moral foundations once Locke was identified as the archetypal liberal. Liberalism's enemies raised Locke from the dead as a means of burying liberalism once and for all. Conversely, for liberals who wanted to stand on liberalism's moral pillar, including some libertarians, going back to Locke's emphasis on natural rights and the social contract was a way to give a moral foundation to liberal "pluralism," even at the cost of eliminating all historical content from Locke's *corpus* (the moral foundation was rarely a Christian one as Locke would have understood it). Since many late twentieth-century liberals wished to ignore liberalism's historical concern with group fears, Locke's individualism was convenient for this purpose as well.[50]

Of all the Locke-conjurers, friends or foes, perhaps the most influential was Louis Hartz, whose *The Liberal Tradition in America: An Interpretation of American Political Thought Since the Revolution* appeared in 1955, and argued that only a single ideology, Lockean liberalism, had ever dominated in America. Despite occasional abortive efforts to contest it, such as by defenders of slavery, Lockean liberalism had always ruled American life and thought according to Hartz. America was the True Pure Land of Liberalism, unpolluted by Europe's vestigial feudalism and rampant class conflict, which deflected European liberals from a Lockean course. American liberalism was unique—Hartz went so far as to claim there were no European counterparts to American Progressivism, dismissing the British New Liberals and the French Solidarists as socialists. He was not enamoured of this situation. In his view the domination of Lockean liberalism in America acted as a form of tyranny of majority opinion—he even managed to blame McCarthyism on Locke.[51]

Hartz's identification of America with Lockean liberalism, and of Locke with "the self-interested, profit-maximizing values and behaviours of liberal capitalism," has had enormous influence, so much so that a chronicler of the history of American political science could write that "political theorists have become so accustomed to talking about John Locke as the founder of the liberal tradition that they forget that Hartz was one of the first individuals to

50. Laski, *The Rise of European Liberalism*, 104–105. On America, see Arcenas, *America's Philosopher*, 107–109, 114–115. I have combined Stanton's four causes for the Locke revival into the first two cited here. See Stanton, "John Locke," 607; Gunnell, "Archaeology of American Liberalism," 136; 140; Stanton, "John Locke," 609.

51. Kloppenberg, "In Retrospect, 461, 464; Gunnell, "The Archaeology of American Liberalism," 130; Hartz, *The Liberal Tradition in America*, 12, 140.

characterize Locke as a liberal, let alone to ascribe to him the role of the founder of a such tradition." Hartz was not one of the first, but he was one of the most influential. His work promoted both Locke's resurrection and the evisceration of any actual Lockean content from the image of Locke used to represent liberalism.[52]

Hartz was followed by many others. In 1960, Sheldon Wolin's highly influential *The Politics of Vision* wrote John Locke's name firmly at the head of the liberal family tree: "If modern liberalism can be said to be inspired by any one writer, Locke is undoubtedly the leading candidate." By the early 1960s the argument was commonly made that liberalism was a "single and continuing entity . . . so extensive that it involves most of the guiding beliefs of modern western opinion" and that Locke was its "founding father."[53]

But the fact is that whatever might be said about the importance of Locke for liberalism post-1950, he might as well never have existed for liberals between 1800 and 1914. Even in the twentieth century, certainly before and even after 1945, a case could be made that a figure today known only to specialists, A. V. Dicey (1835–1920), was far more influential than Locke in framing how liberalism was understood by both its friends and foes (see chapter 7). Once the proto-liberalism of the seventeenth and eighteenth centuries was left behind (and by the mid-eighteenth century, Locke was already a "has-been" outside of the Thirteen Colonies), for the average liberal Locke hardly rose to the status of a minor historical figure.[54]

Does this mean the post–WWII generations that thought Locke was the original liberal were simply wrong? Or did Locke *become* a liberal only centuries after his death?[55] The answer depends on the definition of liberalism chosen and the context in which it is used. A contextualist definition of what liberalism *is* means that Locke was not a liberal in 1690, since no one called themselves one in 1690. But since, from the 1950s, liberals and their opponents (at first more the latter than the former) considered Locke a liberal, however

52. Kloppenberg, "In Retrospect," 460–461; Gunnell, "The Archaeology of American Liberalism," 130; Bell, "What Is Liberalism?," 704.

53. Wolin, *Politics and Vision*, 263; Keith Minogue, cited in Bell, "What Is Liberalism?," 703; 698–699; Macpherson, *The Political Theory of Possessive Individualism*.

54. In fact, even eighteenth-century proto-liberal rights talk typically understood rights very differently than Locke had. See Edelstein, "Enlightenment Rights Talk," 531.

55. The latter is Bell's view. "What Is Liberalism?," 698.

mistaken they may have been in their interpretations of his writings, from the perspective of a contextualist definition of mid-twentieth century liberalism, Locke *was* a liberal, *then*. In his own historical context, Locke was a proto-liberal whose arguments rested on what would become the three pillars of liberalism. But since Locke, proto-liberal though he was, dropped out of the conversation among liberals from the 1780s through the early twentieth century, to begin a history of liberalism with him presents a misleading picture of liberalism's historical development.

Proto-liberals who were far more influential than Locke in the nineteenth century were Montesquieu (1689–1755) and Adam Smith (1723–1790), discussed in chapter 2. To begin with them means beginning with proto-liberals whose works, unlike those of Locke, were of great importance to nineteenth-century liberals. Compared to Locke they were much more directly related, both chronologically and intellectually, to liberalism as it actually took form in the nineteenth century. If the fear of revolution that would create liberalism proper was never their chief motivation, Montesquieu and Smith did have to reckon with the new economic and moral fears that would contribute to the development of liberalism. As proto-liberals, both were afraid of religious fanaticism, the "superstition" and "enthusiasm" the Enlightened loved to hate. But much further removed from the Wars of Religion than Locke, that fear was mostly in the background for them, replaced by more modern fears, whether of the moral and intellectual degradation of the factory worker in Smith, or the difficulty of preserving freedom in societies where honor and virtue were threatened in Montesquieu.

What made their writings especially important for the history of liberalism was not only their fears but their hopes, and the sources of their hopes. Montesquieu and Smith recognized not merely the need to disperse power in society and to separate powers in government, as had been the case among proto-liberals since the Reformation, but also the utility of diversity and conflict for the political, economic, and moral development of individuals and societies. Their thinking was marked by the emphasis on historical change that would be typical of nineteenth-century liberalism. Key to the changes that separated their world from previous epochs, in their view, was the development of commercial society. For Montesquieu and Smith commercial society was, for all the new dangers it presented, a pillar of freedom and resistance to oppression, in a way that thinkers who lived earlier in history could not have perceived for the simple reason that commercial society was much further developed in the eighteenth century. Montesquieu and Smith could and did rely on freedom, markets, and morals in ways that were much closer to liberal thought than earlier proto-liberals. As we will see in chapter 2, there were significant ways in which the late eighteenth century took a long step toward the liberalism of the nineteenth century.

This chapter and the discussion of Montesquieu and Smith in chapter 2, "Before the Revolutions," Part one of the book, are the prologue to the discussion of the first wave of liberalism in chapters 3 through 6, Part two, "The All-Too-Short Nineteenth Century."

Liberals and Liberalisms

After the prologue's discussion of proto-liberalism, chapters 3 and 4, "After the Revolutions" and "Many-Splendored Liberalism," introduce some of the ideas of the leading liberal thinkers of the nineteenth century, ideas that may be familiar to some readers, but that are given a new reading in the context of the fears of first-wave liberalism in general and the writers' own particular fears. The writers examined are Kant, Madison, Constant, Macaulay, Tocqueville, and J. S. Mill, each of whom represents a significant facet of liberal thought. These two chapters deal with the creation of a more or less consensual set of liberal attitudes over the course of the period 1815–1873, the "short" nineteenth century, based on the fear of revolutions (and their shadow, reactions), and on the three pillars of freedom, markets, and morals.

A different approach to the history of liberalism is adopted in chapter 5, "Liberalism on the Front Lines: Freedom, Nation, and God": the chapter looks at liberalism not by reading theoretical texts, but by discussing political controversies over suffrage, nationalism, and Catholicism, struggles essential to the development of liberal democracy, liberal nation-states, and liberal (and illiberal) attitudes toward religion. As with the analysis of liberal thinkers, the case is impressionistic rather than comprehensive. One reason the argument departs from analyzing thinkers is to adopt a broader approach to both issues and the people who responded to them. Understanding the way in which liberals in practice did or did not rely on freedom, markets, and morals / religion to ward off their fears and empower their hopes helps to unpack the arguments liberals made. It shows how they could all be considered liberal in their time even if, from some perspectives, they could be considered contradictory or even illiberal.

Chapter 6, "Liberalism with Something Missing," is the last chapter in part two. It looks at a minority tradition in nineteenth-century liberalism, liberals who preferred to stand on one pillar, whether Benthamite utilitarians, laissez-faire economists like Bastiat, or devotees of the survival of the fittest such as Herbert Spencer. This rejection of moral perfectionism (partial in Spencer's case) and greater reliance on economics foreshadowed what would become mainstream liberalism in the late twentieth century. In describing the development of liberalism and making claims about putatively "mainstream" versus "minority" rhetoric, the argument is again suggestive rather than quantitative. Part two thus covers the development of the first wave of liberalism through about 1873, the year of John Stuart Mill's death.

Part three, "New Fears, New Hopes," chapters 7 through 11, discusses the evolution of the second and third waves of liberalism, and potentially a fourth. It discusses the history of liberalism from the fin de siècle onwards, examining the successive waves of liberalism that arose in response to new fears: the fear of poverty; the fear of totalitarianism; and the fear of populism. While in many respects the approach is transatlantic, the differences that emerge in various times and places between American and European liberalisms play a greater role in this period.

Chapter 7, "Modern Liberalism vs. Classical Liberalism," treats the fin de siècle liberal response to the problem of poverty and the rise of two main competing forms of liberalism, modern liberalism and classical liberalism. The cleavage is considered not as evidence of the decline or even the disappearance of liberalism, but rather as evidence of the way in which liberalism had become the dominant operating system of Western political and social thought by the end of the nineteenth century.[56]

In the fin de siècle, modern liberals sometimes proclaimed themselves socialists in order to fight poverty, liberalize socialism, and / or ward off the threat of revolution or reaction, just as in the short nineteenth century liberals had sometimes joined revolutions in order to end them (see chapter 2). Classical liberals rejected this move, and sometimes called themselves "liberal conservatives" while their opponents described themselves as "liberal socialists" (both always maintained that they alone were the true liberals). The split between modern and classical liberals thus echoed the tension during the

---

56. Contra the arguments for decline to be found in Kahan, *Liberalism in Nineteenth-Century Europe*, and in different forms in Leonhard, *Liberalismus*, and Hazareesingh, *Political Traditions in Modern France*.

short nineteenth century between liberals who aligned themselves with the party of movement or reform and those who chose the party of resistance.[57]

Progressivism in the United States, New Liberalism in Britain, and Solidarism in France, identified with such thinkers as Jane Addams, L. T. Hobhouse, and Léon Bourgeois, represent modern liberalism, while classical liberalism is represented by A. V. Dicey. The chapter closes with a discussion of modern liberals' flirtation with the Hegelian temptation to rely on the state for salvation. Hegel was liberal in most things, except, crucially, in his ultimate rejection of civil society in favour of the state. The modern liberals of the fin de siècle were frequently tempted to follow in his path, a temptation felt even more strongly after the World Wars.

Chapter 8, "Liberalism's Limits," discusses three issues that took on particular salience in the fin de siècle and thereafter: radical nationalism; imperialism / colonialism; and feminism. In contrast to the mostly positive relationship between liberalism and nationalism during the short nineteenth century discussed in chapter 5, the relationship between liberalism and nationalism in the fin de siècle (and thereafter) was increasingly fraught with tension. This tension often crystallized in debates over anti-semitism, which is considered in light of the Treitschke Affair in Germany. The "nation" was a double-edged sword from a liberal perspective: it protected its own members from fear, yet it could be a source of fear for others. This was especially true when "nation" became "nation-state," and even more so when the nation-state became an imperial / colonial power.

The relationship between liberalism and imperialism discussed in the chapter repositions the scholarly debate over liberalism and empire as a discussion of the triad of liberalism, nationalism, and imperialism. The relationship was complicated: liberals took divergent positions, as can be seen in the debates over colonialism in the French legislature. There was no necessary connection between concern with poverty and rejection of imperialism. Modern liberals sometimes drew support from imperialism, as was the case for Friedrich Naumann. Finally, the relationship between liberalism and feminism, which from a liberal perspective was a question of whether or not women's well-justified fear of men ought to be recognized, is discussed over the whole course of the nineteenth century and the fin de siècle, through the writings of Mary

---

57. The relationship between classical liberalism and conservatism continued to be controversial in the twentieth century, when Hayek, who sometimes considered himself a classical liberal, felt compelled to write an essay about "Why I Am Not a Conservative." See chapter 8.

Wollestonecraft, Elizabeth Cady Stanton, and John Stuart Mill, as well as the post–WWI debate over women's suffrage in France.

Chapter 9, "A World in Crisis and the Crisis of Liberalism," describes some of the forms taken by the third wave of liberalism after WWI. Liberalism 3.0 emerged in response to the challenges posed by the emergence of totalitarianism. Fascism and communism in the 1920s and '30s, the Cold War in the 1950s and early '60s, and the more diffuse totalitarian threats of the late twentieth century were the focus of three generations of anti-totalitarian liberals. Totalitarianism became the main focus of liberal fear, although the fears of revolution / reaction or of poverty did not disappear. In many respects the emergence of the third wave of liberalism was epitomized by Walter Lippman's 1937 book, *The Good Society*. The book inspired the 1938 Colloque Lippman, held in Paris and attended by liberal luminaries as diverse as Friedrich Hayek and Raymond Aron. The Colloque was devoted to the question of how liberalism was to respond to its catastrophic failures. The discussions of Hayek, Isaiah Berlin, and Ordoliberalism that follow the examination of Lippman's book and the Colloque present some of the most important third-wave liberal responses to the problem of totalitarianism. They highlight the attempts of the first generation of anti-totalitarian liberals to bridge the fin de siècle divide between modern and classical liberalism, and to overcome the fin de siècle tendency to separate the three traditional pillars of liberalism, freedom, markets, and morals, and in particular to limit appeals to morality and religion.

Chapter 10, "Hollow Victories, 1945–2000," begins by describing the divergence between American and European usage of the word "liberal" that took place in the middle of the twentieth century. While liberals on both sides of the Atlantic remained devoted to creating a world without fear, the way in which they used "liberal" to describe their aims gradually became quite different. Nevertheless, the "end of ideology" movement of the 1950s, which largely encompassed the second generation of anti-totalitarian liberals, was very much a transatlantic phenomenon. It dominated liberal thought and practice in the 1950s and early 1960s, and combined both an acceptance of modern liberal concerns with a determined rejection of any form of moral / religious pillar for liberalism.

The second generation of anti-totalitarian liberalism was also marked by a conference, this one in Rome in 1955. Hayek was one of the few who attended both the Colloque Lippmann and the Rome conference, but his resolutely ideological view of liberalism met with rejection at Rome. Anti-utopianism and the rejection of idealism in favor of practical, limited reforms was the curiously un-utopian path to utopia preferred by the "end of ideology" theorists, whether the liberal American sociologists prominent in the period or European writers like Raymond Aron. Incremental improvements in living standards, education, and culture, directed by the appropriate specialists, were the focus of this generation of liberals. By contrast, they saw ideological commitments as the high road to totalitarianism. In hindsight, they sometimes appear both boring and foolish, but it would be a mistake to underestimate their importance at the time and their influence on the third generation of anti-totalitarian liberals, who in reviving a number of different ideological commitments in liberalism were very much reacting against their immediate predecessors.

The Viet Nam War, the rise of the counterculture in the 1960s, and the collapse of the post–WWII economic boom after the oil shocks of the 1970s was the context in which the third generation of anti-totalitarian liberalism began. This generation was characterized by the revival of liberal ideologies and liberal utopianism. The attempt to reconcile classical and modern liberalism of the first two generations of anti-totalitarian liberalism was abandoned during the last third of the twentieth century, and the gulf between the two became an abyss. John Rawls's egalitarian liberalism moved much further in the direction of state intervention than fin de siècle liberals had ever imagined. Inequality itself and illiberal attitudes were seen as the latest forms of totalitarianism. At the same time Rawls wrestled with the problem of how to persuade a world of plural values, including illiberal values, to accept the legitimacy of a liberal political and social order. On the other side of the spectrum both the libertarian Robert Nozick and the neoliberal Milton Friedman returned to classical liberal positions and regarded liberal egalitarianism itself as a form of despotic totalitarianism.

Despite their strong divergences, all these third-generation liberals had two important things in common. First, they represented the revival of avowedly utopian liberal thought after the attempts by end of ideology thinkers to banish it from liberalism (admittedly, in some ways an equally utopian dream of a world that had never existed). Second, they either eliminated (neoliberals) or greatly narrowed (Rawls, Nozick, and Shklar, in very different ways), the moral / religious pillar of liberalism. Rawls, for all his moralism, renounced any form of liberal perfectionism, as did Nozick and Friedman. There was a general tendency to base liberalism on only one or two kinds of argument.

An exception to the renewed attraction of utopia for liberal thought among the third generation of anti-totalitarian liberals was the liberalism of fear promoted during the same period by Shklar and Bernard Williams. Like the end of ideology movement, they regarded all forms of utopianism as fundamentally totalitarian, or at least very dangerous. The liberalism of fear was also perhaps the only liberalism of the period that still strove to bridge the modern / classical liberal divide, or rather the egalitarian / libertarian divide, in this faithfully reflecting its origins in the end of ideology movement. Williams also broke with the tendencies of the time by regarding a broad moral pillar with a perfectionist component as essential for liberal legitimacy. Shklar and Williams, although far less influential than their contemporaries, foreshadowed some of the issues raised in the early twenty-first century by the rise of populism.

Chapter 11, "Liberalism and Populism," examines how a new fear, the fear of populism, took center stage in the early twenty-first century. In some respects the rise of populism represents the return to prominence of problems previously faced (or suppressed) by liberals, in particular radical nationalism, and more generally the relationship of liberalism to illiberal groups. Nevertheless, populism has left liberals perplexed as to how to respond. Part of the reason for this is historical. There is an important way in which post–WWII liberalisms faced a situation that was unique by comparison with all previous liberalisms and even proto-liberalisms: for all practical purposes, after WWII liberals had no enemies on the right. This temporary blessing, however, left liberals ill-prepared in the early twenty-first century to respond to the growing power and appeal of illiberal populisms. In a number of respects, whether in relation to religious fanaticism, radical nationalism, or mass political participation, populism forced liberals to confront problems they thought had been solved or, if not solved, at least relegated to the dark corners of a liberal Western world. After 2000, as populism has become the new focus of liberal fear, the return of these issues to prominence has left liberals searching for effective responses.

An additional historical reason for the difficulties liberals have encountered in formulating their response to populism has been the reliance of third-wave liberalism on narrowly based arguments, and in particular on the elimination of liberal perfectionism and a broad moral / religious pillar from liberal arguments. The development of Liberalism 4.0 has been especially handicapped by the hollowing-out of the moral pillar of liberalism. A return to three-pillared arguments for liberalism will be necessary, even if not necessarily sufficient for a fourth wave of liberalism to succeed, or even to survive. It will require a return to the combination of perfectionism and utilitarianism common among liberals in the nineteenth century and the fin de siècle. This renewed liberal emphasis on morality calls into question some previous liberal strategies, notably the morally neutral version of pluralism many liberals embraced after WWII. Liberalism 4.0, however, is still seeking firm footing.

There is yet another way in which this history is incomplete: while it is transatlantic, it is not global. Furthermore, even within the limited confines of the United States, Britain, France, and Germany some very important issues are left out, either because they pertain to only one country, or because they have relatively little impact on the evolution of liberalism. For example, the most important issue confronting American liberals for most of the nineteenth century was slavery. Despite the importance the issue had for European politics, there were no European analogues to the American Civil War, Reconstruction, etc., and the struggle against slavery did not really add new intellectual dimensions to liberal thought—there was no such thing as a liberal defense of slavery (Locke, some readers may need to be reminded, was not a liberal as far as the nineteenth century was concerned). This is not the only such exception. The French liberal debate about the compatibility of monarchy with liberalism is left aside because it too had no real analogues in other countries, and did not broadly alter liberal ideas. Both American liberalism's failure to find liberal solutions to slavery and racism, despite a civil war, and French liberalism's long struggle with the idea of monarchy were important chapters in the national histories of liberalism, but they do not have a place here.

The search for a society in which no one need be afraid remains unfinished. The hope that it will one day be achieved remains both alive and unfulfilled. This history, therefore, is necessarily incomplete.

2

Before the Revolutions

THE PROTO-LIBERALISM of the late eighteenth century was still motivated by the fear of religious fanaticism instilled by the Wars of Religion, but had nevertheless evolved considerably. The meaning of the adjective "liberal," not yet political, not yet a noun, was in flux—as so often in its future.

From Cicero to the seventeenth century, the most prominent meaning of the word had to do with generosity, especially on the part of the elite. The antonym for "liberal" was "greedy." A liberal person gave gifts, distributed charity, and spent a lot of money, although liberality was sharply distinguished from prodigality. "Liberal" was also used in an educational sense. A liberal arts education was intended to develop moral excellence in an elite devoted to public service, as befitted a free man—hence the common derivation of "liberal arts" from the Latin "liber," meaning free. John Donne's (1572–1631) use of "liberal" in a sermon dexterously combined generosity with education. He asked his listeners to show their "liberality" by divesting themselves of all "ill affections towards other men" and by spending "all their faculties of mind, of body, of fortune, upon the public." To be liberal thus meant not only to be financially generous, but to take an interest in the community.[1]

In the eighteenth century "liberal" continued to be used in the sense of generosity and public service, but the word's meaning expanded. Eighteenth-century writers discussed not only liberal individuals, but "liberal sentiments," "liberal ideas," and a "liberal way of thinking." One London club described its purpose as being "mutual improvement by liberal conversation and rational

1. Rosenblatt, *Lost History*, 69.

enquiry." It would disseminate freedom of thought and liberality of spirit, which would be conducive to "progress."[2]

Even more significantly, the word "liberal" began to be applied to a society or a period as a whole. People, like those in that London club, described their age as one when liberal sentiments were spreading and liberal ideas becoming general. This liberal movement was linked by proto-liberals to the growth of religious toleration, and tolerance became a meaning of the word "liberal." The *Oxford English Dictionary* states that by 1772, the word liberal had come to mean "free from bias, prejudice, or bigotry; open-minded, tolerant." Beyond the religious and educational spheres, the word liberal, drawing in part on its underlying meaning of generosity, began to be applied to politics, where a "liberal constitution" or "liberal charter" meant one in which the monarch offered a generous helping of autonomy and legal rights to his subjects. A liberal economics was generous in granting the right to work in any trade, in contrast to the monopolies of the guilds, and allowed the import or export of all commodities. In the eighteenth century "liberal" was still only an adjective, and "liberalism" did not exist, but the adjective was being widely applied to politics, economics, and religion / morality. In the context of their times, then, liberal was a word that certainly applied to Montesquieu (1689–1755) and Smith (1723–1790), even though it meant something different than it did later on.

Smith and Montesquieu are crucial to the history of liberalism not because they were liberals in the nineteenth-century sense; they were not. They still focused chiefly on the threat of despotism and religious fanaticism, and they lacked the new fears, new hopes, and new vocabulary that revolutions would bring. They are essential, however, to understanding how and why freedom, markets, and morals seemed to naturally stand together for so many post-revolutionary liberals, and how civil society came to be the basis for liberal hopes of putting an end to despotism. Montesquieu and Smith are not the only eighteenth-century thinkers who might be chosen to illustrate this point, but they were towering figures. Though they came from different traditions of thought, and wrote in full consciousness of their nations' particular problems, they saw freedom, markets, and morals both as necessary elements of analysis and as the foundation for a viable commercial society. As proto-liberals, they are like the last kings of the previous dynasty in a royal genealogy, connected somehow to the new rulers despite the great red line of the revolutions separating them.

2. Rosenblatt, *Lost History*, 27.

Moderating the Modern State: Montesquieu

Montesquieu's work is foundational because of its immense influence and power; because of its focus on combating despotism in modern commercial societies; and because of the pluralism it displays in both values and methods of analysis. Perhaps an additional reason for its influence is that it is so protean in nature that it has something to offer everyone, while seeming to slip the grasp of whoever tries to hold it firmly. Nevertheless, its role in the prologue to liberalism is perhaps greater than any other.

In *The Spirit of the Laws*, Montesquieu reflected not about finding the best form of government, but about avoiding the worst.[3] Despotism, the primeval fear of liberalism, was Montesquieu's great fear. The purpose of his political science was to make us all afraid, so that we would act accordingly: "In a time of ignorance, one has no doubts even while doing the greatest evils; in an enlightened age, one trembles even while doing the greatest goods." Before people acted, they needed to understand how easy it was for power, even with the best of intentions, to become an instrument of evil and cruelty. Freedom for Montesquieu was based on guarantees against the abuse of power, hence the need for limited governments and for political, economic, and moral / religious systems that limited them: they created and preserved spaces in which individuals could live without fear. Montesquieu was hardly the first proto-liberal to emphasize limiting power, a classic theme of liberalism, but he was one of the most important and influential.[4]

Rather than emphasizing eternal natural laws and their effects, Montesquieu spent most of *The Spirit of the Laws* in the realm of the contingent, discussing different possible forms of government, a discussion that rapidly branched into moral, religious, and economic questions. Since Montesquieu chose to build the political frameworks for these discussions first, it is useful to follow his lead and begin with politics before addressing morals and economics.

Montesquieu used two different typologies to describe governments. He did not use the ancient Greek three-part typology of regimes familiar to his readers: democracies, aristocracies, and monarchies, or the rule of the many, the few, or one. His first typology divided governments into republics, mon-

---

3. The analysis of Montesquieu that follows will confine itself to *The Spirit of the Laws*, henceforth *SL*, without referring to either *The Persian Letters* or his other writings.

4. Binoche, *Introduction*, 24; *SL*, xliv.

archies, and despotisms. The republic was further divided into two subtypes, democracy and aristocracy. This effectively brought readers back to Aristotle's three types, with despotism representing all three Classical forms of corruption.[5] Montesquieu's tripartite framework was then overlaid with a second typology, one that divided governments into two kinds: moderate and immoderate. All despotisms were immoderate governments, but not all republics and monarchies were moderate regimes. And then there was the question of freedom, repeatedly introduced by Montesquieu, who noted that not all moderate governments were free and that civil freedom was not the same as political freedom. Moderation and the limitation of power were necessary to establish a society in which people could be free from fear, which Montesquieu identified with freedom and which was the goal of liberalism.

The importance of moderation to Montesquieu came in part from the key role it played in making political freedom possible. Moderation was essential to political freedom, but the relationship was complex. To begin with one of Montesquieu's paradoxes, "Political liberty is found only in moderate governments. But it is not always in moderate states. It is present only when power is not abused. . . . so that one cannot abuse power, power must check power by the arrangement of things." At first glance this seems contradictory. In a moderate government, all powers were limited, so how could power be abused? The answer was that even if institutions, constitutions, and mores limited and moderated power, "it has eternally been observed that any man who has power is led to abuse it." Individuals would strive to evade the limits on their power, and this was dangerous even if their motivations were good. "Who would think it! Even virtue has need of limits." Individuals as well as institutions had to be moderated, whether they were virtuous or not, by the clashing views of other individuals with different conceptions of the public good if they were virtuous, or by clashing personal ambitions if they were not.[6]

Both democracies and aristocracies could be moderate according to Montesquieu, as could monarchies, provided the power of the monarch was moderated. The Spirit of the Laws was an encyclopedic handbook on how to create a moderate government wherever and whenever one lived: "I say it, and it seems to me that I have written this work only to prove it: the spirit of moderation should be that of the legislator; the political good, like the moral good, is always

5. The corruption of democracy is mob rule; of aristocracy, oligarchy; and of monarchy, tyranny.
6. SL, 155.

found between two limits." This applied even to freedom. "The natural place of virtue is with liberty, but virtue can no more be found with extreme liberty than with servitude." The means of moderation would vary: Sometimes political freedom was impossible, sometimes markets could not function, sometimes morals were irredeemably corrupt. Freedoms, markets, and morals needed to take diverse forms, to respond to diverse circumstances. The science of the legislator, as he conceived it, was to calculate the stress each one could bear in specific circumstances. Moderation was a guideline, not a blueprint.[7]

Political freedom nevertheless had a special role to play in moderating governments. It was not the only kind of freedom, and if pursued to the exclusion of all other freedoms it would destroy them and itself. Nevertheless, it had a special status. Political freedom was not, Montesquieu stated, contrary to classical and republican views, the ability to participate in political decision-making. Rather, it was determined by the feeling one had of one's safety. This perspective put him firmly in the proto-liberal camp. From this Montesquieu concluded that political freedom was found in moderate monarchies as well as moderate republics (both aristocracies and democracies), and that a person was free who need not fear that any individual or group could take away their life or property.

Freedom did not exist without laws. However, freedom was not only the product of laws or constitutions, but of how they were practiced. "It can happen that the constitution is free and that the citizen is not. The citizen can be free and the constitution not. In these instances, the constitution will be free by right and not in fact; the citizen will be free in fact and not by right." Montesquieu never privileged one mechanism. Although laws and constitutions were certainly valuable in moderating powers and creating freedom, "it is not enough to treat political liberty in its relation to the constitution; it must be shown in its relation to the citizen. . . . Only the disposition of the laws, and especially of the fundamental laws, forms liberty in its relation to the constitution. But, in relation to the citizen, mores, manners, and received examples can give rise to it and certain civil laws can favour it."[8]

In fact, Montesquieu had more than one definition of political freedom. Two lists of definitions can be found in *The Spirit of the Laws*. The first list

---

7. *SL*, 602, 114. On Montesquieu and moderation, see Binoche, *Introduction*, 2, 7, 25, 245, 354; Aurelian Craiutu, *A Virtue for Courageous Minds*, 40, 68; Larrère, "Montesquieu and Liberalism," 290.

8. Binoche, *Introduction*, 243 ; *SL*, 187.

defined liberty as the citizen's ability to act freely within the law. The second list focused on the individual's *perception* of their freedom—a perception that was in turn fostered by the liberty described in the first series.[9] It was the individual's ability to act as they wished under the law, and their perception of this ability, that constituted freedom. One had to be legally entitled to express one's political opinion, have nothing to fear from expressing it, and be aware of both.[10]

Politics often took first place in Montesquieu's considerations, but often took a back seat. Freedom was not necessarily the goal of a free government, at least not its direct purpose. Freedom, like happiness, was often best acquired by indirect means. Make freedom the purpose of your system of government, and you might end up with despotism (see the French Revolution, liberals would later remark). Try to create a moderate government, and freedom might be a much-cherished by-product. "The monarchies we know do not have liberty for their direct purpose . . . they aim only for the glory of the citizens, the state and the prince. But this glory results in a spirit of liberty that can, in these states, produce equally great things and can perhaps contribute as much to happiness as liberty itself."[11]

How "the spirit of liberty" should be distinguished from "liberty" itself was probably a question of the difference of monarchical versus republican forms, about which Montesquieu was indifferent. Indeed, he emphasized this by flouting the common sense of the Enlightenment and vaunting the merits of the despised "Gothic" post-medieval form of government, a mixture of aristocracy and monarchy. It had the drawback, Montesquieu admitted, that the common people were slaves, i.e., serfs, when it began. But the people were soon liberated, and as a result, "the civil liberty of the people, the prerogatives of the nobility and of the clergy, and the power of the kings were in such concert that there has never been, I believe, government on earth as well-tempered as that of each part of Europe during the time that this government continued to exist."[12]

The political pillar for freedom and for proto-liberalism in Montesquieu thus could be appropriately constructed out of many different materials,

9. Binoche, *Introduction*, 286–289. The first list is found in books XI and XXV, the second in books XL and XII. See for example *SL*, 155, 157.

10. *SL*, 154–155, 187–188.

11. *SL*, 166.

12. *SL*, 167.

depending on circumstances. But some elements were to be found every-where: public controversy that simultaneously bred passions and channeled them; intermediate bodies or decentralized administration; the separation of the executive, legislative, and judicial powers. For similar reasons, many nineteenth-century liberals would adopt the doctrine of *e pluribus libertas*, and stress the importance of a free press, clashing factions, decentralization, and constitutional government.

Montesquieu offered many responses to the question of *how* to be free, but they all involved public controversy and political passion. In a virtuous repub-lic, one debated what was in the public interest; in a monarchy, there were public clashes of ambition and interest. Because freedom always involved mul-tiple conceptions of what should be done, "every time one sees everyone tran-quil in a state which calls itself a republic, one can be assured that liberty does not exist there. . . . True union is a union of harmony which makes all the parts, as opposed as they appear to us to be, participate in the general good of the society, just as dissonances in music participate in the overall harmony . . . , a harmony from which results the happiness which alone is true peace." The point was just as valid for a properly functioning monarchy. Montesquieu's endorsement of diversity was a precursor of its later role in liberalism.[13]

At a different level a free people, whether republican or monarchical, whether motivated by virtue or ambition, was a people of many passions, a nation where "hatred, envy, jealousy, and the ardor for enriching and distin-guishing oneself . . . appear to their full extent, and if this were otherwise, the state would be like a man who, laid low by disease, has no passions because he has no strength." A multiplicity of views and a multiplicity of goods encour-aged moderation, as for example in the state with many religions. Diversity was valuable even in the republic, since in a flourishing republic while all fought for the common good, they conceived of it in many different ways. Debate and discussion were essential limits on power. The ability of a body of representatives to debate in a way that would not be possible for the people as a whole was a great advantage of representative government, according to Montesquieu. Debate was also natural to a monarchy, since the various inter-mediate bodies and the individuals who composed them would all pursue their individual and corporate ambitions.[14]

13. *Considérations*, cited in Larrère, 292; *SL*,168.
14. *SL*, 325, 159. Craiutu, *A Virtue for Courageous Minds*, 49, 63.

Opinion was meant to be divided because society was meant to be divided. For Montesquieu uniformity meant despotism, societies in which everyone was equally the slave of the ruler. Thus Montesquieu does not grant "the people" sole power in democracies. "In a state there are always some people who are distinguished by birth, wealth, or honors; but if they were mixed among the people and if they had only one vote like the others, the common liberty would be their enslavement and they would have no interest in defending it . . . therefore they need to form a body which can check the people, as the people can check them." Since there will always be an elite, the people should not be able to silence the elite, just as the elite must not be able to silence the people. Both people and elite, through their representatives, should form the legislative power, but not only should the legislature check the executive, it should be divided in itself. Montesquieu supported bicameralism.[15]

The theory of the separation of powers, the idea that the executive, legislative, and judicial branches of government should check and balance one another, is the most famous form of pluralism associated with Montesquieu. If the legislative and executive powers are combined, "there is no liberty." According to Montesquieu, although many rulers in Europe possessed both these powers, since they left the judicial power to their subjects the government was still moderate. Perhaps Montesquieu would resolve the tension by distinguishing freedom in relation to the constitution from freedom in relation to the citizen. The judicial power dealt with individuals in civil life, rather than in politics, constitutional life. Therefore an independent judiciary could moderate government in civil life even though the combination of the executive and legislative powers threatened moderation in political life.[16]

Besides the judiciary, there were other political means of moderating a government that combined executive and legislative power, such as decentralization, the existence of intermediate bodies and powers, etc. But this was one of the cases where Montesquieu deliberately left his thought unfinished: "I should like to seek out in all the moderate governments we know the distribution of the three powers and calculate thereupon the degrees of liberty each one of them can enjoy. But one must not always so exhaust a subject that one leaves nothing for the reader to do. It is not a question of making him read but of making him think." The implication was clear enough. The more separation

15. *SL*, 160; I have replaced "voice" with "vote" in the translation of *voix*. Binoche, *Introduction*, 260–261.

16. *SL*, 157.

among and within powers, the more room for freedom, the more freedom from fear.[17]

Like many nineteenth-century liberals, Montesquieu simultaneously insisted on the need for a moral pillar and the diversity of possible moral foundations. People in republics, that is democracies and aristocracies, were motivated chiefly but not exclusively by virtue, according to Montesquieu, whereas people in monarchies were motivated chiefly by honor. Both virtue and honor provided incentives for behavior that was useful, as well as that would lead to moral perfection and greatness. For him the perfection of human character was the same as that of human government, namely moderation. His perfectionism has escaped many observers because they expect the ideal character, whether of an individual or a society, to always look the same. His perfectionism has thus been ignored because of its seeming eclecticism. Montesquieu's one best thing *looked* different every time it was encountered, both in individuals and states, whereas the perfection envisaged by the Church or by Plato looked the same everywhere. One proof that for Montesquieu perfection had many faces is that the sole government to which Montesquieu gave unqualified praise was what he called "Gothic government," the medieval European form of government which in practice he knew was different everywhere. Montesquieu was a liberal pluralist in his own context well before Isaiah Berlin identified liberalism with pluralism and the rejection of monism (see chapter 9). He combined utilitarianism and perfectionism, a combination that would be typical of much later liberalism. Montesquieu's use of both to create and support a moderate society, one without fear, was a prominent example of the endorsement of diverse moral perspectives in support of a common goal. From its proto-liberal beginnings, liberalism thus combined utilitarian and perfectionist perspectives.[18]

This can be seen in his discussion of the moral principles of monarchies and republics. Montesquieu distinguished between the moral principle of monarchy, which was honor, and the moral principle of republics, virtue. To begin with monarchy, honor made people in a monarchy act, motivated them, and made monarchy work. Montesquieu defined honor as "the prejudice of each person and each condition." By "prejudice," Montesquieu meant a prejudice in favor of oneself as an individual and as a member of a specific group. It was

17. SL, 186.

18. Krause contends that honor leads to "self-mastery" rather than to "perfection," but self-mastery is a form of perfection. See Krause, *Liberalism with Honor*, 6.

related to the ambition to distinguish oneself (and one's group) and led to great actions. The honor of the nobility was not the only kind, but it was the archetypal variety, and thus it was only natural that in monarchies, where the nobility flourished, honor "takes the place of the political virtue of which I have spoken. . . . It can inspire the finest actions; joined with the force of the laws, it can lead to the goal of government as does virtue itself."[19]

Honor in a monarchy motivated people to resist despotism and arbitrary authority. Montesquieu told the story of a royal governor during the French Wars of Religion who refused the King's order to murder all his town's Protestants, not because such an order was illegal or immoral, but because it would be dishonorable for him, his soldiers, or indeed any of the town's inhabitants to fill the base and cowardly role of executioner. The governor nevertheless assured the King he would hasten to obey any order that was not contrary to honor. Honor thus served to moderate government because it was more precious than the life one risked by refusing to obey. "In monarchical and moderate states, power is limited by that which is its spring; I mean honor, which reigns like a monarch over the prince and the people." Honor commanded obedience to the ruler, but only as long as the ruler did not command anything contrary to honor.[20]

The governor was not a good man, since he was motivated neither by love of his Protestant fellow citizens nor by love of the nation. Nevertheless the search for personal glory would lead people motivated by honor to risk their lives and fortunes in ways just as useful to the state as the same actions motivated by virtue. One can take two views of Montesquieu's use of honor: either it was effectively a different kind of virtue, or it represented a cynical disassociation of virtue and the common good—and perhaps both readings are correct. If we drop the word cynical, what we see is that Montesquieu used honor in both a utilitarian and a perfectionist way. It made people do great things, even if from motives that from a religious perspective were "false," and it made the state run well.[21]

To avoid criticism in his own time, Montesquieu had to make clear that in basing monarchies on honor and dispensing with virtue he was only talking about *political* virtue, not moral or Christian virtue. In addition, he pleaded

19. *SL*, 21, 26, 22, 24.

20. *SL*, 30, 33, 27; Spector, "Honor"; in *A Montesquieu Dictionary*, http://dictionnaire -montesquieu.ens-lyon.fr/en/article/1376474900/en/; Binoche, *Introduction*, 121.

21. *SL*, 31, 58.

that just because virtue was not the principle of monarchical government, that did not mean that virtue did not exist in monarchies. Nevertheless, in the Catholic monarchy in which he lived, he could not escape censure. His statement that "in well-regulated monarchies everyone will be almost a good citizen, and one will rarely find someone who is a good man; for, in order to be a good man, one must have the intention of being one" attracted the condemnation of the theologians of the Sorbonne, despite the footnote Montesquieu added that "these words, *good man*, are to be taken here only in a political sense." But the point was sufficiently important to Montesquieu that he insisted on making it despite the criticism he knew would follow. It was essential that future lawmakers recognize that "not all moral vices are political vices," just as "not all political vices are moral vices." Honor served to uphold freedom and moderation, not to make people saints or even get them to heaven. And, unlike religion, where it was possible there was one "best" path, "human laws enact about the good" and "there are several goods." Honor was not the only possible moral foundation for freedom, according to Montesquieu. Virtue could play a similar role.[22]

If honor was the moral pillar of monarchy, virtue was the moral pillar of republics, both democracies and aristocracies. Montesquieu defined virtue as the love of the nation and of equality. Virtue was necessary above all in democracies. It was necessary in aristocracies, too, but less so because in aristocracies the people were constrained by the nobility, so they didn't need to be virtuous. The aristocrats themselves, however, needed some degree of virtue, either "a great virtue, that makes the nobles in some way equal to their people, which may form a great republic, or a lesser virtue, a certain moderation that renders the nobles at least equal among themselves, which brings about their preservation."[23]

Virtue required "a continual preference of the public interest over one's own." The only personal ambition one should cherish was that of "rendering greater services to one's homeland than other citizens." Virtue had to be taught, notably by parents to their children. This education was not learning a set of facts, but imbibing emotions. Virtue "is a feeling and not the result of knowledge." Education also had to make sure that each citizen had "the same happiness and the same advantages, must taste the same pleasures, and develop the same hopes." The result was a kind of virtuous circle. "Love of the homeland

22. *SL*, xli, 26, 26n2, 314; 29.
23. *SL*, 21, 26, 22, 24.

leads to good mores, and good mores leads to love of the homeland." Thus virtue would motivate people to strive for the happiness and moral perfection of their society.[24]

In traditional moral accounts, both Christian and republican, it was particularly difficult to reconcile virtue with a commercial society. In ancient Sparta, traditionally considered the epitome of virtue, commerce and money had been banned. In modern commercial societies, therefore, it seemed that virtue would be very hard to achieve. Montesquieu rejected the standard narrative, first by doubting even ancient virtue, which after all people had never actually seen, but had only read about in history books: "all those heroic virtues we find in the ancients and know only by hearsay." But this was not enough. Montesquieu needed to reconcile commerce and virtue in modern societies if virtue was to be a moral pillar for moderation in the modern world and not just an historical curiosity.[25]

Montesquieu argued that this was both possible and real. In modern commercial societies, the market could encourage virtue, rather than corrupt it, as the Spartans thought. For example, if frugality was necessary for virtue, as the ancients and moderns agreed, who could be more virtuous than the Dutch, that modern trading people famous for their frugality? Holland and Sparta were both frugal, and both rejected despotism, despite being radically different societies. The desire to earn money by commerce was not avarice, and the frugality of the merchant was not license. Since wealth and frugality were not opposed, according to Montesquieu, modern commerce was not necessarily a source of corruption. "When democracy is founded on commerce, it may very well happen that individuals have great wealth, yet that the mores are not corrupted. This is because the spirit of commerce brings with it the spirit of frugality, economy, moderation, work, wisdom, tranquility, order, and rule." The market was not opposed to virtue, rather the spirit of commerce was the source of many virtues. Montesquieu explicitly rejected Cicero's claim that a great nation should not also be a nation of shopkeepers. In republics "great commercial enterprises" were possible. Markets could contribute to our greatness as well as satisfy our needs. Commerce and the republic were thus natural allies in the modern world.[26]

24. *SL*, 36, 43, 42.
25. *SL*, 25.
26. Binoche, *Introduction*, 117; *SL*, 23, 25, 48, 340–341. However, "excessive" wealth (the difference between "great" and "excessive" wealth is not explored) led to "disorders of inequality."

The traditional source of virtue was not commerce but religion, and religion was a particularly important subject for Montesquieu to deal with in the circumstances of eighteenth-century France, where the fear of religious fanaticism was central to proto-liberalism. According to Montesquieu, religion in general, and Christianity in particular, could have either good or bad political effects. Religion was potentially both ally and enemy, sometimes the last friend of freedom in despotisms, sometimes its mortal enemy in a monarchy or republic—or its most important ally. Montesquieu was attempting to walk some very fine lines: to avoid condemnation by the Church; to defend the need or at least the utility of a morality founded on religion; and to warn against religious fanaticism. The question was "which is the lesser evil, that one sometimes abuse religion or that there be none among men." Montesquieu preferred to run the risk of religion, at the risk of being condemned for insufficient loyalty to the "true" one. "It is much more evident to us that a religion should soften the mores of men than it is that a religion is true." Like honor and virtue, religion could also be a moral support for moderation and freedom.[27]

Thus Montesquieu argued that religious belief was better for society than atheism, and that a good Christian was a good citizen.[28] On the other hand, the power of religion, like any other power, could be abused. When religion attempted to turn its ideals into laws, for example creating a legal ban on usury because it was good to lend money without charging interest, religion overstepped its bounds and became a force for evil. It was for human laws to decide about such rules, whereas counsels of spiritual perfection were the domain of religion, which should limit itself to the most basic laws. But the role of religion should vary according to circumstances: "the less repressive religion is, the more the civil laws should repress." Montesquieu left open how many religions a state should have. While one should always tolerate existing religions, whether or not to accept new ones depended on how useful the old ones were.[29]

In his discussions of honor, virtue, commerce, and religion, Montesquieu sought to highlight sources of moderation and freedom that were appropriate to different kinds of governments and shared a common ability to serve mod-

---

Montesquieu advised that inherited fortunes should be divided equally among the children in commercial republics in order to prevent this. *SL*, 48.

27. Binoche, *Introduction*, 320; *SL*, 472, 460, 462.

28. He was arguing against the opposite case made by Pierre Bayle.

29. Binoche, *Introduction*, 321, 324; *SL*, 30, 468, 325–326.

ern European societies. All could lead to behavior useful to the state. All could be the basis of moderate government, and all could lead to greatness in the individual and the state. The moral pillar of freedom in Montesquieu was as broad and wide as possible, and its best construction was a matter of circumstances.

The circumstances that were most interesting or at least most instructive to Montesquieu, and certainly of most interest to nineteenth-century liberals, were those of a free commercial society. For his account of one, to see how he portrayed the actual working of freedom, markets, and morals in a contemporary situation, we must turn to his celebrated analysis of England. Many of Montesquieu's readers have thought, unlike Montesquieu, that there was only one good constitutional model, and only one good kind of government. They therefore misread Montesquieu by assuming that England either was or was not the embodiment of that ideal, and that if it was, it was the only incarnation. But for Montesquieu there were many ways to achieve moderation and freedom, and they could be quite different from one another. One country with a free and moderate government might offer some lessons for others, but in important respects every example was unique. Nevertheless, understanding the portrayal of England in *The Spirit of the Laws* is crucial to understanding Montesquieu's proto-liberalism.[30]

From the perspective of the history of liberalism, what is particularly interesting about the English example is that in his account Montesquieu downplayed the importance of the externals of politics, such as whether there was a king, or even whether the government was an aristocracy or a democracy. The political discussion of England, despite being titled "On the constitution of England," focused not on the big constitutional questions about monarchy or republic, honor or virtue, but on the level beneath, on laws and mores. England was a place where arbitrary power was restrained judicially by juries, written statutes, and precedents. Bail and habeas corpus existed. The laws were made not by direct democracy, but by the largely preferable form of representative government, with the representatives elected locally, not nationally. There was a parliament for discussing public business, with a bicameral legislature: the House of Lords prevented the wealthy and distinguished from being oppressed by the masses, who dominated the House of Commons. The monarch had a right of veto, necessary to protect the executive against the legislature, etc. The system was one of freedom founded on law. "It is not for

30. Larrère, "Montesquieu and Liberalism," 297; *SL,* 166–167.

me to examine whether at present the English enjoy this liberty or not. It suffices for me to say that it is established by their laws, and I seek no further."[31]

Montesquieu did not care very much if England was a monarchy or a republic, as long as it was free. A few pages after he concluded his discussion of the constitution of England in Book XI, he suggested that "states are often more flourishing during the imperceptible shift from one constitution to another than they are under either constitution. At that time all the springs of government are stretched; all the citizens have claims . . . there is a noble rivalry between those who defend the declining constitution and those who put forward the one that prevails." England's freedom thus served as proof of Montesquieu's statement that "it is not a drawback when the state passes from moderate government to moderate government, as from republic to monarchy, or from monarchy to republic, but rather when it falls and collapses from moderate government into despotism."[32]

Nevertheless the freedom England experienced during this transition might be too much of a good thing: "I do not claim hereby to disparage other governments, or to say that this extreme political liberty should humble those who have only a moderate one. How could I say that, I who believe that the excess even of reason is not always desirable and that men almost always accommodate themselves better to middles than to extremities." England indeed was at risk of despotism—as had already been seen under Charles I and Cromwell. Its laws established an extreme liberty, and were based on extreme political passions. For Montesquieu extremism of any sort was dangerous, but the genius of the English constitution lay in the way in which it harnessed passions and turned political conflicts to the benefit of the state. In English circumstances, passion motivated freedom: "The customs of a slave people are part of their servitude; those of a free people are part of their liberty." Thus in his exploration of "the mores, manners, and character" of the English nation, Montesquieu discovered that the separation of powers did not moderate political passions. If anything it fanned them because "most people would have more affection for one of the powers than the other." But the moderation of the laws and the government did not allow passions to be satisfied by complete triumph over the other side. These unsatisfied passions, which changed sides as individuals changed allegiances to the executive or the legislature as governments succeeded one another, gave people a real love of freedom, the freedom

31. *SL*, 156, 166.
32. *SL*, 173, 118.

that gave them the opportunity to express their passions. Passions being balanced by each other as well as by laws that maintained everyone's freedom, moderation ensued. Because people loved their freedom, they were willing to pay high taxes to maintain it, and what could be a greater sign of moderation than someone docilely paying high taxes?[33]

England thus showed how political moderation was produced by allowing passions to multiply in the context of the separation of powers; politics and morals reinforced each other. Party passions fulfilled the functions of both aristocratic intermediate bodies and democratic virtue, giving the executive the force to maintain its prerogative against the legislative, and vice versa. Freedom was morally supported not by monarchical honor or republican virtue, but by passion, provided the passions were plural and conflicted with one another. One constant with the rest of Montesquieu's analysis seems to be the importance of diversity / pluralism. But there was one domain where England's passions were not many but one, and thus not moderate: commerce. If England, in its own way, represented political and moral moderation, when it came to markets its moderation was more than dubious.

Its commercial passion did help maintain English freedom domestically. It encouraged the moderate virtues of frugality, order, etc. Internationally, however, English commerce was anything but moderate. Indeed, Montesquieu's account of English commerce took him far from the views of commerce usually attributed to him. Commerce normally had the effect, according to Montesquieu's famous "*doux commerce*" thesis, of leading to peace between nations as they became mutually dependent on one another for trade. But with the English the result was the opposite:

> A commercial nation has a prodigious number of small, particular interests; therefore, it can offend and be offended in an infinity of ways. This nation [England] would become sovereignly jealous and would find more distress in the prosperity of others than enjoyment in its own.
>
> And its laws, otherwise gentle and easy, might be so rigid in regard to the commerce and navigation carried on with it that it would seem to negotiate only with enemies. . . .
>
> It could be that it had formerly subjugated a neighboring nation [Ireland] which, by its situation, the goodness of its ports, and the nature of its wealth,

---

33. *SL*, 166, 325. On Montesquieu's use of the passions generally, see Alberto Hirschman's *The Passions and the Interests*, and the long line of scholarship it has spawned.

made the first [England] jealous; thus, although it had given that nation its own laws, the great dependence in which the nation was held was such that the citizens would be free and the state itself would be enslaved.[34]

This was very different from the well-known argument made a few pages later that "the natural effect of commerce is to lead to peace." English imperialism in Ireland was motivated by commercial jealousy, and its commercial behavior was in general anything but gentle. England was a warlike commercial society, even if it was not interested in conquest for conquest's sake, according to Montesquieu. When it founded colonies, it founded them for commercial profit, not tribute money. England's international commerce was a sort of parallel expression of its party passions, but in a foreign context where they had no need to moderate themselves. They were the motivating force of English foreign policy: "Other nations have made commercial interests give way to political interests: England has always made its political interests give way to the interests of its commerce." If Montesquieu at least provisionally admired England's domestic freedom, his admiration did not extend to its international role.[35]

Thus, as usual in Montesquieu's analyses, passion played a positive and a negative role in England. It is telling that for the proto-liberal Montesquieu, always afraid of religious fanaticism, the one area where, much to it its advantage, England seemed to lack passion was religion. England for Montesquieu was the world leader in religious indifference or, when seemingly passionate about religion, so confused in its preferences that sects multiplied. The clergy of the established Anglican Church, Montesquieu noted, had little power as a body. The result was a clergy that "unable to protect religion or to be protected by it, lacking force to constrain, would seek to persuade; very fine works would come from their pens, written to prove the revelation and the providence of the great being." The English avoided extremes in religion, and Montesquieu approved. Religion soothed the English after the high-pitched excitement of their political and commercial life. The one respect in which they departed from religious moderation, according to Montesquieu, was revealing: they hated Catholicism because they associated it with slavery. Anti-Catholicism was to have a long history in liberalism, one that extended well beyond England (see chapter 5).[36]

34. SL, 328–329.
35. SL, 343.
36. SL, 331, 330.

In summarizing the sources of English moderation, Montesquieu used a formula that bears a strong resemblance to the argument of this book that liberalism is best served when supported by the three pillars of freedom, markets, and morals / religion: "This is the people in the world who have best known how to take advantage of each of these three great things at the same time: religion, commerce, and liberty." Montesquieu's England modeled a version of what would become the three pillars of liberalism. England, of course, has often been considered liberalism's homeland, and this is one reason why.[37]

Montesquieu's three-pillared analysis of England shows why, in one commentator's words, "if there is continuity to be had from before the American founding and the French Revolution to after, we will find it in the transition from Montesquieu to the generation of Madison and Constant."[38] Despite the continuities, Montesquieu was not motivated by the same fears and hopes as the generation of Madison and Constant. Montesquieu's fear of religion was more direct than that of nineteenth-century liberals (his personal experience of book-banning and censorship demonstrates this) while he came too early to see religion as a bulwark against revolution. Nor was his fear of the state similar in kind to that which afflicted liberals after the French Revolution. The American and French revolutions created a new political world that was not foreseen in *The Spirit of the Laws*. Nineteenth-century liberals wrote constitutions. Montesquieu did not. Nineteenth-century liberals confronted a world in which markets played a still more important role than in the eighteenth century, and in which new technologies aggravated all the moral problems of an industrial society, as Smith had already begun to perceive. Nineteenth-century liberals had to find new responses to new fears, and new grounds for new hopes. Nevertheless, Montesquieu pointed to many of the paths they would follow.

History and Human Nature: Adam Smith

Alongside Montesquieu, Adam Smith presents a good example of the ways in which late eighteenth-century proto-liberalism laid the foundation for liberal thought in the nineteenth century. His economic thought rapidly became the canonical description of how markets worked best when governments left them alone, the famous laissez-faire approach, although Smith endorsed some

37. *SL*, 343.
38. Levy, "Montesquieu's Constitutional Legacies," 118.

important politically and morally motivated exceptions to this rule. While not a systematic political thinker in the manner of Montesquieu, Smith paid far more attention to the political basis of a society free from fear than has sometimes been recognized. At the same time his historical and moral justification of commercial society, like that of Montesquieu, married utilitarian with perfectionist perspectives, and together they created an important model for nineteenth-century liberals. Along with his celebrated embrace of free-market economics, it was Smith's blend of history with moral philosophy that made his work such an important part of the prologue to liberalism.

Smith sought to develop "a theory of the general principles which ought to run through and be the foundation of the laws of all nations." These general principles were to be construed historically, through "all the different revolutions which they have undergone in the different ages and periods of society." Smith summarized these "ages and periods" in what is known as the four-stage theory of history—although it is sometimes only three stages. It differed from the two-stage versions of history familiar from Christianity—before and after the Fall, or before and after Christ—and from the two stages of the natural law tradition of political thought—a stage of natural freedom and a stage of civil government. The move to three or four stages allowed Smith to emphasize the most recent stage, commercial society.[39]

The four stages were "the age of hunters; the age of shepherds; the age of agriculture; and the age of commerce." Laws and institutions needed to be adapted to each stage of society because a good law for shepherds would not necessarily make a good law for farmers or merchants. Smith and the other Scottish thinkers who adopted stadial theory thought that the "system of commerce . . . is the modern system, and is best understood in our own country and in our own times." According to Smith, the nature of commercial society shaped the ways in which modern people experienced freedom and markets and molded their characters. The story was one of progress, although regress was historically possible (e.g., from commercial Imperial Rome to the

---

39. Smith, *Lectures on Jurisprudence*, https://oll.libertyfund.org/title/smith-lectures-on-justice-police-revenue-and-arms-1763#lf1647_head_010, henceforth *LJ*, cited in Winch, "Commercial Realities, Republican Principles," 296–297. The four-stage theory was not unique to Smith. See Moore, "Natural Rights in the Scottish Enlightenment," 311. Smith also sometimes used a three-stage version consisting of hunter/gatherers, pastoral, and agricultural stages in which commercial society appears as an advanced stage within the latter. The details are less important than the overall direction.

pastoral / agricultural German barbarians), and Smith was sensitive to potential drawbacks to commercial society itself. The qualified optimism about commercial society, set within a context of progressive historical development, would become a common trait in nineteenth-century liberalism. It was the development of commercial society that permitted people to be freer from fear than they had ever been and experience an unprecedented level of both material and moral progress.[40]

What made human progress possible, according to Smith, was trade. "The propensity to truck, barter and exchange one thing for another is common to all men, and to be found in no other race of animals." From this trait emerged the division of labor, that is the growth of specialized skills and training. "This same trucking [trading] disposition" led the one who was the best arrow-maker to specialize in arrow-making because then he could trade for more meat than he could hunt himself, and so on. It was the division of labor that had brought about "the greatest improvement in the productive powers of labour"; *The Wealth of Nations* begins with an account of the division of labor. In commercial societies, its "very slow and gradual" progress had finally reached the takeoff stage. Eventually, "every man thus lives by exchanging, or becomes in some measure a merchant, and the society itself grows to be what is properly a commercial society." The economic consequence of specialization was ever more wealth.[41]

Smith's story about the division of labor was not, however, an account of unmitigated blessings. The fact that we are all in some measure merchants and specialists had all kinds of consequences, not just economic, but moral, and political. Smith recognized some serious moral problems that went along with material progress. To use Smith's example, the poor person in a commercial society was materially better off than the African king, but might be worse off morally. One unfortunate moral consequence of commercial society was that the over-specialized worker whose life was wholly devoted to making one part of a pin "has no occasion to exert his understanding. . . . He naturally loses, therefore, the habit of such exertion, and generally becomes as stupid and

40. Smith, *Lectures on Jurisprudence*, 538–541; *Wealth of Nations*, ed. Edwin Cannan (London, 1904, available at https://oll.libertyfund.org/title/smith-an-inquiry-into-the-nature-and-causes-of-the-wealth-of-nations-cannan-ed-vol-1), henceforth *WN*, 1:395. The stages are a matter of ideal types, not a straitjacket for historical development. Too much emphasis on them misreads Smith. See Sagar, *Adam Smith Reconsidered*, 10ff.

41. *WN*, 1:15–21, 24.

ignorant as it is possible for a human creature to become. The torpor of his mind renders him, not only incapable of relishing or bearing a part in any rational conversation, but of conceiving any generous, noble, or tender sentiment." Unfortunately, "in every improved and civilized society this is the state into which the laboring poor, that is, the great body of the people, must necessarily fall, unless government takes some pains to prevent it." Marx borrowed passages like this, and they have led some recent commentators to wonder if Smith was not really a moral critic of capitalism, perhaps some kind of "republican," rather than a "liberal." The question is historically misplaced (see below), but the point remains that for Smith the relationship between freedom, markets, and morals was not without tensions. As with Montesquieu's account of England, Smith found mechanisms by which those tensions could be balanced and freedom from fear preserved.[42]

Thus if commercial society had some bad moral effects, they were balanced by good ones: "before we can feel much for others, we must in some measure be at ease ourselves . . . all savages are too much occupied with their own wants and necessities, to give much attention to those of another person." Wealthy commercial societies were more sensitive than previous epochs to poverty, to love, even to death itself. They provided individuals, and especially the poor, with the protection of law: "In commercial countries . . . the authority of law is always perfectly sufficient to protect the meanest man in the state." Of crucial importance, Smith argued that commercial society liberated the pin-maker from dependence, both moral / psychological and political, on his former noble lords. If his intellectual position was poor by comparison with previous stages of society, it was susceptible of being made better through education. Smith cared as much about morals as about productivity, and from his perspective, markets, morals, and freedom could flourish alongside one another.[43]

Smith was concerned about both the material progress (utility) and the moral character (perfection) of the people who live in improved material circumstances. This combination would be common among liberals during the short nineteenth century. His attention to the intellectual and psychological

42. *WN*, 2:267. Meek, "Smith and Marx"; Tribe, "Adam Smith, Critical Theorist?"; Fleischacker, *On Adam Smith's Wealth of Nations*. For a good summary of the negative consequences Smith attributed to commercial society, see Hanley, *Adam Smith*, 52.

43. Smith, *The Theory of Moral Sentiments*, henceforth *TMS*, 205–206, 223; Winch, "Commercial Realities, Republican Principles," 308. On the positive psychological effects of commercial society, see Castiglione, " 'That noble disquiet,' " 65–66.

effects of commercial society, its broad moral effects alongside its economic consequences, indicated his adoption of both utilitarian *and* perfectionist attitudes to the changes brought about by commercial society. But Smith was not only both a utilitarian and a perfectionist personally: he thought everyone else was too. As a utilitarian, he thought people pursued their own interests and sought to maximize pleasure and minimize pain. As a perfectionist, he thought people inherently looked to others for praise and moreover sought to deserve it, to feel that they were praiseworthy whether or not they were praised. In his view the combination of utilitarian and perfectionist motivations had, over the course of human history, created commercial society and continued to shape its effects.

The division of labor for utilitarian purposes was not Smith's sole mechanism for explaining the progress of civilization, even if Marx chose to think so. There was a moral motivation as well, as much founded in human nature as the propensity to exchange. Smith's theory of moral sentiments played a crucial role in his understanding of the development of modern commercial societies, and made a crucial link between human nature and the historical development of markets and morals. It set an example for nineteenth-century liberals who wanted to show how markets contributed to the moral development of individuals and societies, not just their wealth, and how commercial society represented not just material, but moral progress, and laid the basis for political progress as well.

At the heart of Smith's theory of moral sentiments were the ideas of "sympathy" and "propriety." However selfish we might suppose human beings to be, there was something in human nature that interested people in others, and made others' happiness matter to them. Even "the greatest ruffian" felt some pity, compassion, or sorrow when seeing others' pain. This was because people automatically imagined what they would feel in the other's place. This imaginative identification Smith called "sympathy." It was not necessarily directed at actual people, or at what a real person was actually feeling. "We may feel a passion for a person who does not himself feel it, because we would feel it in his place, or they *ought* to."[44]

Thus, our natural feeling of sympathy inevitably led to the crucial notion of propriety, which turned the fact that people felt sympathy into a set of moral values. People learned how they and others *ought* to feel, what was appropriate (thus "propriety), by observation and instruction. "Custom and fashion"

---

44. *TMS*, 9, 10, 12. Emphasis added.

therefore had enormous influence on our sentiments and sympathies. If human beings grew up in isolation, they would have no more idea of morality than of whether they were beautiful. They learned these things by observing others. As they learned by observing others, so "we suppose ourselves spectators of our own behaviour, and endeavor to imagine what effect it would, in this light, produce upon us." They learned to judge what Smith called "propriety," that is, "the suitableness or unsuitableness" of actions and feelings.[45]

It might seem that Smith's ideas about sympathy and propriety have little to do with the development of commercial society or its impact on the personality, but they were crucial to the entire system of human motivations on which *The Wealth of Nations* was built. People strove to have more than others because they wanted the "attention and approbation" of their fellows, which they had internalized through the spectator within and through the spectator's ability to imaginatively sympathize with what others were feeling, not for direct material reasons. Smith's explanation of historical progress was not based on the search for utility in any material sense. While recognizing the power of material self-interest as a motive, Smith nevertheless put utility second in moral importance and motivational power to propriety. Propriety provided Smith with a means of explaining social progress apart from the utility of the division of labor. The poor person looked at the rich person and imagined that they *ought* to be happier than he was. The poor man thus acquired the ambition to rise in the world, at the expense of lots of unpleasant hard work, because he imagined that when he was rich he would have better means for being happy. A palace would be more fit for the purpose of happiness than a hut. This judgment, even though false from the perspective of maximizing pleasure and minimizing pain, motivated human beings to work hard to "better their condition," and ultimately was behind all social progress.[46]

Elsewhere Smith suggested that the attention attracted by the rich and great was in itself a source of satisfaction to them—and thus another motivation to become wealthy. Getting rich might actually result in happiness because "to be the proper object of esteem, is by every well-disposed mind more valued than all the ease and security [forfeited by the ambitious poor man] ... on the contrary to be odious, to be contemptible [like the poor man] is more dread-

45. TMS, 194, 110, 112, 245, 145, 18, 109–110, 112n, 141n.

46. TMS, 181, 50, 51; Winch, *Adam Smith's Politics*, 184; Hanley, *Adam Smith*, 69; TMS, 188–189, 182.

ful." Propriety, the desire for esteem, trumped any material pleasure / pain calculation.[47]

Further, motivated by their sense of propriety, the rich persons bought luxuries, and by purchasing luxuries to attract esteem, the rich person contributed to the employment of hundreds. Thus, even though the rich acted from purely selfish motives, through their purchases they divided their wealth with the poor. It was at this point that Smith made a rare use of his most famous metaphor: the rich were "led by an invisible hand to make nearly the same distribution of the necessaries of life, which would have been made, had the earth been divided into equal portions among all its inhabitants, and thus without intending it . . . advance the interest of the society." The rich man spent, and everyone ate until they were full, even if not the same quality of food.[48]

Smith argued that propriety, not the search for material benefits and personal happiness, i.e., utility, was the primary motivation of much behavior, and that as a result commercial societies could be the scene of as much moral perfection, if not more, than any past stage of human history—propriety was a constant factor in human motivation, as strong in eighteenth-century commercial Europe as in Sparta. This proto-liberal reconciliation of markets and morals was emblematic of the later history of liberalism. But one set of behaviors motivated by our sense of propriety needs to be singled out because it is key to Smith's moral justification of commercial society—the behaviors that lead to the perfection of human character. Smith wanted to do more than show that commercial society could feed more people without being morally vicious; he wanted to show that commercial society could be morally great. This concern would be widespread among later liberals. It was crucial for Smith to show that commercial society, and for later liberals to show that capitalism and free markets, were compatible with moral progress, despite the situation of the pin-maker. Markets and morals were, or should be, friends. Propriety led to prudence, and it could also lead people to combine prudence with the perfection of other virtues, and thus to greatness. Material progress and moral progress could, should, and would go hand in hand, for Smith and for the liberals who followed.[49]

47. TMS, 298. These luxuries existed much more in commercial societies than previously, when the rich hired servants rather than purchasing watches.

48. TMS, 192; WN, 1:421.

49. TMS, 216–217. There is a parallel here with Tocqueville, who faced the same issue with democratic society as Smith did with commercial society. See Kahan, *Tocqueville, Democracy, and Religion*, 49–67.

Smith made this argument by showing that commercial society was compatible with moral improvement. In all stages of human society, "we are pleased, not only with praise, but with having done what is praise-worthy."[50] Everyone wanted to deserve praise, and thus the search for greatness and perfection had roots in human nature and was present in all stages of society. Nature had endowed people "not only with a desire of being approved of, but with a desire for being what ought to be approved of." Both desires were necessary to make humans fit for society, but it was only the second that could "inspire . . . the real love of virtue."[51] The same impartial spectator within who urged people to strive for wealth also spurred them to "the love of what is honorable and noble, of the grandeur, and dignity, and superiority of our own characters."[52]

Most people wanted no more than an average amount of praiseworthiness, or anything else for that matter, which was why most people were not great, but merely prudent. Smith emphasized that people rarely, perhaps never, judged themselves by only one of these two standards, although one of them almost always predominated. For most people that standard was what Smith called "prudence," striving not to fall below the average.[53] Prudence, however, was not a path to greatness. While it might be eminently respectable, it was never "considered as one of the most endearing, or of the most ennobling of virtues. It commanded a certain cold esteem, but seems not entitled to any very ardent love or admiration." Furthermore, it encouraged a certain isolation in one's own affairs (sticking one's head out in public was dangerous). To achieve greatness, we had to apply higher standards. It is essential to bear in mind that Smith was no enemy of prudence. Society could not exist without it. Smith did not despise prudence just as he does not despise the pursuit of self-interest. That commercial society encouraged prudence was, from Smith's perspective, to its moral credit.[54]

Smith's vision of commercial society was optimistic precisely because it could incorporate both prudence and greatness. For Smith commercial soci-

50. *TMS*, 115–116.

51. *TMS*, 117.

52. *TMS*, 137, 309.

53. Smith was not altogether consistent in his use of terms, and also defined prudence as the union of foresight and self-control, a definition that focused more on the means of prudence than on its end.

54. *TMS*, 216–217. The argument of Book VI of *TMS* was a catalog of virtues in ascending order that represented the ladder by which the individual climbed from prudence to a greater perfection. See Hanley, *Adam Smith*, 127–132, 44, 91.

ety had something to offer everyone. On one level his perfectionism reserved virtue or excellence to a minority, on a second it made room for the beneficial effects of vanity and pride, and on a third it gave a respectable place to average prudence.

Smith also provided an alternative utilitarian standard of moral judgment, based on happiness, which was fully egalitarian. "What can be added to the happiness of the man who is in health, who is out of debt, and has a clear conscience?" "This really is the state of the greater part of men." The majority were not virtuous, but they were perfectly happy. And happiness was perfectly appropriate for them, in Smith's view. Alongside an elitist and perfectionist virtue ethic, Smith thus presented a democratic happiness-based ethic that was based on utilitarian considerations first and foremost. According to Smith, people were utilitarians by nature, that is, they possessed a "love of pleasure, and the dread of pain," which "prompt us to apply those means for their own sakes."[55] They thus acted from utilitarian motives, not just from considerations of propriety. But Smith was a very different sort of utilitarian from Jeremy Bentham, whose later and far more reductive version of utilitarianism has all too often been identified with liberalism. Smith would have thought it a gross impropriety to suggest, as Bentham did, that pushpin (a children's game) was as good as poetry. Not all pleasures were equal, nor should utility be the basis of our judgment of all things. "It seems impossible that the approbation of virtue should be a sentiment of the same kind with that by which we approve of a convenient and well-contrived building, or that we should have no other reason for praising a man than that for which we commend a chest of drawers." Utility was a sufficient criterion for judging a chest of drawers. It was insufficient for judging a human being.

Crucially, Smith's concept of propriety thus both incorporated utilitarianism and encouraged moral improvement and perfection. By harmonizing utility, prudence, and perfection, Smith described a kind of harmony of the moral spheres for modern commercial societies, orchestrated in every individual by their personal sense of propriety. Through his theory of propriety, freedom, markets, and morals came to work together, as if by an invisible hand.[56] He thus left behind the opposition between wealth and virtue that had preoccupied so many predecessors, answered the challenge posed by Mandeville in *The Fable of the Bees* by seeing the appropriate pursuit of private interest as no vice at all,

55. *TMS*, 78.
56. *TMS*, 61.

and helped create the liberal consensus of the short nineteenth century that markets and morals were natural allies, not natural enemies.[57]

With regard to Smith's support for markets, the second pillar of what would become liberalism, Smith was the most prominent apostle of free trade and free markets in eighteenth-century Europe. It was natural and good to truck, barter, and exchange, and in most circumstances (there were significant exceptions to his advocacy of laissez-faire, some of which will be discussed below) this was best done without government interference, which was inevitably ignorant of its own effects. Free markets were an essential part of commercial society and serve to promote both freedom and morals. For the purposes of this study, no further discussion of his economic thought as such is necessary. His deviation from a policy of laissez-faire with regard to government intervention in religion and education will be examined in the context of his political views.

Alongside morality and markets, politics played an important role for Smith in relation to the development of commercial society, in encouraging moral perfection, and keeping people safe from despotism and fanaticism. There was no description of an ideal form of government for commercial societies, nor lengthy analysis of the ways in which existing governments were appropriate (at least outside the sphere of their relationship to markets, for which see above). Smith, however, emphatically linked the political and the moral domains. What he called the "natural system of liberty" with regard to markets was not one in which government was morally neutral. If he founded the system of economic liberty on limiting the state's role (for example, no more government-granted trading monopolies), he wanted to preserve or expand it with regard to morals, preserving a state Church and creating publicly funded schools and universal military training. Further, without going into detail, Smith insisted that liberty required the rule of law, the separation of powers, and some form of political participation. In all these respects, Smith foreshadowed the liberalism of the nineteenth century.

For Smith, "according to the system of natural liberty, the sovereign has only three duties to attend to." The roles of government were: (1) national defense; (2) justice, that is, the protection of every member of society against "injustice or oppression" by others, including the government; (3) "erecting and maintaining certain public works and certain public institutions," in particular, depending on circumstances, religious and educational ones. Smith

57. TMS, 45. See also Hanley, Adam Smith, 44.

did not believe in a neutral state that limited itself to procedural justice. A free society ignored the moral state of the people at its peril.[58]

The first duty of government, self defense, is self-explanatory. In order to perform the second, that is to maintain justice, Smith insisted on limiting arbitrary power. It was true, according to Smith, that commercial society itself imposed certain limits on arbitrary authority. Once international bills of exchange were invented, money could flee a tyrant, a thought already found in Montesquieu. But this was not enough, and most commercial societies were not free. One needed institutional and legal means to preserve freedom and justice. Crucially this meant the separation of the executive and judicial power: "Upon the impartial administration of justice depends the liberty of every individual, the sense which he has of his own security."[59] In order to make every individual feel himself perfectly secure in the possession of every right which belonged to him, it was not only necessary that the judicial should be separated from the executive power, but that it should be rendered as much as possible independent of that power." This led to a "right of resistance" against a government that violated its subjects' rights. Even when the boundaries of the government's power were unclear, Smith insisted that "there are certain limits to the power of the sovereign, which if he exceeds, the subject may with justice make resistance." The right to resist was not founded on a contract between government and people, a theory dismissed by Smith, and exactly when resistance is permitted was unclear. Nevertheless, "the raising of a very exorbitant tax . . . the half or even the fifth of the wealth of the nation, would, as well as any other gross abuse of power, justify resistance in the people." It was easier to figure out when one of the branches of government, i.e., the King, has overstepped their legal bounds—this was how Smith justified the Glorious Revolution of 1688.[60]

Smith did not focus on the political limitations on arbitrary power. Rather he devoted attention to the laws that defended people from the exercise of arbitrary power in civil life. This was the subject of his *Lectures on Jurisprudence*, massive in length but not published in his lifetime. In this emphasis on the importance of law Smith joined Montesquieu and the

58. Winch, "Scottish Political Economy," 46; *WN*, II 243–244, see also *LJ*, 313; *LJ*, 271, 275, 284–285.

59. Note the resemblance to Montesquieu's definition of political freedom as our sense of personal security, cited above.

60. *WN*, 2:214; *LJ*, 311, 315, 316, 324.

natural rights tradition on the one hand, and anticipated liberal thinkers like Constant on the other.

In order to maintain legal institutions and the rule of law, Smith strongly encouraged the study of politics, and political participation (by some), if only because it would motivate people to take an interest in the public good. Even the worst political theories were helpful in this respect. "They seek at least to animate the public passions of men, and rouse them to seek out the means of promoting the happiness of society." This was not the language of a thinker uninterested in politics, as has sometimes been alleged of Smith. Nor would someone uninterested in politics suggest that the "greatest and noblest of all characters" was that of a "reformer or legislator of a great state," or propose, as Smith did at the end of *The Wealth of Nations*, what he himself considered a Utopian plan for mending the relationship between Great Britain and its American colonies. If only by exhortation and example, Smith valued political participation just as highly as most nineteenth-century liberals.[61]

What he said about it was suggestive and coherent with his moral perspective on commercial society.[62] Smith thought that all civilized societies consisted, economically speaking, of wage-laborers, landowners, and capitalists / merchants, those who lived by labor, by rent, or by profits. In *The Wealth of Nations* he considered the ability of these three groups to give advice about economic policy, which may stand in for political advice. The workers represented the great majority, and their interest was effectively equivalent to the common interest in economic questions, in Smith's view, because their interest was in jobs and rising wages, and these were only to be found in a prosperous and growing economy. But laborers were "incapable . . . of comprehending that interest." No votes for the workers, therefore. Then there were landowners, who profited when rents went up. Rents increased most in a thriving economy, so they too had a personal interest in the general good. Unfortunately, landlords were naturally lazy: their "indolence . . . renders them too often, not only ignorant, but incapable of that application of mind" needed to understand any economic proposal. So no votes for them. Finally, there were the merchants and manufacturers. Their interests were not necessarily in accord with those of society, according to Smith, because their rate of profit was often unaffected or inversely affected by the general prosperity, and they had

---

61. *TMS*, 187, *WN* 2:418ff.; Winch, "Commercial Realities, Republican Principles," 297.

62. Long, "Adam Smith's Politics," 295, 300; Phillipson, "Adam Smith as Civic Moralist," 179.

a natural tendency to reduce competition, to the detriment of society. So no votes for them.[63]

Philosopher-kings perhaps? Not a viable option, because intellectual and spiritual qualities were so hard to measure that "no society, whether barbarous or civilized, has ever found it convenient to settle the rules of precedency of rank and subordination, according to these invisible qualities." Furthermore, philosopher-kings were subject to particular moral temptations. They possessed a "certain spirit of system," and were in reality motivated less by "pure sympathy" with the public than by love of an ideal perfection. "The perfection of police, the extension of trade and manufactures, are noble and magnificent objects. . . . We take pleasure in beholding the perfection of so beautiful and grand a system." Government ought to be utilitarian—its sole end is to promote the happiness of those who live under it. But the spirit of system made the patriot and the intellectual, like the ambitious poor person and the wealthy purchaser of luxuries, value the means over the end. Even, or rather especially among virtuous patriots and "wise" men of system, propriety took priority over utility, with potentially disastrous consequences for government, which ought to be motivated solely by the happiness / utility of the governed.[64]

Yet although he appeared to think that just about everyone lacked either the capacity or the desire to offer good advice, and thus to be a suitable participant in political life, in practice Smith suffered from no great anxiety. Things would work out as long as freedom was preserved, in politics as in economics. To preserve freedom and limit power one needed a representative body to vote taxes and laws. "The frequency of elections is also a great security for the liberty of the people" because then the representative must serve his country, or "at least his constituents," on pain of losing his job. This kind of representation prevented favors from being showered on the King's favorites. Instead, they were bestowed on "the active, bustling, important men," and "it is not a bad way that power should be conferred on those who have naturally the greatest influence." Although unfortunately the lecture notes are blurred here, he seemed to say that universal suffrage was too democratic, the Scottish suffrage too limited, and the English suffrage (at the time 10–15% of adult English males could vote) sufficient to prevent the monarch from being an absolute ruler. In

63. WN, 1:249–251.
64. WN, 2:204; TMS, 185–187.

sum, Smith was reasonably satisfied with the political arrangements of Britain circa 1776.[65]

When it came to the third role of government, "erecting and maintaining certain public works and certain public institutions," Smith's departure from a laissez-faire perspective is notable with regard to the linked questions of religion and education. Smith's chapter on education in *The Wealth of Nations* began with a consideration of religion, since "the institutions for the instruction of people of all ages are chiefly those for religious instruction." He was sensitive to both the need for religion and the dangers posed by fanaticism. According to Smith, society owed much to the support of religion, which "enforces the natural sense of duty," learned from the impartial spectator within our breasts, through the promise of an afterlife, reinforced by a sense of appropriateness in obeying God—utility and propriety as ever working together. But the social benefits of religion only took place where "the natural principles of religion are not corrupted by the factious and party zeal of some worthless cabal." While Smith called for "the greatest mutual forbearance and toleration" about differences of religious opinion, he was quite hostile to sects that broke this rule. Extreme Protestants were included in his condemnation, but he chiefly had Catholics in mind.[66]

To retain the benefits of religion without the drawbacks, to get its support for society without fanaticism, a state church was often needed. Although the establishment of a religion with a salaried clergy deprived the clergy of any incentive to work hard, or to maintain the attachment of the people to their religion, the opposite course, refusing state support to religion, led not to atheism but to fanaticism. When their only source of income came from the donations of their congregation, clergy wanted as devoted and fanatical a congregation as possible, and "Each ghostly practitioner ... will inspire ... the most violent abhorrence of all other sects. . . . Customers will be drawn to each conventicle by new industry and address in practicing on the passions and credulity of the populace." The wise government should therefore encourage clergy to be lazy by paying them. If they were not paid too much, as was the case with the Presbyterian Church in Scotland which Smith much admired, they would still be diligent enough for the purpose, while being restrained from

65. *LJ*, 273–274.

66. *WN*, 2:273ff; *TMS*, 305, 168–170, 235; *TMS*, 170, 176, 333, 132–134; Smith's personal religious beliefs have been the subject of controversy. See Pocock, "Adam Smith and History," 283; Haakonsen and Winch, "The Legacy of Adam Smith," 385; Hanley, *Adam Smith*, 144, 198n.

fanaticism. "And in this manner ecclesiastical establishments . . . prove in the end advantageous to the political interests of society."[67]

This was only true if there was just one religion, or two or three great sects. If society was divided into "two or three hundred" sects, then the fanaticism of their clergy was no danger, and society might safely do without a state-supported religion. Competition would force the clergy "to learn . . . candour and moderation." Smith even expressed the hope that in time, competition would "probably reduce the doctrine of the greater part of them to that pure and rational religion, free from every mixture of absurdity, imposture, or fanaticism, such as wise men have in all ages of the world wished to see established."[68]

The larger point of Smith's discussion was that he thought the government had an interest in morality in general. The political pillar of the system of liberty was linked to the moral pillar (and to markets, of course). Government should foster morality and reduce fanaticism. This was necessary because fanaticism was not compatible with freedom. Religious fanaticism needed to be discouraged by the government, both directly, through a subsidized and supervised clergy, and indirectly.

Along with state-supported religion, Smith backed state-supported education. Educating the poor was a moral and political necessity. "A man without the proper use of the intellectual faculties of a man, is, if possible, more contemptible than even a coward." The state itself was threatened because the uneducated were subject to "the delusions of enthusiasm and superstition," which "frequently occasion the most dreadful disorders." Educated people were less likely to engage in faction and sedition because they were less easy to fool. Therefore, "in free countries, where the safety of government depends very much upon the favourable judgement which the people may form of its conduct, it must surely be of the highest importance that they should not be disposed to judge rashly or capriciously concerning it." Freedom required an educated people.[69]

The education Smith demanded for the poor was limited to learning to "read, write, and account," including "the elementary parts of geometry and mechanics." Whether education was paid for by the state, by private charity, and / or by those who received it should depend on circumstances. Smith was willing to see the government establish schools, but it should only pay for

67. *WN*, 2:276.
68. *WN*, 2:278.
69. *WN*, 2:272–273.

them in part. A small sum should be paid by the poor directly to the teacher because otherwise the schoolmaster, like the established clergyman, would neglect his business—and there was no good in a lazy schoolmaster, whatever might be the advantages of a lazy clergyman. Small prizes to encourage the best pupils should also be funded by the government. To this little carrot Smith added a rather large stick: the requirement for every man to pass an examination in basic subjects before he could take up a trade in any village or town.[70]

Along with basic education Smith required a course of military training. The question of a militia versus a standing army was much agitated in Scotland in his time. The militia's proponents argued that it was sufficient for national defense and necessary for the preservation of freedom, ever threatened by a standing army. Smith earned the ire of Adam Ferguson and other republican thinkers by asserting that a standing army was militarily superior to a militia, and that therefore it would be folly to replace it with one. Smith nevertheless saw benefits in the creation of a militia in which all able-bodied men participated. As a result of commercial society, the military skills of the people were in decline throughout Europe. An example had been seen in Scotland, when in 1745 "four or 5 thousand naked unarmed Highlanders took possession of the improved parts of this country without any opposition from the unwarlike inhabitants." Two hundred years previously, Smith asserted, they would have roused the nation against them: "Our ancestors were brave and warlike, their minds were not enervated by cultivating arts and commerce." Smith did not hesitate to compare the commercial British to the Indians and Chinese, equally subject to conquest by a handful of Europeans or Tartars, and for the same reason. Even if the martial spirit was militarily useless, Smith wrote, it was necessary to prevent the "mental mutilation" of cowardice from spreading through the population. The government needed to act in this regard just as it would act against a physical plague such as leprosy.[71]

Smith supported state intervention in education on grounds both utilitarian—better military capacity, a less fanatical populace, and perfectionist—the moral improvement of the people, preserving them from negative aspects of commercial society, such as the stupidity of the pin-maker or the lack of martial courage of the population in general. This intervention was necessary,

70. WN, 2:270–271.
71. WN, 2:194; LJ, 540–541. and see Hanley, Adam Smith, 35–36. Cf. Winch, "Scottish Political Economy," 463.

but had to be approached with fear and trembling. It fell under the heading of requiring people to do what was appropriate, such as educate their children or learn to defend their country, rather than simply requiring them to behave with justice, that is to refrain from harming their neighbors. And it required the government (and taxpayers) to behave with beneficence in paying for it. As Smith said of requiring beneficence, "of all the duties of a lawgiver . . . this, perhaps, is that which it requires the greatest delicacy and reserve to execute with propriety and judgement. To neglect it altogether exposes the commonwealth to many gross disorders and shocking enormities, and to push it too far is destructive of all liberty, security, and justice." Like many liberals later on, Smith hesitated in fear and trembling before the question of how much government was too much.[72]

Proto-Liberalism and Republicanism

Smith and Montesquieu were supporters of modernity who saw in commercial society the potential for political, economic, and moral progress. Proto-liberals, they relied on what would become the three pillars of nineteenth-century liberal thought, freedom, markets, and morals, as engines of progress and weapons against despotism. In responding to the fears and challenges of their own times and places, Smith and Montesquieu helped put in place what would become the three pillars of liberal thought.[73]

They were nevertheless not liberals because for all their warnings against government monopolies and religious fanaticism, they were insufficiently fearful, and to some extent fearful of the wrong things. Their fears of religion and of the state were significantly different than those of the next generation. Even Smith, despite being a witness to the American Revolution and the fall of the Bastille, evinced little fear of the spontaneous combustion of the political order at home or in continental Europe, and only to a modest degree in imagining the fate of the former American colonies. From the anachronistic perspective of a history of liberalism, Montesquieu and Smith were "almost modern," that is, "proto-liberal."[74]

72. *TMS*, 116.

73. Long, "Adam Smith's Politics," 315.

74. However, Smith feared that America would be increasingly subject to "those rancorous and virulent factions which are inseparable from small democracies" if the colonies became

In the story as often told by historians writing about eighteenth-century political thought, proto-liberalism struggled against older "republican" ways of understanding the world. Many commentators have tried to distinguish between liberal and republican elements in Montesquieu and Smith and battled over which predominates, and the same is true for many other authors of the period. In this view, an author is either a republican whose theories are based on virtue, or a liberal who is supposed to regard virtue as unimportant.

Despite all the ink spilled fighting it, to a large extent the battle is an imaginary one. Partly this is because, as John Adams put it in 1807, "there is no more unintelligible word in the English Language than republicanism." Still, the interpretive debate is instructive, and something should be said about what is at stake from the perspective of a history of liberalism. To a large extent, it has been a war waged by those who want to reject liberalism, in particular by arguing that liberalism has never had and can never have a moral component. When thinkers usually assigned to the liberal, or in this case proto-liberal, camp do rely on moral arguments, the attempt is made to show that they are really closet republicans, or have incorporated republican elements in their thought. In the process, the history of liberalism is seriously distorted.[75]

In this context, an attempt to define republicanism is necessary. Literally, to be a republican was to be in favor of a republic, originally the Roman Republic, and against the establishment of the Roman Empire or of a monarchy. By the eighteenth century most republicans conceded that under certain circumstances a limited monarchy was, in effect, a republic, but the original term persisted. As republicanism developed from Rome to Machiavelli, Harrington, and their successors, it took on a number of shapes, but always retained a stress on virtue and the overriding importance of politics.

From a republican perspective, freedom was about the ability of the individual to further the common good through political participation. Seventeenth-century republicans had little conception of civil society, of a sphere of life that was and ought to be outside of politics. Everything was about the citizen's relationship to the state and how one could have the civil liberty necessary for participation in government and military defense (strongly linked for republicans, as for the Greeks). If republicans talked about

---

fully independent. *WN* 2:430. In the 1790 additions to *WN*, he implicitly rebuked the French for lack of good judgment. But he died before the Terror.

75. Adams, cited in Appleby, *Liberalism and Republicanism*.

the rule of law or about individuals' need for economic independence, about the role of institutions or the role of individual virtue, it was always in the service of politics. They shared a common fear: that freedom would be lost because of corruption, as historically it always had been. One thing that republicans and liberals had in common was being fearful, sometimes of the same things, which encouraged overlap between them.[76]

What caused the loss of freedom, in the republican view, was the loss of virtue, i.e., corruption. The struggle between virtue and corruption, not altogether dissimilar from the struggle against sin, always had the same long-term result: the triumph of corruption and the downfall of the republic. This did not dissuade republicans from trying to learn lessons and get things right, or at least better, for the next time. Nevertheless, fear of decline and corruption was the leitmotif of every republican story. Corruption was both a moral failure—evil self-interest replacing zeal for the commonwealth, and a failure of rationality—a failure to understand that individual freedom depended on virtue and public service. Republicans often charged laws and institutions with the duty, if necessary, of forcing people to be free, in Rousseau's famous phrase.[77]

This republican view of history and politics was very different from the proto-liberal views of Smith and Montesquieu. Instead of a progressive stage theory of history leading up to commercial society, republicans had a two-stage theory of the rise and fall of the republic. Instead of a recognition of the value and importance of civil society and commerce, for republicans they were at best a necessary foundation for political action, always distractions from politics, and at worst inevitable and incorrigible sources of corruption. Republican political thought had difficulty seeing the rise of commercial society as anything but a kind of corruption. From the republican perspective the commercial spirit would destroy the self-sacrificing virtue needed for political freedom. For Montesquieu and Smith and other proto-liberals, this was not the case. They looked at the overall picture very differently, while discussing many subjects dear to the republican heart.

There was quite a bit of discussion of virtue in Montesquieu and Smith. Smith in particular talked about how important the martial virtues were, how they were threatened by the development of commercial society, and how they

76. Skinner, *Liberty before Liberalism*, 17; Geuna, "Republicanism and Commercial Society in the Scottish Enlightenment," 194.

77. Skinner, "Conclusion," 304–306.

could be revived—impeccably republican topics. Indeed, Smith is sometimes seen by commentators as reconciling republicanism and commercial society. On the other side, republicans debated the extent to which virtue was compatible with the commerce, politeness, and the gentle commercial mores that Montesquieu and Smith, among others, thought had or would replace the ruder, "manly" virtues of republican tradition. The textbook example is Adam Ferguson, a friend of Smith who lamented the decline of the martial virtues (as did Smith), but rejected the idea of a professional army (he broke with Smith over this) and attempted in many respects to reconcile commerce with virtue. By the late eighteenth century, many supposedly republican thinkers accepted commercial society as a fact of life, and even acknowledged some merits in it.[78]

At the same time proto-liberals like Montesquieu and Smith found ways of reconciling self-interest and virtue, utilitarian and perfectionist views. They conceived of the world as a place in which morals and religion (virtue and perfection) could work in tandem with a developing modern market society (based on self interest and utility) to promote, preserve, and encourage freedom (of many kinds, including political). In turn freedom would promote and preserve commerce and morals. Thus conceived, freedom, markets, and morals, working together, could serve to hold off corruption, a traditional republican fear. They would tame religious fanaticism, too often the reaction to corruption or the fear of corruption. They would prevent despotism, whether Enlightened or not, and, by providing bulwarks against all these fears, assure the continued progress of humanity. Any new forms of corruption available in commercial society would be manageable. The modern world would be a better place than the ancient world.

The struggle against despotism and against moral and political corruption was old. Its context—commercial society—was new, and so were some of the means used to pursue it. The distinction between old and new was crucial. Eighteenth-century proto-liberals made an historical distinction between ancient and modern society, identifying modernity with commerce. Historical analysis, along with economic and moral analysis, was crucial to their political analysis. The historical distinction between ancient and modern had implications for everything from slavery to civility to politics. There was no need to

---

78. Winch, "Commercial Realities, Republican Principles," 310; Geuna, "Republicanism and Commercial Society in the Scottish Enlightenment," 180, 182–185; Kalyvas and Katznelson, *Liberal Beginnings*, 51–87; Armitage, "Empire and Liberty," 39–40.

imitate or mourn the virtues of the past if they were no longer appropriate to modernity, although a little nostalgia might be in good taste. The great debate over wealth and virtue and freedom that took place throughout the Western world in the eighteenth century was in large part a debate over what it meant to live in a commercial society. It is only a little anachronistic to say that it was a debate over the meaning and merits of capitalism—a word that, like liberalism, did not yet exist.[79]

The fact is that eighteenth-century thinkers often talked about classical military virtues, modern political institutions, and the benefits (and drawbacks) of commercial society without much regard for the dictionaries of political language drawn up for them by historians. The political equivalents of Spanglish and Franglais were the dominant dialects of political thought. Not for everyone of course: for Baron d'Holbach the virtue and patriotism of the ancient republics was just another form of fanaticism, worthy of no more respect than the religious kind. Nevertheless, it is certainly the case that "Scholars have for too long treated classical liberalism and republicanism as purely discrete political languages." For most republican and proto-liberal thinkers, certainly for Montesquieu and Smith, the moral questions raised by commercial society were no longer seen as black or white. The pursuit of self-interest through commerce and the pursuit of virtue leading to personal and political perfection did not need to be seen as mutually exclusive, for either the society or the individual. One could have both. There was little real difference between republicans concerned with virtue and the "non-domination" of individuals, and proto-liberals / liberals concerned merely with self-interest and their "non-coercion." Smith and Montesquieu were perfectly content to use both concepts, without seeing them as contradictions. For them, a society with the appropriate basis in freedom, markets, and morals would liberate individuals from coercion *and* domination.[80]

A response by those who wish to save republicanism from too much contamination by liberalism has been to propose that there was a "liberal republicanism," "a polymorphous synthesis of classical republican and liberal political

---

79. Berry, *The Idea of Luxury*. See also the work of John Shovlin and Henry C. Clark; Hampsher-Monk, "From Virtue to Politeness," 2:86, 88, 90.

80. Spitz, "From Civism to Civility," 108–109, 112–113; Isaac, "Republicanism vs. Liberalism?." Jainchill, *Reimagining Politics After the Terror*, 15. Cf. Skinner, *Liberty before Liberalism*, and Pettit, *Republicanism*, for distinctions between liberalism and republicanism founded on the supposed difference between non-coercion and non-domination.

languages that first began to emerge between 1794 and 1804," or even before. It is important to reject the suggestion that proto-liberalism was a form or variant of republicanism. The suggestion is motivated by the mistaken view that "liberalism in its purest form is indifferent to politics and more often than not rejects politics as such." From this perspective, the existence of liberals or proto-liberals who evidently cared a great deal about politics must mean that such thinkers were not liberals at all, or were at least tinged with something else, like republicanism. The very limited degree to which this view is anachronistically justified by the history of liberalism in the late twentieth century will be seen in the forthcoming chapters. It is not justified at all with regard to Montesquieu or Smith, as even its proponents admit. Nor is it justified by the liberalism of the nineteenth century, which relied on the three pillars of freedom, markets, and morals to liberate humanity from the new fears, and justify the new hopes, of a revolutionary epoch: the age of revolution, which was also the midwife of liberalism. In the age of revolution it was the revolutionaries who insisted on linguistic purity, and the liberals who preferred to use Franglais to discuss the construction of a world in which no one need be afraid.[81]

81. Winch, "Commercial Realities, Republican Principle," 303–304, 308; Hont and Ignatieff, "Introduction," 44; Jainchill, *Reimagining Politics*, 14; Sullivan, *Machiavelli, Hobbes*; Skinner, "Conclusion," 308. The affinity of radicalism for linguistic purity did not end in 1799.

PART II

The All-Too-Short Nineteenth Century

3

After the Revolutions

HISTORIANS OFTEN SPEAK of a "long" nineteenth century from 1789 to 1914, from the outbreak of the French Revolution to the beginning of the First World War. For liberalism, however, the nineteenth century was shorter. All too short, from a liberal perspective, because the nineteenth century was the period in which liberalism was born, flourished, and dominated Western political discourse as never since. Liberalism's short nineteenth century began in the late 1790s, when the word "liberal" was first used to designate a current of political opinion. It ended in 1873, when the death of John Stuart Mill announced a fin de siècle which brought new fears that evoked a "modern liberalism" in response, and a "classical liberalism" in response to the moderns. This was Liberalism 1.0, the first wave of liberalism to shape Western political thought.

"Liberalism" entered the dictionary in response to revolutions in America and France that led to enormous new hopes and equally enormous new fears. The hope was for freedom. The fear was of political fanaticism, on the part of both revolutionaries and their reactionary opponents, as cruel as religious fanaticism had ever been. Liberals saw themselves as holding the center, trying to steer a safe course down the narrow strait between the rocks of Scylla and Charybdis, to use a classical metaphor that nineteenth-century liberals adored.

For much of the nineteenth century, the liberal movement had unclear boundaries in both politics and intellectual debate. Nevertheless, throughout the century liberals shared common fears and usually responded to them by calling on all three pillars of liberal thought—freedom, markets, and morals. Three towering figures serve here as landmarks to delineate the broad—very broad—current of liberalism as it took shape in the early nineteenth century, and to explore the different ways in which liberals addressed their new hopes and fears: Immanuel Kant, James Madison, and Benjamin Constant.

From some perspectives, there is not much common ground to be found among the East Prussian professor Kant, the American revolutionary and sla-veowner Madison, and the Swiss / French politician, gambler, and novelist Constant. In a strict but misguided sense two of the three, Kant and Madison, might not even qualify as liberals, since Madison's *Federalist Papers* and most of Kant's political works were written before "liberal" became a word. But it would be wrong to be too pedantic. Madison was as liberal in his response to the American Revolution as Kant was in response to it and the French Revolu-tion. The contexts of Kant, Madison, and Constant were very different, and yet very similar in one crucial respect: they were all responding, after revolu-tions, to new circumstances they perceived as presenting new opportunities and new dangers. They did not respond identically. Kant and Constant fo-cused on the fears and hopes of individuals, Madison more on those of groups. Constant wrote a great deal about economics, Kant barely anything and Madi-son little. But all three sought to emancipate human beings from fear and find a way to secure their freedom.

Kant, the oldest of the three, stood on an historical cusp with respect to revolutions and their aftermath, and it is with Kant that we begin. His liberal-ism was an intellectual liberalism if ever there was, founded on the idea of critical thinking.

Immanuel Kant: Liberalism and Critical Thinking

Kant (1724–1804) was arguably the most important Western philosopher after St. Thomas Aquinas. His contributions to epistemology and moral philosophy were the foundation of his reputation, but his writings on politics, if relatively short, were important. Kant's philosophy has always been highly influential among liberals, especially German liberals but also late twentieth-century American liberals, notably John Rawls (see chapter 10). Kant was the godfa-ther of the "secular humanism" of the late twentieth century and as such his liberalism is of particular interest.[1]

Kant's liberalism started where all liberalisms do, with fear. For Kant, human beings were "radically evil," that is, subject to following their inclina-tions without regard for others.[2] Despotism was the ultimate in following

---

1. Galston, "What Is Living and What Is Dead in Kant's Practical Philosophy?," 207–208.

2. Kant also believed in an "original disposition to good in human nature," which was the source of the hope inherent in his liberalism. See Kant, "Religion within the Boundaries of Reason," 50.

one's own inclinations, and hence, given human nature, a permanent temptation. Kant opposed all forms of despotism and wished to liberate people from
the whims of arbitrary authority and secure their freedom. Without freedom,
people could not fulfill what Kant considered their universal duty to act
morally because for Kant, to make a moral choice we had to be able to act freely
and autonomously, which is not the case when we are subject to despotism
and arbitrary authority. Despotism was thus unjust because it prevented
people from acting morally. Kant's idea of an unjust society was in effect the
definition of an illiberal society—a place where fear prevented one from doing
what the moral law permitted, and required one to do what it forbade, as Montesquieu might have put it. Hence, a liberal politics was needed to prevent
despotism and to attain a free and just society. Kant's faith in progress was
based on reason, and in the long run, both critical thought and progress depended on the establishment of a liberal state.[3]

Kant showed how to attain a free society in his 1784 essay, "An Answer to the
Question: What Is Enlightenment." Even though he did not use the word "liberal" and talked about "enlightenment" instead, and even though it was published five years before the fall of the Bastille, it was very much a liberal rather
than a proto-liberal work. If the French Revolution had not yet taken place, the
American Revolution had just ended. The background of the work was the
question of how reforms intended to secure freedom and make people secure
from arbitrary power could take place without provoking violence, rebellion,
anarchy, and despotism—a question raised by the American Revolution. This
was *the* liberal question of the short nineteenth century. Unlike his proto-liberal
predecessors, Kant was preoccupied by the question of revolution: "Perhaps a
revolution can overthrow autocratic despotism and profiteering or power-
grabbing oppression, but it can never truly reform a manner of thinking; instead, new prejudices, just like the old ones they replace, will serve as a leash
for the great unthinking mass."[4] These concerns were absent from the thought
of Montesquieu and Smith and other proto-liberals. By contrast, Kant's fear of
revolution was characteristic of first wave liberalism, Liberalism 1.0.

Kant's response to these fears was destined for a long future. In "What Is
Enlightenment," Kant argued that only if people learned how to think for

---

3. Kant, "Religion within the Boundaries of Reason," 53–54; Riley, "The Elements of Kant's
Practical Philosophy," 20; Onora O'Neill, "Kant and the Social Contract Tradition," 39.

4. Kant, "What Is Enlightenment?," 42. Some eighteenth-century proto-liberals, e.g., Locke,
were also preoccupied by revolution, but it was religious, not secular revolution that concerned
them most.

themselves, to think critically, would despotism be vanquished and human beings no longer have cause to live in fear. Critical thinking was what Kant meant by "enlightenment": "Enlightenment is man's emergence from his self-imposed immaturity. Immaturity is the inability to use one's understanding without guidance from another. . . . *Sapere aude* [Dare to think]! Have courage to use your own understanding."[5]

At the time most people could not think critically, but Kant believed in progress. "If it is now asked, 'Do we presently live in an *enlightened* age?' the answer is, 'No, but we do live in an age of *enlightenment*,'" in which "the obstacles to general enlightenment . . . are gradually diminishing." The way to make progress was through free speech. If the public was allowed "the freedom to use reason *publicly*," then "enlightenment is almost inevitable." Free critical thinking would create a moral political culture: a liberal culture, to use a term he did not. A liberal culture was one that encouraged critical thinking; a liberal government one that both made it possible for people to think critically and let them do it in public (Kant used "enlightened" instead of liberal, here it means the same). Censorship was the great enemy. Nevertheless, in the new, post–American Revolution context of 1784, he also has some concerns about the consequences of free speech: "only a ruler who is himself enlightened and . . . who likewise has a well-disciplined, numerous army to guarantee public peace, can say . . . *Argue as much as you want and about what you want, but obey!*"[6]

Seemingly paradoxically, Kant also said that free governments (which he called "republics," in keeping with eighteenth-century practice) could not afford to permit as much public discussion as less free governments. Kant thus seemed to admit illiberal arguments about the need to enforce virtue and restrain critical thinking / criticism. But in true liberal fashion he then rejected this limitation by saying that a fully enlightened people would not need limits placed on its topics of discussion, and that a republican form of government was appropriate only for an enlightened people.[7]

Kant's fear of revolution was new, but one of the continuities between liberal and proto-liberal thought was hope and faith in progress. Kant believed, not unreasonably for someone living in 1784, that critical thinking was on the

5. Kant, "What Is Enlightenment?," 41.

6. Kant, "What Is Enlightenment," 44–45. Smith had earlier said that only countries with strong, well-regulated armies could tolerate "licentious liberty." *TMS*, 230.

7. Kant, "What Is Enlightenment," 46.

march. He criticized Moses Mendelssohn for saying that although individuals might make progress, the human race as a whole could not. Rather, "the human race's natural end is to make steady cultural progress. . . . This progress may well be occasionally *interrupted*, but it will never be *broken off.*" For Kant, it was our moral duty to believe this because it was our moral duty to strive to improve the world, and we could only have such a duty if it was possible to fulfill it. Hope was built into the moral foundation of Kant's political theory.[8]

Progress was inevitable for reasons that had nothing to do with human desire for it. Political and individual perfection over time was part of nature's plan for human beings: "The history of the human race as a whole can be regarded as the realization of a hidden plan of nature to bring about . . . [a] perfect political constitution as the only possible state within which all natural capacities of mankind can be developed completely." Progress "depends not so much on what *we* do . . . nor on what method we adopt so as to bring it about; instead, it depends on what human *nature does in and with us so as to compel us onto a path that we ourselves would not readily follow.*" This was Kant's Invisible Hand theory of human progress. Like Smith, he thought nature / Providence made us do what we would not intentionally do ourselves—in Smith's case, distribute our wealth more or less equally; in Kant's case, proceed slowly along the path to a world federation with universal peace, universal guarantees for human rights, and universal enlightenment. Kant's invisible moral hand was at work in nature, "in which self-seeking inclinations naturally counteract one another," and were "used by reason as a means to prepare the way for its own end, the rule of right."[9]

Like Smith, Kant appealed to competition to obtain this result. Nature, according to Kant, prevented the formation of universal empires by differences in language and religion which led to mutual hatred and provided pretexts for

8. Riley, "Social Contract Theory and Its Critics," 370–371; Galston, "What Is Living and What Is Dead in Kant's Practical Philosophy?," 209; Kant, "Idea for a Universal History with a Cosmopolitan Intent," 36; Kant, "On the Proverb: That may be true in theory, but is of no practical use (1793)," 85. In one of his last writings, "An Old Question Raised Again: Is the Human Race Constantly Progressing?," Kant admitted that while progress has occurred (so Mendelssohn was still wrong), we cannot prove that it will continue. See Louis Dupré, "Kant's Theory of History and Progress," 821.

9. "Universal History," 41–42; "Proverb," 86–87; "To Perpetual Peace: A Philosophical Sketch (1795)," 124. Irving Fetscher applied the invisible hand metaphor to Kant in "Republicanism and Popular Sovereignty," 589. See also "Universal History," 31, and Ellis, *Kant's Political Theory*, 155.

war. Having ensured that progress was not halted by the establishment of a universal empire, nature then overcame those differences when "the growth of culture and men's gradual progress toward greater agreement regarding their principles lead to mutual understanding and peace. Unlike the peace that despotism (in the graveyard of freedom) brought about by vitiating all powers, this one was produced and secured by an equilibrium of the liveliest competing powers." Diversity thus eventually led to peace and progress. It is hard to imagine a more Scottish or Smithian conclusion, and in some ways a more surprising one from a thinker who is often supposed to ignore human diversity in favor of universal rationality.[10]

Unlike Smith, Kant proposed a unique version of social contract theory to both describe and justify political progress. Kant's approach to contract theory was problematic in that he regarded the idea of an original contract as a potentially harmful fiction. It was *"futile"* as well as dangerous to inquire into an original social contract as if it were real, and it could not be grounds for a lawsuit or a revolution. But the idea of an original contract was important for Kant's liberalism because it led him to the idea that legislators were obligated to formulate their laws "in such a way that they *could* have sprung from the unified will of the entire people." The fiction of the contract created the political equivalent of Kant's Categorical Imperative (act so that your will could become a universal law = write laws in such a way that the entire people could support them), and provided a foundation for treating people equally. Thus, for example, one could not establish a particular class of people as a hereditary ruling class because "an entire people *could not possibly* agree to such a law." On the basis of this contractual fiction, but rarely referring to it, Kant proceeded to create the formal outlines of a liberal state, built to withstand the dangers of religious and political fanaticism and enable all human beings to realize their moral potential.[11]

Progress would lead people to think critically and eventually obtain a "republic," the kind of government Kant thought best. For Kant, governments could be analyzed based either on their "form of sovereignty," the familiar mon-

10. Kant, "Proverb," 87; "Perpetual Peace," 125. For criticism of Kant's lack of appreciation of diversity, see Bernard Yack, "The Problem with Kantian Liberalism."

11. O'Neill, "Kant and the Social Contract Tradition," 27; Kant, *Metaphysics of Morals*, 86, 90, 95, 111–112; Kant, "Proverb," 77. Kant explicitly rejected the idea attributed to liberalism by Mehta (*Liberalism and Empire*) that the moral superiority of civilization justified the conquest of savages in order to civilize them. *Metaphysics*, 53.

archy, aristocracy, or democracy; or more importantly on their "form of government," whether they were republics or despotisms.[12] Naturally, "the only constitution that accords with right, [is] that of a pure republic . . . which makes *freedom* the principle and indeed the condition for any exercise of *coercion*." In the republic, everyone's freedom had to be limited, by coercion if necessary, so that it would be compatible with the freedom of everyone else. This was what the law did. Kant thus set up the framework for a liberal state.[13]

In such a society human beings were free, equal to everyone else as a subject, which meant they obeyed the same laws and were equally independent as citizens. "This is the only constitution of a state that lasts, the constitution in which the *law* itself rules and depends on no particular person." Laws made by a parliament legislating for all alike would not, according to Kant, deliberately do wrong, since no one ever did wrong to himself.[14]

Kant's republic, where critical thinking reigned, was what we may call the liberal "form of government": the opposite of a despotism. What was the liberal "form of sovereignty"? For Kant, democracies were by definition despotisms, since in democracies the people exercised both the sovereign and the legislative power, and in a republic legislative and executive power had to be separate. However, Kant also said that the people themselves were *always* the ultimate sovereign, for in the people "is originally found the supreme authority from which all rights of individuals . . . must be derived." The solution to the riddle of having a sovereign people without having a democratic form of government was the art of representation, an art unknown to the ancients, and thus another instance of political progress. Without representation, government was "despotic and brutish," whatever the form of the constitution.[15]

The parliament, with its elected deputies, was the guardian of the "freedom and rights" of the people. But who should elect them? "The only qualification . . . is being fit to vote. But being fit to vote presupposes . . . independence." Kant distinguished between active citizens, voters, and passive citizens who did not vote. The distinction between active and passive citizens was also used by Abbé Sieyès, the author of several French Revolutionary constitutions

---

12. The double typology of sovereignty and government may owe something to Montesquieu (see chapter 1).

13. *Metaphysics*, 112.

14. Kant, "Perpetual Peace," 113–114; see also *Metaphysics*, 94; "Proverb," 71–72, "Perpetual Peace," 112, "Proverb," 72; *Metaphysics*, 91.

15. Kant, "Perpetual Peace," 114, *Metaphysics*, 94–95, 113, 91; "Perpetual Peace," 115.

(Kant prudently refused to enter into a correspondence with Sieyès on the subject, fearful of arrest as a revolutionary). The criterion of independence was commonplace among nineteenth-century liberals, although the definition varied widely. Non-voters for Kant included children, women, and anyone whose existence was "dependent" on another person, "except the state"— public employees got the vote. Some examples used by Kant: someone employed to work in my yard does not get the vote, but a blacksmith with his own shop does. Private tutors do not, whereas public schoolteachers do. Kant did not say why those who lacked independence should not vote, but we can infer an argument from equality: no one should have more than one vote, and the votes of dependents would be controlled by their employers / husbands / parents, giving the master more than one vote. This was a common nineteenth-century liberal view.[16]

Along with representative government and the separation of powers as securities for freedom, Kant provided for protection against moral or religious constraint. In the republic, "no one can compel me (in accordance with his beliefs about the welfare of others) to be happy after his fashion; instead, every person may seek happiness in the way that seems best to him." In this respect Kant endorsed diversity. A government that decided what ought to make people happy, that treated the people as children, was paternalist, and even with the best of intentions, "the worst despotism we can think of." Paternalism was the opposite of enlightenment, since it rejected critical thinking and insisted that the subject remain under the tutelage of the state.[17]

Kant's rejection of paternalism did not mean that the republic should be indifferent to the morality or religion of its subjects. Churches were "a true need of a state," people needed to "regard themselves also as subject of a supreme *invisible* power to which they must pay homage." Nevertheless, churches should not be paid for by the state, and the state could not make laws about beliefs, whether of individuals or of sects, nor prefer one religion to another. All it could do was police religions so that they did not threaten the public peace. In short, there had to be separation of Church and state.[18]

Kant's politics were designed to encourage human beings to develop their natural capacities without fear and to think and act without the external con-

16. Kant, *Metaphysics*, 96; Reidar Maliks, *Kant and the French Revolution* (Cambridge: Cambridge University Press, 2022); *Metaphysics*, 91.

17. Kant, "Proverb," 72–73; *Metaphysics*, 94.

18. Kant, *Metaphysics*, 101–102.

straints imposed by war, tyranny, paternalism, religious persecution, etc. Government was more than just a way of coping with the flaws of human nature. Politics provided people with a unique opportunity to develop their capacities. The liberal state would thus encourage people to become better human beings in every way. Kant's politics were simultaneously a barrier against tyranny, and the support and enabler of morality, which required freedom. It was, in the manner typical of liberalism in the short nineteenth century, both utilitarian and perfectionist.[19]

Despite the eminently liberal political ideals described above, Kant has been accused of buckling to tyrants. This is because he rejected the right to resist a tyrant by force of arms.

Kant nevertheless hoped, in vain, that "no one . . . will accuse me of flattering the monarchs too much by maintaining their inviolability." Kant rejected as "terrifying" the idea (which he attributed to Hobbes) that people had no rights against their ruler, even though they should not use violence to enforce those rights. He provided for a legislature to refuse to accept the demands of the government. Indeed, if they never did so, it was a sign that the state was despotic. If Kant was an enemy of revolution, he was a partisan of change, which "if it is attempted and carried out by gradual reform in accordance with firm principles, can lead to continual approximation to the highest political good, perpetual peace."[20]

On his own terms, Kant was even prepared to regard the French Revolution as progress. Turning upside down Smith's view that human beings were naturally sympathetic toward the great, Kant concluded that the "universal and disinterested sympathy" people felt for the French Revolution and its goal of freedom proved that moral progress had occurred. Kant effectively justified in practice the resort to force he denied in principle. By calling the Estates General, Louis the XVI had, in Kant's view, chosen to surrender his sovereignty to them. From that moment on, it was royal resistance to the Estates that was illegal rebellion, and the Estates were right to use force against the King. Once a revolution had occurred, the new government had to be considered legitimate, and any attempt to return to the previous constitution was rebellion. Kant rejected only the execution of Louis XVI. Kant was one of the first to articulate a classic liberal standpoint: It is not a good idea to start a revolution,

19. Kant, "Proverb," 124. Kant's moral theory is too vast to be addressed here. Suffice it to say that for Kant, reason is humanity's prime attribute, and morality the acme of reason.

20. Kant, "Proverb," 82; *Metaphysics*, 123–124; "Proverb," 82–83.

but once it has begun, it is often necessary to join it, in order to end it and return to a state of law. This simultaneous endorsement of both resistance—no to revolution—and movement—yes to reform—was a "contradiction" that most liberals endorsed in the short nineteenth century. Indeed, they did not regard it as a contradiction within their position, but as both a moral and practical virtue of liberalism: Kant being a case in point.[21]

Kant's politics combined moral and political pillars that supported the security and freedom of the individual, provided bulwarks against that which might make people afraid, and offered grounds for optimism about the future of humanity. At first glance, Kant's republic did not seem to need a commercial society to work. Kant did think people had an indirect duty to seek prosperity because poverty led to moral temptations, but this was not followed by any detailed study of economics. Perhaps he thought that Adam Smith, whose writings he admired and on several occasions quoted, had said what needed to be said. Most liberal thinkers did not devote equal attention to politics, markets, and morals. Kant was no exception.[22]

He did, however, make some suggestive remarks about the relationship between commerce and morality. In his lecture notes on anthropology (1798), Kant returned to the idea of immaturity evoked in "What Is Enlightenment," and singled out for mockery sumptuary laws, the traditional darlings of virtuous republicans who rejected commercial society and admired Spartan frugality. For Kant they were an example of government paternalism. People should be able to make their own choices about their clothes. By extension, therefore, the market was an arena where, by making their own choices people had the opportunity to develop their judgment. Kant also endorsed Montesquieu's *doux commerce* theory: "The *spirit of trade* cannot coexist with war, and sooner or later this spirit dominates every people. For among all those powers (or means) that belong to a nation, financial power may be the most reliable in forcing nations to pursue the noble cause of peace (though not from noble motives); and wherever in the world war threatens to break out, they will try to head it off through mediation." On the broadest level, when it came to his analysis of progress, Kant relied on the pursuit of self-interest. It was a device of Nature which, if amoral in itself, nevertheless provided a structure that encouraged moral development. To the extent that

21. Kant, *Metaphysics*, 113; "Perpetual Peace," 129, 136.
22. Kant, *Metaphysics*, 152. On Kant and Smith, see Banham, Schulting, and Hems, *Bloomsbury Companion*.

free markets and commercial societies involved the pursuit of self-interest, Kant endorsed their basic motivation, in much the same way and for the same reasons as Adam Smith. All this did not amount to an in-depth exploration of the relationship between liberalism and the market, but at a minimum Kant showed no hostility and some sympathy toward free markets.[23]

It is interesting to note some surprising economic consequences of his moral perspective. In most respects Kant was the opposite of a utilitarian. What mattered morally were good intentions, not good results. Nevertheless, it was our moral duty to care for the happiness of others. This meant, among other things, that for Kant the republic should tax its citizens to "care for the poor" and for orphans. More broadly, there were therefore many areas in which it was appropriate for the government to make decisions on the basis of happiness (provided that happiness did not clash with morality), always remembering that telling people how to be happy was not the business of the state.[24]

Of course, fundamentally Kant was no utilitarian, and happiness was not his main concern. It was human perfection that interested him above all. He defined perfection more broadly than just moral perfection. "Our *natural* perfection is the *cultivation* of any *capacities* whatever for furthering ends set by reason," and people have a duty "to make ourselves worthy of humanity by culture in general". The Kantian citizen was called upon to cultivate all sorts of talents. Kant was not indifferent to the decisions people made about what to do with their lives, even while insisting that these decisions had to be *autonomous*, not forced on them by a paternalistic state or society. His insistence on a combination of individual autonomy and perfectionism, his justification of self-interest combined with concern for the basic material welfare of others, characterized much nineteenth-century liberalism. So did his fear of both revolution and reaction, and his reliance on civil society, in his case through the mechanism of a critically thinking public, to bring about progress and stave off fear. Kant's embrace of critical thinking and faith in progress, as well as his endorsement of a liberal state as the necessary foundation for them both, would remain typical of liberalism, as would be the accusation of timidity and cowardice in pursuing progressive aims that confronted Kant in his lifetime

23. Fleischaker, *Third Concept of Liberty*, 188–189; LaVaque-Manty, "Kant's Children," 365–388; Kant, "Perpetual Peace," 125.

24. Kant, *Metaphysics*, 151; *Metaphysics*, 100–101.

and thereafter. Kant's liberalism was a balancing act based on the classic liberal tripod of freedom, markets, and morals.[25]

James Madison: Liberalism for a New World

There were hardly two more different places in the eighteenth-century Western world than Frederick the Great's Prussia and the thirteen former colonies of British North America. Kant had just enough freedom to dream a liberal dream in Prussia. America was born, in many respects,[26] a proto-liberal society. From the beginning, proto-liberal fears of religious persecution and royal despotism were central to colonial political life, even if some colonists were as avid to persecute as their European brethren. Many colonists had personal or ancestral experience of religious persecution, and all were aware of it as a present danger. In addition, fear of British despotism motivated all the American revolutionaries. Both of these fears were frequently expressed in the seventeenth- and eighteenth-century proto-liberal rhetoric used in America (and England) in the decades leading up to 1776, especially the proto-liberal language of Locke, who was often cited in this period and was a leading inspiration for the Declaration of Independence.[27]

If the colonists' traditional English fears helped bring about a revolution, it was in a social and political context which, even before the revolution, was much more democratic, in every sense of the word, than any European state. After their revolution, Americans, no one more so than James Madison, were highly conscious of the originality and newness of their situation. Madison was among the first political theorists to respond to a democratic, post-revolutionary state of affairs. He did so in full consciousness of the novelty of his situation and of the new dangers and opportunities it presented. More explicitly than Kant, Madison responded to the first wave of historical fears that shaped the history of liberalism, the fear of revolution and reaction after the American and French revolutions.

The post-revolutionary world in which Madison found himself led him to original reflections about the role of factions, a bête noire of eighteenth-century thought; about the dangers posed by a government dominated not by a royal executive, but by an unchecked legislative assembly; and about the

25. Kant, *Metaphysics*, 154.
26. Notable exceptions being slavery and the religious intolerance of many of the colonies.
27. Lutz, "Relative Influence."

ways in which self-interest and virtue could be harnessed alongside one an-other to preserve freedom. He was one of the leading inventors of a new lib-eralism for the new world coming into being on both sides of the Atlantic.

Madison's contributions to political theory, and to liberalism, are evident in the US Constitution, much of which he authored, and in the *Federalist Papers*, the series of essays written alongside John Jay and Alexander Hamilton to persuade Americans to ratify the Constitution in 1787–88. Traditionally the *Federalist Papers*, and in particular Madison's contributions, have been recog-nized as one of the most important, if not the most important, works in the history of American political thought, still frequently cited in US Supreme Court decisions. They are also a landmark in the history of liberal thought, something not sufficiently emphasized by historians. Madison's liberalism left a permanent mark on America and contributed much to the development of Western liberalism.

Madison's contributions to the *Federalist Papers* included both old and new elements, but he justified the new constitution in predominantly new terms, and repeatedly argued that the new American polity would be not just differ-ent, but better, since the ancients were inferior in the art of representative government. "The true distinction between [the ancient] and the American governments lies *in the total exclusion of the people in their collective capacity, from any share*" in government. In America, the popular will was never put directly into effect, it was always mediated by a representative body, which mitigated the danger of enthusiasm. Like both Kant and Constant, Madison rejected direct democracy because of fear that it might result in tyranny by the mob or the majority. Instead, in the modern mode of representative govern-ment, popular sovereignty was not vested in the mass assembly, but in their elected representatives. Representation was fundamental to Madison's repub-lic and his vision of self-government. To those who objected that representa-tion, and especially indirect representation as in the American Senate (which originally was elected by state legislatures) was undemocratic, Madison's lib-eral response was that "liberty may be endangered by the abuses of liberty as well as the abuses of power."[28]

---

28. Kalyvas and Katznelson, *Liberal Beginnings*, 117, 105, 103. Kalyvas and Katznelson refer to Madison (and more dubiously Thomas Paine) as contributing to "a strand of political thought that had not previously existed." The unnamed "strand" was liberalism. See *Liberal Beginnings*, 118. Madison, *The Federalist Papers*, #63, 387.

The purpose of good government, what we may call a liberal government even if Madison wrote before the word was invented, was to protect *all* people against arbitrary and excessive power of all kinds: "Where an excess of power prevails, property of no sort is duly respected. No man is safe in his opinions, his person, his faculties, or his possessions. Where there is an excess of liberty, the effect is the same, tho' from an opposite cause. Government is instituted to protect property of every sort; as well as that which lies in the various rights of individuals, as that which the term particularly expresses. This being the end of government, that alone is a *just* government, which *impartially* secures to every man, whatever is his *own*." Madison rejected both "arbitrary taxes [which] invade the domestic sanctuaries of the rich," and "excessive taxes [which] grind the faces of the poor." He wanted no one to be afraid. The American constitution he defended in the *Federalist* was designed to provide new means of protection against fear. In doing so, Madison developed a series of arguments that were central to and typical of the first wave of liberals, and in many respects continued to be central thereafter. Perhaps the most striking of these was his defense of factions.[29]

Madison is especially significant for the history of liberalism because of his attention to the question of "who is afraid?" as well as "what is to be feared?." He worried about the oppression of groups, even of factions, not just of individuals. For Madison, fear was both a matter of being threatened as an individual by another individual, such as a despot, and about being threatened as a member of a group by another group. Hence his rethinking in liberal terms of an old theme, faction. "It is of great importance in a republic not only to guard the society against the oppression of its rulers, but to guard one part of the society against the injustice of the other part."[30]

A faction, according to Madison, was a group, of any size (but especially dangerous when a majority), pursuing its own self-interest at the expense of the whole, "united and actuated by some common impulse of passion, or of interest, adverse to the rights of other citizens, or to the permanent and aggregate interests of the community." Factions were traditionally viewed as bad, a perspective that persists in the twenty-first century in the occasional laments

29. Madison, "On Property," March 29, 1792, in Philip B. Kurland and Ralph Lerner, eds., *The Founders' Constitution* (Indianapolis: Liberty Fund, 2001), 1:16, Document 23; Madison, Federalist #52, 327; Federalist #63, 386–387; Shklar, "Montesquieu and the New Republicanism," 279; Federalist #43, 279; "Notes," 247, 262; "Notes," 263.

30. Federalist #51, 323.

still heard about the evils of parties and special interests. Madison agreed that factions were evil, but he also argued that they were not merely inevitable, but a useful, indeed an indispensable means of protecting society against itself. Madison rejected the old republican remedy for factions, that of eliminating them by the application of virtue, and if need be terror: "There are two methods of curing the mischiefs of faction: the one, by removing its causes; the other, by controlling its effects. There are again two methods of removing the causes of faction: the one, by destroying the liberty which is essential to its existence; the other, by giving to every citizen the same opinions, the same passions, and the same interests." For Madison, removing the causes of faction, freedom and diversity, were cures worse than the disease. Factions might be religious, political, or especially economic, Madison wrote, but they would always exist. Civilization inevitably created more of them.[31]

The chief task of modern legislation was thus not the elimination of factions, but their regulation. In the modern world "the spirit of party and faction" was part of the "necessary and ordinary operations of government." In a "popular government," the greatest danger would come from a faction supported by a majority (although minority factions could also gain power). Madison's "great object" was to prevent such factional tyranny by the majority while preserving popular government.[32]

There were only two ways of regulating factions, according to Madison. A power independent of society could regulate them, a hereditary monarch for example, but this ran the risk of despotism either by the monarch or by the monarch in alliance with a faction. Alternately, the solution exemplified by American society and encouraged by a federal system of government was that: "the society itself will be broken into so many parts, interests and classes of citizens, that the rights of individuals, or of the minority, will be in little danger from interested combinations of the majority." Security came from "the number of interests and sects." More diversity would make oppression less likely, and the larger the society, the greater the diversity. In particular Madison, attentive to the American religious context, pointed out that if one religious group should succeed in dominating a state or even a region, the wide variety of religious groups elsewhere would prevent danger. The same was true of experiments with paper currency, debt repudiation, and so on, such as had recently been proposed in a number of American states.

31. Federalist #10, 78; "Notes," 201.
32. Federalist #10, 78–80.

Madison therefore rejected Montesquieu's objection to large republics. The larger the society, the more factions there would be, and this was in itself highly useful: "The best provision for a stable and free Government is not a balance in the powers of the Government, though that is not to be neglected, but an equilibrium in the interests and passions of the society itself, *which cannot be obtained in a small society*." The new American constitution was not merely better than that of the Greeks and Romans, it was better than that of other moderns as well because America was a bigger country with correspondingly more factions. The creation of a large republic that considered diversity a blessing rather than a curse was a new thing. "Happily for America, happily we trust for the whole human race, [the Revolutionaries] pursued a new and more noble course. . . . They reared the fabrics of governments which have no model on the face of the globe." Madison's embrace of faction and diversity was a landmark in the history of liberalism.[33]

Another new development central to liberalism was Madison's recognition of the need to fear the legislature and to create obstacles to legislative, rather than royal, despotism. Seventeenth- and eighteenth-century proto-liberals, writing before the American and French revolutions, had thought the monarch the chief source of tyranny. The balance of Madison's fears was different. Even if they liked to talk about bad King George, the American revolutionaries were well aware that it was the British Parliament that had run roughshod over their rights. Post-Revolutionary American experience, even without the lessons of the Reign of Terror in France (1793–94), taught that danger could come not just from the executive branch, on which proto-liberalism had concentrated its attention, but from a tyranny of the legislature. In a republic, indeed, the legislature was the greater danger. Before the Terror, the example that taught Madison's generation to fear the legislature was what was generally considered Pennsylvania's disastrous experiment with a unicameral legislature and a weak executive. The unicameral state legislature of Pennsylvania was the source of several warning examples:

A great number of laws had been passed, violating, without any apparent necessity, the rule requiring that all bills of a public nature shall be previously printed for the consideration of the people; although this is one of the precautions chiefly relied on by the constitution against improper acts of legislature. The constitutional trial by jury had been violated, and powers assumed which had not been delegated by the constitution. Executive powers had been usurped. The salaries of the judges, which the constitution expressly requires to be fixed, had been occasionally varied; and cases belonging to the judiciary department frequently drawn within legislative cognizance and determination.[34]

The example of Pennsylvania showed that a mere "parchment" separation of powers, which existed in the Pennsylvania constitution, was no help. Nor, as Madison gently pointed out, was Thomas Jefferson's remedy—recourse to constitutional conventions to settle disputes over the division of powers—a good solution. The results would be dictated not by reason, but by aroused public passions likely to lead to injustice and tyranny.[35]

To maintain the separation of powers, an essential political bulwark against despotism, Madison relied on factions and personal interests acting within government institutions for checks and balances that would limit legislative despotism. If the self-interests of individuals and factions were attached to different institutions, that would strengthen them. "Ambition must be made to counteract ambition. The interest of the man must be connected with the constitutional rights of the place. . . . Opposite and rival interests [supply] the defect of better motives." In this way "the private interest of every individual may be a sentinel over the public rights." For example, judges had a personal interest in their ability to strike down an unjust law because defending judicial prerogative increased their personal importance and the importance of their group, the judiciary. This was Madison's version of Smith's Invisible Hand applied to politics.[36] Instead of the desire for personal wealth resulting in social and economic benefits, it was the desire for personal political success that helped the public cause. Madison recognized its broad application: "this policy of supplying, by opposite and rival interests, the defect of better motives, might be traced through the whole system of human affairs, private as well as public."[37]

34. Federalist #48, 310

35. Federalist #48, 309–312.

36. As seen above in Kant, and below in Constant, versions of the Invisible Hand argument were ubiquitous in nineteenth-century liberalism, perhaps even more outside economics than inside.

37. Federalist #51, 322.

Officeholders must have their personal ambitions and self-interest linked to that of their branch of government—and not just to the branches of one government, but to the many different governments of a federal system. The great virtue of a federal republic, for Madison, lay in its unique resources for countering despotism on several levels, in state and local governments as well as at the national level. Thus, in the American Senate the representation of the states checked the despotism of the majority represented in the House of Representatives, while state governments naturally would be jealous of national authority—and vice versa, for Madison also saw the national authorities as referees when faction was destroying a state. In fact, Madison feared the encroachment of the states on national authority more than the reverse, and thus a diminution of the power of the national government to counter state-level tyranny (possibly he had slavery in mind). This is why Madison supported a constitutional power for the national government to veto state laws, in order "to secure individuals against encroachments on their rights."[38]

In a "popular government," the greatest danger came from a faction supported by a majority. Madison's "great object" was to prevent such factional tyranny by the majority while preserving popular government. Madison was also concerned that in a popular government, in which the right to vote was widespread, the rich would be oppressed. This was the classic fear that in any kind of democracy, even a democratically elected representative government, the poor majority would take away the money of the rich. Madison's remedy resulted from something not dissimilar to Smith's notion of the sympathy people naturally feel for the great: "If the law allows an opulent citizen but a single vote in the choice of his representative, the respect and consequence which he derives from his fortunate situation very frequently guide the votes of others to the objects of his choice; and through this imperceptible channel the rights of property are conveyed into the public representation." The faction of the wealthy thus found means to influence representative government— and Madison thought this was a good thing.[39]

By attaching individual and factional interest to different branches and levels of government, legislative tyranny could be averted. Madison thus developed a new, liberal analysis of balanced government, based on the encouragement of faction and self-interest. But self-interest and faction alone

38. Federalist #43, 277; "Notes," 216–219; "Notes," 219, 286.
39. Federalist #54, 339.

were not, for Madison, a sufficient remedy for the problems facing post-revolutionary society. Virtue too was needed. Madison was in favor of both prudence and principles.[40]

Neither a multitude of factions, nor a federal system of government in a large republic, nor the self-interest of individuals in preserving the separation of powers were enough to keep life and property safe if virtue was entirely absent. For the public and their representatives to perform their function in a popular government required a certain amount of virtue: "Is there no virtue among us? If there be not, we are in a wretched situation. No theoretical checks—no form of government can render us secure. To suppose that any form of government will secure liberty or happiness without any virtue in the people is a chimerical idea." Republics required more virtue than other regimes: "As there is a degree of depravity in mankind which requires a certain degree of circumspection and distrust, so there are other qualities in human nature which justify a certain portion of esteem and confidence. Republican government presupposes the existence of these qualities in a higher degree than any other form."[41]

However, if Madison considered virtue necessary, he treated it as a weaker force than the gravitational pull exerted by self-interest and expressed by factions. "We well know that neither moral nor religious motives can be relied on as an adequate control" on factions. Nor were they sufficient with regard to individuals: "The aim of every political constitution is, or ought to be, first to obtain for rulers men who possess most wisdom to discern, and most virtue to pursue, the common good of the society; and in the next place, to take the most effectual precautions for keeping them virtuous whilst they continue to hold their public trust." Trust, but verify, as President Ronald Reagan said about the Soviet Union. Virtue was necessary, but even less sufficient on its own than self-interest. When listing things that might restrain a majority from violating the rights and interests of a minority, Madison suggested three possible motives based on virtue, all of which were useful but inadequate: (1) a prudent regard for the general good and a recognition that honesty was the best policy, but this was too often forgotten by nations and individuals alike;

40. Federalist #10, 78–80; Federalist #54, 339. On Madison's support for prudence and principle, see Morgan Smith, "Madison, Religious Liberty and Union," 692.

41. Madison, Speech to the Virginia Ratifying Convention, June 20, 1788, in *The Papers of James Madison*, 11:163; Federalist #55, 346.

(2) respect for character, by which Madison meant respect for how others would see one's actions, but if the majority agreed with injustice, then there was little to be hoped for from this remedy; (3) religion. But religion was subject to enthusiasm, a passion that could lead to injustice, and even "in its coolest state . . . it may become a motive to oppression as well as a restraint from injustice." If religious belief was natural and naturally supported morality and virtue, according to Madison, it was also a source of enthusiasm and fanaticism, and best divided into many sects. The *Federalist Papers* steered clear of any religious sanctification of the new American Constitution, save for the unique and perhaps telling claim that its agreement by the delegates to the Constitutional Convention was proof of divine intervention and a miracle. In any event Madison, while more than willing to criticize religious fanaticism, was unwilling to criticize religion as such, and rather saw it as a possible basis, if an insufficient one, for restraining injustice and promoting virtue.[42]

What made representative government work in America was "the vigilant and manly spirit which animates the people of America." This vigilance was motivated by self-interest and also by virtue. It was what would keep the American Congress, Madison wrote, from discriminating in favor of themselves or some particular faction. Public opinion kept the representatives on the path of virtue. If this vigilant "spirit which nourishes freedom, and in return is nourished by it" disappeared, liberty would be impossible. American self-government was founded on the moral character of the population, but not on their republican self-sacrifice, rather on their liberal vigilance against sources of fear and willingness to express themselves.[43]

If virtue played a crucial role for Madison, even if often in the background, his discussion of economic questions was much more limited in both space and scope. Unlike his *Federalist* co-author Alexander Hamilton, Madison did not believe that economic interest in itself, for all its utility, was a sufficient pillar on which to base either the new nation or a liberal society, although the contribution of the multiple economic interests liberated by a free market to the multiplying of factions was not insignificant.[44] Madison

---

42. Lindsay, "James Madison on Religion and Politics," 1328; "Federalist" #37, 230–231; Federalist #10, 81; Madison to Jefferson, 24 Oct. 1787, in Sheehan, *The Mind of James Madison*, 202–203; Morgan Smith, "Madison, Religious Liberty and Union," 700.

43. "Notes," 134; Federalist #57, 353.

44. Sheehan, "Introduction," in *James Madison and the Spirit of Republican Self-Government*, 10.

praised free trade in language seemingly borrowed from Smith, and *doux commerce* in even stronger terms than Montesquieu, and he rejected the idea of government-sanctioned monopolies, but they were not central to his concerns.[45] Like Kant and Constant, Madison was convinced of the central importance of political guarantees for freedom. It was the most important pillar of his liberalism. Like Constant and Kant, he also saw a necessary relationship between morality / virtue / religion and the maintenance of a liberal order.

Madison's real originality, his greatest contribution to the development of liberal thought, derived from his concern to guarantee the safety of groups as much as of individuals. In a characteristically liberal way, he did so by multiplying their number and promoting diversity, rather than trying to eliminate conflict and impose uniformity. The multiplication of sects and factions was collectively useful, just as it allowed each of them, in its own way, to pursue its own interest or salvation. *E pluribus unum.* In this Madison anticipated the arguments not just of John Stuart Mill but a whole line of European liberals who stressed the diversity of both individuals and groups. Faced with a similar democratic social situation, and similarly post-revolutionary historical conditions, they arrived at comparably liberal solutions.

Constant: Squaring the Circle between Ancient and Modern Freedom

Madison's recognition of new circumstances that demanded new responses was naturally focused on the particular conditions facing the young American state. Benjamin Constant broadened this historical understanding to make it the foundation of modern liberty, and thus liberalism.

---

45. Madison said in a speech to the first American Congress in 1789, "In the first place, I own myself the friend to a very free system of commerce, and hold it as a truth, that commercial shackles are generally unjust, oppressive and impolitic—it is also a truth, that if industry and labor are left to their own course, they will generally be directed to those objects which are the most productive, and this in a more certain and direct manner than the wisdom of the most enlightened legislature could point out." This was pure Smith. The notes for this speech restate the *doux commerce* theory of international trade promoting peace "Notes," 164–165; Speech by Madison on April 9, 1789 on duties on imports, Gales, ed., *The Debate and Proceedings in the Congress of the United States*, 115–116. On monopolies, see Madison, "On Property"; Sheehan, *The Mind of James Madison*, 110, 263.

Benjamin Constant was not the first liberal,[46] but he was possibly the first person to use the word "liberal" in print to designate a set of political positions. He did so in Paris in April 1797. The place and date matter. The word "liberal" was invented in the guillotine's shadow: the French Revolutionary Terror had only just ended, coups d'état were frequent, and political violence, whether revolutionary or reactionary, was very much on French minds. Constant was among the first generation in Europe to directly confront the fear of revolution and reaction that produced liberalism. As a politically active figure living in Paris, he confronted it with personal urgency. He lived, in intensely personal form, the characteristic liberal fear of fighting a war on two fronts. In his case the fear was aroused by the Jacobins on the left, and Napoleon or the Bourbons on the right. From Constant's liberal perspective, "despotism and anarchy are more alike than people think."[47]

His positions evolved considerably over time, sometimes because of changes of opinion, often because the tactical situation so dictated.[48] Constant was sufficiently a political chameleon to support the Directory, then Napoleon's coup d'état, then serve in his government, then go into opposition and exile, and then help Napoleon write the liberal "Acte Additionel" to the imperial constitution during his brief return from Elba, only to once again swear an oath of allegiance to the Bourbons after they returned to power. Nevertheless, there is considerable truth in the preface he wrote to a collection of essays published near the end of his life: "For forty years I have defended the same principle: freedom in everything, in religion, in philosophy, in literature, in industry, in politics: and by freedom, I mean the triumph of individuality, both over the authority which wants to govern by despotism, and over the masses which claim the right to subject the minority to the majority."[49]

One reason Constant could claim to be consistent was that his analysis of freedom was consistently based on freedom from fear: "ask yourselves . . . what an Englishman, a Frenchman, and a citizen of the United States under-

46. Who was? No one—one more bit of evidence that liberalism is the organic political tradition of modern Western culture.

47. Constant, *Principles*, 7.

48. There is some debate over what should be considered Constant's mature position. Stephen Holmes opted for the *Commentary on Filangieri's Work* of 1824, while Jeremy Jennings preferred the *Principles of Politics* in the version of 1806. Here the *Principles* are given preference, partly because of their more comprehensive discussions. See Holmes, *Benjamin Constant*, 269n89; Jennings, "Constant's Idea of Modern Liberty," 73–74.

49. Constant, "Mélanges de littérature et de politique," 519.

stand today by the word 'liberty'. For each of them it is the right to be subjected only to the laws, and to be neither arrested, detained, put to death or maltreated in any way by the arbitrary will of one or more individuals." His list of freedoms continued, but freedom from fear was what began it, and his further specifications were just a list of guarantees against arbitrary power. For Constant, freedom in the modern world means personal security, or there is no freedom at all.[50]

Constant's guarantees against fear were based on a new understanding of historical development derived from his well-known distinction between ancient and modern ideas of freedom. They involved strict limits on the scope of government and emphasized the need for laissez-faire policies in the economy and beyond. At the same time, Constant argued that a liberal state depended on morality and religion. He was indeed one of the few liberal writers who gave nearly equal attention to all three pillars of liberalism. The ensemble of his positions was by no means typical either of his contemporary French liberals or of other liberals, but individually they had enormous resonance in liberal discourse, both in his own time and thereafter.

Fundamentally, for Constant, the Revolution's errors were caused by misunderstanding modernity. Like Kant and Madison, Constant thought it was necessary to understand the way in which the present differed from the past, and his understanding of liberalism was based on this distinction. Constant was familiar with the Scottish three- or four-stage theory of history from his time as a student in Edinburgh. He limited himself, however, to a two-stage version that distinguished between ancient and modern liberty:[51] "The aim of the ancients was the sharing of social power among the citizens of the same fatherland: this is what they called liberty. The aim of the moderns is the enjoyment of security in private pleasures; and they call liberty the guarantees accorded by institutions to these pleasures."[52]

50. Constant, "Speech on Ancient and Modern Liberty" (henceforth AML), in Constant, *Political Writings*, 310; see also *Principles*, 7, 18; *Principles*, 10–11; Holmes, "The Liberty to Denounce," 59.

51. The distinction first appeared in the *Considerations on the Principal Events of the French Revolution* by his friend and lover Mme. De Staël, with which Constant was deeply involved as well.

52. Constant, AML, 317. The discussion here is based on Constant's famous 1824 lecture. However, he presented a very similar discussion of ancient and modern freedom in the earlier *Principles*, 351–365.

Although the ancients were politically free, frequently exercising their political rights in sovereign assemblies, they were, in Constant's judgment, slaves in every aspect of their private lives, subject to state supervision in everything from their religion to their sexuality. By contrast, modern people exercised their political freedom on rare occasions in a voting booth, but were free in their private lives. Ancient freedom was appropriate for a society in which war was the normal state of affairs and politics always a life-and-death affair. Modern freedom was appropriate for a society in which commerce was king and peace the natural state. The business of the moderns required individual independence and suffered from any state intervention. The small republics of the ancient world gave political scope to the individual. Large modern states condemned individuals to the pains and pleasures of political obscurity and private life. Modern people would not, could not, and should not sacrifice their individual liberty for the sake of political liberty in the ancient sense of exercising direct sovereignty. "Individual liberty . . . is the true modern liberty." The great error of the French Revolution, according to Constant, was to try to revive ancient political virtues in a modern society for which they were inappropriate. The revolutionaries' mistake was the cause of "infinite evils," according to Constant, "yet God forbid I should reproach them too harshly. Their error itself was excusable. One could not read the beautiful pages of antiquity, one could not recall the actions of its great men, without feeling an indefinable and special emotion, which nothing modern can possibly arouse." Nostalgia was part of the liberal repertoire. What distinguished liberals from other political movements, at least during the short nineteenth century, was that liberals had less of it, rather than that it was absent from liberalism.[53]

To preserve individual freedom, Constant prescribed some familiar strategies. There is no need to go into detail about his embrace of the separation of powers and of representative government as guarantees against despotism and cruelty. Constant was typically liberal in these respects. There are nevertheless several respects in which his treatment of politics as a guarantee against despotism and fear is significant for illuminating the development of liberalism.

Limiting the sphere of government was part of proto-liberal thought: salvation could no longer be a concern of government if people were to sleep safely in their beds; property had to be secure against the king. Thinkers like Montesquieu and Smith extended the principle beyond religion and property ownership. In the nineteenth century, liberalism proper broadened *noli me*

---

53. *Principles*, 314–315; AML, 318.

tangere to a whole raft of new areas, from freedom of expression to freedom of contract. Constant was one of the most systematic spokesmen for limiting the role of government.[54]

Constant set himself up in opposition to Rousseau, as well as to ancient liberty. Neither Rousseau nor the ancients, in Constant's view, recognized any limit on the power society could exercise over the individual. For Constant, however, "there is a part of human existence which necessarily remains individual and independent, and which by right is beyond all social or legislative competence. . . . [Individual rights] are rights which legislation should never touch, rights over which society has no jurisdiction, rights which it cannot invade without making itself as guilty of tyranny as the despot who has no other title to authority than a deadly sword. The government's legitimacy depends on its purpose as much as its source."[55]

Constant complained that all past writers on political theory, "even in some respects Montesquieu," had attributed too much power to the government. But "political society cannot exceed its jurisdiction without being usurpative. . . . The assent of the majority is not enough in all circumstances to render its actions lawful." Whereas in the *Federalist* Madison concentrated on preventing majority despotism by preventing the formation of a majority faction, Constant concentrated on limiting the majority's scope of action. Unless the scope of government was limited, Constant argued, its organization, the separation of powers, etc., was of little interest. How I may be persecuted is of little importance compared to the question of whether I will be persecuted.[56]

If the government went beyond its sphere, if it became despotic, people had a right to resist, according to Constant, parting company with Kant, although he chose Bentham as his explicit target.[57] Like Kant, Constant was not anxious to encourage revolutions, having lived through too many. Nevertheless, in Constant's view, the more a government overstepped its bounds, the fewer duties one had toward it. People had a positive duty not to execute unjust laws, a duty of passive resistance. Did this right to resistance amount to a right to

54. Craiutu, *A Virtue for Courageous Minds*, 215.

55. Constant, *Filangieri*, 32; *Principles*, 385–386.

56. *Principles*, 47, 31, 33, 35.

57. Constant rarely missed a chance to reject Bentham. Despite their disagreements, he shared too much with Kant to do the same. Cf. Welch, " 'Anti-Benthamism': Utilitarianism and the French Liberal Tradition."

revolution? "It would be a childish endeavor to seek to present individuals with fixed rules relative to revolution." Revolutions were natural catastrophes that took place regardless of individual wills. "It is only to governments that one can give useful advice for the avoidance of revolutions," namely avoiding injustice and the rule of force. When it came to revolution, the longest chapter in Constant's most comprehensive account of his views, the *Principles of Politics*, was "The Duties of Enlightened Men during Revolutions," followed by "Continuation of the Same Subject," where Constant took the opportunity to condemn the Terror and fanaticism. It is worth pointing out that Constant agreed with Kant that if the people had the right to depose a king or to deprive a class of hereditary privileges, they had no right to punish or kill them.[58] Constant and Kant (and for that matter Madison) shared the liberal fear of revolution, for the good reason that what was liable to happen in a revolution was enough to make any sensible person afraid.

Constant's use of "rights" here and elsewhere merits a digression because it is widespread in nineteenth-century liberalism. For Constant and many other nineteenth-century liberals, individual rights were the most effective check on the power of government and of the majority. As he put it, "Individual rights are composed of everything independent of political authority." Constant rejected Bentham's view that the idea of rights was nonsense because no one ever agreed on what they were, not because it was wrong in itself but because it was equally applicable to Bentham's own criterion of utility. Indeed, for Constant the idea of utility was even more vague than that of rights. Nevertheless, Constant wrote that in the end he and Bentham arrived at the same conclusions. Constant, however, preferred the language of rights over that of utility because it was a moral language: it created a feeling of duty, and produced a very different psychology: "Say to a man: you have the right not to be put to death or arbitrarily plundered. You will give him quite another feeling of security and protection than you will by telling him: it is not useful for you to be put to death or arbitrarily plundered." Constant agreed that there was in effect no such thing as an "inalienable" right. The term "inalienable" meant not that a given right could not be taken away, but that it should not be. Rights for Constant, as for many other short nineteenth-century liberals, were a tool that gave a special moral / psychological force to ramparts raised against fear.[59]

<hr>

58. *Principles*, 402, 397, 404–405, 414.
59. *Principles*, 10–12, 31, 33, 39–42.

For Constant, economic rights and freedoms were as valuable as any other civil freedoms, just as much part of modern liberty. The vast majority of nineteenth-century liberals agreed with Constant in seeing commercial society as a pillar of liberalism and a guarantee against despotism in modern societies—as did proto-liberals like Montesquieu and Smith before them. Constant, however, went further than most of his predecessors in systematically enunciating his economic theory and justifying it on liberal grounds.

If permitted to go its way, a free market would work wonders, according to Constant. Laissez-faire economic policy (including the destruction of monopolies, economic privileges, guilds, restraints on trade, etc.) would lead, as if by the work of an invisible hand, to an "egalitarian" result. "Wealth is distributed and divided by itself in perfect equilibrium, when the division of property is not limited and the exercise of industry does not encounter any hindrances." This equilibrium, or the idea often repeated by Constant that human society was tending toward equality, should not be taken to mean that everyone would get the same share. "What is equality? It is distributive justice. It is not the absence of all differences in social advantages. No one has demanded, no one demands that kind of equality. Equality is the aptitude to gain those advantages according to the means and facilities with which one is endowed." He had no objection to unequal wealth as such. "When wealth is the gradual product of assiduous work and a busy life or when it is transmitted from generation to generation by peaceful possession, far from corrupting those who acquire it or enjoy its use, it offers them new means of leisure and enlightenment and consequently new motives for morality."[60]

Constant did not expect his embrace of laissez-faire economics to meet with universal applause, even among liberals, and especially not in France. Hence even though he thought it was intimately connected to all other forms of freedom, he took care to separate his free-market economics from his other views, fearful they might suffer from its proximity. It was for tactical reasons, he admitted, that he left economic freedom out of his list of inalienable individual rights. "I did not wish, although all questions of this kind are interlinked, to put commercial freedom and civil freedom at the same level, for fear that the men who would disagree about the former" would then discredit the latter. Constant took pains to note that "I could be wrong in my claims about the freedom of production and trade without my principles of

60. *Filangieri*, 27; Jennings, "Constant's Idea of Modern Liberty," 78; *Filangieri*, 252; *Principles*, 158, 366.

religious, intellectual, and personal freedom being weakened by this." Nevertheless, private property and the division of labor were "the basis of the perfecting of all the arts and sciences," and without them "the progressive faculty . . . would die." More important, free markets were "one of the principal bases of liberty." Modern society, and modern freedom, rested on an economic pillar.[61]

To return to Constant's economics, Constant's understanding of political economy was not altogether modern. He mixed ancient elements into his modern gospel of laissez-faire. Ancient, for example, was his argument for the political superiority of landownership over other forms of property. "Business property," such as factories or shops, "lacks several of the advantages of landed property and these advantages are precisely those in which the safeguarding spirit necessary for political association consists." The ownership of a particular piece of land encouraged moral ties across generations (a particular concern for Constant), whereas "people never say my parents' workshop or shop counter." "Landed property guarantees the stability of institutions; business property assures the independence of individuals." Thus, Constant concluded, when voting rights were based on property ownership, it was right to deny the right to vote to owners of business property, since it did not provide the same guarantees for stability, and after all those who wanted to vote could always buy land.[62]

Constant was right in thinking that most liberals did not adopt laissez-faire economic views. Most French liberals, and many German, were advocates of protection rather than free trade. Even in England, the putative homeland of laissez-faire liberalism, it was not adopted by all liberals.[63] For much of the nineteenth century, liberalism was not associated with any particular economic theory. It was perhaps as a means of attracting more liberal support for his economic views that Constant attempted to extend the application of "laissez-faire" well beyond commerce: "The greatest service government can do to knowledge is not to bother with it. *Laissez-faire* is all you need to bring commerce to the highest point of prosperity; letting people write is all you need for the human mind to achieve the highest degree of activity." The final sentence of Constant's *Commentary on Filangieri's Work* was: "For thought, for

61. *Principles*, 227–228, Constant, cited in Holmes, *Benjamin Constant*, 54; *Principles*, 168.

62. *Principles*, 175, 177–178. The preference for landownership over business property was fairly common among contemporary liberals.

63. See the discussion of Macaulay, chapter 4.

education, for industry, the motto of government ought to be: *Laissez-faire et laissez-passer*."[64]

Laissez-faire was thus a general guide to the freedom that civil society needed and was entitled to in the modern world. All freedoms were interlinked. For example, restrictions on freedom of thought blighted economic activity, in Constant's view, and he cited the example of Inquisition-ridden Spain as proof: the person who feared the Inquisition was less likely to invest. There was an invisible link between all forms of freedom, all the ways in which people felt secure against despotism and cruelty. Thus, economic activity was not driven only by self-interest, and public opinion played a crucial role: "People often exaggerate the influence of personal interest. Personal interest itself needs the existence of public opinion to act. The man whose opinion languishes, stifled, is not for long excited even by his interests. A sort of torpor seizes him." Commerce thus needed the right moral and political conditions to flourish, and inversely. Liberalism needed all its three pillars to stand.[65]

Constant's greatest concern in the age of modern liberty was not to prescribe how politics or the economy should be structured, as important as that was, so much as to drive home the importance of the moral / religious aspect of liberalism. He wanted political freedom both as a means of guaranteeing civil freedom for individuals, and as a means to a moral end, preventing the degradation of the modern soul. Political freedom was a moral guarantee and a moral technique, and Constant valued it as much for its positive moral effects as for its negative role in preventing despotism.[66]

Political freedom was not simply a device for increasing our chances at happiness. "Is it so evident that happiness, of whatever kind, is the only aim of mankind? If it were so, our course would be narrow indeed, and our destination far from elevated. . . . It is not to happiness alone, it is to self-development that our destiny calls us; and political liberty is the most powerful, the most effective means of self-development that heaven has given us." Political freedom, even among modern people for whom private interests and pleasures came first, encouraged "all classes" to "emerge from the sphere of their usual labours and private industry," and learn to "choose with discernment, resist with energy, brave threats, nobly withstand seduction." Thus a modern, duly limited, representative government could provide modern people the moral

64. *Principles*, 116; Constant, *Filangieri*, 261.
65. *Principles*, 119.
66. *Principles*, 387; Holmes, *Benjamin Constant*, 40.

benefits of political participation that would otherwise have been reserved to the ancients. Constant thus sought, "far from renouncing either of the two sorts of freedom . . . to learn to combine the two together."[67]

Modern humanity's disinterest in politics was dangerous in two ways. First, "the danger of modern liberty is that, absorbed in the enjoyment of our private independence, and in the pursuit of our particular interests, we should surrender our right to share in political power too easily," and soon find ourselves subject to a despotic government. Second, there was the danger that private pleasures would lead to the moral diminution and degradation of humanity.[68]

What Constant wanted was not some historically, sociologically, and economically impossible marriage of the ancient city-state and the modern republic. His speech on ancient and modern liberty showed that that was impossible. What he sought was a means of raising the moderns, by different paths, to the moral peaks attained by the ancients—while at the same time allowing them to pursue an entirely modern personal happiness. The aim of political institutions, Constant said at the end of his speech, was best achieved "if they elevate the largest possible number of citizens to the highest moral position." Political institutions therefore "must achieve the moral education of the citizens," while respecting their individual rights. Constant wished to "combine" ancient and modern freedom. Freedom was priceless "because it gives soundness to our mind, strength to our character, elevation to our soul."[69]

Freedom for Constant, as throughout mainstream liberalism in the short nineteenth century, was thus both negative and positive. Constant came close to saying this himself. He discussed "two moralities." The first ignored people's motivations and was limited to forbidding evil actions. This was the negative morality appropriate for the state to enforce through law. The second was all about individual feelings and motivations, and here the state should never intervene. In twentieth-century terms, the government should remain neutral about differing conceptions of the good life. In Constant's terms, even the imposition of moral truths by the government "is not only useless but harmful, *truths as much as error*," because it denies our intelligence and makes us "wretchedly passive creatures." "Even were the protection of government

---

67. AML, 327. The modern tendency to apathy is discussed above in the context of AML, and is also a theme of his novel, *Adolphe*. See Vincent, "Character."

68. *Principles*, 323, 317, 326; AML 327; *De la religion*, cited in Rosenblatt, *Lost History*, 218.

69. AML, 327–328; Constant, cited in Rosenblatt, *Liberal Values*, 154.

never granted save to virtue, I would still hold that virtue would be better off independent." Constant rejected any official positive morality, whether imposed directly by the government, or indirectly, through a state religion. He favored the strict separation of Church and State.[70]

But negative morality, even if it was the only kind that the state could legitimately enforce, was not enough to defeat apathy and preserve a free state. One could not simply let people pursue their own self-interest, with the state interfering only when that pursuit harmed others in illegitimate ways, and assume this would be enough to maintain freedom. Or rather, while the government must let people pursue their self-interest, if that was all that people did, while looking at their government in a purely instrumental, utilitarian way, then the government would not survive, at least not a free government. Such an ethics of self-interest had led France to political "indifference," and "servility" (Constant had the Empire in mind). Such a society was like a collection of "industrious beavers," ruled by nothing but prudence and an "arithmetic morality" (a jab at Bentham): it had no moral content. Without elevation of soul, freedom could not be preserved.[71]

Thus the second kind of morality, of individual elevation and perfection, was crucial to the existence of a free state. In the end, for Constant, freedom became a kind of religion, or at least a moral gospel within the bounds of reason / modern society. Indeed for Constant, "All that is beautiful, all that is intimate, all that is noble, partakes of the nature of religion." But religion itself was necessary too.[72]

Constant's liberalism, it has been observed, was always informed by religious values. In nineteenth-century Europe, liberals generally regarded religion and freedom as both compatible and mutually reinforcing, providing it was the right kind of religion, duly separated from the state, or at least defanged, as in England, and as a general rule not Catholic (see chapter 5). But while liberals wanted the *government* to be neutral toward religion, that did not mean that *liberals* were neutral toward religion. Constant certainly was not.[73]

---

70. Holmes, *Benjamin Constant*, 9; Constant, cited in Rosenblatt, *Liberal Values*, 129; *Principles*, 307, 134–135 and elsewhere.

71. Constant, cited in Rosenblatt, *Liberal Values*, 194; Constant, cited in Rosenblatt, *Liberal Values*, 193; Jennings, "Constant's Idea of Modern Liberty," 71.

72. Izenberg, "Indivdualism and Individuality in Constant," 223–224; Constant, cited in Garsten, "Constant on the Religious Spirit," 298.

73. Dickey, "Constant and Religion,"313; Garsten, "Constant on the Religious Spirit," 296.

Religion was the royal road to elevating human souls, in Constant's view, a multi-lane highway to perfection. It also had its vulgar utility, helping to repress theft, murder, and so on, but it was not needed for this: "there is a common morality, based on calculation, interest, and security, which can, I think, at a pinch do without religion." But the second and greater kind of morality needed religion: "It is for the creation of a more elevated morality that religion seems desirable to me. I do not invoke it to repress gross crimes but to ennoble all the virtues." Religion, like politics, raised people above the "habits of common life" and the "petty material interests that go with it." A nation without it "would seem to me to be deprived of a precious faculty and disinherited by nature."[74]

Crucially, religion enabled modern people to engage in self-sacrifice. "Liberty nourishes itself on sacrifices. . . . Liberty always wants citizens, and often heroes. Do not let fade the convictions that ground the virtues of citizens and that create heroes, giving them the strength to be martyrs." The need for religious conviction was both political and personal. As the liberal state needed religion, so did the liberal individual: "the more one loves freedom, the more one cherishes moral ideas, the more high-mindedness, courage, and independence are needed, the more it is necessary to have some respite from men, to take refuge in a belief in a God." This was why "among all peoples, religious institutions always have intimate ties with political liberty, and whenever religion itself has the liberty that it deserves, the liberty of nations is firmly in place."[75]

It was not one particular religion that did this, according to Constant, although it was also not every religion that did so. Constant was ferociously anticlerical, and his vision of religion as ennobling and perfecting character owed much to German Protestantism, as he himself recognized. Partly because of this Protestant perspective, Constant thought it was better to have many religions than few. In a society with only one religion, religion became a powerless form. Unlike Smith, Constant approved of the fact that new sects tended to distinguish themselves by a more stringent morality. If previously the advent of new sects had been accompanied by "strife and misfortune," this was because the government had gotten involved. Keep Church and State separate,

74. *Principles*, 141, 142; Rosenblatt, *Liberal Values*, 136, Constant, cited in Rosenblatt, *Liberal Values*, 173; *Principles*, 133.

75. Constant, cited in Garsten, "Religion and the Case Against Ancient Liberty,", 21; *Principles*, 131; Constant, cited in Garsten, "Religion and the Case Against Ancient Liberty," 4.

and the proliferation of sects would result in "mutual checks," and the government wouldn't have to worry about the degeneration of one religion or the combats of two or three because each of the innumerable sects would be too weak to disturb the peace. As Constant put it at the end of his study of religion, "Divide the torrent, or, rather allow it to divide itself into a thousand rivulets. They will fertilize the earth that the torrent would have devastated."[76]

Constant, in part because of his political gyrations, in part because of his ideas, often felt himself isolated on the French political scene and even among French liberals. His canonical stature in histories of liberalism resembles that of Locke, adopted late into a genealogy when it suited their descendants' twentieth-century purposes. In some respects, in particular Constant's commitment to laissez-faire economics, this is surely the case. Nevertheless in many respects Constant's ideas of historical development, of the need to limit government, and even of the fundamental importance of morality and religion were typical of nineteenth-century liberals. Even when that was not the case, as with his economic views, he was not altogether isolated—his sense of isolation came largely from the difficulties he encountered in French political life. Constant was a classic representative of a liberalism that responded to the fears of the age and relied on the three pillars of freedom, markets, and morals to do so.

After the revolutions in America and France, liberalism emerged as a noun and a movement. Kant, Madison, and Constant, three of its founding figures, had very different concerns when viewed from certain angles, but when viewed from the perspective of liberalism, they were engaged in responding to similar problems. They raised common concerns and proposed more or less compatible solutions. They exemplify the overlapping consensus that made up liberal political language and practice in the nineteenth century.

This "consensus" was a very broad agreement about what was to be feared and what kinds of remedies might diminish those fears. Kant, Madison, and Constant shared not only fear but hope, a hope that all of them located in civil society, although the rational / historical / sociological analyses on which their hope was based differed considerably. As liberalism developed, these different analyses served to differentiate various sorts of liberal, both in retrospect and in practice. The liberal consensus always contained tensions, including the relative weights given to the three pillars, and different analyses of the sources

76. Rosenblatt, *Liberal Values*, 194; Garsten, "Constant on the Religious Spirit," 296; *Principles*, 137–139; Constant, cited in Todorov, "Religion According to Constant," 285.

of fear, compatible with the enormous diversity of liberals and liberalisms and of their circumstances. Liberals engaged with the problems at hand, and those problems varied. Some liberals were simply interested in different things. Some were altogether outside the liberal mainstream, in that they explicitly or implicitly rejected the need for a political, or an economic, or a moral basis of liberalism. But these were relatively few in the short nineteenth century (they will be discussed in chapter 5), although they would become increasingly prominent later, especially after WWII. Kant, Madison, and Constant in their time, like Macaulay, J. S. Mill, and Tocqueville in the next generation, were examples of both the kind of consensus and the tensions within it that were typical of Liberalism 1.0.

What is important to recognize is the way in which Kant, Madison, and Constant articulated a set of concerns and responses, of fears and hopes, that can serve as a baseline against which to examine the historical development of, and the tensions within, nineteenth-century liberalism. First-wave liberalism continued to develop over the next two generations, responding to new circumstances and developing new understandings of politics, economics, and morals. Not without the tensions and disagreements typical of any family, Macaulay, Tocqueville, and John Stuart Mill represent the development of liberalism in a society moving further away from the immediate experience of revolution and the more distant experience of the Enlightenment, and entering an increasingly industrial and democratic world. They represent, in many respects, liberalisms that are quite removed from those of Kant, Madison, and Constant, but which continue to respond to similar fears and rely on civil society and on freedom, markets, and morals as the source and bulwark of their hopes.

4

Many-Splendored Liberalism

LIBERALISM 1.0 RUNS from the last decade or so of the eighteenth century through the first three-quarters of the nineteenth century. What set this period apart were the particular fears to which liberals responded: new fears of revolution and reaction, as well as older, proto-liberal fears of religious fanaticism and despotism. Nineteenth-century liberals typically relied on all three pillars of freedom, markets, and morals to fight their fears. Naturally, individual liberals stressed one pillar more than the others. But rather than exclusively relying on any one of them, such as free markets or political rights, all three pillars were consistently part of the mainstream liberal arsenal against arbitrary cruelty. There were prominent exceptions, some of which are explored in the following chapter, but most liberals thought and argued in this way.

Their common fears, and commonly three-pillared arguments, nevertheless allowed for considerable variation in the positions taken by first-wave liberals, sometimes in ways that seem surprising in light of the manner in which liberalism is ordinarily viewed in the twenty-first century. This may not be immediately evident when looking at Kant, Madison, and Constant. Their emphases on freedom of speech, limited government, and laissez-faire economics are all still associated with liberalism today. But, unlike them, many nineteenth-century liberals were partisans of a bigger state, were by no means laissez-faire in economics, were distrustful of commercial society and the middle classes, and were even dubious about permitting socially offensive speech. Freedom, markets, and morals were central to the thought of most nineteenth-century liberals, but they constructed their pillars from very diverse materials. T. B. Macaulay, Alexis de Tocqueville, and John Stuart Mill illustrate the widely different views held by nineteenth-century liberals. Nineteenth-century liberals shared a very broad tent, and there were many facets to nineteenth-century liberalism. It is important not to let the particular shine of one facet in a certain light obscure the others. Liberalism in the short nineteenth century was a many-splendored thing.

Mid-century liberals such as Macaulay, Tocqueville, and Mill diverged conceptually in some respects from the previous generation. One shift was a change in vocabulary and attention from commercial society to the "middle class(es)" or the "bourgeoisie." This common shift did not entail common attitudes, however. While most liberals of the period, like Macaulay or François Guizot, lauded the middle class and made them central to liberal politics, aristocratic liberals, such as Tocqueville and Mill, added fear of the middle classes to the old liberal fear of a revolutionary or religiously fanatic mob. These liberals changed their focus from the proto-liberal "fear of Puritans" to a new "fear of Philistines."[1]

It was admirers of the middle classes like Macaulay, however, who were at the center of mid-nineteenth-century liberal thought. Macaulay articulated the commonsense liberalism of his period. His faith in progress; his flexible attitude toward state intervention and laissez-faire economics; and his pragmatic rejection of both utilitarian and religious enthusiasm represented the center of nineteenth-century liberalism in England, the leading liberal culture of the time. The approach to liberalism taken by the English is therefore especially significant. Macaulay was as close as we can come to the center of English liberalism.[2]

Macaulay: Faith in Progress and the Middle Classes

The reputation of Macaulay, formerly a household name, has fallen into eclipse. His once-popular poetry is unread, and if a few passages from his historical works or essays, bestsellers in their time, are still occasionally quoted, they no longer exercise any great influence. Some of his parliamentary speeches are used as textbook illustrations of themes in British liberalism, but as he was never a politician of the first rank, he is not a leading figure in historical studies.[3] In his time, however, he was a well-known and very popular author. No less a judge than Lord Acton wrote that Macaulay "had done more than any writer in the literature of the world for the propagation of the Liberal faith, and he was not

1. Burrow, *Whigs and Liberals*, 19, 76.

2. See Parry, *Rise and Fall of Liberal Government*, 99–100; Hall, "Macaulay's Nation," 521.

3. This is not true in India, where he is alternately decried as an imperialist and celebrated as author of a penal code that is still the heart of Indian criminal law. See Masani, *Macaulay*, xii.

only the greatest, but the most representative Englishman then [1856] living." An important figure in Britain's administration of India, he was a leading orator in the House of Commons and junior minister in several governments.[4]

Like the great majority of nineteenth-century liberals, Macaulay believed in progress as the natural state of humanity. "In every experimental science there is a tendency toward perfection. In every human being there is a wish to ameliorate his own condition. These two principles have sufficed . . . to carry civilization rapidly forward," despite the obstacles posed by accidents and bad government. Bad government could, however, slow down progress, and sometimes stop or reverse it entirely. Progress was greatest when people were free, when they were not afraid. As Macaulay put it, "We entertain a firm conviction that the principles of liberty, as in government and trade, so also in education, are all-important to the happiness of mankind." Progress was the natural accompaniment of liberalism: "We are reformers: we are on the side of progress . . . we infer, not that there is no more room for improvement, but that . . . immense improvements may be confidently expected."[5]

If progress was natural, except under exceptionally bad governments (which alas were the rule for most of human history), it flourished in England. In his *History of England*, Macaulay portrayed the state of the nation in 1685: "the national wealth has, during at least six centuries, been almost uninterruptedly increasing," and "this progress, having continued during many ages, became at length, about the middle of the eighteenth century, portentously rapid, and has proceeded, during the nineteenth, with accelerated velocity." This rapid progress was due to the fact that England had been exempt from revolutions, from "popular fury" and "regal tyranny," and that there had been "ample . . . civil and religious freedom." "Every man has felt entire confidence that the state would protect him in the possession of what had been earned by his diligence and hoarded by his self-denial." In short, England's exceptional progress was due to its being an exceptionally liberal state, where people had less to fear than elsewhere.[6]

Politics could not remain immobile as society developed: liberalism could encourage progress only if liberalism itself progressed. If it did not, the result

---

4. Lord Acton, *Historical Essays and Studies*. https://oll.libertyfund.org/titles/2201#Acton_1479_728

5. Macaulay, "Chapter 3, *History of England*," 257; Macaulay, "Sir James Mackintosh," 162. The echoes of Adam Smith are clear.

6. Macaulay, "Chapter 3, *History of England*," 258.

would be the classic liberal catastrophes, revolution and reaction. Macaulay made this case in his March 2, 1831 speech in Parliament in favor of what became known as the Great Reform Act, which gave much of the middle class the right to vote in parliamentary elections while diminishing the influence of the landed aristocracy. In his speech he argued that if the political system failed to recognize the changes that had taken place in British society, revolution was inevitable. Very conscious of the 1830 revolution in France, Macaulay concluded that rejecting reform would mean "the wreck of laws, the confusion of ranks, the spoliation of property, and the dissolution of social order." As he put it more concisely in a later speech, "the great cause of revolution is this, that while nations move onward, constitutions stand still." The fear of revolution was central to Macaulay's embrace of political reform.[7]

After the Reform Act of 1832, followed by the major reforms initiated by the Whig / Liberal[8] governments that came immediately afterward, including the abolition of slavery, an improved penal code, and limitations on child labor, Macaulay congratulated British liberals on their successes. "I look with pride on all that the Whigs have done for the cause of human freedom and of human happiness." For Macaulay political progress did not have a terminal point. While more conservative liberals in England (and Guizot in France) argued that once a certain measure of reform had been achieved, in particular about suffrage, there ought to be "finality," Macaulay responded that "I altogether disclaim what has been nicknamed the doctrine of finality. . . . I do not consider the settlement made by the Reform Bill as one which can last for ever." Significantly, his rejection of finality was made in the context of a parliamentary speech attacking the idea of universal manhood suffrage because it would lead to the plunder of private property. Good nineteenth-century liberal that he was, Macaulay combined his endorsement of progress with the fear that universal

7. "Speech on Reform Bill," March 2, 1831, in *Selected Writings*, 180; "Speech on Reform Bill," July 5, 1831, in Macaulay, *Speeches on Politics and Literature*, 19.

8. The relationship between "Whig" and "Liberal" in England is complicated. From the mid-1830s, the term "Liberal party" was increasingly used to refer to the former "Whig Party," without replacing it. By 1847, 175 MPs identified themselves as Liberal vs. 52 Whigs and 55 "reformers." However, the "Liberal Party" was only formally founded in 1859. See Parry, *Rise and Fall of Liberal Government*, 128–132, 167. For Burrow, the Whig / Liberal distinction was based on the degree of connection to eighteenth-century political language (late proto-liberalism, in the terms used here) maintained by nineteenth-century Whigs despite their identification with issues they saw as distinctly modern, such as the French Revolution or suffrage reform. See Burrow, *Whigs and Liberals*, 11–16.

suffrage led to popular despotism. But he did not permanently rule out even universal male suffrage—once the lower classes were in a better position both economically and educationally, as they were in America, then universal suffrage could be adopted without danger. The key was not lowering the franchise, "but . . . raising . . . the great mass up to the level of the franchise."[9]

At the center of Macaulay's narrative of progress was the middle class. In this respect he was typical of most European liberals. For Macaulay, "the higher and middling orders are the natural representatives of the human race." It was they alone, not the masses, who represented the interests of future generations, not just of today's empty stomachs. The middle class was "that brave, honest, and sound-hearted class, which is as anxious for the maintenance of order and the security of property, as it is hostile to corruption and oppression." The middle class "has taken its immovable stand between the enemies of all order and the enemies of all liberty. It will have reform: it will not have revolution: it will destroy political abuses: it will not suffer the rights of property to be assailed." The middle class was thus a natural social bulwark against liberal fears of revolution and reaction, suitably linked to the liberal pillars of political freedom, markets and, especially in England, to good morals and religious practice. Macaulay's ideal government was therefore "the express image of the opinion of the middle orders of Britain." Since the modern world was a middle-class world, it would be a liberal world.[10]

Macaulay was a great optimist; a common breed among nineteenth-century liberals. In the mid-century they often focused on the middle class as both motor and proof of progress. In his optimism, he differed little from the first generation of liberals. But conventional as he was in his optimism, typical as he was in his fears, when it came to some of the means he adopted to encourage progress and preserve society from fear, Macaulay was quite different from earlier liberals such as Madison, Kant, or Constant. If Macaulay was at the center of British liberalism in his time—and he was—then we must revise certain assumptions about what liberalism means.

9. Speech to Edinburgh Electors, May 29, 1839 in *Selected Speeches*, 142; Speech to the House of Commons on the People's Charter, May 3, 1842, in *Selected Speeches*, 193, 192, 194, 197; Speech on Parliamentary Reform of March 2, 1831, in *Selected Writings*, 167–168.

10. Macaulay, "Hallam's Constitutional History," 215, http://oll.libertyfund.org/titles /macaulay-critical-and-historical-essays-vol-1; Speech in the House of Commons on the Reform Bill, December 16, 1831, in *Selected Speeches*, 58; "Utilitarian Theory of Government," in *Selected Speeches*, 465.

In his faith in progress and his wholehearted embrace of the middle classes, Macaulay was typical of many historians and political theorists in how they understood liberalism. In other respects, however, while typical of nineteenth-century Europe and America, his positions were heterodox from the perspective of early twenty-first century liberals. This can be seen in his attitude toward free markets and limited government. Macaulay's ambiguous relationship to laissez-faire views of economics and society was actually more the rule than the exception in mid-nineteenth-century liberalism. This was true even in Britain, the supposed stronghold of laissez-faire, where for many liberals "strong government could check the power of vested interests and could also improve national morals." However, it was also true that other liberals continued "to articulate a libertarian suspicion of a strong state, and one of the great difficulties of Liberal politics [was] to reconcile this suspicion with the exercise of state authority." Macaulay exhibited both these tendencies.[11]

In his 1830 essay on Southey,[12] Macaulay heatedly defended both the progressive nature of the Industrial Revolution (the poor were better off because of it) and the importance of leaving everything possible to the private sector, unhindered by government regulation or high taxes. Macaulay accused Southey of thinking that governments knew better what to do with their money than did individuals. Public works carried out by the government might or might not be useful, but they would always be overpriced. £500,000 "subscribed by individuals for railroads or canals . . . produce more advantage to the public than £5,000,000 voted by Parliament for the same purpose." Therefore, "buildings for state purposes the state must erect. And here we think that, in general, the state ought to stop."[13]

Macaulay also was very firm about the limits of government. He attacked Southey for making it the government's business "to relieve all the distress under which the lower orders labour." When Southey claimed paternal rights for the government, Macaulay rejoined with both practical and theoretical objections: "there is no reason to believe that a government will have either the paternal warmth of affection or the paternal superiority of intellect"; and with regard to religion and morals, "any man in the street may know as much and think as justly as the King." And then, in good Kantian fashion, Macaulay

11. Parry, *The Politics of Patriotism*, 43.

12. Robert Southey (1774–1843) was a well-known conservative essayist and poet.

13. "Southey's Colloquies," in *Macaulay's Essays*, 36–37, 45.

proceeded to laud free debate on all issues, without government interference. He concluded in a way that Constant would have approved: "Our rulers will best promote the improvement of the nation by strictly confining themselves to their own legitimate duties . . . by maintaining peace, defending property, by diminishing the price of law, and by observing strict economy in every department of state. Let the Government do this: the People will assuredly do the rest."[14]

Later, Macaulay revealed another side to his thought, one that favored a larger scope for government. In 1846, Parliament debated a Ten Hours Bill to reduce the labor of children. He supported the Bill, arguing that "I hardly know which is the greater pest to society, a paternal government, that is to say a prying, meddlesome government . . . or a careless, lounging government, which suffers grievances, such as it could at once remove . . . and which to all complaint and remonstrance has only one answer: 'We must let things alone.'" Suggesting that opposition to the Corn Laws had exaggerated laissez-faire sentiment, he said, "I hope we have seen the last both of a vicious system of interference and of a vicious system of non-interference."[15]

Macaulay went on to give examples of "vicious" non-interference by government. Contradicting his own argument against Southey that private investors made better decisions than governments, he complained that the inefficient paths taken by British railroad tracks were due to the absence of government intervention. He was still "as strongly attached as any member of this House to the principle of free trade, rightly understood." But "rightly understood" meant understanding that some trades affected national interests. On this ground Macaulay supported everything from the Navigation Acts (as did Adam Smith) to rules preventing cabs from charging passengers more when it rains. It was also necessary to create minimal heath standards for housing because "it concerns the commonwealth that the great body of the people should not live in a way which makes life wretched and short, which enfeebles the body and pollutes the mind." The state had a right to intervene "where health is concerned, and where morality is justified in interfering with the contracts of individuals." Thus the state should ban pornography and lotteries, and enforce Sunday closing laws. As Macauley stated in an 1847 speech, laissez-faire principles "which are

---

14. "Southey's Colloquies," in *Macaulay's Essays*, 46, 52, 69. See also Speech on the Reform Bill, September 20, 1831, in *Selected Speeches*, 29.

15. Speech on the Ten Hours Bill, May 22, 1846, in *Selected Writings*, 195, 210–211.

sound only when applied to commercial questions" should not be applied to political and moral issues.[16]

Macaulay's willingness to expand the scope of government extended to many issues. In his 1839 review of Gladstone on Church and State, after listing the essential purposes of government, that is, securing persons and property and national defense, Macaulay continued, "But does it follow from hence that governments ought never to pursue any end other than their main end? In no wise." For example, the chief aim of a hospital was to cure the sick, and nothing superfluous to that end should be undertaken until it was fulfilled—but if there was money available to make the hospital building pretty, why not? In the same way, Macaulay suggested that, after accounting for essentials, the government could and should fund museums, the arts, scientific research, and so on. He was no dogmatic advocate of laissez-faire.[17]

Therefore Macaulay supported the Ten Hours Bill and its requirement that child laborers be provided with minimal education and time to receive it: "Education is a matter of the highest importance to the virtue and happiness of a people." While the education of the upper classes should be left alone, "It is the right and duty of the state to provide means of education for the common people." Even the most limited definitions of government, Macaulay noted, agreed that security was a government responsibility. On that ground alone, government support for educating the poor was justified because "the education of the common people is a most effectual means of securing our person and our property." He cited Smith and historical examples in support of his view. The Gordon Riots of 1780 and the Luddites of 1815 were what happened when the poor were left uneducated: the result was religious fanaticism and resistance to technological progress. Thus, "the gross ignorance of the common people is a principal cause of danger to our persons and property," and "I say therefore, that the education of the people is not only a means, but the best means, of attaining that which all allow to be a chief end of government."[18]

Macaulay's defense of government support for education was also based on its economic effects, and therefore represented an endorsement of govern-

16. Speech on the Ten Hours Bill, May 22, 1846, in *Selected Writings*, 196, 197–200, 203; Speech in the House of Commons on Education, April 18, 1847, in *Selected Writings*, 212.

17. "Gladstone on Church and State," in *Critical and Historical Essays*, vol. 2, http://oll.libertyfund.org/titles/macaulay-critical-and-historical-essays-vol-2, 494.

18. Speech in the House of Commons on Education, April 18, 1847, in *Selected Writings*, 200–201, 214–217.

ment economic intervention. Working from his usual claim that government was an experimental science, not one to be decided on abstract principles (against Bentham), he argued that the Scottish system of state-funded education had permitted Scotland to catch up economically with England over the previous century. Based on this, in his view, conclusive experiment, he decided that "it is the duty of the State to educate the people." Nevertheless, Macaulay wanted as little state intervention in education as possible. The state should provide the funds and the obligation for the education of the poor, but it should not choose the teachers. The difference with Smith, who made the same suggestion (see chapter 2) was that in Smith it was the parents who chose the teacher, while in Macaulay it was a group of local notables. It is impossible to say whether this choice represented Macaulay going along with his government's bill, designed to appease religious sentiments, or represented his preference. In any event, the bill failed, as did every other attempt to create a national system of education in England before 1870. Macaulay's centrism was not always successful.[19]

This shows how even in nineteenth-century England, the supposed homeland of laissez-faire economics and government, liberals rarely considered economic or other questions without taking into consideration political and especially moral considerations that might result in considerable deviations from laissez-faire policies. Macaulay's views demonstrate how even in Britain mainstream nineteenth-century liberalism was "never about doctrinaire individualist anti-statism." Good government was seen as a requirement for a functioning market, and "moral arguments could be combined with economic arguments that emphasized the progressive credentials of market society." Resolving boundary questions about when and where government intervention was useful or justified was a matter of experiment as much as of principle. Indeed, those who held too strictly to putatively liberal principles were Macaulay's enemies.[20]

Just as Macaulay and most other liberals during the short nineteenth century rejected a strict view of laissez-faire, so they rejected an insistence that only individuals mattered—an insistence often found among the adherents of pure laissez-faire doctrines. They rarely regarded individuals in an atomistic way.

19. Speech in the House of Commons on Education, April 18, 1847, in *Selected Writings*, 225–227, 228.

20. See Hilton, *The Age of Atonement*; Thompson, "Modern Liberty Redefined," 730, 733, 746; Parry, *Rise and Fall of Liberal Government*, 84, 195–227.

Instead, they emphasized the importance of representing the middle classes (not middle-class individuals) in parliament, and paid significant attention to communities and collective interests that often trumped laissez-faire counter-arguments based on purely individual concerns. The three pillars of liberalism were meant to provide a barrier against fear for every group and class, as well as every individual. Laissez-faire individualism, far from being at the center of liberalism during the short nineteenth century, was a relatively rare position. Macaulay's attacks on Jeremy Bentham and his controversial assault on James Mill are examples of how the liberal center rejected this view.

James Mill was, along with Bentham, the leader of the Philosophical Radicals, a group inspired by Bentham's philosophy. Bentham and his "Philosophic Radical" followers saw only individuals where Whig liberals acknowledged classes and interests. Based on Bentham's "hedonistic calculus," his theory that all policy should be based on maximizing whatever made the most individuals happy, the Philosophic Radicals deduced such radical consequences as the abolition of the monarchy and its replacement by a republic with universal male suffrage, unicameral government, the abolition of the nobility and established churches, etc. The Radicals, by and large, had little fear of the consequences and no respect at all for the fears of minorities or existing interests without logical utilitarian justification for their existence. It was a classic example of the way in which the liberalism of fear distinguished itself from insufficiently fearful—hence illiberal—progressives. Bentham's views and their relationship to liberalism in his day and after will be discussed in chapter 6. Of interest here are the grounds on which Macaulay criticized James Mill's very Benthamite "Essay on Government."[21]

Macaulay minced no words in his response to Mill.[22] His object was "not so much to attack or defend any particular system of polity, as to expose the

21. Although they generally supported Liberal governments in Parliament, many of the Philosophic Radicals were not really liberals at all—they were democrats who did not share liberal fears. Even when they did, they typically relied on only one pillar—strict Benthamite utilitarianism—to support their logic. See chapter 6.

22. There is a semi-legend that Macaulay was later embarrassed by the fierceness of his attack because of his respect for James Mill as an historian of India, and he therefore refused to republish it in his collected essays. See Collini, Winch, and Burrow, *That Noble Science*, 110. However, in an edition of his collected speeches published at an unknown date, dedicated by Macaulay to Lord Lansdowne, Macaulay did include, under the title "Two Political Reviews," both his "Mill on Government" and the follow-up essay, "Utilitarian Theory of Government." I use this edition as the source of quotations from his "Essay on Government."

vices of a kind of reasoning utterly unfit for moral and political discussions . . . Our objection to Mr. Mill is fundamental. We believe that it is utterly impossible to deduce the science of government from the principles of human nature." Against James Mill he upheld "that noble science of politics, which is equally removed from the barren theories of the Utilitarian sophists, and from the petty craft, so often mistaken for statesmanship . . . ; [a science] which draws nutriment and ornament from every part of philosophy and literature." According to Macaulay the Benthamites, like most fanatics and sectarians, were mostly ignorant men whom a little knowledge had driven mad. They had "narrow understandings and little information." Many had "read little or nothing."[23] Mill was an example of how they followed a logical path to perdition. For example, he argued that everyone always pursued their own self-interest, that it was only in democracies that there was an identity of interests between rulers and ruled, and therefore only a democracy could be a just form of government. For Macaulay, this was nonsense. If everyone only pursued their self-interest then, once elected, even by universal suffrage, the representatives would immediately constitute themselves an aristocracy because that was in their interest. In practice, "in no form of government is there an exact identity of interest between the people and their rulers." For Macaulay, the real guarantee against bad government, which worked equally in democracies, aristocracies, and even absolute monarchies, was "the fear of resistance and the sense of shame" (note the typical liberal combination of practical and moral restraint). In his rejection of James Mill and of Benthamism's dogmatic reliance on just one principle of human nature (individual happiness / utility), his flexible views on the limits of government, and his concern for both classes and individuals, Macaulay was typical of mainstream nineteenth-century liberalism. This can be seen with regard to another question of principle as well: his attitude toward religion and especially the separation of Church and State.[24]

While Macaulay's views on politics and laissez-faire were very much those of the liberal center, when it came to morals and religion a distinction must be made between his personal views and the role religion played in his social and political thought. One peculiarity Macaulay, John Stuart Mill (the son of James Mill), and Tocqueville shared was that, unlike most liberals of their time, they

23. "Mill on Government," in *Selected Speeches*, 405.

24. "Mill on Government," in *Selected Speeches*, 422–423, 432, 436. Burrow, *Whigs and Liberals*, 37–38, 67.

personally held heterodox religious views. Tocqueville was more or less a Deist, Mill hesitated between Manichaeanism and atheism, and Macaulay described himself as a nondenominational "Christian" but seemed to be chiefly a skeptic: "his journal . . . shows him believing little or nothing while regularly acting religiously and talking and writing about religion."[25] Macaulay, however, like Tocqueville and unlike J. S. Mill, was convinced of the value of traditional religion as a support for liberalism.

Macaulay supported traditional religion as a barrier against religious fanaticism and as a source of moral improvement. In a speech supporting increased government funding for the Irish Catholic Church, he argued that even if the separation of Church and State was a good idea in principle, since the state was unquestionably going to support Irish Protestantism, the only question was whether Catholicism should benefit as well. Supporting Catholicism was important because the Catholics were not only the majority, but in great majority poor, and therefore most in need of religion. It was not quite a case of any religion would do for Irish peasants: "I heartily wish that they were Protestants. But I had rather that they should be Roman Catholics than that they should have no religion at all." However, Macaulay thought no religion was better than some religions. Hinduism was "a curse to mankind. It is much better that people should be without any religion than that they should believe in a religion which enjoins prostitution, suicide, robbery, assassination." By contrast, Catholicism was a "very corrupt" Christianity, nevertheless it would do much more good than harm, and should therefore be encouraged.[26]

Where Christianity did more harm than good, it should be deprived of state support. Macaulay defended the established Churches of England and Scotland. But, "if there were, in any part of the world, a national church regarded as heretical by four fifths of the nation committed to its care, a church established and maintained by the sword, a church producing twice as many riots as conversions . . . such a church, on our principles, could not, we must own, be defended." Macaulay therefore supported the disestablishment of the Anglican Church of Ireland.[27]

25. Sullivan, *Macaulay*, 351.

26. Speech to the House of Commons on the Maynooth Grant, April 14, 1845, in *Speeches on Politics and Literature*, 277, 278.

27. "Gladstone on Church and State," in *Critical and Historical Essays*, vol. 2, 501, http://oll .libertyfund.org/titles/macaulay-critical-and-historical-essays-vol-2.

Did Macaulay support the separation of Church and State, supposedly a key tenet of liberalism? Like most European liberals, with the exception of the French, Macaulay thought the question was open. Everyone should be free to practice the religion of their choice, or none at all, but this did not debar the government from supporting one. Where religious divisions got in the way of good government and served to diminish freedom, then religion should be excluded from political and even social institutions. Macaulay gave the example of when denominations fought over what religion the hospital chaplain should be. His answer was to either provide multiple chaplains or none at all. Furthermore, the chaplaincy should always be subordinated to the main purpose of the hospital, which was to cure the sick. Similarly, the propagation of religion was not a prime purpose of government: if government made it one, "the most absurd and pernicious consequences . . . follow." However, "a government which considers the religious instruction of the people as a secondary end, and follows out that principle faithfully, will, we think, be likely to do much good and little harm." Whenever such instruction jeopardized public order, then it was worse than useless: hence no evangelization of India. Nor should the government help "to spread a system of opinions solely because that system is pleasing to the majority." The correct conclusion was "that religious instruction which the ruler ought, in his public capacity, to patronise, is the instruction from which . . . the people will learn most good with the smallest mixture of evil. And thus it is not necessarily his own religion that he will select. . . . The question which he has to consider is, not how much good his religion contains, but how much good the people will learn, if instruction is given them in that religion."[28]

Macaulay's attitude was pragmatic, although not divorced from moral principles. Like any good Victorian and most liberals of his time, he put morality alongside utility to guide it: "Undoubtedly it is of the highest importance that we should legislate well. But it is also of the highest importance that those who govern us should have, and should be known to have, fixed principles." In practice religious principles had to be filtered by circumstances that dictated what was to be feared (religious unrest) or hoped (moral improvement) from their application.

The liberal position, for Macaulay, was one of calculating the balance between hope and fear using freedom, markets, and morals to navigate between

28. "Gladstone on Church and State," in *Critical and Historical Essays*, vol. 2, in http://oll .libertyfund.org/titles/macaulay-critical-and-historical-essays-vol-2, 496–497, 499.

revolutionaries and reactionaries. He appealed to both utility and moral principle, he took into consideration groups as well as individuals, he defended free markets while acknowledging many respects in which government intervention was desirable even if not necessary. He held a firm faith in human progress, if not in religious dogma, and regarded the middle classes as the great social bulwark of liberal hopes. However heterodox he might appear from a twenty-first-century perspective, in the nineteenth Macaulay was the epitome of the liberal center. If one is looking for a baseline against which to measure the various forms liberalism took during the nineteenth century, Macaulay is probably as close as one can come.

Tocqueville: The Inventor of Liberal Democracy?

Alexis de Tocqueville was *not* at the center of French liberalism in his lifetime (1805–59). As a politician, he was a more minor figure than Macaulay, and unlike Macaulay, the policies he supported were rarely enacted into law. As a thinker, he was widely respected, but rarely imitated. Many of his positions were unusual. Unlike most nineteenth-century liberals, unlike Kant, Madison, Constant, or Macaulay, Tocqueville was an aristocratic liberal who feared the middle classes as much or more than the mob, if in a different way. His famous discussion of the tyranny of the majority in *Democracy in America* was mostly about the tyranny of the middle classes, who for Tocqueville represented mediocrity, individualism, and a ferocious search for material well-being. They were a dangerous and dominant force whose character was destined to spread to all classes in democratic society. For Tocqueville, the middle classes were potential agents and supporters of despotism, rather than a social foundation for freedom. By contrast, most liberals of the time saw the middle class as naturally liberal and natural opponents of arbitrary power. This was not the case for Tocqueville, which led to his uphill battle to invent liberal democracy and prevent the tyranny of the (middle-class) majority, or of a despot acting in their name.[29]

In some respects it is both anachronistic and misleading to describe Tocqueville as the inventor of liberal democracy. The phrase only came into wide

---

29. Tocqueville, *Democracy in America*, 3:933–934. For Tocqueville, like J. S. Mill, America's entire White population was already essentially middle class; *Democracy* 2:764n. On Tocqueville's attitude toward the middle classes, see Eduardo Nolla, "Editor's Introduction," *Democracy*, 1:cxxviii–ix; Kahan, *Aristocratic Liberalism*, 41–46.

use after his death, and it emphasizes democracy as a political system, which is not how Tocqueville usually used the word "democracy." Nevertheless, at the deepest level, "liberal democracy" is an accurate representation of Tocqueville's goal: creating a world free from fear in a society that was based on "equality of conditions" (his definition of democracy) and the sovereignty of the people. This problem has remained central to liberalism, and it accounts for Tocqueville's continued relevance to the liberal tradition. Indeed, as the phrase liberal democracy has become central to liberals' self-description after WWII, so has Tocqueville's place on Western political thought become ever more important.[30]

In the first half of the nineteenth century, those who called themselves democrats in France rarely recognized the threat that democratic majority tyranny posed to liberty, while those who called themselves liberals rarely recognized the promise democracy could offer as a bulwark against revolution and reaction. Hence Tocqueville's view that he was a new kind of liberal, and his frequent feelings of isolation from all colors of the political spectrum. Tocqueville's first masterpiece, *Democracy in America*, was a long lesson for an uncomprehending world in how to construct a liberal democracy. Oddly, the lesson proved popular even among those who didn't understand it.

In Tocqueville's thought, "democracy" replaced "commercial society" as the essence of the modern environment. He mostly used the word to describe a social situation rather than a political one, a social situation in which everyone was presumed to be equal. Such societies, according to Tocqueville, were the future of the world. Democracy was a "Providential fact" that could not be successfully challenged. The only legitimate human authority that remained in such a society was the majority, whose views were expressed in public opinion. Hence the need to limit the power of the majority to make individuals afraid, and to use political, economic, and moral / religious means to do so. If successful, the result would be a liberal democracy.[31] Liberal democracy,

---

30. The phrase "liberal democracy" was widely used in the early years of the Second Empire in France, when it referred to efforts to make the plebiscitary, hence democratic, regime of Napoleon III more liberal. See Rosenblatt, *Lost History*,162–164, which cites Montalembert. An 1834 use revealingly contrasts the "religious democracy" of the lower classes in Spain with the "liberal democracy" of the Spanish middle class. See *Annuaire historique universel*, edited by A. Thoisnier-Desplaces and Ulysse Tencé, Paris, 1834.

31. Schleifer, *The Making of Tocqueville's Democracy*, 325–329. Tocqueville, *Democracy*, 3:733, 748; 1:9–10. These views were common in France at the time. See Kahan, *Tocqueville, Democracy, and Religion*, 12n3.

however, while in one sense Tocqueville's goal, in another was only a means to a still greater end: human perfection and greatness. His fear was that the result of revolutions and reactions and all forms of democratic despotism would be the same: diminished human beings. Liberalism, for Tocqueville as for many nineteenth-century liberals, was not just a matter of free governments and free markets, but of moral and spiritual development.

For Tocqueville, liberalism had a positive purpose, namely to encourage people to become better human beings. If there was ever a liberal who made nonsense of the categorization of liberalism as purely negative freedom, freedom from coercion, it was Tocqueville. He wanted to free individuals from the fear of despotism in democratic societies in order to make it possible for them to attain greatness. Tocqueville was a moralist above all, and the "new political science" he created was really a compendium of political, social, and spiritual means to preserve human dignity and encourage individual greatness in democracies.[32]

As a moralist, Tocqueville chose a middle path between utilitarianism and perfectionism. In this he was rather like Kant, who wrote that "neither human morality alone nor happiness alone is the Creator's end; instead, that end is . . . the union and harmony of the two."[33] Tocqueville saw that equality was better for the majority. He also valued greatness, human perfection. In both cases it was the individual he was concerned with, "to raise up and make the individual greater, constant goal of great men in democratic centuries," even though he often proceeded by considering groups. To attain greatness, there was only one path: "All my reflections lead me to believe that no moral and political greatness is possible for long without [freedom]. I am therefore as strongly attached to freedom as to morality"; "Freedom is, in truth, a *holy* thing." Tocqueville was one of the first liberals to make liberalism into a religion.[34]

Because Tocqueville was so much a moralist, it is best to understand his liberalism first by discussing his moral / religious methods for making democ-

---

32. *Democracy*, 1:16. It is, by contrast, less relevant from an economic perspective. Tocqueville wrote relatively little about economic issues, but his memoirs on pauperism indicate a thinker who combined generally laissez-faire economic views with a sense that some limited government intervention for the poor, as well as a reform of the tax system to bear less heavily on poor people, were necessary. Tocqueville, *Memoirs on Pauperism and Other Writings*.

33. Kant, "Proverb," 64.

34. *Democracy*, 4:1275, 1275y; 3:722n; "Voyages en Angleterre," *OC*, vol. 5, t. 1:91.

racy liberal, and then proceed to his better-known political prescriptions, decentralization and association, methods that led Tocqueville back to a secular and utilitarian moral pillar for liberalism, enlightened self-interest. Tocqueville saw the role of religion in political life as enormous. A bad religious situation could make liberal democracy nearly impossible, while a good religious situation could greatly promote it. France was the prime example of the former, America, for Tocqueville, of the latter. In France, the friends of freedom were the enemies of religion, and the friends of religion were the enemies of freedom. In America, the friends of freedom were friends of religion, and vice versa. In Tocqueville's view, the right kind of religion, playing the right kind of political and social role, was essential to liberal democracy. Rather than trying to preach a new religion of freedom, Tocqueville looked to the religion that already existed in the West, Christianity, to provide liberal democracy with its most important, if not its only, moral pillar. Liberal democracy, in Tocqueville's view, could not do without religion. One of his greatest concerns was that few French liberals recognized this—a problem that continues to vex liberalism in the twenty-first century.

A crucial element in the relationship between religion and liberal democracy, for Tocqueville, was the separation of Church and State. According to Tocqueville, the hatred for Catholicism in France during the Enlightenment was the product not of hatred for religion, but of animus against the French monarchy and aristocracy. Since the Church was so closely bound to the State and the existing social order, one could not attack the State without attacking the Church. The *philosophes'* "rage against the Church" was essentially a political matter, and "it was much less as a religious institution than as a political institution that Christianity aroused these furious hatreds." In no other country, Tocqueville noted, was the Enlightenment so hostile to religion as in France.[35]

The origin of the French left's struggle against Catholicism was accidental, but once aroused, the anti-religious passion was tenacious: "among the passions born of the Revolution the first lit and the last extinguished was this passion against religion." The fatal accident had had a lasting impact and became so entrenched in French political culture that the Church could not conceive of a republic that was not hostile to Christianity, and neither could republicans. This was fatal to the stability of liberal democracy because it

---

35. Tocqueville, *The Old Regime and the Revolution*, 1:47, 96; Kahan, *Tocqueville, Democracy, and Religion*, 162.

made it impossible for religion to play the role Tocqueville thought crucial, that is, to check and balance the impulses to despotism of a democratic society. This was why, he stressed, it was so important to separate Church and State. His fear was not the proto-liberal fear of the Church persecuting heretics with the aid of the royal army. It was a new fear, that without religion to check and balance secular political passions, they would become murderous and cruel. It was the Jacobins, not the Inquisition, that he feared. But religion would be of no use against the Jacobins so long as it was identified with the Inquisition, and alienated many idealists who ought to be its strongest supporters.

This was why again and again in *Democracy*, in a vain effort to convince the French Church that separation of Church and State was not the Devil's claw, and French liberals that Christianity was not their enemy, Tocqueville emphasized how in the most religious country in the Western world, America, everyone was convinced that the separation of Church and State was necessary for the *sake of religion*. Tocqueville asked all the clergy he met in America, and especially the Catholic clergy, why religion was so strong, and "all attributed the peaceful domination that religion exercises in their country principally to the complete separation of Church and State. I am not afraid to assert that, during my visit to America, I did not meet a single man, priest or layman, who did not agree on this point."[36]

The role of religion in Tocqueville's theory of liberal democracy was not just to act as a check and balance on political practice. Its role as a spiritual check and balance for democratic souls, as an influence on their character, was even more important. For Tocqueville, religion was the chief moral pillar of liberal democracy.

Tocqueville feared democratic people would see themselves as "insignificant." This created a moral and spiritual disposition to accept despotism: "each individual is isolated and weak; society is agile, far-sighted and strong; individuals do small things and the State immense ones." There was then nothing left in society to moderate the ruler(s). Self-interest rightly understood, promoted by free association, could do much to prevent this collapse; religion well understood could do even more. Tocqueville wanted religion in democratic societies to restore a sense of individual greatness to souls who would otherwise be unable to conceive of it, let alone attain it. Only God could stand against the tyranny of majority opinion, only religion could give democratic

36. *Democracy*, 2:480.

people "the taste for the infinite, the sentiment for the grand and the love of non-material pleasures."[37]

Tocqueville took both a utilitarian and a perfectionist view of religion, as he did of politics. When he wanted religion to act as a check he was utilitarian, and he was a perfectionist when he wanted religion to balance materialism by elevating the democratic passions of the soul. "The principal business of religions is to purify, to regulate and to limit the overly ardent and overly exclusive taste for well-being that men feel in times of equality," and simultaneously "to inspire entirely opposite instincts." Religion worked to improve both happiness (utility) and greatness (perfection). Tocqueville summarized: "If religion does not save men in the next world, it is at least very useful to their happiness and to their greatness in this one."[38]

Tocqueville did examine non-religious moral or spiritual sources of human greatness in democratic societies: patriotism; scientific passions; even poetry. However, he considered them inferior moral pillars for liberal democracy compared to religion. Nor did he consider all religions equally good at checking and balancing democracy as Christianity, at least some ideal form of Christianity (Tocqueville had a lively appreciation of the flaws, from his perspective, of all existing forms of Christianity). Tocqueville ruled out Hinduism entirely, because of its caste system. He considered Islam severely handicapped by a lack of separation of mosque and state (but he saw French Catholicism in the same position). Judaism he saw as limited to one people. Pantheism, which Tocqueville considered the religion most natural to democracies, "destroys human individuality."[39]

What happened when religion could not fulfill the role Tocqueville envisaged for it was evident in Europe, where "since religion lost its dominion over souls, the most visible limit that divided good and bad is overturned; all seems doubtful and uncertain in the moral realm, kings and peoples move there haphazardly, and no one can say where the natural limits of despotism and the bounds of licence are." This was why Tocqueville wrote to one of the few Catholic liberals, Montalembert, that "I have never been more convinced . . . that it is only *freedom* . . . and *religion* that can, by a combined effort, lift men above the quagmire where democratic equality naturally plunges them, as

37. *Democracy*, 4:1280; 3:740, 740d, 958.

38. *Democracy*, 3:744, 751.

39. See the discussion in Kahan, *Tocqueville, Democracy, and Religion*, 94–95, 182–93; *Democracy*, 3:758.

soon as one of these supports is lacking them." Liberal democracy for Tocqueville had neither the means to sustain itself nor a reason for existing if it
could not produce great human individuals.[40]

Tocqueville's methods for making individual freedom and greatness possible were always multiple. He had one big goal in mind, liberal democracy, but
many little ideas about how to make it work. He liked to think in parallel lines
and use parallel mechanisms: secular and religious means; individual and
group incentives; institutional devices and political parties. His chief political
and secular methods for making democracy safe, that is liberal, were decentralization, associations, and the idea of self-interest well understood. In these
discussions, one can see his continuity with common liberal concerns and the
very different way in which he responded to them. Political freedom, free markets, and morality / religion were all central to Tocqueville's project of creating
a liberal democracy, but just as his aristocratic liberalism reconceptualized
liberal fears, so his unique understanding of the nature of democratic society
and the need to foster democratic greatness led to new conceptualizations of
liberal institutions.

The power of the state was always a potential danger for liberals. Unfortunately, according to Tocqueville, it was in the nature of democratic society to
make the scope of the state unlimited and centralize its power too much. "In
the democratic centuries that are about to open up, individual independence
and local liberties will always be a product of art. Centralization will be the
natural government." Tocqueville was not opposed to all forms of centralization. Like Constant, he wanted a state that was strong in its proper sphere.
Democratic societies, however, naturally tended to encourage the state to act
outside its proper sphere. Hence Tocqueville's support for political decentralization, increasing the power of local governments, etc., as a means of curbing
and balancing the power of the state.

But local government was still government, and still potentially inclined to
trample on people, hence the need for associations, especially those that engaged in the public sphere: associations for building a school or a road, or
promoting abstention from alcohol, a purpose Tocqueville mocked at first
until he realized its political implications. Tocqueville encouraged the freedom
of association because in a democratic society where everyone was equal, and
all individuals equally powerless, association was the only means by which

40. *Democracy*, 2:474; Tocqueville to Montalembert, December 1, 1852, *OC*, vol. 17,
3:75–76.

individuals could exercise their freedom in and out of politics. On their own, individuals in a democratic society had everything to fear when faced by a government and a mass of public opinion. Joined together in associations and local governments, they could be free from both political and social tyrants. Association had to be developed in proportion to the progress of equality. "Freedom of association has become a necessary guarantee against the tyranny of the majority." In his focus on associations, Tocqueville emphasized the importance of the freedom of groups and collective action. A liberal society could not be maintained without them.[41]

Associations were important for Tocqueville both inside and outside politics—an example of his parallelism and how he nimbly skipped from one pillar of liberalism to another: associations were powerful tools for Tocqueville's liberalism in politics, in economics, and in religion. But the political pillar was often preeminent with him. "Political associations can be considered vast free schools where all citizens come to learn the general theory of associations." Once educated, citizens could use association to free themselves from tutelage in any domain. As the aristocrat had once been able to scoff at majority opinion and sneer at royal authority, "simple citizens, by associating, together can constitute very wealthy, very influential, very strong beings—in a word aristocratic persons."[42] Tocqueville was by no means trying to restore aristocracy, but he was trying to recreate, by democratic means, some of its characteristic functions in order to liberalize democracy.

Association for Tocqueville was more than just a means of counterbalancing power. It had moral effects, and was essential to the moral as well as political and economic pillars of liberalism. It produced psychological effects that were crucial for developing individuals capable of greatness and desirous of independence, willing and able to think critically and concerned with more than purely material and selfish interests. Crucially, association was the enemy of "individualism," the moral curse of democratic societies. Association was a political mechanism for creating a liberal politics and fighting against the tyranny of the majority. But associations were simultaneously a moral weapon against individualism and a means of fostering "enlightened self-interest" to fight it.

Like "democracy," "individualism" is a word with a specific meaning for Tocqueville. "Individualism is a considered and peaceful sentiment that disposes

41. *Democracy*, 2:667; 3:1205; 2:307; Alexander, "Tocqueville's Two Forms of Association."
42. *Democracy*, 3:914; 4:1268.

each citizen to isolate himself from the mass of his fellows and to withdraw to the side with his family and his friends; so that, after thus creating a small society for his own use, he willingly abandons the large society to itself." Like government centralization, individualism was natural to democratic societies. It left the individual with a family, but without a country, without politics. People became "similar and equal men who spin around restlessly in order to gain small and vulgar pleasures with which they fill their souls." Individualism encouraged the middle class's endless pursuit of wealth that Tocqueville despised as antithetical to freedom and greatness and an incentive to the abandonment of liberalism in favor of an orderly despotism.[43]

In Tocqueville's thought individualism was analogous to the modern temptation to concern oneself only with private pleasures (see Constant). Tocqueville, even more than Constant, emphasized that if people became individualistic, their private freedoms would evaporate under the pressure of majority opinion, which they would be unable to resist. Here associations played yet another role in Tocqueville's argument. Even if people associated for selfish reasons, for the convenience of paving the local street, the improvement of a local school, etc., associations brought people out of their individualist shells. Whether used for political purposes, devoted to a seemingly idiosyncratic cause such as the prohibition of alcohol consumption, or used to undertake large industrial projects, the freedom to associate enabled the Americans to fight, "by means of liberty, against the individualism given birth by equality, and [defeat] it." Association broke the habit of individualism and created new ones that had much in common with virtue.[44]

Democratic societies, in Tocqueville's view, tended to isolate people and led them to individualism. But the same concentration on one's own self-interest that led to individualism and disinterest in the community could be used to promote association and political involvement. If properly understood, self-interest could lead to very different behavior, as Tocqueville showed in the chapter of *Democracy* titled "How Americans Combat Individualism with the Doctrine of Self Interest Properly Understood."[45]

A proper understanding of one's interest meant taking a broad, long-term view. A businessman willing to pay higher taxes to support better public schools because this would mean better future employees, displayed enlight-

43. *Democracy*, 3:882; 4:1249.
44. *Democracy*, 3:891.
45. *Democracy*, 3:918.

ened self-interest. According to Tocqueville, this attitude was widespread in America. Americans "show with satisfaction how enlightened love of themselves leads them constantly to help each other and disposes them willingly to sacrifice for the good of the state a portion of their time and their wealth," because it was useful to themselves. This was "a doctrine not very lofty, but clear and sure," one that was highly effective in a democratic society. It was so effective that it could be found in every aspect of American society, even in religion, where one might expect other goals. But in listening to the average American preacher, Tocqueville wrote, "it is often difficult to know, hearing them, if the principal object of religion is to gain eternal felicity in the other world or well-being in this one." Self-interest properly understood motivated Americans to form associations for all kinds of purposes—political, economic, and even religious.[46]

Associations, often motivated by enlightened self-interest, thus limited the scope of government at the same time as they provided a means of resisting social pressures; they increased the sphere of action of the individual while providing material incentives to overcome the psychological barrier of individualism; they solved Constant's problem of how to build a bridge between the public and the private spheres and persuade democratic individuals to cross it. Free associations were essential to liberal politics, to modern liberal economics (the business corporation was, for Tocqueville, very much an association in his sense), and to morality / religion.[47] In a democratic society, none of the three pillars of liberalism could do without them.

Once members of an association, individuals were no longer isolated, they were part of a group. Tocqueville, for all his belief in the value of the individual and in individuality as the basis of human greatness, analyzed society in terms of groups and collective goals as much as he did in terms of individuals and individual goals. In this respect his analyses were typical of most nineteenth-century liberal thought, which usually regarded society in terms of social classes as much as individuals. In Tocqueville's analysis of democracy, there were different kinds of groups. There were artificially created groups, such as associations, and more "naturally" occurring ones (albeit still socially constructed), such as professions, social classes, cultures, and ethnicities. These latter groups also played a significant role in his political thought, sometimes pillars of freedom, sometimes examples of what happened in the absence of

46. *Democracy*, 3:921; 929.
47. See Kahan, "Tocqueville: The Corporation as an Ethical Association."

freedom; they interacted with liberal democracy in important ways. The examples are many, but two significant ones are his treatment of lawyers and his treatment of Black Americans.

Tocqueville devoted a chapter of *Democracy* to "Of the Spirit of the Jurist in the United States, and How It Serves as Counterweight To Democracy." Lawyers, it turned out, maintained in democratic society many traits of the "corporations" (or guilds) of the old regime, which Montesquieu saw as bulwarks against royal despotism and which Tocqueville, in modern circumstances, saw as a limit on democratic despotism. Lawyers were "a kind of privileged class among the intelligent . . . What is more, they naturally constitute a *corporation* . . . in the sense that common studies and like methods link their intellects. . . . One therefore finds, hidden in the depths of lawyers' souls, some of the tastes and habits of aristocracy." If associations were synthetic aristocrats in democratic societies, lawyers were their natural elite. As a result of their democratic origin (lawyers were made, not born), their corporate education, and their political role, lawyers naturally exercised important responsibilities in democratic societies. Lawyers "form the only aristocratic element that can mingle with the natural elements of democracy without effort and combine with them in a happy and enduring way." In Europe, based on the experience of the French Revolution and other radical movements, lawyers were seen as natural radicals. But for Tocqueville law was naturally a barrier against arbitrary government, not its instrument. Thus lawyers in America were a force for moderation. They acted as a brake on democratic passions, imposed rules, and limited democratic tyranny. Tocqueville saw in lawyers a way to preserve certain liberal habits and attitudes from aristocratic societies in democratic ones. Lawyers were an important social building block in the construction of a liberal democracy.[48]

Black Americans were, in a sense, not properly part of Tocqueville's consideration of democracy, precisely because they were American. Unlike lawyers, they were not to be found in every democratic society and nation. But the issues of slavery and racism raised by Tocqueville's discussion of Black Americans,

---

48. *Democracy*, 2:430; 436; 434. Tocqueville was not always so sanguine about law and lawyers, however. He recognized the role of Roman law in encouraging the development of early modern European absolutism and noted that jurists were always to be found at the shoulder of every despot. See *The Old Regime*, 1:257–258. Nevertheless, lawyers had a crucial role to play in preserving freedom in democratic societies. See Kahan, "Aristocracy in Tocqueville / De l'aristocratie chez Tocqueville," 323–348.

while in some respects purely American, in others had broad implications for liberal democracy. As Tocqueville pointed out, the problem of slavery, in itself potentially solvable in a short space of time, was linked in America (and in many other places) to the enduring problem of racism. "After abolishing slavery, modern peoples still have to destroy three prejudices much more elusive and more tenacious than slavery: the prejudice of the master, the prejudice of race, and finally the prejudice of the white." These prejudices have posed challenges to liberalism ever since: how to make a society in which Black people need not be afraid of White people, and vice versa.[49]

Tocqueville made an analogy between racism and the social distinctions between aristocrats and commoners which the French found so hard to overcome. Even in his time, marriages between those who claimed noble blood and commoners were the exception in France. In America, interracial marriages were even more unusual. According to Tocqueville, "those who hope that one day the Europeans will blend with the Negroes seem to me to entertain a chimera. My reason does not lead me to believe it, and I see nothing in the facts that indicates it." Tocqueville noted that the racism of Northern states was even more marked than in those of the South where slavery still existed. In the foreseeable future a mixed-race America was not possible because American racism would remain even after American slavery was abolished.[50]

Tocqueville rejected as impossible a popular solution among abolitionists in his time (c. 1835), the voluntary or forced return of freed slaves to Africa. What instead would happen after liberation, Tocqueville predicted, was some form of institutionalized racism: "The same abuses of power that maintain slavery today" would continue. White racism would grow stronger rather than diminish. Laws enforcing racial segregation would be passed. But, Tocqueville less presciently continued, free Blacks would not stand for this, and the result would be a race war in America, which he thought the Whites would win, unlike in Haiti, because of their greater numbers.[51]

Nevertheless, slavery would end, Tocqueville wrote, regardless of the efforts of White Southerners to preserve it. "It will end by the deed of the slave

49. *Democracy*, 2:550–552. See also Tillery, Jr., "Tocqueville as Critical Race Theorist."

50. *Democracy*, 2:553. In *The Old Regime*, Tocqueville argued that the only way to tell if caste, and by analogy racial, prejudice had ceased was to look at the rate of intermarriage. By this criterion American racism only began to decline in the 1990s.

51. *Democracy*, 2:571, 577, 573–574, 578. Or perhaps this was a prescient forecast of the events of Reconstruction.

or by that of the master. In both cases, great misfortunes must be expected." One can hardly say that Tocqueville was wrong, given the American Civil War and the history of Jim Crow and American racism thereafter. There was, for Tocqueville, *no* possible liberal solution to the problem of American racism in 1835: a racially constructed slavery had made the mutual fear of Whites and Blacks inevitable. He excluded the only solution that occurred to him, intermarriage, as out of the question, as indeed it was in his time. Tocqueville saw in African American slavery and its long-term costs an object lesson in "the most horrible and the most natural consequence of slavery." America provided Tocqueville both the shining example of liberal democracy and the most awful example of democratic despotism.[52]

In his own time Tocqueville's case for liberal democracy was perhaps more prescient than pertinent, although even in the nineteenth century its importance was felt, resulting in his common designation in the reviews of *Democracy in America* as "the modern Montesquieu." The aristocratic nature of his liberalism, his atypical views (for a Frenchman) on the relationship of freedom and religion, and his own somewhat chilly personality all served to make him something of an outsider. But he was an outsider who by virtue of that very fact saw deeper into the nature of democratic society than perhaps anyone since, and who thereby recognized both its promise and its danger from a liberal perspective, and strove mightily to construct a theory of liberal democracy as a result.[53]

John Stuart Mill was as concerned with individuality as Tocqueville, but Mill's English context was very different from Tocqueville's French one. Tocqueville lived in a world in which bitter and destructive political struggles were all too frequent. He valued diversity—hence his theory of associations and fight against individualism—but he did not value conflict nearly as much as Mill felt free to do in peaceful England. In this, Tocqueville, even if he was a liberal of a new kind, was more conventional than Mill. Indeed, Mill stretched the boundaries of nineteenth-century liberalism so far that for some commentators the author of *On Liberty* is not even a liberal. If Macaulay represented the center, almost a generic version of three-pillar liberalism, and Tocqueville was one step away from that center, then Mill was at the extreme edge of the nineteenth-century liberal consensus, and yet somehow central

52. *Democracy*, 2:581.
53. On Tocqueville as Outsider, see Kahan, *Alexis de Tocqueville*.

to it. The spectrum from Macaulay to Tocqueville to Mill is indeed a broad and splendid one.[54]

John Stuart Mill: A World Safe for Struggle

Nietzsche despised John Stuart Mill and called him a "blockhead," yet the two had a good deal in common: they shared a love of struggle and conflict. However, where Nietzsche saw this struggle as the natural preserve of the aristocrat, from which the mass of human sheep were excluded, Mill wanted the sheep—even the ewes—to be given every opportunity to participate, and thus cease to be sheep. Where Nietzsche saw physical force as one, albeit not the only, honorable means of combat, and fear as the appropriate state for sheep, Mill wanted everyone to feel sufficiently safe and empowered to express humanity's glorious diversity in conflict. Only in this way could the individual, the society, and the species progress. The "function of Antagonism" was at the root of Mill's liberalism.[55]

The fact that Mill can plausibly be connected to Nietzsche, the archetype of the *illiberal* theorist, shows just how unusual Mill's liberalism was. Because his name is virtually synonymous with liberalism today, as it was in the nineteenth century, and yet at the same time many of his positions were far from the liberal mainstream of both periods, makes him the perfect case to show just how broad mainstream liberalism was in the short nineteenth century. Many of Mill's fears were not common among the liberals of his time, either with regard to his fear of poverty, which only became the focus of the third wave of liberal fear after his death in 1873, or the oppression of women, where his concerns did not become commonplace until the twentieth century.[56] Still later, his chapter on the "stationary state" became very important for late twentieth-century environmentalists. Thus, outside economics, where for the most part he represented the liberal orthodoxy of his time despite his very heterodox sympathy for cooperatives and the stationary state, his views were

54. A case can be made that Mill's emphasis on struggle was a result of his reading of Humboldt and perhaps other Germans, but that case cannot be made here.

55. Nietzsche, *The Will to Power*, section 30; Mill, "Guizot's Essays and Lectures on History," *Collected Works* (hereafter *CW*), 20:269; Varouxakis, "Guizot's Historical Works"; Mill, *On Representative Government*, in *CW*, 19:119.

56. See the discussion of Mill's feminism in chapter 8.

rejected during his lifetime by most of his contemporaries for the excellent reason that his fears were not (yet) theirs.

Mill was both an enigma and a lodestar to his contemporaries and to posterity. His liberalism is important as much for what it contributed to later liberalisms as for what it says about nineteenth-century liberalism, both its breadth and its limits. The fact that Mill's fears were different from those of most other liberals of his time is what made him seem like no liberal at all to later commentators, who defined liberalism in a doctrinaire way as negative freedom: he was seen as a peculiar sort of socialist instead. But, although Mill indeed proclaimed himself to be a socialist—of a new kind, Tocqueville might have added—he was steadfast in his commitment to liberalism, and even his socialism, such as it was, was purely a means to liberal ends.

What made Mill's liberalism different was also the sort of remedy he offered for liberal fears, both old and new: conflict and antagonism, applied to all the three pillars of his liberalism—political, economic, and moral. Mill was not the first liberal to talk about the utility of difference and conflict (see Montesquieu on freedom in republics, chapter 1, or Madison on faction, chapter 2). But Mill made the "principle of Antagonism" central to his theory of human development and to his liberalism. For Mill, one way in which modern societies were superior to ancient ones was that no ancient society "contained in itself that systematic antagonism, which we believe to be the only condition under which stability and progressiveness can be permanently reconciled to one another."[57] Mostly, people who want to avoid fear and cruelty prefer harmony. It was in part his strong preference for strife that made Mill's classic *On Liberty*, a book designed to make conflict easy, a surprise to Mill's liberal readers when it was published in 1859. They thought there was already quite enough discord in Victorian Britain. Mill did not.

What made Mill unique was his embrace of antagonism not only past and present but in perpetuity. He identified it with "the interests of man as a progressive being," that is, with a perfectionist view of character. Mill was a liberal who for all his fears was still in hot pursuit of utopia, a utopia in which not only would people be free from fear and cruelty, but in which, partly through permanent benign conflict, they would realize their full potential as human beings. His perfectionist utopianism was found in many liberalisms, but rarely

---

57. Burrow, *Whigs and Liberals*, 113, 122–123; Varouxakis, "Guizot's Historical Works"; Collini et al., *That Noble Science*, 157. Mill, cited in Collini et al., *That Noble Science*, 157.

in such a strong form. Mill was in this respect a visionary. Carlyle was not altogether wrong when after reading some of Mill's articles he said to himself that "here is a new Mystic."[58]

In some respects Mill's liberalism was less atypical than he liked to imagine.[59] He relied on freedom, markets, and morals as much as any mainstream liberal, and he did not ignore the commonplace fears of his generation, revolution and reaction, religious intolerance, and despotism. His utopian liberalism expounded liberal commonplaces while highlighting the extreme boundaries of what nineteenth-century liberalism could be. Aspects of Mill's utopian liberalism can be seen in three of his major works. In his *Principles of Political Economy* we see his critique of the market; in *On Liberty*, his critique of bourgeois society and its morality; and in *Considerations on Representative Government*, his critique of political democracy. Each work appealed to more than one of kind of argument and brought his particular vision to each of the three pillars of liberalism. Nevertheless, each focused more on one pillar of liberalism than the others.

Economics is a good place to begin with Mill, both because his *Principles of Political Economy* became the leading English-language textbook of economics from the time of its publication in 1848 to the end of the nineteenth century, and because of the way it is representative of his views not just on economics, but on other issues. The book established Mill's reputation as an economist and became the standard statement of liberal economics, despite containing some quite heterodox elements. It is a good introduction to the way Mill, and for that matter most mainstream nineteenth-century liberals, mixed moral and political considerations with their economic views, even when writing something as seemingly straightforward as an introduction to economic theory. In the book, Mill deployed free-market economics partly for the sake of encouraging efficient production, but equally for the sake of improving people's character. Economic productivity was a potential ally of moral growth. This shifting focus between efficiency and morality has not made Mill easy to understand. As one biographer put it, "Mill could be accepted as a moralist, or

58. See Mill, *CW*, accessed via http://oll.libertyfund.org/titles/mill-collected-works-of-john -stuart-mill-in-33-vols; *Autobiography*, in *CW*, X:181, 181n; Carlyle and Carlyle, *Collected Letters*, 5:216, 235n., 398.

59. His imagination was led astray partly by the stress he laid on two areas in which his views *were* atypical, feminism and birth control.

he could be accepted as an explicator of the market economy, but what he could not get was acceptance as both."[60] But he was both, and it is impossible to understand his economics without accepting him as a moralist. His economics was based on a theory of combined economic and moral progress similar to that of Adam Smith, who served as Mill's acknowledged interlocutor in the book.[61]

In *Principles* Mill discussed several kinds of progress. The first was economic, a "progressive movement which continues with little interruption from year to year and from generation to generation; a progress in wealth." Another was "a continual increase of the security of person and property." A third was that people were safer from "arbitrary exercise of the power of government." This greater security led to more investment and production, for the safer people felt, "the more do industry and frugality become pervading qualities in a people." Mill's description of progress thus far was both conventional and conventionally liberal. Free people from fear and the economy would get better—Constant had argued much the same thing (see chapter 3). Mill's conclusion seemed equally conventional: "The progress which is to be expected in the physical sciences and arts, combined with the greater security of property, and greater freedom in disposing of it, . . . afford space and scope for an *indefinite* [emphasis added] increase of capital and production."[62]

"Indefinite" means without foreseeable end. However, Mill added an additional stage to the Scottish theory of history. After commercial society, Mill imagined a "stationary state." This was unconventional and, in some readings, illiberal. It was indeed curious that forty pages after having pronounced that material prosperity would increase indefinitely, Mill announced that "it must always have been seen, more or less distinctly, by political economists, that the increase of wealth is not boundless."

Even more unconventionally, Mill did not object. "It is only in the backward countries of the world that increased production is still an important object." As far as he was concerned, the wealth of England circa 1850 was enough, provided the population stopped increasing and wealth was more equally dis-

60. Capaldi, *John Stuart Mill*, 358–359.

61. It is tempting to say that Mill's silent discussion partner was Constant, many of whose similes and arguments appear almost verbatim. Yet there is no evidence Mill read Constant, and he would certainly not have concealed his influence, since he loved to cite French sources. See Lachs, "Mill and Constant." Oddly, the same is true of Tocqueville.

62. Mill, *Principles of Political Economy*, in *CW*, 3:706, 709.

tributed. In the stationary state, "while no one is poor, no one desires to be richer." Mill yearned for the stationary state as a place where there was "a well-paid and affluent body of labourers; no enormous fortunes, except what were earned and accumulated during a single lifetime; but a much larger body of persons than at present . . . with sufficient leisure . . . to cultivate freely the graces of life." Mill's utopian vision did not make economic development a priority for the future.[63]

The stationary state was the economic homeland of Mill's utopia. It was, naturally, a liberal utopia—it was still about progress, even if not material progress: the stationary state was not stationary in everything. Material progress would stop, perhaps out of disinterest, but other kinds of progress would continue: "There would be as much scope as ever for all kinds of mental culture, and moral and social progress; as much room for improving the Art of Living, and much more likelihood of its being improved, when minds ceased to be engrossed by the art of getting on."[64]

And yet, in seeming contradiction to this idyll, Mill remained an ardent supporter of economic competition and the free market. "I do not pretend that there are no inconveniences in competition, or that the moral objections urged against it by Socialist writers, as a source of jealousy and hostility among those engaged in the same occupation, are altogether groundless. But if competition has its evils, it prevents greater evils." Competition was necessary to arouse the majority from their laziness, and thus "every restriction of [competition] is an evil, and every extension of it, even if for the time injuriously affecting some class of labourers, is always an ultimate good."[65] This was where Mill's peculiar liberalism came back in: the stationary state was a place that had been made safe for strife and competition, and hence progress, albeit not material progress. There was no contradiction between Mill's endorsement of competition (a form of antagonism, in his view) and his suggestion that a "stationary state" might not be a bad thing. Competition could and should be maintained even when the goal was not an increase in productivity or personal wealth. Mill promoted competition as an agency of economic efficiency and of moral improvement.

Preserving competition was one of the principal reasons for limiting the scope of government, according to Mill. His point of departure when

---

63. Mill, CW, 3:752.
64. Mill, CW, 3:756.
65. Mill, CW, 3:795; 3:933. See also Capaldi, John Stuart Mill, 214.

considering the proper scope of government, whether with regard to economics or broader political and moral questions, was that "in all the more advanced communities, the great majority of things are worse done by the intervention of government, than the individuals most interested in the matter would do them, or cause them to be done, if left to themselves." Only where popular interest and ability was evidently lacking was government intervention permissible. Therefore, "*laisser-faire*, in short, should be the general practice: every departure from it, unless required by some great good, is a certain evil."[66]

Nevertheless, this did not lead Mill to advocate a laissez-faire state. He didn't think even the supporters of laissez-faire really wanted to restrict government only "to the protection of person and property against force and fraud; a definition to which neither they nor any one else can deliberately adhere."[67] Mill suggested many areas in which government action was not only convenient (inheritance laws, common weights and measures, building lighthouses, street cleaning), but could be a positive force for good. Consumers were not always competent judges in Mill's view, and "this is peculiarly true of those things which are chiefly useful as tending to raise the character of human beings. The uncultivated cannot be competent judges of cultivation." Governments might be better judges. "Any well-intentioned and tolerably civilized government . . . should therefore be capable of offering better education and better instruction to the people, than the greater number of them would spontaneously demand." Governments should require parents to educate their children regardless of the parents' wishes.[68]

Indeed, Mill thought a certain level of government intervention in matters of education so important that he repeated it in *On Liberty*: it was "an allowable exercise of the powers of government, to impose on parents the legal obligation of giving elementary instruction to children." In *On Liberty*, this was extended from "elementary" to "good" education: "If the government would make up its mind to *require* for every child a good education, it might save itself the trouble of *providing* one. . . . and content itself with helping to pay the school fees of the poorer classes of children." Mill did not want to see a government monopoly on education, since in his view "a general State education is a mere contrivance for moulding people to be exactly like one another." Nev-

66. Mill, *CW*, 3:941; 3:945–946.
67. Mill, *CW*, 3:936; 3:660.
68. Mill, *CW*, 3:947–948.

ertheless, by insisting on universal education mandated and in part paid for by government, Mill gave the government a voice.[69]

More controversially, Mill thought the government had a right to enforce birth control on the poor. He argued that "it still remains unrecognised, that to bring a child into existence without a fair prospect of being able, not only to provide food for its body, but instruction and training for its mind, is a moral crime, both against the unfortunate offspring and against society." Therefore, "the laws which, in many countries on the Continent, forbid marriage unless the parties can show that they have the means of supporting a family, do not exceed the legitimate powers of the State."[70]

There was a potentially infinite number of such cases for expanding the role of government: "In the particular circumstances of a given age or nation, there is scarcely anything really important to the general interest, which it may not be desirable, or even necessary, that the government should take upon itself, not because private individuals cannot effectually perform it, but because they will not." However, the government should never claim a monopoly, on education or anything else that would limit competition. "It is one thing to provide schools or colleges, and another to require that no person shall act as an instructor of youth without a government licence. There might be a national bank, or a government manufactory, without any monopoly against private banks and manufactories," and so on.[71] Government could thus advance progressive, even utopian ends, within liberal limits—in all senses of the word "liberal," provided the all-important principle of antagonism was allowed to flourish.

Nevertheless, Mill thought there needed to be some absolute limits on government: "There is a circle around every individual human being, which no government . . . ought to be permitted to overstep: . . . I apprehend that it ought to include all that part which concerns only the life, whether inward or outward, of the individual, and does not affect the interests of others, or affects them only through the moral influence of example."[72] Mill thus held that there needed to be some absolute limits on the power of the state in order to protect individuals and groups from oppression and allow them to flourish. More broadly, despite individual instances to the contrary, it was the principle of laissez-faire and of limited government intervention that was his baseline.

69. Mill, *CW*, 18:305; 3:949; 18:302; 3:948.
70. Mill, *CW*, 18:302; 18:304.
71. Mill, *CW*, 3:803; 3:970; 3:937.
72. Mill, *CW*, 3:938.

Laissez-faire was economically efficient, according to Mill. It was also morally important because competition built character. By contrast external direction, whether by the government or by the pressure of public opinion, degraded it. In *On Liberty*, character was Mill's watchword and competition and antagonism were central to the formation of every individual's moral core, as they were to the moral pillar of liberalism.

If there has ever been a liberal Bible, it is *On Liberty*, even if (or maybe because) no two liberals have ever understood it the same way, and few have read it without reservations. Not many liberals have written books explicitly devoted to the question of freedom, and none so influential. *On Liberty* touches on many ways in which people should be free from fear, but it is above all concerned with their moral liberty and the development of their character.

Much of the interpretive debate about the book has centered around Mill's famous "harm principle": "The only purpose for which power can be rightfully exercised over any member of a civilized community, against his will, is to prevent harm to others." The principle is simple enough; determining its justification and application is more difficult. The questions here are who Mill feared would inflict harm; and who / what would be harmed by such violations. In other words, how did fear operate in modern society, and how could liberalism defend against it.[73]

Mill's fears were predominantly of two kinds. One was a fear of bureaucracy that will be addressed below with regard to political institutions. But this fear was often overshadowed by a second fear, of a soft despotism over the thoughts and actions of individuals and groups exercised not by the government, but by the social pressure of the middle class—a fear he admittedly learned from Tocqueville—and perhaps in the future by the proletariat.[74] Mill feared that the middle class would dominate the moral and intellectual world, and that this domination would have potentially disastrous effects on character. In particular he feared for what he considered the highest element of character, individuality, to which he devoted the central chapter of the book. The domination of the middle class and its effects were the central sociological fact and moral concern of *On Liberty*. The soft despotism of modern social pressure was as much to be feared as any tyrannical despot of the past. Liberalism, as Mill saw it, was called upon to combat the new threat to freedom just as fiercely.

73. Capaldi, *John Stuart Mill*, 266; Mill, *On Liberty*, in *CW*, 18:223.
74. On the two fears, see Ryan, *The Making of Modern Liberalism*, 293.

For Mill, "the only freedom which deserves the name, is that of pursuing our own good in our own way." The kind of person one should be was "a person whose desires and impulses are his own—are the expression of his own nature, as it has been developed and modified by his own culture." This kind of person "is said to have a character. One whose desires and impulses are not his own, has no character."[75] Character had to be defended against the oppression of middle-class respectability.

"Character" and "respectability" were the two great moral watchwords of Victorian England. For Mill, unlike for most of his contemporaries, there was significant tension between them. Too much concern for respectability was bad for your character. As a result, "society has now fairly got the better of individuality." This was disastrous. For Mill, the worst that could be said "of any condition of human affairs" was that it prevented the development of individuality. This was the cruelty that Mill feared the middle classes inflicted on themselves and the rest of society. It was a moral cruelty that prevented human beings from performing their highest moral duty, their own self-development: "it is the privilege and proper condition of a human being, arrived at the maturity of his faculties, to use and interpret experience in his own way." For Mill, individuality was a moral obligation, the highest form of individual freedom. If my individuality frightened you, that was a fear that you were obliged to tolerate, for our common good (although Mill made an offhand remark that contraventions of "decency" could be punished).[76]

Mill lamented that "in maintaining this principle [individuality], the greatest difficulty to be encountered ... [lies] in the indifference of persons in general to the end itself." "The majority of moral and social reformers" did not value individuality. Perhaps the most pessimistic comment in *On Liberty* was Mill's acknowledgment that "doubtless, however, these considerations will not suffice to convince those who most need convincing; and it is necessary further to show, that these developed human beings are of some use to the undeveloped." Mill's fears were not those of his time.[77]

Mill did not think that character, or freedom, was only needed by the few. It was not "solely, or chiefly, to form great thinkers, that freedom of thinking is required." On the contrary, it was indispensable to "enable average human beings to attain the mental stature which they are capable of." Everyone needed

75. Mill, *CW*, 18:226; 18:263; 18:264.
76. Mill, *CW*, 18:262; 18:295–296.
77. Mill, *CW*, 18:267; 18:260–261.

character, everyone needed freedom to think, everyone needed freedom to act. "If a person possesses any tolerable amount of common sense and experience, his own mode of laying out his existence is the best, not because it is the best in itself, but because it is his own mode."[78]

Furthermore, individuality required the availability of diverse environments. Everyone needed to be exposed to challenges and arguments. Even if an opinion was true, "if it is not fully, frequently, and fearlessly discussed, it will be held as a dead dogma, not a living truth." The benefits of diversity and conflict were for all. It was because Europe was so culturally diverse and permitted so much cultural competition that it had continued to make progress where other societies had not.[79]

Unfortunately, the growing domination of the middle classes, a phenomenon that had first occurred in the Anglo-Saxon countries but was destined to spread elsewhere with the spread of democratic society (here again Mill spoke as a reader of Tocqueville), threatened to eliminate the diversity once characteristic of Western societies: "England is progressively changing . . . from an aristocracy with a popular infusion, to the regime of the middle class . . . America is all middle class." At least White America: "Those whose opinions go by the name of public opinion, are not always the same sort of public: in America they are the whole white population; in England, chiefly the middle class. But they are always a mass, that is to say, collective mediocrity." It was middle-class mediocrity that dominated public opinion, and that opinion was ever more uniform because society was ever more middle class. In the modern world, "the engines of moral repression have been wielded more strenuously against divergence from the reigning opinion" than ever before. Mill blamed the middle class for that.[80]

Mill not only feared the bourgeoisie: the proletariat also posed a threat, if only in the future. "We have only further to suppose a considerable diffusion of Socialist opinions, and it may become infamous in the eyes of the majority

78. Mill, *CW*, 18:243; 18:270.

79. Mill, *CW*, 18:245; 18:243.

80. Mill; *CW*, 18:226; Mill, cited in Kahan, *Aristocratic Liberalism*, 55; Mill, *CW*, 18:268. Mill is not opposed to the middle classes or even the commercial spirit in all circumstances, however: "The spirit of commerce and industry is one of the greatest instruments not only of civilization in the narrowest, but of improvement and culture in the widest sense. . . . So long as other coordinate elements of improvement existed beside it . . . the benefits which it conferred on humanity were unqualified. But . . . its complete preponderance would commence an era either of stationariness or of decline." *CW*, 18:218.

to possess more property than some very small amount, or any income not earned by manual labour." This was speculative, so Mill suggested a real example of the tyranny of proletarian opinion: "It is known that the bad workmen who form the majority of the operatives in many branches of industry, are decidedly of the opinion that bad workmen ought to receive the same wages as good. . . . And they employ a moral police" to make sure no one worked too hard. Fear of this kind of enforced conformity and restraint on competition was one reason Mill insisted that no one should ever be forced to join a labor union.[81]

When Mill turned to discussing political institutions proper, issues of character remained central: "The first element of good government, therefore, being the virtue and intelligence of the human beings composing the community, the most important point of excellence which any form of government can possess is to promote the virtue and intelligence of the people themselves." This could best be done by creating the freedom and security they needed to develop themselves. His central concern remained the kind of human being fostered by the political system, and his method continued to be the promotion of diversity and individuality through conflict and antagonism. Making the world safe for all to struggle in was Mill's peculiar vision of a liberal utopia. The political means for doing so were at the heart of the political institutions he prescribed in *On Representative Government*.[82]

Mill began the book by marching through history to his own day, when representative government was the best government, although not every modern society was fit for it yet. Mill's arguments for the superiority of representative government combined appeals to utility with appeals to perfection. First, people were only safe from oppression to the extent that they were "self-protecting," and this meant they had to directly participate in government through their representatives. As he developed this idea, it turned out that people chiefly needed to be able to protect themselves from class domination: "the interest of the excluded is always in danger of being overlooked; and, when looked at, is seen with very different eyes from those of the persons whom it directly concerns." This was the basic utility of representative government: preventing class domination.[83]

81. Mill, *CW*, 18:286–287.
82. Mill, *CW*, 19:390. See also Ryan, *The Making of Modern Liberalism*, 314.
83. Mill, *CW*, 19:404–405.

Second, representative government was important to perfect morals: "If we now pass to the influence of the form of government upon character, we shall find the superiority of popular government over every other to be, if possible, still more decided and indisputable." The world was dominated by passive characters, but progress only came from the active and energetic. The conclusion was that "there can be no kind of doubt that the passive type of character is favoured by the government of one or a few, and the active self-helping type by that of the Many."[84]

Thus Mill used political freedom in the same way he used economic and intellectual / moral freedom, namely to create a situation in which individuals could develop themselves without fear, "self-protected" from government interference in all areas by their participation in representative government. Representative government was necessary if people were to be safe from fear and able to pursue their own perfection in their own way. But even under representative government people were still subject to two dangers: class domination and bureaucracy.

Despite representation for all, there was still a danger that one class would dominate politics. At present that class was the middle class, but once one accepted universal suffrage, as Mill did, it would be the lower-class majority that dominated. This was a common liberal fear. A second danger that concerned him, bureaucracy, was more unusual and more for the future than the present: bureaucracy could co-exist with representative government, indeed was necessary to it, but it was dangerous because it was so efficient and the despotism of expert bureaucrats would be as illiberal as any other kind.

Mill attempted to solve both problems at once: he wanted to restrict the scope of legislative authority not only to prevent class tyranny, but to change the way the legislature carried out its duties, so as to combine the virtues of bureaucracy and democracy—or more accurately to combat the fears each aroused in him. Mill thus proposed representative institutions to check and balance a legislative body that would inevitably have a majority based on social class; to make sure minority opinions were heard and intellectual competition maintained; and to retain the benefit of bureaucratic expertise without succumbing to the rule of the experts.

For Mill, the chief duty of a representative assembly was "to watch and control the government: to throw the light of publicity on its acts . . . to censure them if found condemnable, and . . . to expel them from office, and . . .

84. Mill, *CW*, 19:406–407; 19:410.

appoint their successors." But actual lawmaking should be reserved to experts, i.e., bureaucrats, who would form a "commission of legislation." After the laws had been drawn up by the bureaucratic experts, the assembly should vote on them, thus giving national consent. "Nothing but the restriction of the function of representative bodies within these rational limits, will enable the benefits of popular control to be enjoyed in conjunction with the no less important requisites . . . of skilled legislation and administration." Although Mill feared bureaucracy, he also wished to use it to check and balance popular government. Himself a professional bureaucrat in the service of the East India Company, Mill thought that bureaucracy was a necessary part of a modern state: "Government by trained officials cannot do, for a country, the things which can be done by a free government; but it might be supposed capable of doing some things which free government, of itself, cannot do. . . . freedom cannot produce its best effects, and often breaks down altogether, unless means can be found of combining it with trained and skilled administration." Mill wanted a form of representative government that would balance popular and expert influence in its legislation. The bureaucracy was educated, experienced, habituated to the practice of government, etc. But its utility did not make up for its fatal flaws: Compared to representative government, bureaucracy "is not equally favourable to individual energy of mind. The disease which afflicts bureaucratic governments, and which they usually die of, is routine." Thus an additional function of the representative assembly was to act as the nation's "committee of grievances." It should be able to demand legislation on a certain subject, or even make propositions, but without the force of law. In so doing, the representatives would have scope to exercise initiative and break through bureaucratic inertia. Rather than appealing like Max Weber to democratic charisma as the counterweight to bureaucratic routine, Mill appealed to democratic political institutions.[85]

Mill designed a further political institution that was in some measure intended to bring the bureaucracy into the legislature, but in a subordinate role. Although he thought it inevitable that the lower, popularly elected chamber would be the strongest, he thought it useful to create alongside it "a body of which special training and knowledge should be the characteristics," a senate

85. Mill, *CW*, 19:432; 19:430; 19:433; 19:439; Kahan, *Aristocratic Liberalism*, 64; Mill, *CW*, 19:440. Comparing Mill and Max Weber on the dangers of bureaucracy reveals why it is a mistake to consider Weber a liberal. A liberal would be terrified of Weberian "charisma" in a position of political power.

or upper house. Ideally its membership would be composed of former members of the technical committees that drew up legislation; judges; ex-ministers; high-ranking military officers; diplomats; and possibly even a few professors. It is not clear what powers Mill wanted to give this senate. He was content to leave them as hazy as those of the British House of Lords of his day.[86]

When it came to the electoral system, Mill had to reconcile his view that "In all human affairs, every person directly interested, and not under positive tutelage, has an admitted claim to a voice," hence universal suffrage, with the fact that most voters would then be "manual laborers." The domination of any one class would be catastrophic, and universal suffrage thus threatened a tyranny of the majority. "The problem is, to find the means of preventing this abuse, without sacrificing the characteristic advantages of popular government," "foremost" among which was character development: the "education of the intelligence and of the sentiments, which is carried down to the very lowest ranks of the people when they are called to take a part in acts which directly affect the great interests of their country."[87]

Mill had two solutions to the problem of how the representative body should be chosen: how people would vote—the Hare Plan—and differentiating how many votes they would each have. Today the Hare Plan, better known as the "single transferable vote," is used in Ireland and Australia and some American elections. For Mill, its purpose was to ensure that minorities were represented, so that if 80 percent of the voters were members of the lower class, they did not get 100 percent of the representation. The single transferable vote differed from proportional representation in that there were still geographical election districts and that voters chose individual candidates rather than parties. The latter was very important for Mill, who thought it would allow meritorious individuals to be elected without party affiliation. Thus, even though "the superior intellects and characters will necessarily be outnumbered. . . . the influence of these leading spirits is sure to make itself sensibly felt in the general deliberations." As a result, "this portion of the Assembly would also be the appropriate organ of a great social function. . . . This may be called the function of Antagonism." The necessary conflict would be preserved and, Mill hoped, the intellectual and moral influence of the superior intellects might prove decisive.[88]

86. Mill, *CW*, 19:516–517.
87. Mill, *CW*, 19:473; 19:446; 19:467.
88. Mill, *CW*, 19:457–459.

Mill's second solution to the suffrage question was that although everyone would vote, some people would have more votes than others. In fact, Mill did not believe that "everyone" should have a voice. The illiterate, those receiving public assistance, those who had declared bankruptcy or been guilty of tax evasion within the last five years should not vote. At least on matters affecting taxation, those who did not pay taxes should not vote either, although Mill preferred a small universal poll tax to obviate this question. Who should receive extra votes, and how many? The only possible justification was "individual mental superiority . . . If there existed such a thing as a really national education, or a trustworthy system of general examination, education might be tested directly. In the absence of these, the nature of a person's occupation is some test." How many votes should they get? "The plurality of votes must on no account be carried so far, that those who are privileged by it, or the class (if any) to which they mainly belong, shall outweigh by means of it all the rest of the community." Without plural voting, universal suffrage was, according to Mill, an evil. Mill thus adopted what we will see in the next chapter was the standard nineteenth-century European liberal view of the suffrage: votes for all, but not yet. Utopia had to be protected from the ignorant, who otherwise would prevent its realization.[89]

Mill's liberalism marked an evolution from the traditional liberal view of politics, which relied on a "balance" of different interests for the sake of protecting people from fear, to one that valued diversity and antagonism for themselves. His focus on struggle was not universal among liberals in the nineteenth century, however. Madison might have been sympathetic, and Mill's view of history as struggle was widespread among some German liberals, but for Macaulay or Guizot and many other German liberals, social struggles were more in the past than in the future. For these liberals, the battle to be free from fear emphasized that freedom would produce harmony rather than chaos, and they did not endorse the permanent struggle Mill valued. These liberals therefore opposed universal suffrage, unlike Mill, because they wished to exclude from political participation groups considered inherently antithetical to harmony and intrinsic sources of fear. Hence, as the next chapter will show, liberal efforts were made to exclude workers from the vote, "aliens" from the nation, and Catholics from public life. Mill's wholehearted embrace of the principle of antagonism as the source of individual and social perfection and progress

89. Mill, *CW*, 19:473; 19:470–471; 19:474–477. See 19:471 on universal suffrage in America.

was exceptional. It made his liberalism as unusual as it was (and remains), important.

Liberalism and liberals are often taxed with inconsistency. The short list of liberals discussed so far, Kant, Madison, Constant, Macaulay, Tocqueville, and Mill, are evidence of liberalism's diversity. Liberals have always contradicted each other: Macaulay's cautious centrist Whiggism, Tocqueville's bold embrace of liberal democracy, and Mill's visionary liberal utopianism are all examples. Nevertheless, as has been underlined, there is remarkable consistency in the liberal project of making a society where no one need be afraid, and mainstream nineteenth-century liberals stood everywhere on the three pillars of freedom, markets, and morals to battle against fear. However, liberal consistency was obscured by differing circumstances. Comparable fears and functionally equivalent remedies looked very different in different places, whether in politically stable Britain, socially homogeneous White America, post-revolutionary France, or Germany in the throes of national unification. Nineteenth-century liberalism changed its political colors often.

When it comes to practice, rather than theory, the simplest and most direct way of approaching liberalism in the nineteenth century is by asking, in the language of the time, whether nineteenth-century liberals belonged to the "Party of Movement" or the "Party of Resistance." In practice, liberalism in the nineteenth century was *both* a party of movement and a party of resistance, *all the time*—hence the two-front war often noted as characteristic of nineteenth-century liberalism—but one of these aspects was usually foremost and obscured the other, leading to consternation when the other appeared. Both movement and resistance could be appropriate means of ending cruelty and fighting fear, and depending on circumstance both were perfectly liberal positions. Liberals often disagreed with one another about which side of the fence circumstances dictated. It is only through observing liberals' conduct on the ground in various political and social struggles that liberal support for both movement and resistance can be understood. Some of the most important of those questions, liberal positions on the suffrage, on nationalism, on the relationship of liberalism to religion, are discussed in the next chapter, "Liberalism on the Front Lines: Freedom, Nation, God."

5

Liberalism on the Front Lines:
Freedom, Nation, God

ONE OF THE MANY REASONS nineteenth-century liberals acquired a reputation as the party of contradictions was because they straddled the divide between "movement" and "resistance." To the left of liberalism, radicals always favored whatever reform was on the day's agenda. To the right of liberalism, conservatives just as consistently opposed it: the party of movement faced the party of resistance to change. By contrast, for the liberals in the middle, it was often unclear whether the fear of revolution and reaction—hence resistance—or hope for progress—hence support for movement and reform—was foremost in the liberal mind. Liberal waters were further muddied by the fact that sometimes resistance to change seemed the best way of keeping hope alive, for example when fighting to preserve a liberal institution against revolutionaries, and sometimes change seemed the best response to fear, for example to expand the suffrage out of fear of revolution.

Liberalism nevertheless began the short nineteenth century in most places as a party of movement (the exception was England, where liberals were divided between supporting reforms and resisting them as early as 1830) and ended it mostly in ambivalence or resistance, before a renewed burst of support for reform in the fin de siècle. Everywhere east of the English Channel liberals began the period by demanding constitutions to protect people from despotism. The demand took time to be fulfilled, but by the end of the short nineteenth century constitutions were the rule everywhere west of the Russian Empire, and thereafter liberals gradually transitioned to a more ambivalent attitude to reform. As one German liberal put it at the Frankfurt Parliament in 1848, "when we still didn't have freedom of the press, when no Bill of Rights yet spoke of freedom of religion and freedom of association . . . then no one could say he was 'conservative' and the only one who strove for freedom was the one on the destructive side. But . . . if it is rational to strive for a good not yet achieved, so it is still more reasonable . . . to preserve it, to conserve it."[1] This malleable orientation, putting liberals now on the left, now on the right side of change, contributed to giving liberalism its chameleon-like political appearance.

During the short nineteenth century, the political, economic, and moral questions posed by who should be allowed to vote; by the relationship between liberalism and nationalism; and by the issue of liberal anti-Catholicism forced liberals into difficult choices between movement and resistance. In responding to these challenges liberals used all three pillars of their argument, although the market pillar was usually less central to these debates. Analyzing them allows us to grasp the strategies pursued by nineteenth-century liberal politicians in their struggle to keep fear and cruelty at bay.

The Discourse of Capacity: Liberalism and Suffrage in Europe

One crucial issue on which nineteenth-century liberals alternated between movement and resistance was suffrage. European[2] liberals found both reasons for fear and reasons for hope in mass political participation. From the liberal perspective, political participation was necessary to prevent despotism, but could itself result in despotism. In debating the suffrage, liberals had to combine their allegiance to universal freedom from fear—which made them partisans of expanding the vote—with restricting political participation by those who made them afraid. In nineteenth-century Europe, liberals sought to establish a working relationship with the sovereignty of the people as expressed through representative government. The discourse of capacity was the linguistic tool they used to do it.

---

1. Bassermann, *Stenographischer Bericht*, 5253–52 to 5354–41. All translations from German suffrage debates are my own.

2. In America all White men could vote by the early nineteenth century. However, the mid- to late-nineteenth- century development of American variations on the discourse of capacity is an important story not yet fully told. It played a critical role after the Civil War, sometimes opposing women's suffrage, sometimes supporting it as a means of boosting the White vote and supporting Black exclusion. See Kraditor, *Ideas of the Woman Suffrage Movement*. It also came into play against immigrants. Francis Parkman, in "The Failure of Universal Suffrage" (1878), called for a property qualification for local voting for this reason. See Alexander Keyssar, *The Right to Vote*.

Freedom, to nineteenth-century liberals, meant first of all rights guaranteed by a constitution. But for nineteenth-century European liberals, voting was not a right. Voting was a trust. It was a political office, a role that not everyone was capable of fulfilling, and "the electoral office must be limited to those who are presumed capable of making good choices." Even John Stuart Mill, for all his stress on the benefits of political participation, rejected any idea of a right to vote: "no person can have a right to power over others. . . . But the exercise of any political function, either as an elector or as a representative, is power over others."[3]

A characteristic liberal discourse thus emerged in suffrage debates.[4] To the question "Who should vote?," liberals responded: those who have the capacity to participate in politics without bringing about either revolution or reaction. The discourse of capacity dominated liberal discussions of voting. Who possessed the necessary capacity? How could it be determined? Was it individual capacity that mattered, or the capacity of the group of individuals represented? These were the questions liberals characteristically asked.

All liberal Europe spoke the language of capacity from shortly after the French Revolution until the fin de siècle. The words "capacity," "*capacité*," "*Befâhigung*," or "*Kapazität*" were ubiquitous when liberals had to deal with suffrage questions. The discourse of capacity was the common liberal response to the dangers and opportunities of post-revolutionary politics (liberalism is always a combination of fears and hopes). It distinguished liberals from radicals who talked about a universal (male) *right* to vote, and from conservatives who talked about the hereditary ownership of political power. The discourse of capacity, and the limited but expanding suffrage it justified, served to ward off liberal fears of elective tyranny and aristocratic or royal despotism. Capable voters, susceptible neither to demagoguery nor government pressure, would choose representatives who would limit the arbitrary powers of rulers and mobs. Capable voters were the antidote against fear. The language of capacity was flexible enough to express liberal demands for both reform and resistance, as needed, demanding votes for some and refusing it to others.[5]

---

3. Duvergier de Hauranne, during the French parliamentary suffrage debates in 1831, *Moniteur Universel*, 23 February, 1831, 377–2; Mill, *CW*, 19:488.

4. The debates discussed in this chapter were about men's suffrage. For women's suffrage, see chapter 8.

5. See Kahan, *Liberalism in Nineteenth-Century Europe*.

The language of capacity was democratic, in the sense that anyone could possess capacity, earn it, or even lose it. In theory, liberals excluded no one from the vote. For the present, given the lamentable lack of capacity of the majority of men and all women, most people had to be excluded from political participation because their participation would be detrimental to everyone, even to themselves. While it might seem a good idea to a starving man to vote private property out of existence, such a decision in the long run would hurt the starving voter. An uneducated man might be persuaded by a demagogue (Robespierre) or a dictator (Napoleon I or III) that despotism was the solution to his problems. To prevent these disasters, only those with the capacity for good decision-making should be allowed to vote. But once a person or a class possessed the necessary capacity, there was a prima facie case for their political participation—the discourse of capacity, in liberal mouths, always included the promise of future universality when everyone was ready for it.

However, as a perceptive radical opponent noted, "for these clever [liberal] politicians, the people are always going to get their freedom, and are never ready for it." But liberals sometimes supported expanding the suffrage because they thought it could be as dangerous to give the vote to too few people as to too many. Hence the widening of the suffrage seen in Great Britain in 1832 and France in 1830. It is possible to misunderstand the language of capacity as purely a weapon against the left, against radicals who sought universal male suffrage. But it was equally directed against conservative aristocratic claims. As Earl Grey, the British Prime Minister who sponsored a massive expansion of the British suffrage in 1832, put it, "I deny that the power of returning Members of Parliament is to be considered . . . property." This was to reject the conservative / aristocratic theory that political participation should be reserved to an hereditary class. Since the vote was "not a property, but a trust," the goal was to give "the franchise [vote] to a class to whom it might be safely given, and in withholding it from others when the public convenience required it."[6]

In deciding about capacity, liberals addressed linked questions about fear: Are we afraid of dangerous individuals, or dangerous classes? Are we afraid as individuals with unpopular opinions, or as members of a property-owning class? Hence "individualist" or "social" definitions of capacity. The most com-

---

6. Julius Fröbel, cited in Brandt, *Landständische Repräsentation, Politica* v. 31, 277. Earl Grey, *Hansard*, October 3, 1831, 946; Attorney General Sir James Scarlett, *Hansard*, August 30, 1831, 895. All further references to British parliamentary debates come from *Hansard*, which can be consulted online.

mon variety of liberal political discourse in the nineteenth century was one
that had class at its center, that saw the question of capacity as a question of
which class or classes or "interests" ought to participate in politics. Liberals
thought the middle classes should play an important role, although not necessarily a dominant one. In the early part of the century individualist liberalisms were weak, in parliamentary debates if not necessarily among theorists,
but they gained strength over time. However, it is often pointless to stress
the individualist / social distinction strongly. Both frequently appealed to
the same criteria, for example "independence," as a necessary "guarantee" of the
voter's behavior, whether the voter was representing a personal opinion or
those of a class.

The word "guarantee" that liberals liked to use in relation to potential voters
is redolent of the liberal fears. One needs a guarantee against irresponsible
behavior, against violence, against despotism. But it can also be construed in
line with liberal hopes, a warranty that the machine will work as advertised,
bringing about the moral, economic, and political progress that liberals expected and that would also serve to diminish danger. The discourse of capacity
assisted liberals in building a firm political pillar to help ward off their fears, a
political pillar that included economic and moral components. In nineteenth-
century suffrage debates, liberal political arguments were buttressed with appeals to moral education and economic development. In doing so liberals built
an effective appeal that contributed much to making liberalism into a dominant force throughout the Western world.

Liberal use of political, economic, and moral arguments can be seen in
parliamentary debates that are a convenient and broadly commensurable repository of everyday liberal language. Two such parliamentary debates can
serve as examples. One is a well-known and frequently described liberal victory, the other an obscure and rarely discussed liberal failure: the British Great
Reform Act of 1832, and the inconclusive Prussian debate over suffrage reform
that took place in 1861. Together they display the spectrum of liberal hopes and
fears about political participation, the liberalism of movement and the liberalism of resistance.

Suffrage reform in Britain was sparked by revolution in France. In 1830, the
July Revolution in France put a liberal regime in power—nineteenth-century
liberals had no problems joining a revolution if by doing so they could stop
it—and acted as a catalyst for liberal activity elsewhere, if only to prevent more
revolutions. In England, a Whig / liberal government came to power with the
express intention of avoiding revolution by timely reform. The Reform Act of

1832 was meant to transform an electoral system that had remained largely unchanged for centuries. It abolished "rotten boroughs," places that elected members of Parliament despite the fact that almost no one lived there any more. It gave new or additional seats to centers of population and industry—before the Reform Act, neither Manchester nor Birmingham was represented in Parliament, despite their size and enormous role in the Industrial Revolution, and London was grossly underrepresented. London continued to be somewhat underrepresented after the Reform Act, as liberals feared giving too much power to representatives potentially subject to the influence of a revolutionary mob, even if that mob could not vote.

The Reform Act further established uniform national suffrage qualifications based on property ownership. Somewhere between 15 and 20 percent of adult males voted as a result, compared to roughly half that number before, and they voted in electoral districts that were more representative, although far from numerically equal in population. Everyone had only one vote in any local election, although a person who owned property in several electoral districts could vote in all of them.

The reform of 1832 was a liberal project. In defending it, two ideas about political participation were nearly universal among its parliamentary supporters: voting was a "trust," not a right or a possession, and the vote ought to be given only to those who could provide guarantees that they had the capacity to exercise their trust properly. This credo was accepted by all English liberals in 1832, and by the vast majority of European liberals between approximately 1830 and 1880.

The vote was to be given to those who would use it to make the government stronger and society safer. The requirement that voters possess property was first of all a demand that they provide a guarantee that it would be safe to allow them to vote. As Lord Stanley said, the suffrage ought to be broadened "to as low a scale of property as would be consistent with the safety of the State." Or, as Brougham argued, the reason to admit more voters was to "admit those whose interests and feelings . . . were most adverse to any violent change, to assist in giving stability to the Constitution." Suffrage reform should prevent revolution and assist future progress.[7]

To help prevent revolution and promote progress, a voter needed "independence," a criterion found in Kant and one widespread in European liberal

---

7. Lord Stanley, December 7, 1832, 520; Brougham, April 13, 1832, 423, 426. On Whigs and Liberals, see Burrow, *Whigs and Liberals*.

suffrage discussions. The independent voter was a person capable of resisting coercion, whether from a radical mob, a reactionary aristocrat, or a domineering employer. The suffrage should not be given to persons "who, from being in dependent circumstances, were incapable of deliberation, and must act as they were commanded." But independent voters were not the same thing as equal voters even if, in the English system, all had only one vote. The British liberal aim was not to abolish due deference to the opinions of one's betters, and independent voters were voters who could, and should, rationally decide to defer to their social and intellectual superiors. The purpose of the criterion of independence was to encourage the correct kind of deference, voluntary deference to superior wisdom and ability, not coerced deference.[8] By giving the vote to independent individuals or classes, due deference would be encouraged by example among the lower classes who currently lacked it. The Reform Bill offered "an opportunity of reclaiming those misguided individuals, by placing among the persons [now given the vote] capable of controlling them by their influence, and of gaining them over, by their advice."[9]

Property was not the only possible guarantee of independence or capacity. Many liberals did not think property in itself was a criterion or the sole criterion for establishing who might safely vote. Intelligence or education was necessary as well, along with virtue. Nevertheless, property was generally considered the best means of ascertaining other virtues. Thus Lord Russell combined wealth, brains, and morals: "the electors should . . . be intelligent, incorrupt and independent. In other words, they should have the capacity to make a choice, the wish to make a good choice, and the power to carry that wish into effect." As Macaulay argued, it was the incapacity of the lower classes to understand what policies were in their best interest that was the first grounds for excluding them from political participation, but other grounds included their weak morality and lack of economic independence.[10]

A phrase frequently used by speakers supporting reform was "property and intelligence," stated in various formulas that parallel the German usage of *Bildung und Besitz*. They were considered natural allies (this was less true in France, due to the experience of intellectuals' radicalism during the French Enlightenment and Revolution). In England, and to a lesser extent elsewhere,

8. On the distinction between kinds of deference, see Marshall, *Political Deference in a Democratic Age.*

9. Sir James Graham, March 8, 1831, 220–221; Brougham, April 13, 1832, 423.

10. Lord Russell, December 12, 1832, 497; Macaulay, February 6, 1832, 366.

intelligence and education were mostly not defined by formal qualifications. Instead they came from life experience and social situations.[11]

The result in Britain was a consensus that the middle classes, possessed of property and intelligence, hence capacity, ought to vote. In line with the nineteenth-century transformation of the Scottish theory of commercial society into a theory of middle-class society, liberals recast the history of progress and used it as an argument for suffrage reform: "The rapid and astonishing influx of wealth had absolutely changed the whole state of the middle classes of society. Those middle classes now consisted of persons well acquainted with every useful branch of art and science; they were fully capable of forming enlightened views and sound principles upon all political and moral questions [NB political *and* moral] . . . This class of persons had been raised in England into astonishing power, and they now came forward and demanded reform with an irresistible pressure."[12]

The new social and economic importance of the middle class meant it was necessary to give it greater political weight. If political representation did not mirror the real state of society, then the government would be weak and the probability of both revolution and reaction would increase. Variations on this argument were made by liberals throughout Europe: the middle classes wanted reform, and if they did not get it they would foment a revolution. If they did get it, they would aid further progress. By increasing, through suffrage reform, the legitimacy of government, liberals guaranteed political stability and created the preconditions for a government more capable of fulfilling its functions. Regardless of their differences about the scope of government, all liberals wanted it to be strong in its proper sphere. It could only be strong with the participation of the middle classes.[13]

Although the middle class certainly supported suffrage reform, it was not the members of the middle class themselves who reformed the suffrage in England in 1832. The landed gentry and their representatives still controlled Parliament, just as they still accounted for the majority of wealth. It was a testament to the strength of English liberalism in 1832 that it crossed class lines. Liberalism's broad political appeal made it the natural party of government in Britain from 1832 until 1886, when the question of Irish Home Rule split the

11. Frances Jeffrey, March 4, 1831, 62.

12. Lord Plunkett, March 28, 1831, 1044.

13. For British use of the mirror image, see Conti, *Parliament the Mirror of the Nation.* More generally, see Kahan, *Liberalism in Nineteenth-Century Europe.*

Liberal party. The suffrage debates of 1831–32 and the reforms that followed thereafter (abolition of slavery, new poor law, municipal government act, repeal of the Corn Laws, etc.) show British liberalism as the party of movement in England even as it continued to be a party of resistance, not to change, but to revolution.

Prussian liberalism showed German liberals choosing a different path. Prussia emerged from the 1848 revolutions in Germany with a constitution and a parliament, albeit one with limited powers, but until 1858 the powers of the Prussian parliament were largely illusory, since the government manipulated elections. In 1858 the so-called New Era began with the regency of the future Wilhelm I, who called into office a relatively liberal ministry that allowed free elections. Liberals emerged with a strong majority. In 1861 the ministry proposed a law reforming the structure of local government to curb the power of the Prussian aristocracy. The law occasioned a debate over the suffrage for local elections which all sides acknowledged to be a proxy for the Prussian national suffrage law.

The existing suffrage law, created by the reactionary Manteuffel government in 1851 with some liberal support, established almost universal male suffrage for Prussian national elections (95% of adult males could vote), but voting was indirect and weighted. Voters were divided into three classes / groups, each class paying one-third of the taxes of the electoral district. The highest-paying taxpayers made up the first class. In some districts these numbered only a handful of people. A somewhat larger number of individuals made up the second class, and everyone else the third.[14] In most districts, at least 70 percent of voters were in the third class. Each class voted for an equal number of electors, who then voted for the actual representative. In elections for local government, the system was the same in the Rhineland and a few other places, but in most of Prussia there was an equal and direct suffrage with a property-based qualification to vote. The government's bill was an attempt to homogenize the systems.

Although the three-class suffrage in national and local elections initially favored liberals (from the first free elections in 1858 until the late 1870s liberals maintained a majority, sometimes enormous, in the Prussian lower house), many Prussian liberals were dissatisfied with it, and in committee they modified

14. Nevertheless, in 1861 there were 159,000 voters in the first class, and 454,000 in the second. Proportionate to population, this was a larger number of voters than in England in 1866, even when leaving out the third class. Gay, *Cultivation of Hatred*, 270.

the government's 1861 bill to eliminate it for all local (and by implication future national) elections. The reason was that "the three-class suffrage system leads to social and political enmity within the citizenry," in other words to the kind of class struggle that might have dangerous consequences.[15]

But the Prussian liberals could not agree on an alternative. Their parliamentary committee proposed, for local purposes, a suffrage qualification based on taxpaying that varied in proportion to the population of the district, with the largest districts (towns with greater than 50,000 population) requiring double the tax payment of the smallest. This was justified in the language of capacity. According to the committee, the suffrage should be based on "independence, intellectual capacity, and enduring interest," i.e., property and education. The parliamentary debate turned chiefly on "independence" and its relationship to property ownership. Left liberals (the "Progressive Party") supported letting all direct taxpayers vote, which would still disenfranchise a substantial minority, and guaranteeing independence by introducing the secret ballot. But most liberals thought more property necessary for independence. Property was the best approximation for the moral independence of the individual, their capacity to make a free choice. What one Prussian liberal called "true universal suffrage" therefore meant excluding servants, apprentices, men too young to establish households, etc., from the vote. But once an individual was independent, there was no justification for giving different weights to votes: "We want the political *equality* of all really independent men." German liberals were less comfortable with the idea of a rational deference by independent voters to their betters than English, perhaps due to Kantian influence, or to the differences between Junkers and English gentry.[16]

Even opponents of the three-class system like Rudolf v. Gneist, who thought it destroyed social unity and led to class struggle and potentially revolution, did not like the committee proposal. Gneist thought that homeownership was what should count, not paying taxes. He opposed the committee proposal because in Berlin it would mean homeowners being outvoted 2–1 by renters. More broadly, he rejected the proposed new system because, echoing many English arguments in the same period, "self-government" (he uses the English phrase) required people to be involved with "higher political, moral, and educational goals." Homeowners, not renters, were typically involved in

15. Mill to William Rathbone, November 29, 1863; *CW*, 15:905; Max Duncker, *Stenographische Berichte des Haus der Abgeordneten*, May 2, 1861, 1021–1022.

16. Lette, *Stenographische Berichte*, May 3, 1861, 1050, 1065. Emphasis in original.

community service, and therefore should get the vote. But even if the vote was given to all houseowners, von Gneist was not happy with taking away the vote from people who had had it, even if in relatively weak form, under the three-class system.[17]

Gneist thus reluctantly supported retaining the three-class system. He was typical. The Progressives agreed that in most of Prussia the new requirements disenfranchised many citizens, which they opposed. But unlike Gneist they would not accept the criterion of homeownership of any value (nor would have most English liberals at the time). So, as one liberal said, "Gentlemen, even if I too condemn the three-class system, I am nevertheless only willing to get rid of it, now that it has been introduced, if I can replace it with a really good electoral system . . . and such a system, I must state, I cannot see presented before me now."[18]

In 1861 Prussian liberals feared conservative manipulation of the masses— hence their exclusion from the proposed new suffrage as well as liberal hostility to the three-class system, which permitted the lower classes to control one-third of the electors. A few years later, it was socialist influence they feared.

Unlike British liberals who established apparently uniform national property qualification knowing that in large cities they would allow a handful of lower-class voters, German liberals could think of no acceptable mechanism for politically integrating a portion of the lower classes as equals, except for the helpful suggestion that if they drank less and saved their money they too could acquire property. Even Schulze-Delitzsch, the liberal founder of the German cooperative movement, was hostile to lower-class political participation.[19] This social exclusivity dominated German liberalism until 1914. By contrast, English liberal suffrage proposals, and eventually the Second Reform Act of 1867, and still more the Third of 1884, were intended to bring the lower classes, at least those capable of it, into the Pale of the constitution, as Gladstone put it. Unlike English liberalism, Prussian liberalism was exclusively a party of resistance when it came to the lower classes. Liberals in different times and places in nineteenth-century Europe spoke the same language and used the same kinds of argument, but came to very different conclusions.[20]

17. Gneist, *Stenographische Berichte*, May 3, 1861, 1041–1044, 1067.

18. Riedel, *Stenographische Berichte*, May 3, 1861, 1058.

19. Vincke, *Stenographische Berichte*, May 3, 1861, 1055–1056; Kahan, *Liberalism in Nineteenth-Century Europe*, 100–101.

20. Gladstone (Chancellor of the Exchequer), *Hansard*, May 11, 1864.

The discourse of capacity was a utilitarian discourse about whose vote was useful for preventing revolution and reaction, and whose political participation would be most effective in warding off fear. But if the discourse of capacity was predominantly utilitarian, for some it had a perfectionist aspect. Both the acquisition of property and the acquisition of education could be conceived in perfectionist terms, as could political participation itself. Mill and Tocqueville argued that political participation was a form of education, although neither supported universal suffrage, a minimum of preexisting education / capacity being necessary to benefit from the education that politics offered without endangering society. Over time, the argument that voting itself *created* capacity / intelligence / education, and for that reason should be extended as far as possible (eventually to universal suffrage), became an integral part of British liberal politics. In 1884, in the course of debates over the Third Reform Act, Gladstone stated, "I do not think it is easy to dispute the enormous value of the Parliamentary vote as an educating power." Liberal MP Albert Grey agreed: "The good which he anticipated from extension [of voting rights] was the advantage which would be certain to result from the development of that spirit of self-help which the bestowal of the vote was calculated to produce." Political participation could itself create the kind of character necessary for useful political participation. A democratic perfectionist element thus introduced itself into an apparently restrictive utilitarian political discourse.[21]

This perfectionist turn was not unique to the latter part of the century, even among practicing politicians. In France in the 1830s Guizot saw desire to attain the franchise as an incentive to work hard, save money, and become a more moral person, in his (in)famous advice to those who wanted to vote under the July Monarchy, "Gain wealth! By savings and hard work and honesty!"[22] Vincke and others said much the same thing in Prussia in 1861. Most liberals saw political education in moral terms as much as or more than intellectual ones, and many defined the capacity for political participation as attaining a certain moral level (guaranteed, if only approximately, by social situation). What was new in the latter part of the short nineteenth century was the idea that it was safe for education and moral development to follow rather than precede the vote. The idea was found among earlier liberal theorists, but it took time to spread to parliamentary debates, and indeed spread farther in

21. Gladstone, *Hansard*, April 7, 1884, 1839–1840; Albert Grey, *Hansard*, April 1, 1884, 1316–1317.

22. "Enrichissez-vous" is often more tendentiously translated as "Get rich!."

some places than others. It was partly a question of the balance of fear and hope. The greater the fear, the more strictly utilitarian the approach. The more the memory or threat of revolution faded, the more hope was placed in the perfectionist educational powers of political participation. Some English liberals used this language in the failed suffrage reform attempts of the 1850s, but in 1884 it penetrated the party leadership and succeeded. Once capacity followed the vote, rather than preceding it, the justification for any limits on the suffrage was greatly weakened.[23]

Over the last decades of the nineteenth century the language of capacity largely vanished, along with limited suffrage. Although limited or weighted suffrage survived in England and Prussia until WWI, universal manhood suffrage was the order of the day in Germany on a national level, if not on the state level, once the German Empire was founded in 1871. Universal male suffrage was also enshrined in the constitution of the French Third Republic in 1875. Political participation (at least by men, especially White men) was increasingly spoken of as a right even by liberals because it was no longer seen as a danger, and instead became a bulwark against revolution and reaction, a necessity if the representation was to mirror the real nation. By the fin de siècle, liberals came to see the discourse of capacity as irrelevant at best, and counterproductive at worst.

The transition to a more democratic political liberalism after about 1873 was in part a consequence of the rise of nationalism.[24] Nationalism played a crucial role in transforming the liberal idea of the "people." It helped to discredit the idea that capacity was confined to a few, and challenged previous liberal ideas of what constituted oppression and despotism by recasting fear in terms of nations and nationalities. Even more important, perhaps, the rising nationalism of the short nineteenth century was one of the forces propelling liberals to power.

Nationalism

Liberalism and nationalism were twin births, albeit far from identical. Although when nationalism began is hotly debated, it is clear that it greatly increased after the American and French Revolutions, at the same time as liberalism

23. In 1852 John Bright spoke of the increased "self-respect" the vote created. *Hansard*, April 27, 1852, 1213–1214. It was still commonly believed that women and non-Whites were incapable of profiting from this education.

24. Other causes, notably the change in liberal attitudes to poverty, will be discussed in the next chapter.

emerged.[25] Their mutually supportive relationship during the short nineteenth century was an essential part of the history of liberalism, all the more so because it was a relationship that became increasingly difficult in the fin de siècle and thereafter.

The rise of nationalism was not expected by Montesquieu, Smith, or other proto-liberal thinkers of the eighteenth century. The stage theories of history popular among proto-liberals, and the cosmopolitan expectations of much of the Enlightenment did not foresee a nationalist future. On the contrary, commercial society was supposed to diminish distinctions among peoples and local loyalties. But nations did not merely persist and flourish and indeed get born or reborn in the nineteenth century, they attracted ever-increasing loyalty.[26] Constant and Tocqueville feared and prophesied an increasingly individualist society where affections were restricted to family and friends. Instead or rather alongside such developments there was a vast upsurge in nationalism. This had both positive and negative implications for liberalism. During the short nineteenth century, the positive ones dominated, but in the fin de siècle and later the relationship became problematic (see chapters 8 and 11). In the earlier period nationalism helped reconcile liberalism with democratic political movements and mass political participation, and in so doing improve the prospects for liberal democracy.

Nationalism helped liberalism adapt to a more democratic society and politics on several levels: theoretical, psychological, political, and international. On a theoretical level, perhaps the most significant overlap between liberalism and nationalism with regard to democracy had to do with moral equality. *"National identity is, fundamentally, a matter of dignity"* for everyone, just as from a liberal perspective everyone, as a matter of human dignity, should be able to live without fear. Both liberalism and nationalism attributed moral dignity to all human beings—at least the versions dominant in the short nineteenth century.[27.] For the Italian nationalist leader Giuseppe Mazzini (1805–1872), nationalism and liberalism ought to work together to achieve the moral improvement of individuals, society, and the human race. As Mazzini put it, "you

25. For the argument that nations, and perhaps nationalism, are ancient, see Grosby, *Nationalism*, 64–66; Yack, *Nationalism*, 1, 118.

26. A nation is "born" or "reborn" when people choose to see their common cultural legacy as constituting a national community in opposition to some Other.

27. Some forms of nationalism deny dignity to some or all other nations, as did some liberal imperialists. See chapters 7 and 8 for this discussion.

are *men* before you are *citizens* or *fathers*"—but national citizenship was crucial to the development of both the private individual and the world.[28]

Nationality was a form of consciousness in which everyone participated, a "plebiscite," to use the image made famous by the Frenchman Ernest Renan (1823–1892), a plebiscite in which everyone voted, women as much as men, the poor as well as the rich, and the "nation" and its "people" were seen as fundamentally homogenous. The democratic nature of this "nation" was mirrored in the way in which, over the course of the nineteenth century, the term "people," or its equivalent in most European languages, changed from a synonym for the mob to a synonym for the nation as a whole. The change in the word reflected a different psychological attitude. Nationalism preached trust in the people, *all* the people. Liberal freedom from fear could be attained only through association or community, and a national community was a necessary means to achieve the dignity for all to which liberalism aspired.

Nationalism also had the potential to psychologically reassure liberals about the dangers of democracy, while reducing illiberal tendencies in society at large. On a moral / psychological level, according to Tocqueville, individuals in democratic societies were always prey to the fear of losing status, for which nationalism provided powerful reassurance: one could lose one's money or one's reputation, but never one's nationality. In this respect nationalism was a bulwark against fear. To the extent to which the fear of losing status could provoke revolution or reaction, nationalism, by providing reassurance, prevented liberal fears from being realized. This psychological reassurance, simultaneously reducing the fears that caused illiberal revolutions and reaction and reducing liberals' fear of the no longer dangerous masses, helped bring about a rapprochement between liberalism and democracy by the fin de siècle, embodied in the abandonment of liberal opposition to universal male suffrage (although nationalists did tend to run ahead of liberals in this regard, leading to tensions). Nationalism could thus provide a basis for liberal democracy that extended to all the people of the nation. The psychological connection between liberalism and nationalism, however, later revealed itself to be circumstantial rather than fundamental. The twentieth century, for example, showed that an illiberal nationalism, one that excluded minorities and sought to terrify them, could provide even more psychological reassurance for some than

28. Greenfield, *Nationalism*, 487; Mazzini, *On the Duties of Man*, 57. Mill thought similarly. See Varouxakis, "Cosmopolitan Patriotism," 24–25.

liberalism could apparently offer. Nevertheless, during the short nineteenth century, liberalism and nationalism mutually reinforced each other.[29]

The positive relationship was perhaps most clear in the political realm. Politically, both liberalism and nationalism presumed that having a state was an essential tool for realizing their goals. Nationalists were more concerned with the boundaries of the territory the state ruled and the ethnicity of the people in it; liberals with its constitution. Despite these different emphases, "liberal understandings of political legitimacy make an important, if unintended, contribution to the rise of nationalism; and national loyalties help liberals strengthen the principle of legitimacy that supports their political goals." They were mutually supportive, each an essential means for attaining the other's goal. From a liberal perspective, Mill wrote that "among a people without fellow-feeling, especially if they read and speak different languages, the united public opinion, necessary to the working of representative government, cannot exist." Reciprocally, from a nationalist perspective, liberalism strengthened the nation by delegitimizing despots who regarded themselves as exterior or superior to the nation. A nation's liberalism could even be a means for nationalists to assert national superiority over other nations, proclaiming, for example, that their nation was a unique beacon of freedom and liberalism—a view often found among American, British, and even French nationalists.[30]

With regard to international relations, during the short nineteenth century nationalism was often espoused as a means of freeing one's people from the fear of other nations, an essentially liberal goal. One could become a nationalist out of fear of the intervention of a foreign despot, as some German liberals feared the Czar in 1830–50. Theodor Herzl, an Austrian liberal, became a Zionist because, after witnessing the Dreyfus Affair he thought Jews would always have cause for fear until they had a national state. In this national liberal view, in order to be free from fear every people had to have a territory and a state because otherwise one's nation would be oppressed. Nationalism could thus be a means to a liberal end internationally, or even a constituent part of that end.

Liberalism and nationalism could mutually support each other because both liberalism and nationalism were partial, rather than total, worldviews

---

29. Greenfeld, *Nationalism*, 6; Yack, review of Greenfeld, 176.

30. Mill, *On Representative Government*, in *CW*, 19:547, 548–549. Varouxakis, "Cosmopolitan Patriotism," 32. For a comprehensive discussion of Mill's views, see Varouxakis, *Mill on Nationality*; Yack, *Nationalism*, 7.

which left room for the addition of other perspectives. Both left many questions open. For the liberal, there were a wide variety of politics, market systems, and moral / religious views that could help people ward off their fears. Nationalism insisted upon the preeminent importance of the nation but it did not say how the nation ought to act, whether in a liberal or an illiberal fashion. During the short nineteenth century, liberals and nationalists often provided each other with mutual support, and they were frequently allies in the party of movement.

Yet even when liberalism and nationalism were most in harmony, tensions were present. Nationalists were "people who both *feel* a sense of connection to members of a national community and *believe* that nations have a special role to play in human life." The second clause brings into focus the potential tension between nationalism and liberalism. The special role nationalists attributed to the nation could lead them to oppress outsiders, both within the nation and across its borders. The special status of the nation could make it yet another power to be feared. From the nationalist perspective, liberals' defense of ethnic minorities could interfere with the cultural consolidation and nation-building.

Domestically, even during the short nineteenth century it was fundamental for nationalists that the nation was the sole source of political legitimacy. In illiberal versions of nationalism, no limit on the nation's authority was acceptable—hence the possibility of nationalist despotism, whether via the rule of a dictator or through the tyranny of the majority exercised over minorities perceived as outsiders. Nationalism could authorize a new form of tyranny which reminded nineteenth-century liberals all too strongly of the Jacobin cult of the *patrie* during the French Revolution, which they had hoped was a thing of the past. For Constant, the ancient form of liberty as total identification with the (nation) state was supposed to be in decline, not taking on a new identity. This aspect of nationalism came as a surprise to nineteenth-century liberals accustomed to seeing the nation as a benign force: a phenomenon that has been regularly repeated down through the twenty-first century.[31]

The tendency of nationalism to intolerance of ethnic and other minorities was aggravated by the issue of *ressentiment*. *Ressentiment*, an aggravated jealousy

---

31. The definition is derived from two nineteenth-century liberals, Ernest Renan and John Stuart Mill, as well as Benedict Anderson. See Yack, *Nationalism*, 29; Renan, "What Is a Nation. Mill, *On Representative Government, CW*, 19:546; Yack, *Nationalism*, 118; Yack, *Nationalism*, 129, 189, 232; Yack, "The Myth of the Civic Nation," 207.

of superiors, is characteristic of individuals in democratic societies, according to Nietzsche, who coined the French term in its specialized sense, despite being German. Nationalists sometimes cultivated resentment as a means of increasing emotional attachment to the nation, just as in other circumstances nationalism served to reassure people and lessen their resentment over possible loss of status. When instead of reassuring them and thus diminishing illiberalism, nationalism strengthened individuals' sense of grievance and attached it to the nation, nationalism transformed private resentment into political dynamite, encouraging violence and cruelty abroad and at home toward the subjects of that resentment—foreigners and minorities.

Whether based on resentment or not, nationalism posed problems for liberal ideas of international order. National identity was often asserted by calling attention to what made some people different from the ones across the river. "There is no more effective way of bonding the disparate sections of restless peoples than to unite them against outsiders." A nation's identity might be fluid and internally disputed, but it was always formed in distinction from some Other, and that Other was generally a rival or an enemy. As Kipling put it:

Father, Mother, and Me,
Sister and Auntie say
All the people like us are We,
And every one else is They.[32]

To the extent that nationalists saw their nation as built upon conflict with other nations, especially armed conflict, nationalism became motivation for international aggression, and a source of fear that liberals had to combat.[33]

Nationalism could bring liberals closer to the masses, persuade them that universal male suffrage was nothing to fear, or nationalists could use their greater closeness to the masses to outbid liberals for their votes, as happened often in the fin de siècle and afterwards. Nationalism could be a means of defending ethnic groups from oppression, or a justification for oppressing them. It could be seen as the basis of a peaceful international order, or as the inspiration for a permanent battle of all against all. It is impossible to say in the abstract if nationalism is more friend or foe of liberals: it has been both at different times. An illiberal nationalism is perhaps the strongest rival of liberalism

32. *We and They*, Stanza 1.

33. Rogers Brubaker, cited in Colley, *Britons*, xv; Eric Hobsbawm, cited in Colley, *Britons*, xxvi and 376.

in democratic societies—but at the same time a liberal nationalism can be a powerful ally of liberalism.

Despite the tensions present from the beginning of both liberalism and nationalism, the marriage of the two was largely successful in the short nineteenth century. This is evident in cases as different as those of England and Germany.[34] In both countries, during the short nineteenth century liberals made nationalism part of their toolkit, and found that it worked. In Britain, the nation actually became identified with liberalism, and throughout the short nineteenth century asserting British superiority meant asserting British liberalism. In a Germany striving to become a nation in 1848, the role of liberalism in defining the nation itself was much greater than in nineteenth-century Britain, which had been a nation for much longer. In 1848 German liberal nationalists strove to create a liberal understanding of nationality that need not make anyone afraid.

Great Britain was created in 1707 by the Act of Union between England, Wales, and Scotland. Britain at that time was both a new nation and an amalgam of several older ones. British nationalism was made in several ways, two of which were by no means unique. One was the classic means of contrasting the "British" with others who were dangerous, threatening, and inferior: Catholics, Irish, and above all the French (conveniently, the Irish and French were also Catholic). British national identity was forged in war with France, and the French were considered the opposite of British in all things: besides their religion, they were materialist, sensuous, decadent, and given to anarchy, despotism, and revolution. When, over time, anti-French feeling waned, new enemies were available. The word "Britishness" was only invented in the late nineteenth century, when Germany, the United States, Russia, and colonized peoples played the role of Other.[35]

Religion also served to set the British nation apart. In Britain as elsewhere, religion marginalized outsiders and bonded insiders. Although there was a small Catholic minority in England, and a handful of Jews and other religions, the vast majority of the British population was Protestant, and despite their many internal divisions, they were united in their fear and often hatred of Catholics. Wars with France and Spain were perceived in part as religious wars, the defense of true Christianity against papist idolatry. The Catholic / Protestant

---

34. The same is largely true of France. The American case, especially in the twentieth century, is too complex to be discussed here.

35. Colley, *Britons*, xxi, 331–32, xxv, 6, 382, 1, 376; Parry, *The Politics of Patriotism*, 92.

distinction combined neatly with slavery versus freedom in the British national imagination: "Popery and slavery, like two sisters, go hand in hand."[36]

Freedom was thus identified with British national identity from its beginning. The "free" British, in the words of "Rule Britannia," "never, never, never would be slaves." Free in their Protestant religion, free in their politics, free in their nationhood, Britons were not subject to despots, and need not live in fear. Throughout the short nineteenth century and especially after 1830, when for the rest of the nineteenth century Britain was most often ruled by liberal governments, liberalism was a part of British identity and British nationalism.[37]

British thus came to mean liberal, at least as liberals saw it. The Reform Act of 1832 was a good example of the identification of Britishness with liberalism. The reformers almost universally felt part of a British national movement. The Whig / liberal leadership that made the reform was motivated by the characteristically liberal fear of revolution, by their own interest in retaining power, and by "above all—their own brand of patriotism." Reformers of all classes in 1832 called upon the "nation." People spoke of what the reform act would do for the nation more than for what it would do for classes or regions. The *Scotsman*, the leading newspaper of lowland Scotland, ran a column during the fight over reform titled "The National Movement." The year 1832 was a crucial moment in the rise of British liberalism *and* British nationalism.[38] The British, unlike the French and the Americans, had had a reform, not a revolution or a civil war. Reforms were liberal, whereas revolutions were not. After 1832 British nationalism self-identified as a party of movement and reform, the progress of which British liberals were equally proud. The liberal idea of British national identity (and one could just as well say the nationalist idea of British liberalism), became "constitutionalist and religiously pluralist," no longer "narrowly Protestant," as was proved by Catholic Emancipation in 1829 and then Jewish Emancipation in 1858 and thereafter. From 1832 on, liberalism was British, and Britishness liberal.[39]

British liberalism and British nationalism went hand in hand at home and abroad. In the nineteenth century many British nationalists perceived Britain's role in the world to be the defender of liberty. Britain's role as world leader of liberalism was demonstrated by its campaign against the slave trade, and still

---

36. The Earl of Shaftesbury, Speech to the House of Lords, March 25, 1679.

37. Colley, *Britons*, xx, 376.

38. Colley, *Britons*, 352, 346, 348, 350.

39. Parry, *The Politics of Patriotism*, 27.

more the 1833 abolition of slavery in the British colonies. Nineteenth-century British foreign policy, especially under the Liberal party, tended to support liberalism on the Continent, at least once the immediate aftermath of the Napoleonic Wars was over. If wary of the French revolutions of 1848, Britain at first welcomed the revolutions in Prussia and Austria of that year and supported the early efforts of the Frankfurt Parliament, even if it later became disillusioned by the radical tendencies of the revolutionaries. For the iconic liberal foreign affairs specialist, Lord Palmerston, constitutional, liberal states were the "natural allies" of Britain, while it was hard to cooperate with countries like Russia because "their views and opinion are nowadays the reverse of ours." Supporting constitutional government against despotism while rejecting republican democracy was the liberal position and generally the British position during the short nineteenth century. Nineteenth-century Britain regularly encouraged liberal reform movements in various continental states, and blocked or opposed other governments' attempts at repression.[40] Free trade and free markets were themes of Britain's economic and commercial policy, especially after the repeal of the Corn Laws in 1846. The British identified themselves as the archetypal liberal nation.[41]

Liberalism thus became part of the British national identity and was identified with British national pride and self-assertion. Liberalism entitled Britain to rule the world. As Mill put it in 1861, Britain was "the Power which, of all in existence, best understands liberty." As a result, according to Mill, not just the English but all of Europe believed that "the safety, and even the power of England, are valuable to the freedom of the world, and therefore to the greatest and most permanent interests of every civilized people." In a famous speech Palmerston juxtaposed Britain's standing as a liberal nation with the assertion

40. Parry, *Politics of Patriotism*, 147–48; 146; Muller, *Britain and the German Question*; Parry, *Politics of Patriotism*, 241, 249–250, 253–254, 9. The strength of non-interventionism in British liberalism, exemplified by Cobden and Bright, has been exaggerated by historians. It was mostly found in the strand of Radicalism and Nonconformism that tended toward a narrow, one-pillar version of laissez-faire liberalism, a faction always present but rarely ascendant in the short nineteenth century. Non-interventionism, for Mill and his disciple Morley, and even for some Nonconformists, was immoral.

41. Contemporary Americans might have objected, or at least claimed equal status, but from a European perspective American slavery and peculiar American circumstances largely ruled it out as a source of emulation. Even Tocqueville did not want to import American institutions wholesale to Europe. *Democracy in America*, 1:27.

of its right to intervene to protect her citizens anywhere in the world. The famous "civis Romanus sum" conclusion was preceded by "We have shown that liberty is compatible with order; that individual freedom is reconcilable with obedience to the law. We have shown the example of a nation, in which every class of society accepts with cheerfulness the lot which Providence has assigned to it; while at the same time every individual of each class is constantly striving to raise himself in the social scale." For Palmerston, British power, British nationalism, and British liberalism were parts of a whole.[42]

Domestically, after the Reform Act of 1832, British nationalism reinforced liberalism and in some ways helped to broaden its base and prevent nineteenth-century British liberals from adopting the strict laissez-faire policies later associated with classical liberalism. Nationalism provided liberals with justifications for policy initiatives about everything from education to sewers. In an environment in which all liberals, even relatively interventionist ones, wanted to limit state power, nationalism helped reconcile liberals to the exercise of government authority in the name of improving national morals and diminishing class divisions. In the fin de siècle the otherwise laissez-faire liberal Dicey, for example, argued that the spread of education to the masses would increase national feeling. For most nineteenth-century liberals, in Britain and elsewhere, there was no tension "between the defence of constitutional liberty and the strengthening of state authority and social morality." Freedom, markets, and morals were natural allies—of each other and the nation.[43]

The way in which nationalism justified liberals in relaxing their fear of state power leads to the question of whether the nationalist tail was wagging the liberal dog, or vice versa. The question is not easy to answer, since both nationalists and liberals were happy to make use of the other ideology as a tool, or else hold it concurrently, a consequence of the overlapping and partial nature of each worldview. This has led historians to write sentences such as "It was not freedom as such but the desire to maintain an effective national political community and to develop the right virtue in the nation that was at the heart of nineteenth-century liberalism." The sentence is about Britain, but could as easily have been written about Germany. Equally true would be a statement to the effect that it was not nationalism as such but the desire to prevent despotism that led many liberals to embrace a national political com-

42. Parry, *Politics of Patriotism*, 148; Palmerston, "Don Pacifico Speech," June 25, 1850, Wikisource.

43. Parry, *Politics of Patriotism*, 43, 25, 275, 49.

munity, as a useful or even necessary means of preserving the nation and its citizens from the arbitrary cruelties of domestic despots or foreign oppressors. To give a concrete example, the nationalism displayed in the organization of volunteer military units in Britain was seen by many liberals as a lesson in self-government and character-building, as well as a means of lessening tensions among classes that might otherwise have revolutionary or at least unfortunate consequences.[44]

What Jonathan Parry calls "liberal constitutional patriotism" was a successful political strategy for British liberalism in the short nineteenth century. It was not a uniquely British strategy. In fact, it was almost a commonplace of nineteenth-century liberalism, but it did not have the same degree of success everywhere. We can better understand the reciprocal roles of liberalism and nationalism by looking at a traditional sore spot between them: Germany.

Unlike Britain, Germany was a new nation in the nineteenth century. Indeed, one of the signs that the short nineteenth century was coming to an end was the foundation of a German nation-state, the German Empire, in 1871. When the word liberalism was invented circa 1795 there were several hundred German-speaking states, and in 1815 German-speaking Europe was still divided into roughly three dozen states, most of whom were very loosely linked in the powerless "German Confederation." In 1848, a revolutionary movement swept Germany, both liberal and nationalist, which, among other things, sought to create a unitary German state. Precisely because nineteenth-century German liberalism and German nationalism took shape in the absence of a preexisting national state, nineteenth-century German liberalism was faced with a problem that nineteenth-century Britain, America, and France did not face, but that many nations in Eastern Europe and other parts of the world would confront then and later: how to define the nation's membership, whether on ethnic, linguistic, ideological, political, religious, or other grounds. The choices made did much to determine the liberal or illiberal character of the nation. National identity was a consequential question from both nationalist and liberal perspectives. The nineteenth-century German debate over the question is instructive.

In the years between the end of the Napoleonic Wars in 1815 and 1848, liberalism and nationalism appeared together on the German political stage as the lead actors of the party of movement, striving for reform and mutually supporting each other against tyrants both native and foreign. It was very hard

44. Parry, *Politics of Patriotism*, 73, 78, 88.

to distinguish between German liberalism and German nationalism before 1848, in the period historians of Germany anachronistically call the *Vormärz* (from 1815 to March 1848, when revolution broke out). They were seen as inseparable. "Constitution was the cardinal value, then the idea of a nation-state. . . . The national aim had become self-evident for the people. . . . Of course, the nation-state was also a symbol of freedom and of a citizens' state that was opposed to both the evil Confederation (*Bund*) and the familiar authoritarianism."[45] Liberals and nationalists used the same language and made the same demands. According to the nationalists of the time, nationhood required freedom, rights, and political participation. For liberals the nation became another group / class with a right to flourish unafraid. German nationalists often thought of the nation as a collective individual with its own dignity, autonomy, and individuality.[46]

The liberal / nationalist synthesis in Germany nevertheless faced pressure that although overcome in 1848 would become ever more significant as time went on. The crucial question was "who is a German?." During the short nineteenth century, especially in the revolutionary moment of 1848–51, liberals and nationalists (who in practice were mostly the same people) had to work out who was a German and where the boundaries of the German nation lay. These questions were then and later crucial for the relationship between liberals and nationalism in many of the "new" nations of Central and Eastern Europe and beyond, and the German case is paradigmatic in many ways. Ultimately, the definition of who belonged to the nation, and what the consequences might be for those who did not, or who claimed multiple national identities, was crucial in determining whether nationalism would be an illiberal source of fear or a liberal bulwark against it. In the attempts to define the German nation at the Frankfurt Parliament in 1848–49, we can see the potential for both.

German nationalism is often supposed to be especially "ethnic" and thus illiberal, stressing "blood and soil," ancient memories, DNA, and the mother tongue. This is opposed to "civic" nationalism, which is a personal political commitment, one that can be derived from a set of principles, for example loyalty to a constitution or a Declaration of Rights, a liberal nationalism exemplified by France or the United States. But "the now-traditional ethnic versus civic typology of nationalism is inappropriate when applied to the German case" before 1850. German nationalists in the period were as much civic as

---

45. Nipperdey, *Germany from Napoleon to Bismarck*, 352.
46. Vick, *Defining Germany*, 43, 17.

ethnic. The German historical school of law, in which many of the Frankfurt parliamentarians were trained, found in laws, constitutions, and mores constituents of nationality just as important as language or ethnic origin. Carl Mittermaier, future president of the 1848 Frankfurt Pre-Parliament, said in 1846, "who will deny that nationality expresses itself best and most purely in the nation's laws?." Just as the English appealed to an unwritten "ancient constitution," so Germans appealed to a written but uncodified body of German law as a foundation of the state, of nationality, and of freedom.[47]

The combination of ethnic and civic elements in defining a nation was not only German, it was the standard nineteenth-century liberal definition of nationhood, as enunciated by the French liberal nationalist Renan, who wrote that a nation is an entity constituted by two things: "One is the past, the other is the present. One is the possession in common of a rich legacy of memories; the other is present consent," which he famously described as "a daily plebiscite." For Renan, a national community existed only if its members told a common story of their past—*and* if they choose to regard that story, or some part of it, as their national identity (they might still disagree about its details or what were its most important parts—hence the potential for different understandings of what it meant to be American or German). Even in the most "civic" nations, civic identity was regarded as a shared cultural inheritance. All nations were therefore both "ethnic" and "civic."[48]

For German liberals and nationalists, this was the problem. The civic element, a common consciousness, was still missing. They had the language, the DNA, and the old graveyards, but they needed to create the consciousness. The *Staats-Lexikon*, a sort of encyclopedic dictionary of political and historical concepts often referred to as the bible of German liberalism in the 1830s and '40s (and influential until at least 1870), stated in its article on "Nation, People" that not "every group of men that has such things as descent, language, and customs in common is a nation. It only becomes a nation when as opposed to other men they feel and recognize themselves as a entity and a self-contained

47. Yack, "The Mmyth of the Civic Nation," 194, 196; Breuilly, "On the Principle of Nationality," 106. The *locus classicus* of the distinction is Brubaker, *Citizenship*. Vick, *Defining Germany*, 77, 28, 29.

48. Ernest Renan, *What is a Nation?*, http://ucparis.fr/files/9313/6549/9943/What_is_a _Nation.pdf; Yack, "The Myth of the Civic Nation," 194, 196; Yack in "Debate on Bernard Yack's Book *Nationalism and the Moral Psychology of Community*," in *Nations and Nationalism* 20, no. 3 (2014): 409.

totality." This civic element was what German liberals / nationalists sought to develop in Germany. It was a potential opening to ethnic and cultural diversity: if you felt German, identified yourself as German, you were a German, regardless of ancestry. But it was also a potential opening for an illiberal nationalism, that would insist all Germans adopt a single consciousness and a single identity, and oppress or expel those who would or could not.[49]

This tension was implicit in the debates about the extent to which assimilation was required of all. German nationality was open to outsiders, but the Frankfurt deputies required a degree of assimilation, linguistically at least. The so-called Mareck clause in the draft constitution guaranteed non-German speakers the same civil rights as everyone else, and the right to use their own language in schools, church, courts, local administration, but not in Parliament, where it was decided that only German was acceptable. The speakers of other languages had to participate in German.

This applied to individuals. Whether group rights for other cultures and languages should be acknowledged was a matter for considerable debate in Frankfurt in 1848. It posed a problem that liberals have continued to struggle with, as shown in late-twentieth-century debates both theoretical and practical (Quebec language laws, Muslim headscarves and burqas).[50] In Frankfurt, the debates sometimes took on a form familiar to twenty-first century multiculturalism, as when one delegate objected to the formulation "every German" in a proclamation by the Pre-Parliament because it excluded "our millions of Slavic brothers," and proposed replacing it with "every citizen." The proposal was accepted by acclamation. But when the same issue was raised in the Frankfurt Parliament itself, with regard to the constitution, debate was heated, and "every German" was retained. However, the advocates of "every German" insisted that "it is not nationality in its natural sense, but rather nationality in its political sense that is under discussion." The rapporteur, Georg Beseler, said it was the committee's view that "citizenship and nationality will be viewed as coinciding."[51]

This led naturally to debates about who was a German citizen. In the end, the Frankfurt Parliament avoided the question by leaving it out of the constitu-

49. Cited in Vick, *Defining Germany*, 39–40.

50. For the theory, see the work of Charles Taylor, Bruce Kymlicka, and Chandran Kukathas.

51. Vick, *Defining Germany*, 210, 130–132; 110; 111–114; 117–118.

tion. Contrary to later thought and practice, there was no consensus about either citizenship by descent (*jus sanguinis*) or residence (*jus domicilium*) or birth (*jus soli*).[52]

The problem of cultural assimilation of the "non-German German," as one delegate put it, remained. Germany was not just a political concept, it was also a cultural concept (like liberals, most nationalists based their thought on more than one pillar). A delegate made explicit comparison to the British situation: "In England too there are different nationalities, and yet all of these citizens know that they are English." One historian has suggested that this was non-sense, as a Scot would never have claimed to be English in 1848 (or thereafter). But making charitable allowance for foreign terms, and substituting Britain and British for English, the delegate was perfectly correct—Scots in 1848 identified themselves as British, while continuing to be Scotch—and what the delegate was really suggesting was that German identity, like British identity, could be one hat worn atop another.

A good test case for the relationship between German liberals and nationalists and groups that wished to maintain multiple identities, and thus for the liberalism / illiberalism of German nationalism, can be found in the Frankfurt Parliament's treatment of Jews. It is evidence that the influence of nationalism on liberalism could be positive in purely liberal terms. Effectively, German nationalism encouraged German liberals who previously had been willing to let Jews be afraid, to deprive them of civil rights, to accept Jews among those whose fears liberals had to take into account. As German nationalism developed in the years leading up to 1848, it became increasingly open to Jews. "By the early 1840s, at the latest, anti-Jewish images and arguments met with an ever chillier reception and were eventually driven almost entirely from the realm of polite political discourse." At the 1848 Frankfurt Parliament there was virtually no opposition to granting full rights to Jews, signaled by the election of a Jewish deputy as Vice-President of the Assembly (Gabriel Riesser), and the hostile reception accorded the very few anti-semitic speakers. Even though many of the liberal supporters of Jewish Emancipation at Frankfurt had previously expressed anti-semitic opinons, they no longer voiced them. German nationalism trumped anti-semitism. The deputies did not demand or even expect the conversion or disappearance of Jews, Poles, or other groups (Czechs, Slovenes, etc.). They did expect some acculturation, for example the

52. Vick, *Defining Germany*, 133–134, 116–117.

use of German in Parliament, but they did not demand the elimination of all non-German identity. A little *Bildung* would go a long way.[53]

This is not to say that German nationalists or German liberals imagined complete cultural equality, whether the groups concerned were Jews, Poles, or Czechs—they were not quite that liberal. The assumption was that German culture would prove so attractive that others would freely embrace it. This was in accord with the widespread German cultural assumption of progress through struggle, and was sometimes even conceived in economic terms. Heinrich Ahrens, a Frankfurt delegate from the German-speaking portion of the Austrian Empire, analyzed the multicultural, multinational Austrian Empire as a place where freedom would bring struggle, but with a positive result, just as in the economic sphere "free competition" was a struggle that brought improvements for everyone. Naturally, those with greater "material and mental capital" would win, but the "losers" would gain too. As another Austrian deputy put it, "we should rather seek than flee this honorable competition—it will bring profit for victor and defeated." The different national cultures should neither be favored nor hindered, neither preserved nor suppressed by the future German state. "The development of their nationality in cultivation, language and literature must be left to their own power; it should not be hindered, but it cannot possibly be guaranteed." One deputy let the cat out of the bag by predicting the eventual disappearance of all minority nationalities by means of this free competition.[54]

More often, however, the German nationalism of 1848 rejected a cultural monopoly. Cultural competition was to continue for the indefinite future, for mutual benefit. This is not to say that German nationalism in 1848 did not, like all nationalisms, proceed by distinguishing Germans from others and even promoting hostility toward them. The enthusiastic participation of liberal nationalists in the war with Denmark over Schleswig-Holstein (1848–51) was evidence of that. Domestically, the general rejection of women's rights (see chapter 8) was further testimony. Nevertheless, there was also a strong emphasis on inclusion, on making a Germany in which everyone would be free from fear and free to progress. Liberalism and nationalism were joined hand in hand.[55]

53. Vick, *Defining Germany*, 94, 94n27; 83–85; 134; 104.

54. Vick, *Defining Germany*, 135–137.

55. Vick, *Defining Germany*, 135–136; 225.

After the German Empire was founded in 1871 this relatively inclusive attitude on the part of German nationalists changed, and a far greater degree of cultural and national assimilation became the order of the day, causing liberals to resist at least some aspects of nationalism, or else to abandon their liberalism (see chapter 8). In the fin de siècle an increasingly radical and radically illiberal ethnic nationalism grew in Germany (and elsewhere), which German liberalism was unsuccessful in resisting, especially after WWI.

During the short nineteenth century, liberalism and nationalism were fellow travelers in Germany. Their goals lay in the same direction, and they saw each other as necessary partners to get where they wanted to go. Education for liberal freedom was the same as education for nationhood, and the nation was defined in predominantly liberal terms. But in Germany and elsewhere the common path diverged over time. In fact, both liberals and nationalists had difficulty accepting the legitimacy of those who wanted something different, at least if the people who were different insisted on manifesting their differences in public. This was most obvious in the nationalist case, but it was true for liberals as well, as evidenced in the relationship between liberalism and Catholicism. Like nationalists faced with ethnic minorities, nineteenth-century liberals were not necessarily inclined to accept the legitimacy of the "other," especially when what the other wanted made liberals afraid. In the context of the liberal fear of revolution or reaction, this rejection of the other could take the political form of limiting the suffrage, as discussed above. But in moral terms, the most striking example of liberals rejecting those who made them afraid was not so much fear of revolutionaries or reactionaries, nor fear of socialists, nor even of conservative aristocrats, but of the Catholic Church. Throughout the Western world nineteenth-century liberalism struggled with Catholicism. Bismarck's *Kulturkampf*, the "Culture War" he waged against Catholicism in close alliance with German liberals, is perhaps the most famous example. But Bismarck was no liberal, and the most purely liberal examples of anti-Catholicism can be found in America and France—and Norway.

Like Oil and Water? Liberalism and Catholicism

Nineteenth-century liberal anti-Catholicism was heir to the Wars of Religion of the sixteenth and seventeenth centuries. Although most nineteenth-century liberal anti-Catholics would have indignantly denied that it was out of religious animosity that they despised and persecuted Catholics, nonetheless they inherited some of the emotions and echoed some of the language of traditional

Protestant anti-Catholicism. Nineteenth-century liberals also, and more directly, inherited the Enlightenment's often hostile relationship with the Church. Liberals were apt to ape Voltaire's hostility to Catholicism. There were both Reformation and Enlightenment proto-liberal elements in nineteenth-century liberal anti-Catholicism.

There were also "new" forms of anti-Catholicism in the nineteenth century, independent of traditional Protestantism or Enlightened proto-liberalism. Socialist and radical versions of anti-Catholicism shared common sources with liberal hostility to the Church but had different aims. Nationalists, irrespective of whether they were liberals, also found reason to quarrel with the Church. The Church, with its capital in Rome and its claim to universality, was seen as an obstacle to the development of national identity and to the consolidation of national unity, a suspicious foreign and international body. Bismarck was a classic example of this kind of anti-Catholic, but it was not just a German trait. Charges that Catholic education "denationalized" children and that the clergy was unpatriotic were a staple of French anti-Catholicism.[56]

What concerns us here is a specifically liberal anti-Catholicism, an anti-Catholicism that helped define liberalism in the nineteenth century. "Anti-Catholic intolerance was not derivative but constitutive of liberalism; it was not an ancillary expression but, on the contrary, at the core of liberalism." Not all liberals were anti-Catholic all the time: liberals sometimes even joined forces with the Church against socialists. Nevertheless, liberal hostility to Catholicism was omnipresent. It was the result of the fear of Catholicism, but it was aggressive as much as it was defensive. When liberalism was the party of movement, Catholicism was one of the obstacles liberals sought to move out of their way. At the same time, Catholicism was a reactionary force liberals sought to resist. Catholicism posed the general problem of the relationship of liberalism to illiberal beliefs and movements, a problem that has continued to be significant for liberalism. Liberal struggling against Catholicism encountered the difficulties of navigating between a liberal equality and an illiberal homogeneity. From a liberal perspective, the liberal / Catholic relationship was an example of what in 1945 Karl Popper formulated as the "paradox of intolerance": "Unlimited tolerance must lead to the disappearance of tolerance. If we extend unlimited tolerance even to those who are intolerant . . . then the tolerant will be destroyed, and tolerance with them." Popper was thinking about fascists and

---

56. Gross, *The War against Catholicism*, 299; Rémond, *L'anticléricalisme en France*, 56; Dittrich, *Antiklerikalismus in Europa*, 498.

communists. Something like this theory, however, was the basis for the anti-Catholicism of the liberal mainstream in the nineteenth century.[57]

Liberal fear of and intolerance for Catholicism had deep roots and many branches. To examine it, one can only start with John Locke, whose 1686 *Letter on Toleration* made a notable exception for Catholics (and atheists). It was not their religious doctrines that put Catholics beyond the Pale for Locke, it was that they held political and moral positions that, in his view, threatened civil society. Catholics threatened the political order because they obeyed the Pope in preference to civil authority, and on religious grounds felt entitled to engage in all manner of crimes, from bombings (the Guy Fawkes plot in Britain) to assassination (Henri IV in France). As an individual belief, Catholicism did not pose a threat. But as a group that recognized a human source of authority (the Pope) other than that of the government, which in principle did not recognize any non-Catholic political authority and could not be counted on to keep faith with such an heretical government, which claimed a right to commit violence in the name of religion, Catholics were a source of fear: "These therefore, and the like, who attribute unto the Faithful, Religious and Orthodox; that is, in plain terms, unto themselves; any peculiar Priviledge or Power above other Mortals, in Civil Concernments; or who, upon pretence of Religion, do challenge any manner of Authority over such as are not associated with them in their Ecclesiastical Communion; I say these have no right to be tolerated by the Magistrate." For Locke, Catholics should not be tolerated out of fear that they were natural oppressors.[58]

Later, Montesquieu argued that "it is useful for the laws to require of these various religions not only that they not disturb the state, but also that they not disturb each other. A citizen does not satisfy the laws by contenting himself with not agitating the body of the state; he must also not disturb any citizen whatsoever". One origin of *laicité* is here, in Montesquieu's fear of aggressive religion. Montesquieu did not wish to banish religion from the public sphere because religion played a crucial role in restraining governments, especially in

57. Clark and Kaiser, eds., *Culture Wars*, 3; Popper, *Open Society*, 581.

58. Mark Goldie, "Introduction," https://oll.libertyfund.org/titles/2375#Locke_1560_47; Locke, "A Letter concerning Toleration," https://oll.libertyfund.org/titles/2375#Locke_1560_187. Locke's tolerance of Muslims was conditional at best: "It is ridiculous for any one to profess himself to be a *Mahometan* only in his Religion, but in every thing else a faithful Subject to a Christian Magistrate, whilst at the same time he acknowledges himself bound to yield blind obedience to the *Mufti* of *Constantinople*." Locke, A "Letter concerning Toleration," https://oll.libertyfund.org/titles/2375#Locke_1560_188.

despotisms. But he did want to make sure that religion, in particular Catholicism, did not disturb politics or civil society. When a religion became a source of fear, Montesquieu favoured legal restraints on it. A religion could even be banned: when one had a choice about letting a new religion establish itself, "as there are scarcely any but intolerant religions that are greatly zealous to establish themselves elsewhere", "it must not be established". Not that Montesquieu, unlike Voltaire, wanted to *écrasez l'infâme*: once a religion *was* established, he opposed any effort to eliminate it. Still, even for eighteenth-century proto-liberals generally friendly to religion like Montesquieu, there was hesitation about the acceptability of forms of religious life which conflicted with the existence of a liberal society. This hesitation became stronger when it involved a single religion having "a far-reaching, perhaps even irresistible, influence on the state", This was especially the case for many nineteenth-century liberals faced with Catholicism.[59]

The strength and ubiquity of nineteenth-century liberal anti-Catholicism can be illustrated by comparison with anti-semitism. Anti-clericalism served as a common liberal cultural code. If nineteenth-century German anti-semitism has, for good if anachronistic reason, attracted enormous attention, the fact is that even in Germany the nineteenth century was "arguably more a century of anti-Catholicism" than of anti-semitism. German anti-Catholicism, with strong liberal support, culminated in the German *Kulturkampf* of 1872–1886, which included the expulsion of the Jesuits and other religious orders from Germany, the imprisonment of bishops and priests, the closing of monasteries, etc. Despite the Dreyfus Affair, it is not hard to argue a case for the priority of anti-clericalism over anti-semitism in nineteenth-century (and fin de siècle) France. In the United States, as well as England, the nineteenth century saw far more anti-Catholic than anti-semitic violence. Overall, there was more expression of anti-Catholicism than anti-semitism in Western culture during the short nineteenth century.[60]

Actually, the similarities between anti-semitism and anti-Catholicism are striking. They extend to telltale details. Jesuits, like Jews, were frequently depicted as the source of a vast conspiracy to take over the world. If the Jesuit conspiracy was led by the Pope rather than by a committee of bankers, it too

---

59. Montesquieu, *The Spirit of the Laws*, 488; Gross, *The War against Catholicism*, 248; Dittrich, *Antiklerikalismus in Europa*, 316, 327.

60. Volkov, "Antisemitism as Cultural Code," 25–45; Dittrich, *Antiklerikalismus in Europa*, 501; Gross, *The War against Catholicism*, 1.

was typically described as working in the shadows, using subversion and manipulation to corrupt the nation. Both Jews and Catholics were seen as outsiders who could not be assimilated or refused to adopt national values. There was even a transnational anti-Catholic version of the Jewish "blood libel," the legend that on Passover Jews killed a Christian child and used its blood to make matzah. In the anti-Catholic version, Catholic clergy kidnapped or persuaded a beautiful young girl to become a nun. Once safely inside the convent walls, she was imprisoned and used as a sexual plaything for the clergy. When a baby resulted, it was baptized, murdered, and buried inside the convent. Throughout the Atlantic world, "anti-clericals of every shade repeated the same metaphors, pictures, novelistic plots, concepts, and arguments."[61]

One major difference between anti-Catholicism and anti-semitism in the nineteenth century was the fact that liberals were more likely to be anti-Catholic than anti-semitic. The reason for this illuminates the sources of liberal intolerance. To the extent that Judaism was perceived as an individual's faith, or as a community that did not clash with civil or political society, liberals had no fear of Jews. They had no fear that Jews would be either revolutionaries or reactionaries, and defended them from those who would make them afraid. Fairy tales about the conspiracies of the elders of Zion or the Rothschilds found little grace in nineteenth-century liberal eyes, unlike Jesuit horror stories (the fin de siècle would be a different story). If sources of friction remained, they were manageable and tended to remain private. Macaulay is a good example of such management: a fierce defender of Jewish Emancipation in Parliament, he made anti-semitic remarks in private correspondence. By contrast, to the extent that Catholicism appeared as a corporate presence in the public sphere, it appeared dangerous to liberals. Just as dangerous classes had to be excluded from the suffrage, so dangerous religious communities had to be prevented from endangering others. It was a temporary problem from a nineteenth-century liberal perspective because history was on the side of liberalism, and it was assumed that Catholicism was destined to disappear or lose its sting, but it was a real problem nonetheless.

Another difference, even more important, between nineteenth-century anti-Catholicism and anti-semitism was that the hostility between liberalism and Catholicism was mutual. Catholics perceived liberals as their enemy almost as soon as the word "liberalism" was invented. One of the earliest uses of "liberal"

---

61. Verhoeven, *Transatlantic Anti-Catholicism*, 11, 14–15; Borutta, *Antikatholizismus*, 23; Arnstein, *Mr. Newdegate and the Nuns*; Dittrich, *Antiklerikalismus in Europa*, 500, 503.

to be found in print was in a conservative Spanish newspaper in 1813 in an article titled "What does liberalism mean?" The article explained that liberalism was "founded upon ignorant, absurd, anti-social, anti-monarchic, anti-Catholic [ideas]." A series of nineteenth-century Papal Encyclicals, from *Mirari Vos* in 1832 to the *Syllabus Errorum* of 1864, condemned liberalism root and branch.[62] To the dismay and shock of liberals everywhere, including liberal Catholics, in 1870 Vatican I established papal infallibility. Papal infallibility was restricted to matters of faith and morals, but matters of faith and morals were emphatically part of liberalism, so the restriction did not reassure. A French liberal newspaper saw papal infallibility as an "invasion . . . on civil society," and hence on liberalism—as indeed it was intended. The repeated repression of liberal voices within Catholicism—in 1869 the Jesuit journal *Civiltà Cattolica* said it was impossible to be a liberal and a Catholic, and in 1871 Pope Pius IX said he feared the Paris Communards less than liberal Catholics—added to liberal anxiety. In America, the Catholic Church's refusal to support the abolition of slavery in the 1840s and '50s and its flirtation with the Confederacy reinforced Shaftesbury's equation of papacy and slavery.[63]

Liberal hostility to Catholicism was not only defensive, a defense of freedoms against those who would take them away, it was also a way for liberals to display their positive principles and highlight their own aspirations. Against Catholicism, liberals underlined their commitment to the three pillars of liberalism: "individualism, science, education [elements of the moral pillar], constitutionalism, and free market economics." In Protestant countries like England, America, or northern Germany, the moral pillar was in practice identified with a generic Protestantism, in France with secular or unorthodox spiritual (deist, Positivist) tendencies. Everywhere it was a matter of liberals positively asserting their own moral / religious values. If liberals' defensive hostility to Catholicism was essentially utilitarian (Catholics, if given a chance, would oppress people), its positive hostility was essentially perfectionist (Catholics as a community interfered with improving society). In struggling with Catholicism liberals saw themselves both as a party of movement, overcoming backwardness and superstition, and a party of resistance to Catholic despotism, actual or potential. This created a situation in which liberals and

---

62. Indeed, as late as 1910 Pius X's encyclical *Editae Saepe* condemned liberalism without using the word.

63. Cited in Rosenblatt, *Lost History*, 198; cited in Dittrich, *Antiklerikalismus in Europa*, 321, 321n149.

Catholics regarded one another, as more than one nineteenth-century Pope made explicit, as if they were adherents of different and mutually exclusive *religions*. The controversies in France over the question of civil burial are a case in point: secular and Catholic French people held equally elaborate funerals, with their own rituals. As one historian put it, French "Catholics and Republicans [read liberals] were divided by competing religious beliefs. It is thus not surprising to find them capable of similar levels of intolerance." But liberals were not in fact bothered by *all* religious beliefs because not all religious beliefs were in competition with liberalism. Not all religions insisted on the political role that nineteenth-century Catholicism did.[64]

The conflict between liberalism and Catholicism varied in timing and intensity. Particularly violent phases occurred in the United States in the 1840s, Germany in the 1870s, and France around 1900, but the struggles extended beyond the nineteenth century into the Spanish Civil War and Vichy France.[65] They even occurred in places where there were no Catholics, like Norway, where nevertheless the Norwegian Constitution of 1814, written largely by liberals, forbade Jews, Jesuits, and members of monastic orders to enter Norway (with certain exceptions for Sephardi Jews).[66] The ban on Jews was dropped in 1851, and in 1897 on monks, but not Jesuits. When Norway became fully independent in 1905, its new constitution once again banned Jesuits from setting foot in the kingdom, a ban that persisted until 1956.[67]

Throughout the period anti-Catholic writers and writings regularly crossed the ocean, as shown by the success of the Frenchman Jules Michelet's anti-Catholic works in both England and the United States, and by voyages to America by ex-Catholic clergy who denounced the Church in popular lectures.[68] The ways in which liberals struggled with this problem, as well as the ways in which liberals framed their anti-Catholicism in both defensive and

64. Dittrich, *Antikerikalismus in Europa*, 323; Gross, *The War against Catholicism*, 99; Gibson, "Why Republicans and Catholics Couldn't Stand Each Other," 109.

65. See Borutta, *Antikatholizismus*, 13–14.

66. The fact that anti-Catholicism could flourish even in the absence of actual Catholics was another similarity with anti-semitism, which often flourished in the absence of actual Jews, as Shakespeare's and Marlowe's plays demonstrated in seventeenth-century England.

67. Wolffe, "North Atlantic Anti-Catholicism," 9.

68. Wolffe, "North Atlantic Anti-Catholicism in the Nineteenth Century," 23–41; Verhoeven, *Transatlantic Anti-Catholicism*, 23, 27. For Michelet's reception as an anti-Catholic thinker in England, see Alan S. Kahan, "'Through a Looking-Glass Darkly: The Image of England in Michelet and Michelet's Reception in England," Princeton University undergraduate thesis.

aspirational terms, is evident in the American and French experiences. America and France were in different ways leading examples of liberalism, and they were equally good examples of liberal anti-Catholicism.

American anti-Catholicism is one of the great exceptions to American "exceptionalism," the doctrine that America is unique, especially in comparison with Europe. In most respects it is exactly the same as anti-Catholicism everywhere else. Anti-Catholic American literature is filled with the same images of priests, especially Jesuits, corrupting families and institutions; the same hostility to nuns and convents accused of corrupting young women; the same variations on the anti-Catholic libel of imprisoned nuns and surreptitious sexuality. American rioters burned convents and Catholic churches, while serious American liberal thinkers questioned whether Catholicism could ever be compatible with freedom. After all, as the leading Unitarian Minister and abolitionist Theodore Parker put it in 1854, the Roman Catholic Church was "the natural ally of tyrants and irreconcilable enemy of freedom." America is therefore a good place in which to see how "Anti-Catholicism is neither exceptional within nor anathema to liberal democracy." Anti-Catholicism is a window into how American liberals, like liberals elsewhere, while affirming religion as a necessary pillar of liberalism, responded when facing the challenge of what seemed to them a fundamentally illiberal faith.[69]

The American republic offered full civil and political rights to people of all religions. In the early decades of its existence anti-Catholicism was relatively low-key, although in the course of the American Revolution and thereafter a good deal of anti-Catholic sentiment was expressed (especially in reference to Catholic Quebec).[70] From the 1830s, however, the issue of Catholicism came increasingly to the fore, largely as a result of Irish and to a lesser extent German Catholic immigration to America: the words "immigrant," "Catholic," "Irish," and "alien" ware often used interchangeably.[71]

The defense of freedom was frequently linked to defending American borders against Catholic immigration. Typical was Lyman Beecher's 1834 lecture series denouncing Catholic immigrants, which drew a wide audi-

69. Verhoeven, *Transatlantic Anti-Catholicism*, 10, 14–15; Fenton, *Religious Liberties*, 58; Del-Fattore, *The Fourth R*, 23; McGreevy, *Catholicism and American Freedom*, 34; Fenton, *Religious Liberties*, 9.

70. On American anti-Catholicism predating mass immigration, see Fenton, *Religious Liberties*, 40.

71. Verhoeven, *Transatlantic Anti-Catholicism*, 1.

ence.[72] His lecture in Charlestown, Massachusetts sparked a riot that ended in the burning of an Ursuline convent. In 1835 Beecher turned the lectures into a novel, *A Plea for the West*, which imagined a takeover of America's frontier by Catholics "unacquainted with our institutions, unaccustomed to self-government, inaccessible to education," and "easily accessible to prepossession, and inveterate credulity, and intrigue . . . wielded by sinister design." Beecher's fears led him to suggest that universal manhood suffrage in America be limited to prevent Catholics from democratically turning America into a Catholic theocracy.[73]

Not all American liberals endorsed anti-Catholicism. Writing to a friend in 1855, Abraham Lincoln was, as usual, eloquent: "As a nation, we began by declaring that 'all men are created equal.' We now practically read it 'all men are created equal, except negroes.' When the Know-Nothings [populist anti-Catholic and anti-immigrant party] get control, it will read 'all men are created equal, except negroes, and foreigners, and catholics.' When it comes to this I should prefer emigrating to some country where they make no pretence of loving liberty—to Russia, for instance, where despotism can be taken pure, and without the base alloy of hypocrisy." But Lincoln was exceptional. Liberal anti-Catholicism was widespread in America. When a renegade French Catholic priest visited the United States on a lecture tour in 1869 he met with, among others, America's leading poet, Henry Wadsworth Longfellow; the historian, diplomat, son, and grandson of presidents Charles Francis Adams; and the governor of Massachusetts—the liberal elite of America, hardly supporters of the by-then defunct Know-Nothing party. Ralph Waldo Emerson complained of "Romish priests, who sympathize, of course, with despotism." In Cincinnati, marches were held to protest the visit of an Italian archbishop in 1853, with banners proclaiming "No Priests, No Kings, No Popery."[74]

American liberal anti-Catholic rhetoric about Catholic incapacity for freedom echoed European liberal rhetoric about the incapacity of the lower classes. The difference was that liberal rhetoric about the lower classes foresaw

72. Beecher, a well-known author and Presbyterian minister, was the father of Harriet Beecher Stowe, the author of *Uncle Tom's Cabin*, which itself had anti-Catholicism as a subtheme.

73. Fenton, *Religious Liberties*, 53–54.

74. Lincoln to Joshua F. Speed, August 24, 1855, http://www.abrahamlincolnonline.org /lincoln/speeches/speed.htm; Oates, *With Malice towards None*, 141; Citations in McGreevy, *Catholicism and American Freedom*, 36, 23, 25. See also Farrelly, *Anti-Catholicism in America*, 165–167, Verhoeven, *Transatlantic Anti-Catholicism*, 19.

the eventual fitness of the poor. By contrast, a Catholic would always be a Catholic, and no evolution of Catholicism itself could be expected—especially after the repeated repression of liberal Catholics by the Church hierarchy. The poor could be educated; Catholics could not be.

Education was a prominent battleground for liberals and Catholics, in America as elsewhere. American liberals invested their hopes in and promoted their values through education, and created what they believed were nonsectarian public schools to propagate those values. They then found, to their horror, that Catholics did not see the education issue in the same way. Catholics and liberals agreed that freedom required a moral foundation, that moral and even religious training was essential to education, and neither wanted a morally neutral school. But they differed profoundly over the content of the moral and religious education *both* regarded as essential.

The public schools became "a symbol of the history of anti-Catholicism in the United States." Very few people in antebellum America favored a purely secular public school. Before the arrival of large numbers of Catholics, there were battles between conservative Protestants who supported publicly funded denominational education, and liberal Protestants who favored "nonsectarian," generically Protestant public schools. The latter group won, and their victory was embodied in the work of the famous Massachusetts Commissioner of Public Education, Horace Mann, who was the leading partisan of nonsectarian schooling. The new-model public school was to be "the great equalizer of the conditions of men" and "the balance-wheel of the social machinery," integrating and elevating both native-born and immigrant children of all religions and classes. The school was to act as a melting pot, converting everyone into upstanding American citizens.[75]

Although the school had to be nonsectarian, it was not meant to be secular: "The whole influence of the Board of Education . . . has been to promote and encourage, and, whenever they had any power . . . to *direct* the daily use of the Bible in schools." Theology, theoretically, was out. The King James Bible was very much in. However, what nationalists saw as benign cultural assimilation and liberals saw as a common grounding in the three pillars of liberalism—teaching children to be good citizens, successful participants in a market economy, and morally upright people—was rejected by Catho-

75. Long, *The Church-State*, 12; DelFattore, *The Fourth R*, 14; Mann, 12th Annual Report to the Massachusetts State Board of Education (1848).

lics.[76] From the liberal (and nationalist) perspective, reading from the King James Bible and reciting the Ten Commandments was "the key to democracy and Americanism." To Catholics, it was indoctrination in heresy.[77]

In the Catholic view, not only was the translation of the King James Bible biased in favour of Protestant theology, but the Bible should not be read without (Catholic) explanatory commentary, to ensure it was understood in a Catholic sense. Individual, unmediated Bible reading was a Protestant practice imposed on Catholic children. Even the apparently anodyne reading of the Ten Commandments became a source of violent controversy because they differed by religion (as a blow against Catholic images of saints, the Virgin, etc., Protestants made the prohibition of worship of graven images the second commandment, while that did not appear in the Catholic version. Catholics, by contrast, split the Protestant Tenth Commandment in two, separating adultery from theft).

Controversy over reading the Ten Commandments in Boston public schools led in 1859 to confrontation over the corporal punishment of a Catholic schoolboy who, instructed by his priest, refused to recite them. When the case went to court, the verdict was that Bible reading was "no interference with religious liberty." When required reading from the King James Bible was taken to court in Maine in 1854, the court ruled that "A requirement . . . that the Protestant version of the Bible shall be read in the public schools . . . is in violation of no constitutional provision, and is binding upon all." Similar struggles took place in many places. In Philadelphia in 1844, the Catholic bishop asked that Catholic children either be excused from Bible reading or be allowed to read from the Douay Bible, a Catholic translation with commentary. The Board's response was telling: students could use "any particular version of the Bible, without note or comment." The response was open and tolerant—from a Protestant perspective. But from a Catholic perspective, it required their children to read a heretical text—a Bible without Catholic commentary. When, after several months of further controversy in 1844, a Catholic public school director in Philadelphia suggested that Bible reading be suspended until a generally acceptable policy could be devised, the result was rioting, during which more than twenty people were killed, many more injured, and

76. Partly from a deliberate rejection of the nationalist melting pot. Archbishop Hughes in New York insisted on the right of Irish Catholics to preserve their national identity. DelFattore, *The Fourth R,* 19.

77. Verhoeven, *Transatlantic Anti-Catholicism,* 47; Farrelly, *Anti-Catholicism in America,* 148.

two Catholic churches and a seminary burned. The grand jury convened afterward refused to indict any of the riots' leaders, and instead blamed the riots on "the efforts of a portion of the community [i.e. the Catholics] to exclude the Bible from the public schools."[78]

Liberals offered students as *individuals* the freedom to understand the Bible as they chose. The Catholic students were denied the freedom to read the Bible in the manner their *community* approved. But the divide was not the simple one between liberal individualism and Catholic communitarianism sometimes portrayed.[79] In one sense, individual diversity—the student alone with the text without commentary—had to be protected, at the price of excluding group diversity: Catholics could not read their community's version of the Bible. But at the same time liberals viewed education as central to community cohesion, while Catholics viewed it as a private parental prerogative. Both liberals and Catholics thought in terms of *both* the individual and the group, the private conscience and the community. American anti-Catholicism demonstrated liberalism's commitment to a *limited* pluralism, one that did not exclude religion(s) from the public sphere, but that did limit what kind of religion and what kind of religious claims were acceptable.

Catholics who refused to accept the liberal values of the public school were a public danger, all the more so because they were not alone in antebellum America in rejecting public education. They had allies, as American liberals never tired of pointing out, in the slaveowners of the American South. One peculiarly American reason for anti-Catholicism was the strong hostility of the Church and many of its adherents to abolitionism, and Catholic support for slavery. As late as 1866 the Pope declared that, subject to some minor reservations, it was "not at all contrary to the natural and divine law for a slave to be sold, bought or exchanged." Support for slavery was not unique to the Catholic Church, of course. Southern Protestant churches were outspoken in its defense. It nevertheless confirmed American liberals' view that there was something inherently dangerous about Catholicism.[80]

78. McGreevy, *Catholicism and American Freedom*, 187; DelFattore, *The Fourth R*, 45; 33–35; McGreevy, *Catholicism and American Freedom*, 120; DelFattore, *The Fourth R*, 42; Beyer-Purvis, "The Philadelphia Bible Riots of 1844," 365–387. The Philadelphia riots were the result of many factors, yet the predominant factors were religious ones.

79. Cf. McGreevy, *Catholicism and American Freedom*, 37.

80. DelFattore, *The Fourth R*, 157, 167, 170–172, 183, Fenton, *Religious Liberties*, 107, McGreevy, *Catholicism and American Freedom*, 9, 62; Pius IX, cited in Rosenblatt, *The Lost History of Liberalism*, 173.

In response to the perceived danger posed by Catholicism, American liberals used the common Western anti-Catholic vocabulary and reproduced common Western liberal attitudes. As one speaker noted in 1851, it was a cliché to refer to the Catholic as "the ally of tyranny, the opponent of material prosperity, the foe of thrift, the enemy of the railroad, the caucus, and the school." Catholicism embodied the opposite of liberal politics (ally of "tyranny," enemy of "the caucus"), liberal economics (material prosperity, the railroad), and liberal morals (thrift, the nonsectarian school). Catholicism embodied the illiberal, and was to be feared and fought as much as any despot. It was a fear Americans shared with European liberals, perhaps nowhere more strongly than in France.[81]

Germany, courtesy of Martin Luther, may claim to be the homeland of anti-Catholicism, but France, where the word "liberalism" was invented, can claim priority with regard to liberal anti-Catholicism. In France the struggle between liberalism and Catholicism continued with hardly a break from the 1790s to well into the twentieth century. Many observers described the conflict between liberals and the French Church as a war of religion—exactly what liberalism was intended to prevent. Were this point to be suggested to a nineteenth-century French anti-clerical, or for that matter an American, English, Norwegian, or German liberal anti-Catholic, the response would doubtless have been: "but this is self-defense!" After 1871, French liberals summarized this as "defending the Republic." Without going into the details of the French conflict, which largely echoed generic liberal anti-Catholicism, the French case is useful for examining the clash between the positive visions of liberalism and Catholicism in a secular rather than Protestant context. The French case is particularly instructive from a twenty-first century perspective, in which secular sources of liberal anti-religious feeling are the most common.

During the whole period from the invention of the word "*libéralisme*" circa 1795 to the end of the nineteenth century, there were only brief truces between French liberalism and French Catholicism. Arguably this was true throughout the West. What differentiated the French struggle from that in majority Protestant countries like the United States or Germany was the avowedly secular nature of opposition to the Church. And yet, despite its secular orientation, the French liberal tradition was largely spiritualist in its outlook. Traditional Christian belief was not common among leading French liberal politicians,

81. Cited in McGreevy, *Catholicism and American Freedom*, 46, 51, 48.

but religion / spirituality in some form was omnipresent. Many French liberals were influenced either by Saint-Simon or Auguste Comte. Comte's "Religion of Humanity" (building on St. Simon's ideas) was intended to replace Christianity. Comte argued that while Christianity was outmoded, there remained a need for a "spiritual power." The most determined source of French liberal opposition to the Church was the (relatively small) Masonic movement, which despite the existence of a small atheist wing was firmly committed to spiritual beliefs. In France more overtly than elsewhere, liberalism was its own form of religion.

The French conflict's most enduring focus was education, a controversy whose origins dated back to Napoleon I's creation of a secular high school and university system. The conflict swung back and forth, in a liberal direction during the July Monarchy (1830–48), back to the Church after the loi Falloux of 1850, which gave the Church control of elementary education and supervision over higher education. After the end of the Second Empire in 1871, the combination of representative government and secular schooling became the credo of French liberalism. Primary education became free and obligatory from the age of six until age thirteen for both boys and girls, and above all *laic*.

The word *laic* poses a problem for translators, usually solved by the inadequate "secular." In the context of the nineteenth century, at any rate, it did not mean atheist or even agnostic—it meant "liberal." *Laic* education was intended to be an education that no one need fear, like Horace Mann's earlier common school, which greatly influenced Jules Ferry. Ferry was the great apostle of laic schooling in France and a leading figure in French anti-clericalism in the 1870s and '80s. Education, for Ferry as for almost all liberals of the nineteenth century (and thereafter), was the sovereign balm against fear. It was not, contrary to many twenty-first-century interpretations, meant to be directed against religion. Ferry foresaw the "regeneration of humanity"—spiritual language—through universal public education. The rich should be willing to pay for it as a means of morally legitimizing their wealth (hence reducing their fear) and encouraging the moral progress of society (ditto). The old liberal language of capacity was democratized in the French Third Republic to support universal suffrage and require universal schooling. It was moralized and mobilized against the Church, considered the opponent of the Republic, progress, and liberalism. *Laïcité* itself was a political, moral, and even a religious program. As Ferry put it, "My struggle is the struggle against clericalism, but struggle against religion . . . never!

Never!" Ferry's liberalism, and French *laicité*, were far from a simple negation or rejection of religion. Naturally, this made Catholics fear the heretical *laic* school even more.[82]

Universal education would make the poor man the equal of the rich man, teach rich and poor not to fear each other, and make them capable of contracting together as equals, as Ferry said in his great speech on education in 1870. The last third of the speech was devoted to the need for public education for girls, which did not yet exist in France: women too had to be freed from fear. Ferry cited Mill's *On the Subjection of Women*, but significantly his crowning argument was that this was the only way in which women could be liberated from the domination of the Church. For Ferry it was the school, transmitting the values of the Republic, science, enlightenment, and progress, liberal values that would be the foundation of the new post-Catholic spiritual power (Ferry was influenced by Comte), and a pillar of liberalism. Not, heaven forbid, that liberals rejected the idea of competition in education, even spiritual education. Ferry refused to ban private Catholic schools because as a good liberal he thought public schools needed competition, or they would become mere organs of indoctrination (more of Mill's influence).[83]

As Ferry also said in his speech, public education needed a spiritual foundation. Historically, Ferry admitted, that foundation was Catholicism (he used the word "Christianity," but in France this was a synonym for Catholicism). But, since the eighteenth century, that foundation had become the sciences, among which Ferry took pains to include not just the physical and natural sciences, but also "moral science," which had to be taught from primary school and had to combine nationalism with morality—another blow against internationalist Catholicism. Ferry's moral science was in some respects traditionally religious. The new school manuals, whose publication he supervised closely as Minister of Education a few years later, included a section on "Duties to God" and enjoined teachers to cultivate among their pupils "a feeling of respect and veneration" toward the divinity. A student should be taught that "the first allegiance he owes is to the divinity, that is obedience to the laws of God as revealed to him by his conscience and his reason." This laic / liberal formula would doubtless have passed muster with Horace Mann. From a

82. Bauberot, *Histoire de la laicité*, 44.

83. Ferry, "De l'égalité d'éducation," https://gallica.bnf.fr/ark:/12148/bpt6k5695789n/f31 .image.texteImage; Bauberot, *Histoire de la laicité*, 43n2, 49.

Catholic perspective, such generic religious teaching was merely more heresy.[84]

Laïcité asserted that liberalism was the party of hope, movement, and progress, *and* the party of resistance against the permanent threat of Catholic reaction. The supporters of laïcité continually referred to their own moral and even religious values. French liberals who struggled against Catholicism, even at their most "secular," made no pretense of moral neutrality. The struggle was the product of liberalism's own moral commitments, which clashed with Catholicism once Catholicism entered the public sphere. Neither liberals nor Catholics considered education a wholly private matter, as Macaulay, Tocqueville, and Mill made clear from the liberal perspective. When it came to education, in America, France, or anywhere else, nineteenth-century liberals thought in terms of groups and communities, the corporate public, as much as private individuals or families. And they were prepared to oppress Catholics, not as individuals, but as members of a religious community.

Liberals did not abandon pluralism in their struggle against Catholicism, but they limited it. They never forbade the private practice of Catholicism, but they did sometimes banish certain of its practitioners, i.e., Jesuits. They did not want Catholics to be afraid to be Catholic as such, that is, in the privacy of their conscience or within the walls of their church. Nevertheless, the Catholic schoolboy in Boston or Philadelphia faced with corporal punishment for refusing to read from the King James Bible certainly felt fear. Liberalism produced an illiberal result.

The liberal relationship to Catholicism in the nineteenth century was mostly based on fear rather than hope. What hope remained was based on faith that liberal values, science, etc., would triumph in the long run, that history was on the side of liberalism, that Catholicism would disappear. When it came to Catholicism, liberals supported both movement—the creation of liberal public schools—and resistance—expelling Jesuits—to make Catholicism go away or at least stay home, out of the public sphere. As Karl Popper much later observed, which tactic they chose was a matter of circumstances. "I do not imply, for instance, that we should always suppress the utterance of intolerant philosophies. . . . But we should claim the *right* to suppress them if necessary even by force." Just as nineteenth-century liberals denied the right to vote to those who endangered a liberal order, so they were willing to deny the public expression of religion and freedom of speech when such expression

84. Ferry, "De l'égalité d'éducation"; Bauberot, *Histoire de la laïcité*, 47–48.

made other people afraid that *their* security was in danger. In the twenty-first century this became the basis for liberal bans on hate speech. Given the stubborn refusal of Catholicism and analogous religious commitments (e.g., fundamentalist Islam) to disappear, it is no surprise that even in the twenty-first century, liberalism's relationship with religion is fraught.[85]

If, during the short nineteenth century, the need to deal with nationalism pushed liberals to become more democratic, for example more open to expanding the suffrage, the liberal struggle with Catholicism had very different political effects. In places with a Catholic peasantry it reinforced liberal distrust of the devout masses, and vice versa. Just about everywhere it served to make liberals wary of giving the vote to women because women were considered to be under the control of their priests. Anti-Catholicism also pushed some liberals to support more state involvement in education. While a few liberals saw the solution to the "Catholic problem" as the withdrawal of the state from any involvement in religious or moral questions, many more, as we have seen, drew closer to the state as a means to preserve and spread essential values, especially with regard to education. It was not just in Germany that "liberals . . . believed intolerance of Roman Catholicism and of the Roman Catholic Church was a duty, and they believed they were bound by duty to invoke the force of the state to preserve the independence of the state."[86] Compulsory public education made great progress in both Europe and the United States in part as a result of this view.

The liberal *modus vivendi* with nineteenth-century Catholicism was a question not of overcoming fear, but of managing it.[87] Catholicism, like some aspects of nationalism and even democracy, presented a situation in which an effectively permanent aspect of society was illiberal and would not, whatever liberal theories of history predicted for the long run, disappear in the short run.[88] Liberals were faced with a choice between assimilation, accommodation, and opposition with respect to votes for the lower classes, their attitude toward nationalism, and their relationship with Catholicism.

85. Popper, *The Open Society*, 581.

86. Gross, *The War against Catholicism*, 299.

87. Twenty-first-century parallels with Islamic fundamentalism will occur to many readers.

88. Although liberals kept on hoping. An 1861 *New York Times* editorial claimed that "educated minds in every country" thought Catholicism a "fast-vanishing quality." Cited in McGreevy, *Catholicism and American Freedom*, 14.

The choice was not purely theirs, however; much depended on the attitude of the other side.

During the short nineteenth century, liberals crossed and recrossed the lines separating the party of movement from the party of resistance, not because they couldn't make up their minds, but because different circumstances and different issues, such as suffrage, nationalism, and anti-Catholicism, required different responses from them. With regard to suffrage, the vast majority of liberals had crossed over from resistance to movement by the fin de siècle, with the exception of women and, in America, Black people. Almost everywhere, most liberals had little trouble accommodating themselves to nationalism and joining nationalist movements until the fin de siècle. The "Catholic Problem" encouraged both support for and resistance to reform by nineteenth-century liberals, in ways that make twenty-first-century liberals uncomfortable, although very few liberals were bothered at the time. It raised questions about how far liberals would, could, or should go to accommodate what they perceived as an aggressively illiberal community, questions to which later liberals would often have occasion to return.

For a few liberals, the reason for liberal difficulties was mainstream liberals' insistence that freedom from fear could only be maintained with the aid of political, *and* economic, *and* moral / religious pillars. For these liberals, liberalism was better off without any trace of perfectionism, without any moral / religious component, and should stand on only two or even just one pillar, either political or economic. It was in the minority tradition of purely political or purely economic liberalism, discussed in the next chapter, that the strongest liberal adherents of indifference to all religious communities as well as support for political openness and democratic suffrages were often, albeit not always, to be found. Liberals who preferred to stand on two pillars, or even just one, represent a strand of liberalism that was of some significance even in the short nineteenth century, and increasingly so in the twentieth in a multitude of ways.

6

Liberalisms with Something Missing

NINETEENTH-CENTURY LIBERALS FEARED DESPOTS, religious fanatics, revolutionaries, and reactionaries, categories that often overlapped. In response they typically relied on defenses that were simultaneously political, economic, and moral / religious—the three pillars of freedom, markets, and morals. If individual liberals rarely gave equal time to all three, they nevertheless usually acknowledged their importance.

However, there were prominent liberals throughout the short nineteenth century who thought that two pillars, or even one, were all the support liberalism needed. They espoused a "thin" liberalism, based on more narrowly circumscribed arguments, and with correspondingly limited goals as compared to the mainstream liberalisms that rested on all three pillars. In particular, some "thin" liberals excluded all moral or religious ideals from their liberal credo. Others maintained a moral / religious doctrine but walled off morality and religion from political and economic questions so that they no longer acted as a pillar of liberalism. To a large extent, these thin liberalisms were exclusively concerned with "negative liberty," freedom from coercion, and did not combine utilitarian and perfectionist views the way most liberals did.

Thin liberalisms did not much affect liberal policy during the short nineteenth century, and liberal governments rarely adopted their views. Nevertheless it is important to recognize the presence of thin liberal arguments throughout the period. This is partly because they became increasingly influential in the century that followed and partly because they provided some later liberal (and anti-liberal) thinkers with cover for the inaccurate claim that liberalism was always thin and only concerned with freedom from coercion. In this context it should be stressed that from their own perspective what was "missing" from thin liberalism was not a weakness but a strength. The fact that some liberals in the short nineteenth century rejected elements of mainstream liberal argument was not necessarily to their disadvantage, either from their own perspective or from the anachronistic / treasure-seeking vantage point of the twenty-first century. A thin liberalism is not always less theoretically convincing or less adapted to its circumstances than a thick one, even though most of the time this is the case.

Thin liberals were as different from one another as any other kind of liberal, but three elements common in mainstream liberal thought were usually missing from thin liberalisms. One was that history tended to disappear. As opposed to the Scottish stage theories prominent in the proto-liberalisms of the eighteenth century, or the distinctions between ancient and modern freedom or aristocratic and democratic societies found in Constant and Tocqueville, thin liberals tended to make fewer references to historical circumstances or development, outside of a linear concept of progress. This tendency would remain in the thin liberalism of the twentieth century.

More important, thin liberals tended to eliminate discussion of the oppression of groups, classes, and interests in favor of an exclusive focus on individuals. What was later called "methodological individualism" reigned among thin liberals during the short nineteenth century. When it came to calculating happiness or inventorying dangers and fears, only individuals were concerned, not groups or classes. If any groups or classes were discussed, they appeared chiefly as oppressors of individuals. This meant a narrower understanding of all three pillars of liberalism—political, economic, and moral, applying them purely to individuals.

But the most important element that was consistently missing, whittled down to insignificance or walled off in a corner, was the moral pillar of liberalism, and in particular its perfectionist aspect. If there was still a pinch of utilitarian morality in such arguments, it was often that of Jeremy Bentham and his followers: Bentham's version of utilitarianism had no place for the visions of character development characteristic of mainstream liberalism. Religion, if discussed at all, was often purely ornamental, as in the case of Frédéric Bastiat. If any perfectionism remained, as in the case of Herbert Spencer, it was radically separated from politics and economics. In Bentham, Bastiat, and Spencer, the moral / religious pillar of mainstream liberalism was deprived of any real influence if it was left standing at all.

Thin theory was often linked with the advocacy of thin policy, that is of the greatest possible limits on the role of the state. Fear of the state as the most powerful potential source of despotism was universal among nineteenth-century liberals. But the desire to reduce it to a night watchman, whose only business was to discourage criminal assault, or even to eventually see it wither away (in this the evolution of human society was much the same in Spencer and Karl Marx) was much stronger among thin liberals—Bentham, as we will see, was an exception to this rule. From their point of view this "missing" state, severely limited in scope, added to freedom by subtracting the greatest threat to it.

Even those who today regard a night watchman state with less than delight should note that because these thin liberals narrowed down the moral / religious pillar of mainstream liberalism and divorced it from politics, they were less morally judgmental. Thin liberals were also more inclined to condemn imperialism and colonialism because they saw the moral improvement of the victims (the famous *mission civilisatrice*) as none of anyone's business. All three of the thinkers discussed in this chapter, Bentham, Bastiat, and Spencer, were among the relatively few prominent liberals of their time to thoroughly reject any form of colonialism or militarism.

Even if their arguments were more narrowly based, Bentham, Bastiat, Spencer, and others who used thin liberal arguments confronted the same problems and fears, and the same political choices, as other liberals. Their solutions were sometimes different in significant ways, and sometimes not. For example, as we will see below, the narrowness of their arguments paradoxically made them more open to universal suffrage and to complete religious neutrality. On the other hand, they were to be found on the same wide spectrum as mainstream liberals with regard to the question of whether to join the party of movement and reform or that of resistance to change. Bentham, like most English liberals at the beginning of the nineteenth century, was clearly a member of the party of movement, except perhaps when he was briefly terrified by the Jacobins during the French Revolution. Bastiat was too. Spencer was perceived by his contemporaries as a member of the party of resistance, during what was sometimes described as the debate over "individualism vs. collectivism" (a debate in which liberals were to be found on both sides). He himself, however, always rejected this characterization of his views and thought of himself as a proponent of change, albeit change in a direction that was no longer popular with many liberals.

Thin visions of liberalism tended to concentrate on narrow remedies for fear. Thus for Bentham, a politics based purely on individual self-interest, provided all individuals could express themselves, was the only necessary security for a liberal society. Others, like Bastiat, concentrated their attention on the realization of a laissez-faire market economy with a very limited state. Yet others, like Spencer, argued in many respects on the same multiple political, economic, and moral grounds as mainstream liberals. But Spencer effectively separated his liberalism from the mainstream by insisting on a strict separation between the morality appropriate for social life and the morality appropriate for personal behavior, cutting off politics from morals—and paving the way for twentieth-century liberalisms that were thinner and narrower than his.

Bentham, Bastiat, and Spencer were three thin liberals with very different perspectives. Each of them presented a viewpoint that found many adherents when thin liberalisms came into their own in the twentieth century. In some respects, Bentham's laser-like focus on self-interest and purely individual happiness was particularly influential in the twentieth century, and thus it is appropriate to begin with him. Like Kant and Madison, his career spanned the proto-liberal and liberal periods (he was born in 1748 and died in 1832). As a witness of the American and French Revolutions, he responded to the new hopes and fears those events embodied, even if, at times, he maintained a sort of fearless optimism more radical than liberal. Bentham played a role in the history of more than one kind of political thought, and it is his liberalism, and the role it would play in future liberalisms, that is of concern here.[1]

Bentham: Liberalism on the Basis of Happiness

Bentham relied on one principle: utility, which for him meant the search for pleasure and avoidance of pain that, when successful, equaled happiness. In his youth, Bentham was inspired by reading the French Enlightenment figure Helvétius to try to explain "all effects from the simplest and fewest causes". Bentham identified this simple cause as utility: all human judgments were derived from pleasure and pain. To describe his theory, Bentham invented the word "utilitarianism" in 1781. On this single-minded moral theory Bentham

---

1. Bentham's influence in his own time and later in the nineteenth century is a hotly debated question. Depending on the commentator, Bentham's ideas were either irrelevant or crucial to the reform of the English state in the nineteenth century, and either dominated or were largely irrelevant to English intellectual life. For the view that he mattered, see Hamburger, *Intellectual in Politics*. For the opposite perspective see Lubenow, *Politics of Government Growth*, and Parry, *The Rise and Fall of Liberal Government*, 114. Mill thought foreigners tended to greatly overestimate the prevalence of utilitarianism in England. Mill to Dupont-White, 10 Oct. 1861, *CW* 14, 2:745.

built an equally single-minded theory of politics, in which the protection of
the individual pursuit of happiness from interference by others was the sole
purpose of government.[2]

Bentham formally defined utility as "that property in any object, whereby
it tends to produce benefit, advantage, pleasure, good, or happiness ... or ...
to prevent the happening of mischief, pain, evil, or unhappiness." Utility was
the motivation and goal of all human actions, actions whose sole purpose was
the attainment of happiness, defined by Bentham as the greatest possible sur-
plus of pleasure over pain. Hence his principle of "the greatest happiness of
the greatest number" as the proper goal of both legislation and moral judgment. The interest of the community was the sum of the happiness / pleasure
and pain of the individuals who composed it. There was no common good of
the community as a whole, nor of some group within it, since only individuals
felt pleasure or pain. Utility was capable of "almost mathematical" measure-
ment via the "felicific calculus"—how many units of happiness were added or
taken away by a given action.[3]

Within the broad category of utility, the things that give pleasure and avoid
pain, Bentham identified four "subordinate sub-objects": subsistence, abundance, equality, and security, of which security, as will be seen below, held the
position of *primus inter pares*, as was natural for a liberal trying to ward off fear.
Maximizing the pleasures produced by subsistence and abundance gave us the
principles of economics. Equality, for Bentham, meant that everyone's pleasure and pain counted equally with everyone else's ("agent neutrality," in
twenty-first-century terminology). This was a very democratic and fairly common idea. Even more democratic and much less commonplace was Bentham's
insistence that no pleasure was qualitatively different from any other. "Every
person is not only the most proper judge, but the only proper judge of what
with reference to himself is pleasure and so in regard to pain." Therefore, "every
man, being of mature age and sound mind, ought on this subject to be left to
judge and act for himself: and that every thing which by any other man can be
said or done in the view of giving direction to the conduct of the first, is no
better than folly and impertinence." Bentham was not content only to defend
humanity's right to trivial pleasures. He attacked those who thought that there

2. Schofield, *Utility and Democracy*, 52; Long, "'Utility' and the 'Utility Principle,'" 198; de
Champs, *Enlightenment and Utility*, 41–54.

3. Bentham, *Introduction*, https://oll.libertyfund.org/titles/278#bentham_0175_44; Long,
"'Utility' and the 'Utility Principle,'" 182; Rosen, "Reading Hume Backwards," 32.

was anything trivial about one pleasure compared to another. "There is no taste which deserves the epithet good . . . : there is no taste which deserves to be characterized as bad, unless it be a taste for some occupation which has a mischievous tendency."[4]

Bentham's view excluded any relationship between freedom and moral perfection. This was why his fellow utilitarian of a very different kind, John Stuart Mill, later attacked him. Mill had a notion of the perfectibility of human character, the superiority of certain pleasures. Bentham did not. The units of pleasure produced by the child's game of pushpin and by poetry were equal for different people. Thus, "prejudice apart, the game of push-pin is of equal value with the arts and sciences of music and poetry. If the game of push-pin furnish more pleasure, it is more valuable than either." The only reason for fancying a gourmet restaurant or a Shakespeare play better than fast food or video games was that "they are calculated to gratify those individuals who are most difficult to be pleased." But this was hardly a justification for such views.[5]

Bentham's judgment that a dissatisfied Socrates was worse off than a contented drunkard (to reverse Mill's famous example of the distinction between higher and lower pleasures) may seem intuitively unappealing. However, some of the consequences of his refusal to rank pleasures are attractive to some twenty-first-century liberals. He rejected any attempt to make moral distinctions between two starving people. Both deserved to be fed, even if one was a drunkard and the other not. In both cases, the pain they would suffer by starving to death was greater than the pain caused to the taxpayer by having to feed them, so the state was obliged to do so. Nor did the state have any right to lecture the poor about morality, although it did have every reason to encourage them to earn their own living by making the poorhouse as unappealing as possible, so that the pain to the taxpayer would be minimized. He further argued that because no one can know better than the individual what pleases them, no one has a right to intervene in their sexuality. Bentham left his defense of homosexuality unpublished,[6] but he was among the tiny group who

---

4. Bentham, cited in Kelly, "Security, Expectation, and Liberty," 167–169; Schofield, *Utility and Democracy*, 9:25; Bentham, cited in Schofield, *Utility and Democracy*, 48; Bentham, *Rationale of Reward*, https://oll.libertyfund.org/titles/1921#Bentham_0872-02_3586; Schofield, *Utility and Democracy*, 47; https://oll.libertyfund.org/titles/1921#Bentham_0872-02_3587.

5. Bentham, *Rationale of Reward*, https://oll.libertyfund.org/titles/1921#Bentham_0872 -02_3581.

6. The scholarship of the last thirty years has shown a wide gap between the historical Bentham and the one found in his unpublished manuscripts.

rejected all forms of sexual coercion and championed any form of sexual expression that did not cause harm. He went so far as to recommend homosexuality to the poor, since it did not result in the birth of children doomed to starvation.[7]

Bentham was no would-be dictator, of pushpin or of poetry. His commitment to the idea that all pleasures were equal forbade dictatorship. Yet he early acquired a reputation for authoritarianism, which was given new force in the late twentieth century by Michel Foucault's use of Bentham's "Panopticon" project as an example of enlightened despotism. The panopticon was Bentham's never-realized design for a prison where the inmates were, at least potentially, under constant observation, and in which work, sobriety, and discipline were continually enforced. It was to be a "mill for grinding rogues honest."[8]

On Bentham's own grounds, this would seem to be both "impertinent" and illiberal. The answer to the puzzle lies in the fact that for Bentham criminals were not rational adults:

> Delinquents . . . may be considered as persons of unsound mind, but in whom the complaint has not swelled to so high a pitch as to rank them with idiots or lunatics. They may be considered as a sort of grown children, in whose instance the mental weakness attached to non-age continues, in some respects, beyond the ordinary length of time.[9]

Therefore criminals would respond readily to the incentives and punishments provided by the Panopticon. Like small children, they lived only in the present and their prison experience would create in them new habits that would replace their old ones and lead to a reformation of their character. This view was certainly authoritarian, but it was not "impertinent": it did not attempt to dictate to an equal what they ought to like or dislike. The criminals were not Bentham's equals. Nor was this attitude perfectionist. Bentham did not care if the prisoners liked pushpin or preferred poetry. He cared only that they ceased to harm others and acquired the habits necessary to support themselves. The Panopticon was not intended to save souls. Bentham did not want to make

7. Quinn, "Jeremy Bentham and the Relief of Indigence," 403–404, 409, 411.

8. Foucault, *Discipline and Punish*; Bentham, "Panopticon," https://oll.libertyfund.org/titles/1921#Bentham_0872-02_3581, 342.

9. Bentham, "Panopticon," https://oll.libertyfund.org/titles/1925#Bentham_0872-04_1447.

people "better." He wanted to make them safer, the fundamental liberal goal of making people free from fear.[10]

To this end, Bentham relied on law. Law created security, security was assured by the existence and enforcement of law, and this was what people generally thought of as freedom, although Bentham acknowledged that there was such a thing as freedom without security, which was what "Hottentots and Patagonians" had. But in civilized societies, freedom required law, and the making of laws was dependent on politics.[11]

Bentham defined politics thinly, seeing only individuals and disregarding groups. His politics made no use of the usual liberal devices of a balance of power or the representation of group interests because in his view those devices, with their emphasis on the collective, at best distracted from and at worse hindered the pursuit of individual happiness. Public opinion, if free and properly represented, would be more than adequate to keep the government from acting against the interests of the people and engaging in impertinent interventions into their pleasures. Politics, broadly construed to include the operation of public opinion, was the sole pillar of liberalism for Bentham, who eliminated all particular content from his moral pillar (pushpin was as good as poetry) and did not assign markets / economics any special role in his theory.

In his early writings, Bentham assumed that however misguided they might be, rulers and legislators had good intentions, that is, they were trying to increase the happiness of the majority. After his prison reform proposals foundered, Bentham changed his mind and created his theory of "sinister interests." A sinister interest was a motivation to promote the happiness of a particular individual or set of individuals (the king, the aristocracy, the Church of England), and not that of the majority. England was ruled by an alliance of royal and aristocratic sinister interests, with the aid of corrupt soldiers, lawyers, and priests, all motivated by their own happiness, not that of the majority. Since people were always motivated by self-interest, according to Bentham, it was not surprising that sinister interests existed. Rulers and subjects had naturally opposed interests. But in a well-run state, political institutions would be structured so that rulers would find it impossible to further their own interests

---

10. Bentham, "Panopticon," https://oll.libertyfund.org/titles/1925#Bentham_0872-04
_1141.

11. Bentham, cited in Long, "Fundamental Words," 108.

when they conflicted with those of the majority, and it would be disadvanta-geous to them even to try.[12]

When confronted with the problem of restraining rulers, mainstream liber-als tried to create some means to check and balance powers within government and limit its scope. But in language reminiscent of Thomas Paine, Bentham rejected constitutional limits on the scope of government as "the old recipe for enabling the dead to chain down the living." The legislature ought to be "omnicompetent" to do anything that would, in its judgment, benefit the ma-jority. All authority was to be concentrated in the omnicompetent national assembly, and the assembly chosen in such a way that it always represented the interests of the majority. In order for people to hold their rulers responsible, Bentham eventually decided that nothing would do short of a republic whose legislature was elected by the suffrage of all the literate. In private, he went so far as to extend the vote to literate women. Only in this way could everyone be sure that their interests would be taken into account, and that the rulers had the necessary intellectual and moral aptitude, that is, the ability and desire, to rule in the interest of the majority.[13]

The guarantees for ensuring that the rulers would want to rule in the inter-est of the majority had nothing to do with virtue or public spirit. The differ-ence between Bentham and a mainstream liberal such as James Madison was that while Madison too assumed that people were self-interested, and like Bentham attempted to harness their self-interest to the public good, Madison required and encouraged a certain amount of virtue alongside self-interest: otherwise, in his view, the nation was doomed (see chapter 3). Not so Ben-tham. The actions of Bentham's rulers derived purely from self-interest. The amount of utility / pleasure to be gained by acting in the public's interest had to be adjusted so that it was not profitable for the rulers to put their own in-terests first, on pain of anything from losing the next election to beheading. So that their self-interested sins could be detected, the rulers needed above all to be carefully watched. Bentham confided this oversight to public opinion:

> The public compose a tribunal, which is more powerful than all the other tribunals together. An individual may pretend to disregard its decrees—to

---

12. Schofield, *Utility and Democracy*, v, 107, 109–136, 142–145, 250–255, 272–303; Rosen, "Lib-erty and Constitutional Theory," 207–208.
13. Rosen, "Sovereignty and Democracy," 280.

represent them as formed of fluctuating and opposite opinions, which destroy one another; but every one feels, that though this tribunal may err, it is incorruptible; that it continually tends to become enlightened; that it unites all the wisdom and all the justice of the nation; that it always decides the destiny of public men; and that the punishments which it pronounces are inevitable.[14]

Hence what was "indispensable, at all times and everywhere . . . to everything that can with any propriety be termed good government" were "those two intimately-connected liberties—the liberty of the press, and the liberty of public discussion by word of mouth." Freedom of speech about everything, especially "for the purpose of affording . . . every facility for eventual resistance—for resistance to government, and thence should necessity require for a change in government," was the only way to keep rulers in check. Government was a trust, liable to be abused, and publicity and free speech the guarantee that it would not be. The sole remedy against misrule by sinister interests was publicity. The need for continual oversight of the government by society shows how Bentham was a liberal: salvation lay in civil society, not the state, even if Bentham's legislature was omnicompetent.[15]

Bentham liked to refer to public opinion as the "Public Opinion Tribunal," or POT. The POT, as Bentham was aware, might appear to be an imaginary body. It seemed imaginary because it could never be seen or touched, but it was real nonetheless, as those who attempted to run counter would soon learn. Even without elections, public opinion was influential, and in the last instance all-powerful. If the POT was given sufficient political power and scope, it would be easier even for an absolute monarch to keep his promises than to break them. Its ultimate punishment was the withdrawal of obedience and revolution, as demonstrated, according to Bentham, by the execution of Charles I.[16]

Bentham was confident that the decisions of public opinion would generally be good ones, and would improve over time. "Even at the present stage in the career of civilization, its dictates coincide, on most points, with those of the greatest happiness principle; on some, however, it still deviates from them:

14. Bentham, cited in Schofield, *Utility and Democracy*, 259–260.

15. Bentham, cited in Schofield, *Utility and Democracy*, 250, 252; Bentham, "Securities Against Misrule," https://oll.libertyfund.org/titles/2208#Bentham_0872-08_5299.

16. Bentham, "Securities Against Misrule," https://oll.libertyfund.org/titles/2208#Bentham_0872-08_5340.

but, as its deviations have all along been less and less numerous, and less wide, sooner or later they will cease to be discernible." Bentham recognized some exceptions to the beneficence of public opinion. The opinion of the majority could deviate from their own interests because of "delusion." "Honest intellectual weakness" was at the root of popular support for things that were not in the popular interest. Rulers and governments furthermore had a natural interest in suppressing public opinion or preventing the public from being informed. But left free, the POT would not only rule the government, but do so wisely, that is, in accord with the interests of the majority.[17]

Provided public opinion was free to oversee the government, eventually everyone would be free. The citizen had to obey the law, even unjust laws (laws that served the interests of a minority). But if citizens could appeal from the judgment of the government's court to the judgment of the POT, they would eventually win their case. That was why, for Bentham, "Under a government of laws, what is the motto of a good citizen? To obey punctually; to censure freely." This was effectively identical to Kant's famous maxim: "Argue as much as you will, and about what you will, but obey!" (see chapter 3). Starting from radically different presuppositions, Bentham and Kant arrived at the same conclusion about the crucial importance of obedience to the law and of public opinion. Thus, radically different but nevertheless liberal political theories supported core liberal positions, such as the priority of civil society and the necessity of freedom of speech.

The thinness of his politics did not mean that Bentham favored a wholly laissez-faire state, one equally hands-off in economics as in morals. Many readers, as diverse as Marx, Henry Maine, A. V. Dicey, Lord Robbins, and Michel Foucault have seen Bentham as an advocate of laissez-faire economics. Yet it is easy to demonstrate that this is not true. Bentham had no "horror . . . of the hand of government." While he preferred non-intervention by the government because he thought that in practice it usually worked better, that is, was more conducive to the general happiness, he accepted a role for the state that often far surpassed that of a night watchman.[18]

17. Bentham, cited in Schofield, *Utility and Democracy*, Kindle edition, loc 4793; loc 4838.

18. Lieberman, "Economy and Polity," 109: Postema, "Utilitarian Justice and the Tasks of Law," 117; Kelly, "Security, Expectation, and Liberty," 294, 312; Lieberman, "Economy and Polity," 110–111; Kelly, "Security, Expectation, and Liberty," 311; Bentham, cited in Stephen Conway, "Bentham and the Nineteenth-Century Revolution in Government," in Rosen, ed., *Jeremy Bentham*, 601.

Bentham was equally willing for the state to intervene in science. There was no need for the government to subsidize research that could turn a profit, but there was a danger that more theoretical and less immediately profitable research, though perhaps more useful in the long run, would not be privately funded. Therefore "discoveries may at all times be materially accelerated by a proper application of public encouragement" and "the most simple and efficacious method of encouraging investigations of pure theory" was for the government to provide competitive prizes to pay for it.[19]

Strikingly, Bentham was prepared to regulate or even forbid the introduction of new technology. He suggested that while it was desirable that printing presses should be introduced to spread knowledge cheaply, their use should not "throw out of employment any of the existing scribes, except in so far as other employment, not less advantageous, is found for them." Printing presses should be regulated and even forbidden if their introduction would result in unemployment. Far from being the heartless English shopkeeper described by Marx and Foucault, Bentham sometimes sounded more like a socialist lamenting the ravages of technological unemployment: when introducing new technology, "an effect which can never be too scrupulously attended to . . . is its effect on the interest—on the very means of subsistence of the working hands. . . . In various countries of Europe, in England more perhaps than in any other, prodigious is the mass of misery that has been produced by this means."[20]

Bentham's liberalism was simultaneously extremely limited and yet all-embracing in its ambitions. He reduced the traditional moral pillar of liberalism to a form of self-interest that drastically narrowed the grounds on which society and government could act, but which allowed for very far-reaching action on behalf of the general happiness. Sometimes, as with regard to preferring pushpin or poetry, this led Bentham to enjoin the strictest laissez-faire policy on the state as well as society. Usually this applied to economic questions as well. But there were other moments where in Bentham's judgment the balance of utility lay in state intervention. Above all, what mattered for Bentham was politics. Without a political system in which sinister interests were restrained by universal suffrage and the free play of public opinion, a liberal society was impossible.

19. Bentham, *Rationale of Reward*, https://oll.libertyfund.org/titles/1921#Bentham_0872 -02_3598.

20. Bentham, "Securities Against Misrule," https://oll.libertyfund.org/titles/2208#Bentham _0872-08_5510; https://oll.libertyfund.org/titles/2208#Bentham_0872-08_5504.

Bentham is an important figure in the history of liberalism because his work shows that a narrowly based liberalism was present from the beginning of the liberal project of creating a society in which everyone could live without fear. His narrow focus on the political pillar of liberalism set a precedent for a liberalism that relied on only one mechanism to achieve its goals. Regardless of whether it had immediate practical impact, it became part of the intellectual atmosphere of liberalism through Bentham's nineteenth-century British disciples, the Philosophic Radicals, and his many French readers. Furthermore, Bentham's purely utilitarian, individual-focused felicific calculus was the starting point for a whole series of later reflections on liberalism, especially in the twentieth century, when they influenced figures as diverse as Robert Nozick and John Rawls, whether as friend or foe.

Bastiat: Producers versus Plunderers

While Bentham sustained mainstream liberalism's strong interest in politics, other thin liberalisms chose to largely ignore politics and focus instead on what Constant called the purely "modern," essentially apolitical forms of liberty. A good example is the laissez-faire liberalism *à outrance* of Frédéric Bastiat (1801–1850). The history of liberalism, from Bastiat's perspective, was the story of hardworking, peaceful individuals who feared losing the fruits of their labor to lazy, violent people, and sought means to restrain them. Liberalism's goal was to keep the producers safe from those who would plunder them. Bastiat's means of doing so was his own version of utilitarian morality, which was tightly interlaced with laissez-faire economics and a strictly limited role for politics and the state.

Bastiat started from the perspective that everyone naturally pursued their own self-interest, but that contrary to what socialists and Catholics both thought, the natural result of the pursuit of self-interest was social and economic harmony. The struggles between producers and plunderers had led superficial observers to wrongly think that society was based on antagonism, resulting in destructive theories of class struggle and general distrust of free markets and free human beings. But according to Bastiat, individual freedom spontaneously brought about social harmony and liberated people from fear, whereas attempts to limit freedom, based on the view that harmony must be imposed from above, ended up facilitating plunder.[21]

21. Bastiat, *Economic Harmonies*, passim, but especially https://oll.libertyfund.org/titles /79#Bastiat_0187_96

Adam Smith had said much the same thing, as Bastiat acknowledged. But Bastiat stressed a disturbing element in human nature that played little role in Smith: laziness. Sloth, for Bastiat, was the original sin and its product was aggression: "Since work is in itself a burden and since man by his nature is drawn to escape burdens, it follows, and history is there to prove it, that wherever plunder is less burdensome than work, it triumphs over it." The plunderers were those whom hard-working producers had to fear.[22] This led to a version of the usual first-wave liberal fear of revolution and reaction, which in Bastiat's historical circumstances meant a fear of socialist revolutionaries and Catholic reactionaries, both of whom wished to plunder the producers for their own reasons, although socialists, revolutionary and otherwise, played the more prominent role in his writings, natural enough given the context of 1848.

Like Bentham, Bastiat feared the operation of "sinister interests," not just the socialists and the Catholics, but all kinds of plunderers who used the state to disguise their thefts.[23] There were many tricks of "legal plunder" engaged in by the plunderers with the state's help: "Tariffs, protectionism, premiums, subsidies, incentives, progressive taxes, free education, the right to work, the right to assistance, the right to tools for work, free credit, etc. etc. And all of these plans, insofar as they have legal plunder in common, come under the name of socialism" (in lumping these together and calling them "socialism," Bastiat anticipated the classical liberal opponents of the modern liberals of the fin de siècle). Once one admitted "that, in order to be truly free, man needs the POWER to exercise and develop his faculties, it follows that society owes a suitable education to each of its members, . . . together with the instruments of work." In short, one gave plunderers the high-minded excuse that their thefts were in freedom's cause.[24]

The better to oppress the producers, the plunderers had thus perverted law and morality: "When plunder has become a way of life for a group of men living together in society, they create for themselves in the course of time a legal system that authorizes it and a moral code that glorifies it."[25] To defend

---

22. Some readers will see in this an anticipation of the work of Ayn Rand, who in many respects simply rewrote Bastiat.

23. Bastiat, *Economic Harmonies*, https://oll.libertyfund.org/titles/79#Bastiat_0187_61; Bastiat, "Two Systems of Ethics," https://oll.libertyfund.org/titles/276#Bastiat_0182_868; Bastiat, *The Law*, translated by Dennis O'Keeffe and edited by Jacques de Guenin, revised by David M. Hart (Indianapolis, 2012), 7.

24. Bastiat, *The Law*, 50.

25. Bastiat, *Economic Sophisms*, https://oll.libertyfund.org/titles/276#Bastiat_0182_746.

humanity against its plunderers, who came armed with moral and spiritual weapons as well as physical ones, Bastiat developed a moral theory that would enable people to morally justify themselves against the real or professed good intentions of the plunderers. He thus became an eloquent voice for a thin liberalism that relied on a radically non-perfectionist, utilitarian moral vision. Bastiat's was a night watchman morality of sorts, whose function was not to lead people to spiritual perfection, but to help them recognize thieves and defend themselves against them.

Actually, for Bastiat, there were two moralities. One was "religious or philosophical ethics." It was unlimited in its scope and ambitions, it was perfectionist and poetical, and it was ultimately either useless or, when manipulated by plunderers, harmful. This was paralleled by a second kind of ethics, "utilitarian ethics, which I shall permit myself to call economic"—Bastiat's morality was always, even in vocabulary, closely linked to defending free-market economics against the plunderers. Bastiat, in this foreshadowing of Herbert Spencer (see next section), cut all links between religious / philosophical and utilitarian / economic ethics. The two sorts of morals did not contradict, but neither did they reinforce each other—like parallel lines, they never touched.[26]

Bastiat admitted that religious ethics was "more beautiful and . . . more moving" than utilitarian ethics, and that only religious ethics had a perfectionist character and appealed to a positive ideal of human development. He conceded that "the triumph of the religious moralist, when it occurs, is more noble, more encouraging, and more fundamental." Religious ethics were "active," they tried to raise human beings to perfection. "This code of ethics will always be the more beautiful and the more moving of the two, the one that displays the human race in all its majesty, that better lends itself to impassioned eloquence, and is better fitted to arouse the admiration and sympathy of mankind." Religious and philosophical ethics inspired souls. Unfortunately, they had little effect on actions. Bastiat did not wish "to forbid philosophy and religion the use of their own direct methods of working for the improvement of mankind," but he was sure that "the triumph of economics," based on self-interest, "was more easy to secure and more certain."[27]

Religious and philosophical ethics were not only of little use, they could be and had been actively harmful. While morality in the religious or philosophical

26. Bastiat, *Economic Harmonies*, https://oll.libertyfund.org/titles/79#Bastiat_0187_1510.

27. Bastiat, *Economic Sophisms*, https://oll.libertyfund.org/titles/276#Bastiat_0182_872 -884.

sense encouraged virtue, in the eyes of public opinion virtue often meant plundering one's fellow human beings across the border. Christian virtue was no different in this regard than pagan virtue. "Has there ever been a religion more favorable to peace and more widely accepted than Christianity? And yet what have we witnessed for eighteen centuries? The spectacle of men warring with one another not only in spite of religion, but in the very name of religion." The ultimate proof of the uselessness of religious / philosophical morality was the persistence of slavery, a "striking example of the impotence of religious and humanitarian sentiments in a conflict with the powerful force of self-interest." Plunder trumped work whenever people could get away with it "without religion or morality . . . being able to stop it."[28] Between justifying war and plunder and failing to stop slavery, religious / philosophical ethics showed themselves to be useless or worse.

There was a specifically anti-clerical side to Bastiat's thought often ignored by his commentators. Without naming names, Bastiat described Catholicism as a form of institutionalized plunder, despite his own formal (and at the end of his life, real) Catholic faith. He wrote:

> If I tell a man, "I am going to render you an immediate service," I am obliged to keep my word. . . . But suppose I say to him, "In exchange for services from you, I shall confer immense services upon you, not in this world but in the next. Whether, after this life, you are to be eternally happy or wretched depends entirely upon me; I am an intermediary between God and man, and can, as I see fit, open to you the gates of heaven or of hell." If this man believes me, he is at my mercy.[29]

Voltaire could not have said it better.

By contrast, utilitarian, economic ethics helped people defend themselves against plunderers. Unlike the active search for perfection demanded by religious or philosophical ethics, utilitarian ethics were "passive." They worked precisely because they didn't require spiritual perfection first. "The economic, or utilitarian, system of ethics has the same end in view, but above all addresses itself to man in his passive role. Merely by showing him the necessary consequences of his acts, it stimulates him to oppose those that injure him, and to honor those that are useful to him." Without attempting to change people or

28. Bastiat, *Economic Sophisms*, https://oll.libertyfund.org/titles/276#Bastiat_0182_781; Bastiat, *The Law*, 7.

29. Bastiat, *Economic Sophisms*, https://oll.libertyfund.org/titles/276#Bastiat_0182_789.

make them better, the utilitarian ethic "strives to disseminate enough good sense, knowledge, and justifiable mistrust among the oppressed masses to make oppression more and more difficult and dangerous," and thus "dry up the springs of vice." Self-interest did all the work for Bastiat, with religious, philosophical, or poetic ethics serving, at best, a decorative function.[30]

Bastiat apologized for preferring an effective but purely secular utilitarian morality. A society "well-regulated" by a purely "economic system of ethics" still offered "opportunities for the progress of religious morality." Even if it was second best, in a spiritual sense, "perhaps society must pass through this pro-saic stage, in which men practice virtue out of self-interest, so that they may thence rise to the more poetic sphere in which they will no longer have need of such a motive." Nevertheless, utilitarian / economic morality was the only moral weapon really effective against the plunderer. "Political economy re-gards man from one side only," but this side of man turned out to be the only side that really counted.[31]

Bastiat was not the first liberal to distinguish between two sorts of morals. There are parallel distinctions in Smith, Kant, and Tocqueville, among many others. Nevertheless, there was a significant difference between Bastiat's ver-sion of the "two moralities" argument and that of mainstream liberals such as Constant (see chapter 3). They thought some kind of perfectionist moral-ity a necessary complement to a utilitarian ethics, necessary to preserve a liberal society. Not so Bastiat, for whom a utilitarian ethics was perfectly suf-ficient. Constant's version of liberal morality makes an illuminating contrast, and demonstrates the radical nature of Bastiat's move to morally thin out liberalism.

Constant's moral vision was embodied in what he himself called the "two moralities." The first ignored people's motivations and was limited to forbid-ding actions that damaged other people. This was the utilitarian, "passive" (in Bastiat's term), negative morality appropriate for the state to enforce through law: "the functions of government are negative: it should repress evil, and let the good take care of itself." The second, positive morality was equivalent to what Bastiat called "active," "religious or philosophical" moral-ity. It was all about individual feelings and motivations and virtues, and was none of the state's business. Constant rejected any imposed positive morality,

30. Bastiat, *Economic Sophisms*, https://oll.libertyfund.org/titles/276#Bastiat_0182_872.

31. Bastiat, *Economic Sophisms*, https://oll.libertyfund.org/titles/276#Bastiat_0182_904. *Economic Harmonies*, https://oll.libertyfund.org/titles/79#lf0187_footnote_nt029_ref.

whether imposed directly by the government, or indirectly through a state religion.[32]

What distinguished Constant from Bastiat was that for Constant, negative morality, the morality of self-interest, was not enough to prevent despotism, even though it was all that could be legally required. One could not simply let people pursue their own self-interest, with the state interfering only when that pursuit harmed others, and assume this would be enough to maintain freedom. If people saw their government in a purely instrumental, utilitarian way, then the government would not survive, at least not a free government, according to Constant. In his view, an ethics of self-interest had led France to political "indifference," and "servility" under Napoleon. It was morally incapable of preserving freedom. Looking at government or indeed anything *solely* in terms of utility was self-defeating, according to Constant and the mainstream of liberal thought in the short nineteenth century. Alongside a utilitarian morality, an active, perfectionist morality was not merely useful to freedom, it was necessary. By contrast, Bastiat celebrated a morality based exclusively on interest and utility as the only thing needed to keep people safe from their plunderers.[33]

When Bastiat then considered politics, it was only in a negative light, a matter of refraining from evil, preventing plunder, rather than pursuing any positive good via political means. For Bastiat, politics was purely a matter of defending people's interests against plunderers. A good political system, i.e., a strictly limited state, was a means of stopping plunder, not a means of making people better. As with Bentham, there was no perfectionism in Bastiat. Protecting individuals' interests against plunderers was all that mattered, whether in politics or in morals. That was the meaning of justice.[34]

32. Constant, *Commentary on Filangieri's Work*, 248; Holmes, *Benjamin Constant*, 9; Constant, cited in Rosenblatt, *Liberal Values*, 129; Constant, *Principles of Politics*, 307, 134–135 and passim. See chapter 2.

33. Constant, cited in Rosenblatt, *Liberal Values*, 194; Constant, cited in Rosenblatt, *Liberal Values*, 193, Jennings, "Constant's Idea of Modern Liberty," 71. Constant, AML, 327. Unlike Constant, Bastiat was unremittingly hostile to Classical antiquity and wanted French schools to stop teaching Greek and Latin: "The subversive doctrines that have been given the name of *socialism* or *communism* are the fruit of classical teaching." Bastiat, "Baccalauréat and Socialism," https://oll .libertyfund.org/titles/2450#Bastiat_1573-021291. Furthermore, for Bastiat the ancient freedom and virtues acknowledged by Constant never existed.

34. See Leroux, *Lire Bastiat*, 59, 128; Bastiat, *The Law*, 13.

There was nonetheless a link between Bastiat's morality and his politics, or rather his view that the state should be limited to the greatest possible extent. He moved from the morality of self-interest to a minimal state via a theory of responsibility. Responsibility served "to limit the number of our harmful actions and to increase the number of our useful actions." In order for people to learn responsibility, they had to suffer the consequences of their actions. Thus, "let us admit it frankly, evil must, for the moment, exact its severe penalty." State intervention must not get in the way: "Every attempt to divert responsibility from its natural course is an attack upon justice, freedom, order, civilization, or progress."[35] As proof of this proposition Bastiat cited the increased number of abandoned babies. Now that there were "public funds and administrative agencies" to take care of foundlings, there were ever more of them.[36]

Bastiat did not extend the principle of personal responsibility so far as to see no role for the state at all. He was not an anarchist. "The members of society have certain needs that are so general, so universal, that provision is made for them by organizing government services. Among these requirements is the need for security." Without security, people had to live in fear from plunderers. But the state, while necessary, was dangerous: "To assure us [security], it must have at its command a force capable of overcoming all individual or collective, domestic or foreign forces that might imperil it. In combination with that fatal disposition that we have observed among men to live at the expense of others, this fact makes for a situation that is obviously fraught with danger."[37] Bastiat therefore drew the limits of state authority narrowly. "What are the things that men have the right to impose upon one another by force? Now, I know of only one, and that is justice." Justice could be a broad term, but not for Bastiat: "When the law and compulsion hold a man in accordance with justice, they impose on him nothing other than pure negation. They impose only an abstention from causing harm." Bastiat wanted a purely night watchman state. Any attempt by the state to go beyond its limited remit was unjust because it required plundering people either directly, through taxation, or indirectly,

35. Without a theory of evolution, Bastiat came to the same conclusions as Herbert Spencer in this regard. They were moral commonplaces at the time.

36. Bastiat, *Economic Harmonies*, https://oll.libertyfund.org/titles/79#Bastiat_0187_1541; *Economic Harmonies*, https://oll.libertyfund.org/titles/79#Bastiat_0187_1516.

37. Bastiat, *Economic Sophisms*, https://oll.Libertyfund.org/titles/276#Bastiat_0182_819; *Economic Harmonies*, https://oll.libertyfund.org/titles/79#Bastiat_0187_118; Bastiat, *The Law*, 30; Bastiat, "The State," https://oll.libertyfund.org/titles/2393#Bastiat_1573-01_1794.

through tariffs and monopolies. In the case of colonialism, it involved plundering entire nations—Bastiat resolutely opposed the French colonization of Algeria. Such unjustified state action harmed society both directly and indirectly. If we had "noninterference of the state in private affairs, needs, and satisfactions would develop naturally. We would not see poor families seeking literary education before they had bread. We would not see towns growing in population at the expense of the countryside or the countryside at the expense of towns. We would not see those large scale migrations of capital, labor, or populations triggered by legislative measures."[38]

Bastiat, unlike Bentham, did not attribute the desire for plunder chiefly to minorities, to would-be monopolists, established clergies, monarchs and their courts, etc. Everyone had the impulse to plunder. People wanted everything from the state, but they did not want to pay for it. The only way to achieve this was by plundering other people, whether the wealthy, the people in some other industry, the people in a neighboring country, the urbanites, the rural people, etc. All of this, according to Bastiat, was the result of a lack of understanding: "The state has nothing it has not taken from the people, it cannot distribute largesse to the people. The people know this, since they never cease to demand reductions in taxes . . . but at the same time they never cease to demand handouts of every kind from the state." People wanted to plunder others through taxes, but did not want to pay taxes themselves. This was the basic mistake of all forms of socialism, which "consists in demanding everything from the state while giving it nothing, this is illusionary, absurd, puerile, contradictory, and dangerous." A liberal government would need to pay for itself by taxation as well, but since the scope of government would be much smaller, it would require much lower taxation, and the taxation that remained would be justified by the necessary services it provided to all.[39]

For Bastiat, liberalism was essentially a party of opposition to the state. Indeed, opposing the state was the whole purpose of politics from a liberal perspective: "The role of the opposition, and I would even say that of parliament as a whole, . . . consists solely in keeping the government within its limits." For most liberals, representative government was the answer to the problem of how to limit state plunder, since in a representative government the interests of the people checked those of the plunderers. But Bastiat

38. Bastiat, *The Law*, 27; Bastiat, "The State," https://oll.libertyfund.org/titles/2393#Bastiat _1573-01_1799); *The Law*, 4.

39. Bastiat, "The State," https://oll.libertyfund.org/titles/2450#Bastiat_1573-02_739.

doubted the effectiveness of representative government in achieving this goal, at least in the short term: "I am convinced that in the long run the system of representative government will succeed. Yet it must be admitted that up to now it has not done so. Why? For two quite simple reasons: Governments have had too much discernment, and people have had too little." Rulers, elected or not, were always tempted to plunder. And so were the people, who did not realize that they were plundering themselves.[40]

What was needed, therefore, was to educate the people. Hence Bastiat's career as the most brilliant economic journalist in history, as he has been described. Perhaps the most telling comment on Bastiat as a journalist is that of Flaubert, writing to George Sand in 1871: "In three years, everyone in France will know how to read. Do you think we'll be more advanced? Imagine on the contrary that, in every village, there was one bourgeois, just one, who had read Bastiat, and that this bourgeois was a respected person: things would change." But of course things didn't change. Bastiat's political impact in France was nil. Unlike in Britain, where free trade and laissez-faire economic ideas were the political bread and butter of the "Manchester School" of British liberalism, represented by such men as John Bright and Richard Cobden (the latter corresponded on friendly terms with Bastiat), there was little support for laissez-faire variations of liberalism in France.[41]

One can only speculate, but perhaps the thinness of Bastiat's liberalism was one of the reasons why his brilliant advocacy was not successful with contemporaries. Uninterested in "religious or philosophical ethics," seeing political freedom in purely instrumental terms, Bastiat's liberalism was a classic thin liberalism, based on market economics and a narrowly utilitarian morality, even more so than Bentham's who combined his narrow utilitarianism with politics. Relatively rare in his time, Bastiat's kind of thin liberalism would find more adherents in the twentieth century. The impact of Bentham on the liberalism of his time is debated; that of Bastiat is clearly minimal outside the small band of French laissez-faire economists. Herbert Spencer, by contrast, was one of the most famous intellectuals of his era. He was famous in his native Britain, well-known in France where many of his works were rapidly translated, and, if we are to believe Rudyard Kipling's novel *Kim*, popular even in

---

40. Bastiat, *Economic Sophisms*, https://oll.libertyfund.org/titles/2393#Bastiat_1573-01_1799; https://oll.libertyfund.org/titles/276#Bastiat_0182_832.

41. Leroux, *Lire Bastiat*, 11–13, 44, 47, 91, 123, 203–206; Flaubert, cited in Leroux, *Lire Bastiat*, 40.

Bengal, not to mention Russia, China, Japan, and Egypt. In America he was so influential that Justice Holmes found it necessary to remind his fellow Supreme Court Justices that Spencer's *Social Statics* had not been enacted into the American Constitution.[42]

In some ways Herbert Spencer's relationship to liberalism was similar to that of Bentham. Like Bentham, Spencer's career stretched across a watershed in the history of liberal thought, although in his case it went from the short nineteenth century to the fin de siècle (he published his first book in 1851 and his last in 1902). Spencer began as the adversary of Macaulay and Mill, and ended by opposing modern liberalism, as a classical liberal who never recognized poverty as something liberals need fear or invoke the state to ameliorate.

A sociobiologist who added a new, "scientific" layer to liberalism—evolution—an eccentric moralist, and a thorough libertarian, to use an anachronistic twentieth-century term, Spencer was also in many ways far more a mainstream liberal than either Bentham or Bastiat. Yet he was equally a partisan of a kind of thin liberalism that endured well after he himself was largely forgotten.

Spencer and Evolution: For Better or Worse

Spencer is best known in the twenty-first century, if he is known at all, as a Social Darwinist. Strictly speaking, the association is false, but on a deeper level it is not far from the truth. Spencer's notion of evolution was formed before *The Origin of Species* (1859), and owed more to Lamarck than to Darwin. In his time in many respects it was Spencer, not Darwin, who was the great teacher of evolution, and Darwin himself eventually reluctantly adopted Spencer's phrase "survival of the fittest." Spencer's theories on just about everything were derived from evolution. The phrase "Social Darwinism" conveys a eugenicist approach to society, which Spencer shared, and a general hardheartedness toward the poor and unfortunate, more or less tinged with racism. Spencer was no friend of the poor, at least of those he called the "undeserving"

---

42. Duncan Bell, "Empire and Imperialism," 886. One historian wrote that "it would be difficult to overestimate Spencer's popularity in the United States during the quarter-century after the Civil War (over 350,000 copies of his works were sold in America between 1860 and 1903)." Doherty, *Radicals for Capitalism*, 35. And not only in the West. See Bayly, "European Political Thought," 851; Lightman, ed., *Global Spencerism*. Holmes's remark is in his dissent in *Lochner vs. New York*, 1905.

poor, which was most of them. As for racism, Spencer is more difficult to pi-
geonhole: his resolute anti-imperialism was accompanied by a great deal of
sarcasm directed at the supposedly superior "white race," but he also praised
America as a happy blend of "Aryan races."[43]

Spencer's theory of evolution is key to understanding his brand of liberalism, and how it both stands on and overturns the three pillars of mainstream
liberal argument: freedom, markets, and morals. If in the 1850s his emphasis
on biology was relatively rare, by the fin de siècle, with considerable assistance
from his own writings, it was part of much liberal (and illiberal) thought. During the short nineteenth century, when arguments for liberalism appealed to
"science," the sciences they appealed to were typically economics and history,
rather than the sociology and biology prominent in the fin de siècle. When
Kant, Madison, and Constant wrote, biology was in its infancy. Sociology, if
masterfully practiced by proto-liberals like Montesquieu and liberals like Tocqueville, had no recognized disciplinary status, and Auguste Comte, the inventor of the term "sociology," was no liberal. With Spencer, by contrast, history
and even economics took a back seat to sociology, of which he is considered
a founder. But he used sociology merely as an illustration for what he called
"super-organic evolution." In his emphasis on what a later age would call "so-
ciobiology," Spencer was a key transitional figure from the first-wave, Liberalism 1.0, of the short nineteenth century to the second-wave, Liberalism 2.0, of
the fin de siècle (see chapter 7). Along with debates about the new fear, i.e.,
poverty, Liberalism 2.0 integrated new kinds of "scientific" argument into liberalism. In the fin de siècle, scientific arguments based on evolution, such as
Spencer's, became a means of thinning out liberalism through biological reductionism—a role taken over by economics in the second half of the twentieth century. Spencer played a key role in this, even if he was in many respects
less reductionist than often portrayed.[44]

For Spencer, genetic evolution, the result of both random and acquired
characteristics, determined social change. Spencer used both Darwin (random
genetic variation) *and* Lamarck (the passing on of useful traits acquired during

43. Offer, *Herbert Spencer and Social Theory*, 14; Spencer, "The Americans—A Conversation,"
16:480. Even "Darwin's bulldog," T. H. Huxley, thought that in social theory Spencer, not Darwin, was the pioneer of the use of the concept of evolution. See Offer, *Herbert Spencer and Social
Theory*, 14–15.

44. Spencer, *Principles of Sociology*, vol. 1, https://oll.libertyfund.org/titles/2642#lf1650-01
_label_061

an individual's lifetime) to understand evolution: evolution occurred "either by survival of the fittest [Darwin], or by the inherited effects of use and disuse [Lamarck], or by both." It happened slowly. According to Spencer, human beings had still not fully adjusted "to the partially civilized present," but humanity would, "if allowed to do so, slowly adjust itself to the requirements of a fully civilized future," if evolution was not interfered with. Civilization exerted a steady pressure on the evolution of human beings to better equip them for civilized societies. Spencer concluded, rather like Montesquieu and Tocqueville, but with a biological rationale that, over time, laws had genetic, evolutionary consequences: "every law which serves to alter men's modes of action . . . cause[s] in course of time adjustments to their natures." Like his predecessors he regarded this as a slow process.[45]

Spencer made an evolutionary argument for the rise of liberalism, as he understood it, and for its inevitable future triumph. "Militant" illiberal societies reflected a less-evolved human past, and "industrial" naturally liberal ones represented the fully evolved human future. The present was a mixture of the two. Evolution followed a predictable general course, according to Spencer, from homogeneity toward heterogeneity. The progression was from simple societies to complex ones, from human relationships based on status to those based on contract, and from militant societies to industrial ones. It was a biological process. In "man but little civilized there does not exist the nature required for extensive voluntary co-operation." Cooperation had to be compelled by force, for example through slavery and by violence. For militant societies to make war successfully, they needed highly centralized decision-making, strong hierarchies, and governments that intervened powerfully in all aspects of people's lives. They were essentially despotic in nature. "So long as militancy predominates, the constitution of the state had to be one in which the ordinary citizen is subject either to an autocrat or to an oligarchy." In a militant society, it was necessary that people have absolute faith in government. The theoretical reflection of this was the idea of the divine right of kings.[46]

Militant societies gradually, "generation after generation," created human beings capable of voluntary subordination, and as war became less frequent,

45. Burrow, *Evolution and Society*, 200, and passim; Spencer, *Principles of Ethics*, 2:277; Spencer, cited in Offer, *Herbert Spencer*, 79; Spencer, *The Man Versus The State*, 124; Spencer, *The Man Versus The State*, 247.

46. Offer, *Herbert Spencer*, 14; Spencer, cited in Mingardi, 57; Spencer, *The Man Versus The State*, 171.

evolution favored the development of industrial societies whose voluntary means of cooperation were more efficient in producing goods, and thus in reproducing their members. In industrial societies, "whereas of old, the working part existed for the benefit of the fighting part, now the fighting part exists mainly for the benefit of the working part." People grew ever more free, in principle, to make ever more choices, whether it was where they lived, how they dressed, worshipped, or worked, without fear or compulsion. This was reflected, in Spencer's view, following Sir Henry Maine, in a transition from militant societies based on hereditary / hierarchical "status," to industrial societies based on voluntary "contract" between equals.[47]

Militant society was thus by nature illiberal, whereas industrial society was liberal. To the extent voluntary cooperation replaced involuntary cooperation, it "rightly bring[s] about a correlative decrease of faith in governmental ability and authority," and "strengthens the consciousness of personal rights." Thus, "progress to a higher social type is marked by relinquishments of functions" by the state. This was the situation of modern Europe, where "there has been a change from a social order in which individuals exist for the benefit of the State, to a social order in which the State exists for the benefit of individuals." But there was further to go. Like Marx, Spencer foresaw the state withering away as the conflicts that it was the state's vocation to regulate disappeared, as more civilized human beings evolved. Liberalism itself would cease to have a purpose because there would be nothing left to fear, whether from the state or any other source. The utopian element in liberalism was strong in Spencer's evolutionism.[48]

Most nineteenth-century Western societies, according to Spencer, were intermediate forms, with a mix of industrial and militant characteristics. Politically, therefore, governments needed to contain both militant and industrial elements. Getting the proportions right was a matter for debate. The true conservative defended necessary aspects of militant compulsion, while the true liberal fought for the state to move closer to the industrial ideal of limited government. Much to Spencer's regret, after the 1860s he saw a "redevelopment of militancy." As a result, "the spirit of regimentation proper to the militant type has been spreading throughout the administration of civil life."[49]

47. Spencer, cited in Offer, *Spencer*, 232; Mingardi, *Spencer*, 62–63; Spencer, *Ethics*, vol. 2:461.

48. Spencer, *The Man Versus The State*, 172; *Ethics*, 2:520; *Principles of Sociology*, vol. 2, cited in Offer, *Spencer*, 232; Burrow, *Evolution and Society*, 222; Spencer, *Ethics*, 1:290.

49. Spencer, *Ethics* 2:59; *Principles of Sociology*, cited in Offer, *Spencer*, 230, 238; Spencer, *Social Statics*, 288–289; *Ethics*, 2:461–462.

Modern militancy was embodied, for Spencer, in the imperialism and international aggression rapidly increasing in fin de siècle Europe. It was also evident in the rise of socialism, which regimented workers and production through compulsory cooperation. The two were often linked in practice: Wilhelmine Germany, in his view, led the way in both militarism and state socialism. Spencer became quite pessimistic, at least for the intermediate term: "though . . . we are commencing a long course of re-barbarization from which the reaction may take very long in coming, I nevertheless hold that a reaction will come, and look forward with hope to a remote future of a desirable kind. . . . Did I think that men were likely in the far future to be anything like what they are now, I should contemplate with equanimity the sweeping away of the whole race."[50]

In the short run, Spencer was not opposed to the persistence of some militant aspects in social life. Militantism embodied the "worship of power," but "we must admit that this power-worship has fulfilled, and does still fulfill, a very important function, and that it may advantageously last as long as it can," until evolution bred the need for it out of human society, which could then be fully organized for the benefit of the individual, rather than for the benefit of the state.[51]

But for these good things to happen, evolution had to be allowed to pursue its civilizing mission unhindered by misguided attempts to stop it. People had to be "allowed to bear the pains attendant on their defect of character. . . . all interposing between humanity and the conditions of its existence— cushioning-off consequences by poor-laws or the like—serves but to neutralize the remedy and prolong the evil." Spencer thus opposed "Acts of parliament to save silly people from the evils which putting faith in empirics[52] may entail upon them," as well as poor laws which encouraged improvident marriages by relieving parents of the responsibility to feed their children (public education did so to a lesser extent by relieving them of the responsibility to educate them). It was "folly" to try "to protect men against themselves because it would

50. Spencer to Blunt, October 6, 1898, cited in Offer, *Spencer*, 243.

51. Spencer, *Social Statics*, 426. It is going too far to say that this means that "for Spencer, the industrial type of society was *not* the perfect form." His preference for what he called the ethics of amity over the ethics of hate, and his hope that one day the ethic of beneficence would no longer conflict with the ethic of justice, show that for Spencer perfection could only be achieved in an industrial society. Cf. Offer, *Spencer*, 244.

52. Unlicensed doctors and quack medical treatments.

lead to the degeneration of the race. Non-intervention was painful to the observer: evolution was red in tooth and claw. But in the long run it was beneficial. "Partly by weeding out those of lowest development, and partly by subjecting those who remain to this never-ceasing discipline of experience, nature secures the growth" of a better race.[53]

One can see why Spencer was branded a "Social Darwinist." And yet Spencer also thought that "in so far as the severity of this process can be mitigated by the spontaneous sympathy of men for each other, it is proper that it should be mitigated." In order to understand the seeming contradiction, which was at the heart of Spencer's liberalism, it is essential to understand two things, only the first of which is usually emphasized by commentators: Spencer's theory of a laissez-faire state, and Spencer's theory of ethics.[54]

According to Spencer, in an ideal industrial society, the only function of the state was to enforce justice, that is, to preserve individual freedom from infringement.[55] The government was the guardian of neither the physical nor the spiritual welfare of the population. The state's sole duty was enforcement of the "law of equal freedom": "Every man is free to do that which he will, provided he infringes not the equal freedom of any other man."[56]

Government rules and regulations unjustly limited individual freedom. But they did worse: according to Spencer, the "philanthropists" in power "are in many cases insuring the future ill-being of men while eagerly pursuing their present well-being." Every unnecessary interference with laissez-faire did not merely slow evolution toward the good, but encouraged evolution toward the worse. Equity and evolution run in tandem in Spencer's thought. In this as in much else he was almost a mainstream liberal, combining political freedom (at least when exercised properly, to limit government), markets, and morals

53. Spencer, *Social Statics*, 351; see also *The Man Versus the State*, 90; *Social Statics*, 377. Spencer's fear that natural selection would disappear from modern society was very different from Darwin's view. See Stack, "Charles Darwin's Liberalism," 525–554, 538. See also 541.

54. Leonard, "Origins of the Myth of Social Darwinism," 37–51; Spencer, *Social Statics*, 379.

55. Spencer extended the role of the state in a few instances. He regarded land as different from other forms of property, in his youth going so far as to think that landownership ought to be nationalized. He also thought the state should have responsibility for ensuring clean air and rivers. Offer, *Spencer*, 291; Spencer, *Social Statics*, https://oll.libertyfund.org/title/spencer-social-statics-1851#lf0331_label_126.

56. Spencer, *Ethics*, 2:272. *The Man Versus The State*, 125. Spencer discussed at some length the relationship between Kant's view of justice and his. See his appendix A to the *Theory of Ethics*, "The Kantian Idea of Rights."

to anchor a world evolving toward freedom from fear. Only the emphasis on the scientific theory of evolution was new—but it was crucial.[57]

Unfortunately, from Spencer's perspective, rather than letting evolution pursue its course, people increasingly wished to interfere with it. Spencer was appalled that people "speak of Laissez-faire as an exploded doctrine" and "are no longer frightened at the thought of socialism." They "think it wrong that each man should receive benefits proportionate to his efforts. . . . Their doctrine is . . . let there be equal division of unequal earnings." This was a violation of justice. Spencer feared that injustice would be no bar to socialism. "The fanatical adherents of a social theory are capable of taking any measures, no matter how extreme, for carrying out their views: holding, like the merciless priesthoods of past times, that the end justifies the means." They would use coercion, and the better to coerce, they would use the most powerful source of coercion available, the state.[58]

State coercion no longer took the form of torturers and executioners. Society had evolved, and coercion was now embodied in the tax collector, whose services were increasingly necessary as the state went beyond the night watchman function it was justified in performing. All taxation, for Spencer, was coercion—money individuals had been free to spend was no longer available to them. Some minimal taxation was necessary for the government to fulfill its necessary functions, but anything beyond that was slavery. A slave, according to Spencer, was a person who was forced to labor on another's behalf, without their consent (an image later borrowed from Spencer by the late twentieth-century libertarian philosopher Robert Nozick, see chapter 10). To the extent that the government took your income in unjustified taxation, you were a slave, even if the government chose to give back to you more in benefits than you paid. In such circumstances "each member of the community as an individual would be a slave to the community as a whole." What socialists proposed was trading freedom in return for material welfare, and "the final result would be a revival of despotism." Thus Spencer's fear of socialism ended in the classic fear of all liberalisms: despotism—however, socialism was now represented not just by socialists, but also by people who, much to Spencer's annoyance, called themselves liberals.[59]

57. Spencer, *The Man Versus The State*, 174.

58. Spencer, *The Man Versus The State*, 94; *Ethics*, 2:454; Spencer, "From Freedom to Bondage" in the Liberty Fund edition of *The Man Versus The State* (Indianapolis, 1982), 246.

59. Spencer, *The Man Versus The State*, 103, 101.

According to Spencer, liberalism once fought to adapt British politics to industrial society and strove to get rid of coercive laws like the Corn Laws, restrictions on the freedom of movement of the poor, and monopolies. In the past, "Liberalism habitually stood for individual freedom *versus* State-coercion." But in the England of the 1880s, liberals sponsored increased coercion: regulation and tax increases. Instead of setting people free to spontaneously advance, liberal governments were "developing administrative arrangements of a kind proper to a lower kind of society—are bringing about retrogression while aiming at progression."[60] An example of this, for Spencer, was the history of English education:

> On the day when £30,000 a year in aid of education was voted as an experiment, the name of idiot would have been given to an opponent who prophesied that in 50 years the sum spent through imperial taxes and local rates would amount to £10,000,000 or who said that the aid to education would be followed by aids to feeding and clothing, or who said that parents and children, alike deprived of all option, would, even if starving, be compelled by fine or imprisonment to conform, and receive that which, with papal assumption, the State calls education. No one, I say, would have dreamt that out of so innocent-looking a germ would have so quickly evolved this tyrannical system.[61]

In England it was through Parliament that injustice was inflicted. The divine right of kings had become the divine right of parliaments, and "the divine right of parliaments means the divine right of majorities." To prevent unjustified coercion, liberals had to reject unlimited parliamentary authority just as they once rejected unlimited royal authority. Liberals had to use political freedom to limit government's capacity for injustice.[62]

Spencer began as a supporter of universal suffrage, for both men and women, for just this reason, the same as that given by Bentham—that universal suffrage would serve as a check on government. Democratic government meant "less government. Constitutional forms mean this, Political freedom means this. Democracy means this." But as time went on, Spencer decided that a parliament elected by universal suffrage was more likely to expand than limit government. He therefore turned against universal suffrage. Adopting the

60. Spencer, *The Man Versus The State*, 66; *The Man Versus The State*, 174, 61, 69.

61. Spencer, "From Freedom to Bondage," 242–243.

62. Spencer, *The Man Versus The State*, 144; 77, 169.

standard liberal position and dismissing the idea of a "right" to vote, he considered the capacity of the voter to make a good choice. Women came out the losers: they should not be allowed to vote because their greater "love of the helpless" would lead them to support "public actions that are unduly regardful of the inferior as compared with the superior." Women had undue regard for the needy, and if they had the vote it would result "in still more numerous breaches . . . than at present" of the law of equal freedom and the principle of justice. The only thing in politics that mattered to Spencer was "the limitation of the functions of the State." Once women appeared unlikely to agree, they had no place in Spencer's politics.[63]

Spencer's broad political goal of limiting the power of the state was in line with that of mainstream liberalism, although his strict adherence to a night watchman state was not. He also parted company with the mainstream liberal view of politics in rejecting any positive value for political participation in itself. Constant attempted to combine the best elements of ancient and modern freedom; liberals as diverse as Kant, Tocqueville, and Mill thought that political participation was in itself a form of human perfection. But for Spencer, "the giving of a vote, considered in itself, in no way furthers the voter's life, as does the exercise of those various liberties we properly call our rights." Thus "the acquirement of so-called political rights is by no means equivalent to the acquirement of rights properly so called. The one is but an instrumentality for the obtainment and maintenance of the other." As one commentator noted, "for Spencer, unlike Aristotle, politics is not an integral component of the good life." The political pillar of liberalism was a hollow one in Spencer's thought.[64]

Given Spencer's view that evolution should not be interfered with, and that the state had no right or duty to intervene in matters of social welfare, one might be tempted to consider him a latter-day Malthus, a by-word for harsh treatment of the poor and restrictions on their ability to reproduce—as indeed many have done. Yet this is to ignore what Spencer saw as the natural tendency

63. Doherty and Gray, "Herbert Spencer," 476, 481; Spencer, cited in Doherty and Gray, "Herbert Spencer," 478; Spencer, *Ethics*, 2:216; Offer, *Herbert Spencer*, 90; Doherty and Gray, "Herbert Spencer," 488; Spencer, cited in Doherty and Gray, "Herbert Spencer," 480. Spencer had other reasons for reversing his views on women's suffrage, but this was the most important.

64. Doherty and Gray, "Herbert Spencer," 475–490, 484; Spencer, *Ethics*, 196; Doherty and Gray, "Herbert Spencer," 484–485.

of human evolution: altruism. The rise of industrial society with its emphasis on voluntary cooperation was supposed to make people kinder, more able to take pleasure in the pleasure of others, and thus more inclined to help them. To aid this process, Spencer devoted decades to what he considered the capstone of his life's work, the development of an ethics of altruism.[65]

Spencer's theory of ethics was the culmination of his thought and the essence of his idiosyncratic liberalism. For Spencer, there were two kinds of morality: one based on self-interest, which led to justice and the law of equal freedom; the other based on sympathy or "beneficence," which led to altruism. The state must enforce justice. It had to punish murders, require contracts to be fulfilled, repress fraud. The state should have nothing to do with altruism. The first part of an individual's moral development was equally about justice. But without altruism, an individual's moral development was incomplete. "The limit of evolution is consequently not reached, until, beyond avoidance of direct and indirect injuries to others, there are spontaneous efforts to further the welfare of others." This was necessary to achieve "the highest life." Spencer defined progress as the creation of the kind "of man and society required for the complete manifestation of every one's individuality" (a notable example of positive freedom in the "classical liberal" canon). Such a fully developed individuality required the expression of benevolence / altruism.[66]

For Spencer, altruism had to be confined to the private sphere: the government had no business engaging in altruism, and any attempt on its part to do so was unjust and immoral. This was a great departure from much previous liberal moral thought. For Adam Smith, by contrast, on some occasions government was justified in compelling benevolence: "the civil magistrate is entrusted with the power not only of preserving the public peace by restraining injustice, but of promoting the prosperity of the commonwealth . . . he may prescribe rules, therefore, which not only prohibit mutual injuries among fellow-citizens, but command mutual good offices to a certain degree," that is, benevolence. This, Smith continued, was "of all the duties of a lawgiver . . . perhaps . . . that which requires the greatest delicacy and reserve to execute with propriety and judgement. To neglect it altogether exposes the commonwealth to many gross disorders and shocking enormities, and to push it too far is destructive of all liberty, security, and justice." Nevertheless, this was

65. Spencer, cited in Mingardi, *Spencer*, 71, Mingardi, *Spencer*, 71–72.
66. Spencer, *Ethics*, 2:289, 466; *Social Statics*, 379; Offer, *Spencer*, 246.

how Smith justified the government requiring and financing the education of poor children.[67]

This was wholly illegitimate for Spencer. Altruism belonged to the realm of the family, or to civil society, and "even a partial intrusion of the family *régime* into the *régime* of the State, will be slowly followed by fatal results," namely, interfering with the survival of the fittest. It would also be unjust, taking A's money without due cause to give it to B. Therefore, "while enforcement of justice must be a public function, the exercise of benevolence must be a private function." "While the first may be rightly enforced, the second had to be left to voluntary action."[68]

What Spencer meant in practice can be seen in his attitude to charity. He distinguished between three kinds of assistance to the poor: government aid; aid given by private associations; and aid given directly by individuals. Government aid was ruled out because it interfered with the beneficial processes of evolution and because it was inefficient, requiring a large and expensive bureaucracy neither intended to distinguish nor capable of distinguishing between the deserving and undeserving poor. It was also ruled out on grounds of justice. The government had no right to take A's money, via taxes, for the benefit of B. If the state "taxes one class for the benefit of another, it exceeds its functions and, in a measure contravenes the first of them," namely the enforcement of justice and the law of freedom. Sympathy for the poor was no virtue when it resulted in a violation of equity.[69]

Private charity distributed by associations did not violate justice, but it shared the disadvantages of state charity. Because it was given through paid intermediaries, "the transaction, instead of being one which cultivates the moral nature on both sides, excludes culture of the moral nature as much as is practicable, and introduces a number of bad motives." Above all, charity by private associations, like government aid, was incapable of distinguishing between worthy and unworthy recipients. "The worthy suffer rather than ask assistance, while the worthless press for assistance and get it." The very large number of people who used free medical care in London was proof, for Spencer, that most of them were not really indigent and were "able to pay their doctors." Furthermore, he believed, once you gave people free medical care, they soon started demanding free food, and then cash. The result was

67. Smith, *TMS*, 116, Winch, "Scottish Political Economy," 459.

68. Spencer, *The Man Versus The State*, 128; *Ethics*, 2:290, 293.

69. Spencer, *Ethics*, vol. 2:395; *The Man Versus The State*, 136, 131.

once again the frustration of evolution and the degeneracy of the morality of the poor.[70]

Instead, Spencer favored "that charity which may be described as helping men to help themselves," as well as donations to those who truly were the victims of accidents, unforeseeable events, and fraud. "Even the prodigal, after severe hardship . . . may properly have another trial afforded him." For the sake of encouraging altruism, Spencer was willing to interfere to some extent with evolution: "although by these ameliorations the process of adaptation must be remotely interfered with, yet in the majority of cases, it will not be so much retarded in one direction as it will be advanced in another."[71]

That "other direction" was improving the altruism and beneficence of the giver. To the response that few people were charitably inclined, Spencer, oddly enough for a liberal, touted the merits of coercion, albeit not government coercion: "in the absence of a coercive public law there often exists a coercive public opinion." If private voluntary charity were to replace compulsory public charity, public opinion would force "contributions from the indifferent or the callous," who would gradually learn to find generosity pleasurable, thus creating a benefit on both sides. Interest and altruism would eventually coincide, partly because evolution ensured that once human beings and human civilization were sufficiently evolved, "there will disappear that apparently permanent opposition between egoism and altruism. . . . The individual would not have to balance between self-regarding impulses and other-regarding impulses," but would get so much pleasure from helping others that it would be the greatest pleasure to themselves. In these circumstances, Spencer believed, private charity "would go a long way towards meeting the needs" of the poor. It would at any rate be more judicious: it "would, on average, be given with the effect of fostering the unfortunate worthy rather than the innately unworthy."[72]

The most striking thing about Spencer's opposition to government or associational aid to the poor, etc., is that he thought his opposition was useless. He expected people to reply to him that "my conscience shows me that the feeble and the suffering must be helped; and if selfish people won't help them, they must be forced by law to help them. . . . Every man with sympathy in him must feel that hunger and pain and squalor must be prevented." This, Spencer wrote, was "the kind of response which I expect will be made by nine out of ten." His

70. Spencer, *Ethics*, 2:398, 399, 401.

71. Spencer, *Social Statics*, 283.

72. Spencer, *Ethics*, 2:404; *The Man Versus The State*, 128.

expectations were not disappointed. Spencer did not care because he thought he was ahead of his time, and therefore rejection was inevitable. His general argument for the restriction of government power was only appropriate for a purely industrial type of society, and thus "partially incongruous with that semi-militant, semi-industrial type, which now characterizes advanced nations."[73]

One of the ways in which Spencer broke with the mainstream liberalism of the short nineteenth century was that in his work the utopian element that was always part of liberalism was so strongly dominant. Not only was Spencer, in his own mind, a partisan of movement (even though to contemporaries and some readers he has appeared to be a conservative—the parallels with Hayek's "Why I am Not a Conservative" essay are striking), he was the partisan of a movement that he knew could not yet, in the social / evolutionary circumstances, take place.

Spencer's views on aid to the poor are a useful introduction to the moral reasoning at the heart of this thought. As with most mainstream liberals, Spencer's utopianism included an economic and a political doctrine, as well as a moral theory. But there was a crucial difference between his morals and that of the mainstream, a difference that was partly anticipated by Bastiat and persists in many twentieth-century libertarians: an absolute separation between public and private morals. Spencer made an absolute moral separation between state and society, but if the state was forbidden to take any interest in altruism, that did not mean Spencer had none. It surfaced in some surprising connections, for example his discussion of economic competition: "each citizen, while in respect of this competition not to be restrained externally, ought to be restrained internally," not just to refrain from fraud, but if head of a business to refrain from "the ruin of his competitors," because of "sympathetic self-restraint."[74] Deliberately selling at a loss to put a weaker competitor out of business was "commercial murder," and ought to be morally condemned nearly as much as bloodshed. There was some justification to Spencer's view that he was not in the least hard-hearted: "I do not see how there could be ideas more diametrically opposed to that brutal individualism which some persons ascribe to me."[75]

73. Spencer, *The Man Versus The State*, 132.

74. In contrast to Milton Friedman, who famously argued that the only moral duty of a firm was to make profits legally.

75. Offer, *Spencer*, 292; *Ethics*, 2:301, 305. On the other hand, if lowering the price was the result of new technology, and was still profitable, then it was acceptable even if it put the competitor out of business. *Ethics*, 2:302; Spencer, cited in Mingardi, *Spencer*, 71.

Spencer's view of money-making was remarkably similar to that of his friendly enemy, John Stuart Mill. Mill and Spencer were open about their disagreements—and about their mutual intellectual respect. Mill went so far as to offer to subsidize the publication of some of Spencer's works, an offer Spencer felt compelled to decline because of their disagreements. Nonetheless Mill had reason to be sympathetic to Spencer. One of the most quoted passages in Mill's *Principles of Political Economy* is "there would be as much room for improving the Art of Living, and much more likelihood of its being improved, when minds ceased to be engrossed by the art of getting on," that is, of making money and social climbing. Spencer was concerned by the same problem: "And if we ask—Why this intense desire [for riches]? the reply is—It results from the indiscriminate respect paid to wealth. To be distinguished from the common herd—to be somebody—to make a name, a position—this is the universal ambition; and to accumulate riches is alike the surest and the easiest way of fulfilling this ambition." This, for Spencer, was an attitude that should and would be overcome. "When this age of material progress has yielded mankind its benefits," then "the desire for applause will lose that predominance which it now has. . . . when the wish to be admired is in large measure replaced by the wish to be loved; that strife for distinction which the present phase of civilization shows us will be greatly moderated." People should ideally take more time for enjoyment, and what was needed was a "gospel of relaxation."[76]

But for this to occur, a change in public opinion regarding wealth had to happen. This would eventually come to pass, Spencer thought, but not in the near future. Just as in his views about helping the poor, Spencer did not expect public opinion to agree with him—but this time he endorsed, at least temporarily, his own rejection. "We have little hope, however, that any such higher tone of public opinion will shortly be reached. The present condition of things appears to be, in great measure, a necessary accompaniment of our present phase of progress. . . . To subjugate Nature and bring the powers of production and distribution to their highest perfection, is the task of our age, and probably will be the task of many future ages."[77]

Spencer was a moralist, as his strong endorsement of altruism and rejection of materialism demonstrated. He believed that private property and free

---

76. Spencer, *Autobiography* (Arkose Press, 2015), 2:134–36; Spencer, "The Morals of Trade," in *Essays*, 3:143; "Speech at Delmonico's," Nov. 9, 1882, *Essays*, vol. 3.

77. Spencer, "The Morals of Trade," 149–150.

markets were endorsed by both justice and political economy, and were necessary for individual freedom and for moral as well as social development. In these respects he took the stance of a mainstream liberal, as he did when he saw limiting the power and scope of the state as a prime purpose of politics, even if in his nearly pure laissez-faire attitude he was in the minority.

And yet, for all the ways in which Spencer argued like a mainstream liberal, seemingly building his liberalism on the three pillars of freedom, markets, and morals, there were nevertheless crucial differences. The issue was not biology—Spencer's evolutionary biology was highly influential in the fin de siècle, on both the left and right. But when it came to political freedom, his purely negative view of the purpose of political participation already separated him from mainstream liberals. When it came to the relationship between morality and politics, the separation between Spencer and the mainstream became an unbridgeable abyss. Spencer chiseled out much of the political pillar of mainstream liberalism, retaining politics only as a struggle to avoid harm. He did the same with the moral pillar, demanding social justice, in his own sense of the phrase, but rejecting social beneficence. Yet Spencer was a moralist and even a perfectionist who rejected the wholehearted pursuit of material wealth. His was indeed a liberalism with some things missing.

The important ways in which Bentham, Bastiat, and Spencer departed from the mainstream of liberalism shows that the need for all three pillars, freedom, markets, and morals, was always contested within the liberal tradition by those who thought a narrower foundation was stronger. One of the things all three writers were doing was arguing against mainstream liberals who insisted that liberal arguments needed all three pillars for both legitimacy and efficacy. For Bentham, Bastiat, and Spencer, attempts to give liberalism such a broad base, rather than serving to ward off despotism, religious fanaticism, revolution, and reaction, served to provide justifications for coercion and terror to sinister interests, plunderers, or evolutionarily regressive elements. This was a minority view among the liberalisms of the short nineteenth century. Nevertheless, it shows how liberalism always contained dissonant elements who addressed the same fears as other liberals, in the context of the same issues, but used different and thinner arguments to make their case.

It is equally important to note that even the thin liberalisms of the short nineteenth century were not exclusively attached to a narrow view of self-interest that dictated a strict adherence to laissez-faire. Of the three versions considered in this chapter, only Bastiat held this view. Bentham had a very mixed record when it came to laissez-faire, and was open to any state intervention that might increase the greatest happiness of the greatest number. Spencer was as strong an advocate of a laissez-faire state and a laissez-faire economy as Bastiat, but unlike Bastiat was a moralist whose utilitarianism was always complemented by perfectionism, if only in private form. As we will see in the next chapter, many of the "modern liberalisms" of the fin de siècle and the early twentieth century were perfectionist, anti–laissez-faire, and also quite thin, but in a different way. It turned out it was perfectly possible for liberals to combat the fear of poverty with a morality that was the mirror image of Spencer's: one that reserved the pursuit of interest to the private sphere and assigned altruism to government.

The question of whether a broad or a narrow foundation was best suited to building a wall against fear and cruelty grew ever more heated over the course of the fin de siècle and the twentieth century. By the late twentieth century, thin liberalisms had become the majority view. The period from the fin de siècle through the twentieth century was a time when liberalism faced new challenges arising from new fears, and both individuals and groups were subject to new and utterly terrifying threats. The growth of new layers of liberal thought in response, and also in response to the new hopes and opportunities created by a world continually growing in wealth and education, is the subject of part three.

PART III

New Fears, New Hopes

7

Modern Liberalism versus Classical Liberalism

Liberalism in the Fin de Siècle, 1873–1919

On May 8, 1873, John Stuart Mill died, the short nineteenth century came to an end, and the fin de siècle (1873–1919) began. The date is arbitrary, even in terms of Mill's own production, since important work appeared posthumously in 1874. Watersheds in geography may be traced with precision; in the history of political thought their boundaries often meander across a decade or two, depending on local and individual circumstances. The nineteenth-century English jurist A. V. Dicey dated the transition in British opinion to two different years, 1870 and 1865, which he considered respectively the end of "Individualism" and the beginning of "Collectivism."[1] Collectivism was Dicey's way of describing the desire for state intervention to reduce poverty that many liberals began to express around this time. 1875 or 1885 would have been equally plausible for either. What matters is that an important transition took place. Centered on·the fear of poverty, Liberalism 2.0 dominated fin de siècle liberalism.

During the short nineteenth century the fears that had inspired liberalism were the perennial liberal fear of despotism; the fear of religious fanaticism which dated to the proto-liberalism of the seventeenth and eighteenth centuries; and the fear of revolution / reaction, born with the American and French Revolutions. For the most part these fears had been embodied in the state, and thus liberals had directed much of their attention to limiting the powers of the state. Things changed in the fin de siècle: for the first time, many liberals, the

---

1. Dicey, *Law and Public Opinion*, 46.

"modern liberals," began to fear poverty, and to see the state as their tool to end it.

Poverty is different in kind from previous liberal fears. It wears no uniform, demands no allegiance to dogma or despot. A new kind of fear, it both transformed old liberal remedies and called for new ones. Poverty was not invented in 1873, of course. Indeed, by 1873 the most extreme form of poverty, death by starvation after a bad harvest or three, had disappeared from the West. Yet it was clear that if absolute poverty had not increased, and perhaps even decreased (the subject was and is controversial), many people were experiencing new kinds of poverty, and their poverty was more visible. Whether or not the rain would come had always been unpredictable. Whether or not a financial panic would arrive and the factory would close seemed even more random and even more threatening. The boom and bust cycles of nineteenth-century industrial life were frightening, and poverty was more visible than ever before. The new discipline of sociology cut its teeth on studies of the urban poor, and mass-distribution newspapers brought their readers a new consciousness of social ills.[2] Fear was stimulated by growing urban blight, by the supposed immorality of the urban poor, and perhaps most important, by increasing, and increasingly violent, labor strife.[3] Strikes and the growth of socialist political parties reinforced the old liberal fear of revolution, even if most socialist parties were more reformist than revolutionary. All these phenomena combined to put poverty, and reactions to poverty, at the top of the agenda for liberals in a way it had never been before.

The eradication of poverty thus became a liberal goal, a hope that would grow ever greater with time. It was later encapsulated in American President Franklin D. Roosevelt's "Four Freedoms" speech of 1941, which included "freedom from want" alongside political and religious freedoms. As Raymond Aron put it, "the ambition to eliminate [poverty] was new and testified to a pride that neither the Founding Fathers nor Tocqueville would have shared or approved

2. As both the American Progressive Jane Addams and the classical liberal A. V. Dicey pointed out. See Addams, *Democracy and Social Ethics*, Kindle edition, 3; Dicey, *Law and Public Opinion*, 156ff.

3. "Strike rates increased steadily. In 1892 French workers struck 261 times against 500 companies; most of the efforts remained small and local, and only 50,000 workers were involved. By 1906, the peak French strike year before 1914, 1,309 strikes brought 438,000 workers off the job. British and German strike rates were higher still; in Britain, more than 2,000,000 workers struck between 1909 and 1913." https://www.britannica.com/topic/history-of-Europe/The-rise-of-organized-labour-and-mass-protests. Things were similar in America.

of." Since the fin de siècle public opinion, in Aron's view, had equated subjection to impersonal economic forces with despotic coercion, and thus was born the duty of liberal governments to do something about it.[4]

Fin de siècle liberals' reaction to poverty resulted in an abiding cleavage among liberals: modern liberals feared poverty, and "classical liberals" feared the solutions modern liberals proposed to address the new fear. This problem characterized second-wave liberalism. Although liberals had to confront other challenges and issues in the fin de siècle, including radical nationalism, imperialism, and feminism, as the next chapter will show, it was the fear of poverty, and the reactions it provoked, that shaped Liberalism 2.0.

The fear of poverty was actually both old and new for liberals. It was old in the sense that the poor had always been perceived as a repository of religious fanaticism, economic ignorance, and support for despotism which might lead to revolution or reaction. During the short nineteenth century and before, to think that poverty could be alleviated by anything but the slow action of time had been the mark of a revolutionary. The liberal attitude to poverty in the nineteenth century is exemplified by the British liberals who passed the New Poor Law in 1834 aiming at nothing more than palliative care for a chronic problem: the poorest of the poor would be housed and fed, but except for the long-term effect of lowering their birthrate (men and women were housed separately), there was no expectation that poorhouses would reduce poverty. Even when British liberals abolished the Corn Laws in 1846, the resulting drop in the price of bread was seen as a boon to the poor, but not as causing any significant decline in the poverty rate.

This attitude toward the poor was still present in the fin de siècle, encouraged by labor strife and by poor voters who backed socialist or reactionary parties. It remained as a layer within the oyster of liberal thought. But the old fear was transformed by a new layer of hope: modern liberals, instead of focusing on the poor as a threat to freedom, saw poverty as a threat to the freedom of the poor. They hoped to do something about it with the help of the government. A good example of the difference in liberal attitudes to the poor before and after 1873 can be found with regard to education. Liberals had always favored education. Macaulay had wanted the government to educate the poor because he was afraid that ignorant poor people would be violent, whether as common criminals or as agents of revolution or reaction (see chapter 4). Kant had called for universal education to develop critical thinking

4. Aron, *Essai sur les libertés,* 64, 213.

and moral reasoning (see chapter 3). The result might be occasional social mobility, but the point had been to develop the kind of character that would not murder for profit, whether personal or political.

The modern liberals of the fin de siècle had a different goal for education. They wanted to educate the poor, all the poor, so that they would cease to be poor. This unprecedented hope contrasted strongly with previous liberalisms' recognition that while the growth of commercial society might result in more economic growth and less poverty, the poor would nevertheless be with us always. In the fin de siècle education for all became part of a toolkit for the elimination of poverty, a toolkit that relied on state action to a much greater degree than previous liberalisms had been willing to countenance. The fin de siècle saw the beginning of what would later become known as the welfare state, frequently under liberal auspices, a government-operated machine for addressing and solving the problem of poverty.[5]

Many fin de siècle liberals, however, did not share the new fear or the new hope, rejected the new solutions to poverty as worse than useless, and thought that modern liberals were pursuing a mirage. In their view modern liberals' desire to make war on poverty with the help of the government would create a bureaucratic monster willing and able to exercise arbitrary authority and inflict cruelty in a multitude of ways. They feared the way modern liberals wanted to expand the power and scope of the state in their efforts to eliminate poverty. These liberal opponents of the modern liberals, and there were many, needed a term to distinguish themselves. They could have called themselves simply "old liberals," and some did. However, "old" has rarely appeared as a winning rhetorical strategy when contrasted with modern or new. The term "classical liberal" was first used around 1900 to describe this strand of liberal thought.[6]

Classical liberals thought that modern liberals were revolutionaries or reactionaries themselves. Modern liberal concern for what was called "the social question" led both liberals and their opponents, left and right, to speak of "liberal socialism." Classical liberals called the new social engineering "social-

---

5. "Liberal socialism," however, did not aim to eliminate capitalism.

6. I am not aware of any study of the origins of the term. For an inadequate substitute, see https://books.google.com/ngrams/graph?content=%22classical+liberalism%22&case_insensitive=on&year_start=1800&year_end=2000&corpus=15&smoothing=3&share=&direct_url=t1%3B%2C%22%20classical%20liberalism%20%22%3B%2Cc0#t1%3B%2C%22%20classical%20liberalism%20%22%3B%2Cc0.

ism" without any moderating adjective, even if there was no intention to abolish private property or nationalize the means of production, and they saw in it only schemes to redistribute wealth that gave the taxpaying classes reason to fear without giving anyone grounds for hope. In the classical liberal view modern liberals advocated measures that threatened the economic, moral, and political bulwarks that protected freedom and were the heart of liberalism. They were dangerous to true liberalism even if the revolution they favored did not involve violence and their tyranny showed the greatest respect for the law. Instead of fighting fear, from the classical liberal perspective modern liberals had invented new means and justifications for coercion and the exercise of arbitrary power.

By contrast, from modern liberals' perspective, classical liberals failed to provide any remedy for the poverty that afflicted most people in Western nations. Modern liberals wished, to quote one British newspaper sympathetic to them, that "the too narrow Liberal should shed his rooted conviction that there is no real economic problem. " For modern liberals the once inspiring features of Liberalism 1.0 seemed dull: "across a broad front in both the United States and fin de siècle Europe. . . . Suffrage and constitutionalism, the liberties of trade and person as a political program, bare and alone, these [have] lost much of their earlier luster." They thought classical liberals were behind the times, engaged in blind resistance which opened the door for revolution / reaction, precisely because the classical liberals illiberally refused to address society's most pressing fear. It was the old intra-liberal division between the party of movement and the party of resistance, transformed from political to social terms, in which each side described their opponents as revolutionaries or reactionaries.[7]

The revolution feared by fin de siècle liberals, whether modern or classical, was thus not their parents' revolution. Their nightmares did not feature a repeat of the Jacobin Terror of 1793, Napoleonic despotism, or even the Romantic nationalism of 1848. The revolutionary movements both classical and modern liberals feared in the fin de siècle were not aimed at greater political rights, or constitutions, or ending restrictions on trade or religion. Instead, the new revolutionaries aspired to redistribute income, end unemployment, and nationalize industry—in a word (much-contested) they aspired to a revolutionary socialism that went well beyond the modern liberal program.

7. *Daily Chronicle*, April 2, 1897, cited in Freeden, *the New Liberalism*, 64; Rodgers, *Atlantic Crossings*, 41.

Such new forms of revolution were embodied in the Paris Commune of 1871 and the general strikes that troubled the liberal dream of progress in the fin de siècle. Fin de siècle revolutionaries had no qualms about making some people afraid, indeed gloried in the fear of the bourgeoisie. The threat was all the more dangerous because these new revolutionaries took aspects of the liberal program, whether the fear of poverty or nationalism, and made it the core of their new justifications for arbitrary power. The old liberal fear of revolution hence took on a new meaning in the fin de siècle, transformed by the new fear of poverty.

The Liberalism 2.0 that resulted from the fear of poverty revised many aspects of nineteenth-century liberalism. It produced changes in liberal language, with a new attitude toward rights talk and a more prominent role for positive freedoms; it produced changes in how liberals viewed the history of liberalism, with dueling modern and classical liberal versions; and it produced exceptionally deep and lasting cleavages within the liberal camp, between modern and classical liberals, divergences that long outlasted the fin de siècle. It also saw a transformation in the scientific arguments used to defend liberal principles, integrating the new disciplines of sociology and above all biology into the liberal understanding of the world. All these changes, each in its own way, tempted liberals to narrow the basis of their liberalism, that is to abandon one or two of the three pillars of liberal argument that had dominated nineteenth-century liberal debates. Liberalisms with something missing did not dominate the fin de siècle as they would the late twentieth century, but they became more prominent.

New in the fin de siècle and continuing into the twentieth century was that both the fear of poverty and the revised meaning of revolution led liberals to talk more about rights. During the short nineteenth century, most liberals had not discussed rights very much, or even dismissed them. Bentham and other utilitarians had regarded the idea of natural rights as "nonsense on stilts." The social contract had largely disappeared from liberal discourse, and while never denying that people had rights, they had not been the main focus of canonical liberal authors of the period such as Tocqueville or Macaulay. America, where the language of natural rights remained current, mostly because of the unresolved issue of slavery, was something of an exception, although even in the United States Locke was nearly forgotten during the short nineteenth century (see chapter 1). In some areas, such as suffrage, liberals during the short nineteenth century had gone to great lengths to exclude rights talk.

In the fin de siècle, rights became more central to liberal arguments without any consensus about their nature. Hopes became identified with rights. Thus modern liberal discussions of poverty were often framed in terms of rights—a right to self-development or to a living wage, appeals to a "quasi-contract" to justify progressive taxation and government regulation—while classical liberals denied any and all of these in the name of individual rights to property and free contract. Politically, the fear of poverty encouraged modern liberals to accept a right to vote and universal manhood suffrage by transforming the poor from fearful objects to people with justified fears. Modern liberals justified the right of the poor to vote as their right to take political action to free themselves from fear. When providing financial aid to the poor, modern liberal policies typically rejected requiring good character as a prerequisite for financial assistance. This helped further discredit the notion that good character / moral capacity was required for the vote. The discourse of capacity disappeared from liberal politics. Instead, liberals largely recognized the idea of political rights and the right to vote. Women, however (and in America Blacks and sometimes immigrants), continued to be an exception.

More generally, the fear of poverty highlighted liberalism as a vision of positive freedom, that is freedom as a positive ability to do something, which required the ability to make choices that poverty had hitherto prevented. Modern liberals supported positive freedoms, while classical liberals opposed them, but in both cases it moved the discussion in new directions. The result was a new sort of rights talk for addressing the problem of poverty, even by liberals who had no interest in "natural rights" or regarded it as pernicious nonsense. What most modern liberals meant by "rights" was perhaps best summed up in a 1911 statement by the *Nation*[8] that "the proper meaning of a right", should be construed as something that guarantees "fundamental conditions of social welfare." Essentially this meant a right to be protected from the effects of poverty. One American list of "three indisputable rights" included the right to "a decent home . . . in a respectable neighborhood and at a reasonable rental"; the right to education through secondary school; and the right to employment—the final demand borrowed from the socialists, but omitting the idea of the state as employer of last resort. Equally characteristic was the "right to a living wage" as the necessary basis for all such rights, which should include a right to leisure (paid vacations), and even a "right to consume." The

---

8. This is the British *Nation*. One confusing overlap between American Progressivism and British New Liberalism is that both produced periodicals with the same name.

whole discussion was framed as "The Right to a Decent Life," that is, one without fear, in which positive freedom was possible.[9]

While modern liberals expanded the scope of rights talk for the poor, they contracted it for the rich (and vice versa for classical liberals). During the nineteenth century liberals had claimed that the vote was not a right but a trust, and thus had required limits on political participation. In the fin de siècle the same logic was applied to property rights. For modern liberals, "property that gave its owners economic power over others was held in trust, and its regulation was not an infringement of the rights of ownership but a reflection of their social nature." As the American President Theodore Roosevelt put it in his State of the Nation address in 1908, "business power" could not be permitted to be "irresponsible." For the French Solidarists, property owed a "social debt" that had to be paid. In consequence, if "laissez-faire . . . is not done with as a principle of rational limitation of State interference . . . it is quite done with as a pretext for leaving uncured deadly social evils which admit of curative treatment by State action." Therefore "governmental regulation" should be seen as "not merely a temporary resource, but . . . a normal element of the organization of industry." Liberalism 2.0 both expanded and contracted the sphere of rights, and liberals found themselves talking more about rights than had been the case during the short nineteenth century. Liberals of all stripes increasingly found rights talk useful as a means of solving their problems and warding off their fears.[10]

Nevertheless, in keeping with the oyster-like character of liberalism, in which one layer of liberalism is deposited over another without totally obscuring or replacing it, many fin de siècle liberals continued to prefer a discourse of capacity that excluded certain groups, whether on an ethnic, national, religious, or gender basis. Limiting liberalism, however, was not always the reason liberals spoke in terms of capacity in the fin de siècle; many liberal advocates of women's suffrage, for example, appealed to women's capacities as a reason to give them the vote.

9. "The State and the Right to Work," *Nation*, 18.2.1911, cited in Freeden, *The New Liberalism*, 215; Eisenach, *The Lost Promise of Progressivism*, 3; Maureen A. Flanagan, *America Reformed*, 91–95, 127, 195. In France, see Logue, *From Philosophy to Sociology*, 9.

10. Theodore Roosevelt, 1908 State of the Nation address, http://www.let.rug.nl/usa/presidents/theodore-roosevelt/state-of-the-union-1908.php. Rodgers, *Atlantic Crossings*, 28–29. A German equivalent: "We do not regard state welfare as an emergency measure or as an unavoidable evil, but as the fulfilment of one of the highest tasks of our time and nation." Verein für Sozialpolitik, 1873, cited in Rosenblatt, *Lost Liberalisms*, 220.

The common resort of modern and classical liberals to rights talk did little to bring them together, since their catalog of rights was very different. Each group wished to establish an intellectual and political monopoly over the word "liberal." This resulted in a good deal of polemical distortion. Both groups wrote histories of liberalism to bolster their own genealogical title to be the only legitimate heirs of nineteenth-century liberalism, and each distorted the facts to suit their case. Their efforts have remained influential.

Classical liberals identified historical liberalism with a strict laissez-faire attitude in order to strengthen their case for minimizing the role of government, even when they were well aware that this was not accurate. A. V. Dicey engaged in this when constructing his highly influential distinction between "Collectivism" and "Individualism" (see below). Modern liberals more accurately claimed that they were only adapting attitudes to state intervention frequently adopted by mainstream liberals in the past. But they were less quick to point out that their own emphasis on positive freedom, and the role of the state in promoting it, was in many respects a new departure. Modern liberals also departed from the past in their attitude to redistributing wealth, as classical liberals liked to point out. Proto-liberals and nineteenth-century liberals had frequently supported tax exemptions for the poor, as well as poor laws that had redistributive effects. But modern liberals were willing to use far more direct means than previous generations to relieve poverty, from old age pensions to labor laws to progressive taxation. Modern liberals sought to blur the novelty of their views by arguing that they were merely adopting the traditional liberal tactic of steering between extremist views, in this case those of individualism and socialism: "Logically carried out, the one can be nothing less than anarchism, and the other social despotism." This, from the classical liberal viewpoint, was a fundamental violation of liberal faith because a state that engaged in redistribution made the wealthy afraid. For modern liberals, by contrast, redistribution was nothing for the rich to fear. A limited redistribution of wealth was the best possible bulwark, both ethically and practically, against revolution and despotism.[11]

The fin de siècle thus witnessed a sharp contest over the meaning of the word liberal. During the fin de siècle, liberal increasingly became an adjective, as in "liberal socialist," or if it remained a noun was accompanied by one, hence

11. Rodgers, *Atlantic Crossings*, 76. Ryan "Liberalism 1900–1940," 68, Freeden, *New Liberalism*, 96; Edward Caird, "The Present State of the Controversy," 179. Caird was an important influence on Jane Addams.

"advanced liberal," "New Liberal," "social liberal," or "classical liberal." Liberals of all persuasions attached modifiers to their name that would serve as a lifeboat in difficult times, or at least a nostalgic gesture. In this regard classical liberals affixing their nostalgia for an imagined liberal past were no different from liberal socialists or social liberals looking for a way to improve their electoral fortunes with the proletariat: all used adjectives. Less and less often was "liberal" used unadorned. Differences among liberals were nothing new. Mill in the 1840s had remarked on what different kinds of people were to be found under the common denomination "liberal" in France. But during the short nineteenth century, liberals' common fears and hopes, despite their differences, had united them both in their own eyes and in those of their adversaries on the left and right. In the fin de siècle, their differences seemed more important. This difference required verbal distinctions, and hence the greater need for and emphasis on adjectives.

As an adjective, "liberal" in the fin de siècle was sometimes a throwback to an eighteenth-century usage which had never been entirely abandoned, meaning "generous" or "open-minded."[12] Liberal Protestantism and Liberal Catholicism, for example, frequently retained this sense in the fin de siècle. "Liberal," however, mostly retained its political connotation, notably in "liberal socialism" or "social liberalism." Modern liberals of many sorts became fond of adding "social" or "socialist" to their brand label. The word socialism was used to "describe any enlargement of the functions of government."[13] The reason modern liberals used it, whether as an adjective in "social liberal" or as a noun in "liberal socialist," was to show that they regarded poverty as a problem and thought it needed to be addressed by the state. Nevertheless, modern liberals of all stripes, even those who might call themselves liberal socialists, had to struggle against the pejorative connotations liberals traditionally associated with the word "socialist," even when suggesting, as Sir William Harcourt notoriously did, that "we are all socialists now."[14]

12. See the discussion of the history of the word "liberalism" in chapter 1.

13. This usage of "socialism" has remained current among libertarian and other heirs of the classical liberal tradition into the early twenty-first century.

14. Collini, *Liberalism & Sociology*, 17; Hobhouse, *Liberalism and Other Writings*, 80; Collini, *Liberalism & Sociology*, 35, Freeden, *The New Liberalism*, 25. When the term "liberal socialism" entered the vocabulary, it varied nationally, but followed a broadly similar path. In English the phrase appeared in 1867–77, and then disappears until 1900. In French, "*socialisme libéral*" and "*socialiste libéral*" made a modest appearance in 1850, flourished in the 1860s, and then faded

The word "liberal" thus became a source of strife within the liberal camp, with much denial of nouns and flinging of adjectives. "You are not a liberal, you are a socialist!" "I am a *liberal* socialist!" If so inclined, one can see a Hegelian dialectic at work in the progression of "liberal" from adjective to noun and back again between the mid-eighteenth and late nineteenth century, with "liberal" starting as an adjective, passing through a triumphant nominal phase which stated the liberal thesis, and then confronting a new antithesis within itself expressed by competing adjectives, as the Rationality incarnate in liberalism developed itself.

Another innovation of Liberalism 2.0 was that many modern liberal thinkers, and some classical liberals, preferred to draw the "scientific" support for their liberalism not from economics, but from the new disciplines of sociology and evolutionary biology. Sociology, whose invention is often attributed to two very different kinds of liberal, Herbert Spencer and Emile Durkheim, was in a sense *not* new: if one can call Spencer and Durkheim the founders of modern sociology, one can also give the title to Montesquieu. By any definition, Tocqueville was a good sociologist too. But modern liberals like Jane Addams used sociology in a new way: they saw sociological facts as justifications against the economic theory of classical liberalism. Sociology showed that the fears poverty engendered in the poor were real, that laissez-faire did not eliminate poverty, and that it was incumbent on liberals to take action, *pace* classical liberal objections.[15]

As for the role of biology in fin de siècle liberal thought, Darwin's *Origin of Species* was published in 1859, but it was Herbert Spencer's version of the theory of evolution, especially in the 1870s and '80s (see chapter 6), that made it an almost inescapable element of liberal argument in this period. The theory of evolution as liberals used it can be seen as just another theory of progress, to which neither the Enlightenment nor the short nineteenth century was a stranger. But theories of progress before and after Darwin were quite different. The stages of history found in Montesquieu and the Scottish Enlightenment, or the broad faith in scientific and moral progress of nineteenth-century liberals, were rarely as scientifically oriented in their language as the evolutionary biology of the fin de siècle. Evolution added a new twist to liberal thinking for

---

until the 1890s. My thanks to Google Ngram. In both languages increased use accompanied the rise of modern liberalism.

15. Their classical liberal opponents followed or indeed, in Spencer's case, preceded them onto the ground of sociology, but despite Spencer often reluctantly and defensively.

both modern and classical liberals. Spencer was a classical liberal, but the appeal to evolution as arbiter was made just as often by his modern liberal adversaries. Even the great fin de siècle liberal economist Alfred Marshall described himself as taking "the biological view of the science."[16]

Still more than science, ethics were at the forefront of liberal arguments in the fin de siècle. Like science, or rather intertwined with it, they had a tendency to become the sole pillar of much liberal thought. Marshall stated that the distinguishing characteristic of his *Principle of Political Economy* was its concern with "ethical forces." As the English liberal philosopher Henry Sidgwick put it, "human beings will not permanently acquiesce in a social order that common moral opinion condemns as unjust." This meant that, according to one Progressive American economist, modern economics could not "acknowledge laissez-faire as an excuse for doing nothing while people starve, nor allow the all-sufficiency of competition as a plea for grinding the poor." Fighting poverty by individual charity was not enough for modern liberals, while for many of their classical liberal opponents, giving to one's favorite charity was virtuous, but taxing individuals to provide public charity was immoral as well as ineffective. The modern liberal retort was that while private charity was indeed a virtue, practice showed it to be ineffective and that there was a moral duty to fight poverty that could only be performed collectively, by the state.[17]

However, few or no modern liberals "held the 'welfare state' as an end goal." Their focus was on morality, which became the sole supporting pillar of much modern liberalism. They distrusted market competition as unethical, especially when it came to the distribution of income. For modern liberals, the natural harmony of moral and economic interests perhaps had been effective in the past; in the present it created too much social dissonance. A conductor, i.e., the government, was needed in order to give the whole orchestra, rich and

16. Freeden, "Eugenics and Progressive Thought," 144–172. Bourgeois became president of the French Eugenics Society. See Rosenblatt, *Lost Liberalisms*, 237; Ryan, "Liberalism, 1900–1940," 69; Sidgwick, cited in Winch, *Wealth and Life*, 216–217, Winch, *Wealth and Life*, 225–227; Greenleaf, *The British Political Tradition*, vol. 2, *The Ideological Heritage*, 168; Weinstein, Jackson, "Socialism and the New Liberalism," Marshall, cited in Rothschild, "Political Economy," 768.

17. Marshall, cited in Rothschild, "Political Economy," 771; Sidgwick, cited in Kloppenberg, *Uncertain Victory*, 403; Richard T. Ely, cited in Rodgers, *Atlantic Crossings*, 98. On the role of ethics in German social liberalism, see Rosenblatt, *The Lost History*, 220–228. As Rosenblatt put it, "It is in fact impossible to understand new liberalism [she is referring to the British version of modern liberalism] apart from the primacy its advocates gave to ethics." *Lost History*, 234.

poor, the freedom to play their own tunes. To classical liberals all this seemed like a regression to medieval economic coercion.[18]

As the twentieth century went on, more and more liberals chose a narrow basis for their arguments. Modern liberals rejected the market pillar in whole or in part; to a lesser extent they reduced the importance of the political pillar, giving it only instrumental value. Thus the moral pillar of liberalism was called upon to bear all the weight of the struggle against poverty. Sometimes modern liberals found that the moral imperative was so strong as to drive them out of the liberal camp altogether, whether to embrace an illiberal socialism or a conservatism with a social conscience.

From the classical liberal perspective, modern liberals' emphasis on the moral pillar was the equivalent of the imposition of a state religion, albeit this time imposing its rules and taxes in the name of a social gospel rather than a spiritual one. In reaction, even classical liberals who, like Herbert Spencer, were strongly attached to the moral arguments for liberalism cut off a large portion of the moral pillar, restricting it to the private sphere. What Spencer called the morality of altruism was removed from social and political influence. Unlike nineteenth-century liberals, fin de siècle classical liberals like Spencer and A. V. Dicey did their best to wall off morality from political and economic life. In their arguments for limiting the scope of the state and maintaining a laissez-faire attitude to poverty, classical liberals claimed to be upholding the mainstream liberalism of the nineteenth century, but with regard to morality they radically departed from it, largely replacing it by an exclusive reliance on the economic pillar. For classical as well as modern liberals, the political pillar tended to take a lesser, more purely instrumental role: constitutional questions took a back seat for both, and the suffrage issue was largely in the past, except for women. Fin de siècle liberals were much more likely than their predecessors to rely on a single pillar for their arguments, whether moral for modern liberals or economic for classical liberals.

As the twentieth century progressed, both modern and classical liberals sometimes abandoned their identification as liberals. To socialism went former liberals who in their fear of poverty ended up identifying the state itself, or the community as a whole, as needing protection from certain individuals and groups within it who were considered to contribute to poverty—capitalists, landowners, Jews. To conservativism went those whose fears—of financiers, ethnic minorities, Jews—took a different valence, frequently in association with

18. Freeden, "The Coming of the Welfare State," 18–19.

the increasingly radical nationalism of the fin de siècle, as the next chapter shows. Other ex-liberals adopted what one might call the Fabian heresy,[19] which put its faith in the rule of experts and bureaucrats, sometimes in the employ of the state, sometimes outside it, sometimes identifying the state as the only rational solution to fear, sometimes seeing the state merely as the prime agent for solving social and political problems, and always preferring state-oriented to market or civil society-based solutions. Examples of this were the Fabian Socialists and the "expert" wing of American Progressivism. With liberalism left behind, newly minted conservatives and socialists embraced the idea of making some people afraid, whether socialists or the bourgeoisie. Liberalism 2.0 thus paradoxically served to strengthen the centrifugal forces within liberalism. As the argument about poverty developed, it became harder and harder for liberals to maintain their central position, equidistant from revolution and reaction.

In the fin de siècle both modern and classical liberals were found throughout the West. Classical liberalism was much the same everywhere, but modern liberalism took different forms and names in different places: Progressivism in the United States; New Liberalism in Britain; Solidarism in France; and Social Liberalism in Germany. They shared, regardless of geography, a tendency to rely chiefly or exclusively on the moral pillar of liberalism. They typically embodied their moralism in a commitment to furthering the opportunities for the moral perfection of individuals and groups, especially the poor. Some form of perfectionism was often central to modern liberal backing for the nascent welfare state. Modern liberals tended to concentrate their concern on groups as much or more than individuals, and like so many fin de siècle thinkers, liberal and illiberal alike, to make use of some form of the theory of evolution.

Each of the three modern liberals discussed below illustrates common modern liberal themes as well as some of the differences within modern liberalism. The American Jane Addams shows how some modern liberals adapted evolutionism to support a new social ethics, and how they concentrated their attention on the fears and hopes of groups and classes. Unlike many modern liberals, Addams was interested in only a limited expansion of state action. Unlike most, she was committed to the importance of diversity, to an extent

---

19. The British Fabian Socialists favored the slow and democratic creation of a socialist society in which the state, guided by (their) expert advice, would direct the economy and social development.

rivaled only by John Stuart Mill in the short nineteenth century. In France, Léon Bourgeois was a moralist and an evolutionist. He emphasized poor people's right to social assistance via the idea of a "quasi-contract" and a "social debt." In so doing he foreshadowed the return of social contract thinking to the liberal mainstream, where it would find a place in the twentieth century. He occupied a middle ground with regard to government intervention. In Britain, L. T. Hobhouse combined evolutionism and moralism with heavy reliance on state action to make perfection possible, including a considerable dose of nationalization of industry and redistribution of income.

By comparison, classical liberals were relatively uniform, as befitted those who claimed to be defending an orthodoxy. The British jurist A. V. Dicey represents a classical liberalism predominantly interested in the fears of individuals, not of groups, and resolutely opposed to any expansion of the scope of government. He illustrates how classical liberals imagined themselves the true heirs of a laissez-faire economic tradition of liberalism, to a large extent invented by Dicey himself and enthusiastically endorsed by his fellow classical liberals. One reason classical liberals liked to stress their orthodoxy and adopted the label "classical" was that those words implied that they were, or ought to be, the majority. The strategy is similar to Lenin describing his faction of the Russian Social Democratic Party as "Bolsheviks," which means "majority." The Bolsheviks were really the minority faction, and classical liberals too rapidly found themselves in a minority faced by the local branch of modern liberalism. Nevertheless, they played a central role in second-wave liberalism, and continued to be an important strand of liberal thought throughout the twentieth century.

Jane Addams and Progressivism

The period of "Progressivism" in American politics runs from roughly 1880 to 1919. Jane Addams (1860–1935) is in some respects the quintessential American Progressive, in others unique. Those on the right, then and now, typically call her a socialist, while those on the left describe her as a mere reformist. Both usually describe her as a saint: her contributions in social work, sociology, social reform, women's rights, pacificism, etc., have always been well-known. The resulting hagiography, along with some misogyny, has until recently ignored the important role she played as a Pragmatist philosopher.[20]

20. On her Pragmatism, see Seigfried, "The Courage of One's Convictions."

Two respects in which Addams was a typical modern liberal were her evolutionism and her stress on what she called "social ethics." These were found across broad swaths of the modern liberal spectrum. By contrast her profound commitment to diversity and pluralism and her defense of the freedom of minorities, as groups and cultures rather than individuals, were virtually unique.

Addams was typical of modern liberals in her reliance on evolutionary theory. Fin de siècle modern liberals, like classical liberals, often discussed liberty in terms of evolution. They used moral and "scientific" arguments in the manner of Herbert Spencer, but for radically different ends. Addams adopted Spencer's views of evolution and his vocabulary wholeheartedly, and she was far from alone in using Spencerian language and concepts to justify government intervention and regulations that would have horrified Spencer.[21]

The nature of Addams's relationship to Spencer can be seen in her essay "Survivals of Militarism in City Government." The title borrowed the evolutionary perspective of Spencer's sociology. For Spencer, "militarism" belonged to a previous evolutionary stage and ought to be left behind. But thereafter Addams used Spencer's language to turn his conclusions upside down. She assimilated the American Founding Fathers and their idea of inalienable and unchangeable natural rights to militarism—hardly Spencer's view. For Addams the whole idea of inborn rights was crude, and what was worse, according to Addams, anti-progressive compared to the "modern evolutionary conception of the slowly advancing race whose rights are not inalienable, but hard-won in the tragic process of experience." Inalienable rights, codified in constitutions that limited government action, were appropriate to an older, militant era (a good response to its fears), but they showed a lack of confidence in the people—for Spencer the opposite was true, and the idea of natural rights was the sign of the coming of "industrial" society, the opposite of militarism. For Addams the old focus on political and constitutional issues was appropriate to a militant society. The new era required broader scope for government action to achieve positive liberties. Today's problems were "more industrial than political." They therefore needed a different solution—the modern liberal solution of government action to fight poverty, whether

21. Eddy, "Struggle or Mutual Aid," 29; Seigfried, "The Courage of One's Convictions," 163. To the embarrassment of her hagiographers, she was a supporter of eugenics. See Addams, "Moral Education and Legal Protection of Children," in Elshtain, *The Jane Addams Reader*, 192.

through limits on child labor, the encouragement of trade unions, or more directly.[22]

Perhaps even more widespread than the adoption of Spencer's evolutionism in the fin de siècle was the adoption of his ethics.[23] Addams adopted and adapted his ethics in much the same way she had his evolutionism. She argued that formerly people had believed in self-help as the remedy for poverty, and that belief had been appropriate, but this was no longer true: "The virtues of one generation are not sufficient for the next." Both ethics and economics had to be conceived in new, broader, more social terms. The present laissez-faire economic system, as found in factories, in the relationship between employers and workers, and in the effects of poverty in general, made it nearly impossible for the poor to attain positive freedom, to have the resources necessary to be able to develop themselves. This was contrary to the demands of present-day ethics. An ethical advance more in accord with the current evolutionary state should be secured by law, and people must "insist upon the right of state regulation and control." Addams supported legislation to protect factory workers and prohibit child labor, develop municipal water and sewer systems, create decent housing for the poor, educational reform, etc. Her intermingling of ethics and economics was typical of many American Progressives, including many economists. It was an example of the takeover of economics by ethics, the heavy reliance on the moral pillar of liberalism found among modern liberals.[24]

Much more unusual was Addams's rejection of the hegemony of a single, more "advanced" ethical and political system dominated by White European, in this case Anglo-Saxon, culture. Addams maintained her Spencerian evolutionary standpoint, but once again came to different conclusions. Civilization

22. Addams, "Survivals of Militarism," in Elshtain, ed., *The Jane Addams Reader*, 152. Addams was typical of the American Progressive tradition of replacing natural rights with evolutionary understandings of both liberalism and the American constitution. Woodrow Wilson was even more radical in his disdain for constitutional limitations on Progressive policy. The relative weakness of natural rights liberalism outside the United States made this operation less necessary for modern liberals elsewhere.

23. This often passes unperceived—a recent discussion of "Progressivism" in Europe and America has a chapter titled "The Ethics of Rational Benevolence" that does not mention Spencer. Kloppenberg, *Uncertain Victory*, 115.

24. Addams, "A Modern Lear," in Elshtain, ed., *The Jane Addams Reader*, 170; "The Thirst for Righteousness," 140; Jane Addams, *Democracy and Social Ethics*, Kindle edition, 63. Michael Freeden makes a similar point about the British New Liberals. Freeden, *The New Liberalism*, 174–175.

was a complex struggle, with each race and nation contributing, and "the variety and continuity of this commingled life afford its charm and value. We would not, if we could, conform them to one standard." She was conscious that her attitude represented an innovation: "this modern attitude, which may even now subside into negative tolerance, did not exist among the founders of the Republic."[25] Spencer had argued that the progress of civilization was from the simple to the complex, but he viewed the advance of civilization from a single hegemonic vantage point, that of the White English man. Addams paid attention to the diversity of the poor, Black Americans and immigrants, and respected it. For Addams, cultural and moral diversity were "industrial" (Spencer's term for the higher level of human evolution, vs. militant), Anglo-Saxon hegemony was militant.[26]

Most Progressives and modern liberals emphasized the fears of groups, e.g., the poor. But Addams took care to subdivide the poor and oppressed into categories, not the moral categories of the short nineteenth-century and fin de siècle classical liberals, that is the deserving and undeserving poor, but cultural categories—immigrants of different national and religious backgrounds, Black Americans, women. She emphasized their right, as groups, to freedom from fear and from the infliction of arbitrary cruelties. She represented a minority of modern liberals for whom diversity was as central to a liberal society as it was to John Stuart Mill. For Addams, too many Progressive reformers failed to understand the "spiritual implications" of democracy, and looked at everything from a "native American" [she meant WASP—White Anglo-Saxon Protestant] perspective.[27]

For Addams the failure to recognize the different perspectives of immigrants, Blacks, and other groups demonstrated the failure of American democracy, of American liberalism, to accept diversity. "Although we have scrupulously extended the franchise to the varied immigrants among us, we have not yet ad-

---

25. Addams could have used Madison's theory of faction in support of her views and reconciled the *Federalist Papers* with her Pragmatism, but given the dominant formalist interpretation of the American Declaration of Independence and the Bill of Rights in her time, it is understandable that she chose not to.

26. Eisenach, *The Lost Promise of Progressivism*, 138–138. The influence of German economists' moralism on the Americans, who often obtained their PhDs in Germany, was very strong; Addams, "Survivals of Militarism," 148. Both Spencer's and Addams's views of evolving morality in some respects foreshadow the moral cleavage described by Jonathan Haidt and encapsulated in the Somewhere / Anywhere description, for which see chapter 11.

27. Addams, "Survivals of Militarism," 150.

mitted them into real political fellowship. . . . We have persistently ignored the political ideals of the Celtic, Germanic, Latin, and Slavic immigrants who have successively come to us, and in our overwhelming ambition to remain Anglo-Saxon, we have fallen into the Anglo-Saxon temptation of governing all peoples by one standard. We have failed to work out a democratic government which should include the experiences and hopes of all the varied peoples among us."[28]

Addams had a genius for making such abstract statements concrete. When Progressive reformers attacked the immigrants of Chicago for supporting corrupt aldermen, and bemoaned their unfitness for democratic citizenship, she enlightened them with an essay on "Why the Ward Boss Rules" in which she explained the different ethics of North Shore WASP Progressives and South Side immigrants. What the poor cared about was human feeling and generosity. They didn't care about corruption in city contracts, they cared that the alderman was there with a free turkey at Thanksgiving, fixed parking tickets for people too poor to pay them, made sure people could have a decent funeral. There was the same diversity of attitudes with regard to public or private charity: "the poor help each other cheerfully, the charity organization only with inquiry and cruelty." The middle-class inquirer did not understand why it was appropriate for her to spend less than she could afford on clothing, but for a poor woman to spend more, she understood neither the cultural nor the economic imperatives behind the poor woman's choice—if the poor woman was not well-dressed, the middle-class employer wouldn't hire her, and she would lose the respect of her neighbors. From the appropriate age of marriage, to the number of children, to sending a child to work at age fourteen, there was "an absolute clashing of two ethical standards." The WASP middle class was separated by an ethical gulf from the immigrant and Black poor. For Addams, it was the task of modern liberals to bridge that gulf. The recognition of diversity was necessary if ethnic conflict was to be replaced by cooperation. In *Democracy and Social Ethics*, Addams emphasized that one must "learn about" the poor: "One does good *with* people and not *to* them." She opened her famous Hull House Settlement in a poor neighborhood and lived there, so that the poor were not her "clients," but her neighbors.[29]

28. Addams, "Survivals of Militarism," 150, 155. The problem is central to the relationship between liberalism and populism and between liberalism and nationalism.

29. Addams, "Why the Ward Boss Rules," in Elshtain, ed., *The Jane Addams Reader*, 118–124; *Democracy and Social Ethics*, 7, 13–15; 1–3.

According to Addams the solution to the problem of ethical diversity, and the economic and political problems associated with it, was through a new stage in the evolution of ethics. She took Spencer's private "ethics of altruism," reconnected it to politics, and called it "social ethics," or "social morality," by contrast with "individual ethics" (Spencer's "ethics of interest"). What social ethics required was "the complete participation of the working classes in the spiritual, intellectual, and material inheritance of the human race." This participation, as for a change Spencer would have approved, had to take place in a cooperative, industrial manner, not through the confrontation typical of militarist societies. Addams stressed that the emancipation of the working class had to take place in cooperation with employers. Expropriating the wealthy, in her view, would be worse than useless. Addams feared the traditional liberal catastrophe if a revolution took place. Once "the sense of justice" left "the regular channels of established government," the result was inevitably "disaster." She even used the standard nineteenth-century liberal reminder of French Revolutionary terror as a warning. The solution was a process in which industrial social ethics slowly overcame the old, outmoded militant individualism. Her shining example was Abraham Lincoln, and his idea of the "best possible," rather than the best, society.[30]

Addams's views were both very American and very much those of modern liberalism in general. She emphasized the fears of groups and classes, not just individuals. Her arguments relied on evolution and ethics, and the former supported the latter. Her situation amidst an immigrant society was particularly American, but whether or not liberals accepted diversity was an issue that frequently arose during the debates over nationalism and imperialism of the fin de siècle, as we will see in the next chapter. Addams's willingness to accept the entry of new groups into liberal society and her ability to explain them was rare.

Both Jane Addams and the American Progressive movement in which she played a distinguished role are something of a Rorschach test—when you look at the blots on the paper, what pattern, if any, do you see? Defining Progressivism has proved a difficult task for Americanists, almost as difficult as defining liberalism, and for much the same reasons. In 1970 a well-known historian even claimed that there was no such thing as Progressivism, but rather many different things wrongly lumped together. Perhaps the closest thing to a consensus view of Progressivism is the argument that there were three separate

---

30. Addams, "The Chicago Settlements and Social Unrest," in Elshtain, ed., *The Jane Addams Reader*, 216; "A Modern Lear," 173–175.

political programs within American Progressivism, one based on anti-monopolism; a second which favored social reform and emphasized social bonds against the claims of "individualists"; and a third which appealed to expertise to solve social problems. The three were not coherent, and had different origins, but all adopted the label "Progressive." From the perspective of the history of liberalism, the solution to the problem of defining Progressivism is simple: the Progressives were all modern liberals. They embraced state intervention, albeit in varying degree and manner, to solve the problem of poverty.[31]

Furthermore, Addams was typical of the wider Progressive and modern liberal movement in stressing morality. American Progressives, like modern liberals generally, put special emphasis on the perfectionist elements of liberalism. Jane Addams sought "that which will secure the health, the peace of mind, and the opportunity for normal occupation and spiritual growth to the humblest industrial worker, as the foundation for a rational conduct of life adapted to an industrial and cosmopolitan era." The Progressive American sociologist Charles Cooley (1864–1929) defined freedom as "*the opportunity for right development, for development in accord with the progressive ideal of life that we have in conscience.*" This moral / religious emphasis on "spiritual growth" and "right development" in accord with a "progressive ideal of life" illustrated the reliance on the moral / religious pillar of liberalism characteristic of most American Progressives and most modern liberals. It was no accident that in America one of the most important sources of support for Progressivism was the "Social Gospel" movement that energized both Protestants and Catholics at the time, and which had parallels in Europe, especially in Germany and Britain, and in secular form in France, where it was at the heart of Solidarism.[32]

As one classical liberal noted, laissez-faire seemed "to have lost favour chiefly owing to moral considerations."[33] These moral considerations frequently took the form of a common good to be pursued by the community,

31. Connolly, "Review of Shelton Stromquist, 464–466; Rodgers, "In Search of Progressivism," 113–132; Rodgers, *Atlantic Crossings*, 84ff. The reluctance of Americanists to describe Progressivism as the American form of modern liberalism is puzzling, particularly given that fin de siècle British New Liberals themselves recognized the affinity. By WWI, Progressives often used "liberal" as a self-description. See Rodgers, *Atlantic Crossings*, 84ff.; Rosenblatt, *Lost Liberalisms*, 246–247. See chapter 8 for a possible explanation.

32. Addams, *Newer Ideals of Peace*, cited in Fischer, "The Conceptual Scaffolding of *Newer Ideals of Peace*," 189–190, 139, 139n2; Cooley, cited in Kloppenberg, *Uncertain Victory*, 397.

33. Goschen, cited in Collini, *Liberalism and Sociology*, 25.

or individual goods pursued in common, and proved highly attractive to many modern liberals. They saw in collective life, whether embodied in government or private associations, a means of pursuing individual and social perfection and morality. Many modern liberals emphasized the importance of association in pursuit of the common good—Jane Addams's Settlement Houses in poor neighborhoods were an example. A society in which no one need be afraid could only be built in association with others. This was accompanied by an insistence that membership in a community meant paying one's dues, one's "social debt," whether through accepting government regulation or paying a progressive income tax. Only in this way could the risks that people entered society to avoid, and that poverty increased, be overcome. This point was forcefully made in the French variant of modern liberalism, the Solidarism of Léon Bourgeois.

Solidarity Forever: Léon Bourgeois

In France, "Solidarism" was the local brand of modern liberalism. It acted as "an ideological umbrella that unified the diverse approaches of republican social reform." Solidarism became the official philosophy of the Radical or Radical-Socialist party (it used both names), the party most often in the French cabinets of the fin de siècle. Founded in 1901, the Radical-Socialist party was radical only in its anti-clericalism, and socialist only in the most liberal sense. Contemporaries called it "the hyphen between socialism and liberalism." It defended private property while being sympathetic to social legislation. Under Radical auspices France created a Ministry of Labor and instituted a system of pensions for workers and peasants, an income tax, free secondary school education, and a variety of social legislation. The leading Solidarist theorist, Léon Bourgeois (1851–1925), became head of the party and briefly Prime Minister (*président du conseil*) of France in 1895.[34]

The fin de siècle French were quick to adopt the phrase "liberal socialism" (it had already had a brief vogue in France in the 1860s). Bourgeois noted in

34. Logue, *From Philosophy to Sociology*, 2; Horne, *A Social Laboratory for Modern France*, 9, 118; Audier, *Léon Bourgeois*, 13. Audier, "Introduction," 8. It should be noted that the French sociologist Célestin Bouglé, a student of Durkheim, was an almost equally strong presence in Solidarism as Bourgeois, and a discussion of Bouglé would emphasize the sociological rather than evolutionary and philosophical links of the movement. See Logue, *From Philosophy to Sociology*.

1901 that in France the word socialist was used "so broadly that anyone who is concerned, really concerned, with social problems may call himself a socialist." For his own part, "I agree I am a socialist, but a liberal socialist, the most liberal of socialists." Liberal socialism figured strongly in Solidarist vocabulary because in France as elsewhere the problem of poverty took center stage in the fin de siècle. The distinctive contribution of Solidarism to modern liberalism was combining support for a degree of government intervention and taxation in accordance with one's means to pay for it, with an emphasis on private association, supplemented by government action only if necessary. These ideas were by no means restricted to French modern liberalism, but they were expressed most systematically by Léon Bourgeois in the form of Solidarism.

What makes Solidarism interesting is how it addressed these problems ideologically. The key concept was the "quasi-contract" that bound all members of society to pay their "social debt," and thus resolved the apparent contradiction between social justice and individual rights. The quasi-contract expressed and established solidarity between individuals, communities, and generations, and enabled people to pursue a common good. It turned out to justify a considerable amount of state intervention, more than Addams supported, but considerably less than Hobhouse foresaw. Rather than state intervention, the Solidarists emphasized free association.[35]

The Solidarist argument began, as with so much fin de siècle thought, with evolution, which encouraged the mutual exchange of services among human beings.[36] Evolution led to increasing human interdependence, and eventually to increasing consciousness of the moral obligations people had to one another: solidarity. Thus Bourgeois combined the "scientific method and the moral idea." As a result of their growing solidarity, people acknowledged the existence of what Bourgeois called the social debt. "Man living in society, and unable to live without it, is always a debtor towards it. This is the base of his duties, the tax on his freedom." People were bound to repay this debt by what Bourgeois called, borrowing from the liberal philosopher Alfred Fouillée (1838–1912), a "quasi-contract."[37] The government, in its role as the enforcer of

35. Horne, *A Social Laboratory*, 9–11; Bourgeois, *Solidarité*, Amazon reprint, 7.

36. Bourgeois made explicit reference to Bastiat and Proudhon, an eclectic combination, as ancestors of Solidarism. He even borrowed Bastiat's language of a society based on the exchange of mutual services. Bourgeois, *Solidarité*, 26–28.

37. It is only a "quasi" contract because, unlike Rousseau's social contract, it comes into operation *after* society is created, not before. Above all, Bourgeois wrote, chastising Rousseau,

contracts, had the right and duty to force people to pay their debt to society, that is, to pay their taxes. By paying our social debt, by fulfilling our "quasi-contract," we arrive at "social justice."[38]

Bourgeois also provided an additional explanation for the social debt and the resulting quasi-contract, intended to demonstrate that the social debt included an individual's responsibility to alleviate others' poverty. According to Bourgeois, the reason people agreed to enter into society was to avoid or limit the risks, not just of being murdered, but of being poor, of being unemployed or ill or too old to care for oneself, etc. And "if, as I believe, the mutualization or putting in common of the burdens I have listed figures incontestably among the conditions without which individuals would not have agreed to associate, or would voluntarily agree to remain associated, it follows that any associate who refuses to fulfil one of the social burdens incumbent on them violates the contract." To enforce the contract, the government had a right to create elements of a welfare state, paid for by taxation.[39]

The question to be determined was what portion of our wealth or income was needed to pay the social debt. Bourgeois admitted that the problem of deciding which wealth was of social origin was difficult. Would it not mean the return of "the arbitrary and the a priori," the fear of government confiscation that nineteenth-century liberalism was meant to banish? In response, he said that the laws of physics and chemistry were still laws even when it was difficult to apply them. A social debt was a debt, even when its amount was hard to determine. Indeed, he never resolved the question.[40]

There were a number of pitfalls to be avoided here, and not all modern liberals avoided them. Owing a debt to society for one's wealth is rather like owing a debt to one's parents for one's existence. The commandment to honor thy father and mother can be construed to mean an infinite obligation or annual New Year's cards. When a sometime New Liberal like J. A. Hobson went

---

one did not surrender any rights to be part of society, rather one gained increased ability to exercise all one's rights. Bourgeois, *Solidarité*, 30n1. But this must be paid for, and the quasi-contract was the legally enforceable promise to pay society for benefits received.

38. Bourgeois, *Solidarité*, 24, 9; 31, Audier, *Léon Bourgeois*, 32; Bourgeois, *Solidarité*, 35; 41, 44; Audier, *La pensée solidariste*, 289.

39. Audier, *La pensée solidariste*, 289.

40. Bourgeois, "Les risques sociaux et l'assurance maladie," in Audier, *La pensée solidariste*, 290; Bourgeois, *Solidarité*, 33. Many other modern liberals were faced with the same problem. In Hobhouse's words, the "function of taxation is to secure to society the element in wealth that is of social origin." But how much was that?

so far as to support the quasi-nationalization of most British industry, it is easy to see why fin de siècle classical liberals feared that the modern liberals were sliding rapidly down a greased slope to a socialist economy and the abolition of private property.[41]

But Bourgeois intended to stay on the high ground. Solidarism took aim at poverty, not property. Bourgeois's goal was "without harming individual freedom . . . to give every member of society, within the limits of inevitable natural inequality, the greatest amount of economic independence." There was no question of abolishing private property. "Individual property" was "the continuation and the guarantee of freedom," and therefore "the development of private property, not its elimination, is the goal for me, and my social ideal is one in which everyone will arrive in just measure at individual property." Unlike many British New Liberals, the Solidarists had no interest in nationalizing industries. If they supported redistributive measures, it was not redistribution for its own sake that interested them. When Bourgeois's government proposed a progressive income tax in 1896, it created brackets in the range of 1–5 percent. Hardly a confiscatory and barely a redistributory level of taxation. Regardless of practice, in theory the doctrine of the quasi-contract and the social debt provided moral justification for the creation of a liberal welfare state funded by progressive taxation. The wealthy, since they made more use of tools furnished by society than the poor, should pay more for them; the poor, in the name of solidarity and the social debt, had an enforceable claim to have their poverty diminished.[42]

However, to focus exclusively on the "welfare state" aspect of Solidarism, as its classical liberals critics did, is to draw an inaccurate picture. The means that the Solidarists aimed to employ against poverty, although they included state regulation and expenditure, were largely independent of the state. Bourgeois's preferred method of demonstrating solidarity was not taxation and regulation, but free association. While he thought that the state had a necessary role to play in fighting poverty, it had no place whatsoever in his understanding of the ultimate goal of a liberal society: the freedom of the individual.

Bourgeois did not cite Tocqueville, but like Tocqueville and Jane Addams he believed strongly in decentralization and the importance of associations

41. On Hobson, see Jackson, "Socialism and the New Liberalism," 41ff.

42. Audier, *Léon Bourgeois*, 21; Bourgeois, "La justice sociale," in Audier, *La pensée solidariste*, 253.

within civil society.[43] For Bourgeois, associations acted as intermediaries be-tween the individual and the state. It was desirable that there be "institutions based on private initiative," which were more flexible and adaptable than the government could be. They were the only institutions that could lighten the state's burden—and the state had to see them as friends, not, as so often in French history, as rivals (a very Tocquevillian point): "It is necessary that the State see in the mutuality [the independent association]—what in truth it is—the only institution that can stand in for it and lighten its burden, the only one which can take care of some of its responsibilities and, in a word, give it less to do." Bourgeois preferred the French to the German system of workers' insurance because it was based on associations rather than the state, and sup-ported laws giving associations more legal rights.[44]

Despite the superiority of associations, the state had to provide backup when private associations did not furnish the necessary insurance against old age, sickness, etc. As Bourgeois pointed out, the French had always been a nation of savers. Nevertheless, this had not prevented great suffering due to unemployment, and thus a national system of obligatory, state-supported un-employment insurance was necessary. Thus, by paying the social debt, by ful-filling the "quasi-contract," society arrived at "social justice."[45]

This common project, Bourgeois repeatedly stressed, was not some great overarching vision imposed by the state. The state had no rights because the state was not a person. Society was nothing but individuals—but individuals with a mutual obligation, the quasi-contract, to help limit the risks all faced, and to give everyone the opportunity for self-realization through solidarity. Society had to intervene, if necessary through government action, preferably through private associations, to make sure poverty did not limit individual freedoms, allowed people opportunities for self-development, and did not leave them subject to arbitrary coercion, whether by other individuals or the government. The French Solidarists represented themselves as a kind of middle way—the most liberal of socialists, that is of those who concerned themselves with the social problem, the problem of poverty. To a large extent

43. Audier's argument for dividing Solidarism into two currents, one emphasizing associa-tions, the other the social debt, seems to me overly abstract. Solidarists like Bourgeois fre-quently switched from one track to the other. Cf. Audier, *La pensée solidariste*, 61–62.

44. Audier, *Léon Bourgeois*, 74 ; 67–68, 70.

45. Bourgeois, "Le mal du chômage," in Audier, *La pensée solidariste*, 301; Bourgeois, *Soli-darité*, 44.

they were successful in this, in that their political success, nationally and lo-cally, was perhaps the greatest of any modern liberalism. But if their success was great, their ambitions were modest. The latter could not be said of the British New Liberals.

Hobhouse and Liberal Socialism

British New Liberals shared with Addams a desire for a moral refoundation of liberalism. But they did not much discuss the cultural diversity that Addams, living in an immigrant neighborhood in Chicago, highlighted. By contrast they emphasized the role of the central government far more than Addams, who maintained her allegiance to the decentralized environment of American poli-tics, and surprisingly also more than the French Solidarists. Perhaps because they lived in the country where the laissez-faire tradition and free trade on the one hand, and the cooperative movement on the other, had the longest history, they were the most skeptical of the possibility of alleviating poverty without considerable state intervention, and the most inclined to expand the functions of the state. L. T. Hobhouse is a good example of New Liberalism.

L. T. Hobhouse (1864–1925), sociologist and political theorist, was one of the leading New Liberal theorists in fin de siècle Britain. Author of the classic *Liberalism*, written in 1910–11, he is often described as the leading liberal theo-rist of his time. In some ways, as in his evolutionism, he was quite typical of liberalism. And yet, it has been suggested that even in his self-described New Liberal phase his work "cannot easily be categorized as liberal" and that there was "some doubt as to whether it is . . . illuminating to label Hobhouse as a 'Liberal' . . . at all, at least without considerable qualification." The reason was the extent to which Hobhouse supported government intervention, which indeed left him uncomfortably close, from a classical liberal perspective, to the socialist abyss. The reasons Hobhouse was both a leading New Liberal and from some perspectives only doubtfully a liberal at all make him a good rep-resentative of modern liberalism.[46]

Hobhouse's *Liberalism* epitomized the modern liberal concern with pov-erty. "People," he wrote, "are not fully free in their political capacity when they

---

46. On his evolutionism, see James Meadowcroft, "Introduction," xiii, and Collini, *Liberalism and Sociology*, 212. Hobhouse's evolutionism was eclectic rather than rigorously Spencerian, but this too was common. For his dubious status as a liberal in some eyes, see Collini, *Liberalism and Sociology*, 121, 121n2, 4–5, 4n7, 4n8, 96, 235.

are subject industrially to conditions which take the life and heart out of them. . . . The social problem must be viewed as a whole." To be free from fear politically, an old liberal demand, required being free from poverty—a new liberal demand. Hobhouse did not have a complete solution to the problem of poverty, but that did not matter. "A right is a right none the less though the means of securing it be imperfectly known."[47] The struggle against poverty was, in Hobhouse's view, the logical extension of earlier liberal campaigns for freedom: "At bottom it is the same conception of liberty and the same conception of the common will that prompts the regulation of industry and the severance of religious worship and doctrinal teaching from the mechanism of State control."[48]

In *Liberalism*, Hobhouse tried his best to show that state intervention to solve the poverty problem had a liberal genealogy. Where classical liberals turned the history of liberalism into the consistent advocacy of laissez-faire, Hobhouse pointed out, with rather more fidelity to the truth if not to the whole of it, ways in which canonical liberals of the short nineteenth century frequently departed from strict laissez-faire principles of limited government. The "older doctrines led, when carefully examined, to a more enlarged conception of State action than appeared on the surface." Hobhouse used these exceptions, as proponents of laissez-faire might view them, as a jumping-off point for justifying far more extensive state action on behalf of the poor than his predecessors had ever imagined. While he cited the British liberal philosopher and icon T. H. Green (a sort of academic secular saint of the Jane Addams variety) to the effect that the New Liberals were merely fighting under "altered names" for "the same old cause of the social good against class interests, . . . as they were fifty years ago," Hobhouse recognized that there was a difference and that he was going much further down the road. For New Liberals, the state should be enlisted directly in the good old cause, and "this is the point at which we stand furthest from the older Liberalism."[49]

For Hobhouse, the old liberal policy prescriptions for laissez-faire had had insufficient effect. "Gladstonian" liberals[50] had to recognize "that while Free

47. Like Jane Addams, Hobhouse and the New Liberals often used rights talk, even though like her they were hostile to natural rights views.

48. Hobhouse, *Liberalism*, 120, 77, 74.

49. Hobhouse, *Liberalism*, 64; Sidgwick, *Elements of Politics*, 1897, cited in Collini, *Liberalism and Sociology*, 21.

50. A Gladstonian liberal, for Hobhouse, was what is here called a classical liberal.

Trade laid the foundations of prosperity it did not erect the building." Wages had risen, but so had expectations. "The very provision of education has brought with it new needs and has almost compelled a higher standard of life in order to satisfy them." As things stood, "the system of industrial competition fails to meet the ethical demand embodied in the concept of the 'living wage.'" The state was ethically compelled to act.[51]

Thus Hobhouse arrived at what he called "liberal socialism." He distinguished liberal socialism from illiberal socialism, either the "mechanical" kind, which was state control of the economy, or "official" socialism, by which he meant the Fabian Socialists and their ideas of bureaucratic rule by experts. The liberal, according to Hobhouse, knew people would rather manage their own lives. But the modern liberal knew that this was not possible for those in poverty, and that it was the state's duty to make it possible for citizens to maintain and develop themselves.[52] The state had to act to assure equal opportunity for self-development for everyone, in particular the poor. Equal opportunity for Hobhouse meant not just abolishing constraints, but giving poor people a real opportunity to freely develop themselves, hence what was beginning to be called positive freedom (empowerment, the opportunity for self mastery and self-development) as well as negative freedom (freedom from coercion, or being left alone). Hobhouse summed it up in a short passage: "The common good ... postulates free scope for the development of personality in each member of the community. This is the foundation not only of equal rights before the law, but also of what is called equality of opportunity."[53]

To achieve the old liberal goal of *la carrière ouverte aux talents* required that everyone have an equal opportunity for factors like a good education. To give all people the opportunity for self-development, absolute poverty had to be eliminated, which would require regulation as well as direct intervention by the government. Ensuring equal opportunity meant it was a function of the state to make it possible for everyone to earn their own living. "The 'right to work' and the right to a 'living wage' are just as valid, as the rights of persons or property." The state should not feed, clothe, and house people, but make it possible for them to do so themselves. There was a minimum level of material welfare that had to be guaranteed by the state to "secure the elementary and

51. Hobhouse, *Liberalism*, 109, 78.
52. Hobhouse, *Liberalism*, 80–82, 84.
53. Hobhouse, *Liberalism*, 64.

essential conditions of a good life." Otherwise, "liberty without equality is a name of noble sound and squalid result."[54]

In fighting poverty, "the function of State coercion is to override individual coercion, and, of course, coercion exercised by any association of individuals within the state." For example, the state should act to prevent poor people from being coerced by poverty to accept a salary which did not allow any opportunity for self-development, and intervene against the factory-owner to assure a "living wage" and healthy working conditions. For fin de siècle modern liberals, poverty was a cruel means of taking away the opportunity for self- development. Hobhouse was not engaged in economics for the sake of material equality. It was the moral effect of redistribution that motivated him. While it was not the role of the state to perfect people, it was the role of the state to make it possible for people to perfect themselves.[55]

Because this would be expensive, Hobhouse endorsed progressive taxation. He took pains to justify this morally, rather than economically: wealth, according to Hobhouse, was the joint product of society and the individual, it "has a social as well as a personal basis." The wealthy, no matter how they had come by their wealth, did not owe it all to individual effort. Therefore, taxing them was justi-fied. Hobhouse favored high inheritance taxes and a progressive income tax. Liberals had always endorsed these to some extent. From Smith and Constant onward, liberals had frequently argued that the poor should not be taxed, which necessarily meant taxation had a progressive element. The English Poor Law was a form of redistribution of wealth. What distinguished the modern liberals was a far greater willingness to redistribute wealth both directly and indirectly, through taxation and regulation. Modern liberals agreed with first-wave liberals that private property was a good thing, a necessary bulwark of freedom, but they were not so sure about the virtues of the free market, and above all how it dis-tributed wealth. The government had to intervene to compensate for this market "failure" in the name of a moral imperative to liberate the poor.[56]

The market pillar of liberalism was thus diminished, sometimes to the point of elimination, in favor of a greatly expanded moral pillar. Hobhouse's vision of moral perfection and happiness, enabled where necessary by the state, re-

54. Hobhouse, *Liberalism*, 76, 154. Hobhouse, "The Individual and the State," in *Liberalism*, 154. Hobhouse, *Elements of Social Justice*, 54; Morrow, "Private Property, Liberal Subjects, and the State," 109. Hobhouse, *Liberalism*, 40–42.

55. Hobhouse, *Liberalism*, 71.

56. Hobhouse, *Liberalism*, 90, 97.

placed the role once occupied during the short nineteenth century by the market in the mainstream vision of liberalism. It was the task of society to uphold all rights that enhanced opportunities for self-development without harming the development of others—Hobhouse's version of Mill's harm principle. Every individual's development, Hobhouse was confident, "fits in with and contributes to the development of others." Such harmony of human goals and ideals might not yet exist, "but . . . there is a possible ethical harmony, to which, partly by discipline, partly by the improvement of the conditions of life, men might attain, and that in such attainment lies the social ideal." A liberal society, in his view, had a duty, just as liberal individuals had, to promote morality in the form of self-development.[57]

For Hobhouse, therefore, increasing state intervention to alleviate poverty was above all a moral duty, rather than a political or even economic one. Hobhouse saw modern liberals' emphasis on a perfectionist morality, and concomitantly on positive freedoms, as a contrast to the classical liberals' emphasis on negative liberties, and a natural historical development. Negative freedoms, as represented by restraints on state coercion, had had to come first: "Liberalism appears first as a criticism . . . its negative aspect is for centuries foremost," and only later were positive freedoms plausible liberal goals. For example, first liberals abolished aristocrats' monopoly of government jobs (negative freedom), then they required civil service examinations to ensure impartiality (more negative freedom), and finally they required free education for all so that all could have the opportunity to compete for those jobs (positive freedom). Hobhouse's history of liberalism was meant as both a proof and an argument: Liberalism, Hobhouse was telling socialists and classical liberals, should now endorse a positive program, a moral one. Its work was not yet finished. Liberalism was "a movement of liberation, a clearance of obstructions, an opening of channels for the flow of free spontaneous vital activity."[58]

---

57. See Weinstein, *Utilitarianism*, 65–70; Hobhouse, *Liberalism*, 59; Hobhouse cited in Weinstein, *Utilitarianism*, 70, and see 70n16; Hobhouse, *Liberalism*, 62. Hobhouse, like T. H. Green, tried to meld our development as individuals with the development of the community(ies) to which we belong. Collini, *Liberalism and Sociology*, 125. For Green, pursuing the common good was much the same as pursuing our own individual good, properly construed because it consisted of the "disposition on each man's part to make the most and best of humanity in his own person and in the persons of others." Green, cited in Weinstein, *Utilitarianism*, 115; see also Collini, *Liberalism and Sociology*, 127, Weinstein, *Utilitarianism*, 50, 69, 71.

58. Weinstein, *Utilitarianism*, 6–7; Hobhouse, *Liberalism*, 8, Collini, *Liberalism and Sociology*, 46–47; Hobhouse, *Liberalism*, 10–12, 15; Hobhouse, *Liberalism*, 22.

If the modern liberal idea of self-development was largely secular, it never-theless bore a certain resemblance to the illiberal project of a society dedicated to saving the souls of its members. For classical liberals, it revived one of liberalism's first fears, that of a state bent on confiscating one's wealth and freedom in the name of someone else's moral / religious vision. The ideal of self-development enabled by the state could lead modern liberals astray from liberalism, when they gave in to the Hegelian temptation to invest the state with moral value in itself, instead of regarding it as merely an instrument, and a secondary one at that. Hobhouse himself did not fall for the temptation to force people to endorse the state's moral vision. He did not attribute any moral value to the state. It was only the individual personality that counted. "Society consists wholly of persons. It has no distinct personality, separate and superior to those of its members." Nor was he tempted to make the state an agent for directing the individual's development—hence his rejection of Fabian social-ism and the rule of experts / bureaucrats.[59]

To a large extent, modern liberals won the competition for the crown of virtue against classical liberals. Classical liberals' moral rebuttal of modern liberalism, that state assistance would demoralize the poor and deprive them of the opportunity for self-development rather than encourage it, had limited traction in the fin de siècle, although it would have greater success in the twen-tieth century (see chapter 10). Fin de siècle classical liberals regularly lamented the dominance of modern liberal ideas, and although quantitative proof is hard to find, the evidence, electoral as well as intellectual, suggests that by WWI modern liberals were the majority within liberalism.

Hobhouse, Bourgeois, and Addams do not represent the entire spectrum of modern liberal responses to the problem of poverty, but they give a broad view of its most important characteristic: moral commitments replacing mar-kets as a pillar of liberalism and reducing politics to a purely instrumental role, in which an expanded state was justified by a moral duty. From the classical liberal viewpoint, this meant that modern liberalism was frequently illiberal in both its ends and its means. Even when fin de siècle classical liberals feared poverty, they denied that the means to combat it included a broader scope for government or limiting the role of markets on moral grounds.

The new fear of fin de siècle classical liberals was their fear of modern liber-als. Just as the new fear of poverty led modern liberals to abandon the three

59. Hobhouse, *Liberalism*, 61. His further discussion of the "collective life" of the community can be compared to Tocqueville's discussion of associations.

pillars of nineteenth-century liberalism to rely on only one, the moral pillar, so the new fear of the classical liberals drove them on to a different pillar, the economic. The result was fierce conflict within the liberal camp, in which the classical liberals were generally forced to beat a slow retreat. Their tactics in retreat were much the same throughout the West. Eugen Richter in Germany, Gustave d'Eichthal and Emile Faguet in France, or the many opponents of the Progressives in the United States presented similar arguments to the British figure who will stand here for all of them: A. V. Dicey (1835–1920).

Dicey's Despair: The Rise of Collectivism

At any point after 1873, classical liberals could be found throughout the Western world lamenting the decline of liberalism and the rise of socialism.[60] Rather than surrendering to what they perceived as the socialism of modern liberals, classical liberals chose resistance. They feared modern liberals more than they feared poverty because, from their perspective, the fight against modern liberalism was the old struggle against despotism and arbitrary authority. The modern liberals' fight against poverty might seem superficially attractive but it was really just another scheme of state-sponsored salvation, carried out by bureaucrats rather than by the clergy, and if no longer accompanied by burning at the stake, all the more suffocating in its gentle and all-pervasive fiscal and regulatory pressure, a modern form of the soft despotism of democracy that Tocqueville had feared. The modern Inquisitor worked for the tax office, and the preferred instrument of torture was the audit. If modern liberals maintained the traditional liberal optimism that history was on their side, classical liberals felt beleaguered, not merely by the usual sources of liberal fear, revolutionary and counter-revolutionary despotisms, but also by the desertion of modern liberals from the cause. As a result, their mood oscillated between pessimism and outrage.

Dicey is a good example. In his *Lectures on the Relation between Law and Public Opinion in England during the Nineteenth Century*, first published in 1905 and revised in 1914, Dicey confronted the new challenges faced by fin de siècle liberalism. The book was considered a major contribution when first published, but fell into obscurity thereafter, only to be revived after WWII by a later generation of classical liberals and libertarians who found its telling of the history of liberalism congenial and therefore convincing. When Hobhouse

---

60. This trend extends beyond the fin de siècle to the time of writing.

constructed his modern liberal genealogy of liberalism in 1911, it was a counter-history to the one constructed by Dicey. But the curious thing is that *Law and Public Opinion* was actually not intended to be history at all—Dicey had no use for history. Nevertheless, although *Law and Public Opinion* was bad history, frequently inaccurate or contradictory, it was highly influential history, and is an excellent introduction to classical liberalism in the fin de siècle. Both for its role at the time, and its enormous, if sometimes subterranean, influence thereafter, it merits an extended account.[61]

In an important sense Dicey was not only typical of classical liberalism, but correct in his understanding of modern liberalism, or Collectivism, as he called it. He put his finger on what was at stake: the problem of poverty and the role of the state in dealing with it. Because he was right about this, his historical errors and textual misreadings have been largely overlooked or minimized. Dicey's vision of liberalism continued to influence twentieth-century liberals, especially those on the right of the liberal spectrum, as much or more than the twentieth-century revival of Locke.[62]

Law and Public Opinion was a lawyer's attempt to discover the laws of liberalism based on very selective precedents. Dicey reduced nineteenth-century liberalism to a single principle, "Individualism," which he identified with negative freedom (freedom from coercion) as embodied in a laissez-faire state and a laissez-faire society. That this impoverished the history of liberalism by leaving out most of what passed for liberalism during the short nineteenth century, even in England, omitting or distorting contradictory elements in the thought and action of figures he cited extensively (notably Macaulay), was of little concern to Dicey. What mattered was elucidating the lawlike principles behind Individualism and its rival, Collectivism.

In this view, liberalism started out with a consensus in favor of Individualism / laissez-faire, but in the fin de siècle it split into two. Modern liberals took the road to serfdom, to adopt a latter-day phrase, which Dicey called Collectivism. Dicey preferred to use the term Collectivism rather than socialism because he thought Collectivism was broader, even though he did "on occa-

---

61. Cosgrove, *The Rule of Law*, xiii, 79, 189, 191–192. In Dicey's view the purpose of history was "to deduce from past events the general principles on which their course has depended." But according to him historians had completely failed in this task, and it is "extremely doubtful whether a single principle has yet been ascertained which can even metaphorically be termed a historical law." Cited in Cosgrove, *The Rule of Law*, 172–173.

62. On the Locke revival, see chapter 1.

sion use the more popular and current expression socialism as equivalent to collectivism." Meanwhile, classical liberals remained on the path of freedom, which Dicey called Individualism. The history of the two divergent principles formed the framework for his defense of classical liberalism. Dicey's vocabulary and its history were thus conceived (like Hobhouse's history of liberalism) as a weapon in the battle between modern and classical liberals. Dicey's history of liberalism became highly influential in the twentieth century, when for different reasons both classical and modern liberals, in their twentieth-century, antitotalitarian versions, preferred Dicey's history to Hobhouse's. They preferred it because each, for their own reasons, wanted to emphasize the laissez-faire elements in the liberal past, as Dicey had, rather than the departures from laissez-faire, as Hobhouse had.

During the short nineteenth century, which Dicey called "the period of Benthamism or Individualism (1825–1870)," Individualism, backed by public opinion, swept "away restraints on individual energy, and . . . exhibit[ed] a deliberate hostility to every historical anomaly or survival, which appear[ed] to . . . in any way place a check on individual freedom." Benthamism was "little else than the logical and systematic development of those individual rights, and especially that of individual freedom which has always been dear to the common law of England." The restraints removed were primarily legal in nature. For Dicey the lawyer, liberalism was about law reform.[63]

Dicey identified liberalism in its heyday with Jeremy Bentham, a somewhat idiosyncratic choice. Bentham, in Dicey's view, was a legal philosopher and law reformer, not a "utilitarian moralist" or a "philanthropist." At first glance, this would seem to be a very narrow view of liberalism as well as of Bentham, but because Dicey identified the law with the protection of individual freedom, for him legal reform translated into the creation of a laissez-faire state. It was the principle of laissez-faire which, according to Dicey, "really governed Benthamite legislation." "Faith in laissez faire . . . was in practice the most potent and vital principle of Benthamite reform." That this was not an accurate description of Bentham (see chapter 6) did not disturb Dicey despite the fact that, as we shall see, he was conscious of the problem.[64]

Bentham himself was only a convenient shorthand for Dicey, who was aware that most of the reforms of his Benthamite period were carried out by people who did not look to Bentham as their inspiration, and that "some of

63. A. V. Dicey, *Lectures on the Relation between Law and Public Opinion*, 46.
64. *Law and Public Opinion*, 92, 105n22, 104.

them would have certainly repudiated the name of utilitarians." Indeed, he went on to include among his Individualist reformers Macaulay, who was neither a Benthamite, nor a utilitarian, nor a supporter of laissez-faire. And just as he was aware that most liberals were neither Benthamites nor even utilitarians, Dicey recognized that "this dogma of laissez faire is not from a logical view an essential article of the utilitarian creed," and thus that utilitarianism was not necessarily liberal, and allowed for benevolent despotism—Dicey cited Mill's passage about how an ignorant people could hope for no better than dictatorship by an Akbar or a Charlemagne. But during the period of Individualism this didn't matter, since public opinion supported Individualism. All the reformers, Dicey claimed, were firm believers in a "common-sense utilitarianism," which is to say supported a limited, laissez-faire state. They accepted "that Benthamism of common sense which, *under the name of liberalism*, was to be for thirty or forty years a main factor in the development of English law."[65]

What mattered was boiling down the varied historical precedents to the legal principle that lurked behind them, which according to Dicey was laissez-faire, and thus discovering the correct principle on which to reach a legal judgment about who was a liberal. For Dicey, true liberalism meant Individualism, both historically and in the fin de siècle, with the difference that in the fin de siècle classical liberal Individualists had to add modern liberal Collectivists to their list of enemies.[66]

Dicey's description of the heresy of Collectivism, the "hope of social regeneration" brought about by the state, i.e., modern liberalism, was just as influential, if not more so, than his history of liberalism's laissez-faire and utilitarian origins. In his view, Individualism had cleared a path for Collectivism in several ways: through the dogma of utility, to which he thought both appealed; through the idea of parliamentary sovereignty, which both made their instrument and which could be a powerful tool of democratic despotism; and through the improved efficiency of government administration, engineered by Benthamite reforms, which made Collectivist government intervention possible. The Collectivist possibilities of these elements had remained latent

65. *Law and Public Opinion*, 120; 121; 128; 126; 121. See also 49: "Benthamite individualism, which in accordance with popular phraseology, may often be conveniently called liberalism." Emphasis added.

66. *Law and Public Opinion*, 104, 105n23. See also 368n8, where Dicey recognized that even Bentham might have been prone to violate laissez-faire dogma.

during the short nineteenth century because the current of public opinion was strongly individualist, fearful of state-sponsored coercion. Once that changed, and social regeneration, motivated by the fear of poverty, became the order of the day, Collectivism found little to oppose it: hence the title *Law and Public Opinion*.[67]

Collectivism, Dicey acknowledged, had a less clear meaning than Individualism. He cited a dictionary to the effect that the word was only invented in 1880, and meant state ownership of the means of production. But Dicey intended it in a much broader sense: "Collectivism . . . favours the intervention of the State, even at some sacrifice of individual freedom, for the purpose of conferring benefit upon the mass of the people." Since 1865, according to Dicey, the Collectivist current of opinion had been growing, to such an extent that by 1900 "the doctrine of laissez faire, in spite of the large element of truth which it contains, had more or less lost its hold upon the English people." Even though many of the actions taken by British governments in 1865–1900 might individually be justified by laissez-faire arguments, taken as a whole they showed that hostility to state interference had, at the very least, greatly decreased.[68]

The reasons Dicey gave for the change varied over time, but in the end he made something close to the argument of this chapter, that it was the question of poverty and how to deal with it that brought about the fin de siècle split between classical and modern liberals, or in his terms Individualists and Collectivists. It is therefore particularly interesting to see how his understanding changed over time as he came to recognize the central role poverty played for liberals in this period.

In Dicey's original account, three things were behind the change in public opinion from Individualism to Collectivism: first, "faith in laissez faire suffered an eclipse." Second, the broadening of the suffrage in 1867 and 1884 meant greater political pressure for state intervention.[69] Finally, improved administrative machinery made Collectivism possible. Later Dicey gave reasons *why* faith in laissez-faire declined. Perhaps the most interesting is the revival of nationalism, and for Dicey, "the opposition between Benthamism and nationalism is obvious." The fashion for historical studies had aggravated nationalist

67. *Law and Public Opinion*, 50, 215, 217; 218.

68. *Law and Public Opinion*, 46–47; 47n5; 364.

69. Dicey hesitated over which suffrage reform was fatal. See Weill, "Dicey Was not Diceyan," 485–486.

sentiments and had "produced racial divisions and animosities, which are not only in themselves a gigantic evil and an impediment to all true progress," but could not be assuaged by any kind of rational reform. In this Dicey recognized some of the tensions discussed in the next chapter and, as will also be seen, there is something to be said for Dicey's linkage of modern liberalism to nationalism.[70]

Elsewhere, Dicey added a different reason for declining belief in laissez-faire. He pointed out that the growth of trade and commerce had been the backbone of faith in the benefits of unlimited competition, that is, of the market pillar of liberalism. But the growth of large corporations owned by myriad shareholders "has gradually become the soul of modern commercial systems." This "has in more ways than one fostered the growth of collectivist ideas." He suggested "that every large business may become a monopoly, and that trades which are monopolies may wisely be brought under the management of the State. The characteristics of modern commerce . . . make for socialism." From a modern liberal perspective, this would be an argument about the *need* for "socialism" to counter oppression by private monopolies, but for Dicey this was not the case. Here Dicey anticipated points made by the Ordoliberals in the 1930s (see chapter 9).[71]

By 1914, however, Dicey had decided that the only thing that mattered for the rise of Collectivism was the fear of poverty: "Now, for the last sixty years and more, the needs and sufferings of the poor have been thrust upon the knowledge of middle-class Englishmen." Consciousness of poverty had led to a desire to do something about it: "Against this evil of poverty the State ought, it is felt by collectivists, to protect the wage-earning class, and . . . must go a good way towards securing for every citizen something like the same advantages, in the form of education, or of physical well-being, as the rich can obtain by their own efforts." Dicey was conscious that poverty was the issue of the day, and that the moral status of poverty had changed. Modern liberal policies implemented by the state in the fin de siècle had deliberately removed the stigma attached to poor relief, for example by giving pensions to all poor elderly people, regardless of their character, thus negating the idea that it was "the duty of every citizen to provide for his own needs, not only in youth, but in old age." Laws to protect women and children from working long hours, or to protect society against the adulteration of food, were based on the idea "that

70. *Law and Public Opinion*, 220; 307–329; 328–329, Cosgrove, *The Rule of Law*, 178–179.
71. *Law and Public Opinion*, 174; 176.

the State is a better judge than a man himself of his own interest, or at any rate of the right way to pursue it." Dicey was as perceptive about what motivated his contemporaries as he was blind to what had actually motived mainstream liberals during the short nineteenth century.[72]

For Dicey and for classical liberals in general, modern liberals had perverted liberalism and justified coercion. Creeping despotism was revealed by rising taxation. Prior to the fin de siècle, liberals had thought lowering taxes was good in principle. But since 1870, in the period of Collectivism, this was no longer true: "Indifference to the mere lightening of taxation, as an end absolutely desirable in itself" was characteristic of a period in which people "expect far more benefit for the mass of the people from the extension of the power of the State than from the energy of individual action." For Dicey, progressive taxation, introduced in 1910, set the precedent of taxation for the sake of redistributing wealth and "the aim of promoting social or political objects." "Such taxation may easily become the instrument of tyranny.... Revolution is not the more entitled to respect because it is carried through not by violence, but under the specious though delusive appearance of taxation imposed to meet the financial needs of the State." The laudable desire to help the poor had turned into an illiberal revolution quietly led by the British Internal Revenue Service.[73]

From Dicey's classical liberal perspective, modern liberals' stress on morality and their attempt to address poverty with the help of the state had had only illiberal consequences. Dicey presented the characteristic slippery slope argument of classical liberals: first, free elementary education for the poor, supported by Adam Smith and many mainstream liberals during the short nineteenth century; then free elementary education for everyone; then free school lunches for the poor; then free secondary education to offer equal opportunity; then progressive and confiscatory taxation to pay for it all and bring about real equality and an illiberal revolution—very much the argument Hayek, a prominent twentieth-century reader of Dicey, would later make in *The Road to Serfdom*. Dicey and his fellow fin de siècle classical liberals were not alone in this view. Around the same time as Dicey wrote, the revisionist German Marxist Eduard Bernstein was arguing that revolution was unnecessary because liberalism was evolving into socialism anyway.[74]

72. *Law and Public Opinion*, 378–382; 383; 195; 186, see also 383, 386; 198.
73. *Law and Public Opinion*, 209; 292; 377.
74. Cosgrove, *The Rule of Law*, 184; on Bernstein, see Rosenblatt, *Lost History*, 232.

The classical liberal response to modern liberalism represented by Dicey looked forward to the twentieth century even more than it looked back to the past, a nineteenth-century past it had reconstructed for itself in light of its very fin de siècle concern with poverty and the modern liberal response to it. The fear of poverty motivated modern liberalism, and the fear of modern liberalism motivated classical liberalism. The result was Liberalism 2.0, a second wave of liberalism in which the fear of poverty and the responses to it were central. Once modern liberals had decided that poverty could and should be fought, to a large extent the story of Liberalism 2.0, at least within liberalism, became a battle about the role of the state. There was always a temptation for modern liberals to put so much trust in the state that the growth of the state would end up becoming the end rather than the means, and this Hegelian temptation led more than one modern liberal to abandon liberalism in favor of socialism.

It was not only the fear of poverty that tempted fin de siècle liberals to embrace the state, however, and it was not necessarily those on the left, the modern liberals, who were most tempted. Radical nationalism and imperialism / colonialism could have much the same effect. One challenge all liberals faced in the fin de siècle was the radical nationalism that swept over Europe and the United States, often associated with imperialism and colonialism. The increasing radicalism of nationalism brought politics back to center stage, sweeping aside or swallowing up economic and moral considerations. It was a different sort of politics (and a different sort of nationalism) than the constitutionalism and concern with political institutions that had preoccupied mainstream liberals during the short nineteenth century. Many ex-liberals embraced the state in the fin de siècle for nationalist and imperialist reasons, a problem of which Dicey had had a premonition. They became conservatives or even, later on, "national socialists" (Nazis).

Even when they remained liberals, some liberals embraced colonialism and imperialism as an extension of what they viewed as a liberal nationalism. In itself imperialism had nothing particularly liberal about it. But there was a distinctively liberal colonialism in the fin de siècle, at least in the view of some liberals. This colonialism relied heavily on a moral "civilizing mission" and also displayed the characteristic modern liberal willingness to rely on the state as a moral agent, at least in foreign lands. Of course not all liberals reacted in this way. Many modern liberals who embraced the state to fight poverty were resolute opponents of imperialism and colonialism, and there were classical liberals on both sides of colonial questions.

Poverty, radical nationalism, and imperialism were not the only issues that liberals confronted in the fin de siècle. Another was less widely acknowledged and rarely took center stage in liberal politics or reflection. This was the question of gender, the question of whether liberals should address women's fear of male arbitrary power and cruelty. The question had a history that predated the fin de siècle: in one sense, it reenacted old liberal battles for negative freedom—freedom from coercion—and reprised liberal fights of the short nineteenth century and even proto-liberals before then. On the other hand, questions of positive freedom for women as a group, and about whether the self-development of women was essentially different from that of men, and if so, how to encourage it, raised a new set of issues which once again called into question the role of the state versus civil society. To what extent did or ought the state to have a special role in the protection, oppression, or emancipation of women?

The fin de siècle marked the beginning of a new period of liberalism. Alongside poverty, the challenges posed by nationalism, imperialism, and gender raised important questions for liberals of all stripes.

8

Liberalism's Limits

LIBERALISM IS THE SEARCH for a society in which no one need be afraid. Starting with the fear of religious persecution and absolutist despotism after the Wars of Religion, liberals added other fears to their concerns over time: revolution and reaction; poverty; and, as future chapters will show, totalitarianism and populism. Liberals also broadened their understanding of whose fears mattered, eventually including slaves, the poor, women, nations beyond the West, and ethnic minorities within. It is very tempting to see liberalism as recapitulating Hegel's history of freedom: first for a few, then for many, and finally for all. Liberalism's story seems like one Hegel himself might have written, with the important caveat that the liberal struggle for freedom from fear is based on civil society rather than on Hegel's beloved state.

Tempting though it is, this story does not fully stand up to historical scrutiny—what good story does? Liberals did expand their understanding of what people feared and whose fears mattered. But the expansion of liberal concerns was incomplete and reversible. In particular times and places liberals became less liberal, that is, their sympathy for fear became less wide or generous, and liberals drew narrower conclusions about what was to be feared and whose fears should matter.[1] When liberal fears trumped liberal hopes, liberals became more narrow-minded. The history of liberalism is not just a story of progress, even if from certain perspectives it *does* progress.

This chapter treats both the expansion and the contraction of liberal fears in relationship to nationalism, imperialism, and feminism in the fin de siècle. In contrast to the relatively happy marriage of liberalism and nationalism in

---

1. It should also be noted that progress in terms of fending off one fear, for example that of arbitrary state power, might be threatened by progress in another direction, for example warding off poverty. This was the classical liberal criticism of modern liberalism.

the short nineteenth century, after 1873 the relationship grew more difficult. During the short nineteenth century nationalism encouraged liberals to expand and democratize their concerns, and liberals helped nationalists overthrow despotic regimes. After 1873 radical nationalists made increasingly illiberal demands, demands that called for liberals to limit those whose fears mattered to those of the right nationality or ethnicity, demands that liberal nationalists sometimes found hard to resist.

If nationalism posed problems as to the limits of liberalism domestically, it also confronted them with the problem of the limit of liberalism internationally. The development of imperialism in the fin de siècle raised uncomfortable questions for liberals. Did liberalism stop at the water's edge? Liberals were forced to confront whether or not liberal colonialism was possible, and if so what might distinguish it from illiberal colonialism. Fin de siècle liberals mostly endorsed the West's "civilizing mission," at the expense of drawing a sharp line between where and when liberalism was or was not appropriate.

Another fear that, alongside poverty, took on new urgency for liberals in the fin de siècle, even if it only came into its own after WWII, was women's fear of the arbitrary power of men, domestic, economic, political, and social. Although proto-liberalism and nineteenth-century liberalism were far from being strangers to issues of gender, gender questions took on new salience in the fin de siecle, and for the first time women's own hopes and fears became the main issue for (some) liberals, rather than the fears that women had aroused in past generations of (male) liberal thought. Like the questions of poverty and nationalism and imperialism, the "Woman Question" showed a tendency to break apart the liberal consensus about what there was to be afraid of, and how to protect people from fear. With some prominent exceptions, most fin de siècle liberals rejected the idea that women had reason to be afraid of male despotism and that something should be done about it. Their liberalism was limited to the fears of heterosexual males. Most feminists were liberals in the nineteenth century, but most liberals were not feminists, either in the short nineteenth century or the fin de siècle. Feminism was an opportunity to widen the scope of liberalism few liberals took advantage of.

All three issues, nationalism, imperialism, and feminism, posed the question of what liberalism's limits should be. These relationships were highly contested and demonstrate yet again how liberalism is a party of contradictions, in which hopes and fears ebb and flow. An important indicator of whether hope or fear predominated, of whether liberals wanted to expand their concerns or not, was whether liberals continued to use the discourse of capacity or switched to talking about rights. The discussion of the modern liberalisms of the fin de siècle in the previous chapter showed a democratizing liberalism in the process of abandoning the discourse of capacity in favor of an expanded list of economic rights, rights that were tools in the fight against poverty that was the characteristic trait of modern liberalisms—and in contrast a different list of rights, e.g., freedom of contract, property, etc., that served classical liberals as tools to reject an expanded state.

However, fin de siècle liberals also continued to speak in terms of capacity when they wanted to limit those whose fears they had to take into account. They often used the discourse of capacity with regard to groups they feared—-e.g., immigrants, African Americans, Jews; foreign nations; colonies; and perhaps especially women. When the discourse of capacity was mixed with evolutionism in the fin de siècle, it could become quite illiberal: not a means to keep people from being afraid, of providing guarantees against despotism, but a justification for terrorizing the "inferior."

The liberal relationship with the increasingly radical nationalism of the fin de siècle provides the first case in point. In this period radical nationalists pressured liberals to contract their concerns, to leave certain people out of account, or even to make them afraid—and thus to abandon liberalism altogether. Jews were one of the first targets of illiberal nationalism in the fin de siècle.

Liberalism, Nationalism, and the Jewish Problem in Fin de Siècle Germany

Nationalism insists upon the preeminence of the nation, but does not determine in advance whether the nation will be liberal or illiberal. Liberalism and nationalism are not necessarily contradictory, but they can be. In the fin de siècle the question became acute, as old problems relating to ethnicity, religion, or both (anti-semitism) became more divisive. The challenges they posed raised intellectual and practical questions about the extent to which liberalism could accommodate nationalism while retaining the commitment to diversity that had been central to some liberalisms during the short nineteenth century (Mill) and played at least some role in almost all.

This question arose everywhere, but it appeared very strongly in Germany, where liberalism and nationalism had been tightly bound during the short nineteenth century. In 1848, nationalism had served to overcome prejudices against Jews, Catholics, and other minorities, and to encourage liberals to accept diversity.[2] In the fin de siècle, if anything the opposite was true. German liberals did not become less nationalist in the fin de siècle, but many nationalists became increasingly illiberal, increasingly intolerant of diversity and unwilling to comprehend the fears of minority groups—and attracted many former liberals to abandon their previous liberalism. The relationship between German liberalism and anti-semitism in the fin de siècle provides a case in point.

Anti-semitism was not characteristic of liberalism in the short nineteenth century, rather the opposite: Jews gained full civil and political rights everywhere in Western Europe during the period, largely under liberal auspices and always with liberal support. German liberalism more or less followed the European pattern, with a sharp drop in anti-semitism in 1846–71, when nationalism repressed anti-semitism and subordinated it to the need for national unity. German conservatives and Catholics began to bring anti-semitism back into the public sphere as early as 1874, in response to the liberal electoral victories of that year: they identified liberalism with the Jews as a means of discrediting liberalism. After Heinrich von Treitschke's 1879–80 articles in the *Preussischer Jahrbücher*, a leading liberal journal, anti-semitism became a significant problem *within* German liberalism for the first time since 1848. The three kinds of response he received from German liberals who continued in varying degrees to oppose him are equally significant. They included those who found their liberalism embarrassing when put in opposition even to radical nationalism (the "notable liberals"), those who were forthright in their liberalism but uninterested in defending diversity (Ludwig Bamberger), and those who maintained that the defense of diversity was central to liberalism and ought to be to any liberal nationalism (Moritz Lazarus).

Treitschke (1834–96) was a well-known and important figure. Professor at the University of Berlin at the time of the dispute, as an historian he was highly successful with both the public and his academic colleagues. He was an editor of the liberal *Preussische Jahrbücher* from 1866 to 1889, and a member of the German Reichstag from its creation in 1871 until 1884. In parliament he was a member of the National Liberal party until 1879, when he left the party to become first an independent and then a member of a conservative party. Politically, as his Reichstag career indicates, he moved from left to right. In the early1860s he argued against the idea of annexing Alsace-Lorraine to Germany because it was contrary to the will of the inhabitants; in 1871 he supported it

2. See chapter 5.

based on its German history which he had previously regarded as "irrelevant." Originally a member of the National Liberal party, the largest of the German liberal parties, he left it in 1878 because it would not support tariffs, which Treitschke considered necessary for German economic development. A ferocious opponent of socialism, he also became increasingly contemptuous of business ("there can be no business activity without swindle and quackery") and respectful of the bureaucracy and aristocracy. The anti-semitism controversy of 1879–80 took place when Treitschke was on the cusp of leaving liberalism behind, but when he was still identified in the public mind as a liberal nationalist. Liberal responses addressed him as one of their own. The anti-semitism dispute thus took shape primarily as a dispute within German liberalism and within German nationalism—which most German liberals thought of as closely linked, if not identical.[3]

It began with an article by Treitschke in the *Jahrbücher*. Treitschke's essay "Our Prospects" consisted of three parts. The first two were devoted to international relations, primarily discussion of the Berlin Congress of 1878 and its results. The third part was about the Jews. It began with a discussion of liberal defeats by conservatives in the recent elections (liberals lost nearly 30 seats, but remained the largest party), which Treitschke attributed to liberal opposition to tariffs, followed by a call to reemphasize morality, culminating in an endorsement of longer prison sentences for criminals. It was from this foundation that Treitschke commented on what he described as "the passionate movement against Jewry." Until just a few months previously, he claimed, philosemitism dominated public discourse. Now, finally, it was acceptable to criticize the Jews. This was a good thing: "the instinct of the masses has in fact recognized a grave danger."[4]

It was especially a German question, according to Treitschke, because the number of Jews further West was too small to matter, and besides, Treitschke thought, they were mostly the superior Spanish variety of Jew, not the inferior Polish version that Germany had to deal with. The difference was important because, in Treitschke's opinion, Spanish Jews could "become good Frenchmen, Englishmen, Italians," whereas Polish Jews were, as a result of "centuries of Christian tyranny," "incomparably more alien to the European, and especially to the Germanic character." Clearly, to be alien, to be different, had nothing

3. On Treitschke see Dorpalen, "Heinrich von Treitschke," 21–35.
4. Treitschke, "Our Prospects" (1879), in Stoetzler, *The State, the Nation, & the Jews*, 311.

to recommend it for Treitschke, for whom diversity was no part of liberalism, or if it was, then liberalism had no role in nationalism.[5]

By blaming the flaws of Polish Jewry on past Christian tyranny, Treitschke separated himself from old religious prejudice and established his liberalism. He also established the Jews as aliens who were called upon to surrender their difference: "What we have to demand from our Jewish fellow-citizens is simple: that they become Germans, feel themselves simply and justly as Germans—regardless of their faith and their old sacred memories which all of us hold in reverence; for we do not want thousands of years of German civilization to be followed by an era of German-Jewish mixed culture." Treitschke's bow in the direction of Jews' sacred memories served to reinforce his objectivity, but the demand was clear. Jewish difference was not to be tolerated.[6]

Treitschke went on to say that it was possible for Jews to become Germans, giving historical examples of both "baptized" and "unbaptized" Jews who had been good Germans as more proof of his fairness. But, Treitschke claimed, the problem was that there was a "dangerous spirit of arrogance" among Jews now (blaming the victim). And then Treitschke turned to traditional anti-semitic imagery: the Jews were materialists, usurers, dishonest businessmen. They controlled the press, "which gives far too much scope to Jewry." Above all, the Jews' crime was to insist on "literal parity" with Germans, "forgetful of the fact that we Germans are, after all, a Christian nation, and the Jews are only a minority in our midst; we have witnessed that the removal of Christian pictures in mixed schools was demanded." The German reaction against this "alien element" was justified, and the most fair-minded, unprejudiced people, those "who would reject with horror any thought of Christian fanaticism [Christian fanaticism = Catholicism, for the very Protestant Treitschke] unite" in saying the phrase Treitschke popularized, and that would become a Nazi slogan: "the Jews are our misfortune" (*Die Juden sind unser Unglück*). By logical extension, the reader may conclude, those who defended diversity equally had no place in the German nation or German nationalism. Rejection of any liberalism that did so was implicit.[7]

Treitschke then once again became the apostle of reason, denied any wish to reverse Jewish emancipation, and repeated his call for the Jews to become fully German. Crucially, however, at the same time he stressed that "the task

5. Treitschke, "Our Prospects," 312.
6. Treitschke, "Our Prospects," 312.
7. Treitschke, "Our Prospects," 314.

can never be solved completely. There has always been an abyss between occidental and Semitic being . . . there will always be Jews who are nothing but German-speaking Orientals." There was a permanent, ineradicable "antagonism," between Jews and Germans, but it could be mitigated if the Jews would show proper "respect." "The complete absence of such respect in a section of our commercial and literary Jewry is the ultimate reason for today's passionate bitterness." In short, the Jews, insofar as they retained a Jewish identity, ought to be afraid, and show it by their respectful attitude. In later responses to critics, Treitschke went even further: differences in religious *"denomination"* (emphasis added), that is between different kinds of Protestant or perhaps even Protestants and Catholics, could be overcome, but different *religions* could be part of one nation "only as a transitional state" and only if one religion "clearly predominates."[8]

Treitschke's demand for complete assimilation in return for citizenship was typical of much of the liberal rhetoric about Jewish Emancipation in Germany and elsewhere. It was not necessarily a demand restricted to Jews— identification with the nation was implied by all versions of nationalism, and demands for the renunciation of other identifications were not uncommon. This rhetoric had been abandoned in 1848 and the years thereafter, but it returned with a vengeance in the fin de siècle. Indeed, if always dubiously liberal, it became explicitly illiberal in the hands of Treitschke and his ilk. What was illiberal was that Treitschke questioned whether Jews could *ever* acquire the capacity to become Germans. Treitschke argued that there was a permanent antagonism between Jews and Germans, and that Jews lacked the capacity to become fully German / fully human, despite the rare exceptions to this rule Treitschke cited in order to appear objective. The language of capacity took on an illiberal character in the fin de siècle it had not possessed in the short nineteenth century. It became a justification for instilling fear—and *never* taking it away.

This illiberalism with regard to diversity was not restricted to Jews. Treitschke's anti-semitic rhetoric mimicked the anti-Catholic language of the *Kulturkampf,* the war against Catholicism waged by Bismarck of which Treitschke, along with most liberals, was a fervent supporter, and which was just beginning to be legally reversed in 1879. Catholics and liberals were still extremely hostile to one another. Indeed, as late as 1912, the left liberal Progres-

---

8. Treitschke, "Our Prospects," 315; Treitschke, cited in Stoetzler, *The State, the Nation, & the Jews,* 108.

sive party vaunted itself as the anti-Catholic party, and proposed banning nuns from working as nurses in public hospitals. Liberal parties helped reject Bills of Toleration for Catholics in the Reichstag in 1900, 1903, and 1905. Anti-Catholicism remained a central part of German liberal identity right through the early twentieth century—just as it did in France.[9] In a sense, the radical anti-semitism of 1880 and thereafter was just playing catch-up.[10]

Yet there was an important difference between Treitschke's anti-semitism and liberal anti-Catholicism. If many liberals would have liked to see Catholicism disappear, as Treitschke would have liked to see Jews disappear, they thought it was possible for Catholics to cease to be Catholic, whereas Treitschke doubted that Jews could ever become German. Further, liberals did not attack the Catholic presence in civil society, as Treitschke attacked the Jewish presence in civil society, as businessmen or journalists. As much as liberals disliked Catholicism in the public sphere, they did not raise objections to it in the private sphere. Liberal anti-Catholicism had in this respect been limited. But the radical nationalist rejection of diversity in the fin de siècle went further. Jews and others perceived as national minorities were not to be permitted to express their diversity even in private if they wished to belong to the nation. For Treitschke, while Jews might be able to keep their "sacred memories," they had better keep them locked in a drawer, for fear of being accused of lack of "respect" for German Christendom. It was not Jewish actions in the public sphere that endangered Germany, but the very presence of Jews because of their essential "Oriental" essence, which must not be mixed with German culture. This was illiberal, and to the extent this view became identified with nationalism, it marked a definitive cleavage between liberalism and nationalism.

The spectrum of liberal responses to Treitschke reveals a good deal about the relationship between liberalism and nationalism in the fin de siècle: that of embarrassed liberal nationalists; that of unembarrassed liberals who nevertheless did not see it as their task to defend diversity; and that of Mill's heirs, who saw accepting diversity as central to both liberalism and liberal

---

9. And in a different context in America, where it remained part of anti-immigrant feeling. Anti-liberalism and anti-Protestantism also remained part of the Catholic repertoire. A Papal Encyclical of 1897 compared Protestants to the Black Plague. See Thompson, *Left Liberals*, 109.

10. Michael B. Gross, Review of Stoetzler, *The State, the Nation, & the Jews, Journal of Modern History* 82, no. 4 (December 2010): 987–989; Thompson, *Left Liberals*, 129–130, see also 163; Smith, *German Nationalism*, 137–138; Thompson, *Left Liberals*, 190; 8.

nationalism. To begin with, while Treitschke's essay called forth a storm of liberal opposition, Treitschke's liberal opponents mostly did not call it illiberal. In 1880 the Declaration of the Notables, signed by seventy-three leading non-Jewish liberal politicians, academics, lawyers, businessmen, etc., expressed a liberal opposition to Treitschke that did not dare identify itself as liberal: nowhere in the brief, four-paragraph Declaration did the word "liberal" appear. Rather, it opened with a tribute to German unity, and a *nationalist* rejection of Treitschke as someone who incited disunity and "punishes those who honestly and seriously strive to overcome their particularity and to achieve true amalgamation with the nation." There was thus a meeting of the minds between Treitschke and his liberal opponents on the ground of assimilation. For both, the ideal German was one who had no other group identity (Protestantism was seen, courtesy of Martin Luther, as another kind of Germanness, and by a stretch this might even extend generally to Christianity). Heterogeneity was not acceptable within the national community as these nationalists imagined it.[11]

What Treitschke and the notables had in common was a certain kind of liberal nationalism that refused to accept diversity; what separated them, according to the signatories of the Declaration, was that Treitschke added to it an illiberal nationalism that refused to allow certain kinds of people, in this case Jews, to ever be part of the nation. The Declaration condemned how "the racial hatred and fanaticism of the Middle Ages are currently revived and directed against our Jewish fellow citizens in an unexpected and deeply embarrassing fashion." It demanded that Jews be treated equally not just by the law, but in the mind of every citizen. It warned that attitudes like Treitschke's would have practical, not just theoretical consequences. Even if Treitschke himself did not call for an end to Jewish emancipation, his attitudes would inevitably lead to "exceptional laws and the exclusion of Jews from this or that profession or kind of property, from distinctions and positions of authority." The Declaration went on to demand "Respect for every confession, equal right, equal sun in competition, equal recognition of merit and achievement for Christians and Jews"—a liberal credo. In short, the Declaration demanded that Jews should have no cause for fear in Germany. But it did so without mentioning "liberalism" by name, or by confronting the fact that Treitschke was not a liberal. As a nationalist, Treitschke was still within the liberal camp as far as the notables were concerned. In Germany, the period around 1879 was

11. Cited in Stoetzler, *The State, the Nation, & the Jews*, 48.

the last moment when nationalism and liberalism could still be uncontroversially identified.[12]

The Anti-Semitism Dispute showed that this identification was now subject to challenge. For Ludwig Bamberger, a prominent Jewish figure within liberal ranks and a veteran supporter of German unification, the reason the Jews were being attacked had nothing to do with nationalism. Rather, "the attack on the Jews is only a smoke screen diverting attention from today's great campaign against liberalism." Bamberger was proudly liberal, and unlike the notables, willing to openly distinguish between liberal and illiberal nationalisms. For Bamberger, Treitschke's main target was not the Jews, but liberalism, and Treitschke was no longer a liberal.[13]

Bamberger was a nationalist, but for Bamberger, "exaggerated nationalism" was the outright enemy of liberalism: "The cult of nationality more than anything else carries within itself this temptation [to hate everything alien]. . . . From this hate of the alien beyond the border, it is only a step to the hate of what can be found to be alien within one's own country." Bamberger compared Treitschke to the American Know-Nothings and their rejection of immigrants. He rejected Treitschke's attempt to differentiate new from old antisemitism, racial and / or cultural rather than religious: both were just illiberal justifications for hereditary inequality. Instead of distinguishing between kinds of antisemitism, Bamberger distinguished between "the cult of nationality," which liberals must reject, and what he called "modern nationality," i.e., liberal nationality, which he supported. This was not really an innovation. John Stuart Mill, a nineteenth-century liberal nationalist, also distinguished between good and bad forms of nationalism, in which the bad forms were based on the hatred of Others. But if the issue was not new, in the fin de siècle it became increasingly prominent.[14]

What was missing from Bamberger too, however, in contrast to Mill, was a positive evaluation of the role of diversity as intrinsic to a liberal society. For that one must turn to the Jewish community leader, nationalist, and sometime

12. Cited in Stoetzler, *The State, the Nation, & the Jews*, 48; German text of the "Erklärung-Notabeln," https://de.wikipedia.org/wiki/Notabeln-Erkl%C3%A4rung. One of the signatories of the Declaration, the eminent liberal historian Mommsen, also wrote his own reply that emphasized Trietschke's "good intentions." See Stoetzler, *The State, the Nation, & the Jews*, 50; 162; 164.

13. Bamberger, cited in Stoetzler, *The State, the Nation, & the Jews*, 43.

14. Bamberger, cited in Stoetzler, *The State, the Nation, & the Jews*, 98–100; Varouxakis, " 'Patriotism', 'Cosmopolitanism', and 'Humanity,' " 101–102.

lecturer at the Prussian Military Academy, Moritz Lazarus. In "What Does National Mean?," Lazarus argued that "we German Jews can and ought to contribute to this most supreme ideal of German nationality in full accordance with ourselves. In order to be perfect, most efficient Germans, we not only can but must remain Jews." "True culture . . . consists in *diversity*" (emphasis original), and Lazarus continued in a footnote that could have been written by Mill: "How will truth grow if not through spiritual struggle, through the struggles of different insights, through the competition of forces?" For Lazarus the historical role of the Jews was to introduce diversity into every nation. Effectively, Lazarus identified the acceptance of unassimilated Jews in national culture with liberalism. At the same time, this diversity was placed in service of the "supreme ideal of German nationality."[15]

The Anti-Semitism Dispute presented a variety of nationalisms and liberalisms. As its most recent chronicler notes, the Dispute was as much about liberal (and illiberal) views of Germans as it was about the Jews, as much about the status of diversity in the nation-state as about Judaism. It showed how in the fin de siècle certain kinds of nationalism led altogether out of the liberal orbit and transformed the discourse of capacity from a bulwark against fear into a terrifying weapon against "aliens." Even confirmed liberal politicians and opponents of anti-semitism such as the signatories of the Declaration of the Notables found themselves using the same language as what Bamberger called "the cult of nationality," fellow travelers who struggled to remain simultaneously liberal and nationalist. Other liberal nationalists, including Bamberger and Lazarus, managed to stay out of these dangerous rapids for the most part, but at the price of being left high and dry by certain currents of nationalist thought. In Germany and elsewhere, nationalists and liberals were pried apart by wedge issues in the fin de siècle, of which anti-semitism was a leading example (tariffs and colonialism were others). When they remained together, it was not always to follow a liberal course. Nationalism provided a chorus of Sirens that led many liberals onto the rocks of Scylla and Charybdis (to use one of nineteenth-century liberals' favorite metaphors), that is, nationalism made illiberalism attractive in a modern, trendy, fin de siècle way, suitable for erstwhile liberal adherents of progress and enemies of Catholics.[16]

The relationship between liberalism and nationalism in the fin de siècle shows that the history of liberalism is not necessarily one of progress, neither

15. Lazarus, cited in Stoetzler, *The State, the Nation, & the Jews*, 14, 343; 345–346.
16. Stoetzler, *The State, the Nation, & the Jews*, 3.

progress toward making a liberal world nor toward a liberalism that gives equal respect to the fears of all groups. For illiberal or ex-liberal nationalists, some groups lacked the capacity to ever become full citizens, and there was no universal right to citizenship, even potentially (one can see the parallel reasoning of the infamous 1857 Dred Scott Decision of the US Supreme Court, which denied any possibility of American citizenship to African Americans). The extent to which fin de siècle nationalists rejected liberalism varied with time and place, but everywhere radical forms of nationalism became, and remained, a standing temptation to illiberalism for many liberals, in a way it had not been during the short nineteenth century. Imperialism presented liberals with a similar problem.

Liberalism and Colonialism

Despite the efforts of many commentators, the only defensible perspective on the relationship between liberalism and colonialism is that it is indeterminate, much like that between liberalism and nationalism. The article on "Empire and Imperialism" in *The Cambridge History of Nineteenth-Century Political Thought* titles the relevant section "Liberalism and empire: ambivalence and critique." This is true of all strands of liberal thought, from utilitarianism to British Idealism to classical liberal economists, and even to Social Darwinism (Spencer was a firm opponent of colonialism). Liberals were always and everywhere divided about colonialism. The proportion of liberals on one side or the other of the argument changed over time and place.[17]

Western imperialism and colonialism (both terms are used here, but the emphasis is on colonialism) were, to say the least, overdetermined. As one historian put it, describing the surge in colonialism during the fin de siècle, "as for its causes, all the positive explanations," there follows a long list, "are true and apply at various points; none is the sole or main answer." This is as true with regard to liberalism as anything else. Liberal attitudes toward colonialism, however, tell us a lot about the history of liberalism in the fin de siècle.[18]

---

17. Bell, "Empire and Imperialism," 882; 886; 875, 881, Pitts, *A Turn to Empire*, 4. David Armitage's claim that "it is now a commonplace of the history of political thought that there has long been a mutually constitutive relationship between liberalism and colonialism" is based on the common error of thinking that Locke was constitutive of both. Armitage, "John Locke," 602.

18. Schroeder, "International Politics, Peace, and War," 189.

It is not clear when liberalism became more colonialist. One view is that this occurred during the mid-nineteenth century, when thinkers like Mill and Tocqueville adopted more or less pro-colonialist views (with an emphasis on the "more or less"), compared to proto-liberals like Smith or Montesquieu. That view has tended to be rejected in favor of the notion of liberal ambivalence to colonialism at mid-century. But in the fin de siècle liberal opposition to colonialism weakened, without disappearing. Many fin de siècle liberals endorsed colonialism as a *liberal* activity, and found political, economic, and moral reasons for supporting it.[19]

It is not obvious at first glance, or even second, how colonialism could be a step toward making a world in which no one need be afraid. There were both liberal and illiberal arguments for colonialism in the fin de siècle, and while it is only the liberal ones that matter here, it must be recognized that some liberals accepted illiberal arguments in this regard (often out of nationalism), and some non-liberals used the liberal one. Thus, as will be seen below, the liberal Jules Ferry also used nationalist arguments to justify the expansion of the French colonial empire, while also making a liberal argument for it: France's *mission civilisatrice*. The mission civilisatrice, or civilizing mission, was the argument liberal imperialists characteristically embraced as a means of exporting liberalism.

The phrase is French, but it was found throughout the West. The mission civilisatrice embodied the idea that those doing the civilizing were superior to those being civilized, and that they had a right and even a duty to pass on to their inferiors whatever it was that made them superior—regardless of whether there was any corresponding desire for improvement on the part of the inferior. The phrase had a religious origin—the Christian mission to save souls. The missionaries of liberalism felt equally justified in imposing "civilization" on barbarians evidently in need of it. If civilization was a prerequisite for liberalism, then perhaps the only liberal thing to do with uncivilized peoples was to civilize them, whether they liked it or not. This involved uplifting them economically, morally, and politically, usually in that order.

19. For the view, see Pitts, *A Turn to Empire*, for rebuttal, see Bell, "Empire and Imperialism," passim, and A. G. Hopkins, "Overseas Expansion," 220. Mill's and Tocqueville's relationship to imperialism is much debated. On Tocqueville, see Kahan, "Tocqueville: Liberalism and Imperialism," 152–168; on Mill, see Tunick, "Tolerant Imperialism," 586–611, and Varouxakis, " 'Patriotism', 'Cosmopolitanism', and 'Humanity.' " The most relevant citation from Mill is "I am not aware that any community has a right to force another to be civilized." *On Liberty, CW*, 18, 1:291.

However, to the extent civilization was forcibly imposed, it conflicted with the liberal impulse to respect diversity (relatively weak in the fin de siècle) and the liberal impulse to limit power (relatively strong). Thus not all fin de siècle liberals thought they had a mission to civilize. Nevertheless, the progressive impulse and the sense of cultural superiority inherent in the civilizing mission were characteristically liberal.[20] One of the initial forms taken by the civilizing mission (and an early example of liberals expanding their understanding of whose fears counted) was the abolition of slavery. Later, liberal colonialists often imposed legal norms that limited despotic power, insisted on equality before the law for lower castes, abolished *suttee*, etc. If these examples were usually accompanied by rights talk, the civilizing mission lent itself even more to expression in terms of capacity: just as individuals and groups within Western societies would one day or recently had acquired the capacity for political participation, so might individuals and peoples overseas, once civilized.[21]

The civilizing mission required certain authentically liberal attitudes. One could not be racist in a strong sense and pursue the mission: if others were fundamentally and ineradicably inferior, they were incapable of civilization. The civilizing mission presumed the unity and equality of the human race. To succeed in the civilizing mission thus meant the end of colonialism: from Macaulay onward, liberal civilizers recognized that equality was the goal, and that once achieved, independence was its natural and necessary consequence. "It may be that . . . by good government we may educate our subjects into a capacity for better government; that, having become instructed in European knowledge, they may, in some future age, demand European institutions. Whether such a day will ever come I know not. But never will I attempt to avert or to retard it. Whenever it comes, it will be the proudest day in English history."[22]

This was a liberal imperialism. Rather than representing a hypocritical contrast with liberal practices at home, it was largely coherent with them. There were parallels with what fin de siècle Christians call the "internal" and "external" missions. The mission civilisatrice was usually associated with extra-European colonialism, but it had a wider application. How liberals thought about Chinese, Indians, or Africans was not so different from how they thought about immigrants or Catholics at home (or the poor, before modern

20. As Pitts notes. See *A Turn to Empire*, 5.

21. Mehta, *Liberalism and Empire*, 74.

22. T. B. Macaulay, "Government of India," parliamentary speech of 1833, cited in Metcalf, *Ideologies of the Raj*, 34.

liberals redeemed them from accusations of moral turpitude). Jane Addams's Hull House was in its way an example of the civilizing mission; some nineteenth-century German liberal nationalists thought of themselves as having a mission to civilize Poles living in eastern Prussia; French peasants had to be turned into Frenchmen by obligatory state primary education; and at the end of the twentieth century some Americans thought they had a mission to civilize Iraq. The means need not be violent, as the example of Jane Addams shows. The mission civilisatrice, at home or abroad, has been a permanent feature of liberalism; in the early twenty-first century it is often indicated by the word "development."[23]

The "educational" means used to civilize clearly had not always been liberal. Progress might be encouraged, illiberally, by Terror—the Jacobin technique liberalism was intended to forestall. Or by monarchical despotism, as the somewhat more ambiguous example of Napoleon spreading the Civil Code had demonstrated. Even the abolition of slavery, "the quintessential civilizing mission of the pre-Victorian age," had "created all sorts of pretexts for interference and intervention across the globe," which often had had little to do with abolishing slavery. In the fin de siècle Kipling wrote "The White Man's Burden" to encourage the Americans to colonize the Philippines after the Spanish-American War (1899), and President McKinley justified America's war against the Filipino resistance in terms that identified, in a way common among American, British, and German liberals, liberalism and Protestant Christianity: "There was nothing left for us to do but to . . . educate the Filipinos, and uplift and civilize and Christianize them [they were already Catholic], and by God's grace do the very best we could for them." There was an unprecedented amount of liberal enthusiasm for the civilizing mission and for colonialism, a change that was coherent with the radical nationalism of the period.[24]

23. Conrad, German Colonialism, 246, 248–249, Osterhammel, "Europe, the 'West' and the Civilizing Mission," 23, 29. The civilizing mission does not apply to all forms of colonialism, in particular "settler colonialism," in which the dominant population of the colony consisted of European settlers whose civilization was that of the metropole, and who themselves typically had little or no interest in "civilizing" such natives as might survive their coming. See Osterhammel, "Europe, the 'West' and the Civilizing Mission," 34–35.

24. Osterhammel, "Europe, the 'West' and the Civilizing Mission," 16–18; 25–27; McKinley cited in Osterhammel, 28; Metcalf, Ideologies of the Raj, 6. Outside the West, there were counter-efforts everywhere from Egypt to Japan at "self-civilization," that is the adoption of whatever Western techniques and methods were needed to preserve an independent state. This included the sprouting of indigenous liberalisms, which identified themselves as such and considered

By 1890 or 1900, liberals "almost all believed it was the responsibility of civilized nations to promote civilization among primitive peoples with the objective of preparing them for self-government." The debate among British liberals about the Second Boer War (1899–1902) was not a debate about whether colonialism was acceptable so much as a debate about what kind of colonialism was acceptable. Many of the pro-Boers were as colonialist as the anti-Boers in other contexts. Context was crucial. Shortly after WWI the distinguished British historian and modern liberal R. G. Collingwood differentiated between "insane imperialism" and "sane imperialism." "Insane" imperialism was the conquest of one civilized nation by another civilized nation attempting to impose its own culture and way of life. This was "false and evil," and exemplified by Germany starting WWI. "Sane" imperialism was the conquest of uncivilized nations by civilized ones, i.e., colonialism, which conferred the benefits of the higher civilization on the lower. According to Collingwood, "such conquest was that which formed the Roman Empire, and that which in more recent days extended the power of European nations over Africa. Conquest in this sense is a necessary and in the long run a beneficent factor in the advance of mankind." Collingwood was only echoing what Renan had said in 1871: "The conquest of the country of such an inferior race by a superior race . . . is not at all shocking. England practices this kind of colonization in India, to the great advantage of India, of humanity in general, and to its own advantage." By 1900 the great majority of liberals had reached a consensus in favor of some forms of colonialism, but it did not happen without a fight. A striking example of such a fight took place in the French Parliament in 1885.[25]

In some respects France is an odd place to look for a watershed moment about liberalism and imperialism. It did not possess the largest colonial empire, being well behind the British. Unlike Britain (the Second Boer War), America (the annexation of the Philippines), or even Germany (the "Hottentot election" of 1907), colonial questions were never a leading electoral issue in France. As in the rest of the West, but even more so, French public opinion was usually indifferent to colonial questions.[26]

---

the creation of a liberal state and society, including some form of representative government, as the best means of resisting Western pressure. See the essays about Asian and Middle Eastern liberals in *Liberal Moments*, ed. Atanassow and Kahan.

25. Boucher, "'Sane' and 'Insane' Imperialism," 1190.

26. Girardet, *L'idée coloniale*, 23–24, Betts, *Assimiliation and Association*, vii, xiv.

Nevertheless, France had possessed a considerable colonial empire since the eighteenth century—and many French proto-liberals and liberals had opposed it: Voltaire, d'Alembert, Raynal, Diderot, Turgot, all rejected any suggestion of a mission civilisatrice. Moving to the short nineteenth century, when France had lost most of her first colonial empire, it should be remembered that the conquest of Algeria in 1830 had originally been the work of the Bourbon Restoration, not of a liberal government. While the liberal July Monarchy had retained Algeria, Guizot had rejected the proposed conquest of Madagascar. The anti-colonialists of the time included the leading French liberal economists of the period, Say and Bastiat (see chapter 6). Even liberals who had supported the retention of Algeria, such as Tocqueville, did not necessarily do so on liberal grounds—Tocqueville was from an early date dubious about the idea of a French civilizing mission in Algeria. On the other hand, while Guizot had rejected the French occupation of Madagascar, he had strongly endorsed the idea of European cultural superiority and a global European civilizing mission. Say eventually supported the British colonization of India from admiration for its "civilizing qualities."[27]

French liberal ambivalence about imperialism peaked during the first ten years of the Third Republic, 1875–1885, when the liberal ideology of the mission civilisatrice was fully developed in France. One of the French liberal parties, led by Jules Ferry, ardently supported the civilizing mission and expanding the French colonial empire. But the other major French liberal faction, led by Georges Clemenceau, rejected the civilizing mission along with colonialism. Clemenceau's factions were for the most part modern liberals, in favour of using state action to address the problem of poverty. But the generally classical liberal French economists also mostly opposed colonialism. While Paul Leroy-Beaulieu, the leading French liberal economist of the day, was a colonialist, according to his contemporary Charles Gide he was the only French economist of whom this could be said in 1885. One, Yves Guyot, mocked the whole idea of a civilizing mission in 1900: "We, we do not doubt that besides European civilization, there are other civilizations, such as Hindu civilization, Chinese civilization, Arab civilization, which constitute advanced social states: rather than condemning them, we should study them." For Gustave de Moli-

---

27. Ageron, *L'anticolonialisme*, 6–7; Girardet, *L'idée coloniale*, 33; 26–27; Ageron, *L'anticolonialisme*, 8; Kahan, "Tocqueville: Liberalism and Imperialism," 152–168; Todd, *A Velvet Empire*, 60–64. Remarkably, the word "liberalism" does not appear in Todd's book, and the word "liberal" hardly ever.

nari, colonies were just an excuse for hiring more bureaucrats and had no economic justification. With respect to colonialism, economistic liberalisms that
had little interest in liberalism's moral or political pillars were sometimes saved
from illiberal conclusions by their narrow focus, although economic apologies
for colonialism as being of economic benefit to the colonized existed. Until
1885, colonialism was a controversial issue in French liberal circles.[28]

The issues surrounding imperialism came to a head in the French parliament in July 1885. Ostensibly, the issue being debated was the vote of money
for a military operation in Madagascar, already partly colonized by the French.
In fact, as everyone was well aware, the future of French colonial policy was at
stake. The debate was largely a debate among liberals. Ferry was Prime Minister, and Clemenceau was his chief opponent.[29] Ferry was among the founding
fathers of the Third Republic. More to the point he was the grand champion
of laïcité (see chapter 5), the French version of liberal anti-Catholicism. The
vocabulary used to defend laïcité and that used to defend the civilizing mission
was much the same—including a lot of the discourse of capacity in preference
to rights talk.[30]

Ferry's arguments for colonialism were based on the three pillars of liberalism: "The policy of colonial expansion is . . . based on three orders of ideas:
economic ideas, ideas about civilization of the greatest signficance [morals],
and ideas of a political and patriotic nature." First came economics. French
colonialism was a response to the failure of free trade and the rise of protectionism. Because there was no free trade in Europe, France had to find markets
for its exports elsewhere: its own colonies. Second, Ferry advanced a moral
argument, "the humanitarian and civilizing aspect of the question." Anti-
colonialist liberals argued that civilization could not be imposed with artillery,
and that even inferior races possessed equal rights. When one challenged him
with a reference to the Declaration of the Rights of Man, he responded: "If the
Declaration of the Rights of Man was written for the blacks of Equatorial Africa, then by what right do you go and impose commerce on them? They did
not ask you to come!" When it was pointed out that to impose and to offer are
two different things, Ferry continued, "I repeat that the superior races have a

28. Girardet, *L'idée coloniale*, 52; Ageron, *L'anticolonialisme*, 8–9; Guyot, cited in Ageron,
L'anticolonialisme, 11; Ageron, *L'anticolonialisme*, 53.

29. Girardet, *L'idée coloniale*, 146–148; Ageron, *L'anticolonialisme*, 15, 20, Girardet, *L'idée coloniale*, 149; Betts, *Assimilation and Association*, 7, Conklin, *A Mission to Civilize*, 139–140.

30. Betts, *Assimilation and Association*, 30–31.

right, because they have a duty. They have the duty to civilize the inferior races." Ferry thus concluded: "Gentlemen, we must speak louder and more truthfully! We must say openly that in fact the superior races have a right vis-à-vis the inferior races." Ferry concluded his argument for the moral justification of colonialism by noting that since the Congress of Berlin in 1878 it was the legal duty of every European nation to put an end to slavery and the slave trade. Thus appeared the mission civilisatrice, red in tooth and claw.[31]

At this point Ferry moved on to the third pillar on which he justified French imperialism, namely "the political side of the question," and left liberalism behind for nationalism. In the competitive international environment of 1885, to abstain from colonialism meant accepting decadence. France must be a world power or decline: "Nations, in our time, are great only through their actions, it is not by the reputation of [their] institutions that they are great today." There followed interruptions from both left and right—not surprising, when Ferry had just abandoned representative government and the Declaration of the Rights of Man as the source of French glory in favor of colonial expansion. He argued that it was impossible to influence the world without colonial expansion, and that failing to expand would leave France a third- or fourth-rate power. France, Ferry argued, could not be a Belgium or a Switzerland, "it cannot be merely a free country, it must also be a great country," spreading everywhere "its language, its mores, its flag, its arms, its genius." Freedom had to take a back seat.[32] Ferry thus simultaneously made liberal and illiberal appeals, and endorsed both a liberal and an illiberal colonialism. Perhaps Ferry's schizophrenia was deliberate. For a vote-seeking politician, it was naturally best to confuse sane and insane imperialism, exaggerated and modern nationalism so as to attract the most voters, at the price of sometimes leaving liberalism behind. But the lack of clarity was dangerous, and not only intellectually. As a form of nationalism, colonialism, like other forms of nationalism, tempted liberals to embrace power and terror and renounce liberalism. Fear was to be projected on one side of the Ocean, while being fought on the other.

This was why Clemenceau rejected colonialism, mission civilisatrice included. "Superior races! Inferior races! It is quickly said. As for me, I have en-

31. http://www2.assemblee-nationale.fr/decouvrir-l-assemblee/histoire/grands-discours -parlementaires/jules-ferry-28-juillet-1885. All citations from the speech come from this document and all translations are my own.

32. In German terms, one might describe Ferry as a National Liberal.

tirely given up that kind of language since I saw German professors scientifically demonstrate that France would lose the war with Germany, because the French race was inferior to the German race. Since then, I confess, I look twice before turning to a man or a civilization and saying: inferior man or inferior civilization!" For Clemenceau, the idea of the civilizing mission was just another way of saying power trumps justice. Against Ferry, he proclaimed that the "genius of the French race" had been "to generalize the theory of rights and of justice," "that the problem of civilization is to eliminate violence [fear] from the relations between individual men in the same society, and to tend to eliminate violence . . . from the relationships between nations." Clemenceau went on to cite the history of Western imperialism from Cortez to Warren Hastings as proof that European civilization had no superiority over others, and to reject any notion of superior nations having rights over inferior ones. "To speak of civilization," in this context, "is to combine violence with hypocrisy."[33]

It was not that Clemenceau rejected nationalism. Clemenceau was fiercely nationalistic. Just as in Britain, Little Englanders confronted Imperialists, so in France in 1885, Clemenceau argued that colonial expansion was a luxury France could not afford, that to maintain her status as a great power France needed to spend all its money at home, on schools, economic investments, dealing with its social problems, etc. For Clemenceau, national greatness had nothing to do with colonialism, and his liberal nationalism could embrace an anti-colonialist position.

Notably, however, in 1885 both pro- and anti-colonialist French liberals talked about national greatness, and it is hard to claim that one group was "insane." Nationalism, like liberalism, is open-ended, and thus the nationalist attitude to colonialism was no more predetermined than the liberal one. When it came to colonialism, for and against, fin de siècle nationalism and liberalism were intertwined, but in the end colonialism was the winner among liberals. Although in 1885 Ferry's victory margin was only four votes, in the following years opposition to French colonialism largely evaporated, despite brief upswings. After 1895 the Radicals, including Clemenceau, moderated their opposition, and when they took over the government in 1902 they became supporters of French colonial expansion. As was true elsewhere in Europe, even French Socialists showed an increasing amount of sympathy for colonialism in the first decades of the twentieth century.[34]

33. Clemenceau, cited in Ageron, L'anticolonialisme, 59–60.
34. Girardet, L'idée coloniale, 97–98.

Liberal colonialism meant a limitation of liberal concerns—some people's fears mattered; others' didn't. When Ferry discussed Algeria, he said that the French colonists there should be given "guarantees which ensure freedom, security, and the dignity of the citizen against arbitrary power." Liberalism should apply to them. The Arab and Berber inhabitants, however, did not deserve the same treatment, according to Ferry: liberalism did not apply to them. Charles Gide, whom we have seen above as an opponent of colonialism, later invented a legal category of "worldwide public utility," *utilité publique mondiale*," to justify expropriating the natives since "the necessities of the existence of the human species do not permit lands to be indefinitely left fallow by inhabitants who do not know how to put them to use." Gide thus legitimized taking "under-used" native lands without compensation.[35] In this interpretation of the civilizing mission, Bastiat might have suggested that what "civilization" meant was "legalized plunder." Guarantees such as the Declaration of the Rights of Man and the Citizen provided were not for the natives.[36]

The doctrine of separate and maybe or maybe not one day equal was the base policy of liberal colonialism. The colonies were considered to be "prepolitical," too immature to be able to choose their own path. The discourse of capacity was used to exclude them from liberal economic, political, and moral consideration. This in certain respects was no different from liberalism at home, when liberals used the discourse of capacity to exclude the majority of men and all women from the suffrage, and evinced little concern with poverty. But within the West the discourse of capacity, as long as it was liberal, was always "assimilationist": those excluded could, should, and would one day acquire equal capacity with everyone else (although the Anti-Semitism dispute provides a counter-example). With regard to non-White colonies, assimilation rapidly declined as a liberal goal, to the extent it was ever present, i.e., that Senegalese were ever supposed to become fully French, or Indians fully British—and even "association," that is equality while remaining different, was increasingly challenged by illiberal imperialists. In this there were parallels with the way in which many liberals abandoned support for diversity and supported cultural homogeneity at home.[37]

35. This argument is also found in Locke, but Locke is not cited by Gide.

36. Girardet, *L'idée coloniale*, 102, 135 ; Ferry, cited in Grandmaison, *La République impériale*,130; Gide, cited in Grandmaison, *La République impériale*, 28, 238.

37. Conklin, *A Mission to Civilize*, 75, 77–78; 136–138; Mantena, "The Crisis of Liberal Imperialism," 21–22; Metcalf, *Ideologies of the Raj*, 43, 58, 203–206, 208–211.

French "associationist" treatment of Africans also resembled the treatment of French women at home. As one historian put it, "women, like Africans, were excluded from the franchise on grounds of natural inferiority," but "in excluding women from the vote, French legislators were also careful to assign them an alternative political role: that of constructing the nation through reproduction and domesticity." Like Africans, French women could be civilized, which in liberal eyes meant weaned away from clerical domination, by education. Like Africans, they would remain associated with French men, but not assimilated to them. And, as with Africans, the language of capacity was used to justify limiting the application of liberalism to women. Colonialism certainly did not invent patriarchy. But it encouraged the use of language and ideas that supported it, and helped prevent liberals from seeing it as a problem—even though it was also possible to be a feminist colonialist.[38]

The civilizing mission became a liberal mission (even if some conservatives or socialists also accepted it), and liberalism became an ever more important aspect of Western colonialism over the course of the fin de siècle. The colonial project helped cement ties between liberalism and nationalism, with all the dangers this implied for liberalism because colonialism and all the attitudes it implied were hard to restrict to the colonies. The civilizing mission was susceptible to being diverted from the liberal project of eventually liberating all humanity from fear, in favor of racism, *realpolitik*, and "insane" nationalism. The sane and insane, liberal and illiberal variations of imperialism (and nationalism) are hard to disentangle, and so are imperialism's effects on liberalism. Clearly, however, imperialism frequently played the role of yet another nationalist siren calling on liberals to change their course, or at least to steer away from large portions of humanity.

Yet colonialism sometimes played a democratizing role in the metropolis in the fin de siècle, encouraging liberals to abandon the discourse of capacity at home even while reinforcing it abroad. Compared to Africans or Chinese, the local poor seemed more respectable, and their fears, especially their fear of poverty, more deserving of consideration. Colonialism sometimes was the ally of modern liberalism, encouraged people who might otherwise have been less concerned with the poor to take an interest in their situation. In Britain, Joseph Chamberlain, the inventor of "municipal socialism," was a

---

38. Conklin, *A Mission to Civilize*, 85, see also 114–115; 105. See also Josep Fradera on the notion of dual constitutionalism, a liberal one for the metropole, an illiberal one for the colonies. Fradera, *The Imperial Nation.*

modern liberal, as was Winston Churchill in the fin de siècle: they were both ardent colonialists. They had many analogs, in Britain and elsewhere. Perhaps the clearest case of imperialism and modern liberalism walking hand in hand was in Germany.

Colonialism and Modern Liberalism:
The Case of Friedrich Naumann

The discussion of modern liberalisms in the previous chapter omitted Germany in order to discuss German modern liberalism in the context of German colonialism. Germany was not unique in this regard; in many countries, there were modern liberals who associated the fight against poverty with imperialism, such as Chamberlain and Churchill in England and Theodore Roosevelt in the United States. In Germany, however, the association was particularly close. German "social liberalism" was a form of liberal colonialism and what was called *Weltpolitik* often wore liberal colors. In Germany as elsewhere, there was an increasingly general endorsement of colonialism at the end of the century, extending to all the liberal parties (and even to many German socialists). Among the German liberal parties the more moderate National Liberal party endorsed imperialism after 1894, and the left liberal Progressives followed in 1907. Liberal support for colonialism was popular with the voters: although it was not the only reason, in the last elections of the German Empire in 1912 the liberal parties received 26 percent of the vote, their highest score since 1893, partly because of their newfound enthusiasm for German colonialism.[39]

Growing liberal support for colonialism in Germany was combined with a turn to modern liberalism that was embodied in the ideas and career of Friedrich Naumann (1860–1919). Naumann is usually discussed in the context of Christian socialism or social imperialism, rather than how he saw himself for most of his career, which was as a liberal nationalist or nationalist liberal. In a sense he attempted to undo Treitschke's work and make it possible for German liberalism and German nationalism to be fellow travelers again without an "exaggerated" nationalism leading the train off the liberal track. Naumann pursued this seemingly anodyne project by unusual means.

39. Schroeder, "International Politics, Peace, and War," 190; Hewitson, "Wilhelmine Germany," 42; Thompson, *Left Liberals*, 22; Mommsen, "German Liberalism in the Nineteenth Century," 428, Hewitson, "Wilhelmine Germany," 45; Thompson, *Left Liberals*, 196.

He was one of very few figures of his time to begin as an anti-semite and become a leading opponent of anti-semitism. For Naumann, anti-semitism, and even anti-Catholicism, strengthened only the Conservatives, the Pope, and the Zionists, not liberals or true German nationalists. He backed trade unions, state economic intervention on behalf of workers, and Germany's struggle to be a world power. Although he failed in his attempt to create a new liberal party, he was very influential as a journalist, editing a new liberal weekly, *Die Hilfe*, and eventually joining a left liberal party and becoming a member of the German parliament in 1907. He was a strong supporter of German colonial policy. During WWI, he became known for his book *Mitteleuropa* (1915), which proposed the creation of a German-led federal empire in central and eastern Europe.[40] One of the fathers of the Weimar Constitution, he died soon after it was written in 1919.[41]

Naumann's attempt to arouse liberal support for colonialism along with state economic and social intervention usually completely engrosses historians, so it is useful to stress the persistence of traditional liberal elements in his thought. His arguments always rested on the three pillars of liberalism, and he insisted that liberalism had to make political, moral, and economic appeals if it was to succeed. The state had to remain secondary. "*The progress of human culture is a consequence of the progress of individual people.* This sentence is necessary against all those mistaken people who think that the world can be reformed by laws alone." The state should be seen merely as "an auxiliary organization for private enterprise." It was "a political big business based on the German people for their benefit." Despite his nationalism, he was a friend of *doux commerce*, the idea that international trade benefited everyone. He called on his compatriots to shake off "the evil dust of fear, the fear of every foreign ship, foreign goods, foreign opinion, foreign constitutions," to reject "material and intellectual protectionism." He supported a large German navy, but justified it as a guarantee of free trade. For Naumann, the essence of freedom was the equality of all citizens, and no violation of the rights of individuals was permissible—all had to be protected from fear.[42]

40. Which he hoped that one day France and Britain would join voluntarily, so that Europe could compete against Russia and the United States.

41. Zimmermann, "A Road Not Taken,", 690; 699–701,702.

42. Naumann, cited in Zimmermann, "A Road Not Taken," 694; 695; Naumann, *Das Blaue Buch*, 83, 46; 80. The "Blue Book" was essentially a collection of articles Naumann wrote for his weekly *Die Hilfe*.

Equally typical of much nineteenth-century liberalism was Naumann's attitude toward self-interest. The pursuit of self-interest was a valuable agent of progress, but it was not the highest motivation, as Tocqueville and Mill, among others, would have agreed. Too narrow a focus on self-interest led to indifference toward the poor, and, like Tocqueville, Naumann required self-interest to be enlightened: "*The question is whether in future we can have men whose private interests will not be small and narrow, but will adapt themselves to an enlarged view of the world.*"[43]

But Naumann drew fin de siècle consequences from these commonplaces of nineteenth-century liberalism. German liberals needed to unite in a single liberal political party in which "democracy and national feeling live together." To succeed in this, "foreign policy is in general even more important and consequential than internal policy." Here Naumann turned the traditional interpretation of German history upside down. Instead of the evil Conservative / Junkers manipulating the hapless liberals and the masses by using imperialism to divert them from domestic issues, it was Naumann, a liberal, who wanted to use foreign policy as a stick to beat the Junkers and Conservatives. He reminded his readers that the national idea was most powerful as a liberal and democratic idea. Only when the old declining aristocracy had been defeated would "the German spirit . . . conquer the world." For Naumann, politics was a "question of world power," and only through a combination of liberalism and nationalism would Germany be able to give the correct answer.[44]

A German modern liberalism was a means to this end, or rather, a constituent part of it. Nauman did not invent modern liberalism in Germany. Although German liberals in the 1880s had mostly resisted Bismarck's creation of the welfare state, later there was an evolution toward modern liberalism, if less so at the national level than in other countries, then at least as strong locally. German liberal mayors introduced what in Britain was known as "municipal socialism." A National Liberal mayor of Frankfurt built city-owned water purification plants, improved housing for the poor, and favored the recognition of labor unions in the 1880s; the 1907 liberal electoral program for Schöneberg, a Berlin suburb and liberal stronghold, included municipal housing, municipal kindergartens and midwives, cheap tickets on public transport for the poor, and progressive taxation. The Schöneberg program

---

43. Naumann, *Das Blaue Buch*, 156; 201. Emphasis original—Naumann was *very* fond of italics.

44. Naumann, *Das Blaue Buch*, 35; 33; 99; 32.

became the model for liberal municipal programs all over Germany. In a further sign of the progress of modern liberalism, German liberal parties were happy to attack the Conservatives as false patriots for their unwillingness to back an inheritance tax as a means of paying for military expansion in 1909. That German liberals were willing to back such a tax is a good indication of the progress of modern liberal ideas about progressive taxation. And German liberals were increasingly willing to form coalitions with moderate socialists after 1900 at the state and local levels.[45]

Naumann worked to make German modern liberalism into an ideology as well as a policy. Liberalism, Naumann argued, did not only stand for independent individuals, but also for the desire that one's neighbor should be independent. This meant that one could not be politically liberal without being willing to fight poverty. The right to vote needed to be supplemented by economic rights. As Naumann put it, in 1900 the proletarian needed to be freed the way the peasant had needed to be freed a hundred years before. Hence his call for the representation of white-collar employees and assembly-line workers in management, and his endorsement of trade unions as a means of recognizing the freedom of individual workers to associate. Therefore, *"liberalism must in its own self interest be in favour of industrial constitutions, for free coalitions, for union wage settlements, for the protection of workers, for everything, which increases the value of the individual person among the crowd of workers and white-collar employees."* But it was not the state that should do all this—Naumann remained a liberal. State regulation for the benefit of workers, the poor etc., was only a second-best, necessary in present circumstances, especially for the poorest, but not ideal. *"Had we given more freedom to the development of trade unions, we would have needed fewer laws, penalties and bureaucrats."*[46]

All this was to respond to the question of Germany as a world power. Naumann maintained the pre-Unification German liberal view that German freedom and German power were inextricably linked. *"Nothing helps in world history, education, culture, morals, nothing, if it is not protected and supported by power!* He who wishes to live must struggle. That goes for individuals, for classes, for a nation." For this reason it was German power in foreign affairs, its military power, that mattered. And this power had to be directed not so much toward Europe, important as that was, as outside. Thus, after visiting the

45. Thompson, *Left Liberals*, 224; Mommsen, "German Liberalism in the Nineteenth Century," 431; Thompson, *Left Liberals*, 47; 109–110, 113; 212, 217.

46. Naumann, *Das Blaue Buch*, 38; 95; 39; 86; 176–177. Emphasis, sigh, original.

World's Fair in Paris in 1900, Naumann wrote: "Between us and the French there are no profound differences. . . . Despite different languages and history, we are basically the same kind of people. You only have to take a look at the Orientals in the exhibition to know what distinguishes racial difference from variation within the race." Germany shared with France and England a colonial mission.[47]

Naumann identified nationalism with colonialism: "What is nationalism? It is the motive power of the German people to spread its influence all over the globe." This meant building a navy big enough to challenge Britain. It also meant colonies. Like Ferry, he saw the failure of free trade in Europe as a justification for acquiring colonies abroad that would serve as export markets. If acquiring such colonies caused harm to the natives, so be it: the struggle for national survival could brook no limits. He took this view so far as to endorse, against the vast majority of German public opinion, Britain's suppression of the Boer states in South Africa: the British drive for world power naturally trumped the Boers' desire for sovereignty.[48]

Thus it is perhaps not so surprising that for all the ways in which Naumann turned Treitschke upside-down, whether with respect to Jews, women (Naumann was a feminist, Treitschke decidedly not), or electoral alliances with socialists, when push came to shove, in 1914 Naumann was more similar to Treitschke than different. In October 1914, he signed the "Manifesto of the 93," a document produced by 93 leading German intellectuals defending Germany's invasion of Belgium and accusing France, England, and Belgium of having colluded to attack Germany. If Naumann was hardly alone in his "exaggerated" wartime nationalism, neither can he be considered a shining example of liberal sanity. Interestingly, however, in his 1915 book *Mitteleuropa*, Naumann turned away from colonialism, which would involve Germany in too many conflicts with Britain and the United States, in favor of a German imperialism directed toward continental Europe.

Nationalism proved to be a good servant but a poor master for liberals in the fin de siècle. Unfortunately, it was a servant who learned insubordination from its erstwhile associate. In the fin de siècle, nationalism and imperialism

47. Naumann, *Das Blaue Buch*, 34; Naumann, cited in Guettel, " 'Between Us and the French There Are No Profound Differences,' " 32.

48. Naumann, *Werke* (Cologne: Westdeutscher Verlag, 1964), vol. 5, p. 201; William O. Shanahan, "Liberalism and Foreign Affairs: Naumann and the Prewar German View," *Review of Politics* 21, no. 1 (Jan. 1959): 205–208.

tempted liberals to limit their concerns far more than they broadened them. Feminism, or rather opposition to feminism, had much the same effect— despite the liberalism of many of feminism's leading representatives.[49]

Liberalism and Feminism in the Nineteenth Century and the Fin de Siècle

Just as most nationalists during the short nineteenth century were liberals, so were perhaps an even greater proportion of feminists. Insofar as feminism was about the reasons women had to fear men, domestically, socially, and politically, and what might be done about it, the "Woman Question" was a fundamentally liberal question, even if until the fin de siècle very few liberals saw it that way. In the late twentieth century, however, liberalism was often considered an enemy of feminism, an inherently patriarchal form of political thought and practice. The eminent feminist theorist Carole Pateman, for example, identified liberalism with contract theory and saw the exclusion of women from the social contract as inherent to liberalism. By the early twenty-first century this view was less prevalent, however, and the possibility of liberal feminism, or feminist liberalism (a noun / adjective problem similar to that of liberalism and nationalism), was again recognized.[50]

However, liberalism and feminism are historically more distinct than liberalism and nationalism. Most liberals were nationalists at various times and places in the nineteenth century; it cannot be said that most nineteenth-century liberals were feminists. During the short nineteenth century, nationalism and feminism in some respects had opposite effects on liberalism. While the rise of nationalism initially tended to democratize liberalism and encourage liberals to abandon the discourse of capacity in favor of rights talk (see chapter 5), feminism at first had the opposite effect. With regard to women, the discourse of capacity persisted long after liberals endorsed universal male suffrage: "the opposition to women's suffrage was much stronger, longer lived, and ran much deeper than the opposition to manhood suffrage, even black manhood suffrage." Indeed, debates over votes for women were

49. On Naumann's feminism, see Zimmermann, "A Road Not Taken," 698–699. Naumann saw raising women's consciousness as related to raising national consciousness, as did Jules Ferry.

50. Taylor, "Mary Wollstonecraft," 199; Pateman, *The Sexual Contract*; for liberal feminism, see Susan Moller Okin's work.

often the occasion for liberals to express nostalgia over limiting male suffrage.[51]

The relationship between liberalism and feminism is made no easier to describe by the fact that feminism's definition and history is much debated. The terms "feminism" and "feminist" have been used to describe everything from biblical characters to medieval women saints. Most historians shy away from this level of anachronism, but clearly the thing preceded the word, and seems to begin in the late eighteenth century, just around the time when "liberalism" was being coined. Without being dogmatic, we can use one historian's recent working definition of feminists as people who "recognize the validity of women's own interpretations of their lived experience," and who are conscious of and oppose the institutionalized oppression of women by men. It becomes easier to identify such people after 1760 or so. Once identified, most of those people could be described as proto-liberals or liberals. If nineteenth-century liberalism was not feminist, nineteenth-century feminism was liberal. During the short nineteenth century, feminism often adopted liberal language and thought very much in liberal terms, as the examples of Mary Wollstonecraft, Elizabeth Cady Stanton, and John Stuart Mill demonstrate.[52]

Mary Wollstonecraft (1759–1797) died in childbirth around the time the word "liberalism" was born. But her activity was essentially post-revolutionary, a response to the fears aroused by revolution and reaction, and hence fully liberal. She entered the political scene with her reply to Burke in defense of the French Revolution, *A Vindication of the Rights of Men* (1790). This was followed by *A Vindication of the Rights of Woman* (1792), often regarded as the first feminist manifesto, at least in the English language. In some ways, however, her feminist liberalism, or liberal feminism, was better displayed in her unfinished novel, *Maria: or, The Wrongs of Woman*, and her essay, *An Historical and Moral View of the Origin and Progress of the French Revolution* (1795). She was a leading figure in both respects. Contextualists will shudder at the suggestion that Wollstonecraft was ahead of her time because who can be, without being out of context? But certainly, both in her debate with Burke, where she emphasized the fear of poverty few liberals felt before the fin de siècle, and in her feminism, where she evoked the fears to which men subjected women, she

51. Carole Pateman, "Women, Nature, and the Suffrage," review of Ellen Carol DuBois, *Feminism and Suffrage: The Emergence of an Independent Women's Movement in America 1848–69*; Harrison, *Separate Spheres*, 567.

52. Offen, "Defining Feminism," 152, 151.

embodied a kind of liberalism more common in 1900 than 1800. Nevertheless, she was well known, both during her brief life and afterward. William Blake may have quoted her, and she was widely read by feminists, and non-feminists, in both Europe and America.[53]

Wollstonecraft argued that women had good cause to be afraid of men, and that it was urgent to make them safe, to find political, economic, and moral solutions to protect women from male oppression. She used what were later called "individualist" as well as "relational" feminist arguments to make this point. Individualist feminist arguments start from the abstract individual, emphasizing personal independence and autonomy, and minimizing the importance of sex-linked differences; relational feminist arguments propose a "gender-based but egalitarian vision of social organization." They start with the couple or the family as their basic unit of analysis, rather than the individual, and argue for women's rights as women, as opposed to as ungendered abstract individuals. Feminists often adopt both perspectives. The parallel to the similar liberal demand for freedom from fear for both individuals and groups is striking. In the same vein Wollstonecraft, like most nineteenth-century liberals, used all three pillars of liberal argument, political, economic, and moral, to buttress her liberal feminism.

Wollstonecraft's combination of liberalism and feminism can be demonstrated by looking at her analysis of the French Revolution, which displayed the classic features of a liberalism trying to steer between anarchy and despotism, and her novel *Maria*, which situated her feminism in the context of the liberalism of fear and the struggle against arbitrary cruelty.[54]

For Wollstonecraft, the French Revolution was a step toward liberalism and creating a society free from fear. But because the French were still warped by their feudal and absolutist past, it was only to be expected that "after they had once thrown off the yoke, which had imprinted on their character the hateful scars of servitude, that they would expect the most unbridled freedom, detesting all wholesome restraints, as reins they were not now bound to obey." The

53. Taylor, "Mary Wollstonecraft," claims this for Wollstonecraft, but ignores Olympe de Gouges's French manifesto; G. E. Bentley Jr., " 'A Different Face,' " 349–350; Botting, "Wollstonecraft in Europe," 503–527; Botting, *Wollstonecraft, Mill & Women's Human Rights*.

54. Offen, "Defining Feminism," 150; Engster, "Mary Wollstonecraft's Nurturing Liberalism," 557–578, 587; Offen, "Defining Feminism," 136. It can be added that Wollstonecraft, equally typically, used both republican and liberal language. See Engster, "Mary Wollstonecraft's Nurturing Liberalism," 582.

lack of political experience of the lower classes, and the depravity of the upper, meant that when the lower classes finally achieved a degree of freedom, they were "easily caught by the insidious arts of the contemptible anarchists."[55]

Thus, while in the long run Wollstonecraft favored a democracy with a unicameral legislature, democracy was for the future, and for the present she was a liberal, looking to fend off despotism from the top and from the bottom. Change needed to take into account the way people actually were, not the way they ought to be: "The revolutions of states ought to be gradual; for during violent or material changes it is not so much the wisdom of measures, as the popularity they acquire by being adapted to the foibles of the great body of the community, which gives them success." As for the French, "no people stand in such great need of a check," because they were "totally destitute of experience in political science." Wollstonecraft thought France needed an executive with some kind of veto, and an upper house because inexperienced popular assemblies would be prone to being carried away by eloquence. Instead, they tried to jump at once into "a system proper only for a people in the highest stage of civilization," with predictably disastrous results in the form of the Terror (Wollstonecraft did not live long enough to see the reign of Napoleon).[56]

So far, Wollstonecraft's thought was typical of mainstream nineteenth-century liberalism, if more inclined to praise the eventual virtues of democracy than most. But from this garden variety liberalism she went on to cultivate a very exotic flower, namely the idea that liberalism ought to protect women from their everyday fear of men. For Wollstonecraft, indeed, the connection between what happened in government and what happened at home was intimate: "the power relationships that structured the institutions and processes of government were coterminous with those existing within the family." She held bad government responsible for "leaving women unprotected in the power struggles within their homes." It was therefore the duty of a liberal government to protect them. Wollstonecraft presented women's fears, and the urgent need for a political, economic, and moral response to them, in her novel *Maria*. The purpose of the book, according to the author, was "exhibiting the misery and oppression, peculiar to women, that arise out of the partial laws and customs of society." The story followed two heroines, Maria, an educated, middle-class woman, and Jemimah, the lower-class woman who befriended

55. O'Neill, "John Adams versus Mary Wollstonecraft," 458–463.
56. O'Neill "John Adams versus Mary Wollstonecraft," 468–471.

her while acting as her guard in the insane asylum / prison to which her husband had committed her. The prison was a metaphor for the larger world, for "was not the world a vast prison, and all women born slaves?"[57]

In prison Maria and Jemimah recounted their histories to one another, which presented a catalog of the ways in which women had cause to fear men, sexually, morally, economically, and because of their lack of political power, their complete inability to do anything about it—all three pillars of liberal argument were engaged. Plot and character development were, by Wollstonecraft's deliberate choice, as she made clear in the preface, subordinated to making larger points about the crippling consequences of being a woman. Jemimah, seduced and abandoned, could find no other means of earning a living than prostitution. When, after many vicissitudes, she left prostitution and became an entrepreneur as a laundrywoman, she faced "a wretchedness peculiar to my sex. A man with half my industry, and I may say, abilities, could have procured a decent livelihood . . . whilst I . . . was cast aside as the filth of society." In response Maria, "thinking of Jemimah's peculiar fate and her own . . . was led to consider the oppressed state of women, and to lament that she had given birth to a daughter" and to pray that she might "prepare her body and mind to encounter the ills which await her sex."[58]

These ills were just as much the fate of middle-class women as poor ones. Through Maria, Wollstonecraft lamented the emotional damage done to mothers, sisters, and younger sons by entail and the inability of English married women to own property. In the novel Maria's husband marries her for her money, and then is only interested in whores or sexually promiscuous women; her brother finds a legal flaw in the property settled on her by her father and takes it. Enslaved by a legally unequal marriage, where a wife is "as much a husband's property as his horse," forced to have sex with a disgusting husband, Maria may not be a former prostitute like Jemimah, but she is equally a prisoner of her sex: "marriage had bastilled me for life." She concludes: "Born a woman—and born to suffer."[59]

Maria was all about fear and arbitrary cruelty. It presented women's claims to freedom from fear as central to liberalism. Despite being couched in impeccably liberal terms, however, Wollstonecraft's arguments did not meet with

---

57. Gunther-Canada, *Rebel Writer*, 151; Walker, "Review of Wendy Gunther-Canada, *Rebel Writer*," 405; Wollstonecraft, *Maria, or the Wrongs of Woman* (1798) Kindle edition, 2; 6.

58. Wollstonecraft, *Maria*, 33; 36–37.

59. Wollstonecraft, *Maria*, 40, 48–49; 40, 48–49, 53–54, 58–59, 63, 79.

success. This did not discourage, or at least prevent, other liberal feminists from continuing the debate. Nineteenth-century liberalism saw a number of efforts to make liberals take women's fears into account. Very different from Wollstonecraft, the American Elizabeth Cady Stanton's (1815–1902) long political career bridged the nineteenth century and the fin de siècle. Her thought, like Wollstonecraft's, integrated feminism and liberalism.

Like many American women activists of the period, Stanton cut her political teeth, both feminist and liberal, in the anti-slavery movement in the 1840s. After 1848 she shifted her main attention to women's issues, notably the suffrage, but also marriage and property law, as well as temperance—then largely considered a women's issue. For Stanton, the link between the abuse of alcohol and men's abuse of women was clear, as was the link between suffrage and temperance: once women had the vote, they would use it to restrict liquor. In 1853, Stanton broke with a leading Temperance organization when it would not support women's suffrage.[60]

Stanton was an important figure in American political thought in many regards, but the foundation of her renown was the "Seneca Falls Declaration" of 1848, the manifesto of American feminism, which she co-authored. The Declaration was representative of Stanton's thought right through to the end of her long career. Historians have had difficulties analyzing her ideas largely because they have lacked an adequate conception of liberalism. Hence the claim that Stanton expressed three or even four different and partly contradictory American political traditions, whereas in fact she consistently wrote and spoke in terms familiar to most nineteenth-century European liberals. She relied on universal arguments for individual rights based on natural law (which her American commentators usually identify as the sole liberal tradition), *and* republican virtue-based arguments, *and* emphasized the unique qualities of women and their special relationship to the family, *and* argued for the superior political and moral capacity of some individuals (native-born, middle-class White women), and the lesser capacity of others (immigrant and Black men). This combination of arguments was common among both American and European feminists. It was also a typically liberal combination. The simultaneous use of the language of natural rights and virtue, of utility and perfection, of arguments based on equality and arguments based on capacity, was standard fare in nineteenth-century liberalism. It was the liberal toolkit for building

60. Davis, *Political Thought of Elizabeth Cady Stanton*, 28, 85; 87; 91.

political, economic, and moral barriers against fear, and Stanton used it for liberal feminist purposes.[61]

What is particularly interesting about Stanton from the perspective of a history of liberalism are her post–Civil War writings, Stanton used the discourse of capacity to defend women's right to vote. She combined positive assertions of the abilities of women, both as a group and as individuals, with negative evaluations of the capacities of "ignorant Irishmen," "drunkards, idiots, horse-racing, rum-selling rowdies," and "ignorant negroes and foreigners." In 1867 she warned the New York State legislature that they "need the moral power of wise and virtuous women in [their] political councils, to outweigh the incoming tide of poverty, ignorance, and vice that threatens our very existence as a nation," presumably referring to immigrants and perhaps African Americans as well. Stanton and Susan B. Anthony famously split from their allies in the former abolitionist movement over the question of the Fourteenth and Fifteenth Amendments to the US Constitution, insisting they should guarantee a right to vote for women as well as African Americans, and refusing to support them when they did not.[62]

It was common for both American and European supporters of women's suffrage in the fin de siècle to denigrate lower-class men. At various points Stanton supported an educational qualification for the suffrage for both men and women, perhaps English-language literacy. Late in life, influenced by Herbert Spencer and Francis Galton, she adopted eugenicist views and became interested in Social Darwinism. At the same time, however, she also inclined toward some modern liberal positions, calling on the upper classes to address the problem of poverty, in 1898 describing herself as a "philosophical socialist," and becoming interested in experiments in cooperative socialism in the United States and in Fabian socialism in Britain. These positions involved a certain amount of contortion from a twenty-first-century perspective, but were paralleled in the thought of Jane Addams and other Progressives (see chapter 7). Indeed, although her career began well before the Progressive movement, by the end of her life Stanton probably ought to be characterized as one.[63]

If liberal American feminists like Stanton were comfortable with the discourse of capacity and often used it in preference to rights talk, the fact remains

61. Davis, *The Political Thought of Elizabeth Cady Stanton*, 30, Offen, "Defining Feminism," 135; Davis, *The Political Thought of Elizabeth Cady Stanton*, 1, 3; Davis, 53.
62. Davis, *The Political Thought of Elizabeth Cady Stanton*, 22, 137; 132; 138.
63. Davis, *The Political Thought of Elizabeth Cady Stanton*, 25, 149; 150–151, 213; 162, 206.

that American liberals, like Europeans liberals, more commonly used the discourse of capacity to reject women's suffrage. The editor of the *New York Times* wrote in 1858, in good European liberal fashion, that the vote was not a right but a privilege—one that women had not earned, and never would. Continuing to use the discourse of capacity, John Stuart Mill's *On the Subjection of Women* responded to this very common attitude toward women's abilities by suggesting that no one knew what women were capable of because women had been forbidden to find out. "I deny that anyone knows, or can know, the nature of the two sexes, as long as they have only been seen in their present relation to one another." We do not know "whether there are any natural differences at all." We have an "artificial" situation, in which women have always been oppressed and men have always been oppressors.[64]

Mill was arguably the author of the most influential text in the history of liberalism, *On Liberty* (1859), and the most influential text in the history of feminism, *On the Subjection of Women* (written 1860–61, published in 1869). The latter, however, was not taken nearly as seriously by liberals at the time of publication because its claims were considered to be so outrageous and implausible.

On the Subjection of Women argued that the current relationship between men and women, based on "the legal subordination of one sex to the other—is wrong in itself, and now one of the chief hindrances to human improvement; and that it ought to be replaced by a principle of perfect equality." The legal subordination was, in Mill's view, oppression pure and simple. It was a coercive power dear to the hearts of all men, regardless of social class, because "everyone who desires power, desires it most over those who are nearest to him." This was one difficulty in getting rid of it.[65]

A second difficulty was posed by the oppressed themselves. Among women, "each individual of the subject-class is in a constant state of bribery and intimidation combined." Fear was joined with an education in submission and gifts of jewelry. Men generally wanted "not a forced slave, but a willing one . . . they have therefore put everything into practice in order to enslave [women's] minds. . . . They turned the whole force of education to effect their purpose." According to Mill, many women accepted the status quo, or wanted only minor alterations. Just as the institution of chattel slavery once seemed natural

64. Davis, *The Political Thought of Elizabeth Cady Stanton*, 96; Mill, "On the Subjection of Women," in *On Liberty and Other Writings*, 184.

65. Mill, "On the Subjection of Women," 119; 128.

to nearly everyone, so the enslavement of women seemed natural to all, even to most women. Mill drew many analogies between the situation of the slave and that of women. Thus, "whether the institution to be defended is slavery, political absolutism, or the absolutism of the head of a family, we are always expected to judge of it from its best instances." He also referred to the male position as the primordial liberal evil of despotism. "At present. . . . The family is a school of despotism."[66]

Women were the victims, partly the willing victims, of oppression and fear. But Mill also chanted the other liberal mantra, hope. Social change was the essence of modernity, according to Mill, so progress was possible. Progress in the situation of women was even likely because "every step in improvement has been . . . invariably accompanied by a step made in raising the social position of women. . . . Through all the progressive period of human history, the condition of women has been approaching nearer to equality with men."[67]

In the absence of reliable evidence to the contrary, the only possible assumption for Mill was that men and women were equals. He thus rejected the widespread Victorian idea that women were morally superior to men, and even turned it upside down. Against the notion, enshrined in a very popular poem of the time, that women were the "angel in the house," ever encouraging their men to moral uplift, Mill saw women, as a result of their corrupt education, as the household enforcers of mediocrity: "The wife's influence tends . . . to prevent the husband from falling below the common standard. . . . It tends quite as strongly to hinder him from rising above it. The wife is the auxiliary of the common public opinion." Perhaps this was a response to the fact that among Mill's acquaintances, women were even more unwilling to accept his relationship to Harriet Taylor than men. Thus Mill's judgment that "whoever has a wife and children has given hostages to Mrs. Grundy" (a fictional character who represented conventional propriety).[68]

Mill also criticized contemporary women's morality in other respects. Women, he said, were generally considered to be more "philanthropical" than men. But, in his view, their philanthropy typically took two forms: they were often involved in efforts at religious conversion which mostly just led to religious hatred; and they were involved in charity work, but—and here he agreed with Spencer, although unlike Spencer he did not consider it a reason

66. Mill, "On the Subjection of Women," 129; 132; 129; 151; 160.
67. Mill, "On the Subjection of Women," 134; 138.
68. Mill, "On the Subjection of Women," 193; 205; 206.

to withdraw support for women's suffrage (see chapter 6)—their charity was generally misplaced. Because women's education was exclusively "sentimental," most women did not realize that any charity "which, taking the care of people's lives out of their own hands, and relieving them from the disagreeable consequences of their own acts, saps the very foundations of the self-respect, self-help, and self-control which are the essential conditions both of individual prosperity and of social virtue" was bad. But since women were hardly encouraged to be "self-dependent," why should they see the value of independence? "She forgets that she is not free, and that the poor," at least the male poor, "are." The remedy was better education for women.[69]

Given that people were ignorant of whether there was any natural distinction between men and women, Mill concluded that there were no grounds for any legal inequality, and supported the transformation of women's position in both public and private life. Women should be able to vote and hold office, exercise any profession, have full property rights, and above all married life should be transformed into a friendship between equals. It was natural that partners should create a "division of powers" between themselves, but these separate spheres would be unique to every marriage. Nevertheless, Mill thought it desirable that the man have primary responsibility for earning an income because otherwise the wife, who had to bear all the bodily suffering of childbirth and usually superintended household management and childrearing, would be overburdened. On the other hand, 'the *power* of earning [rather than its exercise] is essential to the dignity of a woman." Marriage should be considered a choice of profession on the woman's part, at least until the children were grown. But Mill made clear that "the utmost latitude ought to exist for the adaptation of general rules to individual suitabilities."[70]

These attitudes toward family relationships have led many twentieth-century feminists to reject Mill, and liberal feminism with him. They blame him for seeing childrearing as an exclusively feminine activity, and for failing to recognize that this view harmed women and conflicted with his own larger vision of marriage. In his lifetime the criticism came from the other direction. Mill held back publication of *The Subjection of Women* for eight years, hoping for a propitious moment when it might be taken seriously. Nevertheless the reviews were negative. While reviewers, both men and women, often agreed that the legal situation of married women, and women's education generally,

69. Mill, "On the Subjection of Women," 204–205.
70. Mill, "On the Subjection of Women," 164–165.

needed improvement, they thought that most women were happy (which Mill would not have denied), and that equality between the sexes was a chimera that if put into practice would destroy marriage and family life. *The Subjection of Women* was largely rejected by British liberals—just as Mill expected it would be, based on the hostility his long-held and widely known position on women's suffrage had aroused. When he ran for Parliament in 1868, and supported women's right to vote, Walter Bagehot, the essence of Whig liberal respectability, commented that "no party, and scarcely any individual politician except himself holds this theory." Bagehot went on to make the commonplace criticism, found among liberals and non-liberals alike, that giving votes to women would only be giving extra votes to "their fathers, their husbands, their masters, their lovers, or their priests." Only a few of Mill's closest acolytes, such as Morley and Fawcett, and a handful of feminists, supported women's suffrage in Britain in the 1860s.[71]

Liberalism as a whole never identified itself with feminism during the short nineteenth century, even if such prominent feminists as Wollstonecraft and Stanton were liberals, and such a prominent liberal as John Stuart Mill was a feminist. Most fin de siècle liberals refused to acknowledge women's fears, and did not accept the argument that women as a group had something to fear from male hegemony. Or if they did accept it, it was only at the margin— married women's rights to own property expanded during the period. On the other hand, liberals increasingly seemed to fear women, especially their potential political power—one reason why the discourse of capacity, a traditional liberal means of defending the exclusion of potentially dangerous groups from power, remained current in liberal discussions of feminism and women's suffrage.[72]

None of this was unique to liberals, who were no more anti-feminist than any other group. Nevertheless, it seems paradoxical. Fin de siècle liberals by and large embraced political democracy, many developed a concern for poverty, and in both respects liberals abandoned the discourse of capacity. But with regard to feminism, the discourse of capacity became if anything more

71. Pyle, *The Subjection of Women*; Nicholson, "The Reception and Early Reputation of Mill's Political Thought," 473; Shanley, "The Subjection of Women," 397; 404; Nicholson, "The Reception and Early Reputation of Mill's Political Thought," 471–473; Bagehot, cited in Nicholson, 472; Nicholson, "The Reception and Early Reputation of Mill's Political Thought," 495n80.

72. Offen, *European Feminisms*, 188–196.

prominent. It was used to reinforce traditional gender roles, even by modern liberals like Hobhouse. Many of the ways in which liberals continued to deploy the language of capacity with regard to women in the fin de siècle can be seen in the history of French feminism, and the failure of French women to get the vote until 1945.[73]

Historians have seen French "republicans," that is, the partisans of a republic rather than a monarchy, as especially hostile to women's rights. But at least with regard to the liberals among them, this is incorrect. If anything, they were more open to feminism—which is not saying very much—than those to their left or right. Jules Favre, a prominent liberal republican, endorsed women's suffrage as early as 1868. And Jules Ferry, in his famous 1870 speech on public education, insisted to his audience that women's education was as important as men's. Ideas of male superiority, Ferry said, were even worse than the class privileges of the aristocracy—about the worst insult a republican could offer. Ferry cited Mill's *Subjection of Women* (published the previous year, and immediately translated into French) at length. His concluding line was "Citizens, women must belong to either Science or the Church!," science being the preferred option. For Paul Bert, a leading anti-clerical and Minister of Education, women deserved the same education and the same access to professions as men. Once they had been educated, they would deserve the same access to the vote. Women were not yet ready for the vote because, under the influence of the clergy, they were enemies of the republic. But in theory, "no one has the right to limit . . . the role of women." Turning words into action, in the 1880s French liberals introduced obligatory public elementary education for girls as well as boys—making France the first country in Europe to do so. However, while France was a leader in women's education, the French were laggards when it came to women's suffrage, which did not arrive in France until 1945, last among major European countries.[74]

Why did it take so long for French women to get the vote? One historian has suggested that whereas British and Americans thought of women as a class which might or might not possess the capacity to vote, in France voters were seen as individuals, and as the French understood only men to be true individuals, women were excluded. Whereas for the French feminist philosopher Genevieve Fraisse, the explanation is that, again unlike the Anglo-Saxons, the

---

73. Gerson, "Gender in the Liberal Tradition," 700, 701.

74. Offen, *Debating the Woman Question*, 8; 15; 43n71; Ferry, https://gallica.bnf.fr/ark:/12148/bpt6k5695789n/f31.image.texteImage; Offen, *Debating the Woman Question*, 65, 103, 136.

French feared confusing the genders, and reserved laws for men, and mores for women. Neither explanation bears scrutiny. Throughout the nineteenth century, French liberals typically considered political capacity in class or group rather than individual terms (see chapter 5). As for the supposedly French idea of laws made by men and mores made by women, there was nothing especially French about it. For example, the best-selling Victorian author Sarah Stickney Ellis made the same argument in her widely read *The Women of England, Their Social Duties, and Domestic Habits* (1839). What does shed light on the history of women's suffrage in France is a combination of the common history of Western liberalism with the particularities of French liberal anti-clericalism.[75]

Although French feminists began demanding the vote during the Revolution, the issue generally remained on a back burner until late in the fin de siècle. Some feminists complained that few French women cared about it. In the late 1870s the French feminist movement split between those who wanted to concentrate on civil and marital rights for women and those who insisted on the vote as well. After 1896, French feminists united in demanding votes for women, and the question became a subject of mainstream debate, along with women's rights generally. Even the most stodgy liberal newspaper, *Le Temps*, began to support gradual reform in the civil law. In the 1890s women gained the right to vote for chambers of commerce and professional organizations.[76]

French fin de siècle supporters and opponents of women's suffrage both used the discourse of capacity. No longer deemed appropriate when applied to men, it remained commonplace when discussing women, in France and elsewhere. All the arguments based on capacity used against women's suffrage, including that women themselves didn't want it (desire for political participation was considered a necessary but not sufficient sign of capacity for it), had been used by liberals against universal male suffrage before 1848. Even those who in principle accepted women's right to vote worried, as nineteenth-century liberals had with respect to men, that without further educating women, both formally and practically, giving them the vote would be disastrous. It was the standard nineteenth-century liberal argument—democracy later, when people were ready for it, not now.[77]

The argument from capacity cut both ways, however. For opponents of women's suffrage, women were either by nature politically incompetent, or

75. Bouglé-Moalic, *Le vote des Françaises*, 16–17.
76. Bouglé-Moalic, *Le vote des Françaises*, 19, 25; 96–97, 122; 133, 139, 136; 153.
77. Bouglé-Moalic, *Le vote des Françaises*, 217; Offen, *Debating the Woman Question*, 534.

were not yet competent because they lacked sufficient education. But supporters cited the right to vote of illiterate, alcoholic, and even Black men to prove that women possessed the capacity for political participation. For the classical liberal Emile Faguet, the French male suffrage was comprised of one-third alcoholics, one-third unconvicted criminals, and one-third people with no moral sense (for Faguet this meant people inclined to redistribute wealth).[78] Women's suffrage would improve things because women were morally superior to men. One argument for women's capacity based on their gender was associated with alcoholism, as in the United States: give French women the vote, and they would see that alcohol consumption was limited. The campaign for women's suffrage slowly picked up steam: in 1914 one newspaper gathered 500,000 women's signatures in favor of their right to vote. Even if many supporters of women's suffrage thought it should be given to some rather than all women (again mimicking the liberal course with respect to men), support was growing.[79]

WWI crystallized the issue. In 1916, the conservative nationalist novelist Maurice Barrès called for a "vote for the dead": war widows and mothers of dead soldiers should be allowed to vote as their representatives, an idea that was widely taken up by conservatives. Liberals were also galvanized into action. In 1918 a member of the Radical party introduced a measure for women's suffrage in the Chamber of Deputies (the lower house of the French parliament), although it restricted women to the right to vote, not to hold office, and excluded prostitutes. Another proposed giving the vote to women over age thirty (the British solution in 1918). The leading parliamentary arguments for women's suffrage in 1919 were (1) it represented progress, (2) it would keep up with foreign countries, and (3) it would compensate for the contributions and sufferings of women during the war, in that order. Even if the war was not directly referenced, however, it was the war that created the mood in which women's suffrage became part of the political agenda.[80]

A typically liberal aspect of the 1919 suffrage debates was the combination of ideas of both individual and group / class representation, often in the same speech. On the one hand, women should vote because all individuals should be treated the same way. On the other hand, women should vote because as a

---

78. By contrast, Spencer revoked his earlier support for women's suffrage when he decided women were more likely than men to favor government intervention to help the poor.

79. Bouglé-Moalic, *Le vote des Françaises*, 176–177; 164–165; 183, 197–198.

80. Bouglé-Moalic, *Le vote des Françaises*, 206–213.

group they possessed certain capacities peculiar to themselves, usually moral superiority. Instead of rights talk, almost absent from the Chamber debates, liberals returned to the discussion of the capacities and the group interests of the sexes, arguing that women needed the vote to defend their particular interests. The liberal political rhetoric of the short nineteenth century, focused on capacity, persisted when it came to women.

As in July Monarchy suffrage debates about men, fin de siècle liberals divided over women's suffrage. Indeed, not just liberals—"confusion seemed to reign within the political groupings." Nevertheless, a bill giving limited voting rights to women was amended to give all women the right to vote, and finally passed 344–97. The "clinching argument" was WWI. It was nationalism that, as in the nineteenth century, helped to democratize liberalism.[81]

However, French women did not get the right to vote because the French Senate rejected the law. Significantly, a leading liberal anti-clerical, Senator Emile Combes, immediately called for its rejection in May 1919. He may have been motivated in part by the fact that the Italian People's Party, established with the Pope's endorsement in January 1919, had women's suffrage as part of its party program. Indeed, in October 1919 Pope Benedict XV appeared to call for women's suffrage. The result was an anti-female suffrage backlash on the part of French liberals. Their fear of Catholicism trumped their sympathy for women.[82]

The women's suffrage bill was held up in committee in the Senate for some time. When it finally emerged in 1920, the French Senate had a liberal majority, and at a superficial glance might have been expected to support women's suffrage. The committee's rapporteur, Alexandre Bérard, was a Radical, a Solidarist, and previously had supported women's right to vote for and serve in chambers of commerce. He was, nevertheless, a firm opponent. Three arguments were primarily used in the Senate against women's suffrage: (1) it was premature because women lacked education and political experience; (2) it was useless because women didn't want the vote; and (3) it was excessive because women would become the majority of the French electorate, due to the casualties suffered by French men during WWI.[83]

There were two crucial assumptions behind these arguments, assumptions made by both pro- and anti-women suffrage liberals. First, women would vote

81. Bouglé-Moalic, *Le vote des Françaises*, 218; Verjus, "Entre principes et pragmatisme," 68–69. Bouglé-Moalic, *Le vote des Françaises*, 215; 201.

82. Verjus, "Entre principes et pragmatisme," 55; Offen, *Debating the Woman Question*, 605.

83. Verjus, "Entre principes et pragmatisme," 57n5; 57–58.

as a bloc, not as individuals, and second, this bloc would vote as their priest told them. Virtually all French politicians, regardless of party or ideology, accepted these views. In the first respect the 1920 French debate about women recapitulated the 1866 British debate about giving votes to lower-class men. In that debate Robert Lowe had argued that the proposed Second Reform Bill would make the poor the majority of voters, that they were not very interested in the vote anyway, but that if given the vote they would vote en masse to redistribute wealth. Significantly, the rejoinder by Austen Henry Layard had no parallel in the French debate. Layard had argued that there was no risk because the poor were individuals who held many different opinions, belonged to many different classes, and therefore would not all vote the same way. In the French Senate in 1920, no one suggested the same of women. Senators on both sides were convinced that women would vote as a bloc, and that they would vote as the Church told them. Even pro-suffrage senators accepted the argument of a clerical women's bloc vote.[84]

Thus if nationalism made liberals vote in favor of women's suffrage in 1919, anti-Catholicism did the opposite in 1920. In 1919, the specter of a majority of women voters was overshadowed by the vivid memory of their wartime sacrifices. In 1920 this had faded, leaving only the picture of their faithful attendance at Mass. Bérard's report denounced female clericalism. Giving women the vote would "seal the tombstone of the Republic." The day women got the ballot, "the Church, more than ever, will risk becoming a political club and the pulpit a political platform." The Radical Senator J. Philip, former secretary to Frederick Buisson (leading Solidarist and supporter of women's suffrage), proclaimed himself a supporter of women's suffrage, was certain that it would come to pass, and opposed putting it into practice, except in some limited form (he did however vote in favor of a second reading). This was typical of the attitude of Senate liberals, even those who favored some kind of vote for women. The result, in a Senate with roughly 154 liberal members, was a 156–134 vote against proceeding to a second reading of the bill, in which about 60 percent of the liberals voted against, while 70 percent of conservatives voted in favor. Since the conservatives too thought that women would vote as their priests told them, for most of them the prospect of more pro-clerical votes outweighed any female lack of capacity.[85]

84. Verjus, "Entre principes et pragmatisme," 61, 72, 77.

85. Bérard, cited in Bouglé-Moalic, *Le vote des Françaises*, 231; Verjus, "Entre principes et pragmatisme," 62, 58n2; 75; 57n4, Bouglé-Moalic, 235–236; Verjus, 58.

Fin de siècle French liberals did not entirely dismiss women's fears and hopes. French women gained more civil and marital rights and more educational and professional opportunities. Nevertheless for most French liberals, as for most fin de siècle liberals generally, women's fears had very limited legitimacy, and women's concerns did not play a major role in the construction of most liberalisms of the period. Other fears, including men's fear of women—that they would vote for clerical despotism, or for socialism (Spencer's fear, and even Mill's)—mattered more. Many liberals did not think that expanding women's rights would lead to greater freedom / security for either women or men. Fin de siècle liberals mostly did not choose to become feminists.

Before the Deluge

Fin de siècle liberals were confronted with many temptations. Nationalism and imperialism from one perspective, and the problem of poverty from another, were most dangerous to the liberal project of a world in which no one need be afraid, precisely because they were simultaneously temptations and potential tools for furthering liberal aims. They tempted liberals to embrace the state and to limit whose fears should matter (foreigners, minorities, the wealthy, women), while simultaneously creating opportunities for liberalism to become more universal and diverse. They provoked intra-liberal controversy, whether the modern / classical liberal debate over poverty, or the debates over whether nationalism and imperialism or women's suffrage were liberal or illiberal projects. Fin de siècle liberalism was very divided, both intellectually and politically. This was not new. It was fiercely contested, from both left and right. This too was not new. But the context was different and new fears had entered into the picture while old ones had been transformed. The challenge of socialism had been largely tamed, or so it appeared, and socialism no longer was identical with violent revolution. But in taming socialism, modern liberalism had generated a new and unprecedently deep cleavage within liberalism, breaking with classical liberalism far more profoundly than first-wave liberals had differed over who should vote. Nevertheless, liberalism was no less vital, and no less central, throughout the West in the fin de siècle than it had been throughout the short nineteenth century. Liberal optimism seemed on strong grounds: from the abolition of American slavery and Russian serfdom to the development of constitutional government, and expanded suffrage throughout the West. The nascent development of the welfare state might be accounted as progress by modern liberals and deplored by classical liberals, but as most liberals shared the modern perspective, most liberals thought that this too was evidence of progress. Even if all liberals had to acknowledge the challenges the fin de siècle presented, for the great majority there was every reason for confidence. Louis XV supposedly foretold the coming French revolution on his deathbed, proclaiming "after me, the deluge." Fin de siècle liberals did not see storm clouds on the horizon, or if they did, thought that continued reform would keep the rainy day away, as it essentially had for many decades, allowing for occasional downpours such as the American Civil War and the Paris Commune. Liberals did not foresee WWI. Neither did almost anyone else. Like all great failures, the First World War provoked a transformation in attitudes—for a while, everything "pre-war" seemed like ancient history. Liberalism faced new fears, a new set of problems. Liberalism 3.0 was the response.

The first problem third-wave liberals had to confront was that of perceived failure, failure perceived by liberals at the time and by historians since. It has been argued that liberalism failed in the fin de siècle, on two grounds. First, the temptations discussed in this chapter and the previous one: many liberals followed the siren songs of nationalism, colonialism, and the power of the state to do good for the poor so far that they left liberalism behind. In the right circumstances many liberals showed themselves to be comfortable with certain forms of oppression. As a result, they either ceased to be liberals or discredited liberalism. In this view, by WWI liberalism had lost its reason for existence, since it was no longer capable or even desirous of preserving people from fear. The result was the decline of liberal parties after WWI, and the increased reliance throughout the Western world on the state rather than civil society as the source of salvation.

Second, both in the immediate aftermath of WWI and since, many claimed that liberals failed to prevent WWI, and even more damningly failed to make sure that a liberal society resulted from it. Not only did the so-called war to end all wars (which if it had really ended war would have been a fundamentally liberal endeavor, and was announced as such by a leading American liberal, Woodrow Wilson) not end war, it was swiftly followed by communism, fascism, Nazism, Depression, and WWII, none of which were testimony to the power or attraction of liberalism. Liberalism thus revealed itself to be politically, economically, and morally bankrupt. The three pillars of liberal argument proved to be weak fulcrums for the liberal lever. People increasingly thought a single, really big fulcrum, most often the state, would be more efficient, even if less liberal, or even illiberal.

Liberals had responses to these arguments available to them. To the first, the weakness of liberals faced with temptation was proof that they were human, not proof of the weakness of liberalism. The hope of a world without fear continued to inspire liberals after WWI as before, if necessarily in different guise. To the second, liberals might reply that liberalism should not be condemned for the sin of not being always victorious. Liberals themselves did not worship at the altar of success, and were well aware that the odds often favored the despot. Nevertheless, it is striking that in the period circa 1920–1950 most liberals agreed with one or both of these critiques. Throughout the interwar period and into the immediate postwar years, many liberals perceived liberalism to be in crisis, in need of new approaches and new solutions. That crisis, and liberal reactions to it, are the subjects of the next chapter.

9

A World in Crisis and the Crisis of Liberalism, 1919–1945

SOMEWHERE BETWEEN THE VALLEY of the Somme in 1916 and the chateau of Versailles in 1919, liberal optimism faded to a whimper. There followed a time of anxiety and suffering in Europe, which after 1929 became worldwide. The world was in crisis, indeed in multiple crises, as was liberalism, often held responsible for the world's troubles, as would be the case in every crisis thereafter. By 1938, liberal political parties hardly existed in Italy, Germany, eastern Europe, or Russia. They had been replaced by communist, fascist, and radical nationalist dictatorships. Even where dictatorship was avoided, liberals lost power. In France their influence waned compared to both the left and the right. In Britain, their traditional stronghold, the Liberals became a barely relevant third party. In the United States, Roosevelt's New Deal veered from one course to another, and not always in a liberal direction. Illiberal movements were everywhere.

In this fearful time liberals, whether classical or modern, seemed impotent—parrots of the past, squawking tired old slogans and shrieking in alarm, with nothing to offer but fatigue and failure. The exciting banners and slogans were waved by Fascists, Nazis, and Communists. People of conviction accepted the dogma that salvation lay in making their enemies more afraid of them than they were of their enemies. In a frightening world, fear seemed the best weapon and the best ally.

There was no place in such a world for the liberal project of a society where none need be afraid. In 1920 the Italian dictator Benito Mussolini coined a new word, "totalitarianism," to describe the form of society he wished to create: "all within the state, none outside the state, none against the state." It is hard to imagine anything more illiberal, but Hitler and Lenin succeeded where ordinary imaginations fail. Whether totalitarianism was conceived as an all-powerful state or an all-powerful political party, whether it was a return to an ancient dream of "freedom" in Constant's terms, or a purely modern invention, it terrified liberals.

Liberalism 3.0; the third wave of liberalism, started in the early 1920s, when Fascism took power in Italy and the Bolsheviks triumphed in the Russian Civil War. It was characterized by the fear of totalitarianism. This was embodied by fascism and communism during the first generation of anti-totalitarian liberalism, from 1920 to 1945. The second and third generations of anti-totalitarian liberals after WWII would never forget this period, but mercifully faced less immediate threats. Anti-totalitarian liberals in the 1920s and '30s feared for the survival of liberalism, and many doubted their old certainties about the relationship among freedom, markets, and morals. John Maynard Keynes spoke for them when he wrote that it was problematic to combine "economic efficiency, social justice, and individual liberty." There was widespread doubt about whether the pillars of liberalism were really compatible with one another, and especially whether markets were compatible with morals. Keynes defended free markets, but in terms that invited contradiction: "I think that Capitalism, wisely managed, can probably be made more efficient for attaining economic ends than any alternative system yet in sight, but that in itself it is in many ways extremely objectionable."[1]

There was an outpouring of liberal self-doubt and pessimism, ranging from Walter Lippmann's *The Phantom Public* (1925) and Julien Benda's *The Treason of the Intellectuals* (1927) to Ortega y Gasset's *The Revolt of the Masses* (1930). In 1933, University of Chicago economist Frank Knight wrote that it was inevitable that the United States would adopt some kind of controlled economy, and that the only question was "whether any sort of liberty, especially freedom of consumption and intellectual freedom, can be maintained to a significant extent." The German Ordoliberal Wilhelm Röpke stated flatly in 1935 that "the case of liberalism and capitalism is lost strategically even where it is still undefeated tactically."[2]

If liberalism in general was in difficulty, classical liberalism, identified with laissez-faire, seemed almost dead. Those who were willing to defend free

1. Keynes, "The End of Laissez Faire," in *Essays in Persuasion*, 174, 169; "Liberalism and Labour," 187.

2. Knight, cited in Burgin, *The Great Persuasion*, 4; Röpke, cited in Burgin, *The Great Persuasion*, 13; Jackson, "At the Origins of Neo-Liberalism," 150.

markets, and *a fortiori* laissez-faire, were marginalized. Knight and his fellow Chicago economist Henry Simons mocked Ludwig von Mises's and Lionel Robbins's attempts to defend a laissez-faire state. Simons called Robbins's work a "disservice to liberalism." Lippmann regarded the idea of laissez-faire public policy as "so obvious an error that it seems grotesque." Robbins compared the remaining defenders of free markets to Elijah the prophet lamenting in the wilderness that "Only I, of all the prophets of God, remain." And even Robbins could be critical of classical liberalism, writing to Lippmann that "I am entirely at one with you in rejecting laissez-faire." These ex-classical liberals who now criticized laissez-faire were also, however, skeptical about modern liberals' faith in the beneficence of state economic intervention, which they accepted with reluctance and only in moderation.[3]

What resulted, and characterized the first generation of anti-totalitarian liberals, were strenuous efforts to overcome the split between classical and modern liberals that had emerged in the fin de siècle. These "neo-liberals,"[4] as they occasionally described themselves, adopted three positions that they thought necessary to successfully confront totalitarianism: they rejected laissez-faire; they emphasized the common values of classical and modern liberalism; and they supported a social safety net and a permanent state role in regulating economic development.[5] The narrowing gap between liberalism and the left was visible in this period both among figures closer to classical liberalism, such as Hayek or the Ordoliberals, and those closer to modern liberalism, such as Keynes or Berlin. Liberals adopted a Popular Front policy against totalitarianism.[6]

3. Burgin, *The Great Persuasion*, 14; 33; Jackson, "At the Origins of Neo-Liberalism," 134–135; Jackson, "Freedom, the Common Good, and the Rule of Law," 57. Robbins's position disavowing laissez-faire and endorsing an Ordoliberal-like role for the state in establishing a competitive framework can be found in *The Theory of Economic Policy in English Classical Liberal Political Economy*, 11–12, 55–61. I am indebted to Paul Lewis for the reference.

4. The term "neo-liberal," as has often been noted, was invented for purposes diametrically opposed to the commitment to laissez-faire it came to mean in the 1980s.

5. These criteria are similar but not identical to those proposed by Ben Jackson for what he calls the "neo-liberal" movement that crystallized at the colloque Lippmann. See Jackson, "At the Origins of Neo-Liberalism," 134.

6. Jackson, "At the Origins of Neo-Liberalism," 150. The traces of this policy extended to the formation of the Mt. Pélerin Society after WWII. See Karl Popper's letter to Hayek, March 15, 1944, cited in Jones, *Masters of the Universe*, 39n19 and Popper to Hayek, Jan. 11, 1947, cited in 39n20.

The fear of totalitarianism did not entirely sweep away older liberal fears. Unreconstructed classical liberals like Ludwig von Mises (1881–1973) continued to pound the drum of laissez-faire, while old-fashioned American Progressives like Justice Brandeis and the British New Liberal Hobhouse persisted with modern liberal views. The liberal oyster continued to add overlapping layers, displaying ever more strata. Liberalism 1.0 and 2.0 continued to find users who preferred them to the update, and responded to Hitler and Stalin in terms of the fear of revolution and reaction and / or the fear of poverty, without seeing totalitarianism as a new fear requiring a fundamentally different response. But first- and second-wave liberals content to stand on the old foundations in the 1920s or 1930s were a relatively small group among the shrinking number of liberals.

The anti-totalitarian third wave of liberalism will be examined here from West to East, from America to Central Europe and Russia, although the geographical perspective is complicated by the frequent movement of liberals from place to place, not always of their own free will. Walter Lippmann was a very American figure who made many professional trips to Europe. Friedrich Hayek began his career in Vienna, transferred his base to Britain and the United States, and then returned to Austria and ended up in Germany. Isaiah Berlin was permanently marked by his youthful Russian experience before emigrating to Britain and making many sojourns in America. The German Ordoliberals divided, some remaining in Germany under Hitler, while others left, sometimes permanently, as Wilhelm Röpke did for Switzerland. But whatever their national origin, their liberalism was marked by the fear of totalitarianism. Even if they moved on to other concerns, as was arguably the case for Hayek, that fear was central to their orientation in the 1920–1945 period, and usually considerably longer. It motivated their attempts to reconcile classical and modern liberalism.

Walter Lippmann and His Conference

To a surprising degree, the thought of the first generation of Liberalism 3.0 was encapsulated in a single book, rarely read after WWII, by an author who is remembered mostly as a journalist: *The Good Society*, published in 1937 by Walter Lippmann (1889–1974). In his early career, Lippmann was a maverick Progressive. In the 1920s he was mostly concerned with the relationship between liberalism and democracy. He doubted the ability of the public to understand complicated issues, and thought they lacked the time and interest necessary to learn about them. When the Great Depression struck in 1929, he opposed direct aid to the unemployed on the classical liberal ground that it would morally corrupt them. He also objected to government restrictions on child labor and the early payment of WWI veterans' bonuses. On the other hand, he was a supporter of trade unions, although not without reservations, and privately expressed support as early as 1917 for some kind of social safety net.[7]

Until around 1930, Lippmann was a mildly interesting figure who straddled the line between classical and modern liberalism on some issues, without making their contradictions central to his ideas. But under the continuing impact of the Great Depression and still more of totalitarianism, a revolution occurred in his thought, as it did for many liberals. In 1932 Lippmann told the newly elected FDR that he might have to assume dictatorial powers if Congress balked at the radical measures necessary. In 1934 he wrote that "responsibility for the successful operation of a nation's economy is now just as much a function of the government as national defense. . . . I wish it were not the case . . . But I don't think we live in that kind of world any longer." It was not chiefly the economy, however, that worried Lippmann, it was the threat of fascism and communism. The economy had to be taken care of by a liberal state because otherwise it would be replaced by a totalitarian one. This was the leading message of *The Good Society*, which described the intellectual framework within which a generation of liberals would rethink liberalism.[8]

The preface to *The Good Society* stated the crisis of liberalism: "Everywhere the movements which bid for men's allegiance are hostile to the movements in which men struggled to be free. The programmes of reform are everywhere at odds with the liberal tradition." Nowhere was the liberal insistence that civil society was the primary source of hope respected. Whether they "call themselves communists, socialists, fascists, nationalists, progressives and even liberals," they rely "upon the increased power of officials to improve the condition of men. . . . the only instrument of progress in which they have faith is the coercive agency of government." This was "the dominant dogma of the age." It was "the doctrine that disorder and misery can be overcome only by more and more compulsory organization." Totalitarian societies represented the ultimate development of the idea of "the state as saviour."[9]

7. Steel, *Walter Lippmann*, 180–182, 212; 388–389; 65, 80; Goodwin, *Walter Lippmann*, 204–205, 207.

8. Steel, *Walter Lippmann*, 300; 311; Burgin, *The Great Persuasion*, 63. It is unclear to what extent Lippman influenced people or merely served as their spokesperson.

9. Lippmann, *The Good Society*, xliv, 3, 5, 53.

Lippmann took the history of this new dogma from Dicey. Adopting Dicey's vocabulary, he dated the rise of "collectivism" to 1870, a collectivism that would, over the course of decades, become totalitarianism.[10] For Lippmann, collectivism began with economics, but soon went beyond it, for "in so far as men embrace the belief that the coercive power of the state shall plan, shape, and direct their economy, they commit themselves to the suppression of the contrariness arising from the diversity of human interests and purposes." The result was "intellectuals who expound what now passes for 'liberalism,' 'progressivism,' or 'radicalism,'" but who "are almost all collectivists in their conception of the economy, authoritarians in their conception of the state, totalitarians in their conception of society." These intellectuals deceived themselves that collectivist economics could be reconciled with political freedom. The real totalitarians, the fascists and communists, knew better: "The fascist conception of life, says Mussolini, 'accepts the individual only in so far as his interests coincide with those of the state.' Does communism accept the individual on any other terms?"[11]

Lippmann then took a new course characteristic of third-wave liberals: he blamed the rise of collectivism and then totalitarianism on its most fervent opponents, that is, on classical liberalism. If the question was "why liberalism lost its influence on human affairs," the fault lay with "the later liberalism," incarnated in "the aging Herbert Spencer" and the doctrine of laissez-faire. Lippmann took Dicey's history and turned its moral compass 180 degrees. Laissez-faire was a perversion of liberalism just as much as collectivism. Lippmann appealed to Adam Smith against Spencer, lamenting that "the doctrine which has come down from him [Smith] and from the great liberals of the eighteenth century has in our time become the intellectual defense of much injustice and oppression. In Herbert Spencer's old age, liberalism became a monstrous negation raised up as a barrier against every generous instinct of mankind." If liberalism could not, to use Spencer's language, bring altruism back into politics, then liberalism would die, and deserve it. Liberalism, however, had to bring altruism back not by arbitrary government policies, but by a revitalized notion of law.[12]

10. Quite possibly the seeds of Hayek's "road to serfdom" are found in Lippmann, rather than Tocqueville.

11. Lippmann, *The Good Society*, 46; 45–91; 51; 49; 51.

12. Lippmann, *The Good Society*, 240, see also 182; xlvii. As will be seen below, this emphasis on law brought Lippmann close to Ordoliberal ideas.

Lippmann wanted the law to step in, not to replace the market, but to compensate for its inevitable collateral damage, to pay for what economists call "externalities." When globalization moved industries from one place to another, "in the long view this is industrial progress, but in the close view its human evil is tragic." It was entirely proper to tax the winners to indemnify the losers. Lippmann also endorsed "large social expenditure" on "education; the conservation of the people's patrimony in the land and natural resources; the development of the people's estate through public works . . . providing the organization of markets by information, inspection, and other services." In *The Good Society* he rejected the idea of a minimum income, but by 1934 he was no longer opposed, and by 1938 endorsed at least a strong form of unemployment insurance: "To have economic independence a man must be in a position to leave one job and go to another; he must have enough savings of some kind to exist for a considerable time without accepting the first job offered. . . . The more I see of Europe the more deeply convinced do I become that the preservation of freedom in America, or anywhere else, depends upon maintaining and restoring for the great majority of individuals the economic means to remain independent individuals."[13]

Besides a misguided idea of the role of the state, the laissez-faire theorists had, in Lippmann's view, a misguided notion of property rights. Fin de siècle liberalism had become "a collection of querulous shibboleths invoked by property owners when they resisted encroachments on their vested interests." Private ownership did not mean that an "individual can or should exercise a sole and despotic dominion over any portion of the earth or of the things therein. . . . the rights of any man upon the earth must be reconciled with the equal rights of other men, not only of living men but of the unborn generations." Thus Lippmann justified what in the late twentieth century would be described as environmental measures.[14]

It was essential that laissez-faire property rights be limited not by arbitrary bureaucratic intervention, nor by direct state action, but through law. Lippmann used an image later borrowed by many others, including Hayek, to distinguish liberal ideas from those of collectivists:

13. Lippmann, *The Good Society*, 223; 226; 227–228; Lippmann, *The Method of Freedom* (1934), cited in Audier, *Le colloque Lippmann*, 99, 99n2, Lippmann, July 16, 1938, *New York Herald Tribune*, cited in Goodwin, *Walter Lippmann*, 250.

14. Lippmann, *The Good Society*, 183; 276.

Officials can, for example, regulate the traffic on the roads. . . . But if, instead of defining the rights of all the drivers, the officials seek to prescribe the destination of each driver . . . some few, those who have the ear of the authorities, will undoubtedly go just where they want to go, more swiftly, more pleasantly, than under a free system of equal rights. But the rest will be going where they do not wish to go.[15]

Lippmann continued in a fashion the later Hayek would probably have rejected, but which the younger Hayek enthusiastically endorsed: "under the laissez-faire delusion it was supposed that good markets would somehow organize themselves or, at any rate, that the markets are as good as they might be. That is not true. The improvement of the markets had to be a subject of continual study in a liberal society." As an example, Lippmann suggested reforming corporate law in order to restrain the growth of quasi-monopolies.[16]

Lippmann concluded *The Good Society* with a restatement of liberalism as the search for a society in which none need be afraid. After recounting the story of Sir Edward Coke telling King James I that the King himself was subject to the law, Lippmann pointed out that "the essential and enduring part of Coke's reply is the denial that the King may act arbitrarily. The denial that men may be arbitrary in human transactions *is* the higher law." He then gave what probably remains the best short definition of a liberal conception of human rights: "*The development of human rights is simply the expression of the higher law that men shall not deal arbitrarily with one another*" (emphasis added). Contrary to contractarians and natural law theorists, this did not mean that human rights were fixed for all time. "The ideal of a society in which all are equally free of all arbitrary coercion is a receding goal. From each new plateau in the ascent higher levels become visible."[17]

To this negative conception of liberty as freedom from coercion Lippmann added, in traditional liberal fashion, a positive component. He distinguished the anarchist, who held a purely negative conception of liberty, from the liberal: "the liberal . . . holds that mere unrestraint does not give . . . freedom . . . , that unrestraint merely inaugurates a competitive struggle in which the

15. Lippmann, *The Good Society*, 283. Both Hayek and Rawls, among others, take up the analogy.

16. Lippmann, *The Good Society*, 221; 266; 218.

17. Lippmann, *The Good Society*, 346; 348; 352.

ruthless will exploit the rest." Hence the need for government expenditures and regulations. "Liberalism, therefore, is not the doctrine of laissez-faire, let her rip, and the devil take the hindmost." In order to fight totalitarianism, liberalism had to reinvent itself, "by developing the abiding truth of the older liberalism after purging it of the defects which destroyed it."[18]

Lippmann's call found responsive ears on both sides of the Atlantic. Henry Simons in Chicago, Lionel Robbins and Friedrich Hayek in London, Louis Rougier in France, and William Rappard in Switzerland were all enamoured of *The Good Society*. They saw it as a program for renovating liberalism, and as a result the Walter Lippmann Conference, usually known as the Colloque Lippmann, took place in Paris on August 26–30, 1938. Among those present were Lippmann himself, Raymond Aron, Friedrich Hayek, Ludwig von Mises, Michael Polanyi, Wilhelm Röpke, Louis Rougier, Jacques Rueff, and Alexander Rüstow. Invited but unable to attend were Luigi Einaudi, Johan Huizenga, José Ortega y Gasset, and Lionel Robbins. Many of these liberal luminaries played important roles after WWII.[19]

The term "neoliberalism" was probably invented at the Colloque Lippmann, where many of the participants endorsed it. But it was not a synonym for laissez-faire economics as it became in the 1980s. Almost all the participants in the conference rejected laissez-faire (Mises being a notable exception). When Louis Rougier organized the conference and invited Lippmann to participate, he stressed that its purpose was "to discuss . . . the conditions of a return to a renovated liberal order distinct from Manchester [i.e., laissez-faire] liberalism." For the neoliberals of the Colloque Lippmann, neoliberalism meant reconciling modern and classical liberalism, with a noticeable tilt toward the modern side.[20]

The program of the colloque is a good introduction to what liberals were thinking in 1938:

    I. Is the decline of liberalism due to endogenous causes?
       (a) As a result of the trend of the corporate concentration . . .
       (b) As a result of the trend of economic nationalism.

---

18. Lippmann, *The Good Society*, 356; 355; 345.

19. Burgin, *The Great Persuasion*, 55; Reinhoudt and Audier, eds., *The Walter Lippmann Colloquium*, 12.

20. Burgin, *The Great Persuasion*, 71.

II. Is liberalism capable of fulfilling its social tasks?
    (a) Security. Does liberalism lead to structural crises? ...
    (b) The vital minimum for all. ...
III. If the decline of liberalism is not inevitable, what are its true causes (exogenous causes)?
    (a) Psychological and sociological causes ...
    (b) Political and ideological causes. ...
IV. If the decline of liberalism is not inevitable, what are the remedies to draw from the analysis of its causes? The Agenda of liberalism.
V. Conclusions: Future action.[21]

Lippmann gave a keynote speech which described the contemporary situation: "From the outset, we come up against a brutal fact: the century of progress toward democracy, toward individualism, toward economic freedom, toward scientific positivism, ended in an era of wars, of revolution, and of reaction." Liberals had to acknowledge that "freedom would not have been annihilated in half of the civilized world, so seriously compromised in the other half, if the old liberalism had not possessed critical defects." Calling for a return to (pre–WWI) liberalism was therefore foolish. So was adherence to one of the "liberal sects," which "confuse the cause of freedom with doctrines such as that of natural law, that of popular sovereignty, the rights of man, of parliamentary government, the right of self-determination of peoples, of *laissez-faire* or free trade. Those are concepts that men have used ... under certain historical circumstances. ... the fate of freedom is linked to none of the liberal theories."[22]

The speech was followed by a discussion of the true meaning of liberalism. Some participants wanted to abandon the word on the grounds that it was identified with laissez- faire. Nevertheless, the debates continued under the liberal flag, and ultimately, as Alexander Rüstow pointed out, the participants sorted themselves into two groups. There was a minority, which "does not find anything essential to criticize or to change in traditional liberalism ... In their view, the responsibility for all the misfortune falls exclusively ... on those who, out of stupidity or out of malice, or through a mixture of both, cannot or do not want to discern and observe the salutary truths of liberalism."[23]

21. Audier, *Le colloque Lippmann*, 94–95.
22. Audier, *Le colloque Lippmann*, 103; 105.
23. Audier, *Le colloque Lippmann*, 111; 168–170.

The majority, however, saw that "if the unwavering representatives of old liberalism were right, the practical prospects [for liberalism] would be almost hopeless. . . . If they have not listened to Moses and the prophets—Adam Smith and Ricardo—how will they believe Mr. von Mises?" Rüstow's solution to the problem of "why humanity . . . has brusquely turned itself away from [liberalism]," was that laissez-faire liberals weakened liberalism by regarding it as the solution to a purely economic problem. But a satisfying life could not be obtained by bread alone, and liberalism needed to offer a method of social integration. Neither Rüstow nor anyone else at the Colloque Lippmann referred to Tocqueville or any of the other nineteenth-century thinkers who had addressed exactly this kind of problem—an indication of how strongly Dicey's classical liberal vision of liberal history had imprinted itself on the liberal consciousness. But while the majority was clear that shouting classical liberalism from the rooftops was not a viable solution, it was not capable of agreeing on a program. Nevertheless, these three positions, the rejection of laissez-faire, the appeal to common values, and support for some form of social safety net, attracted something close to a consensus. Under the pressure of crisis and dictatorship, Liberalism 3.0 was born from the appraisal of past failures and from the new fear of totalitarianism.[24]

Liberalism 3.0 was as varied in its approach to fighting totalitarianism as previous liberalisms had been in their struggles. This can be seen in the works of Friedrich Hayek, Isaiah Berlin, and the Ordoliberals. Hayek's appeal to our ignorance, Berlin's call for pluralism, and the Ordoliberals' insistence on a "competitive order" represent three overlapping yet distinct strategies for defeating totalitarianism by reconciling classical and modern liberalism. They departed from the tendency of Liberalism 2.0 to rest its arguments on a single foundation by returning to liberalism's traditional three pillars of freedom, markets, and morals.

Of the three, Hayek's liberalism was simultaneously the most original and the most traditional. Unlike fin de siècle liberalisms, it was based not on presumed scientific knowledge, but on unconquerable ignorance; reconciling classical and modern liberalism, it allowed for the creation of a social safety net alongside a free-market economy; and it rejected nationalism in favor of international federalism in a manner rarely seen since Kant.

24. Audier, *Le colloque Lippmann*, 170, see also Burgin, *The Great Persuasion*, 75; 157; 162; Reinhoudt and Audier, eds., *The Walter Lippmann Colloquium*, 24.

The Hayek Equation: Freedom = Ignorance
Properly Understood

Friedrich Hayek (1899–1992) was born at just the "right" time to serve in the Austrian army in WWI. He began his academic career as an economist in Vienna, and moved to London in 1931 in the middle of the Great Depression, having already witnessed the rise of Italian Fascism and Russian Communism, shortly followed by Hitler taking power in Germany in 1933 and his annexation of Austria in 1938. It is hardly surprising that for Hayek totalitarianism was "the main problem confronting the modern world." Throughout his life his liberalism largely retained its pre–WWII problematic—he hardly ever mentioned the Cold War in his later work.[25]

What made Hayek unique was the foundation he chose for his struggle against totalitarianism. His distinctive contribution was his stress on "our irremediable ignorance." This is known as Hayek's "knowledge problem": when it comes to social phenomena, unlike natural ones, we are condemned to only a limited, local knowledge, no matter how educated we may be. Hayek therefore rejected any application of the predictive methods of the natural sciences to social questions, and asserted our need to leave individuals maximum freedom to act on the limited knowledge at their disposal, consistent with others having equal freedom. Wisdom lay in recognizing our limits: "All political theories assume, of course, that most individuals are very ignorant. Those who plead for liberty differ from the rest in that they include among the ignorant themselves. . . . the difference between the knowledge that the wisest and that the most ignorant individual can deliberately employ is comparatively insignificant."[26] Based on our "unavoidable ignorance," Hayek turned nineteenth-century liberalism upside-down and built a theory of universal political and economic *incapacity*. No individual or group was capable of designing a well-functioning society or economy because everyone was too ignorant. Civilization was not the product of anyone's plan. It was a "spontaneous order," as were languages, and markets. Such spontaneous orders were superior to planned or imposed orders because they could take advantage of the bits of truth that each individual possessed, instead of relying on the necessarily faulty universal knowledge of the planner. Because of the limits of their

25. Kukathas, *Hayek and Modern Liberalism*, 196; Slobodian, *Globalists, Globalists*, 264.

26. The Humean origins of this position have been explored in Kukathas, *Hayek and Modern Liberalism*.

knowledge, people needed the freedom to be spontaneous: "the case for individual freedom rests chiefly on the recognition of the inevitable ignorance of all of us concerning a great many of the factors on which the achievement of our ends and welfare depends." We could and should identify useful broad patterns and principles, e.g., competition is good, and constitutional and legal frameworks are helpful, but any attempt to specify the details, such as fixing prices, was doomed to failure.[27]

Unfortunately, even those who did not embrace centralized price controls were subject to the delusion that it would be useful to plan all or part of the economy. In Hayek's view of the West in the 1930s and '40s, there was an "increasing similarity of the economic views of the Right and Left," characterized by "increasing veneration for the state, the admiration of power, and of bigness for bigness' sake, the enthusiasm for the 'organization' of everything (we now call it 'planning')." All too many people were unwittingly setting out on *The Road to Serfdom*, as Hayek called it in his 1945 book that became a bestseller and influenced generations of twentieth-century liberals.[28]

Hayek thought he knew why people were taking this road, and how and why for decades past many liberals had been their fellow travelers. *The Road to Serfdom* gave a history of the decline of liberalism, as Hayek saw it, largely borrowed from Dicey (with acknowledgment).[29] Hayek suggested that because of its very economic success, by the fin de siècle liberalism had created a situation in which "man became increasingly unwilling to tolerate the evils still with him which now appeared both unbearable and unnecessary." The fear of poverty became central, and people began to demand "a complete remodelling of society." The "new freedom," i.e., the positive "economic freedom," championed by socialism, was "embraced by the greater part of the liberal tradition" after 1870. Hayek attempted to purge what he considered socialism from liberalism, for fear that otherwise totalitarianism was inevitable.[30]

Hayek's broader point was that our ignorance was not only economic. It extended to such things as what ought to be the true scale of values (as it did to

27. Hayek, *The Constitution of Liberty, The Collected Works of Friedrich Hayek*, 1:82, 80; Gamble, "Hayek on Knowledge, Economics, and Society," 111; Hayek, "The Use of Knowledge in Society," 519–530, http://oll.libertyfund.org/title/92, 6, 8; *The Constitution of Liberty*, 73; 80; Lewis, "Editor's Introduction."

28. Hayek, *Road to Serfdom*, 59; 67; 193; 194; 40, see also 180.

29. Although unlike Dicey, Hayek wisely did not attribute laissez-faire views to Bentham.

30. Hayek, *Road to Serfdom*, 72; 77; 78, see also 72, 84.

the true means of saving our souls, to rephrase Hayek's concerns in the terms of Liberalism 1.0). Thus, in rejecting the idea of a central authority setting prices and determining production, Hayek argued that "to direct all our activities according to a single plan presupposes that every one of our needs is given its rank in the order of values . . . It presupposes, in short, the existence of a complete ethical code in which all the different human values are allotted their due place." But no such ethical code existed, only individual, "partial scales of values." Since no one knew enough to set everyone else's values, "individuals should be allowed . . . to follow their own values and preferences rather than somebody else's . . . the individual's system of ends should be supreme and not subject to any dictation by others."[31] Our ignorance justified our freedom. Hayek defined freedom as a "state in which a man is not subject to coercion by the arbitrary will of another or others." Coercion could not be eliminated, but the goal should be to "minimize coercion or its harmful effects."[32]

Freedom was thus, in Hayek's view, a purely negative concept. It was a dangerous error to confuse freedom from coercion with "the power to satisfy our wishes, or the extent of the choices open to us," an identification of freedom with the positive "power to [do x]" which for Hayek had been "deliberately fostered as part of the socialist [and modern liberal] argument." "Once this identification of freedom with power is admitted, there is no limit to the sophisms by which the attractions of the word 'liberty' can be used to support measures which destroy individual liberty." This was how "in totalitarian states liberty has been suppressed in the name of liberty." Hayek attributed the same confusion to modern liberals, notably American Progressives like John Dewey. He rejected the idea that the lack of equal opportunity was coercion: "Whether or not I am my own master and can follow my own choice and whether the possibilities from which I must choose are many or few are two entirely different questions," even if limited possibilities might lead to unhappiness. Fundamentally, for Hayek, freedom was not about happiness: "Above all . . . we must recognize that we may be free and yet miserable."[33]

The first necessity of a free society, for Hayek, was the rule of law. "The Rule of Law . . . excludes legislation either directly aimed at particular people or at enabling anybody to use the coercive power of the state for the purpose of such

31. The ellipses mark qualifications regarding when individuals' preferences result in conflict with others.
32. Hayek, *The Road to Serfdom*, 102; *The Constitution of Liberty*, 58, 60.
33. Hayek, *The Constitution of Liberty*, 59; 65–68.

discrimination." Once limits to legislation were recognized, this created or at least operationalized "inviolable rights of man," rights that would prevent totalitarianism. The reason people objected to the rule of law, according to Hayek, was that if the law remained within its proper limits, it "cannot determine the material position of particular people or enforce distributive or 'social' justice." Doing so would violate equality before the law because people would be treated differently, and suffer coercion.[34]

The classical liberal would have stopped here, with a rejection of social justice, but his fear of totalitarianism prompted Hayek to legitimate a social and regulatory safety net. Hayek distinguished between two kinds of desire for economic security. One, illegitimate, which "far from increasing the chances of freedom, becomes the gravest threat to it"; and the legitimate kind, "which can be achieved for all, and which is therefore no privilege but a legitimate object of desire". The illegitimate kind of demand for economic security was "the security of a particular income a person is thought to deserve," or "the relative position one person or group enjoys compared with others," which inherently violated equality under the law. The legitimate kind was "security against severe physical privation, the certainty of a given minimum of sustenance for all." Because this security applied universally, it was within the legitimate scope of law. Whereas the bad kind of security required "controlling or abolishing the market," and using "the coercive power of government to insure a more even or more just distribution of goods," the good kind of security could and should be provided "outside of and supplementary to the market system."[35] Thus:

> There are good reasons why we should endeavour to use whatever political organization we have at our disposal to make provision for the weak or infirm or for the victims of unforeseeable disaster. It may well be true that the most effective method of providing against certain risks common to all citizens of a state is to give every citizen protection against those risks. The level on which such provisions against common risks can be made will necessarily depend on the general wealth of the community.[36]

34. Kukathas, *Hayek and Modern Liberalism*, 154, Hayek, *The Constitution of Liberty*, 221–223; Hayek, *The Road to Serfdom*, 120; 122; *The Constitution of Liberty*, 340, see also *Road to Serfdom*, 131; *Road to Serfdom*, 117, see also *The Constitution of Liberty*, 150; *The Constitution of Liberty*, 340, see also *Road to Serfdom*, 131; *Road to Serfdom*, 117, see also *The Constitution of Liberty*, 341.

35. *The Road to Serfdom*, 147; repeated almost verbatim in *The Constitution of Liberty*, 376; *The Constitution of Liberty*, 37; *The Road to Serfdom*, 147–148, 156.

36. *The Constitution of Liberty*, 165.

Hayek did not specify, at this point in *The Constitution of Liberty*, the "good reasons" for providing for the "weak and infirm." The ultimate reason was that a minimum social safety net was a necessary bulwark against totalitarianism / socialism. Liberalism *must* respond to the desire for material security prevalent throughout the Western world, on pain of making totalitarianism inevitable. Hayek had lived through the 1920s and 1930s, and he knew that "*some security is essential if freedom is to be preserved*, because most men are willing to bear the risk which freedom inevitably involves *only so long as that risk is not too great*" (emphasis added). In fact, more than the bare minimum was needed: "The one thing modern democracy will not bear without cracking," wrote the man who had seen it crack, "is the necessity of a substantial lowering of the standards of living in peacetime or even prolonged stationariness of its economic conditions." As Hayek repeated in *The Constitution of Liberty*, "the amount of relief . . . in a comparatively wealthy society should be more than is absolutely necessary to keep alive and in health." Compulsory insurance for old age, sickness, unemployment, etc., state aid for the victims of floods and earthquakes, were also justified because otherwise people risked becoming a public burden. A considerable part of the modern liberal social program thus found its way into Hayek's legal framework.[37]

Hayek objected to his friend Karl Popper's endorsement of what Popper called "piecemeal social engineering," but all in all Hayek was not far from it himself. For Hayek, "probably nothing has done so much harm to the liberal cause as the wooden insistence of some liberals on . . . the principle of laissez faire." He thought that the classical liberals should have paid more attention to delimiting "the field within which collective action was not only unobjectionable but actually a useful means of obtaining the desired ends . . . To remedy this deficiency must be one of the main tasks of the future." He endorsed a social safety net and an extent of government regulation anathema to fin de siècle classical liberalism.[38] He recognized the political necessity of making

37. *The Road to Serfdom*, 156; 215. Hayek backed the provision of parks, museums, theaters, and sports facilities by government, as well as the creation of large public nature reserves. *The Constitution of Liberty*, 405; *The Road to Serfdom*, 148; *The Constitution of Liberty*, 406, 408ff.; *The Constitution of Liberty*, 376, 497; *The Road to Serfdom*, 88, repeated in *The Constitution of Liberty*, 333. However, in a sign of his increasing ambivalence, although Hayek endorsed public old age insurance in *The Constitution of Liberty* at 406, he questioned its legitimacy on 429.

38. Shearmur writes that "In the light of the active role that he gives to government in *The Road to Serfdom*, one might wonder about the extent to which he can be described as a classical liberal." Shearmur, *Hayek and After*, 63. The answer is clearly no, as was recognized by Jones,

sure that the benefits of freedom, political, economic, and as we shall see below moral, reached everyone, and thus assuaged everyone's fears.[39]

Liberal societies did not exist in isolation. To be safe, they had to be part of a liberal world order. Kant's plan for perpetual peace found an advocate in Hayek, whose position on nationalism broke with most first- and especially second-wave liberalisms. Hayek was not alone in this attitude, which paralleled the views of a number of other Lippmann Conference attendees. Hayek and others appealed to supranational institutions as a brake on illiberal nations. Hayek was persistently internationalist and, what is more, anti-nationalist. This was one of the reasons he refused the label of "conservative." He criticized conservatism for "its hostility to internationalism and its proneness to a strident nationalism." He maintained the common fin de siècle liberal distinction between a bad "nationalism" and a good "patriotism." Nevertheless, he was unsympathetic to any form of nationalism, suggested that criticizing an idea as "un-American," or "un-German," was absurd, and he attacked imperialism—in particular the idea that a civilizing mission could be imposed on unwilling others—as a nationalist deviation from liberalism. Furthermore, in Hayek's view nationalism and socialism naturally went together because no one could "realistically conceive of a collectivist program other than in the service of a limited group . . . be it nationalism, racialism, or classism." Hayek's nightmare, of course, was National Socialism, aka Nazism. He wrote in 1939 that "even within [the] democracies, the socialists are becoming steadily more nationalist and the nationalists steadily more socialist." In response he argued that "the idea of interstate federation as the consistent development of the liberal point of view should be able to provide a new *point d'appui.*"[40]

Masters of the Universe, 67. But Hayek later adopted a more classical liberal position. The 1976 preface to *The Road to Serfdom* stated that when he wrote the book, "I had not wholly freed myself from all the current interventionist superstitions, and in consequence still made various concessions which I now think unwarranted," 55.

39. Hayek, *The Road to Serfdom*, 70–71. Hayek, "The Trend of Economic Thinking," in the eponymous volume of his collected works, p. 31. On Hayek and Popper see João Rodrigues, "The Political and Moral Economies of Neoliberalism: Mises and Hayek," 1001–1017, 1009n7.

40. On Hayek's fellow travelers, see Rohac and Mingardi, "Hayek's Europe: The Austrian School and European Federalism," 67–80; Slobodian, *Globalists*, 9, 15. Kukathas, "Hayek and Liberalism," 198–203; Jorg Spieker, "F.A. Hayek," 919–942. Hayek, *The Constitution of Liberty*, 526–528; Kukathas, "Hayek and Liberalism," 193; Hayek, *The Road to Serfdom*, 161; *The Constitution of Liberty*, 526; "The Economic Conditions of Interstate Federalism," 131–49; republished at fee.org/articles/the-economic-conditions-of-interstate-federalism/, without pagination.

Internationalism was central to Hayek's early liberalism in a way in which it had not been central to liberalism since Kant. His essay on interstate federalism was essentially a plea for the organization, not of a world government (although that was not excluded) but of supranational federations that bore a certain resemblance to the later European Union. Their primary purpose, as in Kant's world federation, was "to secure peace." The means by which this was to be achieved was through some kind of political union, but the essay, as its title implied, was more interested in the economic structure of the future federations. Hayek was a proponent of what a later generation would call globalization, not simply as a matter of traditional liberal free-trade policy, but as a source of legal constraints on illiberal political and economic policies. His federalism was a regional approach to the rule of law that combined moral and political incentives with economic ones.

Of particular interest to Hayek was that "in a federation, certain economic powers, which are now generally wielded by the national states, could be exercised neither by the federation nor by the individual states, [which] implies that there would have to be less government all round," a conclusion devoutly to be wished. Hayek counted on diverse values within the federation acting as a restraint on economic planning. In strictly economic terms, individual countries would not be able to impose tariffs or create monopolies, and while the federation would be able to, it would face much stronger opposition than national governments did; individual nations would also find it difficult to interfere with markets because they would be subject to both competition from, and supervision by, the federation. The free movement of people, capital, and goods, which Hayek, like the EU, saw as essential, would further limit the powers that could be exercised by the federation and the nations that composed it. Hayek saw a common currency as an essential component that would enforce fiscal restraint, as much or more than the gold standard. Typical, however, of the early Hayek was the reminder that there would be "ample room" for local economic experimentation and that "there will . . . be ample scope for economic policy in a federation and that there is no need for extreme laissez faire in economic matters."[41]

But perhaps the most striking part of the essay was not its anticipation of the European Union, but its conclusion "that nineteenth-century liberalism did not

---

Slobodian raises the question of whether Hayek's rejection of nationalism was a reference to the Austro-Hungarian empire of his youth. See *Globalists*, 105.

41. "The Economic Conditions of Interstate Federalism."

succeed more fully is due largely to its failure to develop in this direction; and the cause is mainly that, because of historical accidents, it successively joined forces first with nationalism and later with socialism." The embrace of nationalism and even "socialism" by nineteenth-century liberalism was essentially a moral failing. For Hayek, the moral pillar of liberalism, its Kantian universalism, was as important as its political and economic aspects.[42]

Hayek thus presented both economic and political arguments. His knowledge problem had moral and even religious implications, and he also addressed moral issues directly. Hayek thought liberal values were under threat from totalitarianism. The basic moral pillar of liberalism, in Hayek's view, was the idea of "individual responsibility," without which neither moral virtue nor freedom could exist. Hence the chapter of *The Constitution of Liberty* titled "Responsibility and Freedom," because "liberty and responsibility are inseparable." Unfortunately, people were not fond of responsibility, and thus the "fear of responsibility . . . necessarily becomes also a fear of freedom." and "the burden of choice that freedom imposes, the responsibility for one's own fate that a free society places on the individual, has under the conditions of the modern world become a main source of dissatisfaction." Responsibility entailed risks. To make those risks bearable, Hayek endorsed a social safety net, as much to help people bear the moral pressures of a liberal society as their possible economic hardships, and thus preserve democratic political institutions from intolerable strain. Nevertheless, individuals had to accept responsibility for their own risks.[43]

Morally speaking, however, this was not enough. If the free markets essential to moral development were to continue to exist, they had to be morally justified. Hayek therefore provided such justification from both a utilitarian and a perfectionist perspective. From the liberal perspective, this was a feature, not a flaw. Thus "the market, defined by the institutions of justice, is to be praised not merely for making production cheaper; for what is discovered in the market process is not only 'economic' knowledge, but knowledge of the world, of others, and even of oneself." Free markets helped people get both cheaper bread (useful) and greater self-knowledge (perfection). It was true that economic progress, indeed progress of any kind might not make us *happier*: it was "unanswerable," Hayek thought, whether we were "in any significant sense better off or happier than if we had stopped a hundred or a thousand

42. "The Economic Conditions of Interstate Federalism."
43. *The Road to Serfdom*, 216; *The Constitution of Liberty*, 133, 143.

years ago"—it was not a Benthamite sort of utility that was in question. But, Hayek went on, "the answer . . . does not matter. What matters is the successful striving for what at each moment seems attainable. It is not the fruits of past success but the living in and for the future" in which "man enjoys the gift of his intelligence." Striving for perfection was what mattered.[44]

The market encouraged striving for perfection, and markets were effectively a matter of continual "experiments in living" as Mill called it, a process of discovery that not only brought knowledge of correct prices, but created the opportunity for discovering one's own priorities and values, and thus attaining greater self-knowledge. *The Constitution of Liberty* described human beings as people who pursued knowledge of the good life. Freedom from coercion meant freedom to pursue our perfection in our own way, and only a free market could produce moral results in terms of individual perfection and self-knowledge. For Hayek, "liberty is not merely one particular value but . . . the source and condition of most moral values." There was thus, in moral terms, a defense of positive freedom in Hayek, the freedom *to discover ourselves*. For Hayek, Western civilization was characterized by "respect for the individual man *qua* man, that is, the recognition of his own views and tastes as supreme in his own sphere . . . and the belief that it is desirable that men should develop their own individual gifts and bents."[45]

According to Hayek, outside of a few misguided rationalists (e.g., Bentham), it had always been recognized that "freedom has never worked without deeply ingrained moral beliefs and that coercion can be reduced to a minimum only where individuals can be expected as a rule to conform voluntarily to certain principles." Hayek cited Madison that "to suppose that any form of government will secure liberty or happiness without any virtue in the people, is a chimerical idea." He dissented from *On Liberty*, suggesting that Mill "probably overstated" the case against private moral coercion.[46]

For this reason Hayek endorsed something like a common curriculum in schools, while recognizing its dangers. "There is a need for certain common standards of values, and, though too great emphasis on this need may lead to

44. Kukathas, "Hayek and Liberalism," 192, Shearmur, *Hayek and After*, 57, Kukathas, "Hayek and Liberalism," 194; Kukathas, *Hayek and Modern Liberalism*, passim; Shearmur, *Hayek and After*, 177; Kukathas, *Hayek and Modern Liberalism*, 101; *The Constitution of Liberty*, 95.

45. Kukathas, *Hayek and Modern Liberalism*, 128; Hayek, *Constitution of Liberty*, 6; *The Road to Serfdom*, 68; 126.

46. *The Constitution of Liberty*, 123; 123n38; 213–214.

very illiberal consequences, peaceful common existence would be clearly impossible without any such standards." This was particularly the case in countries like the United States with large immigrant populations, where Hayek endorsed "a deliberate policy of 'Americanization' in the school system." Despite the dangers of government-run educational systems, "up to a point, the arguments that justify compulsory education also require that government should prescribe some of the content of this education," even if it should probably not dispense the education itself. Hayek insisted that a common moral foundation was required for a liberal society to function, even as the moral purpose of liberal society was to allow individuals to pursue their own moral perfection in their own way.[47]

And yet, Hayek narrowed the moral pillar of liberalism and limited the weight it could bear. In a free society there was no "proportionality of reward to moral merit," even as an ideal, because there was "no human being who is competent to reward all efforts according to merit." Any conception of a morally grounded social "justice" could only be based on some individual's, or majority's, arbitrary decision. "A society in which the position of individuals was made to correspond to human ideas of moral merit would therefore be the exact opposite of a free society." Criteria foreign to the market could not and should not determine economic rewards. As the American neoconservative Irving Kristol pointed out, such a divorce between moral merit and material reward, even in theory, would have appalled the average nineteenth-century liberal.[48]

Hayek strained mightily to reconcile classical and modern liberalism. Yet, with regard to the moral basis of liberalism, the reconciliation was limited. He found in the experience of totalitarianism reasons to adopt certain modern liberal positions on grounds that were partly prudential, and partly a matter of accepting, to a greater degree than Spencer, room for altruism and interest to work alongside one another in the public sphere, as long as the two were not confused. Ultimately Hayek's moralism was thin. It hardly provided sustenance or encouragement for anything like Tocqueville's vision of moral greatness or the reconciliation of ancient and modern freedom envisaged by Constant. There was a moral pillar to Hayek's liberalism, but what he presented was something of an empty shell: common school curricula that were

---

47. *The Constitution of Liberty*, 500; 502.

48. *The Constitution of Liberty*, 156–157, 159; 161; Kristol, *Two Cheers for Capitalism*, 245–246; *The Constitution of Liberty*, 162–163.

not described; the freedom to discover ourselves with the help of the market—but no discussion of what kind of selves those might or should be; an acknowledgment of the necessity of social altruism combined with a demand for personal responsibility. He depended on unspecified "deeply ingrained moral beliefs." Hayek stressed the need for a moral pillar for liberalism rather than actually building one. The same might be said of his view of politics. Although Hayek continually appealed to political institutions, whether national constitutions or supranational bodies, he thought, as he stated in his later work, that "generally politics has become much too important, much too costly and harmful, absorbing much too much mental energy and material resources, and that at the same time it is losing more and more the respect and sympathetic support of the public at large." As a moral problem, Hayek had no remedy for this. As a political problem, it was a restatement of Constant, without Constant's attempt to bring ancient and modern liberty together. The political pillar of Hayek's liberalism, even in his elaborate late constitutional work, thus rang hollow. Law acted as a pallid stand-in for politics.[49]

It is significant that by the end of his essay "Why I Am Not a Conservative," Hayek was unsure how to characterize his position. He was aware that he was neither a modern nor a classical liberal, and that "what I have called 'liberalism' has little to do with any political movement that goes by that name today." He wanted to connect with the broadly conceived liberalism of the eighteenth century, or that of Madison, Tocqueville, and Lord Acton in the short nineteenth century, and wished he could call himself an "Old Whig," since Whiggism, in Hayek's judgment, was "the name for the only set of ideals that has consistently opposed all arbitrary power." At the same time, he rejected any return to the past, and embraced the Utopian element of liberalism because "the belief in integral freedom is based on an essentially forward-looking attitude." Had he read a little more Tocqueville, he might have said he was "a liberal of a new kind." But he was not altogether alone—and in the second half of the twentieth century his brand of anti-totalitarian liberalism became very influential, although often overlaid with an economism foreign to his own thought.[50]

For Hayek the embodiment of evil was the person who claimed to know the correct price of everything, and was willing to impose their price on

49. Hayek, *Law, Legislation, and Liberty,* 482.

50. Hayek, *The Constitution of Liberty,* 529; 531–532. On economism and neoliberalism, see chapter 10.

anyone who disagreed. For Isaiah Berlin the great evil was the monist, the person who claimed to know what everyone should value, and was willing to impose their values on everyone else. Hayek's solution to the knowledge problem was the free market; Berlin's was "pluralism." Berlin's theory of moral pluralism represented another important strand in the development of anti-totalitarian liberalism, and had enormous influence in the late twentieth century. It was a moral theory that, like Hayek's, had the paradoxical effect of both emphasizing and narrowing the moral basis of liberalism. Sometimes running in parallel and sometimes clashing, Hayek's and Berlin's thought represent two major contributions to Liberalism 3.0.

Isaiah Berlin

Isaiah Berlin was born to a Jewish family in Riga (then Russia, now Latvia), which moved to St. Petersburg in 1916, where he witnessed the Russian Revolution and Civil War until the family moved to Britain in 1921. Britain remained his home for the rest of his life, with professional intervals in America. He began his academic career at Oxford in 1932, and although he is often described as a Cold War Liberal, that is, a post–WWII thinker, the roots of his thought were set well before, including his transition from analytic philosopher to the study of political philosophy and the history of political thought. He finally became Chichele Professor of Social and Political Theory at Oxford.[51]

For Berlin, two factors had shaped the twentieth century: technological development, and the "totalitarian tyrannies of both right and left" accompanied by "the explosion of nationalism, racism and in places, religious bigotry" which no one in the nineteenth century had predicted. Beginning with WWI and the Depression, a series of crises had led to the rise of totalitarianism, crises that could neither be avoided nor explained by the old liberalisms— Berlin shared the consensus of the Colloque Lippmann (although he wasn't present). "The result" of these crises "was a loss of faith in existing political activities and ideals, and a desperate desire to live in a universe which, however

---

51. For Berlin's biography, see Ignatieff, *Isaiah Berlin*. For his Cold War context, see James Tully, "Two Concepts of Liberty in Context," and George Crowder, "In Defence of Berlin: A Reply to James Tully," in *Isaiah Berlin and the Politics of Freedom: "Two Concepts of Liberty" Fifty Years Later*. Reframing Berlin as a second- rather than first-generation anti-totalitarian liberal would only marginally affect the conclusions drawn here.

dull and flat, was at any rate secure against the repetition of such catastrophes." The demand for security led to "the progressive and conscious subordination of political to social and economic interests," and "a tacit acceptance of the proposition that the responsibilities of the state to its citizens must and will grow." A new liberalism was needed to confront a situation unimagined by the liberals of the nineteenth century or the fin de siècle.[52]

The moral of Berlin's story was that "unless the champions of [liberalism] find ways to diminish the insecurity that feed people's susceptibility to such appeals, all bets are off." Tellingly, Berlin thought the solution—providing people with security—was actually a dilemma, and "the dilemma is logically insoluble: we cannot sacrifice either freedom or the organisation needed for its defense, or a minimum standard of welfare. The way out must therefore lie in some logically untidy, flexible and even ambiguous compromise." Berlin did not prescribe the details of the "compromise," but he cited the American New Deal as "the most constructive compromise between individual liberty and security which our own time has witnessed." More generally, he opined that "the case for intervention by the State and other effective government agencies, to secure conditions for both positive, and at least a degree of negative liberty for individuals, is overwhelmingly strong."[53]

This would seem to make Berlin a liberal in the twentieth-century American sense of the word, more or less a modern liberal in the fin de siècle way. But he was hostile to the thought of T. H. Green, and "not deeply impressed" by L. T. Hobhouse. Berlin gave only a qualified endorsement to the welfare state: he was in favor of feeding the hungry and clothing the poor, providing people with the minimum conditions for the exercise of freedom, but hostile to bureaucratic experts proposing to turn society into a therapy center under their direction. This would be degrading and destructive of the human personality. By 1950 he no longer supported Britain's Labor government because he considered Labor a bunch of morally narrow-minded levelers. Berlin was always worried about a technocratic despotism run by experts, depriving people of freedom of choice—he was no Fabian socialist or technocratic American Progressive. At the same time he saw "the bloodstained story of

52. Berlin, "The Pursuit of the Ideal," in *The Crooked Timber of Humanity*, 1; "Political Ideas in the Twentieth Century," in *Liberty*, 61; "The Pursuit of the Ideal," 6, 76–78; 81; 77; "Political Ideas in the Twentieth Century," 79; 80.

53. Shapiro and Steinmetz, "Negative Liberty and the Cold War," 211; Berlin, cited in Crowder, *Isaiah Berlin*, 177.

economic individualism and unrestrained capitalist competition"; he remained, as he put it, on "the extreme right-wing of the Left movement," or perhaps more accurately, the extreme left wing of the Right movement. To situate Berlin's liberalism, and the important strand of third-wave liberalism he represents, comparison with Hayek is illuminating.[54]

The two were aware of one another and of the similarities in their thoughts, but they had no personal relationship, and moved in very different political circles, Berlin mostly on the moderate left, Hayek on the right, which doubtless contributed to their lack of contact. The similarities in their ideas go well beyond their common anti-totalitarianism. Like Hayek, Berlin rejected the application of the methods of the natural sciences to the social sciences (he even said that Hayek was better on this than Popper).[55] Their perspectives on historical causation ran in tandem, and both rejected any form of determinism. For Hayek, the market was a spontaneous order, not the product of a plan, and social and political progress generally proceeded likewise, spontaneously and unplanned. For Berlin, too, "when we examine the history of human happiness, toleration, peace, of all those ideals . . . we realise that they have not often come about as a benefit of the consciously thought-out, rational application of universal plans made by infinitely wise social engineers or technologists." Both rejected social engineering and feared bureaucratic despotism in the guise of rule by experts, "the reduction of all questions and aspirations to dislocations which the expert can set right," or rather erroneously thought so.[56]

Most important of all, the parallels with Hayek was Berlin's adoption of something that functioned in his work much like Hayek's "knowledge prob-

54. Berlin, cited in Crowder, *Isaiah Berlin*, 178; Berlin, cited in Aurelian Craiutu, "Isaiah Berlin on Marx and Marxism," in *Cambridge Companion*, 114.

55. He wrote apropos of Hayek's *The Counter-Revolution of Science*: "There is a curious book I am reading now by Hayek who is accounted a reactionary by everybody and indeed to some extent is and yet the strictures he has to pass on the indiscriminate application of scientific analogies beyond their proper sphere seem to me to be exaggerated but just." He confessed a secret sympathy for Hayek and Popper, whom he described as "reactionary liberals who have somehow put on sheep's clothing." Berlin to Burton Drebeen, January 22, 1953, *Enlightening Letters, 1946–1960*, ed. Henry Hardy and Jennifer Holmes (New York: Pimlico, 2011), 496.

56. Berlin to Herbert Elliston, editor of the *Washington Post*, Dec. 30, 1952, in Berlin, *Enlightening Letters, 1946–1960*, 488; Hayek, *Constitution of Liberty*, 69n29. Berlin, "Historical Inevitability," in *Liberty*, 101n2; Steven B. Smith, "Isaiah Berlin on the Enlightenment and Counter-Enlightenment," in *The Cambridge Companion*, 137; Berlin, "The Pursuit of the Ideal," 6; Berlin, "The Lessons of History," in *The Cambridge Companion*, 268; Hayek, *The Constitution of Liberty*, 261ff., 295–297, 304–305; "Political Ideas," 87–88.

lem." Berlin's equivalent of Hayek's knowledge problem was his theory of pluralism. For Berlin, there was no way to overcome the incompatibility of different human values. Justice and mercy, for example, would inevitably clash, and there was no single scale upon which they could be universally ranked without forcibly imposing personal views, and therefore one must renounce the possibility of a unique solution to moral dilemmas, although in specific cases of conflict people could make rational arguments for which value ought to count most. Berlin's great enemy was the person who claimed to know how to rank all values, whom he called the "monist." Analogously for Hayek there was no way to rationally impose an economic plan or dictate prices. Hayek's great enemy was the person who claimed to know how to rank all prices—the socialist. Berlin appealed to a "precarious equilibrium" among conflicting values as a solution, with decisions about conflicts made rationally on a case-by-case basis; Hayek relied on the spontaneous order of the market, aided and abetted by an appropriate constitutional legal order.[57]

A final similarity was their fear that no one, or at least very few, would prioritize freedom. Freedom, according to Berlin, was boring. The need to make a maximum effort to "preserve some kind of precarious equilibrium between varieties of goals and men. . . . This a very difficult and a very undramatic thing to do." Berlin described his liberalism as one "in which one is not over-excited by any solution claiming finality or any single answer." It was much more exciting to be a revolutionary, a Communist or a Fascist than a liberal. Liberal pluralism was "not the kind of thing that the idealistic young would wish, if need be, to fight and suffer for." But the problem was more than that liberalism was dull. "Men do not really all seek liberty—security, yes, but liberty? . . . all men seek security, only some seek liberty." Hayek agreed: many people would not want the responsibilities that came with freedom.[58]

The differences that remained display some of the major variations within third-wave liberalism. They differed with regard to the welfare state, although less than might be supposed at first glance. They also differed with regard to

57. Berlin, "The Pursuit of the Ideal,", section VI, passim; Hayek and Bernard Williams, "Pluralism and Liberalism: A Reply," *Political Studies* 41 (1994): 306–309. Hayek is also arguably a moral pluralist. His justification of a social safety net constructed independently of market forces is an example, as is his rejection of economic planning as undemocratic in *The Road to Serfdom*. I owe the *Serfdom* reference to George Crowder.

58. "The Lessons of History," *Cambridge Companion*, 209; "The Pursuit of the Ideal," 18–19; Berlin to Michael Walzer, cited in Shapiro and Steinmetz, "Negative Liberty and the Cold War," 219.

politics: for Berlin political theory was a branch of moral philosophy. Unlike the later Hayek, he devoted almost no attention to how government institutions and representation should be structured. In this respect, Berlin was more typical of anti-totalitarian liberalism. Perhaps most important, they differed with regard to nationalism. Hayek was a cosmopolitan, a citizen of the world who acknowledged no special loyalty to one community over another, only to freedom. He who gave at best grudging legitimacy to nationalism. Berlin was a liberal nationalist in the style of the short nineteenth century and condemned cosmopolitanism. A final important difference was that Berlin developed an innovative moral theory that was central to his liberalism, namely pluralism, a moral theory that would become widely adopted by later generations of anti-totalitarian liberals.

Three concepts are key to understanding Berlin's liberalism: the distinction between positive and negative freedom, which he popularized; his rehabilitation of nationalism for a post-fascist world; and his rejection of "monism," that is the establishment of any all-encompassing order of values, in favor of pluralism, the recognition that there were many human values and many valid ways of ordering them. All three were significant for the development of twentieth-century liberalism, many of whose leading figures either adopted them or responded to them. The negative / positive liberty distinction took center stage until around 1990, after which his pluralism became more central. His ideas appealed to all schools of liberal: not many contemporaries were quoted with approval by both Hayek and Rawls and their followers. Berlin's ideas were basic to the pluralism, the multiculturalism, and the revived liberal nationalism of the late twentieth century, even if he did not necessarily approve of the latter two.

The unique strengths and weakness that Berlin's ideas brought to liberalism start with his distinction between negative and positive freedom. It became a staple, if oft-disputed, point of departure for late twentieth-century political thought. For Berlin, fundamentally, freedom was freedom from coercion by others. He called this "negative freedom." But there was another, positive meaning of freedom, which was also very important even if not quite as fundamental. Berlin stated the difference between negative and positive freedom in different ways. Negative freedom was freedom *from* coercion, and positive freedom the freedom *to* do something, whether to vote or become an astrophysicist. But perhaps the simplest variation was one Berlin stated in question form: Negative and positive freedom responded to two different questions: "How much am I governed?" (negative freedom's question), and

"By whom am I governed?" (positive freedom's question). The questions, Berlin admitted, were not wholly distinct, but the differences mattered very much. As Berlin put it, the defenders of negative liberty "want to curb authority as such," while those who supported positive liberty "want it placed in their own hands."[59]

These "Two Concepts of Liberty," as the title of Berlin's essay put it, have been both enormously influential and highly controversial. As distinctions, they are most useful as tools to describe the political thought of the totalitarian era, especially the 1930s and '40s; by contrast they are often misleading when applied to earlier thought. During the Cold War, Berlin and many others put particular emphasis on negative freedom, and Berlin is often read as supporting negative liberty against positive liberty, much in the manner of Dicey or Hayek. Berlin later admitted that his essay could be understood this way, but maintained, with some justification, that this was not correct, and that he had always acknowledged the necessity for a degree of positive freedom.[60]

The issue would be academic but for the fact that a conception of positive freedom was, according to Berlin, a major contributor to fascism, communism, and many other forms of oppression. In the name of enabling human beings to attain their true purpose, their salvation in heaven or on earth, hell was born. As Berlin put it, the question, who is Master? was answered: your higher self was master over your lower self, or should be, and "the higher self duly became identified with institutions, churches, nations, races, states, classes, cultures, parties, and with vaguer entities, such as the general will, the common good, the enlightened forces." The result was "what had begun as a doctrine of freedom turned into a doctrine of authority and, at times, of oppression, and became the favored weapon of despotism."[61]

Berlin later pointed out that negative liberty "could equally" be used to justify oppression, and that "belief in negative freedom is compatible with,

59. Berlin, "My Intellectual Path," in Berlin, *The Power of Ideas*, 15; "Introduction," in *Liberty*, 35, "Two Concepts of Liberty," 212.

60. "Two Concepts of Liberty," in *Liberty*, 166–217; Crowder, *Isaiah Berlin*, 64; Shapiro and Steinmetz, "Negative Liberty and the Cold War," 209. While the negative / positive liberty distinction goes back at least to Hobbes, Berlin popularized it, and to some extent is responsible for its overly schematic application. An example of his overdrawing the distinction between the two, in contrast to his later qualifications, can be found in "Two Concepts of Liberty," where he states that "these are not two different interpretations of a single concept, but two profoundly divergent and irreconcilable attitudes to the ends of life." "Two Concepts of Liberty," 212.

61. "Introduction," in *Liberty*, 37.

and (so far as ideas influence conduct) has played its part in, generating great and lasting social evils," for example the "bloodstained story of economic individualism and unrestrained capitalism." Berlin condemned Cobden and Spencer, apostles of a purely negative idea of liberty, and cited on his own behalf Tocqueville, Mill, and Constant. Constant, "who prized negative liberty beyond any modern writer," nevertheless insisted that a dose of the ancients' positive political liberty was necessary to the preservation of negative freedom. Berlin also argued that for "any degree of significant 'negative' liberty [to] be exercised by individuals or groups," minimum conditions of material welfare needed to be provided—hence Berlin's endorsement of the welfare state.[62]

The reason Berlin emphasized negative versus positive freedom was the experience of totalitarianism. Although "each concept seems liable to perversion into the very vice it was created to resist. . . . whereas liberal ultra-individualism could scarcely be said to be a rising force at present, the rhetoric of 'positive' liberty . . . continues to play its historic role (in both capitalist and non-capitalist societies) as a cloak for despotism in the name of a wider freedom." The perversion of "positive freedom into its opposite—the apotheosis of authority . . . has for a long while been one of the most familiar and depressing phenomena of our time." Berlin nevertheless maintained that "positive liberty, conceived as the answer to the question 'By whom am I to be governed?', was a valid universal goal." Thus, for Berlin, while for the past 150 years positive freedom had been, in practical terms, a catastrophe, positive freedom and its component values were real human values, and potentially paths to human perfection, not just to perdition.[63]

This is not to say that Berlin saw negative and positive liberty in natural harmony. They were not two sides of the same coin. "Both are ends in themselves. These ends may clash [NB *may*, not must] irreconcilably." Democracy may clash with individual freedom, just as mercy may clash with justice. No increase in our "skill or knowledge" will eliminate these conflicts. The one unalterable point for Berlin, as a liberal, was that despotism was never acceptable, no matter how much negative liberty it might offer, not just because negative freedoms would always be insecure under a despot, "but because despotism is irrational and unjust and degrading as such: because it denies human rights

---

62. "Introduction," in *Liberty*, 38, and 35–43 more generally.
63. "Introduction," in *Liberty*, 35–43.

even if its subjects are not discontented; because participation in self-government is, like justice, a basic human requirement."[64]

In the end, Berlin found a common source for both positive and negative freedom: all those who have valued freedom have agreed that "to be free to choose, and not to be chosen for, is an inalienable ingredient in what makes human beings human . . . this underlies both the positive demand to have a voice in the laws" of one's society, and the demand to be accorded "a 'negative' area in which a man is not obliged to account for his activities to any man." Despite this common origin, positive and negative freedom are different things, sometimes incompatible, and some degree of both is needed to live our lives without fear. "The essence of the notion of liberty, both in the 'positive' and 'negative' senses, is the holding off of something or someone—of others who trespass on my field or assert their authority over me . . . intruders and despots." Freedom was essentially a defensive value, a weapon to wield against the fear of arbitrary authority in a totalitarian age.[65]

It is thus all the more striking to find in Berlin a consistent defender of one of the more dangerous forms of positive freedom on the modern world, nationalism, and an opponent of cosmopolitanism. First- and second-wave liberals did not necessarily prioritize humanity over their own nations, but nevertheless they mostly had good things to say about cosmopolitanism. Not Berlin: "I regard cosmopolitanism as empty, people can't develop unless they belong to a culture." In practice, for Berlin, modern culture meant nationality: "the desire to belong to a community or to some kind of unit . . . has been national for the last 400 years." It was "a basic human need or desire" that had been "gravely underestimated" by liberals.[66]

Berlin was also very much aware of the dark side of nationalism, which "in its inflamed condition . . . is a form of pathological extremism which can lead, and has led, to unimaginable horror." He thus emulated the liberal nationalists of the fin de siècle and distinguished a good, necessary, sane, or "non-pathological" nationalism that responded to a basic human need, from its evil (identical?) twin. So far this merely repeated the analysis of fin de siècle liberals. But Berlin added a new twist by analyzing *why* nationalism had taken a turn for the worse. If a nation or nationality felt "in some way insulted or

64. "Introduction," in *Liberty*, 42; 50.

65. "Introduction," in *Liberty*, 52.

66. Galston, "Liberalism, Nationalism, Pluralism," 251; Berlin, cited in Oz-Salzberger, "Isaiah Berlin on Nationalism, the Modern Jewish Condition, and Zionism," 180.

humiliated, or some kind of pressure is brought against it, then I think it be-comes inflamed, and this is what is called nationalism," the bad kind. His oft-cited essays "The Bent Twig: A Note on Nationalism," and "Nationalism: Past Neglect and Present Power," were based on this insight. Inflammation could result from defeat in war or because of disruptions caused by modern-ization. Regardless of the cause, it was at best dangerous, at worst catastrophic in its results.[67]

Nationalism could not be abolished because both its good and bad forms responded to a powerful and probably, in Berlin's view, permanent need of humanity (just as negative and positive conceptions of freedom did). Liberals had to learn to live with it. This was not merely putting up with the inevitable: the good kind of nationalism possessed real value. It helped people achieve a feeling of "belonging," of being "recognized," and of equality, a feeling so valu-able to them that they were willing to give up much for it (including, at the evil extreme, their freedom). But this satisfaction should not be bought at the cost of individual freedom. What Berlin's liberalism required was a right of "exit," the absence of compulsion to belong, combined with the positive freedom for people to choose to associate on a cultural or ethnic basis within the nation, otherwise nationalism would inflict fear rather than prevent it.[68]

Berlin's attitude sounds almost like twenty-first-century multiculturalism. But Berlin was willing to accept a limited level of repression of difference. "I believe that the common culture that all societies need [will] be disrupted by more than a moderate amount of self-assertion on the part of ethnic or other minorities conscious of a common identity." How much minority assertion was acceptable or desirable? The answer was unclear. Berlin was a resolute opponent of Jewish assimilation as embodied in his view by the German Jews of the fin de siècle. They were not self-assertive enough. On the other hand, the citation above is preceded by a negative reference to "Black studies, Puerto Rican studies, and the rest. I suppose this too is a bent-twig revolt of minorities which feel at a disadvantage in the context of American polyethnicity." Chari-

---

67. "My Intellectual Path," 13, and see Smith, "Isaiah Berlin on the Enlightenment and Counter-Enlightenment," 142, 145; Oz-Salzberger, "Isaiah Berlin on Nationalism, the Modern Jewish Condition, and Zionism," 177; Berlin, cited in Oz-Salzberger, "Isaiah Berlin on National-ism, the Modern Jewish Condition, and Zionism," 175, see also Crowder, *Isaiah Berlin*, 108–112.

68. Crowder, *Isaiah Berlin*, 111; Crowder, *Isaiah Berlin*, 112, Berlin "Two Concepts of Liberty," in *Liberty*, 203; Crowder, *Isaiah Berlin*, 40.

tably interpreted, as one commentator puts it, what Berlin meant was that minority cultures should not become aggressive in their turn and attack the culture of the majority. Berlin valued both individual choice—the right of exit from a culture—and national unity, which he, like his fin de siècle predecessors, thought an essential basis for liberalism, which would find it difficult to prevail in too conflictual a society.[69]

The issue, however, is not clear-cut. The reason it is not has to do with Berlin's greatest contribution to liberal thought, his theory of pluralism. Pluralism was at the heart of Berlin's anti-totalitarian liberalism, and was the common thread that ran through his works. But for reasons that probably derive from the end of ideology debates discussed in the following chapter, with a few exceptions Berlin's theory of pluralism took a back seat to the negative / positive liberty distinction until the 1990s. Since then pluralism has been widely debated.[70]

Berlin defined pluralism as "the conception that there are many different ends that men may seek and still be fully rational, fully men." Such ends were incommensurable, in the sense that there was no single, objective way to rank them in all situations. Since human ends were many and incommensurable, "then the possibility of conflict—and of tragedy—can never wholly be eliminated from human life, either personal or social." "Some among the Great Goods cannot live together. That is a conceptual truth. We are doomed to choose." From this perspective, liberalism meant permitting the greatest possible scope for the pursuit of different values, and accepting the conflict this implies, without allowing the conflict to degenerate into violence and oppression.[71]

By contrast, "the enemy of pluralism is monism—the ancient belief that there is a single harmony of truths into which everything . . . must fit." Formally, monism was the belief that "1) every moral question has a single correct answer; 2) that answer can be found; 3) all correct answers are compatible." Berlin saw monism as monstrously dangerous, productive of mass murder and torture—and yet he recognized that monism was the traditional belief of mankind: for millennia people had believed that there was one true answer to all

69. Oz-Salzberger, "Isaiah Berlin on Nationalism, the Modern Jewish Condition, and Zionism," 170ff.; Berlin, cited in Galston, "Liberalism, Nationalism, Pluralism," 253; Berlin, cited in Crowder, Isaiah Berlin, 184; Galston, "Liberalism, Nationalism, Pluralism," 260.

70. Crowder, Isaiah Berlin, 4; 65.

71. Berlin, "The Pursuit of the Ideal," 11; "Two Concepts of Liberty," 213; "The Pursuit of the Ideal," 14.

moral / religious / political questions; the spontaneous order was a monist order. Hence, one might add, why it took so long for liberalism to be invented, and why it still is so precarious. The main point of Berlin's argument was the claim that "pluralism *entailed* liberalism."[72]

From the beginning, Berlin's pluralism was accused of being a form of relativism. Berlin rejected the charge. For Berlin, a relativist was someone who believed that values were not only incommensurable, but unintelligible to one another, so that mutual understanding was impossible, and differences merely matters of taste: "I prefer coffee, you prefer champagne. We have different tastes, there is no more to be said." Berlin disavowed the relativist's view. For Berlin, because we are all human, we can understand all human values, even if we can't reconcile them. We can understand justice and mercy, freedom and equality, without subsuming one under the other. It was crucial that liberalism have a moral pillar, but Berlin argued that this had to be understood to mean a multitude of possible moral pillars, and with them a multiple of scales for the calculation of utility and the attainment of perfection. In practice, although a permanent order of rank could not be established among human values, in particular cases an order could be established: justice and loyalty could not be ranked in the abstract, but a trial judge could make a rational determination about which should take precedence in a given case (like Hayek, Berlin preferred common law cases to universal legislation).[73]

Berlin thus advocated a sort of "cautious empiricism, . . . I think that what I am pleading for is really what used to be called Liberalism, i.e. a society in which the largest number of persons are allowed to pursue the largest number of ends as freely as possible, in which these ends are criticised as little as possible and the fervour with which such ends are held is not required to be bolstered up by some bogus rational or supernatural argument to prove the universal validity of the end." It was crucial that the end not be considered universally valid, monism was too dangerous: "I do not believe in general

72. "My Intellectual Path," 14; Crowder, "Pluralism, Relativism, and Liberalism," in *The Cambridge Companion*, 233; "My Intellectual Path," 6; Berlin, "The Pursuit of the Ideal," 8; *The Power of Ideas*, 8–11; Cherniss, *A Mind and its Time*, 286. Berlin's history of pluralism was quite shaky. As Kloppenberg points out, "Dilthey, James, and Sidgwick believed that we must sacrifice some convictions to satisfy others. Moral action, they maintained, involves painful but inescapable choices between competing conceptions of the good." Kloppenberg, *Uncertain Victory*, 116. None played any role in Berlin's account.

73. Smith, "Isaiah Berlin on the Enlightenment and Counter-Enlightenment," 147; Berlin, cited in Smith, 147; Smith, 148; Ryan, citing Berlin and Williams, "Isaiah Berlin," 221–222.

principles myself, because they bear down too cruelly on actual human beings in actual situations too often." What was needed, he wrote, was "less Messianic ardour, more enlightened scepticism . . . more room for the attainment of their ends by individuals and by minorities whose tastes and beliefs find (whether rightly or wrongly must not matter) little response among the majority. What is required is a less mechanical, less fanatical application of general principles.." Mill would have agreed with the conclusion while lamenting the lack of ardor. Perhaps Mill would have been less inclined to admire "Messianic ardour" had he witnessed the Holocaust and the Gulag.[74]

Pluralism therefore implied liberalism. "If pluralism is a valid view . . . toleration and liberal consequences follow, as they do not either from monism (only one set of values is true, all the others are false) or from relativism (my values are mine, yours are yours, and if we clash, too bad)." Pluralism furthermore required a certain minimum degree of negative liberty, and was a "truer and more humane ideal than the goals of those who seek in the great disciplined, authoritarian structures the ideal of 'positive' self-mastery by classes, or peoples, or the whole of mankind."[75]

Unfortunately, pluralism was intrinsically less satisfying than monism. If values conflicted, and one could not have everything one might want, and still worse "if human creativity may depend upon a variety of mutually exclusive choices; then . . . , 'What is to be done'?" Berlin's answer was not very inspirational: "claims can be balanced, compromises can be reached . . . priorities, never final and absolute, must be established." Berlin's goal, as a properly fearful liberal, was "to avoid extremes of suffering." Revolutions were rarely worth the cost. "The best that can be done, as a general rule, is to maintain a precarious equilibrium that will prevent the occurrence of desperate situations, of intolerable choices—that is the first requirement for a decent society." Monism could not make the world safe, only pluralism could. That was why pluralism was a liberal solution to the problem of totalitarianism.[76] But who would be willing to die for a "precarious equilibrium"? Berlin's solution reminds one of the old

74. Berlin To Herbert Elliston, Dec. 30, 1952, in *Enlightening Letters, 1946–1960*, 488, see also 489; "Political Ideas in the Twentieth Century," 92.

75. "My Intellectual Path," 13; "Two Concepts of Liberty," 216.

76. John Gray, *Berlin*, argues that pluralism was actually a conservative solution. This view can be rejected, first because there was no particular value pluralism wished to conserve, and second because Berlin's pluralism remained utopian: for a writer who, like Berlin, lived almost his entire life in a WWII / Cold War World, the idea that pluralism might be put into practice was utopian indeed.

saying that "a liberal [at least a pluralist one] is someone who won't take his own side in an argument."[77]

Berlin preferred a society in which not only were many ends pursued, "but in which these ends are criticised as little as possible." This was to advocate not so much a vigorous diversity of opinion as a state of terrified exhaustion, people too frightened and tired to criticize other people's moral or religious views—but such a state, after all, was what brought about the first truces in the Wars of Religion. If there was a saving grace, it was that in fact the situation was not usually so dramatic. "There is a great deal of broad agreement among people in different societies over long stretches of time about what is right and wrong, good and evil," or in liberal terms, about what people feared. Thus liberalism stood a fighting chance against monism and totalitarianism. In the end, despite pluralism's recognition of individual and group differences, Berlin relied on people's common humanity—the common desire to be able to live a life without fear, and to be willing to fight for such a life—for liberalism's appeal and its ability to inspire.[78]

Coming after WWI and WWII this appeal was, from the perspective of anti-totalitarian liberalism, stronger than ever. But by his own conclusion, in pluralizing the moral pillar, Berlin weakened it, at least potentially. Pluralism did not support liberalism if people were indifferent to freedom, or distracted from freedom by other values—and Berlin himself thought they would be. "All men seek security, only some seek liberty. And even if Rousseau denounces the former as a disgraceful choice of slavery, still they are as they are. I cannot pretend that human beings as such (even if I do), put liberty as a primary value, with a special status. I think that simply as a fact that is not the case." Liberalism was only weakly attractive in a multipolar moral world, and that might not be enough for its survival. Berlin splintered the moral pillar in order to deprive fanaticism of monist moral justification, but in so doing also weakened the moral force of freedom.[79]

With pluralism, Berlin solved one problem and raised another. He solved the problem posed by the colloque Lippman, the problem of reconciling classical and modern liberalism in the face of the crises of the 1930s. Pluralism reconciled the two by acknowledging the validity of conflicting values,

77. "The Pursuit of the Ideal," 17–18; On Berlin's moderation, see Craiutu, *Faces of Moderation*.

78. Berlin to Herbert Elliston, Dec. 30, 1952, in *Enlightening Letters, 1946–1960*, 488; "The Pursuit of the Ideal," 19.

79. Berlin, cited in Shapiro and Steinmetz, "Negative Liberty and the Cold War," 209.

whether negative and positive liberty, nationalism, or the search for social justice, while according none of them absolute priority. It subjected all of them to the need for compromise in a liberal spirit designed to preserve freedom from fear for the individuals and groups making choices. Pluralism was a way of retaining a moral / religious basis for liberalism, while avoiding murderous monist impulses. At the same time, however, pluralism could lead to a hollowing out of the moral pillar. From the perspective of those still pursuing the classical liberal or modern liberal variants of second-wave liberalism, or the struggle against revolution and reaction of first-wave liberalism, all of which continued to find adherents after WWII, Berlin's pluralism was a weakness rather than a strength. Non-liberals like Leo Strauss shared this view, insisting that pluralism had to be a form of relativism. By splitting the moral pillar into so many separate values, the result was the weakening of all of them. But from the perspective of third-wave liberalism, Berlin's pluralism represented an effective strategy for opposing totalitarianism, reconciling classical and modern liberalism, and continuing to wage liberalism's simultaneous battle against revolution and reaction. By sharply distinguishing negative and positive freedom and by promoting pluralism, Berlin took the wind out of totalitarian sails while justifying a limited welfare state.

Alongside Hayek and Berlin, a third attempt to overcome the cleavages of fin de siècle liberalism in order to defeat totalitarianism is much less well-known outside of its native Germany: Ordoliberalism. Ordoliberalism built a bridge between classical and modern liberalism by stressing the responsibility of the state to maintain the "competitive order." More than either Hayek or Berlin, Ordoliberalism relied on the state to perform an active role in maintaining a liberal society. Highly influential in postwar German and European politics, Ordoliberalism was a relatively successful example of third-wave liberalism in practice. It was also an example, however, of the lack of attention to political institutions typical of third-wave liberalism, all the more flagrant in the Ordoliberal case because of its emphasis on the role of the state.

Ordoliberalism

Ordoliberalism played an instrumental role in the post–WWII German "economic miracle," and in setting the terms on which the European Economic Community (EEC, now the European Union, EU) was founded.[80]

---

80. This was true despite the fact that the Ordoliberals split about the merits of the EEC, with some seeing it as a barrier to global free trade. See Slobodian, *Globalists*, 182–183, 214.

Ordoliberalism, and the "Social Market Economy" with which it was closely associated, have been touchstones for early twenty-first-century German politicians: Chancellor Merkel proclaimed in 2016 that "Ordoliberal principles . . . have lost nothing in currency and importance." Ordoliberalism, however, should not be considered a purely German form of liberalism. The French Colloque Lippmann participant Louis Rougier, the Italian journalist Luigi Einaudi, and the American economists Frank Knight and Henry Simons all can be described as Ordoliberals. In 1947, two leading German Ordoliberals (Wilhelm Röpke and Alexander Rüstow), along with Hayek, helped found the Mt. Pèlerin Society, perhaps the leading liberal think tank of the second half of the twentieth century (see chapter 10), and at least until the early 1960s the Mt. Pélerin Society provided an international forum for Ordoliberal views. Nevertheless, although scholarly discussion of Ordoliberalism was found in America as early as 1955, Ordoliberalism has remained obscure outside its native Germany, even though Michel Foucault devoted several lectures to it at the College de France in 1978 (and suggested it was the occult inspiration for the Giscard d'Estaing / Raymond Barre government), and some scholars have tried to identify the far better-known neoliberalism as a form of Ordoliberalism.[81]

As a coherent movement Ordoliberalism flourished from roughly 1930 to 1960.[82] It originated during the Great Depression, partly as a response to the German hyper-inflation of the 1920s and the Nazis, and partly in response to the general crisis of Western liberalism. Its intellectual origins were both very German—the Ordoliberals were heavily influenced by Goethe, Schiller, and Kant, and by the debate within German economics between the Historical School and the Austrians—and broadly liberal—they were avid readers of

81. Dyson, *Conservative Liberalism, Ordo-Liberalism, and the State*, 11–13; Commun, *Les Or-doliberaux* (Paris, 2016, Kindle edition) loc 5779; Nicholls, *Freedom with Responsibility*, 336–37; Commun, *Les Ordoliberaux*, loc 5944ff.; Ebner, "The Intellectual Foundations of the Social Market Economy," 217; Goldschmidt and Wohlgemuth, "Social Market Economy"; Friedrich, "The Political Thought of Neo-Liberalism"; Angela Merkel, cited in Kluth, "Ordoliberalism and the Alleged Aberration of German Economics," https://www.handelsblatt.com/today/politics/handelsblatt-explains-ordoliberalism-andthe-alleged-aberration-of-german-economics/23580920.htm. Foucault, *The Birth of Biopolitics*, 194; Slobodian, *Globalists*. See Dyson, *Conservative Liberalism*, 265–348 on the wider influence of Ordoliberalism.

82. Dyson, *Conservative Liberalism*, 123ff., suggests a second and even third generation afterward, but the relationship of the later generations, especially the third generation, identified with Public Choice theory, to the earlier Ordoliberalism is sometimes tenuous.

Adam Smith, if with varying degrees of engagement / comprehension, as well as of Tocqueville and Ortega y Gasset. It is not always clear how to characterize their liberalism—their first American commentator compared them to the American Progressives, Hobhouse, and Mill, which was certainly incorrect.[83]

The Ordoliberal program can be divided into three parts: one based on the preservation of economic competition through government and legal intervention; a second emphasizing the necessity of a social safety net; and a third showing the need for a moral foundation for both economics and politics. It seems at first glance a repetition of the traditional three pillars of liberalism: politics, economics, and morals. But although politics was implicitly involved in the Ordoliberal program through law, in the 1930s the Ordoliberals largely despaired of democratic political institutions as effective guarantees of freedom, having witnessed first-hand the self-destruction of Weimar democracy. At its most extreme, this was exemplified by Walter Eucken (1891–1950), professor at the University of Freiburg and one of the leading Ordoliberals, writing that "The state must find the strength to free itself from the influence of the masses," although he later retreated from this view. By appealing to an "economic constitution" and government institutions independent of the elective process, the Ordoliberals sought to protect their program from the vagaries of elections. Their use of a political pillar for liberalism was limited to law and the economic constitution. How this form of non-democratic politics was to find political legitimacy was not a question they addressed.[84]

<hr>

83. Dyson, *Conservative Liberalism*, 128–208; Nicholls, *Freedom with Responsibility*, 13; Fèvre, "Le marché sans pouvoir, " 123; Friedrich, "The Political Thought of Neo-Liberalism," 509; Fèvre, "Le marché sans pouvoir," 145; Sally, "The Social Market and Liberal Order,", 464; Horn, "Difficult Relationship"; Friedrich, "The Political Thought of Neo-Liberalism," 512; Commun and Fèvre, *Walter Eucken*, 229. German as their context was, their work had a number of parallels with the so-called First or Old Chicago School of Economics. See Köhler and Kolev, "The Conjoint Quest for a Liberal Positive Program."

84. Eucken, cited in Dyson, *Conservative Liberalism*, 39. See also Eucken, "Structural Transformations of the State and the Crisis of Capitalism," in *The Birth of Austerity: German Ordoliberalism and Contemporary Neoliberalism*, ed. Thomas Biebricher and Frieder Vogelmann (London: Rowman & Littlefield, 2017), 63, 65, 69. Eucken's aristocratic liberalism ran deep—he even quoted Jacob Burckhardt. See Ptak, "Neoliberalism in Germany," 98–138, and Bonefeld, "Freedom and the Strong State," 633–656. For critical discussion, see Nientiedt and Köhler, "Liberalism and Democracy," and Dyson, *Conservative Liberalism*, 128–160.

A good place to begin to understand the Ordoliberal program is Eucken's 1948 text, "The Political Problem of Order." Eucken began by citing Kant as an exemplar of those for whom individual freedom and autonomy was the basis of a fully human existence, to be attained by liberating human beings from their intellectual immaturity and dependence. Progress in this direction, according to Eucken, once seemed natural, proved by the abolition of serfdom and legal distinctions of status. But then came the growth of an industrial proletariat, which rapidly became dependent on factory owners. The legal privileges of the past were replaced by "private powers" which threatened individual freedom today: factory owners, labor unions, and cartels.[85] Freedom of contract became the right to oppress others, and the concentration of power in private hands created dependence. Economic power groups, such as the coal industry or grain producers, made laws to suit themselves. According to Eucken, this was the source of the social problems of the nineteenth century. Liberalism therefore needed to build its economic pillar out of something other than laissez-faire.[86]

For the Ordoliberals, the basic problem of modernity was the growth of private sources of arbitrary economic power, which translated into arbitrary political power through the formation of political pressure groups, who captured the state and abused political power to suit themselves. This was not just bad for the economy, it led to the destruction of political competition and hence political freedom as well. As Röpke, along with Eucken, the leading Ordoliberal thinker of the period, stated at the Colloque Lippmann, "it is special interests that dissolve the State. It is this disintegration of the State by the same parties, out of their interests, which deserves our attention." Only by promoting competition could the arbitrary power of special interests be restricted. The Ordoliberals insisted that the state must serve as the guardian of the "competitive order," based on the market, the economic pillar which for the Ordoliberals was central to limiting private economic power and maintaining freedom. As the Ordoliberal German jurist Franz Böhm (1895–1977) put it: "Competition is by no means only an incentive mechanism but, first of all, an instrument for

85. Eucken however also saw a positive role for unions: "The role of unions is to compensate for the unequal market position of workers and employers. It is an important role." Cited in Fèvre, "Le marché sans pouvoir," 129.

86. Eucken, "The Political Problem of Order," in Commun and Fèvre, *Walter Eucken*, loc 1747ff.; Franz Böhm, Walter Eucken, and Hans Grossmann-Doerth, "The Ordo Manifesto of 1936," in Peacock and Willgerodt, eds., *Germany's Social Market Economy*, 17; Eucken, "The Political Problem of Order," loc 1761.

the deprivation of power, . . . the most magnificent and most ingenious instrument of power deprivation in history." If competition was maintained, the concentration of economic power would be limited and freedom preserved.[87]

The goal was to emancipate the individual from fear of the economic power of other individuals, groups, and the state. The twentieth-century totalitarian state concentrated economic power either in its own hands or in the hand of its favorites. Röpke, in a 1935 article on "Fascist Economics," noted how the Italian Fascists, the Nazis, and the New Deal were alike in encouraging the formation of cartels. Eucken resorted to the "Scylla and Charybdis" metaphor dear to nineteenth-century liberals, but no longer did Scylla and Charybdis represent revolution and reaction; now they represented economic power concentrated in either government or private hands. In the twentieth century, in the Ordoliberal view, concentrated economic power and the power of the state had combined, and this combination posed the "maximum danger" to freedom. The great question was whether it was "possible to preserve individual freedom in an industrialized economy."[88]

This problem was first of all economic, according to Eucken. No political or religious movement could help unless the economic problem was solved. Solving the economic problem was made harder by the fact that in the mid-twentieth century very few people understood how the economy worked, regardless of their social position and education, unlike in past eras when economic questions were within everyone's grasp. Contemporary misunderstandings of economics were partly due, in Eucken's view, to the influence of classical liberal laissez-faire thinkers whose ideas no longer applied. Competition might have been the natural order of things in Smith's time, but it no longer was. Hence a laissez-faire approach to the relationship between government and economics was no longer appropriate. Retaining it was a recipe for disaster.[89]

87. Röpke, *Colloque Lippmann*; Böhm et al., "Ordo Manifesto," 17; Böhm et al., "Ordo Manifesto," cited in Viktor J. Vanberg, "The Freiburg School: Walter Eucken and Ordoliberalism," Freiburg Discussion Paper, 2011, 12; Eucken, "Structural Transformations of the State and the Crisis of Capitalism," 59–60. These arguments were fundamentally democratic.

88. Eucken, "The Political Problem of Order," loc 1761; Fèvre, "Le marché sans pouvoir," 122; Sally, "The Social Market and Liberal Order," 463; Röpke, "Fascist Economics," 97; Eucken, cited in Commun and Fèvre, *Walter Eucken*, loc 989; Eucken, "The Political Problem of Order," loc 1791.

89. Commun and Fèvre, *Walter Eucken*, 1664ff.; Eucken, "The Political Problem of Order," loc 1817; 1846, 1853; Nicholls, *Freedom with Responsibility*, 46; Eucken, "The Political Problem of Order," loc 1866, 1874.

This problem led Eucken to appeal to government experts in almost Fabian fashion, except unlike the Fabian Socialists these experts would understand the benefits of competition and free markets: "Men of science," i.e., economists, "by virtue of their profession and position being independent of economic interests, are the only objective, independent advisers," otherwise "interested parties" would take over.[90] But Eucken, unlike the Fabians or Keynes, did not think that economists should advise how to "fine-tune" the economy. Rather, together with jurists they should help shape an "economic constitution" for the nation. This economic constitution would be the instrument for the preservation of competition, and through competition, individual and political freedom. A competitive order in politics could not be combined with the absence of a competitive order in the economic sphere. Although the Ordoliberals never made clear how they thought political competition should take place, they were clearly in favor of it, and did not want it captured by economic interests trying to establish or protect monopolies.[91]

The Ordoliberal competitive order was thus not natural or Providential, as in Smith, nor wholly spontaneous, as in Hayek. "The problem will not solve itself simply by our letting economic systems grow up spontaneously. The history of the last century has shown this plainly enough. The economic system has to be consciously shaped." Hence the importance of laws and lawyers and the close cooperation of law and economics. As Röpke put it, "it is now advisable, to make courts, more than in the past, organs of the economy and to entrust to their decision tasks that were previously entrusted to administrative authorities," i.e., the state. Conversely, bad laws could destroy the competitive order. The Ordoliberals emphasized what they thought was a disastrous 1897 decision of the German Supreme Court which upheld the right of private parties to form anti-competitive cartels as a turning point in German history.[92]

To maintain a competitive economic order, the natural urge of all entrepreneurs to become monopolists had to be restrained. Eucken developed Smith's

90. Eucken and Ordoliberalism in general had no tolerance for the Madisonian notion of contests between factions, "interested parties," leading to a good result.

91. Böhm et al., "Ordo Manifesto," 15.

92. Commun, *Les Ordolibéraux*, loc 1641, 1943, 316; Eucken cited in Vanberg, "The Freiburg School," 8; Böhm et al., "Ordo Manifesto," 24; for the early Hayek acknowledging a less than fully spontaneous development of markets, see his 1936 "Free Enterprise and Competitive Order," in *Individualism and Competitive Order* (Chicago, 1996). Röpke, cited in Foucault, *Biopolitics*, 176; Böhm et al., "Ordo Manifesto," 18. One will search standard histories of Germany in vain for any reference to this decision.

conviction that "people of the same trade seldom meet together, even for merriment and diversion, but the conversation ends in a conspiracy against the public, or in some contrivance to raise prices." For Eucken, "there is always and everywhere a deep, irresistible instinct to eliminate competition and acquire a monopoly position" among entrepreneurs. It was a mistake for laissez-faire economists to leave it to the spontaneous forces of individual competition to overcome this instinct, and to allow entrepreneurs to write the rules of the game, not realizing that they would write rules to favor monopoly. Individual economic initiative needed protection against both state and private power because both were likely to restrain competition. "All private power must be subject to a certain number of laws and duties, similar to those which prevail with regard to the public administration and above all against the two working hand in hand."[93]

The struggle against monopoly was the keystone of competitive order. The government had to repress cartels and monopolies through a government department created for the purpose. The department had to be independent of the elected political authorities, for example the Economics Ministry, because otherwise it would be captured by special interests: it should be regulated only by law, and possess considerable power. The Ordoliberals were fond of citing Constant's maxim that "the government outside its proper sphere should not have any power; within its sphere, it cannot have too much." The "economic constitution" needed to forbid private contracts, cartels, or non-competition agreements that limited economic freedom, in the same way as the political constitution limited the arbitrary power of government.[94]

Ordoliberalism thus gave the state a crucial economic role as the guardian of competition. But government intervention in the economy was limited to this. The government was not a social engineer, but a gardener whose job it was to uproot weeds. As Eucken wrote, "It is the task of the state to influence economic forms, but not to direct the economic process itself . . . State planning of forms, yes; state planning and management, no."

But "even if complete competition is realized, it contains weaknesses and flaws which require correction" by government action. A competitive economic

93. Smith, *Wealth of Nations*, 1 :130; Eucken, cited in Fèvre, "Le marché sans pouvoir," 127–28; Böhm, cited in Commun, *Les Ordolibéraux*, loc 1405.

94. Fèvre, "Le marché sans pouvoir," 139 ; Eucken, cited in Fèvre, "Le marché sans pouvoir," 141, see also Commun and Fèvre, *Walter Eucken*, loc 1289; Commun, *Les Ordolibéraux*, loc 1405; Commun and Fèvre, *Walter Eucken*, loc 751.

order would hinder the development of social problems, but it would not altogether prevent them. If social questions were not dealt with, neither competition nor freedom would long be able to survive. The second part of the Ordoliberal program therefore made the case that if freedom was to be preserved, the state had to address the problem of poverty. They feared poverty as much as any fin de siècle modern liberal, for both old and new reasons. According to Eucken, in the nineteenth century, while "the freedom of person and equality of status seemed secured in political and legal terms, industrial workers were not, economically and socially, effectively free," due to the economic insecurity in which they lived. He argued that without freedom there was no security, and without security there was no freedom, and that German history after WWI demonstrated this. Therefore, to prevent totalitarianism, social policy had to secure a minimum income for everyone, whether through a minimum wage or some other means, for example trade unions bargaining over wages to prevent employers forcing workers to accept abnormally low wages. It had to include health and safety and environmental regulation. It was not the state's job to ensure full employment, which could only be achieved at the cost of a planned economy, but neither could the state tolerate mass unemployment because "the social consequences forbid it, equally with the political." When Ordoliberals had real influence in Germany after WWII, they made building a social safety net a priority. As Chancellor Ludwig Erhard maintained, "he and his friend Röpke had reversed the adjective and the noun in 'liberal socialism' so that it became 'social liberalism.'" The safety net provided by social liberalism was integral to the Ordoliberal program.[95]

Along with legal / political and economic foundations, Ordoliberalism also recognized the necessity of a moral foundation for the competitive order. As Eucken wrote, "Liberalism declined because it lost its metaphysical and religious content." The Protestant spirituality of many of the Freiburg Ordoliberals was echoed here and elsewhere. Erhard took it up in the 1950s, in the midst of

95. Vanberg, *The Freiburg School*, 13; Eucken, "Five Lectures on Economics," 1951, cited in Myra Posluschny, *Walter Eucken und Alfred Müller-Armack*, 72; Eucken, cited in Fèvre, "Le marché sans pouvoir," 125; Posluschny, *Walter Eucken und Alfred Müller-Armack*, 187; Commun and Fèvre, *Walter Eucken*, loc 1217ff.; Eucken, cited in Fèvre, "Le marché sans pouvoir," 126; Nicholls, *Freedom with Responsibility*, 101; 102; 155, Sally, "The Social Market and Liberal Order,", 472–473; Nicholls, *Freedom with Responsibility*, 75.

the German economic miracle, condemning materialism and consumerism. There was a strong perfectionist element in Ordoliberalism, an emphasis on character development and discipline, often though not always attached to Protestantism. Röpke went the furthest in this direction, after 1960 adopting a moral conservatism that had little that was liberal about it.[96] But already in 1937 he wrote in a manner typical of Ordoliberals that "the capitalist impregnation of all sectors of life in our society is a curse which we must banish, and the free expansion of the economy must not lead to the perversion of genuine human values." He favored a decentralized economy as well as a decentralized politics on moral grounds. From Röpke's perspective, this moral foundation was not merely a decorative flourish on a competitive market economy. It was essential to the acceptance of a competitive order. "Economic liberty" could not "be expected to arouse enthusiasm" unless society would "become stable economically and socially" and "work and life recapture more sense and dignity." The competitive order needed to make moral sense to be accepted.[97]

The Ordoliberals presented a different form of anti-totalitarian liberalism, unique in its view of the role of the state, yet sharing many features with the other liberalisms of the period. Like them, it returned to the three-pillared liberalism of the nineteenth century; like them, it devoted relatively little attention to rethinking the political pillar of liberalism, although the notion of an "economic constitution" might be considered a partial exception to this. But above all they shared the common feeling of the first generation of anti-totalitarian liberals that a liberalism in crisis must disenthrall itself from the orthodoxies of first- and second-wave liberalism, which had failed to rise to the challenges of the post–WWI era.

The anti-totalitarian liberals of 1920–1945 who initiated the third wave of liberalism did so in near despair. After WWI the previously strong association between liberalism and theories of progress vanished: the liberals of the 1920s and '30s were anything but triumphalist. By contrast, after WWII Western liberals started from a position of relative confidence, stability, and influence

---

96. Witness his endorsement of South Africa's apartheid regime in 1964. See Röpke, "South Africa."

97. Dyson, *Conservative Liberalism*, 47ff.; Commun and Fèvre, *Walter Eucken*, loc 1402; Eucken, cited in Commun, *Les Ordolibéraux*, loc 1756n35; 1625; Röpke, cited in Nicholls, *Freedom with Responsibility*, 96; Commun, *Les Ordolibéraux*, loc 351; Röpke, cited in Nicholls, *Freedom with Responsibility*, 99.

which they continued to enjoy until the end of the twentieth century. Many distinctive traits of third-wave liberalism—a social safety net; rejection of economic planning; acceptance of the link between free markets and political freedom—achieved far more acceptance than the participants of the Colloque Lippman had dared hope. They permeated the leading political parties of the West. Despite the Iron Curtain and the threat of nuclear annihilation, the situation of the world after 1945 was far safer from a liberal perspective than it had been in 1938. For the second generation of anti-totalitarian liberals, from 1945 to 1968, fascism and communism no longer seemed like forces that might sweep liberalism aside as an antique. Indeed, to many post–WWII liberals, communism, the sole survivor, seemed the antique view, right down to the day the anachronistic Berlin Wall fell in 1989. From the 1950s, to the proclamation of the "Age of Aquarius" by the hippies of the 1960s, through the fall of the Wall and the "end of history" proclaimed in 1992, liberal optimism progressed from strength to near delirium.

It was natural that this optimistic second generation of anti-totalitarian liberals express their opposition to totalitarianism differently from their frightened and depressed elders. The "End of Ideology" movement prominent during 1945–68, while still concerned to reconcile modern and classical liberalism, insisted on a particularly thin sort of liberalism as the only way to ward off liberal fears, from religious fanaticism, to revolution / reaction, to poverty, to totalitarianism. All forms of ideological commitment were rejected in favor of sober rational policy adjustments. After 1968, however, events overtook this view. Ideology took its revenge on the liberal technocrats, and the third and last generation of anti-totalitarian liberals (1968–2000), whether egalitarians like John Rawls, libertarians like Robert Nozick, or neoliberals like Milton Friedman, had deep ideological commitments and nourished new utopian hopes. Judith Shklar and Bernard Williams reacted against this new utopianism by developing the "liberalism of fear."

One common feature shared by second- and third-generation anti-totalitarian liberals was the abandonment of the limited return to three-pillar liberalism seen in the first generation, replaced by an even stronger tendency to use one-pillar arguments than that of the fin de siècle. The second-generation End of Ideology liberals explicitly rejected moral / religious foundations for liberalism. In the third generation, Robert Nozick's libertarianism, based on contractarian rights, was almost entirely moral in character, but was equally narrow in a different sense—and indeed characterized by a narrow construction of morality itself, as was that of John Rawls, although very differently oriented. Milton Friedman, by contrast, had no use for a moral pillar in his liberalism, and relied solely on economics. The liberalism of fear advocated by Shklar and Williams took, particularly in the latter, some timid steps toward a return to three-pillared arguments for liberalism, but had limited influence in the period. The development of anti-totalitarian liberalism after 1945, and the way in which it weakened liberalism in what seemed at the time a moment of liberal triumph, is the subject of the next chapter.

10

Hollow Victories, 1945–2000

AFTER WWII, American liberalism exerted something close to hegemony over liberalism worldwide, at the same time as America became the world's leading economic and political power. But American hegemony did not extend to the meaning of the word liberal, which came to diverge on the two sides of the Atlantic, and this requires explanation. Generally speaking, from the late 1930s on, the word liberal came to mean modern liberalism in the United States, while in Europe it signified laissez-faire economics and classical liberalism. The different understandings attached to the word by Americans and Europeans were emblematic of the collapse of the attempt to reconcile modern and classical liberalism during the first generation of anti-totalitarian liberalism. This linguistic difference between the two continents has caused confusion which continues to this day.

One of the particularities of American liberalism before the 1930s was that "liberal," as a partisan political term, played only a small, if gradually increasing political role. American usage of "liberal / liberalism" was distinguished from its European analogs chiefly by its relative scarcity. But American usage changed in 1932 and the years immediately following, and not only because liberal became, for the first time, a common slogan in American partisan political debate.

In the election campaign of 1932 between the Republican Herbert Hoover and the Democrat Franklin D. Roosevelt, both men battled for the title of liberal, Hoover using the word in a classical liberal sense and Roosevelt in a modern liberal sense. Initially the waters were muddy. Hoover was known as "the Great Progressive," and many of the politicians who used the label "Progressive" in the 1920s were members of Hoover's Republican party.[1] Although

1. Rotunda, *The Politics of Language*, 15, 60; 58.

the term liberal had been creeping into American political discourse for decades, for most Americans the word only acquired political meaning during the New Deal.

Roosevelt had never described himself as a liberal before 1932, and even in the 1932 campaign more often referred to himself as a Progressive. Roosevelt adopted the liberal label for several reasons. For one, in 1932 "liberal" was not attached to any particular political party, or rather was attached to both. As a liberal, Roosevelt could appeal to Republicans and Progressives as well as to Democrats. Independently, many of Roosevelt's associates felt close to the modern liberal wing of the British Liberal party represented by Lloyd George and Keynes. Regardless of motivation, Roosevelt's choice to use the liberal label was made early in his presidential campaign: in his acceptance speech at the Democratic Convention he described his party as "the bearer of liberalism and of progress," a neat combination. By 1933 progressive was largely abandoned in favor of liberal. Liberal and liberalism became and remained standard terms in American politics.[2]

Three points distinguished American usage from European: First, liberalism in America was identified with modern liberalism. Americans learned to think that a liberal was someone who supported state intervention in the economy to combat poverty and provide opportunities for individuals to improve their lot, a supporter of the welfare state. In contrast, by 1936 most American classical liberals had stopped calling themselves liberals and begun to call themselves conservatives.[3]

Second, beginning around 1935 and culminating with the end of WWII, being a liberal in America meant supporting civil rights for Black people and rejecting racism. During the 1932 presidential campaign, civil rights were not part of FDR's agenda. When surveys were taken to discover if people were liberals or conservatives, racial questions were not included—the questions were all about economic issues and government centralization. Being a New Deal liberal in 1933 35 implied nothing about one's views of Jim Crow and segregation. In 1934, when *The New Republic* became dissatisfied with the pace of reform and published a program for a new party, civil rights and racial issues were not part of it. At the time there appeared nothing inconsistent with

---

2. Rotunda, *The Politics of Language*, 14; 22; 60–61; 62; 16.

3. Rotunda, *The Politics of Language*, 73. In continental Europe, during this period, liberals also moved to conservative parties (as had already begun in England during the fin de siècle), but continued to describe themselves as liberals.

Woodrow Wilson having been being both a Progressive / modern liberal and a racist because liberalism had not previously implied a position on civil rights for Black people.[4]

After 1935, the pro–civil rights elements of the New Deal coalition grew in importance, beginning with the Congress of Industrial Organizations (CIO), the more liberal labor organization founded in that year. Unlike the older American Federation of Labor (AFL), the CIO strongly supported civil rights as well as the New Deal. The CIO / civil rights wing of the Democratic Party became known as the "liberal wing," and by the end of WWII, support for civil rights had become as much a mark of American liberalism as support for the welfare state. The process was lengthy, but by 1950 "liberal" had inevitable connotations in American racial politics. The word thus acquired a double economic / racial meaning unique to the United States.[5]

Finally, though only episodically important, beginning in the late 1950s "liberal" in America took on the meaning of someone willing to compromise with the Soviet Union, and above all adopting a dovish position on the Vietnam War. Liberal opposition to the war was in some respects an internecine conflict: President Johnson, despite being the great liberal force for civil rights and the War on Poverty, was a leading Vietnam hawk. During his term (1964–68) American liberalism became associated with a dovish, pro-compromise position in international affairs generally. However, the fall of the Soviet Union greatly weakened the association of liberal with particular foreign policy views, barring a concern for human rights around the globe as a natural extension of American liberalism's domestic association with civil rights.

The meaning of liberalism in Europe followed a very different path. Even though a British liberal, William Beveridge, wrote the 1945 report that led to the massive expansion of the British welfare state, and despite the fact that in the 1950s the German Ordoliberals had developed a Social Market Economy which adopted many features of modern liberalism, in Europe the word liberalism became strongly associated with classical liberal views and a laissez-faire stance. Separately from the classical / modern distinction, in Europe "liberal" never acquired the foreign policy or civil rights connotations that were part of its meaning in the United States. To add to the confusion, in the late twentieth century the Americans Robert Nozick and Milton Friedman, exemplars respectively of libertarianism and neoliberalism, adopted or wanted to adopt the

4. Schickler, *Racial Realignment*, 42–43, 13, 27, 19; 35; 43.
5. Schickler, *Racial Realignment*, 14, 5.

European meaning (liberal as classical liberal), and Nozick was driven to use "libertarian" as a description of his position to attempt to avoid confusion. While the usage in this book remains consistent—liberalism as the search for a world where no one need be afraid—the different regional meanings of the word after WWII must be borne in mind. Despite transatlantic difference in word usage, however, post–WWII Western liberalisms followed common paths. Totalitarianism continued to be the leading liberal fear, but took on new forms alongside old ones.[6]

In the 1950s and '60s, the end of ideology movement dominated the second generation of anti-totalitarian liberals. It consummated the fusion of modern and classical liberalism to which the Colloque Lippman's participants had aspired. Untroubled by previously deep divisions within liberalism, even more significantly it was uncontested by illiberal ideologies. The disappearance of virtually all opposition to liberalism from the right, and the marginalization of left-wing illiberalism, allowed end of ideology liberals to celebrate the death of socialism and fascism and the arrival of a new world in which liberal progress would be a matter of reforms undisturbed by revolution. The historical context of the end of ideology movement was, in the view of its adherents, the final triumph of Western liberalism. No competitor remained standing in the West, or so it seemed.

A third generation of anti-totalitarian liberalism began when this mirage was dispelled by the events of 1968 and the following years. For the liberals of the last third of the twentieth century, totalitarianism remained the prime focus of their fears, but the chiseled moustaches of Hitler and Stalin were no longer in the foreground as in the 1930s, or even in the background as in the 1950s. In the 1970s and thereafter the totalitarian threat became more general: injustice / inequality for Rawls, the state as such for Nozick or Friedman. The third generation of anti-totalitarianism, circa 1968–2000, saw the revival of liberal ideology and liberal utopianism, and the abandonment of the grand project of reconciliation between classical and modern liberalism of the first two periods of anti-totalitarian liberalism. Modern liberalism was taken to an extreme in the egalitarian liberalism of John Rawls, who envisaged a world in which life was fair, thanks to government-enforced equality, and society was stable, thanks to support from an overlapping consensus of moral views. His utopia was built on a new liberal politics and a limited liberal morality.

---

6. How this happened in Europe is unclear. For a step toward such a history, see Jackson, "Currents of Neo-Liberalism," 823–850.

Libertarians like Robert Nozick and neoliberals like Milton Friedman, similar to classical liberals looking at modern liberalism in the fin de siècle, saw despotism where Rawls saw freedom; Nozick imagined a libertarian utopia with a minimal state in reaction to what he saw as the egalitarians' immoral and illiberal project. Where Nozick took a narrow moral position against egalitarian liberalism (other libertarians used other arguments in support of the same goal), neoliberals reacted against what they saw as egalitarian totalitarianism by making free markets the central or the sole pillar of liberalism.

But the third generation of anti-utopian liberalism was not simply a matter of dueling liberal utopias. The "liberalism of fear" espoused by Judith Shklar and Bernard Williams called for a much more modest liberalism, in contrast to the end of ideology movement and to egalitarian, libertarian, and neoliberal utopianism. The liberalism of fear happened when the end of ideology movement ceased to have any credibility as a statement of fact, and instead became a goal to be pursued, at least for some liberals. It limited its utopianism to the seemingly modest aim of limiting cruelty. For Shklar, liberalism had to be a purely political operation because high moral aspirations were too likely to have cruel consequences. Williams, by contrast, thought it was only realistic to admit that liberalism was based on and required moral arguments as well.

With the exception of Williams, all these late twentieth-century, third-generation liberals, whether egalitarian, libertarian, or neoliberal, shared with the end of ideology movement a tendency to rely on only one or two of the three pillars of liberal argument, which contributed greatly to hollowing out liberalism. As a result, none of the leading currents in liberalism were well-positioned to take on the challenge to liberalism that appeared in the early decades of the twenty-first century: the rise of populism.

The End of Ideology Movement

In the 1950s and early 1960s, the end of ideology movement saw itself as the triumphant consummation of liberalism, embodying the values enshrined by victory in WWII—very much the opposite of the situation liberals had faced after WWI. Yet in many ways the 1950s seemed a strange time for liberal triumphalism. Hitler and Mussolini were dead, but Stalin wasn't. The Soviet Union and the People's Republic of China held sway over a considerable portion of the planet, including most of Eastern and Central Europe. In Western Europe, significant communist parties existed in Italy and France, while fascism ruled Spain and Portugal. Nevertheless liberals, even European liberals, largely felt that they had passed through their time of trial and emerged into something that was, if not exactly the Promised Land without Fear—after all, there were nuclear warheads just minutes away from launch—was still politically, economically, and intellectually a far safer place for liberalism than the 1930s. Instead of Depression, coups d'état, and Blitzkrieg, there were free elections, full employment, and a manageable Cold War. In addition, the intellectual competition was bankrupt: Nazism and fascism were by-words for evil; socialism was no longer revolutionary, nor conservatism reactionary; and Marxism-Leninism's magnetic pull was growing weaker by the day. No one, including liberals, seemed interested in turning the world upside-down. The end of ideology liberals thought that in the brave new post-ideological world all that would be needed were some relatively minor technical adjustments, for example an increase in the minimum wage. Passionate commitment to utopian ideologies was seen as the real danger to liberalism. The best way to prevent totalitarian threats from returning was to banish all ideology and all utopian dreams in favor of technical solutions to practical problems.

It was a time when liberal political thinkers and actors alike, from Raymond Aron and Daniel Bell to President John F. Kennedy, proclaimed the end of ideology and its replacement by technical socioeconomic adjustments that did not inflame anyone's passions. Kennedy was known for soaring rhetoric, but this masked a very mundane and consensual vision. He made this clear in 1962: "The central domestic problems of our times. . . . do not relate to basic clashes of philosophy and ideology, but to ways and means of reaching common goals—to research for sophisticated solutions to complex and obstinate issues . . . What is at stake . . . is not some grand warfare of rival ideologies which will sweep the country with passion but the management of a modern economy . . . political labels and ideological approaches are irrelevant to the solutions."[7]

The end of ideology movement had pre–WWII roots. Perhaps the earliest statement of its theme came in 1929, when the Hungarian / German sociologist Karl Mannheim argued that Western culture was approaching "a situation in which the utopian element . . . has completely (in politics, at least) annihilated itself," a phenomenon embodied in "the gradual reduction of politics to economics . . . the conscious brushing aside of every 'cultural ideal,' " and the "disappearance of every form of utopianism from the political arena." Mannheim went on to suggest—still in 1929—that he lived in "a

7. John F. Kennedy, cited in Bell, "Afterword," *The End of Ideology*, 419.

world which is attaining one of the high points of its existence." He looked on the disenchantment of the political world and found it good. Alas, there was still a lot of magic left. Four years later, Mannheim would be a refugee from Nazi Germany.[8]

The notion that ideological struggle was a thing of the past took off in the 1950s with the rising economies of the West. There was general agreement among liberal end of ideology theorists in the 1950s about two points. First, they recognized the disappearance of ideological politics from what they called "modern industrial society." Political parties were arguing over details, not ideals. In a country like France, this was the first time in the history of liberalism that this had ever been the case. Even in relatively consensual America the situation represented a sharp break from the 1930s.[9]

Second, they thought the end of ideology was a good thing because the end of ideology meant the end of totalitarianism. Liberals thought they were well on the road to "the Good Society," as Lippmann had called it in 1937, and that ideology would only get in the way. A prominent American liberal sociologist, Seymour Martin Lipset, suggested that "the fundamental problems of the industrial revolution have been solved: the workers have achieved industrial and political citizenship; the conservatives have accepted the welfare state; and the democratic left has recognized that an increase in overall state power carries with it more dangers to freedom than solutions to economic problems." In this ideal world, liberalism could progress best without benefit of any grand theory of progress. As another writer put it: "Liberal civilization begins when the age of ideology is over."[10]

It is striking that in the 1950s liberals didn't even want to suggest that history was on their side because that would have been too ideological a claim.[11] But the cause is not hard to find: Nazis and Marxists had so often appealed to historical inevitability and other grand theories in the 1930s that liberals could not wait to see them disappear. Once the illiberals exited, taking their predic-

---

8. Mannheim, *Ideology and Utopia*, in Waxman, ed., *The End of Ideology Debate* (New York: Funk and Wagnalls, 1968), 19; 13.

9. Waxman, "Introduction," in Waxman, ed., *The End of Ideology Debate*, 3–5. Was the French debate over Algeria a detail? Apparently Aron thought so.

10. Lipset, "The End of Ideology?," 73; Feuer, "Beyond Ideology," in Waxman, ed., *The End of Ideology Debate*, 66.

11. This distinguished the end of ideology argument from the 1992 suggestion by Francis Fukuyama that history had ended in a liberal victory. See Fukuyama, *The End of History and the Last Man*. Daniel Bell made a similar distinction in the 2000 edition of *The End of Ideology*, xii.

tions of the future with them, the present belonged to the liberals, to tinker
with as they liked.

This view was almost universal at the 1955 Rome conference on "the future
of freedom," which played a similar role for the end of ideology movement as
that played by the 1938 Colloque Lippman for the first generation of anti-
totalitarian liberals. At the Rome conference, Edward Shils reported, "almost
every paper was in one way or another a critique of doctrinairism, of fanaticism, of ideological possession." Shils thought the conference had the atmosphere of a "post-victory ball." The feeling was that "there was no longer any
need to justify ourselves vis-à-vis the Communist critique of our society." The
intellectual and political appeal of fascism and communism had greatly diminished, despite the continuing military threat. There was broad optimism that
the integration of the working class, and *sotto voce* of Catholics and Jews, into
the liberal democratic consensus meant that no important cultural battles were
left. There was willful blindness to racism, no consciousness of feminism, and
very little attention paid to the world beyond the West.[12]

There was a pointed rejection of classical liberalism at the conference. Most
participants, Shils noted, were hostile to the thought that political freedom
depended on a free-market economy. Hayek spoke, but received an unfavor-
able reception. The need for government to intervene in the economy in a
moderate, Keynesian way was taken for granted. Nationalism was brought up
chiefly by the non-Western attendees, rather to the surprise of the Europeans
and Americans. It did not, apparently, arouse any apprehension. Asia and Africa seemed far away and of little importance. The American civil rights movement was completely ignored. The class struggle was over and there was no
other struggle of sufficient importance left to replace it.[13]

This moral vacuum was a great thing when the alternative, so lately demonstrated, was fanaticism. Nevertheless, Irving Kristol pointed out a real
element of moral weakness in end of ideology liberalism, one which many
liberals at the time were convinced was a strength: morality and religion
were identified with ideology and evacuated from liberalism. Most of the
liberals at the Rome conference no longer felt any need for "a comprehensive

12. Edward Shils, "The End of Ideology?," in Waxman, ed., *The End of Ideology Debate*,
54–55.

13. ; Lipset, "The End of Ideology?," 71; Shils, "The End of Ideology?," 57. A good example
of the blindness to racism as a serious problem was Raymond Aron, who saw American racism
as a problem sure of solution, albeit not immediate. See *Essai sur les libertés*, 112.

explicit system of beliefs" (one can see how John Rawls, then a young assistant professor, might have picked up the desirability of doing without such systems in political life). Shils himself expressed some desire for new beliefs, but only "without yielding to the temptation—which can never completely die out among intellectuals—to construct new ideologies, as rigid, as eager for consistency and for universal obedience as those which have now been transcended." There was a general faith that, as Lipset wrote in 1960, democracy naturally leads to liberalism. Forgotten were Tocqueville's fears and those of the other liberals of the short nineteenth century about democracy's illiberal potential.[14]

Ironically, however, for all the claims of end of ideology advocates that utopia was dead, the end of ideology movement was itself an example of utopia in grey, in which somehow an unplanned liberal victory (very much unplanned—no liberal intended the Great Depression or WWII) had resulted in the revolution to end all revolutions: a post–WWII world in which neither revolution nor reaction need be feared. Liberalism appeared to be the spontaneous order of Western society. From this perspective, the Cold War period was a liberal Paradise. Amid the global disorder of the early twenty-first century, this attitude no longer seems as foolish as it once did.

The Rome conference participants incarnated the consensus about the value of the end of ideology. The extended arguments of Raymond Aron from a French perspective, and Daniel A. Bell from an American viewpoint, provide insight into why so many liberals did not merely want ideology to go away but thought it dead. At the same time the writings of Aron and Bell, more perceptive than many of the other end of ideology theorists, hint at the renewed conflict between classical and modern liberalism that would burst out in the 1970s in the disagreements between the egalitarian liberalism of Rawls and the libertarian and neoliberal views of Nozick and Friedman.

As a young man, Raymond Aron (1905–1983) attended the Colloque Lippmann. Later, after fleeing to London with De Gaulle in WWII, he became a university professor and a prominent political journalist, writing for a number of prestigious French newspapers and magazines. Chronologically he could be classed with the first generation of anti-totalitarian liberals, and in 1981 he was still arguing that "in modern societies, what we must fear above all is the single-party system, the totalitarian system." But, while continuing

14. Shils, "The End of Ideology?," 60; Lipset, "The End of Ideology?," 69–70; Dennis H. Wrong, "Reflections on the End of Ideology," 118; 119, 121.

to fear totalitarianism, by the mid-1950s Aron no longer feared the pre–WWII ideologies associated with it—a situation very different from the atmosphere of the Colloque Lippmann. The final chapter of his 1955 *The Opium of the Intellectuals* was titled "The End of the Ideological Age?." The chapter left no doubt about the answer: the age of ideology was over. "Neither Marxism-Leninism, nor fascism, nor liberalism awake the faith which moves mountains any more." And a good thing too, for this faith, this ideology, had served to justify the mass murders of the twentieth century. Aron was delighted by the fact that "fanaticism is not for us," and thought that "indifference will not harm us" (Aron's Jewishness is probably relevant to understanding the "us"). The Western world had settled into a new conformism, "of which the end of ideology slogan is the expression."[15]

Aron concluded his *Essay on Freedoms* (1965) by rejecting both democratic and liberal dogma. Democratic dogma consisted in unlimited acceptance of the will of the majority—a view always rejected by liberals. Liberal dogma, for Aron, insisted on a set of absolute limits on the sphere of government activity. For Aron, all such limits depended on circumstances. He pointed out that whereas liberals had traditionally been suspicious of the action of a central government, in the United States it was essential for the central government to act to preserve the rights of Black people against oppressive local and state governments.[16] Whether the end of dogma / ideology meant that liberalism had triumphed depended, for Aron, on how one understood liberalism. If it was purely the "fear of arbitrary power," perhaps it had. But to the extent that liberalism also embodied a "Promethean ambition" of hope and transformation that now seemed to be missing, the question was less clear. In his distrust of Prometheus and rejection of ideology, Aron weakened liberalism's moral or spiritual pillar. As one critic put it, "If one really gives up trying to convert the 'pagans,' does not this entail reservations about the value as well as the possibility of converting them?" It was similar to the charge of relativism brought against Berlin, a complaint that liberals had lost their old faith in moral progress. Aron himself admitted it was "perhaps regrettable" that contemporary liberalism was exclusively anti-totalitarian and negative, unlike

15. Schnapper and Gardel, eds., *L'Abécédaire de Raymond Aron*, 17; Aron, *Essai*, 74; Aron, cited in Mahoney, *The Liberal Political Science of Raymond Aron*, 82; Aron, *Essai*, 62; 212; Aron, *Le spectateur engagé*, 204, 184; Aron, *L'Opium*, 323; 324; 334–335.

16. Aron, *Essai*, 76; *Essai*, 74; *Essai*, 209–210; Aron, "Democratic and Totalitarian States," in *The Dawn of Universal History*, 175.

previous liberalisms which had had their own philosophical doctrines, effectively regretting liberalism's loss of a moral mission.[17]

Aron did make occasional moves toward finding a moral basis for liberalism. He suggested that political and economic freedom were necessary to attain the highest spiritual values, and that intellectual and political freedoms offered, above all, a means of educating people, of developing their character, thus suggesting a traditional liberal perfectionism. He identified liberalism with Western civilization and summed it up as a "triple ideal": "bourgeois citizenship, technical efficiency, and the right of every individual to choose their own way to salvation": in other words, politics, economics, and morality / religion, the familiar three pillars of liberal argument. Aron warned that none of these three ideals should be sacrificed, "but let us not have the naiveté to believe that it will be easy to accomplish all three."[18]

All of this was a variation on the first-generation anti-totalitarian liberalism of the 1920s and '30s, modified by Aron's later historical situation as a Cold Warrior and participant in the end of ideology movement. But in an essay originally written in 1956, Aron foreshadowed the issue that would preoccupy Rawls and the egalitarian liberals of the late twentieth century: "the reconciliation of justice with growth requires a compromise between equality and the adjustment of retribution to merit." The final pages of the essay were a meditation on the idea of justice, an inevitably ideological question. But neither Aron nor Daniel Bell understood the continuing role of real or secular religions or moralities. They were part of a process that pushed liberalism's moral and perfectionist commitments to the side. Bell, however, unlike Aron or most of the other end of ideology theorists, understood the danger that this potentially posed.[19]

For Daniel Bell (1919–2011), as for many of the other second-generation anti-totalitarian liberals, the end of ideology meant the end of "the tendency to convert concrete issues into ideological problems, to color them with moral fervor and high emotional charge." This became clear in Bell's 1960 work, *The End of Ideology: On the Exhaustion of Political Ideas in the Fifties*. What interested Bell was the fact that "the basic political drift of the former Left intelligentsia in the US in the forties and fifties has been anti-ideological—that

---

17. Aron, *Essai*, 67; Aiken, "The Revolt Against Ideology," 240; Aron, *Liberté et egalité*, 48, see also 58.

18. Aron, *Le spectateur engagé*, 295–297; *Essai*, 215; 70.

19. Aron, *L'Opium*, 346. On Aron and religion, see Gordon, "In Search of Limits."

is sceptical . . . of socialism." Political millenarianism was no more, and ideology had come to a "dead end." *All* the "nineteenth-century ideologies," left and right, "are exhausted," they "have lost their 'truth' and their power to persuade." There was a post-ideological liberal consensus: "the acceptance of a Welfare State; the desirability of decentralized power; a system of mixed economy and political pluralism . . . the ideological age has ended." Africa and Asia had new ideologies, Bell admitted, but they had no appeal in the West and he devoted little attention to them.[20]

What distinguished Bell from most ideology theorists was that he saw this situation, for all its benefits, as one that presented its own danger: the lack of a strong moral commitment to liberalism presented a problem, especially for intellectuals. Western intellectuals were searching for a cause. They found the middle way of technocratic tinkering and social scientific expertise boring, and intellectuals hate to be bored. Aron, too, thought the revolutionary fly in the ointment was the intelligentsia: revolution was the opium of the intellectuals. For Aron, "intellectuals want neither to interpret nor to change the world, they want to denounce it."[21] For Bell, intellectuals needed the emotional jolt only an ideology could provide. Bell, like Isaiah Berlin, reminded intellectuals of Herzen's warning against sacrificing the present generation to a revolution for the sake of the Utopian future, and preferred a safe, boring politics and economics.[22]

Bell, however, believed that "the end of ideology is not—should not be— the end of utopia as well. . . . There is now, more than ever, some need for Utopia, in the sense that men need—as they have always needed—some vision of their potential, some manner of fusing passion with intelligence." However, Bell made no move to provide such a Utopia. He lamented the absence of a moral / religious pillar in the dominant version of anti-totalitarian liberalism, but had no vision of how to replace it. Arthur Schlesinger, another prominent second-generation anti-totalitarian American liberal, wrote in 1956 that liberals had to move beyond a "quantitative liberalism" aimed at poverty, to a "qualitative liberalism," oriented toward civic virtues and cultural investment. The largely empty moral space of anti-totalitarian liberalism needed filling, but

20. Bell, *The End of Ideology*, 310; 280–281; 402–403.

21. For an analysis of the reasons for this, see Kahan, *Mind vs. Money: The War Between Intellectuals and Capitalism*, on the pseudo-clerical habits of the intellectual class.

22. Aron, *Le spectateur engagé*, 180; Bell, "Afterword," *The End of Ideology*, 402, 404–405; 407.

even when end of ideology theorists glimpsed the need, their attempts to fill it ranged from feeble to non-existent.[23]

The end of ideology movement was terminated by the massive outburst of political, economic, and moral / religious ideology that went under the name of the counterculture and was encapsulated by the year 1968, followed by the blow to Western economies caused by the oil shock of 1973. Ideology returned with a vengeance, in a fashion highly uncongenial to Aron, Bell, and Schlesinger. What was the hippy movement, with its message of universal love and rejection of social inhibitions, but an ideological demand for the realization of a liberal utopia in which fear had no place? What could be more anti-totalitarian than Woodstock? This was dimly recognized by conservatives' use of "liberalism" to describe the hippies, much to the horror of most liberals.[24] The counterculture was in part a reaction to the hollowing out of the moral pillar in anti-totalitarian liberalism between WWI and the 1960s. The contemporary American Civil Rights movement also shoved the moral imperative to confront racism under the noses of complacent liberals. Liberal triumphalism did not survive these events.

The return of ideology meant the return of ideological conflict. From the end of WWI through the early 1960s, the first two generations of anti-totalitarian liberals, Lippman, Hayek, Berlin, the Ordoliberals, and end of ideology theorists such as Aron and Bell, had attempted to bridge the fin de siècle divide between classical and modern liberalism. They had adopted an attitude of moderation, preferred pluralism, and rejected ideological purity. By contrast, late twentieth-century liberals revived conflicts that had been set aside. One was ideology itself: they abandoned the idea that liberalism could do without utopia. Liberal political philosophy was once more a lively subject of controversy, and conflicts over competing visions of a liberal utopia flourished. The compromise between modern and classical liberalism to which the anti-totalitarian liberals of the 1930s aspired, and which by the 1950s seemed a fait accompli, collapsed. In the third generation of anti-totalitarian liberalism, egalitarian liberals on the one hand, and libertarians and neoliberals on the other, resumed the fin de siècle struggle between modern and classical liberalism, but in more radical form. Despite their differences, however, the egalitar-

23. Bell, *The End of Ideology*, 400–402; "Afterword," 441; Matusow, *The Unraveling of America*, 8–10.

24. The application of the term liberal to the hippies accorded with its earlier sense of unorthodox and broad-minded.

ian, libertarian, and neoliberal movements shared the tendency to limit their liberalism to only one of liberalism's three traditional pillars.

The egalitarian utopia of the Harvard professor John Rawls (1921–2002) deserves pride of place in any discussion of liberal utopianism. It is Rawls, after all, who is generally credited with single-handedly reviving Western political philosophy. He incarnated a new egalitarian liberalism that went well beyond the struggle against poverty of the fin de siècle, and utterly rejected the complacency of the end of ideology movement.

Egalitarian Liberalism: Rawls

Rawls has been called the most important political philosopher since John Stuart Mill, and testimonies to his influence are not hard to find. One from 1974 by his friend and libertarian critic Robert Nozick is illustrative: "political philosophers now must either work within Rawls' theory, or explain why not." Before Rawls, political philosophy was a moribund field, much like physics just before Einstein arrived. Rawls's egalitarian theory of justice initiated the third generation of anti-totalitarian liberalism with a bang. His identification of justice with fairness became and remains through the early twenty-first century the leading view in Western academia. Rawls's argument that the only justification for any inequality is if it will make the least well-off better off than they otherwise would be has become the background assumption for policies as varied as requiring access for people with disabilities to national monuments to progressive income taxes. In 2016, a political opponent decried his "formidable" influence on American political life and "astounding" influence on the American mind. Rawls's work is central to any discussion of liberalism after 1970, even though it arguably exerted less influence on policy than neo-liberalism or even libertarianism.[25]

Rawls's dominant role began with the 1971 publication of *A Theory of Justice* (henceforth *TJ*), a 560-page tome that rapidly acquired a level of commentary equaled only by the Bible or Kant.[26] Rawls, however, did not rest on his laurels. In 1991 he published *Political Liberalism* (henceforth *PL*), and in 2001 both *Justice as Fairness: A Restatement*, and *The Law of Peoples*, a book

---

25. Dreben, "On Rawls and Political Liberalism," 316: Nozick cited in Forrester, *In the Shadow of Justice*, xv; Forrester, *In the Shadow of Justice*, xvi; Foss, "The Hidden Influence of John Rawls on the American Mind."

26. More than 5,000 commentaries in article and book form. Fawcett, *Liberalism*, 339.

applying liberalism to international relations. *PL* and the *Restatement* considerably revised his earlier views, and are the main basis for the discussion that follows.[27]

For Rawls, society was structured unfairly, giving many people reason to fear injustice, and the rest no alternative but to profit from it. He broadened modern liberals' fear of poverty into a quest for equality, to be achieved by redistributing wealth and opportunities so as to make them fair. As Rawls himself put it, his was "an egalitarian form of liberalism."[28] His second fear was of political and social instability. There was a danger that a liberal society, even when based on justice, would nevertheless be illegitimate in many eyes and therefore unstable, ending in revolution or reaction. The threat of instability could come from several sources, but above all from those who held illiberal "comprehensive world views." These people were totalitarians, whether from secular or religious motives, and they wished to impose their totalitarianism on society. Rawls did not use the word "totalitarianism" himself, partly because it was out of fashion by the end of the twentieth century, partly because its use had become associated in America with conservative figures. Nevertheless, an illiberal comprehensive doctrine that orders state and society to suit itself can only be described as totalitarian. To combat the danger of such totalitarian doctrines, Rawls called for "political liberalism," which relied on a moral appeal, but one strictly limited in scope.

Rawls started out from the essential dignity and inviolability of the individual, and what the individual might have to fear was thus central to his project.[29] For Rawls the ultimate source of fear for individuals was inequality, and throughout his work "inequalities are our primary concern." This went well

27. This is controversial. Whereas for his colleague Burton Dreben, *PL* was even more important than *TJ*, largely because its subject was different (legitimacy rather than justice), for Katrina Forrester it did not represent a significant change of position. Rawls himself thought *PL* corrected and replaced part three of *TJ*, but he did not, as Dreben noted, emphasize the extent to which *PL* was addressed to a different question, or from the perspective of this book responded to a different fear. Dreben, "On Rawls and Political Liberalism," 316–317, Forrester, *In the Shadow of Justice*, 259, 271, Rawls, *Political Liberalism*, expanded edition, xv–xvi.

28. *PL*, 6, describing his "two principles of justice."

29. This is why Rawls rejected utilitarianism, which he identified with the idea "that the loss of freedom for some is made right by a greater good shared by others," *TJ* 3, See also *Restatement*, 96, 107–20. Our equal dignity meant no one should be afraid, even if it was for the greater good. Equal human dignity was also why Rawls argued that "the Right is Prior to the Good" (no one can be forced to be made a means for someone else's good), later qualified by the argument in *PL* that for the sake of stability, the Right, as embodied in justice, needed to accord with the views of the Good held by a substantial majority of citizens. See below.

beyond the provision of the minimum necessary for a decent life endorsed by modern liberals since the fin de siècle. Egalitarian liberalism made a broad vision of equality central to an extent no previous liberalism had done. It was at the heart of what Rawls called "justice as fairness."[30]

For Rawls any socioeconomic difference between people, any deviation from equality, required justification to be considered fair. The "Difference Principle" was central to determining what was a fair degree of equality. All social and economic inequalities had to "be to the greatest benefit of the least advantaged members of society." It had to be for the benefit of the poorest that the boss was paid one hundred times what they were, otherwise the boss's salary was unjust. There had to be a "decent" distribution of wealth because otherwise the wealthy would dominate political life, which would be unjust— Rawls's moral argument sometimes has political consequences, although political institutions themselves are of little interest to Rawls.[31]

Although Rawls thought fair competition would help, maintaining fairness would require regulation of "the inequalities in life prospects between citizens that arise from social starting positions, natural advantages, and historical contingencies." And not just the most glaring of these, such as racism or sexism: even smaller inequalities in people's starting points would over time "have significant cumulative consequences." Therefore, "adjustments" by the government would always be necessary. Ensuring a just distribution of wealth by continuously redistributing it was central to Rawls's egalitarianism. Examples of such redistributive adjustments included inheritance taxes, progressive income taxes, action in favor of women and ethnic minorities, etc. Unemployment eroded individuals' sense of self-worth, and therefore had to be eliminated, with society acting "as employer of last resort through general or local government, or other social and economic policies." Laws and institutions needed to be constantly active to preserve the level of equality necessary for a fair and just society. Society had to be egalitarian because this was necessary for individual dignity and self-respect, and thus it was worth paying a high price, first to attain fairness and thereafter to prevent equality from eroding. Justice as fairness was Rawls's way of achieving an egalitarian society in which no one need be afraid, and it required the subordination of both politics and economics to a moral imperative.[32]

30. *Restatement*, 41.

31. *PL*, 5–6, *Restatement*, 42–43.

32. *PL*, lvii; *PL*, 271; 284, see also *Restatement*, 53. *PL*, 267; 298, 338; 365; 6; 456, *Restatement*, 73; *PL*, 166; *Restatement*, 44.

Rawls was confident in human ability to regulate large parts of economic life—Hayek's knowledge problem found no echo in Rawls. Rawls was familiar with the objections of Hayek and other defenders of laissez-faire who criticized "the ineffectiveness of the so-called welfare state and its tendencies toward waste and corruption." But Rawls assumed these objections could be overcome: "here we focus largely . . . on right and justice, leaving the other [questions] aside." As Hobhouse put it, and Rawls doubtless would have agreed, "a right is a right none the less though the means of securing it be imperfectly known." He evinced little concern for whether his morality could actually be put into economic practice. And if it turned out that it could not be, so much the worse for humanity: "If a reasonably just society that subordinates power to its aims is not possible and people are largely amoral [. . .] one might ask with Kant whether it is worthwhile for human beings to live on the earth?" This, like the "Veil of Ignorance" discussed below, demonstrates Rawls's lack of respect for history, since judged by this standard, human history up to the present has not been worthwhile, or else worthwhile only as prologue to a utopian future.[33]

Equality was Rawls's benchmark. However, the difference principle justified inequality if it would help everyone, including the worst off, be better off than if everyone was equal. This would often be the case. Many "social and economic inequalities [are] necessary, or else highly effective, in running an industrial economy in a modern state. Such inequalities . . . cover the costs of training and educating, act as incentives, and the like." Too much redistribution of wealth was counterproductive. Thus, although Rawls wanted to regulate the market and greatly diminish the economic inequalities it produced, he did not wish to abolish it or private property. On the contrary, the right to own personal property was a "basic right." It was necessary "to allow a sufficient material basis for personal independence and a sense of self-respect." Personal property included the right to own one's house and the land it was on. It did not include ownership of "natural resources and means of production generally," because in Rawls's view this would lead to too much inequality, both between individuals and across generations. It was an open question for Rawls whether these should be owned by individuals, cooperatives, or the state.[34]

---

33. *Restatement*, 77–78; 44; 47; *Restatement*, 137; For Hobhouse, see chapter 7; Rawls, *PL*, lx.

34. *Restatement*, 132; *PL*, 282; *TJ*, revised edition, 142, cited in John Meadowcroft, "Nozick's Critique of Rawls," 173; x; *Restatement*, 114; 114n36.

This kind of egalitarian society, and only this kind of egalitarian society, was just / fair because it was what any rational person would choose if they were put behind a "veil of ignorance," knowing nothing of their future social position, religion, status, etc., and asked to create a new society.[35] Having eliminated from the deliberations any actual history or culture, Rawls returned to the idea of a social contract made by those behind the veil, a view largely absent from political thought for generations. This contract would, naturally, establish a just / fair society.[36]

Rawls thus revived liberal utopianism and created an egalitarian liberal utopia. But because he was a liberal, and therefore ultimately relied on civil society, not the state, to maintain and preserve justice, he was faced with the problem of how civil society could be persuaded to do so. Otherwise a liberal society would be unstable and fall victim to revolution or reaction. Hence the concern of the later Rawls with the problem of stability, and his solution: political liberalism. Rawls's discussion of stability has received relatively little commentary, but it is arguably the more important and original, and perhaps the more liberal part of his work. It was less influential because at the time he wrote the problem of stability was less interesting than the question of equality. It was only in the twenty-first century that it became salient, rivaling equality in importance.[37]

In his early work Rawls argued that stability would be attained because every reasonable person in a liberal society would adopt a comprehensive philosophical doctrine that would lead them to support justice as fairness and thus egalitarian liberalism. A comprehensive doctrine was a set of beliefs, including "conceptions of what is of value in human life, and ideals of personal character," potentially including "all recognized values and virtues." Rawls later recognized that unanimous or near-unanimous agreement about a single comprehensive doctrine was impossible. Even in modern Western societies, there always would be "a pluralism of incompatible yet reasonable comprehensive

35. The veil of ignorance acts like Smith's impartial spectator, with the important difference that Smith's spectator's attitudes are determined by social and historical circumstances (see chapter 2). Rawls's choosers know "the general circumstances of society," but their attitudes are not influenced by any particular worldview.

36. *Restatement*, 87; *PL*, 22–28. Discussion of the veil of ignorance has led to a large literature, which will be left aside here.

37. *PL*, 35; *Restatement*, 177. On the lack of commentary, see Nussbaum, "Perfectionist Liberalism and Political Liberalism," 6.

doctrines." The later Rawls thus accepted Isaiah Berlin's pluralism of incompat-ible values, and cited Berlin on several occasions.[38]

The fact of pluralism presented major obstacles to building a stable lib-eral society.[39] For example, how could those who held an illiberal religious doctrine support "a just democratic regime"? If they didn't, it might have serious consequences for stability. Rawls opened and closed *Political Lib-eralism* with this question, and "political liberalism" was the answer. Adopt-ing political liberalism meant giving up the idea that there was a single moral basis for liberalism. Liberalism had to "stay on the surface, philo-sophically speaking," limiting its purview to only those moral questions essential to getting support for justice as fairness.[40] If its scope was limited to this, it would find support from an "overlapping consensus" of majority opinion.[41] Political liberalism meant getting groups that had different moral views to agree that justice as fairness, and the egalitarian society it required, deserved their support.

Political liberalism was in a sense the traditional liberal solution of limiting the sphere of government: in order to maintain stability, governments would have to refrain from meddling with illiberal worldviews and those who held them. But in another respect, political liberalism addressed a different ques-tion. It was not a matter of limiting government in order to increase the sphere of individual or group freedom. Rather it was a matter of limiting govern-ment's moral claims so that individuals and groups holding incompatible moral views would nevertheless all have positive moral reasons to support liberalism. A democratic regime had to be supported by "*at least* a substantial majority of its politically active citizens" (emphasis added). For liberalism to survive, people had to love it.[42]

---

38. Freedman, "Introduction," in *Cambridge Companion*, 21, Dreben, "On Rawls and Political Liberalism," 316–317; *PL*, xvi; 13; Voice, "Comprehensive Doctrine," 126, *PL*, xvi; As Bernard Williams noted, "this [change in] emphasis does not only limit the ambitions of the original theory, it also rewrites its basis." Williams, *In the Beginning*, 30.

39. Jan-Werner Müller's remark is apt: "For nineteenth-century European liberals the decline of diversity and pluralism was a problem . . . for late-twentieth-century liberals pluralism was the problem." Müller, "Rawls, Historian," 331–332.

40. *PL*, 395.

41. Liberals, even Rawls, always limit the scope of power to some degree.

42. *PL*, xxxvii, 490; *PL*, 36, repeated verbatim in *Restatement*, 34, *PL*, 38; *PL*, 36, *Restatement*, 37; *PL*, 38. For Rawls, supporting liberalism for merely pragmatic reasons, e.g., you can't be sure of beating your enemies, so you should tolerate them, a *modus vivendi* view, is not enough.

Rawls wavered between optimism and pessimism about his chances of establishing political liberalism. On the one hand, "historical experience suggests that it rarely is" possible, but he also supposed "that one task of political philosophy . . . is to focus on deeply disputed questions and to see whether, despite appearances, some underlying basis of philosophical and moral agreement can be uncovered. Or if such a basis of agreement cannot be found, perhaps the divergence of . . . opinion at the root of divisive political differences can at least be narrowed." It is not surprising that an aged Isaiah Berlin objected to this, questioning Rawls's "optimism in the possibility of offering your views . . . as a permanent basis within which disagreements can be resolved," since such would effectively negate Berlin's own pluralism. Overall, Rawls's goal was "to formulate a liberal political conception that . . . nonliberal doctrines might be able to endorse." This was, in hindsight, a startling anticipation of the problems populism and religious fundamentalisms would pose for twenty-first-century liberalism. For Rawls, liberal democracies, in order to be stable, required cultural support they would not get unless liberal democracy was seen as being morally virtuous (not just momentarily useful) by nonliberal people.[43]

Political liberalism had to accomplish three tasks in order to achieve stability: The first, most important task, was winning over the adherents of reasonable secular and religious comprehensive doctrines, while resisting the unreasonable / illiberal ones, a problem Rawls addressed at length. The second task was overcoming the hostility to egalitarianism of those well-endowed with money or brains, thus avoiding reaction. Rawls said very little about this problem, and what he did say was not very convincing. The third task, about which he said a little more, was the problem of winning over the least advantaged, the poorly endowed. A mere minimum income would never, in Rawls's view, make the poor love their society. Only through the recognition of each individual's inherent equal dignity, embodied in justice as fairness, would the least advantaged feel the necessary positive attachment to society, and thus revolution from below would be avoided. In trying to give both rich and poor reason to support liberal democracy, Rawls participated in the liberal project of a society in which no one, neither rich nor poor, need be afraid. He also in a sense recapitulated the problematic of Liberalism 1.0,

43. *PL*,134; *PL*, 4; *PL*, xlv, xxxvii–xxxviii; *Restatement*, 1–2; Berlin, cited in Teresa M. Bejan, "Rawls's Teaching," 1077–1078; *PL*, 147; 420.

avoiding both revolution and reaction, but in an egalitarian context altogether foreign to nineteenth-century liberalism.[44]

Rawls focused mostly on the chief task facing political liberalism, achieving support from those who held nonliberal, or even merely different comprehensive doctrines: His solution was that political liberalism should not offer its own comprehensive moral doctrine, even though it did promote certain moral virtues. Political liberalism, e.g., politically liberal governments, should not endorse any view of the overall purpose or good or perfection of human life, not that of Aristotle, nor Kant, nor Mill, nor St. Augustine, nor Buddha. Political liberalism "has no final ends and aims." Rawls saw his own view as being able to "define an ideal of the person without invoking a prior standard of human excellence" and that the principle of perfection ultimately failed the test of the original position, providing an "insecure foundation for the equal liberties." More broadly, Rawls defined his problem as stability in a world of plural goods, which is "a problem for political justice, not a problem about the highest good." However, political liberalism did promote the moral virtues of civility, tolerance, and fairness because they were necessary for its own survival. Political liberalism had to have a moral pillar, but it had to be one that renounced any comprehensive view (unlike his earlier position, which insisted that every rational person would adopt a similar comprehensive view).[45]

This very narrow moral pillar, devoid of perfectionism for fear of alienating those whose vision of perfection was illiberal, was necessary to create a stable liberal regime in a society in which there were many different comprehensive doctrines held by many people. Rawls wanted to be able to count on all of them for active support for political liberalism. Yet a liberal state could not be completely neutral. "Unreasonable" and anti-democratic comprehensive doctrines, both religious and secular, were a "permanent fact of life" (a lesson Rawls learned from Berlin). They had to be somehow contained, "like war and disease," "so that they do not undermine the unity and justice of society."[46]

This containment extended to more than just preventing sects from chopping off their children's hands or forbidding girls to learn to read. While political liberalism would not attempt to indoctrinate children with any com-

44. *Restatement*, 125; 129–130. Ontogeny recapitulates phylogeny?

45. *PL*, xviii; 41; 176; 374; *Restatement*, 40; Dreben, "On Rawls and Political Liberalism," 333; *Restatement*, 143; *Restatement*, 201, *PL*, 201–206; *PL*, 194; *PL*, 208; 404n39; *TJ*, 287, 290; *PL*, 6, 188, 295. xii, xv.

46. *PL*, 486; 39; 64n19, xvii; 92–93; 144, xix–xx; 209.

prehensive doctrine, it required that children's education "include such things as knowledge of their constitutional and civil rights so that, for example, they know that liberty of conscience exists in their society and that apostasy is not a legal crime. . . . Moreover, their education should also . . . enable them to be self-supporting; it should also encourage the political virtues [civility, tolerance, and fairness]." Although he did not use the term, Rawls insisted on a right of exit as both a positive and a negative freedom: children couldn't be locked up or coerced, and all had to be given, through education, the means to leave.[47]

The actions necessary to contain illiberalism would give rise to opposition. Fundamentalist groups were likely to lose adherents in a liberal society, and were likely to object. Rawls's response was that "the unavoidable consequences of reasonable requirements for children's education may have to be accepted, often with regret." He was willing to accept conflict with the "unreasonable." The question of how to make sure liberalism would win this conflict was a problem early twenty-first century liberalism was left to answer.[48]

His liberal opponents would say that his egalitarianism might backfire. Markets, the third traditional pillar of liberalism, were never central for him, except in the negative sense that their outcomes needed to be continually adjusted. They were not independent supports for liberalism. When the word "capitalism" occurred in Rawls, it was rarely if ever with positive connotations. He condemned even what he called "welfare-state capitalism." By contrast, free-market capitalism was central to the main rivals of egalitarianism in the liberal camp, libertarianism and neoliberalism. For at least some libertarians, such as Robert Nozick, this was for moral reasons, obviously based on a very different view of morality than that held by Rawls. By contrast, neoliberals like Milton Friedman relied on purely economic justifications for liberalism. For both libertarians and neoliberals, markets were a crucial means of keeping the world a place where no one need be afraid. Rawls's regulating egalitarian state filled them with terror.[49] In all three cases, reliance on a single pillar, whether moral

47. *PL*, 193; 199.

48. *PL*, 200; Rawls's political liberalism essentially viewed comprehensive doctrines instrumentally, as a means of helping to create a stable liberal society. See Fortier, "Can Liberalism Lose the Enlightenment?," 1008–1009.

49. And vice versa: for Rawls, libertarianism "does not combine liberty and equality in the way liberalism does; it lacks the criterion of reciprocity and allows excessive social economic inequalities as judged by that criterion." *PL*, lvi. The same would be true of neoliberalism.

or economic, was characteristic of their arguments. Perhaps this narrow basis was linked to the fact that in the late twentieth century, as with the fin de siècle strife between modern and classical liberals, one kind of liberal tried to read the other out of the liberal camp—and the favor was generously returned by the other side.

Libertarianism: Nozick

For libertarians, any state was a would-be totalitarian state. If they admitted the need for one because it was absolutely necessary to avoid certain fears, it had to be as small as possible, otherwise people would have even more cause to be afraid than if the state did not exist. Libertarianism was in some respects a return to the classical liberalism of Spencer in the fin de siècle, or to Bastiat's idea of the night watchman state in the short nineteenth century. Libertarians, however, were more thorough than either. Unlike anarchists, libertarians accepted the need for a state, yet only the most minimal possible state, with the most limited sphere of action and the lowest tax rates.[50] In order to maximize the freedom of the individual and minimize coercion, the tasks of the state were limited to national defense, criminal justice, and the enforcement of contracts. Libertarianism was a hedgehog sort of liberalism: it knew only one big fear, the danger that the state might trample on individual rights.[51]

This fear, in the context of the late twentieth century, commonly was a fear that the state would redistribute wealth in the name of equality. But alongside the rejection of redistribution was fear that the government would unjustifiably regulate personal behavior, hence libertarian defense of recreational drug use, consensual sexual behaviour, rejection of professional licensing, etc. Many of these converged with the sex, drugs, and rock 'n roll aspects of the counterculture, and libertarianism drew some of its strength from it.

Libertarian arguments against state power were made in many different ways. Some appealed to both utility and moral perfection, and used all three pillars of liberal argument: politically, emphasizing the importance of giving the state no more power than absolutely necessary; economically, arguing for

50. Anarchism will be left out of account here as elsewhere in this incomplete history of liberalism.

51. As Isaiah Berlin, citing the ancient Greek poet Archilochus, put it, the fox knows many things, but the hedgehog knows one big thing.

free markets as central to a liberal society; and morally, arguing that laissez-faire was the only way to honor the inherent rights and dignity of human be-ings and / or further their happiness or perfection of character. Nevertheless, most libertarians tended to emphasize only one or two pillars. Which one they chose varied, but libertarians were unanimous in stressing the need to limit the power of the majority over the individual, which made some libertarians reject democracy, while others defended consensus as the only appropriate form of government.[52]

One difference between late twentieth-century libertarianism and fin de siècle classical liberalism is the extent to which libertarianism is American. Most of its leading advocates resided in the United States. To some extent this was true of most of the post-1970s versions of anti-totalitarian liberalism, in-cluding its egalitarian and neoliberal variants. But libertarianism was extreme in this as in so much else. Perhaps the relative stability of the American context was the source of libertarian radicalism: it allowed libertarians to ignore the question of political stability in their quest to remake the world into a place where no one need fear state coercion.[53]

Robert Nozick (1938–2002), Rawls's Harvard colleague and fellow philos-opher, was a libertarian thinker who set out to directly oppose Rawls's egalitar-ian liberalism, and in the process made libertarianism academically respectable and himself academically famous. Nozick published *Anarchy, State, and Utopia* three years after Rawls's *Theory of Justice*. It won America's National Book Award in 1975, and in Britain the *Times Literary Supplement* named it one of the "hundred most influential books" since WWII. It has been a classroom staple ever since.[54]

Nozick made individual rights central, adopting something like Locke's view of rights (like Rawls, Nozick was part of the back to Locke movement, and indeed made much more use of him). As the first lines of *Anarchy, State, and Utopia* put it, "individuals have rights, and there are things no person or group may do to them." At the time, this was a startling statement. As one commentator wrote, "with the exception of Robert Nozick, no major theorist in the Anglo-Saxon world for almost a century has based his work on the concept of a right." This led Nozick, and libertarians generally, to take a stricter view of laissez-faire than many fin de siècle classical liberals. To some

52. Doherty, *Radicals for Capitalism*, 189, 567; 192; 220.
53. Doherty, *Radicals for Capitalism*, 121.
54. Bader and Meadowcroft, *Robert Nozick*, 2, 4.

extent libertarianism is to classical liberalism what egalitarian liberalism is to modern liberalism.[55]

Nozick did not pretend to develop a unified theory of rights, of justice, or anything else. *Anarchy, State, and Utopia* consisted of three parts, addressing how a state might come into being without coercion, what its powers ought to be, and what a libertarian utopia might look like. The middle part, which most directly presented his critique of egalitarian liberalism, is crucial to understanding the conflict between egalitarian and libertarian liberalisms.

Because people had rights, others, whether individuals or states, were limited in how they could behave toward them. Rights, in Nozick's phrase, acted as "side-constraints": Rights were moral limits on what individuals or governments could do to attain their goals. Our rights reflected "the underlying Kantian principle that individuals are ends, and not merely means; they may not be sacrificed or used for the achieving of other ends without their consent." As a result, "the principle of fairness," as stated by Rawls (although it too was based on the principle that individuals had to be treated as ends, not means), was "objectionable and unacceptable." Reciprocity was not enforceable. One could not give people a benefit, say a just society, and then demand that they pay for it whether they wanted it or not. For Nozick, creating "fair" equal opportunity always involved hurting someone, even if only by taxing them to educate the poor. Talking about the common good was merely hiding the fact that some individual's rights were being violated. "There is no *social entity* with a good that undergoes some sacrifice for its own good. There are only individual people, with their own individual lives." For Nozick, "group rights," or the rights of society as a whole, did not exist.[56]

Nozick therefore rejected using the state to mitigate social and economic inequality. In the context of a laissez-faire economy—the only kind of economy sanctioned by Nozick's conception of individual rights—the only morally appropriate role for the state was to enforce the voluntary contracts made by individuals, and to prevent them from violating others' property rights. Legislating social and economic equality was a morally illegitimate activity for government to perform. "Moral philosophy sets the background for, and boundaries of, political philosophy. What persons may and may not do to one another limits what they may do through the apparatus of a state." The state

55. Nozick, *Anarchy, State, and Utopia*, xix. All references to Nozick will be to this work; Richard Tuck, cited in Bader, *Robert Nozick*, 112.
56. Nozick, 29; 31; 93, 95, 102; 235; 32–33; xix.

was limited to its night watchman function of protecting individuals against violations of their rights by other individuals because anything more than this violated individuals' rights. Any violation of individual rights by the state was the moral equivalent of totalitarianism / socialism, words libertarians tended to use without much discrimination, although this was not true of Nozick himself.[57]

On this basis Nozick rejected a key element of egalitarian liberalism, the redistribution of income and wealth. He described this as a "patterned" distribution, in which the desired pattern might vary, that is, whether income and opportunity were distributed based on merit, productivity, virtue, etc. Nozick insisted on an "unpatterned" distribution: whatever distribution of wealth resulted from free contract, from uncoerced acquisition and transfer of wealth, was just, whereas any form of redistribution was "not achievable by any morally permissible available means." A patterned distribution of wealth made the state the part-owner of the individual, and "involves a shift from the classical liberals' notion of self-ownership to a notion of (partial) property rights in *other* people." Furthermore, patterned distributions were inherently unstable. Egalitarian liberalism meant that the rich and talented enslaved themselves to the poor and stupid. For Nozick, "whether or not people's natural assets are arbitrary from a moral point of view, they are entitled to them, and to what flows from them." The assets belonged to the individual, not to society. A society that allowed you to keep them only to the extent that this benefited the least advantaged was morally illegitimate. Furthermore, the rich and well-endowed wouldn't like this. Even if, as Rawls suggested, they too gained from participating in a just society, they gained much less from the difference principle than did the poor. They would therefore seek to overturn an unfair bargain.[58]

Nozick noted that in practice most writers rarely bothered to justify taking from the rich to give to the poor. They assumed it was self-evident that some level of concentration of wealth was bad, and proceeded to discuss how best

57. Thomas Nagel, "Foreword," in Nozick, xiii; Nozick, 6.

58. This is the plot of Ayn Rand's *Atlas Shrugged*. Nozick, 156; 208; 160; 172; 169, 172; 226; 225–228. Nevertheless, it has been argued that the differences between Nozick and Rawls are less than meet the eye, and that the logical solution would be for Rawls to support market economics and take a consequentialist attitude to redistribution. See Fried, "The Unwritten Theory of Justice," 430–449. Nozick, 194–195. The point about the resentment of the wealthy is a consequentialist / utilitarian argument, of which there are many in Nozick (and Rawls). To the extent that either touches on questions of stability, such arguments are impossible to avoid.

to use the state to alter it. But for Nozick, "one *cannot* decide whether the state had to do something to alter the situation merely by looking at the distributional profile. . . . If these distributional facts *did* arise by a legitimate process, then they themselves are legitimate." There was no moral presumption in favor of equality. Morality applied only to the procedure by which the asset was obtained.[59]

There was, however, one great exception to Nozick's defense of laissez-faire, which requires notice even if it was peripheral to most other versions of libertarianism: the "principle of rectification." What if someone's wealth was stolen? Or was stolen by a grandparent? Or stolen 200 years ago? Or 2000 years ago? There was then potential moral justification, in Nozick's view, to return the wealth to its rightful owners. In such circumstances one could not rule out some form of transfer payments from the current to the former owners, or to society in general, enforced by the state. "Although to introduce socialism as the punishment for our sins would be to go too far, past injustices might be so great as to make necessary in the short run a more extensive state in order to rectify them." As many have pointed out, this was potentially a very broad exception. Nozick left its details hazy: "these issues are very complex."[60]

Libertarians, Nozick recognized, faced the same problem of stability as the just society imagined by Rawls, but in more acute form. Who would man the barricades for a minimal state?, he asked. One might add the lesser question of who would vote for it. Probably not a majority. The last and shortest section of *Anarchy, State, and Utopia* was devoted to describing how a libertarian utopia might "thrill or inspire people to struggle or sacrifice." Nozick's response, his "framework," was in a sense not utopian at all. There could not be just one utopia for Nozick because there was no one best possible world to fit everyone's preferences. So utopia had to have many neighborhoods ("worlds," Nozick called them). Provided all offered a right of exit, it was acceptable that many of these neighborhoods have rules that violated Nozick's moral premises—because all were based on his primary premise, universal consent: "in a free society people may contract into restrictions which the government may not legitimately impose upon them." Individuals could even sell themselves into slavery.[61] It was the possibility of diversity, or at least of creating their own neighborhood, that would inspire people to support the libertarian

59. Nozick, 240; 232; 233.
60. Nozick, 231.
61. Nozick later retracted this position.

framework. In his libertarian fashion, Nozick recreated the traditional liberal appeal to free association. He suggested that the appeal to free association against coercion would give sufficient luster to libertarianism to make it attractive.[62]

Nozick's was essentially a one pillar liberalism, based on a vision of morality, but of a purely negative morality, without any perfectionism, with nothing to say about how one should lead one's life, without even the encouragement to tolerance, civility, and fairness that Rawls provided. Nozick's liberalism required free markets, but he barely discussed economics except to illustrate moral rights claims. His politics of universal consent could hardly be considered a political pillar, since once there was such consent, politics ended, and without such consent, it was illegitimate. Nozick's libertarianism focused solely on the narrow version of the moral pillar of freedom provided by his conception of rights.

Like egalitarian liberalism and libertarianism, neoliberalism, the third main component of third-generation anti-totalitarian liberalism, also offered a narrow justification of its position. Instead of morality, however, the common denominator of Rawls and Nozick, it was the market economy that neoliberals relied on to fend off totalitarian threats.[63]

Neoliberalism and Milton Friedman

The word "neoliberalism" presents certain difficulties. First coined at the Colloque Lippmann or a little earlier, the word led a low-key existence (used more in French than in English), before going underground after 1960. During its period in the shadows, the term shed its original meaning of reconciling modern and classical liberalism to connote a liberalism based on market economics, largely to the exclusion of moral and political elements. The term re-emerged in the late 1970s in both Europe and the United States, becoming steadily more common until taking off around 1990.[64] By then it was generally a pejorative. Since the beginning of the twenty-first century, neoliberalism has served as a

62. Nozick, 297; 330, 320; 331.

63. As noted above, some versions of libertarianism were based on primarily economic / utilitarian considerations, rather than moral rights. This led to a certain overlap between libertarianism and neoliberalism, but in practice it was limited by the pragmatism of the neoliberals and the absence of pragmatism among libertarians.

64. See Google Ngram results in both English and French.

scapegoat for all liberalism's opponents. Partly in consequence, very few neo-liberals ever identify themselves as such, preferring to call themselves liberals, classical liberals, or something else that seems more respectable.

Nevertheless the term neoliberalism remains useful, first because it avoids the confusion caused by the divergence in the meaning of "liberal" between the United States and the rest of the world. Neoliberalism has roughly the same meaning everywhere: it means liberalism identified with laissez-faire economics. Second, neoliberalism, like egalitarian liberalism and libertarian-ism, represented a liberalism standing on one pillar, but instead of politics or morality, neoliberals based themselves almost exclusively on arguments de-rived from economics.[65] Sometimes it was defined a little more broadly, as a "free market ideology based on individual liberty and limited government that connected human freedom to the actions of the rational, self-interested actor in the competitive marketplace." Even the broader definitions essentially see neoliberalism as based on an economic pillar.[66]

Neoliberals were part of the anti-totalitarian third wave of liberalism: when they expressed their fear of totalitarianism, they did so in economic terms. Thus, when in 1975 Milton Friedman expressed his fear that Britain might succumb to dictatorship like Chile, only from the left rather than the right: "even if you were back on a 2 or 3 percent per year rate of inflation with reasonable levels of employment, the basic problem of the fraction of income being taken by government and its tendency to drive you in a totalitarian direction would remain."[67]

Neoliberalism meant not just economism, that is reducing all questions to economic ones, but an economism deliberately designed to exclude politics and morals as independent domains from the liberal purview. One could therefore describe neoliberalism as characterized by "the pursuit of the disenchantment of politics by economics," an effort to "replace political judgement with eco-nomic evaluation." Market forces and competition became the most important means of obtaining liberty, and freedom was constituted in purely economic terms. If there was a social or political problem, the market was seen as the only possible bulwark against fear. Any moral value other than the efficient use of

65. This is also the view taken in Thorsen and Lie, "What Is Neoliberalism?," 15, http://folk.uio.no/daget/What%20is%20Neo-Liberalism%20FINAL.pdf.

66. The broader definition is that of Jones, *Masters of the Universe*, 2. For the Ordoliberal-leaning version see Plehwe, "Introduction,", and Slobodian, *Globalists*.

67. Cited in Burgin, *The Great Persuasion*, 240.

resources was displaced. And it was only individuals who were to be taken into account: neoliberals did not think in terms of the fears of groups.[68]

The elimination of the moral pillar from the writings of neoliberalism's champions did not go wholly unnoticed. One historian has claimed that "morality was almost always absent in the writings of Hayek, Friedman, and Buchanan." While this was not true of Hayek (one reason Hayek should not be considered a neoliberal), it was, generally speaking, accurate. In some respects this did not seem to be a problem, at least in the short run.[69]

According to a few of its friends and far more of its foes, neoliberalism was "the Weltanschauung of the late twentieth century," or at least "the most important movement in political and economic thought." It was "hegemonic," a "universal ideology." These are relatively neutral descriptions. For some on the left, neoliberalism was another name for the international conspiracy run from Switzerland by the Mont Pèlerin Society. In terms strongly reminiscent of nineteenth-century Catholics blaming the French Revolution and all succeeding liberal / radical movements of the nineteenth century on the Freemasons, or anti-semites talking about the Conspiracy of the Elders of Zion, such commentators described neoliberalism as a secret international plot run from a Swiss mountain. "Any person or group that bears any links to the Mont Pèlerin Society . . . since 1947" was viewed "as falling within the purview of the neoliberal thought collective." They were thus participants, or at least fellow travelers, in the alleged conspiracy.[70] This radical intellectual core somehow ruled the world: "From the 1990s onward . . . we are effectively 'post-democracy.' Governments are now left 'ruling the void' where an impotent *Staatsvolk* [voters and politicians] is left open to the vagaries of a *Marktvolk* comprising the transnational investor class."[71]

68. Davies, *The Limits of Neoliberalism*, 3–4; Tribe, "Liberalism and Neoliberalism in Britain, 1930–1980," 75; Becchio and Leghissa, *The Origins of Neoliberalism*, 12; 4, 17.

69. Jones, *Masters of the Universe*, 112.

70. Full disclosure: the author has participated, with great intellectual profit, in many conferences organized by the Liberty Fund, an organization with tenuous links to the Mont Pèlerin Society (MPS), and thus may be considered a fellow traveler or worse. Furthermore, after this chapter was written, he participated in an MPS conference.

71. Becchio and Leghissa, *Origins of Neoliberalism*, 1, Mirowski, "Postface," 426; Plehwe, "Introduction," 2, 3; 4; 7; Mirowski, "Postface," 441; Plehwe et al., *Nine Lives*, 5. Mirowski, "Postface," 432, Plehwe, "Introduction," 6; Plehwe et al., *Nine Lives*, 70. The last-named book is dedicated "to all those who struggle with and against neoliberalism," x. A more sober history of the MPS concludes that "it is easy to describe what it has done since 1947 but very difficult to say what it has achieved." Hartwell, *A History of the Mont Pèlerin Society*, 191.

The neoliberal conspiracy theory, like most such theories, did have a tenuous link to reality: neoliberals did have some success in influencing public policy, and more in influencing public debate, far more than libertarians and, if evaluated in concrete results rather than academic publications, far more than egalitarian liberals. The way for neoliberal influence on policy was paved by the economic problems of the 1970s: stagflation; strife between employers and governments on the one hand and unions on the other; the failure of the anti-poverty strategies pursued in the United States and elsewhere; the slowing growth of economic productivity. In the 1970s inflation was the headline problem, rather than the unemployment that had obsessed (with reason) the economists of the 1930–1950s, and neoliberal economists seemed to have the remedy that had escaped the Keynesian economists of the end of ideology era. The end result was "a broad breakdown of the characteristic mid-twentieth-century belief in the efficacy and moral superiority of government and collective action." The crisis provided an opening for neoliberal economic theories to get a hearing and often a trial. By the 1980s, neoliberal ideas influenced many global economic institutions. They were adopted politically by many even on the left, notably Clinton Democrats in the United States and Blair's New Labor in Britain. The creation of the Word Trade Organization in 1994, endowing free trade with an international court system to protect it from the whims of governments, even democratic ones, is sometimes considered the culmination of neoliberal domination, although it might equally be considered proof of its weakness, given the checkered history of the WTO.[72]

In stark contrast with egalitarian liberalism, the pursuit of equality was nowhere to be found in neoliberalism. This point is often obscured by charges from the left that neoliberals were indifferent to poverty, and by indignant neoliberal rebuttals. Neoliberals were not indifferent to poverty: they disagreed strongly with those to their left, both liberals and non-liberals, about the best method to fight poverty, preferring to rely on free markets rather than government intervention, but neither Milton Friedman nor any other neoliberal ever professed indifference to poverty. Neoliberals, however, were not interested in eliminating or minimizing inequalities of wealth, or in fostering what Rawls called "fair equality of opportunity." This was not because their economic views excluded reducing material inequality—liberals had always argued that one of the natural consequences of free markets was a reduction

---

72. Jones, *Masters of the Universe*, 5; 102; 334; 269; 7; Davies, Jackson, and Sutcliffe-Brathwaite, *The Neoliberal Age?*; Slobodian, *Globalists*, 25.

in inequality—but rather because they did not see reducing inequality as the role of government, just as classical liberals had not seen reducing poverty as the government's role. It should also be noted that while some neoliberals supported a basic social safety net, others did not.[73]

Neoliberalism's reliance on free-market economics as the sole or chief basis of liberalism, its disdain for the moral pillar of liberalism, and its utter rejection of egalitarianism can be illustrated by the writing of one of the most influential of them, the American Milton Friedman (1912–2006). That Friedman never called himself a neoliberal during the time when he incarnated neoliberalism is typical.[74] But he was a model econocentric neoliberal, and his public influence was considerable. He served as an advisor for Goldwater's American presidential campaign in 1964, and was influential with President Ronald Reagan and many other policy-makers, controversially including the Pinochet government in Chile. He received the Nobel Prize in economics in 1976. Many of the economic policies he supported were either put into practice or seriously considered in the United States, UK, Chile and elsewhere.[75]

Capitalism and Freedom (1962) was Friedman's recipe for how to avoid totalitarianism. The viewpoint of the book, as Friedman described it, was liberalism—but not in the American sense of the word, as Friedman was well aware. The major focus was a full-throated defense of free markets and capitalism, and of the benefits to both freedom and efficiency of limiting government in favor of markets. Its minor theme was what roles government still ought to play, and how. The proper orchestration of major and minor themes would lead to a utopia of economic prosperity and personal freedom.[76]

Friedman's liberalism was based on economics, with rare references to politics and only disdainful remarks about morals.[77] Friedman maintained moral neutrality even with regard to what he called the "capitalist ethic," the view that

73. Jones, *Masters of the Universe*, 12.

74. For the exception that proves the rule, see Bowman, "Coming Out as a Neoliberal," cited in *Nine Lives*, 5n12.

75. Burgin, *The Great Persuasion*, 150; 206–207.

76. Friedman, *Capitalism and Freedom*, 5. All references to Friedman's writings, unless otherwise noted, are to this work.

77. Any faint appeal to political freedom was removed in the 2002 preface, where Friedman said the example of Hong Kong had taught him that political freedom was not necessary for economic and civil freedom. He went on to suggest that political freedom could be either positive or negative for civil and economic freedom—hardly a ringing endorsement. Friedman, ix–x.

one should be paid according to how the market values what one produces. This "ethic" was not ethical: it "cannot in and of itself be regarded as an ethical principle; that it must be regarded as instrumental or a corollary of some other principle such as freedom." The capitalist ethic therefore had no ethical justification, and needed none, in Friedman's view. Friedman's "freedom" was substantively empty of moral content except for the necessity of free choice. "Freedom has *nothing to say* about what an individual does with his freedom; it is not an all-embracing ethic" (emphasis added). He went even further than Rawls: not only should liberalism not impose its comprehensive worldview on people, it did not have one. What individuals ought to do with their lives was consigned to "individual ethics and philosophy," about which evidently neither Friedman nor liberalism need speak.[78]

For Friedman, economic freedom was both an end in itself, that is a constituent part of freedom, and "an indispensable means toward the achievement of political freedom." His priority was economic: "The direct importance of economic freedom is at least comparable in significance to the indirect importance of economic freedom as a means of political freedom." According to Friedman, liberalism was founded on this recognition. Competition protected people from coercion by giving them choices. The market was the source of cultural diversity (people would buy diverse cultural products, given the opportunity to choose), government the source of coercion and uniformity.[79] The only freedoms were those of individuals: even when discussing racial and religious discrimination, Friedman thought purely in terms of individuals, never in terms of groups.[80]

Nevertheless, Friedman was not an advocate of pure laissez-faire. He was not a libertarian, that is, he did not wish to limit the functions of the state to those of a night watchman, or those of a rule-maker and umpire.[81] Notably, Friedman supported two specific government policies that became significant subjects of political debate in America and elsewhere. The first was the "negative income tax," under which the government would guarantee a minimum income for all. This way, the poor were helped with the least cost—little bureaucracy was required to administer it—and given the most freedom—there

78. Friedman, 165; 12.
79. Friedman, 8–10; 10–11; 4; 14–5; 16; 8–9.
80. Friedman, 110; 111; 113; 109.
81. Friedman, 30; 190, 34; Doherty, *Radicals for Capitalism*, 466.

were no strings attached to how the money was spent. Meanwhile, all other programs to assist the poor should be eliminated.[82]

Second, Friedman thought government had a duty to make sure that all children received an education. For a stable democratic society, literacy and a certain minimum amount of general knowledge were necessary, as was "widespread acceptance of some common set of values."[83] This justified government requiring and paying for non-vocational education, including elementary and high schools, and even liberal arts colleges, but not medical school or plumbing training—unless vocational students paid back any subsidy they received. But while the government had a duty to make sure all received an education, it should not provide education itself. Instead, "vouchers" should be given to every parent, worth a certain amount of money, to be given to the school of their choice, provided the school offered a minimum curriculum.[84]

Though he made these exceptions to deal with the problem of poverty, Friedman favored a rollback of the welfare state: no more social security, government health or unemployment insurance, minimum wage, or public housing. Above all Friedman opposed any form of economic egalitarianism. "The liberal will . . . distinguish sharply between equality of rights and equality of opportunity, on the one hand, and material equality or equality of outcome on the other." The test of whether one was for or against freedom, in Friedman's view, was whether or not one accepted the inegalitarian principle of market rewards. "Some key institutions must be accepted as 'absolutes', not simply as instrumental. I believe that payment in accordance with product has been, and, in large measure, still is, one of these accepted value judgements or institutions." There was no justification for "taking from some to give to others" on the grounds of justice: "At this point, equality came sharply into conflict with freedom; one must choose. One cannot be both an egalitarian, in this sense, and a liberal." From Friedman's perspective, Rawls was no liberal. In practice, capitalism led to greater material equality than any other economic system, but that was a "desirable by-product of a free society, not its major

82. Friedman, 191–192; 194. He regarded universal suffrage as a cloak for rule by special interests, who were more motivated to vote. See Slobodian, *Globalists*, 178–179. Hayek also raised this question without resolving it in *The Constitution of Liberty*, citing Mises to the same effect. See *The Constitution of Liberty*, 411 and 411n10.

83. This is one place where Friedman and Rawls more or less agreed. Education has typically been a panacea for liberals at all times. In this liberalism really is the scion of the Enlightenment and indirectly of the Protestant Reformation.

84. Friedman, 86; 88, 105; 89; 90.

justification." One could have one's egalitarian cake while rejecting egalitarian principles of how it should be cut. But Friedman viewed material inequalities positively: an unequal distribution of wealth helped provide alternative foci of power to the state and offset centralization. Concentrations of wealth in individual hands further promoted civil freedom by creating patrons for different ideas.[85]

Just as much as Rawls or Nozick, Friedman was a utopian, even if this might not be obvious at first glance. When he wrote, there was no country that exemplified his views, and even though he had the satisfaction of seeing some of his ideas, like school vouchers, put into place, it was always in the context of a far bigger state and a far less free-market economy than he envisaged. Neoliberals like Friedman, rather than seeing themselves as the world's puppet-masters, more often saw themselves as an embattled minority. At least within the walls of academia, that was certainly true, with the possible exception of departments of Economics. Friedman saw utopia as a world in which every individual was free to make as many choices as they wished, limited only by the rights of others and their own means. This is certainly not a world that has ever existed.

The utopias imagined by Rawls, Nozick, and Friedman were all built on very narrow foundations. In their very different ways, Friedman, Nozick, and Rawls all contributed to the hollowing-out of liberalism in the second half of the twentieth century. They wanted to limit its basis, constructing its foundations on a single pillar (with a stub of politics remaining in Rawls), whether by separating it from comprehensive moral views and a market economy, narrowing its scope to the protection of the individual's moral rights, or focusing purely on economic freedom. The narrow view of what liberalism meant taken by both egalitarian liberals and their libertarian and neoliberal opponents led to the weakness that third-wave liberalism experienced after 1992. To some extent, the same was true of the liberalism of fear, which against the utopianism common to Rawls, Nozick, and Friedman claimed to be the only truly realistic liberalism.

Liberal Fear and Liberal Realism: Shklar and Williams

Rawls, Nozick, Friedman, Judith Shklar, and Bernard Williams were contemporaries (Shklar died in 1992, the others 2002–2006). And yet, perhaps because it rejected all the utopian projects of egalitarians, libertarians, and neoliberals

85. Friedman, 35–36; 67; 73; 180; 184–185; 187; 100; 167; 169; 172–174; 168.

alike, the "liberalism of fear" as Shklar and Williams described their views seems like something that comes after, even though in fact it was in contemporary dialog with the leading forms of third-generation anti-totalitarian liberalism. It was never as prominent or as influential, either in academia or outside it, as its rivals. Shklar and Williams were prominent academic figures, but they were far from equaling Rawls's renown. Williams's brief forays into policy-making bear no comparison to those of Milton Friedman—as chair of a royal commission he was a leading influence on the decriminalization of pornography in Britain. The liberalism of fear was a movement of academic theorists of some intellectual and little practical importance. It nevertheless merits its place here because its approach sheds light on the problems populism poses for liberals in the early twenty-first century, and on liberals' potential responses.

Although Shklar and Williams's anti-utopianism superficially resembled that of the end of ideology movement, the resemblance is deceiving: when the liberalism of fear rejected utopianism as dangerous, it took this approach from pessimism, not the optimism of the end of ideology movement. It was not liberal progress that provoked the liberalism of fear, it was the decline of liberalism between 1914 and 1945, and the corresponding rise of cruelty. The liberalism of fear was preoccupied with liberalism's failures and potential failures. Nothing could be farther from the triumphalism of the end of ideology movement.

The liberalism of fear was exceptional in that Shklar and Williams departed from most late twentieth-century liberal thought by making history central to their account of liberalism. As a result, they were far more attuned to the importance of context in formulating liberal policy than egalitarians, libertarians, or neoliberals. They disagreed with each other, however, on the role that hope and morality should play in liberalism. Williams, unlike Shklar, thought that liberalism needed to offer something more than pragmatism in order to be an effective barrier against fear. But his morality was very different from that of Rawls or Nozick. Unlike them, he appealed to a liberal perfectionism that had more in common with Mill than with most twentieth-century liberals.[86]

---

86. Shklar's first book, *After Utopia: The Decline of Political Faith*, was a not uncritical contribution to the end of ideology movement. In it she complained that liberalism had become "unsure of its moral basis," but concluded that "a reasoned skepticism is consequently the sanest attitude for the present." She retained this attitude throughout her career. *After Utopia*, 272.

Like Nozick, Judith N. Shklar (1928–92) was John Rawls's colleague at Harvard, but in the Government department rather than Philosophy. The title of her 1989 essay, "The Liberalism of Fear," helped inspire this book, but her idea of liberalism was very different in some ways. For Shklar, pursuing the goal of a society in which no one need be afraid meant eliminating or side-stepping many considerations, such as autonomy or personal development, central to other forms of liberalism. The pursuit of moral greatness, whether for individuals, groups, or nations, was not on her agenda. Her sole agenda item, the prevention of fear, was much more modest; too modest, perhaps, to attain its aims. She counseled that a purely utilitarian politics which abandoned any hope of utopia on the grounds that such hopes were too dangerous to be entertained.

For Shklar, "liberalism has only one overriding aim: to secure the political conditions necessary for the exercise of freedom."[87] Freedom was defined by the absence of fear: "every adult should be able to make as many effective decisions without fear . . . as is compatible with the like freedom of every other adult." She followed Montesquieu in her conclusion that "fear destroys freedom." And that, for Shklar, was the whole content of freedom.[88]

Shklar usually focused on a narrow kind of fear, the fear of cruelty. Cruelty was absolute evil, and preventing cruelty was the aim and purpose of liberalism as she saw it. Historically, this idea began for Shklar with her heroes Montaigne and Montesquieu, and more generally in reaction to the sixteenth- and seventeenth-century European Wars of Religion. In her view this experience of cruelty, not the Enlightenment, nor new understandings of natural law or human rights, gave birth to liberalism.[89] Citing Dicey, Shklar noted that the recognition of the cruelty inflicted on slaves spread by Harriet Beecher Stowe's *Uncle Tom's Cabin* had more to do with the abolition of American slavery than the idea of natural rights embodied in the Declaration of Independence.[90]

Because political power was a prime source of fear and cruelty, Shklar's liberalism of fear took a deep interest in the construction of political systems and constitutions, and insisted, like Constant, on the need for political guar-

87. Beginning after WWII, "freedom" began to replace "liberty" in the liberal vocabulary, although by no means entirely. Toward the end of the century, liberty was increasingly used only by those on the anti-egalitarian end of the liberal spectrum.

88. Shklar, *Ordinary Vices*, 2; "The Liberalism of Fear," 21.

89. One may wonder what the cruelties Europeans inflicted in Africa and the New World in the sixteenth century also contributed—Montaigne provides evidence for this—but this was not a line of thought the Eurocentric Shklar pursued.

90. Shklar, "The Liberalism of Fear," 23; 35.

antees and for political participation to make them work. She thus argued for
the natural alliance of liberalism and democracy. Political rights were a necessary tool for preserving people from fear, as were pluralist political institutions: "without the institutions of representative democracy and an accessible,
fair, and independent judiciary . . . in the absence of a multiplicity of politically
active groups, liberalism is in jeopardy. . . . It is therefore fair to say that liberalism is monogamously, faithfully, and permanently married to democracy—
but it is a marriage of convenience."[91]

Shklar was aware that the stability of this alliance was subject to strain. The
liberalism of fear recognized the need for democratic political institutions, but
also that democratic government could not be only of laws, but had to at least
sometimes be of men. "Personal political authority is based on something
close to love which is unstable and incalculable, and it has made the liberal
state far less procedural and far less predictable than its first designers had
hoped." What Shklar called leadership and what Max Weber had called charisma was an "inescapable" part of politics, and Montesquieu and James Madison, who felt they could ignore charisma once "absolute rulers and their
confessors were replaced by an institutional 'system,' " were too optimistic. In
times of crisis, liberal democracies would appeal to persons rather than
procedures—there was in this argument an anticipation of the recurrent nature of populism's appeal. Therefore these persons, Shklar insisted without
elaboration, had to "be subject to a process of selection that will moderate the
most unacceptable vices and the worst characters." It was not clear how democracy fit this bill.[92]

Nevertheless, "impersonal government," which seemed to Shklar to have
been embodied in pre–WWI Western governments, with all their faults, was
"the least cruel and the least oppressive of known regimes. But even its best
impulses could not survive the shocks of the First World War." While more
sensitive to history than Rawls, Nozick, or Friedman, Shklar was not really interested in historical details. Nevertheless, she implied that her conceptualiza-
tion of the liberalism of fear in the late twentieth century owed something to
its historical context. After what seemed a terminal decline during the nineteenth century, torture flourished in Europe after WWI. Even if one could trace
its origins to the seventeenth century, the liberalism of fear appealed in the
twentieth century far more because of experiences like the Holocaust and the

---

91. Shklar, "The Liberalism of Fear," 36; 31; 28; 37; *Ordinary Vices*, 48.
92. Shklar, *Ordinary Vices*, 220–221; 244–245.

Gulag than the Wars of Religion. In response to the Holocaust, Shklar, herself a child refugee from Nazi Europe, conceptualized the liberalism of fear.[93]

Shklar took pains to distinguish the liberalism of fear from perfectionism and the liberalism of personal autonomy which she associated with Mill. The liberalism of fear "must avoid any tendency to offer ethical instructions in general." The purpose of freedom, in Shklar's view, was not to make us good or even to encourage us to develop our character, it was to make us safe. Shklar's liberalism of fear went even further than did her friend Rawls's in limiting liberalism's connection with any positive morality. His notion of "political liberalism" encouraged certain specific virtues, e.g., tolerance, civility, and fairness. For Shklar the purpose of liberalism was solely to remove "the most horrible obstacles to any ethical undertaking that we might conceivably have." She contrasted Locke (whose rights-based liberalism she rejected) with her preferred patriarch Montesquieu, who spoke the language of fear and did not use the language of rights or of personal autonomy (at the price of ignoring inconvenient perfectionist elements in Montesquieu—see chapter 2).[94] Shklar's rejection of perfectionism applied to groups just as much as to individuals. Liberalism had to be suspicious of the "ideologies of solidarity" that attracted those who found the liberalism of fear emotionally unsatisfying—making liberalism emotionally satisfying was not part of Shklar's vision. Hence her rejection of nationalism: there was no such thing as "liberal nationalism" from the perspective of the liberalism of fear. The moral pillar of liberalism was thus narrowed to the point where it consisted solely of abhorring cruelty. "The liberalism of fear "does not . . . offer a *summum bonum* . . . but . . . a *summum malum* [cruelty]."[95]

In the view of Bernard Williams (1929–2003), Shklar's liberalism of fear was both the "least ambitious and most convincing justification of liberalism." Williams was an Englishman, a professor of Philosophy at Oxford and Cambridge, with an interval at the University of California, Berkeley. He came to political philosophy only in the 1980s, having previously made his reputation as a spe-

93. Shklar, *Ordinary Vices*, 221; "The Liberalism of Fear," 27.

94. Shklar, *Ordinary Vices*, 237.

95. Shklar, "The Liberalism of Fear," 27; 36; *Ordinary Vices*, 237–239; "The Liberalism of Fear," 31; *Ordinary Vices*, 239; 236; "The Liberalism of Fear," 29. Shklar at most gestured toward Rawls's embrace of civility, tolerance, and fairness by suggesting that liberal systems of government, law, and education would inevitably have unspecified "psychological effect." See "The Liberalism of Fear," 33; Shklar, *Ordinary Vices*, 221.

cialist in ethics. He was also peripherally involved in politics, serving on a number of commissions appointed by Labor governments in Britain, and married for a time to the politician Shirley Williams, a right-Labor MP and then a leader of the short-lived Social Democratic Party. Williams strongly endorsed a version of the liberalism of fear which he acknowledged owed much to Shklar, but also departed from her in significant ways, notably in his recognition that liberalism needed to base itself on all three pillars of liberal argument, in particular morality.[96]

Williams described his political philosophy as "political realism." It was realistic, in his view, because it recognized that in order to survive in the modern world, governments needed to be legitimate in the eyes of their people, and for governments to successfully convince people of their legitimacy, they needed to provide them both political and moral reasons (Williams labeled this process the BLD, or "Basic Legitimacy Demand"). Legitimacy meant that people regard the order imposed by the state as acceptable, and that the state must justify itself to its subjects. For politics to exist, there had to be legitimacy. Williams himself raised the question of whether or not the demand for legitimacy was a moral principle, and his response was "if it is, it does not represent a morality which is prior to politics. It is a claim that is inherent in there being such a thing as politics." In despotism, there was neither politics nor legitimacy, only fear. From the perspective of legitimacy, however, might did not make right. Politics and morals were effectively simultaneous; neither took precedence.[97]

The demand that governments be legitimate in the eyes of their people was a modern demand, according to Williams, and legitimacy was an appropriate criterion to apply only to modern governments. Unlike Friedman, Nozick, Rawls, and even Shklar, Williams strongly insisted that political theories only made sense in specific historical contexts. Thus even today, "to some extent, we may regard some contemporary non-liberal states as [legitimate]," depending mostly on whether there was internal demand for legitimation. But there were limits to Williams's liberality: "some kind of democracy, participatory politics at some level, is a feature of [legitimacy] for the modern world." In the modern world legitimacy required something like representative government and a bill of rights. Just as liberals could not tolerate certain moral outlooks, they could not regard certain forms of government, e.g.,

96. Williams, *Truth and Truthfulness*, 208, cited in Hall, *Value, Conflict, and Order*, 155.
97. Williams, *In the Beginning*, 12; 4; 5, 23.

totalitarian dictatorships, as legitimate. How much toleration liberals should extend to such governments was a question of judgment. From Williams's perspective, the marriage of democracy and liberalism was unavoidable. In current historical circumstances, liberalism had to be democratic or it would not be legitimate.[98]

Discussion of the demand for legitimacy in the twentieth century brought Williams to the discussion of politics and civil rights, although he did not discuss them in detail. Liberals had raised the standard of what was required to make a government legitimate, and giving people rights was an essential part of legitimacy. But these rights did not exist because of some abstract set of principles. Any real, historically appropriate idea of "rights" would require "taking the path which Rawlsian liberalism has resisted, of putting a desirable human life before, or at least level with, a theory of the right." Succinctly put, for Williams the right did *not* have priority over the good. In other words, the rights people should have were inextricably linked to the kind of life they wanted to lead. The right to vote, for example, was tied to the idea the political participation was part of a good life. Against Rawls, Nozick, Friedman, and Shklar (and Berlin), Williams thought liberals had to take a stand about what kinds of life were best, and therefore that liberals "simply cannot avoid present-ing 'another sectarian doctrine' " in order to make liberal government legiti-mate. This meant that "liberals will have to advance to the stronger views that have been part of their Enlightenment legacy, which claim the absolute value of individual autonomy and self-determination against the values of tradition-alist cultural homogeneity." Liberalism was morally committed to giving people the right to independently decide how to live their own lives. When traditionalists claimed that making people conform to their views of what was proper was more important, liberals could not merely shrug their shoulders and regard this as just another moral perspective in a pluralist world. They had to insist on their own understanding of morality.[99]

Historically, liberals had continually broadened what counted as "a threat to people's interests," i.e., what they might fear. In the contemporary Western world, this meant requiring all hierarchies to be justified, and rejecting any justifications based on race or gender. Thus, Williams arrived at the conclusion that in Western societies today the demand for legitimacy could only be met by liberalism, or as he inelegantly put it, "LEG [Legitimacy] + Moder-

98. Hawthorn, "Introduction," in Williams, *In the Beginning*, xiv, xvi; 55; 59; 9; 13; 15.
99. Williams, *In the Beginning*, 137; 39.

nity = Liberalism." To anticipate the following chapter, what Williams did not anticipate was that populism would challenge this equation.[100]

Liberals therefore had to coerce groups who limited the autonomy and self-determination of their members. Toleration was not necessarily the correct policy toward a group that "structurally offends" such as against gender equality. Perhaps they had to be forced to give equal rights to women—or perhaps not. The right response would depend on "political good sense": considering how things looked from the others' point of view, and weighing the costs of coercion, including costs that the precedent of coercion might impose on the future. It was not a question of making traditionalist groups afraid, but of limiting the fear to which they could subject their own members. It was a political question, and Williams's answer referred to "what the late Judith Shklar called the liberalism of fear."[101]

There was nothing utopian about this kind of case-by-case decision: it was a messy sort of common law solution based on historical circumstances, rather than a bright line of utopian idealism. In Williams's view, utopias were not very useful, and utopian discourse about liberty did "not do much for the more specific construction of liberty as a value for us." Against utopia, Williams cited Constant's ancient versus modern liberty speech: attempting to apply a model of utopia not adapted to circumstances, as the French revolutionaries did, could only be a recipe for disaster (see chapter 3). Williams thus rejected most contemporary political philosophy, including both egalitarian liberals and libertarians.[102]

But rejecting utopia did not mean excluding morality as a basis for liberalism. This was Williams's most important difference from Shklar, and it articulated a path by which twenty-first-century liberalism could maintain its legitimacy against populism. For Williams, the contemporary world demanded from liberals a renewed attachment to the moral foundations of liberalism, to the moral ideal of personal development and autonomy, in a word, perfectionism. His political realism was as far as can be from moral neutrality, but he also rejected, versus Rawls, "the priority of the moral over the political" and the

100. Williams, *In the Beginning*, 7; 11; 10.

101. Williams, *In the Beginning*, 137; 39. From a rather different basis, Joseph Raz reached the same conclusion about the necessity of a certain amount of coercion, that is, inflicting fear "to secure an environment suitable for autonomous life." *The Morality of Freedom*, 156. On Raz, see chapter 11.

102. Williams, *In the Beginning*, 25; 90.

notion that "political theory is something like applied morality." Williams made a point of giving equal and independent weight to the moral and the political pillars of liberalism.[103]

Williams's liberalism of fear thus departed from Shklar. He wrote in his commentary on Shklar, also titled "The Liberalism of Fear," that while Shklar was right that liberalism should be resolutely non-utopian, liberalism should be about something more than fear. "It can be, in good times, the party of hope as well." Williams thus heroically tried to repair the damage wrought on liberalism by the hollowing-out or elimination of its traditional pillars by so many post–WWII anti-totalitarian liberals. Fear *and* hope, freedom, markets, *and* morals were realistically all necessary to satisfy modern demands for legitimacy and build a stable liberal society. Such is the case for liberals faced with the challenge of populism in the early twenty-first century.[104]

As for the third pillar of liberalism, free markets, there was little in Williams. There were a few hints, however, of a positive view. Williams argued, following Montesquieu, that people could look to global markets to restrain international aggression: "The line between a politics of legitimate community, and blank tribalism, is going to be held, if at all, by the influence of a world commercial order." He also suggested that "the presumptions in favour of equal and extensive liberty are intimately connected with the central activities of modern societies, in particular their forms of economic organization," i.e., capitalist market economies. The market pillar of liberalism was recognized by Williams, even if he did not have much occasion to discuss it.[105]

Williams's three-pillar liberalism with its strong emphasis on a perfectionist morality was rare among late twentieth-century liberals. When so many liberals reduced liberalism to a single argument or a single perspective, liberalism was hollowed out, and was unbalanced without the three pillars it needed for support. When in the early twenty-first century liberals needed responses to the moral challenges raised by populism, they found themselves with impoverished resources and only thin arguments to make. Late twentieth-century liberalism was in many respects a very fruitful period, and Rawls, Nozick, and Friedman were all powerful influences in the world of ideas and / or the world

103. Williams, *In the Beginning*, 2, 77; Hall, *Value, Conflict, and Order*, 41; Williams, *In the Beginning*, 61; Williams, *In the Beginning*, 3, Hall, *Value, Conflict, and Order*, 5; Williams, *In the Beginning*, 25; 90.

104. Williams, *In the Beginning*, 61.

105. Williams, *In the Beginning*, 39; 95.

of policy. Nevertheless, their ideas and policies were not sufficient when, in the twenty-first century, populism became the leading fear of most liberals. To ward off this new fear, liberals were challenged to develop a fourth wave of liberalism, Liberalism 4.0. Describing fourth-wave liberalism presents a different sort of challenge, however, because it is not yet history. The discussion of liberalism and populism in the following chapter is therefore of necessity the most incomplete of the stories told here.

11

Liberalism and Populism: The Search for a Solution

Defining Populism

After the Berlin Wall fell in 1989, followed by the collapse of the Soviet Union three years later, it seemed as if liberalism had achieved a decisive victory. Liberal democracy spread rapidly throughout Eastern Europe, Latin American dictatorships fell one after another, and a little later there was an "Arab Spring." Neoliberal economic policies were on the ascendant. Egalitarian liberals, if less successful practically, dominated academic culture. Libertarian cultural demands such as the legalization of recreational drugs and the acceptance of sexual diversity made rapid progress, and people had less reason to fear torture and cruelty. Francis Fukuyama was inspired to write about the "end of history," a term reminiscent of the end of ideology movement forty years before.[1]

Liberal triumph did not last long. The World Trade Center attacks of 2001 brought to the fore the challenge of Islamic fundamentalism; the financial crisis of 2007–2008, blamed by many on neoliberalism, shook the world economy; and radical nationalism revived and flourished. These circumstances have conspired to promote the worldwide growth of populism. In Eastern Europe, several liberal democratic regimes have been replaced by illiberal populist ones, and in Latin America left-wing populisms have arisen alongside right-wing ones. Even some of the most established liberal democracies, including France, Sweden, the United States, and the United Kingdom have been shaken by populist successes. The wave of populism that has flooded the

---

1. Fukuyama, *The End of History and the Last Man*.

globe in the early twenty-first century has deeply shaken liberal confidence and fractured the liberal consensus.

Third-wave liberalisms have proven unable to respond to the challenge. There are long-term and short-term historical reasons for this. Ever since the fin de siècle, the moral pillar of liberalism, particularly liberal perfectionism, has been weakened and hollowed out. As a result, faced with what is in large part a moral challenge by populists, liberals find themselves lacking intellectual resources they once commanded. In the short run, for the first time in the history of liberalism, after WWII liberals had no significant enemies on the right. This temporary blessing, however, left liberals in the early twenty-first century unprepared to respond to the growing power and appeal of right populism. Populism has forced liberals to confront problems that they thought they had resolved or at least relegated to the far corners of the world, whether religious fanaticism, radical nationalism, or the dangers of mass political participation. As populism has become the new focus of liberal fear, liberals have been flummoxed, without clear responses. Throughout the world, twenty-first-century liberalism is on the defensive. The situation appears all the more menacing because the nature of populism remains hazy, a menacing specter glimpsed through fog.

If liberalism is to find a way to overcome the fears populism creates, and diminish the fears populists experience, a fourth wave of liberalisms, Liberalism 4.0, is needed to create a world in which no one need be afraid. In order to build Liberalism 4.0, liberals must understand what populism is, why it has become so powerful, and what liberals can, and cannot, do about it.

There is agreement about part of what constitutes populism, and significant disagreement about the rest. Populism cannot be defined by its policy choices because there is little overlap between the policies of left populists like Hugo Chavez in Venezuela or Evo Morales in Bolivia, and right populists like the French Marine Le Pen or the American Donald Trump. This policy variance creates much of the uncertainty surrounding populism. What populists have in common is not their policies, but whom they fear and hate, and who supports them.

At the illiberal heart of populism is its rejection of pluralism, diversity, and difference. The "core claim of populism" is that "only some of the people are really the people," and the others are the enemy. Populisms, whether on the left or the right, are all monisms in Isaiah Berlin's terms (see chapter 8). As monists, they believe in one supreme value, in their case the people, understood monolithically. The people are indivisible, and have only one authentic will or vision—language that reminds liberals of the Jacobin Reign of Terror and of fascism. Populists' desire to make this authentic will prevail against all outsiders, whether homosexuals, foreigners, infidels, people of the wrong ethnicity, and especially the elite, who have chosen to become "aliens" and thus betrayed the people. Populists routinely seek to banish a significant part of the population from the nation, either metaphorically, or sometimes physically in the case of immigrants. As pluralists, liberals can, at least in theory, accept that populists represent real values that must be recognized. Populists neither can nor wish to do the same for liberals.[2]

Populists use the term liberals as shorthand to cover all their enemies. They fear that liberals intend to shut the true people and their values out of public life. They do not intend to let this happen. Instead, they attempt to do to their enemies what they think, not without reason, their enemies would like to do to them: they consign liberals and other groups who do not belong to the fate of medieval Jews: to be walled off in ghettoes—in the twenty-first century the ghetto includes a few select research universities alongside the major urban centers. Populists describe liberals and liberalism as the one true enemy of the people. This powerful liberal elite is always, in populist eyes, "corrupt," both financially and morally. Corruption is perhaps the oldest charge in the Western political book, going back to the Roman Republic and the Greek city-states. In the early twenty-first century populists identify liberalism with corruption, and rejecting them as a bloc attracts adherents. One manifestation is populist rage against the media, typically attacked as the "liberal" media, and typically headquartered in those ghettoes (exceptions are naturally made for populist media that represent the true voice of the people). Populists see the mainstream press not as the servant of the people, providing it with education and information, but as an intermediate body, an elite that interposes itself between the people and the enactment of their will.

Whether in the United States, the UK, France, Austria, Hungary, Poland, Russia, Venezuela, Ecuador, Bolivia, Israel, or India, populists see their enemy as a liberal elite.. Numerous proclamations by populist parties and leaders state that populists represent a democratic but "illiberal state," or a "non-liberal nation," as the populist Hungarian prime minister Viktor Orban put it in 2014.

2. Canovan, "Trust the People!," 14; 4–5; 13, Mudde, "The Populist Zeitgeist," 543; Eatwell and Goodwin, *National Populism*, 78, Mudde, "The Populist Zeitgeist," 543; Müller, *What Is Populism?*, 82; 21; Mudde, "The Populist Zeitgeist," 543–54; Galston, *Anti-Pluralism*, 127; Müller, *What Is Populism?*, 3, 21.

Outside Eastern Europe, such frank declarations have been less frequent, but the content of the American Steve Bannon's manifestos has been substantially similar, and there are many parallels elsewhere. Both populists and anti-populists often describe populism as "illiberal democracy."[3]

Pace Judith Shklar, who proclaimed their marriage unbreakable, populists thus attempt to divorce liberalism and democracy, so as to marry the latter and deny any claim to democracy by the liberal ex-spouse. If democracy means majority rule, and populists are the true majority, while liberals always represent an elite minority, then liberal democracy becomes an oxymoron. By contrast, for some critics of populism, the notion of an illiberal democracy is an Orwellian fraud, a misuse of language to hide its true meaning. For these critics, authentic democracy can only be liberal democracy, and therefore the honorable title of "democrat" should be withdrawn from populist imposters. But it is not easy to claim populists are not democrats when they constantly appeal to the sovereignty of the people, rail against elites, demand frequent referendums, and sometimes even hold more or less free elections. The democratic nature of populism is highlighted by the kinship between the rhetoric of participatory democracy as it emerged from the 1960s, with its emphasis on the direct participation of the people and the priority of winning the street over winning elections, with populist rhetoric. Both advocates of participatory democracy and populists claim that liberal democracy has failed to live up to democratic ideals because the real voice of the people has been smothered by elites.[4]

Populists are recognizable by seeing whom they hate and fear. Populist parties can also be identified by looking at the kind of people who support them, even though their support rarely has a single source. Populist parties are typically coalitions of several different kinds of voter. Their voters are characterized by the anti-elitism already noted, by radical nationalism, and by fundamentalist or conservative religious views.

Nationalism has been a consistent source of populist support, and populists derive much of their charisma, energy, and support from it. They "prioritize the culture and interests of the nation, and promise to give voice to a people

---

3. Mudde, "The Populist Zeitgeist," 546; https://budapestbeacon.com/full-text-of-viktor-orbans-speech-at-baile-tusnad-tusnadfurdo-of-26-july-2014/.

4. Mudde, "The Populist Zeitgeist," 543; Müller, *What Is Populism?*, 6; Canovan, "Trust the People!," 2; 9; 15; 7; 8 Galson, *Anti-Pluralism*, 37; Canovan, "Trust the People!," 3; Müller, *What Is Populism*, 3.

who feel that they have been neglected, even held in contempt" by globalist elites who look down on nationalism as the preserve of provincial bumpkins. Populists reject all transgressions of national boundaries, whether by immigrants and refugees, the European Union, or international trade, all seen as impositions by a liberal elite.[5]

In many countries, the support populism draws from nationalism has come in tandem with support from conservative forms of religion. In India, populists wave the banner of Hinduism; in the West, of Christianity, whether Catholic, Protestant, or both; in Israel, of Judaism. A common problem for both populists and liberals in many places in the West has been the rise of Islamic fundamentalism, but in the Muslim world it has often been identified with populist movements.[6] For populists, "our way of life" is often equated with a certain kind of religion as much as with the nation. Thus old Enlightenment fears of religious fanaticism have come back to haunt liberals. In the West, populist politics have become a zone where a certain kind of Catholic, a certain kind of Protestant, and a certain kind of Jew find common ground with secularists and unbelievers. Populism has become the center of an overlapping consensus of illiberalisms, anti-elitist, nationalist, and religious in origin, the rival of the liberal overlapping consensus appealed to by Rawls. The populist consensus challenges the whole basis of liberal ideals and values: pluralism, diversity, and cosmopolitanism chief among them. It assaults the liberal political and economic establishment and especially liberal culture / morality, attempting to overthrow all three pillars of liberalism.[7]

Finally, as with all would-be Samsons intent on overthrowing the pillars of the establishment, it must not be overlooked that populists display a hostile attitude toward institutional structures. The populism that began to reemerge in the late twentieth century and has dominated liberal fears in the twenty-first opposes many of the characteristic political structures created by liberals. Since the nineteenth century, liberals have favored fragmented, legally constrained forms of power to prevent illiberal takeovers. To prevent revolution and reaction, liberals had tried to moderate democracy, at least in its most direct and participatory forms: constitutions were intentionally difficult to change, the suffrage was restricted to a minority of propertied men, and the

5. Eatwell and Goodwin, *National Populism*, ix.

6. It will be interesting to see if the rise of Pentecostal Christianity in sub-Saharan Africa eventually provides support for populism there.

7. On Rawls, see chapter 10.

courts were not subject to the voters except in the most indirect ways. If later liberals abandoned limited suffrage, the most direct way of limiting democracy, they invented others, such as central banks largely insulated from popular pressure. Populism is a democratic reaction against this liberal legalism. Insofar as all three pillars of liberalism have been embodied in institutions as various as the World Bank, the United Nations, and constitutional courts, populists have found occasions for attacking all of them because they associate all of them with liberalism.[8]

Understanding the Rise of Populism

Although its role as liberals' leading fear is unique to the twenty-first century, populism has a history. Like its definition, however, that history is disputed. Populism has been given historical origins as diverse as the Jacksonians in 1830s America, Bonapartists in the French Second Empire of Napoleon III, and the American People's Party, also known as the Populist Party, prominent in the 1890s. It is a recurrent phenomenon, "erupting whenever significant sections of 'the silent majority' feel that the 'elite' no longer represents them." Populism appeared in force after WWI, when movements with strong populist elements flourished: fascism and Nazism in Europe, Huey Long's followers in the United States, Cardenas in Mexico, and Vargas in Brazil. After the Second World War populism seemed to be in abeyance (with a few exceptions such as Peronist Argentina), frozen out by the Cold War, which generally forced populists to ally with liberals against the common Communist enemy, and accept a subordinate position. This historical circumstance inclined liberals to think that populism was merely a passing childhood disease of democracy rather than a chronic problem. It was one of the developments that encouraged the liberals of the end of ideology movement in their views.[9]

By contrast, one of the developments that brought down the end of ideology movement was the return of populism in the 1960s. In the 1960s and '70s, populists were often found in the New Left and the counterculture; although right-wing populism was also present, for example George Wallace in the United States and Jean-Marie Le Pen in France, it did not dominate. Liberals gave left populism only passing attention, possibly because it was easy for liberals to see the New Left as just another bunch of Reds like the ones they were

8. Eatwell and Goodwin, *National Populism*, xi–xii; Müller, *What Is Populism?*, 94–95.
9. Mudde, "The Populist Zeitgeist," 562–563.

used to defeating. Only in the 1980s and 1990s when populism started to become a leading force on the right did it become central to liberal fears. However, the prominence of right-populist movements in the twenty-first century should not obscure the fact that left populism continues to exist, and outside North America and Europe has been more successful. Even in Europe, the left populists of Syriza briefly ruled Greece, and the Spanish left-populist party Podemos has entered the government. But it is in Latin America where left-populist governments have succeeded most. Hugo Chavez's regime in Venezuela is the clearest example, along with the governments of Evo Morales in Bolivia and Rafael Correa in Ecuador. Right populism, however, also exists in Latin America, as shown by the example of Bolsonaro in Brazil. In the United States, the presidency of Donald Trump has concentrated attention on the right-populist spectrum, but there exists an episodically influential left-populism, represented by the Occupy Wall Street and Black Lives Matter movements. Because the discussion below concentrates on populism in Europe and the United States, it focuses on right populism, although much of what is said about the right applies equally to the left.

By 2020 it could plausibly be claimed that "the rise of populism is the most fundamental challenge to the postwar order since the fall of the Berlin Wall and the collapse of the Soviet Union." Why has populism become the leading fear of liberals around the globe and menaced the survival of liberal democracy? Tocqueville's discussion of the problems of maintaining a "democratic republic," that is a liberal democracy, can be usefully applied here. The most important reason for America's success, Tocqueville argued, was not laws or historical circumstances, but "habits and mores." The most important changes that have led populism to become the great rival of liberalism in the early twenty-first century have been changes in Western mores. Here the many different explanations for why populism has flourished since 1990 can be boiled down to one: cultural alienation.[10]

The current wave of populism is the result of cultural alienation caused by changes in mores at both the bottom and the top of Western and some non-Western societies (e.g., India). Populism is the spearhead of an overlapping illiberal consensus, a consensus of those who have suffered fear and pain that they blame on liberals. The consensus extends from nationalists, to the rela-

10. Mudde, "The Populist Zeitgeist," 548; 541; Galston, *Anti-Pluralism*, xxi; Tocqueville, *Democracy in America*, 1:452. He repeats himself at 1:494–495, attributing the survival of "democratic institutions" in America to "circumstances, laws and mores"; *Democracy*, 1:466.

tively deprived, to traditional religious believers (often the same people), all those who feel culturally alienated for one reason or another. There is "a profound sense of loss" among the supporters of populism, one that combines both cultural and economic factors that are often geographically concentrated. Rural areas, small towns, and industrial centers have been losing in terms of population, economics, and cultural and political influence. They have been the victims of what might be described as an "hourglass culture," in which a certain portion of the population is pinched not just in material terms but even more in terms of social esteem and status.[11] The problems posed by cultural alienation have been multiplied by the geographical and sociological concentration of those who have experienced it. But populist cultural alienation cannot be understood by looking only at populists: changes in the culture of those who support liberalism have also played an important role. This is why it is as important to examine the attitudes of those whom populists describe as the liberal elite as those of the supporters of populism.[12]

For example, nationalism is one of the hallmarks of the supporters of populism. Nationalism's return to prominence since the fall of the Berlin Wall in 1989 has been one of the main expressions of the rise of populism in the twenty-first century. But to understand the role nationalism has played in the rise of populism, the cosmopolitan internationalism, both perceived and real, of late twentieth and early twenty-first-century liberalism must be taken into account. It is the cultural alienation caused by the combination of these two factors that has been crucial to populist success. Nationalism is both a cultural affirmation by populists and an expression of cultural alienation from globalist liberalism.

In the early twenty-first century, populist nationalisms are on the rise everywhere. The cosmopolitan expectations of the Enlightenment and of Kant, cherished again by many liberals after WWII, have once again been disappointed. Some of the reasons for this are explored by the social psychologist

11. This is the opposite of what Rawls had in mind when imagining "political liberalism." Newton's "Second Law of Sociology" has been at play: for every bit of progress for some under liberal auspices, there has been an equal and opposite reaction of loss among others. Newton is to be modified by Einstein's "theory of sociological relativity": the loss is relative to the perspective of the observer, and accordingly may be either greater or less than the progress achieved.

12. Another way of looking at cultural alienation is through the lens of a decline in rational deference to institutions on the part of much of the population, entailing a loss of legitimacy. On this see Marshall, *Political Deference in a Democratic Age.*

Jonathan Haidt in "When and Why Nationalism Beats Globalism." According to Haidt, as nations grow richer, their values evolve in predictable ways. They move away from traditional and religious-based values toward "secular rational" values. They no longer stress economic and personal security, and instead emphasize self-expression. They "prioritize freedom over security, autonomy over authority, diversity over uniformity, and creativity over discipline." Since the world is continuing to grow richer, if one were an economic determinist this would prove that liberalism's triumph over populism was predestined: ever more people would espouse liberal values. Many liberals still think along these lines. But even if this were true, it would not exclude a backlash, potentially catastrophic in scope.[13]

Haidt sees such a backlash in progress. Not everyone perceives liberal values as good, and some people respond in illiberal ways to the spread of liberalism because they perceive liberalism as a threat.[14] It is not threats to their personal economic well-being that make them react. Populists feel that liberalism is threatening the culture of their group / society / nation, and they see growing diversity, or even the possibility of diversity, as an attack on their group, the "real" Americans, or Poles, or Swedes. In particular, increasing immigration, or even the threat of increased immigration, brings on this protective reflex.[15] As a result, "intolerance is not a thing of the past it is very much a thing of the future" as well as the present. Populists see those who support diversity as at best fools, but more likely traitors.[16]

In the populist imagination, growing globalization is identified with liberalism. Thus the growing success of globalization has brought about growing and increasingly passionate populist nationalism—its antithesis, as Hegel might have put it. Populism is likely to flourish precisely because of the relative success of globalization. Cosmopolitanism is in conflict with nationalism. In principle there is nothing illiberal about the coexistence of cosmopolitan

13. Haidt, "When and Why Nationalism Beats Globalism."

14. A point repeatedly stressed by Goodhart, *The Road to Somewhere*, vii, 2–3, 9, 12.

15. An imagined threat can substitute for a real one, as Polish or Hungarian attitudes toward Muslim immigration show, in a manner reminiscent of nineteenth-century Norwegian liberals' fear of Catholics. See chapter 5.

16. Haidt, "When and Why Nationalism Beats Globalism"; Christian Welzel, cited in Haidt, "When and Why Nationalism Beats Globalism," 2. See also Mudde, "The Populist Zeitgeist," 547; Eatwell and Goodwin, *National Populism*, 132, 146; Goodhart, *The Road to Somewhere*, 47, 216, 218. The applicability of this explanation to Latin American and non-Western countries needs further investigation.

and nationalist values in the same society—what could be better proof of pluralism? But there are strict limits to this argument, and therefore to what liberals can offer populists. When populists want recognition for their national culture and their values, pluralist liberals may be able to offer it. But when populists take a monist position, insisting that their definition of the people is the only one, that their identity is the only acceptable identity, liberals cannot assimilate populism.

As for whose notion of identity is likely to win, the monist populist version or the multilayered liberal one, this was a fight from which Isaiah Berlin himself was not sure liberals would emerge victorious. He quoted Schumpeter: "To realize the relative validity of one's convictions and yet stand for them unflinchingly is what distinguishes a civilized man from a barbarian," but not enough people, in Berlin's view, were civilized. For populists, by contrast, Schumpeter's casual identification of civilization with pluralist cosmopolitanism and populism / nationalism with barbarism is a good example of the problem with liberalism. Populist nationalism is not willing to live with cosmopolitanism, and on the liberal side some of the more cosmopolitan liberals want nothing to do with any form of nationalism beyond loyalty to a soccer team. Populism's success is evidence that the alliance between liberalism and sane, moderate nationalism characteristic of the short nineteenth century (see chapter 4) is once again in trouble. Populists reject it and—a new element compared to the nineteenth century, resulting from changes at the top of society—cosmopolitan liberals do too. Those liberals who want to renew the alliance between liberalism and moderate nationalism face a difficult fight.[17]

There is one aspect of twenty-first-century populist nationalism, however, that might help liberal patriots reconcile with populists. At first glance, the populist nationalism of circa 2020 might appear to be just a revival of the radical nationalism of the fin de siècle and the early twentieth century. But it differs in one very significant way: the populist nationalism of the twenty-first century is expressed above all domestically. It is not internationally aggressive. There is an enormous difference between wanting to send people of Algerian origin

17. Schumpeter cited in Berlin, *Liberty*, 217, see also 207, where the demand for freedom by Mill and Constant is described as far beyond the desires of most people. Liberal "patriots" include Yael Tamir, *Liberal Nationalism*; Yoram Hazony, *The Virtue of Nationalism*; and Stephen B. Smith, *Reclaiming Patriotism in an Age of Extremes*. For an incisive critique of this effort, made almost before it began, see Canovan, "Patriotism Is Not Enough," 413–432.

back to Algeria and wanting to conquer Algeria. This nevertheless seems a slim reed for liberal patriots to grasp.[18]

Along with nationalism, another aspect of the cultural alienation behind populism is the sense of relative deprivation, of being politically, economically, and morally left behind, felt by a considerable portion of the Western population. The relatively deprived are distributed, if unequally, across all social classes, but are more commonly situated nearer the bottom. They exist everywhere, but they tend to be concentrated in rural areas and provincial towns, and it is these who make up the bulk of populist electoral support. The cultural gap between urban and rural areas has existed for thousands of years: the word "pagan" is derived from the latin *pagani*, meaning people who live in the country, who maintained their polytheism long after the cities became Christian. Today the situation is reversed. Populist territory is the land of churchgoers. Today's rural / urban cultural and religious divide may or may not be as great as that of 300 CE. Nevertheless, evidence suggests that in the early twenty-first century the divide is much greater than in the not-so-distant past, and that it feeds the sense of relative deprivation.[19]

This can be demonstrated by the different ways Americans refer to the once-archetypal town of Peoria, Illinois, population 108,000 in 2020. When Richard Nixon was President of the United States (1968–72), he liked to ask of any particular policy, "will it play in Peoria?" Peoria represented "Middle America," and its values were considered a reliable indicator of the country in general. Today, Peoria is no longer located in Middle America because Middle America no longer exists. Usage of "Middle America" took off around 1940, peaked around 1980, and has declined precipitously since. Where Peoria is located in 2023 is a matter of contention. For populists, it lies in the "Heartland." For liberals, it is in "flyover country," a term that first appeared in the early 1980s and whose usage spiked dramatically between 2000 and the 2020s. Peoria is one of the places that don't exist in the liberal mind, and where liberals never voluntarily stop. For populists, it represents the true nation the liberals despise. Those overflown resent being looked-down upon. Analogs to Peoria can be found in many countries: in Europe, where the fast trains don't stop.[20]

---

18. Putin's 2022 invasion of Ukraine was a sign that if he ever was a populist, he was one no longer. The language used to justify it was that of nineteenth-century and fin de siècle Russian radical nationalism.

19. Galston, *Anti-Pluralism*, 16.

20. Google Ngram; Galston, *Anti-Pluralism*, xvii.

The sense of relative deprivation and the cultural alienation of populism from liberalism is linked to "one of the major fault lines that runs beneath national populism across the West—the educational divide." Those who lack higher education, regardless of income level, feel excluded and alienated. There are a lot of these people. In 2016, those aged between twenty-five and sixty-four without the equivalent of a university degree comprised 66 percent of the population in the European Union and 55 percent in the United States. People without a degree make up a smaller percentage of the population than at any other time in history. It is partly because of this that higher education generates greater resentment: as educational credentials became both more widespread and more important, those without them feel a greater sense of relative deprivation. Emphasis placed on formal education and expertise has devalued knowledge gained from "the school of hard knocks," from ordinary experience, from the "common sense" to which populist politicians regularly appeal. Those whose education was informal and uncertified, even if financially successful, feel disrespected. When education became the "gold standard" of status, self-esteem became unavailable to a large portion of the population. Education was the greatest determiner of whether one voted for Brexit or Trump in 2016. The uneducated, whether American Trump voters, British Brexiteers, or French *gilets jaunes*, feel unrepresented in liberal cosmopolitan policy-making, and unfairly deprived of equal influence with their better-educated peers.[21]

To say that populists feel "unrepresented" is putting the matter mildly. Populist masses feel *oppressed*. They are afraid. Relatively deprived of cultural influence, especially compared to what they feel entitled to, with fewer educational credentials, less political influence, nationalists in a world in which national identity gets short shrift, geographically rooted in a culture dominated by globe-trotting expatriates with fancy degrees, they are fearful of liberalism and resent being excluded from the liberal overlapping consensus by their choices. Liberal pluralism accepts them only as second-class citizens. They are at best tolerated, never equally respected, never equally recognized. Already in the 1990s, and increasingly in the early twenty-first century, many liberals repeat Enlightenment mantras about ignorant fanatics, whether nationalist peasants or Bible-beating preachers. Neither the peasants nor the pastors like it. More than one liberal feminist has pronounced some version of Voltaire's

21. Eatwell and Goodwin, *National Populism*, 24; 106; 283; 108–109; 30–31; Goodhart, *The Road to Somewhere*, 20; https://fivethirtyeight.com/features/education-not-income-predicted -who-would-vote-for-trump/.

écrasez l'infâme against traditional religion: religious orthodoxy has been ex-communicated from liberal circles once willing to respect or even welcome it. The situation is one that would have been familiar to Tocqueville, who saw it in nineteenth-century France and hoped America would provide a counter-example.[22]

While there is nothing to prevent populists from being secular in orientation, and many are (neither Donald Trump nor the Le Pen family are noted for their religious devotion, and left populists are somewhat less likely than right populists to practice traditional religions), it is clear that the sense of relative deprivation felt by populists extends to many adherents of traditional / fundamentalist religious views, who feel that they are looked down upon by godless cosmopolitans. A good example is American populists' recurrent complaints about liberal assaults on the freedom of religion. From the populist perspective, banning the crèche from public buildings at Christmas, or prayer at the opening of a public meeting, is an assault on the freedom of religion. It testifies to a lack of respect. According to Isaiah Berlin, "The lack of freedom about which men or groups complain amounts, as often as not, to the lack of proper recognition." Berlin saw this as a fight over status. In a democratic society, Tocqueville would have added, everyone is entitled to equal status with everyone else. Relatively deprived populists feel they are deprived of the equal status that is their democratic birthright. To add to their sense of injury, populists see equal status being accorded to groups that they do not believe are properly part of the people—immigrants, homosexuals, atheists. This feeling is multiplied by every liberal cultural success—and despite the rise of populism, liberals have been winning the culture wars for decades. Liberal cultural success goes hand in hand with liberal globalization in explaining the rise of populism. The sense that both are inevitable leads to even more populist anger at the liberal elites who support both.[23]

Some liberals and even more socialists like to insist that economic issues, not cultural alienation, are at the root of early twenty-first-century populism.

---

22. Béla Greskovits, "Rebuilding the Hungarian Right," 257–259, is a striking example. On Tocqueville and religion, see Kahan, *Tocqueville, Democracy, and Religion.* It is remarkable that some of the most prominent commentaries on populism fail to discuss the relationship between populism and religion. Eatwell and Goodwin, *National Populism*, 136, see the relationship as only regionally important, but their evidence is dubious.

23. Berlin, *Liberty*, 201, 200.

It is often claimed that populism was the result of the Great Depression of the 1930s or the Financial Crisis of 2007–2008. However, to paraphrase Bill Clinton's 1992 American presidential campaign slogan, "it's *not* the economy," at least not directly (indirectly it is part of the populist sense of relative deprivation). Nigel Farage's populist UKIP (United Kingdom Independence Party) party scored its first major successes in 2014 on the heels of a period of record British economic growth, at least as measured by aggregate GDP. Austria, the Netherlands, Poland, and Switzerland, despite relatively strong economies, have all seen the rise of successful populist parties. Liberal insistence that the economy was all that really mattered possibly caused Remainers to lose the Brexit referendum in 2016, when 60 percent of Leavers thought significant damage to the British economy would be a "price worth paying for Brexit," while the economy was all that Remainers talked about. Money is not the main root of populist feeling. Nevertheless, even if economic grievances are neither a necessary nor a sufficient explanation for the rise of populism, real or perceived economic deprivation has provided populism with energy in many places. Anger over banks getting bailed out in 2008 when "innocent people" lost their homes did nothing to reinforce the legitimacy of liberal democracy, and the real or perceived stagnation of middle-class incomes in many Western countries from 1990 to the 2020s has stoked dissatisfaction with professional classes, that is, liberal elites, who were less subject to it.[24]

The existence of a large number of unhappy, relatively deprived, culturally alienated people has serious consequences for the legitimacy of liberalism, and hence for its continued dominance, if not existence. As Tocqueville put it, "if liberty is ever lost in America, it will be necessary to lay the blame on the omnipotence of the majority that will have brought minorities to despair and will have forced them to appeal to physical force. Then you will see anarchy, but it will arrive as a consequence of despotism." The events surrounding the inauguration of American President Biden on January 6, 2021 are a case in point. Whether liberal governments elected by a majority are actually exercising omnipotence is debatable. From the populist side, so is their majority status: they do not represent a majority of the "people" as defined by populists. What is unquestionable is that populists often feel a sense of desperation. The perceived omnipotence of a minority of Blacks, immigrants, and homosexuals, abetted by traitorous cosmopolitans and other liberal elements, engenders populist

24. Eatwell and Goodwin, *National Populism*, xxv, 4, 6, 8, 35, Galston, *Anti-Pluralism*, xv, xvi.

despair, and the accompanying rage endangers freedom: it gives many people cause to fear. It produces a situation where both sides make the other afraid, which threatens the liberal order. This is not to suggest a moral equivalence between liberals and populists, but only to state the fact of mutual fear.[25]

The cultural alienation that provokes populist anger is also the result of changes among the relatively advantaged. Two kinds of changes have taken place at the top: a change in attitudes or mores, and a relative increase in the number of people who share these attitudes, an increase that has helped produce the backlash noted by Haidt.

In *The Revolt of the Elites and the Betrayal of Democracy*, published in 1995, Christopher Lasch, an American historian originally from the socialist left, attacked the educated professional elite as a group that had betrayed the masses. For Lasch the elites had betrayed "the values, or what remains of them, of the West." "Upper-middle-class liberals . . . fail to reckon with the class dimension of their obsession with health and moral uplift." The elites didn't understand why everyone did not agree with them about the value of self-expression, globalization, immigration, and the embrace of rapid change. In their contempt for the culturally "backward" the elites "find it impossible to conceal their contempt for those who stubbornly refuse to see the light— those who just 'don't get it.' " They "regard the masses with mingled scorn and apprehension"—sentiments, as Lasch did not say, returned with interest, and which testified to the cultural alienation between liberals and populists. Lasch diagnosed the revolution in elite mores that was a prime cause of populist / liberal mutual cultural alienation.[26]

Two decades later, David Goodhart analogously summed up the cultural divide in Britain as the liberal, cosmopolitan, "Anywheres" vs. the populist "Somewheres." In his view the populist Somewheres have not changed nearly as much as the liberal Anywheres. The Somewheres are relatively deprived and more culturally alienated because the Anywheres looking down on them are a larger and more important group than ever before. Precisely because there are so many more of them, their obtrusive cultural domination is that much more provocative to populists, who respond by doubling-down on their anti-elitism.[27]

---

25. Tocqueville, *Democracy*, 1:425.
26. Lasch, *The Revolt of the Elites*, 25, 28–29.
27. Goodhart, *The Road to Somewhere*, passim.

Goodhart updates Lasch's sociology by stressing the extent to which elite liberal Anywheres define themselves by individual achievement. They place "a high value on autonomy, mobility and novelty and a much lower value on group identity, tradition and national social contracts (faith, flag and family)." According to Goodhart, the Anywheres see work as a venue for "individual self-realization." They are comfortable with the idea of meritocracy, hold egalitarian views of race, gender, and sexuality, embrace change and adore diversity—except when it comes to the attitudes of Somewheres, which they regard as irrational or stupid (the conflict over COVID vaccinations 2019–22 is a good example of this).[28] The meritocratic elites are highly urban, and usually got there from somewhere else. The new elites leave home for their education, and rarely end up living near where they grew up. If they do, it is only after having spent considerable time somewhere else. They have created the ERASMUS program in Europe and have made "Study Abroad" a rite of passage at American universities as a means of reproducing themselves. Some commentators have claimed that there is a budding hereditary aristocracy here, but in the early twenty-first century there is still quite a bit of social mobility in this group. It does not matter. Lasch and Goodhart show how the growth of a meritocracy based on education and culture, not just as fact, but as value, has helped give rise to populism. Populists perceive an undemocratic moral unfairness in the distinction between the educated and uneducated, the meritocracy and the rest. This is the essence of the populist rejection of meritocracy.[29]

One should not oversimplify. Many well-educated people are populists, and some of them live in cities. Particularly when populists are allied to traditional conservatives, the picture is complicated. Whatever the traditionalist faction of the Catholic Church may be, it is not uneducated. However, to stress the social openness of the Anywhere meritocratic elite or to point to the

---

28. Goodhart, *The Road to Somewhere*, 5; 24; 34.

29. The populist case made by Lasch and Goodhart is made even more forcefully in Michael Young's 1958 *The Rise of the Meritocracy*, which invented the English word. The book is a dystopia which culminates in a revolution made by those of average intelligence against the top 20% in IQ. Galston, *Anti-Pluralism*, 34; Lasch, *The Revolt of the Elites*, 79; Goodhart, *The Road to Somewhere*, xiv; Eatwell and Goodwin, *National Populism*, 171; 286. A good example of left-populist rejection of meritocracy is Daniel Markovits, *The Meritocracy Trap: How America's Foundational Myth Feeds Inequality, Dismantles the Middle Class, and Devours the Elite* (New York: Penguin, 2019). On the populist left, meritocracy is further identified as the latest form of capitalism. For how this attitude is typical of intellectuals, see Kahan, *Mind vs. Money*.

existence of people with PhDs who hold conservative cultural views would be to miss the root of populist discontent. Somewheres feel no need for Anywhere culture—they have their own. But they resent the loss of dignity (recognition) and the evident lack of respect from Anywheres for their cultures and their jobs—a prime source of Somewheres' relative deprivation of status and cause of their resentment. The problem is only aggravated by the fact that people with liberal attitudes make up a much greater part of the population than ever before (liberal Anywheres numbered about 25 percent of the UK population in 2010, up from much smaller numbers previously).[30]

Meritocracy, it should be stressed, is not equivalent to liberalism, even if some populists think so. Meritocratic ideas have often been identified with bureaucratic / socialist tendencies that are not friendly to free markets, with the hollowing-out of the moral pillar of liberalism, and with questioning the value of political freedom. Some liberals, from John Stuart Mill to Friedrich Hayek, have always denounced what Mill called *pédantocratie*. In this, a certain strand of twenty-first-century liberalism can find common ground with populists. The relationship of liberalism to rule by bureaucrats who claim to have all the expert knowledge necessary to decide the price and value of everything may well move to the forefront of liberal concerns by the late twenty-first century, should liberalism be fortunate enough to survive the populist challenge. But compared with the illiberalism of the populists, bureaucratic illiberalism provokes considerably less fear among liberals.

The rise of populism, of a new democratic illiberalism, has taken liberals by surprise. That they have been surprised is testimony to the extent of cultural alienation that has taken place, and to liberal inability to hear the populist motors growling across the space that separated the average liberal geographically, socially, and culturally from the average populist voter. But mass demonstrations and elections have brought the din close enough to be heard. Fear of populism has dominated the early twenty-first-century liberal imagination and provoked a wide range of responses.

30. Goodhart, *The Road to Somewhere*, xv; Goodhart, *The Road to Somewhere*, 25; Goodhart, *The Road to Somewhere*, 38–46. Lasch cites R. H. Tawney: "opportunities to rise are no substitute for a general diffusion of the means of civilization," for the "dignity and culture" that are needed by all "whether they rise or not." *The Revolt of the Elites*, 41. For a similar analysis with a divergent conclusion, see Kahan, "And What if Tocqueville Was Wrong?"

Liberal Responses to the Problem of Populism

Populism has forced twenty-first-century liberals to once again confront some old nightmares: religious fanaticism, radical nationalism, and even insurrectionary violence. Since the rise of populism has been accompanied by the renewed salience of earlier liberal fears, it is not surprising that it has provoked similar responses, ranging from calls to limit the impact of universal suffrage,[31] to appeals to supranational institutions or global commerce to tame nationalist passions, or on the contrary attempts to revive the nineteenth-century liberal strategy of co-opting nationalism for liberal purposes. But populism is a new fear and presents new problems that require new solutions. To overcome populism a fourth wave of liberalism, Liberalism 4.0, must find a way to reduce the fears of populists, overcome their cultural alienation, and regain, to the extent that it is possible, legitimacy in their eyes. Where it is not possible, liberals must find a way to defeat them. Unfortunately, to date liberal responses to populism have often been vague, and always ineffective, in both respects. For all their weaknesses, the responses nevertheless demonstrate the continued vitality of the liberal project of building societies in which no one need be afraid.[32]

Populism has performed one salutary task from a liberal point of view: it has reminded liberals of truths they had half-forgotten: of the need for a moral and even religious pillar for liberalism, and the necessity for liberal governments to possess a broad *moral* legitimacy. This means expanding liberalism to include those who feel excluded from the liberal promise of a world without fear: the populists. New political, economic, and moral strategies have to be pursued in the service of greater liberal inclusivity. The thin liberalisms prevalent in the last generation of anti-totalitarian liberalism in the late twentieth century need to be replaced by thick liberalisms capable of operating simultaneously on the

---

31. For language worthy of any nineteenth-century liberal, consider these remarks on Britain's 1975 referendum over membership in Europe by Jean Rey, ex-President of the European Commission: "A referendum on this matter consists of consulting people who don't know the problems instead of consulting people who know them. I would deplore a situation in which the policy of this great country should be left to housewives. It should be decided instead by trained and informed people." Cited in Eatwell and Goodwin, *National Populism*, 98. What Rey would have said about Brexit can easily be imagined.

32. The weakness of liberal reaction is noted by Rosanvallon, *Le siècle du populisme*, 81. Rosanvallon's own suggestions are not immune from this criticism.

political, economic, and moral fronts. Over the first two decades of the twenty-first century something along all these lines has been attempted, as yet without success. Liberalism 4.0 remains inchoate at best. Nevertheless, the failed approaches offer hints of future directions to be pursued and paths to be avoided. Whether eventually successful or not, they are part of the history of liberalism, a very much unfinished part.[33]

Conceptually, the relatively easiest if by no means easy means of inclusion advocated by liberals is economic. There have been a multitude of suggestions by twenty-first-century liberals that the solution to populism is to redistribute wealth, through guaranteed minimum incomes, encouraging entrepreneurship, including workers on company boards, giving priority to full employment, and so on. Often a dose of economic nationalism / protectionism, thought to encourage employment, is included in the prescription. This program differs from fin de siècle modern liberalism or post-1968 egalitarian liberalism less in its chosen means than its end. The target is not poverty, as in the fin de siècle, nor even equality, as in the late twentieth century, but relative deprivation of both cash and status, which contribute greatly to the cultural alienation at the heart of populism.

This tactic is especially attractive to American liberals, who often think that their relatively undeveloped welfare state is the root of the problem of populism, forgetting that highly developed welfare states have not stemmed the rise of populism in countries like the Netherlands or Denmark. Indeed, the growth of the welfare state that has occurred throughout the Western world may have exacerbated the rise of populism by creating a revolution of rising expectations which, when a certain portion of the population feels unsatisfied, helps to power populist claims of elite corruption because if the elite were not corrupt or ineffective, surely the welfare state would have prevented their distress.

More money is not the solution because cultural alienation cannot be overcome with cash. Subsidies do not make rural people more accepting of cultural diversity. Even granting that there is an economic element involved, cultural alienation is not primarily a product of insufficient incomes. Indeed, the rhetoric that accompanies such efforts at economic inclusion often seems better-designed to exacerbate the problem of populism than to contain it. To the injury of low financial reward has been added the insult of withholding "psychic pay," lacking respect for putting food on the table and a roof over the head:

33. Müller, *What Is Populism?*, 99.

to talk about "dead-end jobs" is to devalue those who hold them and to deprive such workers of the respect, dignity, and recognition that only seem attainable by those with a higher education. It is clear that "solving the problem of relative deprivation . . . is not simply a question of trying to raise wages or employment levels, but relates to much wider issues about social integration and respect."[34]

This is not to dismiss the idea that some measures of economic inclusion might help to overcome populism. Reaffirming liberal commitment to an economic safety net as a means of freeing people from fear would probably have some effect. Providing both individuals and groups (the skilled trades, for example) with an increase in psychic pay / recognition might well be useful and would represent a return to the mainstream nineteenth-century liberal practice of considering groups and communities as well as individuals. Finally, a renewed emphasis on the idea of facilitating opportunity for people (whether "equal" or not) may also help the relatively deprived to feel more included. Provided, that is, that such efforts at economic inclusion do not require Somewheres to become Anywheres, to get educated and get out of Peoria.

This last point raises the question of whether some form of liberal meritocratic ideal is still viable. Meritocracy has been associated with liberalism ever since "careers open to talent" became a slogan during the French Revolution. Although many liberals from Mill to Hayek to Rawls have had serious reservations—moral, political, and economic—about meritocracy, it is still closely associated with the liberal ethos, and to the extent liberalism associates moving up with moving out, populists will fight it. For many observers of populism, populist rejection of the elite is equivalent to rejection of meritocracy.

This is to judge the question too narrowly. Meritocracy is more attractive to populists than some of its egalitarian detractors are willing to admit. Populists will never embrace elitism, but this does not mean that they reject the idea that the fastest runner deserves to win the race. Most human beings think they, or at least their children, possess merit. As the American comedian Garrison Keilor put it, speaking of his fictional Minnesota town of Lake Wobegon, "all the children are above average." The dream of merit-based upward social mobility is inherently a democratic dream, provided it can be attained by the plumbers of Peoria, and silencing it does not seem like an effective response to populism.

34. Eatwell and Goodwin, *National Populism*, 283.

At the same time, the historical strand in liberal thought that sees bureaucracy and rule by experts as something to fear can be of use to a prospective fourth-wave liberalism by recasting meritocracy in a form populists can accept as legitimate. The preservation of what the Ordoliberals called a "competitive order" (see chapter 9) in economic life requires limits on mandarin rule and credentialism. Without surrendering a commitment to competition or to merit, liberals may well find it useful to reemphasize these elements. Whether this means, as libertarians or neoliberals might suggest, eliminating many forms of occupational licensing and limiting the scope of administrative rule-making, or as an Ordoliberal might propose, subjecting both to strict legal standards, or somehow making sure that in a pluralist society the plumber's credentials are as respected as the PhD's, remains to be seen. The last point is the one most likely to have an impact on the cultural alienation at the root of populism, but it is also the hardest one to implement.

Political inclusion seems a perhaps more promising way to counter the appeal of illiberal populisms and overcome some of the cultural alienation at their root. Growing political apathy with regard to liberal political institutions and mainstream political parties has accompanied the rise of populism everywhere. The parties and institutions concerned have clearly failed in their liberal democratic task of cultural integration, and liberal attempts to respond to this problem have been ineffective.

This is particularly the case when it comes to nationalism. Nationalism is a cultural problem that has to be approached politically, since that is where nationalism is most a problem. It is an open question whether liberalism can respond to the challenge of populism while taking aboard what fin de siècle liberals called sane nationalism and twenty-first-century liberals sometimes call patriotism. Becoming patriots demands a good deal of sacrifice on the part of liberals who like to think of themselves as citizens of the world. If nationalism / patriotism is not necessarily illiberal, appeasing nationalist populism requires language and policy that potentially make many people—immigrants, for example—afraid. Patriotism as a means of moral inclusion has considerable potential drawbacks from a liberal perspective.[35]

---

35. Tocqueville strongly preferred religion as the moral spring of democracy to patriotism for precisely these reasons. See Kahan, *Tocqueville, Democracy, and Religion*, 109–110. Arguments for and against this course raised by previous generations of liberals have been examined in chapters 5 and 8.

Nevertheless, perhaps patriotic liberals and patriotic populists can find common ground again in the twenty-first century. This argument harks back to the relationship of liberalism to nationalism during the short nineteenth century, when liberals by and large succeeded in identifying nationalism with liberalism. In the early twenty-first century, some liberals argue that liberalism has to "make its peace with national sovereignty," and liberals must not lose "sight of national allegiances while obsessing over transnational ones." At the very least they should not see "the desire to belong to a nation . . . as some sort of pathological perversion" and / or proof of stupidity. Liberal patriotism has the additional merit of being geographically and educationally inclusive. One can be a patriot in London or in Hull, in Peoria or in New York City, and patriotism neither requires a diploma nor excludes those who possess one. Yet such attempts face the same problem liberal nationalists faced in the fin de siècle: it is always easy to get outbid by the illiberals, who are not hindered by liberal constraints. No liberal solution to immigration, for example, has yet convinced populists. If liberals, or two world wars, have by and large convinced populist nationalists to abandon dreams of conquest abroad, they have not had any such success in diverting them from their domestic mission of ethnic cleansing. Liberal patriotism has had little success in overcoming the cultural alienation expressed by populist nationalism.[36]

Nationalism is not the only political arena in which populists feel alienated from elites, and for which liberals have attempted to find solutions. The workings of representative government also loom large on the list of populist grievances. From a populist perspective, liberal political institutions seem rigged in favor of those who have the kind of credentials, experiences, and attitudes they do not. One suggestion has been to turn the concerns of Mill and many other nineteenth-century liberals upside down: nineteenth-centuy liberals worried about finding a place for the educated to exercise influence within a democratic political system. In the early twenty-first century the issue is finding political niches for the uneducated. There have been suggestions for lottery mechanisms for political offices and other devices to "make our political systems more representative of groups that, despite their large size, are largely absent from legislatures and the corridors of power." It is argued that by seeing people who look and sound like them in the corridors of power, populists will

---

36. Galston, *Anti-Pluralism*, xviii, Eatwell and Goodwin, *National Populism*, 169; Eatwell and Goodwin, xxix.

feel a greater sense of belonging. This applies the idea of "role models" long familiar to egalitarian liberals to populists. If it worked for women and people of color, why not for others? These proposals remain purely theoretical with regard to populism, however, and since it is far from clear that this solution has been effective for women or people of color, it is not likely that it will work better for populists. Reforms in political institutions may well have a place in overcoming populist cultural alienation, but the reforms in question have not as yet been convincingly formulated.[37]

Another suggested means of politically including populists has been to find more ways to encourage local, decentralized political participation. Handing power and influence to local populist majorities would include them directly. Alternately, encouraging inclusive techniques such as "town hall" style meetings, or giving more power to local governments, or encouraging local referenda or direct democracy, might have similar results. Such local political changes have a greater impact on the daily life of the average person, and help them feel more included. This is a traditional liberal means to a traditional liberal end, familiar to Tocqueville and Mill. But these solutions also have serious flaws. The problem of fostering a sense of political inclusion is real, but lotteries hardly seem like a serious means of including large numbers of people in the political process. The more people are included by analogous methods, the more government takes on the character of a random sample of public opinion, with all the dangers that plebiscitary despotism poses. Populists will not be satisfied by being given dignified roles without power. As for giving populists power locally, or encouraging more direct local political participation, even in the most decentralized Western countries, Switzerland or the United States, decentralization has not been very effective in containing populism. Populists themselves are not enamored of decentralization when it does not serve their agenda, witness the actions of Orban in Hungary, or of American populists who often deprive cities of autonomy when they control state governments—no freedom for the corrupt! Advocates of decentralizing measures concede this, while arguing decentralization still has important marginal effects. But such measures can have illiberal local consequences—witness French mayors who attempt to ban burkinis from local beaches, and American local library boards who ban books. Empowering populists in local government often comes at the price

---

37. Rosanvallon, *Le siècle du populisme*, 195, 205, Eatwell and Goodwin, *National Populism*, 106–107.

of frightening others, and traditionally liberal institutions have been transformed to serve populist purposes.

The American judicial system is a case in point. In the traditional liberal theory of checks and balances, judicial review limits arbitrary political power, and the court system serves as a check on all forms of majority tyranny, including populism. But the American judicial system has been transformed in a populist direction. On the right, "Originalism" and on the left, the theory of the "living constitution" have been used to make courts into instruments of fear rather than protections from it. The ever-increasing politicization of the American Supreme Court since the 1970s has shown that liberal faith in a judicial model to restrain political power has increasingly less justification.

No one has yet imagined political devices that seem likely to be effective in making groups like the *gilets jaunes*, Brexiteers, or Donald Trump supporters feel included at a price liberals might be willing to pay. The work of creating new political means of overcoming the cultural alienation of populists has barely begun, and Liberalism 4.0 remains a blank page in this respect. Arguably, however, this work is not the most crucial task facing twenty-first-century liberals attempting to reduce populist cultural alienation. The glaring weakness of late twentieth-century liberalism was its moral pillar. Any project to rebuild liberal legitimacy in the twenty-first century must begin with its moral foundations. Populism is not so much the result of a political deficit, or the alleged failure of free markets, as of a moral deficit. Economic and political measures will be necessary to broaden liberal legitimacy among populists, and to help liberalism withstand the challenge of illiberal democracy, but responding to cultural alienation, the biggest contributor to populism, is a moral question, one about values and feeling valued, that requires moral solutions bolder than joining populists in singing the national anthem. The populist rejection of liberalism is a moral rejection—liberals and liberalism are seen as morally corrupt—and in the absence of a strong moral pillar, liberal defenses against this charge fail to carry conviction.[38]

Liberals, as Lasch already argued, must have arguments about "the moral preconditions of a good life" and be prepared to make them—and make sure those preconditions are such that a person without a college degree can satisfy them. To give populists a moral reason to support or even tolerate

38. Müller, *What Is Populism?*, 82; 21; Mudde, "The Populist Zeitgeist," 543–544; Galston, *Anti-Pluralism*, 127; Müller, *What Is Populism?*, 3, 21, Galston, *Anti-Pluralism*, 37; Canovan, "Trust the People!," 11; Mudde, "The Populist Zeitgeist," 561.

liberalism, liberalism must offer populists means of moral perfection that can be pursued in Peoria as well as in Paris. Liberal conceptions of the good must be made attractive or at least comprehensible to populists. This point would have been familiar to Tocqueville, who was not shy about talking about the need to pursue moral greatness in democratic societies, and who made the case for a liberal comprehensive moral understanding of the world. In Tocqueville's view, a liberal democratic society could not survive without such a moral perspective. As Williams put it 150 years later, "Liberals will have to advance to the stronger views that have been part of their Enlightenment legacy, which claim the absolute value of individual autonomy and self-determination against the values of traditionalist cultural homogeneity." To paraphrase Montesquieu, "who would think it? Even pluralism has need of limits": liberals must promote their own values, their own views of the good life, of moral perfection, and human greatness, not just allow others to express theirs. The resulting conflicts will need to be contained within a liberal framework—hence the need for both political and economic pillars to help do that work—but without liberal engagement on the moral front, it is hard to see liberals succeeding in their struggle with populism. Indeed, liberals' refusal to engage, their pretense of a superior neutrality that has no need to engage with, for example, traditional or fundamentalist moral / religious arguments, because liberal understandings of personal autonomy are clearly superior, has only served to alienate populists further.[39]

A revival of liberal perfectionism is necessary to reconcile populists to liberalism, even if attempts so far have been inadequate, just as they have with respect to political and economic remedies for populist cultural alienation. Many populists are perfectionists, often from religious motives. A liberalism that excludes perfectionism excludes them, which is why a liberal government that claims to be morally neutral is anathema to them.

Perfectionism mostly disappeared from liberal language in the late twentieth century, to the point that historians and philosophers have had to struggle for it to be recognized as a form of liberalism at all. Thus the complaints that "liberalism has become passive, planetary, and private. It needs to become passionate, patriotic, and public-minded . . . What modern liberalism seeks—

39. Lasch, *The Revolt of the Elites*, 87; Eatwell and Goodwin, *National Populism*, 171, see also Goodhart, *The Road to Somewhere*, 30; xvi, 180. Williams, *In the Beginning*, 137; 39; Galston, *Liberal Purposes*, 305. Montesquieu, *Spirit of the Laws*, 155. The original reads virtue, rather than pluralism.

and needs to be seen to seek—is not a middle way but a distinct way." And it is surely the case, as the American liberal perfectionist philosopher William Galston wrote, that "Liberalism contains *within itself* the resources it needs to declare and to defend a conception of the good and virtuous life."[40]

A promising if flawed example of a liberal perfectionist response to populism can be found in the work of Joseph Raz, who thought of himself as reviving Millite liberalism. He identified freedom with the ideal of individual autonomy, but his was a perfectionist vision of autonomy. For Raz, pushpin was not as good as poetry, and autonomy was only valuable if people used it to pursue worthwhile, if diverse, ideals and relationships. This was an old liberal view, held by many nineteenth-century liberals, but so long abandoned that when Raz announced it, his perfectionism appeared to be a departure from liberalism. Raz argued that liberalism required liberals to identify, and liberal governments to support, morally worthy ideals and cultures. He rejected the view that promoting good lives was not part of the government's job: liberal governments should never be morally neutral. Governments could and should promote liberal values and practices and discourage illiberal ones. Even if the liberal vision of autonomy meant the government must protect people's right to pursue "immoral or ignoble" ends, even if it must tolerate racists rather than imprison them, the government was free, indeed duty-bound, to discourage racism. Liberalism had to make clear that it had a moral agenda.[41]

Raz laid the foundation for what might be called a liberal intolerance, which brought with it complications faced by nineteenth-century liberalisms. He raised the question in its sharpest form: "Can coercion be used to break up [illiberal] communities, which is the inevitable by-product of the destruction of their separate schools, etc.?" In response Raz amended Mill's Harm Principle. In Mill's version, "the only purpose for which power can be rightfully exercised over any member of a civilized community, against his will, is to prevent harm to others. His own good, either physical or moral, is not a sufficient warrant." In Raz's version, harm to anyone's autonomy, including their own, was sufficient warrant for coercive intervention because autonomy was an essential element of any good life. However, respect for the autonomy of individuals and groups meant refraining from well-meaning manipulation ("libertarian paternalism") as an affront to an individual's independence. One

---

40. Gopnik, *A Thousand Small Sanities*, 221, 223; Galston, *Liberal Purposes*, 304.

41. Norman, "The Autonomy-Based Liberalism of Joseph Raz," 151; Raz, *Morality*, 367; 417; 415; 416; 108, 136; 162, 417.

must provide the "background conditions" that enabled a person to choose autonomy, one could not force people to give up a traditional religion which limited the goods that were available to them by limiting their adherents' freedom to choose: people could not be compelled to be free / autonomous. The idea of autonomy meant that both groups and individuals had rights that could not be violated.[42]

This sounds, despite the rights granted the illiberal, as if it made the state the arbiter of what was morally valuable and produced a satisfying life. That was not Raz's intention. Raz adopted the liberal view that salvation could only come from civil society. It was never the state that should define morality. "The fact that the state *considers* anything to be valuable or valueless is no reason for anything. Only it being valuable or valueless is a reason." Even if it was government's function to take "measures which encourage the adoption of valuable ends and discourage the pursuit of base ones." it was not the government's place to decide what was valuable and what was base. Autonomy could only be generated by individuals and groups, not the state.[43]

Raz's vision of liberal perfectionism thus laid out a moral program of both carrots and sticks. The carrot was the recognition of the moral value of Peoria and the lives people lived there, the recognition that traditional religion, traditional communities could offer satisfying lives to people who were free to choose them and whose choices had to be respected. The stick was the limits placed on this recognition. The illiberal would be tolerated, not approved, and if they went too far, their autonomy would be curbed for the sake of their own and above all their children's autonomy. Education and insistence on the right of exit were the means.

It may be doubted whether the populists of Peoria would be willing to accept toleration in lieu of endorsement, and thus a morally second-class status. Raz's liberal perfectionism is, however, a step forward in that it puts populists and liberals in the same moral arena. Populists would at least know that liberals had convictions, instead of despising them as people without any morals at all, at best relativists, at worst pure hedonists. Liberals would have to admit that the people of Peoria were as authentic in their search for moral improvement as the habitués of any Paris café. The liberal perfectionism of Raz or others is potentially attractive to Peoria, and to many who support

---

42. *Morality*, 156–157, 377; 423; Mill *CW*, 18:223; *Morality*, 412–417; 420; 422; 423, 412.

43. Raz, *Ethics in the Public Domain*, 36; 54–55; 120; *Morality*, 420; 378–379; 407–408; 258; 262.

populism from religious motivations because many populists are perfectionists. But it seems unlikely that Raz's liberal intolerance would lead to a society
in which no one need be afraid. It seems more a prescription for combat than
for compromise.

It is not yet clear what, if any, liberal perfectionist moral solution to the
problem of making liberalism legitimate in populist eyes might be effective. In
any event it is a path that relatively few liberals have taken in the first decades
of the twenty-first century, although there seems to be some movement in this
direction. A return to perfectionism in some new form offers an opportunity
for an effective liberal response to populism, but there is no actual example of
one, at least none whose effectiveness has been demonstrated.

Toward Liberalism 4.0

The argument throughout this book has emphasized the importance of all
three pillars of liberalism, restoring to the moral / religious pillar its traditional
parity with politics and economics. The point has been partly to show its role
in the historical development of liberalism, which has frequently been neglected or underemphasized, and partly to suggest why moral arguments will
have a special role to play in the creation of Liberalism 4.0. It is crucial to respond to populism morally, without neglecting political and economic solutions, and liberalism is capable of doing so. However, there may be limits to
the effectiveness of any liberal response. The problem is that populists fear
liberalism in all its forms: liberal politics, liberal economics, and liberal morals. The liberal project of creating a society where none need be afraid fright-
ens those who think that some people and / or some groups ought to be afraid.
That some people fear a liberal freedom is not a criticism of freedom, nor of
liberalism, nor is it a new problem. But to concede to the illiberal the power
to make others afraid is not a liberal option, and no other is likely to satisfy
some of them.

Liberals must find a solution that will prevent the illiberal from making
others afraid without giving the illiberals themselves avoidable causes of fear.
To the extent that the illiberal consensus led by populists demands respect for
Peoria and recognition for Peoria's religion, liberals can and should make room
for them. When populists demand that the Gay Pride parade in New York City,
or in Peoria itself, be cancelled, they cannot. Liberals must give populists a
voice and a vote, but not a veto. Yet it is highly unlikely that, as some have

suggested, the illiberal will be grateful for the privilege, and therefore regard liberal regimes as legitimate.[44]

It is always darkest before the dawn. The illiberal will be with us always, as they always have been. It was not by eliminating religious fanaticism that proto-liberals put an end to the Wars of Religion; not by eliminating revolutionaries and reactionaries that the first wave of liberals created liberal government during the short nineteenth century; not by eradicating poverty that the second wave of liberalism solved the social question in the fin de siècle. The de facto elimination of totalitarianism in the second half of the twentieth century may be a bad model for twenty-first-century liberals: it required enormous bloodshed. Reducing and limiting fears, not eliminating them, has been the usual liberal method in the past. Liberalism 4.0 needs to reduce and limit the problem of populism, acknowledging that it is unlikely to be able to solve it. Piecemeal, partial solutions may be the only ones available to making Peoria feel less deprived compared to New York, Poitiers less excluded by Paris. Finding new grounds to make a sufficient number of populists feel sufficiently included to support or tolerate a liberal society is an urgent task. Liberals can only defeat populists by presenting an alternative that can be supported by a majority and tolerated by most of the rest. For the remainder, as in their own ways Williams and Raz both recognized, liberals must be willing and able to refuse to tolerate an intolerant minority.

In building a fourth-wave liberalism, liberals have good reason to reflect on many of the layers of previous liberal thought. Understanding the problems liberals have faced in the past and their solutions to those problems is relevant to the different but not entirely dissimilar problems liberals face today. There are many possible solutions to be found in liberalism's history, especially that of the short nineteenth century: diligent mining has already begun, and the history presented here is intended to further that effort. History does not repeat itself, but this does not mean it is devoid of lessons. Many things are very different today than they were in 1830, but not all things, and the differences can be as instructive as the similarities. Understanding liberalism for what it is and has always been, the struggle for a world in which no one need be afraid, is crucial for understanding the situation in which it finds itself today.

In conclusion, the liberal project of freedom from fear cannot be understood in the abstract. It only takes on meaning in the context of the particular fears liberals have addressed in different times and places. Each wave of liberalism

---

44. For the suggestion, see Galston, *Anti-Pluralism*, 118n13.

responds to the fear of its time. These fears have structured the layers and patterns that characterize the oyster of liberal thought. In the beginning, the fear of despotism and religious persecution concerned proto-liberals ("proto" because the word liberalism had not yet been invented as a political term). The first wave of liberalism, Liberalism 1.0, began in the nineteenth century, an era when liberals feared revolution and reaction above all, and those fears structured the liberalism of the period. In the fin de siècle, during the second wave of liberalism, Liberalism 2.0, modern liberals saw poverty as a fear that could be addressed with the aid of the state, and classical liberals rejected that conclusion, resulting in a great schism among liberals. After WWI a third wave of liberalism, Liberalism 3.0, focused on the struggle against totalitarianism, whether fascist, communist, or more diffuse in origin. In the twenty-first century, a fourth wave of liberalism, Liberalism 4.0, still struggles to take shape in response to populism. The previous waves of liberalism can provide resources for that effort.

Some of those resources are summarized by the three pillars of liberalism: freedom, markets, and morals, or politics, economics, and religion / morality. Yet although the three pillars have been central to liberalism from the beginning, throughout the history of liberalism there have been liberals who have chosen to abandon one or more of them—an example of the contradictions characteristic of liberalism. While liberalism has often been identified with diversity and pluralism, there has also been a monist strand in liberalism. The stronger that strand, often the thinner the arguments for liberalism, and the weaker its conclusions.

But it would be a mistake to tell the story of liberalism as a simple history of decline from three-pillared strength to single-pillar weakness. Liberals who prefer to stand on one pillar have played important roles in liberalism from its inception, and not necessarily to its detriment. It is because Bentham so single-mindedly focused on the criterion of happiness and the moral equivalence of push-pin and poetry that he could defend homosexuality, for example. Narrowing one's field of vision sometimes enables one to see further and more clearly.

Nevertheless, since WWI, and especially since WWII, the tendency of twentieth-century liberalism to ignore, hollow out, or greatly narrow the moral pillar of liberalism has contributed significantly to liberal weakness, undermining support for free political institutions as well as for free markets. In particular, the hollowing out or outright elimination of the moral pillar of liberal argument has added greatly to the difficulty of finding effective liberal responses to populism.

Another reason liberals have found it difficult to respond to populism is the view that liberalism should only take individuals into account, not groups. But for most of its history liberalism included the fears of groups as well as individuals within its purview, including over time religious sects, social classes, women, ethnic groups, and oppressed nationalities. The importance of thinking in collective as well as individual terms was clear to most liberal thinkers and actors in the short nineteenth century, and many thereafter. In every period and every context, some and sometimes most liberals have mixed concern for the freedom of the individual with concern for the freedom of groups. Historically the groups that benefited from liberal concern varied, and women, people of color, sexual minorities, certain religious groups, etc., did not always have their fears taken into account. The story of the expansions and contractions over time of the circle of fear is central to the history of liberalism.

After WWI there was a decline in the importance most liberals assigned to groups rather than individuals. The methodological individualism native to certain liberal economic theories led to an overall narrowing of perspectives. Often all good was attributed to the individual, all evil and oppression to the group, the special interest, the party, the faction. As might be expected, such one-sided views in the long run failed as both descriptions of reality and prescriptions for liberal success. The rise of populism has helped redirect liberals' attention to groups.[45]

To ward off their fears and further their hopes, liberals, even those who want to build a welfare state or an egalitarian social system, have ultimately relied on civil society as the source of legitimation, and seen it as the place in which human goods and happiness are ultimately determined. This has been a consistent theme in liberalism, even if it has waxed and waned in prominence over time, as the struggle between modern and classical liberals during the fin de siècle showed. For liberals, the state is never the source of salvation, and never constitutes the ultimate reference by which to judge human progress. Civil society is made up of individuals and groups. What matters is their political freedom, their economy, their morality and religion. It is the fears of individuals and of groups with which liberals are concerned. Hence liberalism is never and can never be about the state, except when it is a ques-

45. For example, a recent call for a new liberal understanding of elections endorses the abandonment of Benthamite individualism in favor of a Madisonian perspective on politics as the domain of factions and groups. See Achen and Bartels, *Democracy for Realists*.

tion of being afraid of it. Civil society is the source of liberal hope. In building Liberalism 4.0 in response to populism, it is civil society on which a solution must be based.

Although liberalism exists as a response to fear, hope is as central to liberalism as fear. While liberal fears are eternal, that is to say that despite changes over time there has always been *something* liberals fear, and always will be until utopia is reached, so are liberal hopes. Hence liberalism always has a utopian element. This is why liberalism has so often been referred to as the "party of progress." There is always something liberals think they can do about fear, whether it is to write a constitution or to build or dismember the welfare state. Liberal fears strike the eye first, but it would be a mistake to overlook the utopian element even in relatively pessimistic liberals like Tocqueville who, after all, endorsed the possibility of "democratic greatness."

Fear is to negative freedom as hope is to positive freedom—always recognizing that there is some overlap between the two. Individual liberals have often advocated for both negative and positive freedom, for freedom from and freedom to, against coercion and for self-mastery, motivated by both fear and hope. Logically distinct, in most liberal thought negative and positive freedom are rarely separated very far. This is a fundamental reason why liberalism has been the party of (useful) contradictions. It has often gotten into difficulty when it tried to be too consistent, yet it has been consistently tempted in that direction. This is nowhere more evident than in the contrast between liberal utilitarianism and liberal perfectionism, often correlated with negative and positive freedom. Philosophically hostile to one another, in practice utilitarianism and perfectionism are often found together in liberal thought and practice in the nineteenth century and the fin de siècle. Separating them was usually the sign of a near-sighted, one-pillar liberalism. One aspect of the decline in the importance or breadth of the moral pillar in post–WWI liberalism was a decline in liberal perfectionism that would have greatly disheartened John Stuart Mill and Tocqueville, and has been a vulnerability in liberalism's struggle with populism. Perfectionism has made something of a comeback in thinkers such as Raz at the end of the twentieth century, as part of attempts to renew emphasis on the moral arguments for liberalism, but it has yet to return to its former prevalence. If Liberalism 4.0 is to succeed, however, it will need a strong perfectionist as well as utilitarian basis. Peoria must be paid: it must be respected in economic terms and in terms of political influence. Liberalism, as usual, must have a utilitarian element. Peoria must also feel itself to be on a path of moral uplift, an autonomous moral path that is equally respected. Liberalism, to persuade and to succeed, must have a perfectionist element.[46]

In summary, liberalism has historically been based on four fears, three pillars, and hope. Proto-liberalism feared religious fanaticism; Liberalism 1.0 feared revolution / reaction; Liberalism 2.0 feared poverty; and Liberalism 3.0 feared totalitarianism. In all periods, liberalism has been concerned with the fears of groups as well as individuals. The three pillars of liberalism, sometimes honored in the breach, have been freedom, markets, and morals. Liberals of all kinds and periods have been sustained by the hope of a world in which no one need be afraid, and they have founded their hopes on civil society.

The history of liberalism recounted here is a history of liberal problems and of liberal solutions to those problems. It is by no means inclusive of all liberal fears, or hopes, or problems. Many readers will be able to name several that in their view ought to have been included. Many of them will be right. It is notably a history missing important geography: the fears and the issues and individuals used to explore them have been American, British, French, and German. Yet liberalism was the first global ideology, and the picture presented here may require modification when liberalism is examined elsewhere. The liberalisms of Latin America, North and sub-Saharan Africa, the Middle East, and Asia may have differed in both content and chronology. Anti-colonialism and nationalism have had very different relationships to liberalism in those places, motivated by different fears. To parrot the usual academic conclusion, more research is necessary.

What is said in chapter 1 about definitions of liberalism is true of this book as a whole: its illocutionary intentions are of four kinds: is, ought, explanation, and contradiction. This incomplete history attempts to describe what liberalism is and has been; to say something about what liberalism ought and ought not to be; to explain liberalism's changes and continuities over time; and to contradict many past and present accounts of all of these. Whether or not it has been successful in fulfilling one intention is not necessarily relevant to another.

To the extent that this history is meant to contribute to the search for means of renewing liberalism in the twenty-first century, helping to formulate Liberalism 4.0, there is an element of treasure-hunting, a search for what Michael Oakeshott called a practical rather than an historical past. By reemphasizing

---

46. To the point that people have to be reminded that it was once common for liberals to be perfectionists. See Lefebvre, "Liberalism and the Good Life," 153.

elements liberalism has recently neglected, but did not neglect in the past, today's liberals can learn something useful today. But attempting to create a fourth-wave liberalism is well beyond the scope of a history such as this one. Developing a theory of democratic liberalism as a counter to populism, present and future, will have to await another occasion.[47]

This is where this history of liberalism stops, rather than finishes, because liberalism has not yet come to an end. As Tocqueville already pointed out, "I see two distinct roads open at the same time before the men of today . . . The one leads to liberty and the other to servitude." This is the perennial liberal problem, and liberalism, like all living traditions, is permanently engaged in problem-solving. Of course, this is an optimistic way of looking at things. The pessimist might say that faced with populism, liberalism is not making progress, and that liberalism is in crisis, a crisis which it may not survive. In truth, from a liberal perspective every crisis means failure because a crisis is a moment when more people are afraid. But every crisis is also an opportunity to take another step toward a society in which no one need be afraid. Liberal thought and practice are thus called upon to build a fourth-wave liberalism, to be reborn, or else to disappear for the foreseeable future.[48]

Liberalism could die. Populism could win and populists could decide that some people need to be afraid for the sake of the cohesion of the rest. Some liberals might come to the same conclusion for fear of populism, and in doing so abandon their liberalism. If this happens, it will be a poor reflection on human nature in general and Western civilization in particular. But I, for one, am not willing to make that assumption. This history of liberalism is written by a liberal. That is another reason, perhaps the most important, why it is incomplete—because liberalism is still, as it must always be, a work in progress.

47. The treasure-hunting analogy is attributed to Derek Parfit. For Oakeshott, see *Experience and Its Modes*, 102–105, and *On History and Other Essays*.

48. Tocqueville, *Democracy*, 4:1284J.

APPENDIX

THE HISTORY OF LIBERALISM presented is summarized in Tables 1 and 2. They are meant as an outline, not as a complete representation.

TABLE 1. The History of Fear

Chronology	Liberalism	Variations	Fears (cumulative)
European Wars of Religion–Atlantic Revolutions	**Proto-Liberalism**		Religious Fanaticism & Despotism
		American and French Revolutions	
Short Nineteenth Century 1815–1873	**Liberalism 1.0**		Revolution & Reaction
		Mill Dies in 1873	
Fin de Siècle 1873–1914	**Liberalism 2.0**	Modern Liberalism Classical Liberalism	Poverty Modern Liberalism as Socialism
		WWI and Great Depression	
1919–1950	**Liberalism 3.0**	Reconciliation of Modern and Classical Liberalism	Totalitarianism
1950–1968		End of Ideology	
1968–1992		Egalitarian Liberalism Libertarianism Neoliberalism Liberalism of Fear	
		End of Cold War	
2000–	**Liberalism 4.0**	To Be Determined	Populism

TABLE 2. The Historical Pillars of Liberalism

Chronology	Chapter	Pillars	People or Issues
Eighteenth Century	2	All three: freedom, markets, and morals	Montesquieu, Adam Smith
Short Nineteenth Century	3	All three pillars	Kant, Madison, Constant
	4	All three pillars	Macaulay, Tocqueville, Mill
	5	All three pillars	Suffrage, Nationalism, Anti-Catholicism
	6	One pillar (varies)	Bentham (politics), Bastiat (economics), Spencer (morality)
Fin de Siècle through Twentieth Century	7	One pillar: morality	Jane Adams, L. T. Hobhouse, Léon Bourgeois
		One pillar: markets	A. V. Dicey
	8	Varies	Nationalism, the Jewish "problem," Feminism, Imperialism, Friedrich Naumann
	9	Some return to three-pillar argument	Lippman, Hayek, Berlin, Ordoliberalism
	10	One pillar (varies)	Rawls, Nozick, Friedman, Shklar
		Three pillars	Williams
Early Twenty-First Century	11	All three pillars?	Responses to Populism

WORKS CITED

Achen, Christopher H. and Larry M. Bartels. *Democracy for Realists: Why Elections do Not Produce Responsive Government.* Princeton, NJ: Princeton University Press, 2016.

Acton, Lord John Dalberg. *Historical Essays and Studies.* Edited by John Neville Figgis and Reginald Vere Laurence. London: Macmillan, 1907.

Adams, John. Letter, "From John Adams to John Stockdale, 12 May 1793," Founders Online. Washington, DC: National Archives.

Addams, Jane. *Democracy and Social Ethics.* San Bernardino, CA: Feather Trail Press, 2009.

Ageron, Charles-Robert. *L'anticolonialisme en France, de 1871 À 1914.* Paris: Presses Universitaires de France, 1973.

Aiken, Henry David. "The Revolt Against Ideology." In *The End of Ideology Debate,* edited by Chaim Waxman. New York: Funk & Wagnalls, 1969.

Alexander, Jeffrey C. "Tocqueville's Two Forms of Association: Interpreting Tocqueville and Debates over Civil Society Today." *Tocqueville Review* 27, no. 2 (2006): 1–16.

Appleby, Joyce. *Liberalism and Republicanism in the Historical Imagination.* Cambridge, MA: Harvard University Press, 1992.

Arcenas, Claire Rydell. *America's Philosopher: John Locke in American Intellectual Life.* Chicago: University of Chicago Press, 2022.

Armitage, David. "Empire and Liberty: A Republican Dilemma." In *The Values of Republicanism in Early Modern Europe,* edited by Martin van Gelderen and Quentin Skinner, 29–47. Vol. 2 of *Republicanism: A Shared Heritage.* Cambridge: Cambridge University Press, 2002.

———. "John Locke, Carolina, and the 'Two Treatises of Government.'" *Political Theory* 32, no. 5 (2004): 602–627.

Arnstein, Walter L. *Protestant versus Catholic in Mid-Victorian England: Mr. Newdegate and the Nuns.* Columbia: University of Missouri Press, 1982.

Aron, Raymond. *L'Opium des intellectuels.* Paris: Calmann-Lévy, 1955.

———. *The Dawn of Universal History: Selected Essays from a Witness of the Twentieth Century.* Trans. Barbara Bray. New York: Basic Books, 2002.

———. *Le spectateur engagé.* Paris: Le Livre de Poche, 2005.

———. *Liberté et égalité.* Paris: Editions de l'Ecole des Hautes Etudes en Sciences Sociales, 2013.

———. *Essai sur les libertés.* Paris: Calmann-Lévy, 2014.

———. *L'Abécédaire de Raymond Aron,* edited by Dominique Schnapper and Fabrice Gardel. Paris: L'observatoire, 2019.

Atanassow, Ewa and Alan S. Kahan, eds. *Liberal Moments: Reading Liberal Texts*. London: Continuum, 2017.

Audier, Serge. *Léon Bourgeois: Fonder la solidarité*. Paris: Michalon, 2007.

———, ed. "Introduction." In *La pensée solidariste: Aux sources du modèle social républicain*. Paris: Presses Universitaires de France, 2010.

———. *Le Colloque Lippmann: Aux Origines Du "Néo-Libéralisme. Précédé de Penser Le "Néo-Libéralisme*. Lormont: Le Bord De L'eau, 2012.

Bader, Ralf M. and John Meadowcroft. *Robert Nozick*. London: Continuum International, 2010.

Banham, Gary, Dennis Schulting, and Nigel Hems, eds. *The Bloomsbury Companion to Kant*. London: Bloomsbury, 2015.

Barrera, Guillaume. *Les lois du monde: enquête sur le dessein politique de Montesquieu*. Paris: Gallimard, 2009.

Bassermann, F. D. *Stenographischer Bericht über die Verhandlungen des deutschen constituirenden Nationalversammlung zu Frankfurt am Main*. Frankfurt, 1849.

Bastiat, Frédéric. *Economic Harmonies*. Irvington-on-Hudson: Foundation for Economic Education, 1850.

———. "The Law." In *The Collected Works of Frédéric Bastiat. Vol. 1: The Man and the Statesman: The Correspondence and Articles on Politics*. Indianapolis, IN: Liberty Fund, 2011.

———. "The State." In *The Collected Works of Frédéric Bastiat. Vol. 1: The Man and the Statesman: The Correspondence and Articles on Politics*. Indianapolis, IN: Liberty Fund, 2011.

———. "Baccalauréat and Socialism." In *The Collected Works of Frédéric Bastiat. Vol. 2: The Law, The State, and Other Political Writings, 1843–1850*. Indianapolis, IN: Liberty Fund, 2012.

———. "Two Systems of Ethics." In *The Law*, translated by Dennis O'Keeffe and edited by Jacques de Guenin, revised by David M. Hart. Indianapolis, IN: Liberty Fund, 2012.

———. *Economic Sophisms*. Indianapolis, IN: Liberty Fund, 2015.

Bauberot, Jean. *Histoire de la laicité en France*. Paris: Que Sais Je, 2000.

Baum, Bruce and Robert Nichols. *Isaiah Berlin and the Politics of Freedom: "Two Concepts of Liberty" Fifty Years Later*. New York: Routledge, 2013.

Bayly, Christopher. "European Political Thought and the Wider World during the Nineteenth Century." In *The Cambridge History of Nineteenth-Century Political Thought*, edited by Gareth Stedman Jones and Gregory Claeys, 835–863. Cambridge: Cambridge University Press, 2011.

Becchio, Giandomenica and Giovanni Leghissa. *The Origins of Neoliberalism: Insights from Economics and Philosophy*. New York: Routledge, 2016.

Bejan, Teresa M. "Rawls's Teaching and the 'Tradition' of Political Philosophy." *Modern Intellectual History* 18, no. 4 (March 2021): 1058–1079.

Bell, Daniel. *The End of Ideology: On the Exhaustion of Political Ideas in the Fifties*. Cambridge, MA: Harvard University Press, 2000.

Bell, Duncan. "Empire and Imperialism." In *The Cambridge History of Nineteenth-Century Political Thought*, edited by Gareth Stedman Jones and Gregory Claeys, 864–892. Cambridge: Cambridge University Press, 2011.

———. "What Is Liberalism?" *Political Theory* 42, no. 6 (December 2014): 682–715.

Bentham, Jeremy. *An Introduction to the Principles of Morals and Legislation*. Oxford: Clarendon Press, 1823.

———. *The Rationale of Reward*. London: John and H. L. Hunt, 1825.

———. "Constitutional Code" in *The Works of Jeremy Bentham, vol. 8*. Edinburgh: William Tait, 1843.

———. "Panopticon" in *The Works of Jeremy Bentham, vol. 2*. Edinburgh: William Tait, 1843.

———. "Securities Against Misrule" in *The Works of Jeremy Bentham, vol. 8*. Edinburgh: William Tait, 1843.

Bentley, Jr., G. E. "'A Different Face': William Blake and Mary Wollstonecraft." *The Wordsworth Circle* 10, no. 4 (1979): 349–350.

Berlin, Isaiah. *The Power of Ideas*, edited by Henry Hardy. Princeton, NJ: Princeton University Press, 2000.

———. *Enlightening: Letters, 1946–1960*, edited by Henry Hardy and Jennifer Holmes. London: Chatto & Windus, 2009.

———. *The Crooked Timber of Humanity: Chapters in the History of Ideas*, edited by Henry Hardy. Second revised ed. Princeton, NJ: Princeton University Press, 2012.

———. *Liberty*, edited by Henry Hardy. Oxford: Oxford University Press, 2017.

Berlin, Isaiah and Steven Lukes. "In Conversation with Isaiah Berlin and Steven Lukes." *Salmagundi*, no. 120 (Fall 1998): 52–134.

Berlin, Isaiah and Bernard Williams. "Pluralism and Liberalism: A Reply." *Political Studies* 42, no. 2 (1994): 306–309.

Berry, Christopher J. *The Idea of Luxury: A Conceptual and Historical Investigation*. Cambridge, UK; New York: Cambridge University Press, 1994.

Betts, Raymond F. *Assimilation and Association in French Colonial Theory, 1890–1914*. Lincoln: University of Nebraska Press, 2005.

Bevir, Mark, ed. *Modern Pluralism: Anglo-American Debates since 1880*. New York: Cambridge University Press, 2012.

Beyer-Purvis, Amanda. "The Philadelphia Bible Riots of 1844: Contest Over the Rights of Citizens." *Pennsylvania History: A Journal of Mid-Atlantic Studies* 83, no. 3 (2016): 366–393.

Bibby, Andrew Scott. *Montesquieu's Political Economy*. Basingstoke, UK: Palgrave Macmillan, 2016.

Binoche, Bertrand. *Introduction à de l'esprit des lois de Montesquieu*. Paris: Presses Universitaires de France1998.

Blease, Walter Lyon. *A Short History of English Liberalism*. London: Adelphi Terrace, 1913.

Bonefeld, Werner. "Freedom and the Strong State: On German Ordoliberalism." *New Political Economy* 17, no. 5 (2012): 633–656.

Borutta, Manuel. *Antikatholizismus Deutschland und Italien im Zeitalter der Europäischen Kulturkämpfe*. Göttingen: Vandenhoeck & Ruprecht, 2011.

Botting, Eileen Hunt. "Wollstonecraft in Europe, 1792–1904: A Revisionist Reception History." *History of European Ideas* 39, no. 4 (2013): 503–527.

———. *Wollstonecraft, Mill & Women's Human Rights*. New Haven, CT: Yale University Press, 2016.

Boucher, David. "'Sane' and 'Insane' Imperialism: British Idealism, New Liberalism and Liberal Imperialism." *History of European Ideas* 44, no. 8 (2018): 1189–1204.

Bouglé-Moalic, Anne-Sarah. *Le vote des françaises: Cent ans de débats, 1848–1944*. Rennes: Presses Universitaires de Rennes, 2012.

Bourgeois, Léon. *Solidarité*. Cork: Primento Digital Publishing, 2015.

Bowman, Sam. "Coming Out as a Neoliberal." *Adam Smith Institute Blog* (October 11, 2016).

Brandt, Hartwig. *Landständische Repräsentation im Deutschen Vormärz: Politisches Denken in Einflussfeld des Monarchischen Prinzips*. Berlin: Neuwied, 1968.

Breuilly, John. "On the Principle of Nationality." In *The Cambridge History of Nineteenth-Century Political Thought*, edited by Gareth Stedman Jones and Gregory Claeys. Cambridge: Cambridge University Press, 2011.

Brubaker, Rogers. *Citizenship and Nationhood in France and Germany*. Cambridge, MA: Harvard University Press, 1998.

Burgin, Angus. *The Great Persuasion: Reinventing Free Markets since the Depression*. Cambridge, MA: Harvard University Press, 2012.

Burrow, J. W. *Evolution and Society: A Study in Victorian Social Theory*. London: Cambridge University Press, 1966.

———. *Whigs and Liberals: Continuity and Change in English Political Thought*. Oxford: Oxford University Press, 1988.

Caird, Edward. "The Present State of the Controversy between Individualism and Socialism." In *The British Idealists*, edited by David Boucher. Cambridge: Cambridge University Press, 1997.

Canovan, Margaret. "Trust the People! Populism and the Two Faces of Democracy." *Political Studies* 47, no. 1 (1999): 2–16.

———. "Patriotism Is Not Enough." *British Journal of Political Science* 30, no. 3 (2000): 413–432.

Capaldi, Nicholas. *John Stuart Mill: A Biography*. Cambridge: Cambridge University Press, 2004.

Carlyle, Thomas and Jane Welsh Carlyle. *Collected Letters of Thomas and Jane Welsh Carlyle*. Edited by Charles Richard Sanders and Clyde De L. Ryals. Durham, NC: Duke University Press, 1970.

Castiglione, Dario. "'That Noble Disquiet': Meanings of Liberty in the Discourse of the North." In *Economy, Polity, and Society: British Intellectual History 1750–1950*, edited by Stefan Collini, Richard Whatmore, and Brian Young, 48–70. Cambridge: Cambridge University Press, 2000.

de Champs, Emmanuelle. *Enlightenment and Utility: Bentham in French, Bentham in France*. Cambridge: Cambridge University Press, 2015.

Cherniss, Joshua L. *A Mind and Its Time: The Development of Isaiah Berlin's Political Thought*. Oxford: Oxford University Press, 2013.

Clark, Christopher and Wolfram Kaiser. 2003. *Culture Wars: Secular-Catholic Conflict in Nineteenth-Century Europe*. Cambridge: Cambridge University Press, 2003.

Colley, Linda. *Britons: Forging the Nation, 1707–1837*. New Haven, CT: Yale University Press, 2014.

Collini, Stefan. *Liberalism and Sociology: L. T. Hobhouse and Political Argument in England, 1880–1914*. Cambridge: Cambridge University Press, 1979.

Collini, Stefan, Donald Winch, and John Burrow. *That Noble Science of Politics: A Study in Nineteenth-Century Intellectual History*. Cambridge: Cambridge University Press, 1983.

Commun, Patricia. *Les Ordolibéraux: Histoire d'un libéralisme à l'allemand*. Paris: Les Belles Lettres, 2016.

Commun, Patricia, Raphaël Fèvre, and Walter Eucken. *Walter Eucken, entre Économie et Politique*. Lyon: ENS Éditions, 2019.

Conklin, Alice L. *A Mission to Civilize: The Republican Idea of Empire in France and West Africa, 1895–1930*. Stanford: Stanford University Press, 1997.

Connolly, James T. Review of Shelton Stromquist, *Reinventing "The People": The Progressive Movement, the Class Problem, and the Origins of Modern Liberalism* in *The Journal of the Gilded Age and Progressive Era* 6, no. 4 (Oct. 2007): 459–463.

Conrad, Sebastian and Sorcha O'Hagan. *German Colonialism: A Short History*. Cambridge: Cambridge University Press, 2012.

Constant, Benjamin. *Principles of Politics Applicable to All Governments*. Indianapolis, IN: Liberty Fund, 1815.

———. "Mélanges de littérature et de politique." In *De la liberté chez les modernes: écrits politiques*, edited by Marcel Gauchet. Paris: Le Livre de Poche, 1980.

———. "The Liberty of the Ancients Compared with That of the Moderns." In *Constant: Political Writings*, edited by Biancamaria Fontana, 302–308. Cambridge: Cambridge University Press, 1988.

———. *Commentary on Filangieri's Work*. Edited and translated by Alan S. Kahan. Indianapolis, IN: Liberty Fund, 2015.

Conti, Gregory. *Parliament the Mirror of the Nation: Representation, Deliberation, and Democracy in Victorian Britain*. Cambridge: Cambridge University Press, 2020.

Conway, Stephen. "Bentham and the Nineteenth-Century Revolution in Government." In *Jeremy Bentham*, edited by Frederick Rosen. New York: Routledge, 2022.

Cosgrove, Richard. *The Rule of Law: Albert Venn Dicey, Victorian Jurist*. Chapel Hill, NC: University of North Carolina Press, 1980.

Craiutu, Aurelian. *A Virtue for Courageous Minds: Moderation in French Political Thought, 1748–1830*. Princeton, NJ: Princeton University Press, 2012.

———. *Faces of Moderation: The Art of Balance in an Age of Extremes*. Philadelphia: University of Pennsylvania Press, 2016.

Croce, Benedetto. *History as the Story of Liberty*. Indianapolis, IN: Liberty Fund, 2000.

Crowder, George. *Isaiah Berlin: Liberty and Pluralism*. Cambridge: Polity, 2004.

Curti, Merle. "The Great Mr. Locke: America's Philosopher, 1783–1861." *Huntington Library Bulletin* 11 (April 1937): 107–151.

Damico, Alfonso J. "What's Wrong with Liberal Perfectionism?" *Polity* 29, no. 3 (Spring 1997): 397–420.

Davies, Aled, Ben Jackson, and Florence Sutcliffe-Braithwaite, eds. *The Neoliberal Age?: Britain since the 1970s*. London: UCL Press, 2021.

Davies, William. *The Limits of Neoliberalism: Authority, Sovereignty and the Logic of Competition*. London: SAGE, 2014.

Davis, Sue. *The Political Thought of Elizabeth Cady Stanton: Women's Rights and the American Political Traditions*. New York: New York University Press, 2008

DelFattore, Joan. *The Fourth R: Conflicts over Religion in America's Public Schools*. New Haven, CT: Yale University Press, 2004.

Dewey, John. "Liberalism and Social Action." In *The Papers of John Dewey: The Later Works, 1925–1953*, edited by Jo Ann Boydston, 1–67. Vol. 11. Carbondale: Southern Illinois University Press, 1987.

———. *Individualism Old and New*. Amherst, NY: Prometheus Books, 1999.

Dicey, A. V. *Lectures on the Relation between Law and Public Opinion in England, during the Nineteenth Century*, edited by Richard VandeWetering. Indianapolis, IN: Liberty Fund, 2008.

Dickey, Laurence. "Constant and Religion: Theism Descends from Heaven to Earth." In *The Cambridge Companion to Constant*, edited by Helena Rosenblatt, 313–351. Cambridge: Cambridge University Press, 2009.

Dittrich, Lisa. *Antiklerikalismus in Europa: Öffentlichlichkeit und Säkularisierung in Frankreich, Spanien und Deutschland (1848–1914)*. Göttingen: Vandenhoeck & Rupprecht, 2014.

Doherty, Brian. *Radicals for Capitalism: A Freewheeling History of the Modern American Libertarian Movement*. New York: Public Affairs, 2007.

Doherty, G. and T. Gray. "Herbert Spencer and the Relation between Economic and Political Liberty." *History of Political Thought* 14, no. 3 (1993): 475–490.

Dorpalen, Andreas. "Heinrich von Treitschke." *Journal of Contemporary History* 7, no. 3–4 (July 1972): 21–35.

Douglass, R. Bruce and Gerald M. Mara. *The Search for a Defensible Good: The Emerging Dilemma of Liberalism*. London: Routledge, 1990.

Dreben, Burton. "On Rawls and Political Liberalism." In *The Cambridge Companion to Rawls*, edited by Samuel Freedman. Cambridge: Cambridge University Press, 2004.

Dunn, John. *Western Political Theory in the Face of the Future*. Cambridge: Cambridge University Press, 1979.

———. "Measuring Locke's Shadow." In *Two Treatises of Government and A Letter Concerning Toleration: John Locke*, edited by Ian Shapiro, 257–286. New Haven, CT: Yale University Press, 2003.

Dupré, Louis. "Kant's Theory of History and Progress." *Review of Metaphysics* 51, no. 4 (June 1998): 813–828.

Dyson, Kenneth. *Conservative Liberalism, Ordo-Liberalism, and the State: Disciplining Democracy and the Market*. Oxford: Oxford University Press, 2021.

Eatwell, Roger and Goodwin, Matthew. *National Populism: The Revolt against Liberal Democracy*. London: Pelican, 2018.

Ebner, Alexander. "The Intellectual Foundations of the Social Market Economy: Theory, Policy, and Implications for European Integration." *Journal of Economic Studies* (Bradford) 33, no. 3 (2006): 206–223.

Edelstein, Dan. "Enlightenment Rights Talk." *Journal of Modern History* 86, no. 3 (2014): 530–565.

Eddy, Beth. "Struggle or Mutual Aid: Jane Addams, Petr Kropotkin, and the Progressive Encounter with Social Darwinism." *The Pluralist* 5, no. 1 (Spring 2010): 21–43.

Eisenach, Eldon J. and Project Muse. *The Lost Promise of Progressivism*. Lawrence: University Press of Kansas, 1994.

Elshtain, Jean Bethke. *The Jane Addams Reader*. New York: Basic Books, 2002.

Engster, Daniel. "Mary Wollstonecraft's Nurturing Liberalism: Between an Ethic of Justice and Care." *American Political Science Review* 95, no. 3 (2001): 577–588.

Eucken, Walter. "Structural Transformations of the State and the Crisis of Capitalism," in *The Birth of Austerity: German Ordoliberalism and Contemporary Neoliberalism*, edited by Thomas Biebricher and Frieder Vogelmann. London: Rowman & Littlefield International, 2017.

Farrelly, Maura Jane. *Anti-Catholicism in America, 1620–1860*. Cambridge: Cambridge University Press, 2018.

Fawcett, Edmund. *Liberalism: The Life of an Idea*. Second ed. Princeton, NJ: Princeton University Press, 2018.

Feder, J. Lester. n.d. "This Is How Steve Bannon Sees the Entire World." BuzzFeed News. https://www.buzzfeednews.com/article/lesterfeder/this-is-how-steve-bannon-sees-the -entire-world.

Fenton, Elizabeth A. *Religious Liberties: Anti-Catholicism and Liberal Democracy in Nineteenth-Century U.S. Literature and Culture.* Oxford: Oxford University Press, 2011.

Ferry, Jules. "De l'égalité d'éducation: conférence populaire faite à la Salle Molière le 10 avril 1870."

Fetscher, Iring. "Republicanism and Popular Sovereignty." In *The Cambridge History of Eighteenth-Century Political Thought,* edited by Mark Goldie and Robert Wokler, 573–598. Cambridge: Cambridge University Press, 2006.

Feuer, Lewis S. "Beyond Ideology." In *The End of Ideology Debate,* edited by Chaim Waxman. New York: Funk & Wagnalls, 1969.

Fevre, Raphael. "Le Marché Sans Pouvoir: Au Cœur du Discours Ordolibéral." *Revue d'Économie Politique* 127, no. 1 (2017): 119–151.

Fischer, Marilyn. "The Conceptual Scaffolding of Newer Ideals of Peace." In *Jane Addams and the Practice of Democracy,* edited by Marilyn Fischer, Carol Nackenoff, and Wendy Chmielewski. Carbondale: University of Illinois Press, 2009.

Flanagan, Maureen A. *America Reformed: Progressives and Progressivisms, 1890s–1920s.* New York: Oxford University Press, 2007.

Fleischacker, Samuel. *A Third Concept of Liberty: Judgment and Freedom in Kant and Adam Smith.* Princeton, NJ: Princeton University Press, 1999.

———. *On Adam Smith's Wealth of Nations: A Philosophical Companion.* Princeton, NJ: Princeton University Press, 2005.

Forbes, Duncan. "Sceptical Whiggism, Commerce, and Liberty." In *Essays on Adam Smith,* edited by A. S. Skinner and Thomas Wilson. Oxford: Clarendon Press, 1975.

Forrester, Katrina. *In the Shadow of Justice: Postwar Liberalism and the Remaking of Political Philosophy.* Princeton, NJ: Princeton University Press, 2019.

Fortier, Jeremy. "Can Liberalism Lose the Enlightenment?" *Journal of Politics* 72, no. 4 (2010): 1003–1013.

Foss, Jerome C. "The Hidden Influence of John Rawls on the American Mind." Heritage Foundation Report, September 22, 2016.

Foucault, Michel. *Discipline and Punish: The Birth of the Prison.* New York: Vintage Books, 1977.

———. *The Birth of Biopolitics: Lectures at the Collège De France, 1978–79,* edited by Michel Senellart. Houndmills, Basingstoke, Hampshire: Palgrave Macmillan, 2008.

Fradera, Josep M. *The Imperial Nation: Citizens and Subjects in the British, French, Spanish, and American Empires,* translated by Ruth MacKay. Princeton, NJ: Princeton University Press, 2018.

Freeden, Michael. *The New Liberalism: An Ideology of Social Reform.* Oxford: Clarendon Press, 1978.

———. "The Coming of the Welfare State." In *The Cambridge History of Twentieth-Century Political Thought,* edited by Terence Ball and Richard Bellamy. Cambridge: Cambridge University Press, 2003.

———. "Eugenics and Progressive Thought: A Study in Ideological Affinity." In *Liberal Languages: Ideological Imaginations and Twentieth-Century Progressive Thought.* Princeton, NJ: Princeton University Press, 2005.

Freeden, Michael. *Liberalism: A Very Short Introduction*. Oxford: Oxford University Press, 2015.

Freeman, Samuel Richard. *The Cambridge Companion to Rawls*, edited by Samuel Freeman. Cambridge: Cambridge University Press, 2004.

Fried, Barbara. "The Unwritten Theory of Justice: Rawlsian Liberalism Versus Libertarianism." In *A Companion to Rawls*, edited by Jon Mandle and David A. Reidy. Chichester: Wiley-Blackwell, 2013.

Friedman, Milton. *Capitalism and Freedom*. Chicago: University of Chicago Press, 1962.

Friedrich, Carl J. "The Political Thought of Neo-Liberalism." *American Political Science Review* 49, no. 2 (1955): 509–525.

Fukuyama, Francis. *The End of History and the Last Man*. New York: Free Press, 1992.

Gales, Joseph, ed. *The Debates and Proceedings in the Congress of the United States: With an Appendix Containing Important State Papers and Public Documents and All the Laws of a Public Nature*. Vol. 1. Washington, DC: Gales and Seaton, 1834.

Galston, William A. *Liberal Purposes: Goods, Virtues, and Diversity in the Liberal State*. Cambridge: Cambridge University Press, 1991.

———. "What Is Living and What Is Dead in Kant's Practical Philosophy?" In *Kant and Political Philosophy: The Contemporary Legacy*, edited by Ronald Beiner and William James Booth, 207–224. New Haven, CT: Yale University Press, 1993.

———. *Anti-Pluralism: The Populist Threat to Liberal Democracy*. New Haven, CT: Yale University Press, 2018.

———. "Liberalism, Nationalism, Pluralism: The Political Thought of Isaiah Berlin." In *The Cambridge Companion to Isaiah Berlin*, 250–262. Cambridge: Cambridge University Press, 2018.

Gamble, Andrew. "Hayek on Knowledge, Economics, and Society." In *The Cambridge Companion to Hayek*, 111–131. Cambridge: Cambridge University Press, 2006.

Garsten, Bryan. "Constant on the Religious Spirit of Liberalism." In *The Cambridge Companion to Constant*, edited by Helena Rosenblatt, 286–313. Cambridge: Cambridge University Press, 2009.

———. "Religion and the Case against Ancient Liberty: Benjamin Constant's Other Lectures." *Political Theory* 38, no. 1 (February 2010): 4–33.

Gaus, Gerald F. *The Modern Liberal Theory of Man*. New York: Routledge, 1983.

Gay, Peter. *The Cultivation of Hatred: The Bourgeois Experience: Victoria to Freud*. Vol. 3. New York: W. W. Norton, 1994.

Gerson, G. "Gender in the Liberal Tradition: Hobhouse on the Family." *History of Political Thought* 25, no. 4 (2004): 700–728.

Geuna, Marco. "Republicanism and Commercial Society in the Scottish Enlightenment: The Case of Adam Ferguson." In *The Values of Republicanism in Early Modern Europe*, edited by Martin van Gelderen and Quentin Skinner, 177–197. Vol. 2 of *Republicanism: A Shared Heritage*. Cambridge: Cambridge University Press, 2002.

Geuss, Raymond. "Liberalism and Its Discontents." *Political Theory* 30, no. 3 (June 2002): 320–338.

Gibson, Ralph. "Why Republicans and Catholics Couldn't Stand Each Other in the Nineteenth Century." In *Religion, Society, and Politics in France since 1789*, edited by Frank Tallett and Nicholas Atkins. London: Bloomsbury, 1991.

Girardet, Raoul. *L'idée Coloniale en France de 1871 a 1962*. Paris: La Table Ronde, 1972.

Goldie, Mark. "Introduction." In John Locke, *A Letter Concerning Toleration and Other Writings*. Indianapolis IN: Liberty Fund, 2010.

Goldschmidt, Nils and Michael Wohlgemuth. "Social Market Economy: Origins, Meanings and Interpretations." *Constitutional Political Economy* 19, no. 3 (2008): 261–276.

Goodhart, David. *The Road to Somewhere: The Populist Revolt and the Future of Politics*. London: Hurst, 2017.

Goodwin, Craufurd D. *Walter Lippmann: Public Economist*. Cambridge, MA: Harvard University Press, 2014.

Gopnik, Adam. *A Thousand Small Sanities: The Moral Adventure of Liberalism*. New York: Basic Books, 2019.

Gordon, Daniel. "In Search of Limits: Raymond Aron on 'secular Religion' and Communism." *Journal of Classical Sociology* 11, no. 2 (2011): 139–154.

Grandmaison, Olivier Le Cour. *La République impériale: politique et racisme d'état*. Paris: Fayard, 2009.

Gray, John. *Isaiah Berlin*. Princeton, NJ: Princeton University Press, 1996.

Greenfeld, Liah. *Nationalism: Five Roads to Modernity*. Cambridge MA: Harvard University Press, 1992.

Greenleaf, W. H. *The British Political Tradition*. London: Methuen, 1983.

Greenstone, J. David. *The Lincoln Persuasion: Remaking American Liberalism*. Princeton, NJ: Princeton University Press, 1993.

Greskovits, Béla. "Rebuilding the Hungarian Right through Conquering Civil Society: The Civic Circles Movement." *East European Politics* 36, no. 2 (2020): 247–266.

Grosby, Steven. *Nationalism: A Very Short Introduction*. Oxford: Oxford University Press, 2005.

Gross, Michael B. *The War against Catholicism: Liberalism and the Anti-Catholic Imagination in Nineteenth-Century Germany*. Ann Arbor: University of Michigan Press, 2005.

———. *The State, the Nation, and the Jews: Liberalism and the Antisemitism Dispute in Bismarck's Germany*. Chicago: University of Chicago Press, 2010.

Guettel, Jens-Uwe. " 'Between Us and the French There Are No Profound Differences': Colonialism and the Possibilities of a Franco-German Rapprochement before 1914." *Historical Reflections* 40, no. 1 (2014): 29–46.

Gunnell, John G. "The Archaeology of American Liberalism." *Journal of Political Ideologies* 6, no. 2 (2001): 125–145.

Gunther-Canada, Wendy. *Rebel Writer: Mary Wollstonecraft and Enlightenment Politics*. DeKalb: Northern Illinois University Press, 2001.

Haakonssen, Knud. *Natural Law and Moral Philosophy: From Grotius to the Scottish Enlightenment*. Cambridge: Cambridge University Press, 1996.

Haakonssen, Knud and Donald Winch. "The Legacy of Adam Smith." In *The Cambridge Companion to Adam Smith*, edited by Knud Haakonssen, 366–395. Cambridge: Cambridge University Press, 2006.

Haidt, Jonathan. "When and Why Nationalism Beats Globalism." *American Interest* 12, no. 1 (2016): 1.

Hall, Catherine. "Macaulay's Nation." *Victorian Studies* 51, no. 3 (Spring 2009): 505–523.

Hall, Edward. *Value, Conflict, and Order: Berlin, Hampshire, Williams, and the Realist Revival in Political Theory*. Chicago: University of Chicago Press, 2020.

Hamburger, Joseph. *Intellectuals in Politics: John Stuart Mill and the Philosophic Radicals*. New Haven, CT: Yale University Press, 1965.

Hamilton, Alexander, John Jay, and James Madison. *The Federalist Papers*. New York: Penguin, 1961.

Hampsher-Monk, Iain. "From Virtue to Politeness." In *The Values of Republicanism in Early Modern Europe*, edited by Martin van Gelderen and Quentin Skinner, 85–107. Vol. 2 of *Republicanism: A Shared Heritage*. Cambridge: Cambridge University Press, 2002.

Hanley, Ryan Patrick. *Adam Smith and the Character of Virtue*. New York: Cambridge University Press, 2011.

Hansard. UK Parliament. https://hansard.parliament.uk/. 1802–Present.

Harrison, Brian. *Separate Spheres: The Opposition to Woman Suffrage in Britain, 1867–1928*. New York: Holmes & Meier, 1978.

Hartwell, R. M. *A History of the Mont Pèlerin Society*. Indianapolis, IN: Liberty Fund, 1995.

Hartz, Louis. *The Liberal Tradition in America: An Interpretation of American Political Thought since the Revolution*. New York: Harcourt Brace and Co., 1955.

Hawthorn, Geoffrey. "Introduction." In *In the Beginning was the Deed*, edited by Geoffrey Hawthorn. Princeton, NJ: Princeton University Press, 2009.

Hayek, F. A. "The Economic Conditions of Interstate Federalism." *New Commonwealth Quarterly* 5, no. 2 (Sep. 1939), 131–149.

———. "The Use of Knowledge in Society," *American Economic Review* 35, no. 4 (Sep. 1945): 519–530.

———. *The Collected Works of F. A. Hayek, Volume 3*, edited by W. W. Bartley III and Stephen Kresge. Chicago: University of Chicago Press, 1991.

———. "Free Enterprise and Competitive Order." In *Individualism and Competitive Order*. Chicago: University of Chicago Press, 1996.

———. *The Collected Works of F. A. Hayek, Volume 2*, edited by Bruce Caldwell. Chicago: University of Chicago Press, 2009.

———. *The Collected Works of F. A. Hayek, Volume 1*, edited by Ronald Hamowy. Chicago: University of Chicago Press, 2011.

———. *The Constitution of Liberty: The Definitive Edition*. Chicago, University of Chicago Press, 2011.

———. *Law, Legislation and Liberty: A New Statement of the Liberal Principles of Justice and Political Economy*. New ed. London: Routledge, 2013.

Hazareesingh, Sudhir. *Political Traditions in Modern France*. Oxford: Oxford University Press, 1994.

Hazony, Yoram. *The Virtue of Nationalism*. New York: Basic Books, 2018.

Hearn, J., C. Kukathas, D. Miller, and B. Yack. "Debate on Bernard Yack's Book *Nationalism and the Moral Psychology of Community*." *Nations and Nationalism* 20, no. 3 (2014): 395–414.

Hewitson, Mark. "Wilhelmine Germany." In James Retallack, *Imperial Germany 1871–1918*. Oxford: Oxford University Press, 2008.

Hilton, Boyd. *The Age of Atonement: The Influence of Evangelicalism on Social and Economic Thought, 1785–1865*. Oxford: Oxford University Press, 1992.

Hirschman, Albert O. *The Passions and the Interests: Political Arguments for Capitalism before Its Triumph*. Princeton, NJ: Princeton University Press, 1977.

Hobhouse, L. T. and James Meadowcroft. *Liberalism and Other Writings*. Cambridge: Cambridge University Press, 1994.

———. *The Elements of Social Justice*. New York: Routledge, 2009.

Holmes, Stephen. *Benjamin Constant and the Making of Modern Liberalism*. New Haven, CT: Yale University Press, 1984.

———. "The Liberty to Denounce: Ancient and Modern." In *The Cambridge Companion to Constant*, edited by Helena Rosenblatt, 47–69. Cambridge: Cambridge University Press, 2009.

Hont, Istvan and Michael Ignatieff, eds. *Wealth and Virtue: The Shaping of Political Economy in the Scottish Enlightenment*. Cambridge: Cambridge University Press, 1983.

Hont, Istvan and Michael Ignatieff. "Introduction." In *Wealth and Virtue: The Shaping of Political Economy in the Scottish Enlightenment*, edited by Istvan Hont and Michael Ignatieff, 1–45. Cambridge: Cambridge University Press, 1983.

Hopkins, A. G. "Overseas Expansion, Imperialism, and Empire, 1815–1914." In T.C.W. Blanning, *The Nineteenth Century: Europe 1789–1914*. New York: Oxford University Press, 2000.

Horn, Karen. "The Difficult Relationship between Historical Ordoliberalism and Adam Smith." Freiburg Discussion Papers on Constitutional Economics 19/03, Walter Eucken Institut e.V., 2019.

Horne, Janet R. *A Social Laboratory for Modern France: The Musée Social & The Rise of the Welfare State*. Durham, NC: Duke University Press, 2002.

Hunt, Eileen M. *Wollstonecraft, Mill, and Women's Human Rights*. New Haven, CT: Yale University Press, 2016.

Ignatieff, Michael. *Isaiah Berlin: A Life*. New York: Metropolitan Books, 1998.

Isaac, Jeffrey C. "Republicanism vs Liberalism? A Reconsideration." *History of Political Thought* 9, no. 2 (Summer 1988): 349–377.

Izenberg, Gerald. "Individualism and Individuality in Constant." In *The Cambridge Companion to Constant*, edited by Helena Rosenblatt, 206–225. Cambridge: Cambridge University Press, 2009.

Jackson, Ben. "At the Origins of Neo-Liberalism: The Free Economy and the Strong State, 1930–1947." *Historical Journal* 53, no. 1 (2010): 129–151.

———. "Freedom, the Common Good, and the Rule of Law: Lippmann and Hayek on Economic Planning." *Journal of the History of Ideas* 73, no. 1 (2012): 47–68.

———. "Socialism and the New Liberalism." In *Liberalism as Ideology: Essays in Honor of Michael Freeden*. Oxford: Oxford University Press, 2012.

———. "Currents of Neo-Liberalism: British Political Ideologies and the New Right, c. 1955–1979." *English Historical Review* 131, no. 551 (2016): 823–850.

Jainchill, Andrew. *Reimagining Politics after the Terror: The Republican Origins of French Liberalism*. Ithaca, NY: Cornell University Press, 2008.

James, William. "The Moral Philosopher and the Moral Life." *International Journal of Ethics* 1, no. 3 (1891): 330–354.

Jardin, André. *Alexis de Tocqueville*. Paris: Gallimard, 1984.

Jennings, Jeremy. "Constant's Idea of Modern Liberty." In *The Cambridge Companion to Constant*, edited by Helena Rosenblatt, 69–91. Cambridge: Cambridge University Press, 2009.

Jones, Daniel Stedman. *Masters of the Universe: Hayek, Friedman, and the Birth of Neoliberal Politics*. Princeton NJ: Princeton University Press, 2012.

Kahan, Alan S. *Aristocratic Liberalism: The Social and Political Thought of Jacob Burckhardt, John Stuart Mill, and Alexis de Tocqueville.* Oxford: Oxford University Press, 1992.

———. "Defining Opportunism, the Writings of Eugène Spüller." *History of Political Thought* 15, no. 3 (1994): 423–445.

———. *Liberalism in Nineteenth-Century Europe: The Political Culture of Limited Suffrage.* London: Palgrave Macmillan, 2003.

———. *Alexis de Tocqueville.* London: Continuum Books, 2010.

———. "Tocqueville: Liberalism and Imperialism." In *French Liberalism from Montesquieu to the Present Day*, edited by Raf Geenens and Helena Rosenblatt, 152–166. Cambridge: Cambridge University Press, 2012.

———. *Tocqueville, Democracy and Religion: Checks and Balances for Democratic Souls.* Oxford: Oxford University Press, 2015.

———. *Mind vs. Money: The War Between Intellectuals and Capitalism.* London: Routledge, 2017.

———. "Tocqueville: The Corporation as an Ethical Association." In *Wealth, Commerce and Philosophy: Foundational Thinkers and Business Ethics*, edited by B. Heath and E. Kaldis, 283–300. Chicago: University of Chicago Press, 2017.

———. "And What if Tocqueville Was Wrong?," *Tocqueville Review*, June 2018, 235–244.

———. "From Basel to Brooklyn: Liberal Cultural Pessimism in Burckhardt, Röpke, and the American Neoconservatives." In *Wilhelm Röpke (1899–1966)*, 157–164. Cham, Switzerland: Springer International Publishing, 2018.

———. Review of *Parliament the Mirror of the Nation: Representation, Deliberation, and Democracy in Victorian Britain*, by Gregory Conti. Cambridge: Cambridge University Press, 2020. *Perspectives on Politics* 19, no. 2 (2021): 598–599.

Kalyvas, Andreas and Ira Katznelson. *Liberal Beginnings: Making a Republic for the Moderns.* Cambridge: Cambridge University Press, 2008.

Kant, Immanuel. *The Critique of Judgment*, translated by J. H. Bernard. London: Macmillan, 1914.

———. "An Answer to the Question: What Is Enlightenment? (1784)." In *Perpetual Peace and Other Essays*, 41–49. Indianapolis, IN: Hackett, 1983.

———. "Idea for a Universal History with a Cosmopolitan Intent (1784)." In *Perpetual Peace and Other Essays*, 29–41. Indianapolis, IN: Hackett, 1983.

———. "On the Proverb: That may be true in theory, but is of no practical use (1793)." In *Perpetual Peace and Other Essays*, 61–93. Indianapolis, IN: Hackett, 1983.

———. "To Perpetual Peace: A Philosophical Sketch (1795)." In *Perpetual Peace and Other Essays*, 107–145. Indianapolis, IN: Hackett, 1983.

———. "Religion within the Boundaries of Mere Reason." In *Religion within the Boundaries of Mere Reason: And Other Writings*, edited by Allen Wood and George di Giovanni, 37–231. Cambridge: Cambridge University Press, 1998.

———. *Anthropology from a Pragmatic Point of View.* Edited and translated by Robert B. Louden. Cambridge: Cambridge University Press, 2006.

———. *The Metaphysics of Morals.* Edited and translated by Mary Gregor. Cambridge: Cambridge University Press, 2012.

Kelly, P. J. "Security, Expectation, and Liberty." In *Jeremy Bentham*, edited by Frederick Rosen, 161–193. New York: Routledge, 2022.

————. "Utilitarianism and Distributive Justice: The Civil Law and the Foundations of Bentham's Economic Thought." In *Jeremy Bentham*, edited by Frederick Rosen. New York: Routledge, 2022.

Keslassy, Eric. *Le Libéralisme de Tocqueville à l'épreuve du paupérisme*. Paris: L'Harmattan, 2000.

Keynes, John Maynard. *Essays in Persuasion*. London: Palgrave Macmillan UK, 2010.

Keyssar, Alexander. *The Right to Vote: The Contested History of Democracy in the United States*. Cambridge, MA: Harvard University Press, 2000.

Kipling, Rudyard. *We and They*. London, 1936.

Kloppenberg, James T. *Uncertain Victory: Social Democracy and Progressivism in European and American Thought, 1870–1920*. New York: Oxford University Press, 1986.

————. *The Virtues of Liberalism*. Oxford: Oxford University Press, 1998.

————. "In Retrospect: Louis Hartz's 'The Liberal Tradition in America.'" *Reviews in American History* 29, no. 3 (September 2001): 460–478.

Kluth, Andreas. "Handelsblatt Explains: Ordoliberalism and the Alleged Aberration of German Economics." www.handelsblatt.com. January 31, 2018.

Köhler, Ekkehard A. and Stefan Kolev. "The Conjoint Quest for a Liberal Positive Program: 'Old Chicago,' Freiburg, and Hayek." In *F. A. Hayek and the Modern Economy*, edited by Sandra J. Peart and David M. Levy, 211–228. New York: Palgrave-Macmillan, 2013.

Kraditor, Aileen S. *The Ideas of the Woman Suffrage Movement: 1890–1920*. New York: Norton, 1981.

Krause, Sharon R. *Liberalism with Honor*. Cambridge, MA: Harvard University Press, 2002.

Krieger, Leonard. *The German Idea of Freedom: History of a Political Tradition from the Reformation to 1871*. Chicago: University of Chicago Press, 1957.

Kristol, Irving. "Keeping Up With Ourselves." In *The End of Ideology Debate*, edited by Chaim Waxman. New York: Funk & Wagnalls, 1969.

————. *Two Cheers for Capitalism*. New York: Basic Books, 1978.

Krug, Wilhelm Traugott. *Geschichtliche Darstellung des Liberalismus: Alter und Neuer Zeit*. Leipzig: Brodhaus, 1823. https://ia800500.us.archive.org/30/items/geschichtlicheda00krug/geschichtlicheda00krug.pdf.

Kukathas, Chandran. *Hayek and Modern Liberalism*. Oxford: Clarendon Press, 1989.

Lachs, John. "Mill and Constant: A Neglected Connection in the History of the Idea of Liberty." *History of Philosophy Quarterly* 9, no. 1 (January 1992): 87–96.

Lapalombara, Joseph. "Decline of Ideology: A Dissent and an Interpretation." In *The End of Ideology Debate*, edited by Chaim Waxman. New York: Funk & Wagnalls, 1969.

Larmore, Charles. "Political Liberalism." *Political Theory* 18, no. 3 (August 1990): 339–360.

Larrère, Catherine. "Montesquieu and Liberalism: The Question of Pluralism." In *Montesquieu and His Legacy*, edited by Rebecca E. Kingston, 279–303. Albany: State University of New York Press, 2009.

Lasch, Christopher. *The Revolt of the Elites and the Betrayal of Democracy*. New York: W.W. Norton, 1995.

Laski, Harold. *The Rise of European Liberalism*. London: George Allen & Unwin, Ltd, 1936.

LaVaque-Manty, Mika. "Kant's Children." *Social Theory and Practice* 32, no. 3 (July 2006): 365–388.

Lefebvre, Alexander. "Liberalism and the Good Life." *Journal of Social and Political Philosophy* 1, no. 2 (2022): 152–168.

Leonard, Thomas C. "Origins of the Myth of Social Darwinism: The Ambiguous Legacy of Richard Hofstadter's Social Darwinism in American Thought." *Journal of Economic Behavior & Organization* 71, no. 1 (2009): 37–51.

Leonhard, Jörn. *Liberalismus: Zur historischen Semantik eines europäischen Deutungsmusters.* Munich: Oldenbourg Wissenschaftsverlag, 2001.

Leroux, Robert. *Lire Bastiat.* Paris: Hermann, 2008.

Levy, Jacob T. "Liberalism's Divide, after Socialism and before." *Social Philosophy and Policy* 20, no. 1 (January 2003): 278–297.

———. "Montesquieu's Constitutional Legacies." In *Montesquieu and His Legacy*, edited by Rebecca E. Kingston, 115–139. Albany: State University of New York Press, 2009.

———. "From Liberal Constitutionalism to Pluralism." In *Rationalism, Pluralism, and Freedom*, 233–253. Oxford: Oxford University Press, 2017.

Lewis, Paul. "Editor's Introduction." In *Hayek, Essays on Liberalism and the Economy*, Vol. 18 of the *Collected Works of F. A. Hayek.* Chicago: University of Chicago Press, 2021.

Lieberman, David. "Economy and Polity in Bentham's Science of Legislation." In *Economy, Polity and Society. British Intellectual History 1750–1950*, edited by Stefan Collini, Richard Whatmore, and Brian Young. Cambridge: Cambridge University Press, 2000.

Lightman, Bernard, ed. *Global Spencerism: The Communication and Appropriation of a British Evolutionist*, Vol. 1. Boston: Brill, 2016.

Lincoln, Abraham. Letter to Joshua F. Speed, August 24, 1855. https://www.abrahamlincolnonline .org/lincoln/speeches/speed.htm

Lindsay, Thomas. "James Madison on Religion and Politics: Rhetoric and Reality." *American Political Science Review* 85, no. 4 (December 1991): 1321–1337.

Lippmann, Walter. *The Good Society.* New York: Routledge, 2017.

Lipset, Seymour Martin. "The End of Ideology?" In *The End of Ideology Debate*, edited by Chaim Waxman. New York: Funk & Wagnalls, 1969.

Logue, William. *From Philosophy to Sociology: The Evolution of French Liberalism, 1870–1914.* Dekalb: Northern Illinois University Press, 1983.

Long, Douglas. " 'Utility' and the 'Utility Principle': Hume, Smith, Bentham, Mill." *Utilitas* 2, no. 1 (1990): 12–39.

———. "Adam Smith's Politics." In *The Cambridge Companion to Adam Smith*, edited by Knud Haakonssen, 288–319. Cambridge: Cambridge University Press, 2006.

———. "Fundamental Words." In *Jeremy Bentham*, edited by Frederick Rosen. New York: Routledge, 2022.

Long, Emma. *The Church-State Debate: Religion, Education, and the Establishment Clause in Postwar America.* New York: Bloomsbury, 2011.

Lubenow, W. C. *Politics of Government Growth: Early Victorian Attitudes Towards State Intervention, 1833–1848.* Newton Abbot, UK: David & Charles, 1971.

Lutz, Donald S. "The Relative Influence of European Writers on Late Eighteenth-Century American Political Thought." *American Political Science Review* 78, no. 1 (March 1984): 189–197.

Macaulay, Thomas Babington. "Gladstone on Church and State." In *Critical and Historical Essays contributed to the Edinburgh Review*, 5th ed. in 3 vols. London: Longman, Brown, Green, and Longmans, 1848. Vol. 2.

———. "Hallam's Constitutional History." In *Critical and Historical Essays contributed to the Edinburgh Review*, 5th ed. in 3 vols.(London: Longman, Brown, Green, and Longmans, 1848. Vol. 1.

———. "Southey's Colloquies." In *Critical and Historical Essays contributed to the Edinburgh Review*, 5th ed. in 3 vols. London: Longman, Brown, Green, and Longmans, 1848. Vol. 1.

———. *Speeches on Politics and Literature*. London: Dent, 1912.

———. "Sir James Mackintosh." In *Critical and Historical Essays: Thomas Babington, Lord Macaulay*, edited by Hugh Trevor-Roper. London: McGraw-Hill, 1965.

———. "Chapter 3, History of England." In *Selected Writings: Classics of British Historical Literature*, edited by John Clive and Thomas Pinney. Chicago: University of Chicago Press, 1972.

Macpherson, C. B. *The Political Theory of Possessive Individualism: Hobbes to Locke*. Oxford: Oxford University Press, 1962.

Madison, James. *The Federalist Papers*. New York: New American Library, 1961.

———. "*The Papers of James Madison*, edited by William T. Hutchinson et al. Chicago and London: University of Chicago Press, 1962–77 (vols. 1–10); Charlottesville: University Press of Virginia, 1977– (vols. 11–).

———. "Notes" in Sheehan, Colleen A. *The Mind of James Madison: The Legacy of Classical Republicanism*. Cambridge: Cambridge University Press, 2015.

Mahoney, Daniel J. *The Liberal Political Science of Raymond Aron: A Critical Introduction*. Savage, MD: Rowman & Littlefield, 1992.

Mann, Horace. Twelfth Annual Report to the Secretary of the Massachusetts State Board of Education. 1848.

Mannheim, Karl. *Ideology and Utopia*. London: Routledge, 1997.

Mantena, Karuna. "The Crisis of Liberal Imperialism." *Histoire@politique* 11, no. 2 (2010).

Marshall, Catherine. *Political Deference in a Democratic Age: British Politics and the Constitution from the Eighteenth Century to Brexit*. Houndmills: Palgrave Macmillan, 2021.

Masani, Zareer. *Macaulay: Britain's Liberal Imperialist*. London: Random House India, 2014.

Matusow, Allen J. *The Unraveling of America: A History of Liberalism in the 1960s*. New York: Harper & Row, 1984.

Mazzini, Giuseppe. *On the Duties of Man*. New York: Funk & Wagnalls, 1898.

McGreevy, John T. *Catholicism and American Freedom: A History*. New York: W.W. Norton, 2004.

Meadowcroft, James. "Introduction." In L. T. Hobhouse, *Liberalism and Other Writings*, edited by James Meadowcraft. Cambridge: Cambridge University Press, 1994.

Meadowcroft, John. "Nozick's Critique of Rawls: Distribution, Entitlement, and the Assumptive World of A Theory of Justice." In *The Cambridge Companion to Nozick's Anarchy, State, and Utopia*, 168–196. Cambridge: Cambridge University Press, 2011.

Meek, Ronald L. "Smith and Marx." In *Smith, Marx, and After: Ten Essays in the Development of Economic Thought*, 1–18. London: Chapman and Hall, 1977.

Mehta, Uday Singh. *Liberalism and Empire: A Study in Nineteenth-Century British Liberal Thought*. Chicago: University of Chicago Press, 1999.

Metcalf, Thomas R. *Ideologies of the Raj*. Cambridge: Cambridge University Press, 2008.

Michnik, Adam and Irena Grudzińska-Gross. *Letters from Freedom: Post-Cold War Realities and Perspectives*. Berkeley: University of California Press, 1998.

Mill, John Stuart. "Principles of Political Economy." In *Collected Works of John Stuart Mill*, edited by John Robson. Vols. 2 and 3. Toronto: University of Toronto Press, 1965.

———. *Essays on French History and Historians*, Vol. 20. Edited by John Robson. Toronto: University of Toronto Press, 1985.

———. *On Liberty and Other Writings*. Edited by Stefan Collini. Cambridge: Cambridge University Press, 1989.

Mingardi, Alberto. *Herbert Spencer*. New York: Bloomsbury, 2013.

Mirowski, Philip. "Postface: Defining Neoliberalism." In *The Road from Mont Pèlerin*, edited by Mirowski, Philip and Dieter Plehwe, 417–456. Cambridge, MA: Harvard University Press, 2009.

Mommsen, Wolfgang J. "German Liberalism in the Nineteenth Century." In *The Cambridge History of Nineteenth-Century Political Thought*, edited by Gareth Stedman Jones and Gregory Claeys, 409–432. Cambridge: Cambridge University Press, 2011.

Montesquieu, *The Spirit of the Laws*, translated by Cohler, Miller, and Stone. Cambridge: Cambridge University Press, 1989.

Moore, James. "Natural Rights in the Scottish Enlightenment." In *The Cambridge History of Eighteenth-Century Political Thought*, edited by Mark Goldie and Robert Wokler, 291–317. Cambridge: Cambridge University Press, 2006.

Morgan Smith, S. A. "James Madison, Religious Liberty and Union." *History of Political Thought* 39, no. 4 (2018): 690–718.

Morrow, John. "Private Property, Liberal Subjects, and the State." In *The New Liberalism: Reconciling Liberty and Community*, edited by Avital Simhony and D. Weinstein. Cambridge: Cambridge University Press, 2001.

Mudde, Cas. "The Populist Zeitgeist." *Government and Opposition (London)* 39, no. 4 (2004): 541–563.

Muller, Frank Lorenz. *Britain and the German Question: Perceptions of Nationalism and Political Reform, 1830–63*. Houndsmills: Palgrave, 2002.

Müller, Jan-Werner. "Rawls, Historian: Remarks on Political Liberalism's 'Historicism.'" *Revue Internationale de Philosophie* 60, no. 237 (3) (2006): 327–339.

———. *What Is Populism?*. Philadelphia: University of Pennsylvania Press, 2016.

Murdoch, Iris. *The Sovereignty of Good*. London: Routledge, 1970.

Nagel, Thomas. "Foreword." In *Anarchy, State, and Utopia*, by Robert Nozick. New York: Basic Books, 1974.

Naumann, Friedrich. *Das Blaue Buch von Vaterland und Freiheit. Auszüge aus Seinen Werken*. Leipzig, 1913.

Nicholls, Anthony James. *Freedom with Responsibility: The Social Market Economy in Germany, 1918–1963*. Oxford: Clarendon Press, 1994.

Nicholson, Peter. "The Reception and Early Reputation of Mill's Political Thought." In *The Cambridge Companion to Mill*, edited by John Skorupski, 464–496. Cambridge: Cambridge University Press, 1998.

Nientiedt, Daniel and Ekkehard A. Kohler. "Liberalism and Democracy—a Comparative Reading of Eucken and Hayek." *Cambridge Journal of Economics* 40, no. 6 (2016): 1743–1760.

Nietzsche, Friedrich. *The Will to Power*, translated by Walter Kaufmann and R. J. Hollingdale. New York: Random House, 1968.

Nipperdey, Thomas. *Germany from Napoleon to Bismarck*. Princeton, NJ: Princeton University Press, 1996.

Norman, W. J. "The Autonomy-Based Liberalism of Joseph Raz." *The Canadian Journal of Law and Jurisprudence* 2, no. 2 (1989): 151–162.

Nozick, Robert. *Anarchy, State, and Utopia*. New York: Basic Books, 1974.

Nussbaum, Martha C. "Perfectionist Liberalism and Political Liberalism." *Philosophy & Public Affairs* 39, no. 1 (2011): 3–45.

Oakeshott, Michael. *Experience and Its Modes*. Cambridge: Cambridge University Press, 1933.

———. *On History and Other Essays*. Oxford: Basil Blackwell, 1983.

Oates, Stephen B. *With Malice Toward None: A Biography of Abraham Lincoln*. New York: Harperperennial, 2011.

Offen, Karen. "Defining Feminism: A Comparative Historical Approach." *Signs: Journal of Women in Culture and Society* 14, no. 1 (1988): 119–157.

———. *European Feminisms, 1700–1950: A Political History*. Stanford, CA: Stanford University Press, 2000.

———. *Debating the Woman Question in the French Third Republic, 1870–1920*. Cambridge: Cambridge University Press, 2018.

Offer, John. *Herbert Spencer and Social Theory*. New York: Palgrave Macmillan, 2010.

O'Neill, Daniel I. "John Adams Versus Mary Wollstonecraft on the French Revolution and Democracy." *Journal of the History of Ideas* 68, no. 3 (2007): 451–476.

O'Neill, Onora. "Kant and the Social Contract Tradition." In *Kant's Political Theory: Interpretations and Applications*, edited by Elisabeth Ellis, 25–42. University Park, PA: Penn State University Press, 2012.

Orbán, Viktor. "Speech at the XXV. Bálványos Free Summer University and Youth Camp." 26th July, 2014.

Osterhammel, Jürgen. "Europe, the 'West' and the Civilizing Mission." Annual Lecture, German Historical Institute, London, 2005.

Oz-Salzberger. "Isaiah Berlin on Nationalism, the Modern Jewish Condition, and Zionism." In *The Cambridge Companion to Isaiah Berlin*, edited by Joshua L. Cherniss and Steven B. Smith, 169–191. Cambridge: Cambridge University Press, 2018.

Parry, Jonathan. *The Politics of Patriotism: English Liberalism, National Identity and Europe 1830–1866*. Cambridge: Cambridge University Press, 2006.

———. *The Rise and Fall of Liberal Government in Victorian Britain*. New Haven, CT: Yale University Press, 2009.

Pascal, Blaise. *Pensées*, translated by A. J. Krailsheimer. New York: Penguin Books, 1966.

Pateman, Carole. *Women, Nature, and the Suffrage*. Chicago: University of Chicago Press, 1980.

———. *The Sexual Contract*. Cambridge: Polity Press, 1988.

Peacock, Alan, Hans Willgerodt, and A. J. Nicholls. *Germany's Social Market Economy: Origins and Evolution*. Cambridge: Cambridge University Press, 1990.

Pettit, Philip. *Republicanism: A Theory of Freedom and Government*. Oxford: Oxford University Press, 1997.

Phillipson, Nicholas. "Adam Smith as Civic Moralist." In *Wealth and Virtue: The Shaping of Political Economy in the Scottish Enlightenment*, edited by Istvan Hont and Michael Ignatieff, 179–203. Cambridge: Cambridge University Press, 1983.

Pitts, Jennifer. *A Turn to Empire: The Rise of Imperial Liberalism in Britain and France*. Princeton, NJ: Princeton University Press, 2005.

Pius X, *Editae Saepe* (1910).

Plehwe, Dieter. "Introduction." In *Nine Lives of Neoliberalism*, edited by Dieter Plehwe, Quinn Slobodian, and Philip Mirowski. Brooklyn, NY: Verso, 2020.

Pocock, J.G.A. "Adam Smith and History." In *The Cambridge Companion to Adam Smith*, edited by Knud Haakonssen, 270–288. Cambridge: Cambridge University Press, 2006.

Popper, Karl R. *The Open Society and Its Enemies*. New One-Volume Edition. Princeton, NJ: Princeton University Press, 2013.

Posluschny, Myra. *Walter Eucken und Alfred Müller-Armack: Ein Vergleich ihrer Konzeptionen des Ordoliberalismus und der Sozialen Marktwirtschaft*. Norderstedt, Germany: GRIN Verlag, 2007.

Postema, Gerald J. "Utilitarian Justice and the Tasks of Law." In *Jeremy Bentham*, edited by Frederick Rosen. London: Taylor and Francis, 2017.

Ptak, Ralf. "Neoliberalism in Germany: Revisiting the Ordoliberal Foundations of the Social Market Economy." In *The Road from Mont Pelerin: The Making of the Neoliberal Thought Collective*, edited by Philip Mirowski and Dieter Plehwe. Cambridge, MA: Harvard University Press, 2009.

Pyle, Andrew. *The Subjection of Women: Contemporary Responses to John Stuart Mill*. Bristol: Thoemmes Press, 1995.

Quinn, Michael. "Jeremy Bentham and the Relief of Indigence." In Frederick Rosen, ed., *Jeremy Bentham*, 2018.

Rawls, John. *Political Liberalism*. New York: Columbia University Press, 1993.

———. *Justice as Fairness: A Restatement*. Cambridge, MA: Harvard University Press, 2001.

———. *Political Liberalism*. Expanded ed. New York: Columbia University Press, 2005.

Raz, Joseph. *The Morality of Freedom*. Oxford: Clarendon Press, 1986.

———. *Ethics in the Public Domain: Essays in the Morality of Law and Politics*. Oxford: Oxford University Press, 1994.

Reinhoudt, Jurgen and Serge Audier. *The Walter Lippmann Colloquium: The Birth of Neo-Liberalism*. Cham, Switzerland: Palgrave Macmillan, 2018.

Rémond, René. *L'anticléricalisme en France: De 1815 à Nos Jours*. Paris: Fayard, 1999.

Renan, Ernest. "What Is a Nation?" 1882.

Riley, Patrick. "The Elements of Kant's Practical Philosophy." In *Kant and Political Philosophy: The Contemporary Legacy*, edited by Ronald Beiner and William James Booth, 9–38. New Haven, CT: Yale University Press, 1993.

———. "Social Contract Theory and Its Critics." In *The Cambridge History of Eighteenth-Century Political Thought*, edited by Mark Goldie and Robert Wokler, 347–379. Cambridge: Cambridge University Press, 2006.

Ripstein, Arthur. "Kant and the Circumstances of Justice." In *Kant's Political Theory: Interpretations and Applications*, edited by Elisabeth Ellis, 42–74. University Park: Penn State University Press, 2012.

Robbins, Lionel. *The Theory of Economic Policy in English Classical Political Economy*. London: Macmillan, 1965.

Robin, Corey. *Fear: The History of a Political Idea*. New York: Oxford University Press, 2004.

Rodgers, Daniel T. "In Search of Progressivism." *Reviews in American History* 10, no. 4 (1982): 113–132.

———. *Atlantic Crossings: Social Politics in a Progressive Age*. Cambridge, MA: Harvard University Press, 2000.

Rodrigues, João. "The Political and Moral Economies of Neoliberalism: Mises and Hayek." *Cambridge Journal of Economics* 37, no. 5 (2013): 1001–1017.

Rohac, Dalibor and Alberto Mingardi. "Hayek's Europe: The Austrian School and European Federalism." In *The Liberal Heart of Europe: Essays in Memory of Alberto Giovannini*, edited by Francesco Giavazzi, Francesco Lefevbre D'Ovidio, and Alberto Mingardi, 67–80. Cham, Switzerland: Springer International Publishing, 2021.

Roosevelt, Theodore. State of the Union 1908. December 8, 1908.

Röpke, Wilhelm. "Fascist Economics." *Economica* 2, no. 5 (Feb. 1935).

———. "South Africa: An Attempt at a Positive Appraisal." *Schweizer Monatshefte* 44, no. 2 (May 1964).

Rosanvallon, Pierre. *The Demands of Liberty: Civil Society in France Since the Revolution*, translated by Arthur Goldhammer. Cambridge, MA: Cambridge University Press, 2007.

———. *Le siècle du populisme: histoire, théorie, critique*. Paris: Seuil, 2020.

Rosen, Frederick ed. *Classical Utilitarianism from Hume to Mill*. London: Routledge, 2003, 29–57.

———. ed. *Jeremy Bentham*. New York: Routledge, 2018.

———. "Liberty and Constitutional Theory." In Rosen, ed., *Jeremy Bentham*, 2018.

———. "Sovereignty and Democracy." In Rosen ed., *Jeremy Bentham*, 2018.

———. "Reading Hume Backwards: Utility as the Foundation of Morals." In Rosen, ed., *Jeremy Bentham*, 2018.

Rosenblatt, Helena. *Liberal Values: Benjamin Constant and the Politics of Religion*. Cambridge: Cambridge University Press, 2008.

———. *The Lost History of Liberalism: From Ancient Rome to the Twenty-First Century*. Princeton, NJ: Princeton University Press, 2018.

———. "The Rise and Fall of 'Liberalism' in France." In *In Search of European Liberalisms*, edited by Michael Freeden, Javier Fernandez-Sebastian, and Jörn Leonhard. New York: Berghahn Books, 2019.

Rosenblum, Nancy L. *Liberalism and the Moral Life*. Cambridge, MA: Harvard University Press, 1989.

Rothschild, Emma. "Political Economy." In *The Cambridge History of Political Thought, 1450–1700*, edited by J. H. Burns. Cambridge: Cambridge University Press, 1991.

Rotunda, Ronald. *The Politics of Language: Liberalism as Word and Symbol*. Iowa City: University of Iowa Press, 1986.

Ryan, Alan. *The Making of Modern Liberalism*. Princeton, NJ: Princeton University Press, 2012.

———. "Liberalism, 1900–1940." In *The Cambridge Companion to Liberalism*, edited by Steven Wall. Cambridge: Cambridge University Press, 2015.

———. "Isaiah Berlin: Contested Conceptions of Liberty and Liberalism." In *The Cambridge Companion to Isaiah Berlin*, edited by Joshua L. Cherniss and Steven B. Smith, 212–228. Cambridge: Cambridge University Press, 2018.

Sabine, George H. *A History of Political Theory*, 3rd edition. Oxford: Oxford University Press, 1960.

Sagar, Paul. *Adam Smith Reconsidered: History, Liberty, and the Foundations of Modern Politics.* Princeton, NJ: Princeton University Press, 2022.

Sally, Razeen. "The Social Market and Liberal Order: Theory and Policy Implications." *Government and Opposition* (London) 29, no. 4 (1994): 461–476.

Schickler, Eric. *Racial Realignment: The Transformation of American Liberalism, 1932–1965.* Princeton, NJ: Princeton University Press, 2016.

Schleifer, James T. *The Making of Tocqueville's 'Democracy in America.'* Chapel Hill: University of North Carolina Press, 1980.

Schofield, Philip. *Utility and Democracy: The Political Thought of Jeremy Bentham.* Oxford: Oxford University Press, 2006.

Schroeder, Paul W. "International Politics, Peace and War, 1815–1914." In *The Nineteenth Century: Europe 1789–1914*, edited by T.C.W. Blanning. Oxford: Oxford University Press, 2000.

Seigfried, Charlene Haddock. "The Courage of One's Convictions or the Conviction of One's Courage?: Jane Addams's Principled Compromises." In *Jane Addams and the Practice of Democracy*, edited by Marilyn Fischer, Carol Nackenoff, and Wendy Chmielewski. Urbana: University of Illinois Press, 2009.

Shanley, Mary Lyndon. "The Subjection of Women." In *The Cambridge Companion to Mill*, edited by John Skorupski. Cambridge: Cambridge University Press, 1998.

Shapiro, Ian and Alicia Steinmetz. "Negative Liberty and the Cold War." In *The Cambridge Companion to Isaiah Berlin*, edited by Joshua L. Cherniss and Steven B. Smith, 192–211. Cambridge: Cambridge University Press, 2018.

Shaw, George Bernard. *St. Joan.* Victoria, BC, Canada: Reading Essentials (1923), 2010.

Shearmur, Jeremy. *Hayek and After: Hayekian Liberalism As a Research Programme.* London: Taylor & Francis Group, 1996.

Sheehan, Colleen A. *The Mind of James Madison: The Legacy of Classical Republicanism.* Cambridge: Cambridge University Press, 2015.

Shils, Edward. "The End of Ideology?." In *The End of Ideology Debate.* edited by Chaim Waxman. New York: Funk & Wagnalls, 1969.

Shklar, Judith N. *After Utopia: The Decline of Political Faith.* Princeton, NJ: Princeton University Press, 1957.

———. *Ordinary Vices.* Cambridge, MA: Belknap Press of Harvard University Press, 1984.

———. "The Liberalism of Fear." In *Liberalism and the Moral Life*, edited by Nancy L. Rosenblum, 21–39. Cambridge, MA: Harvard University Press, 1989.

———. "Montesquieu and the New Republicanism." In *Machiavelli and Republicanism*, edited by Gisela Bock, Quentin Skinner, and Maurizio Viroli, 265–280. Cambridge: Cambridge University Press, 2011.

Sidgwick, Henry. *Elements of Politics.* London: Macmillan, 1891.

Sigmund, Paul E. "Introduction." In *The Selected Political Writings of John Locke: A Norton Critical Edition.* New York: W.W Norton, 2005.

Silver, Nate. "Education, Not Income, Predicted Who Would Vote for Trump." November 22, 2016. https://fivethirtyeight.com/features/education-not-income-predicted-who-would-vote-for-trump/.

Skinner, Quentin. "Meaning and Understanding in the History of Ideas." In *Meaning and Context: Quentin Skinner and His Critics*, edited by James Tully, 29–68. Princeton, NJ: Princeton University Press, 1988.

———. *Liberty before Liberalism.* Cambridge: Cambridge University Press, 1998.

———. "Conclusion." In *Machiavelli and Republicanism,* edited by Gisela Bock, Quentin Skinner, and Maurizio Viroli. Cambridge: Cambridge University Press, 2011.

Slobodian, Quinn. *Globalists: The End of Empire and the Birth of Neoliberalism.* Cambridge, MA: Harvard University Press, 2018.

Smith, Adam. *An Inquiry Into the Nature and Causes of the Wealth of Nations,* edited by Edwin Cannan. Indianapolis, IN: Liberty Fund, 1982.

———. *Lectures on Jurisprudence,* edited by R. L. Meek, D. D. Raphael, and P. G. Stein. Indianapolis, IN: Liberty Fund, 1982.

———. *The Theory of Moral Sentiments,* edited by D. D. Raphael and A. L. Macfie. Indianapolis, IN: Liberty Fund, 1982.

Smith, Helmut Walser. *German Nationalism and Religious Conflict: Culture, Ideology, Politics, 1870–1914.* Princeton, NJ: Princeton University Press, 1995.

Smith, Steven B. "Isaiah Berlin on the Enlightenment and Counter-Enlightenment." In *The Cambridge Companion to Isaiah Berlin,* edited by Joshua L. Cherniss and Steven B. Smith, 132–148. Cambridge: Cambridge University Press, 2018.

———. *Reclaiming Patriotism in an Age of Extremes.* New Haven, CT: Yale University Press, 2021.

Spector, Céline. "Honor." In *A Montesquieu Dictionary,* edited by Catherine Larrère and Catherine Volpilhac-Auger. Lyon, France: École normale supérieure de Lyon, 2013.

Spencer, Herbert. *The Principles of Sociology, vol. 1* (1898). New York: D. Appleton and Company, 1876.

———. "The Americans—A Conversation." In *The Works of Herbert Spencer,* Kindle Edition, loc 81870. October 20, 1882.

———. "Speech at Delmonico's." November 9, 1882.

———. *From Freedom to Bondage.* n.p., 1891.

———. *The Principles of Ethics, vol. 1,* London: Williams and Norgate, 1892. Indianapolis: LibertyClassics, 1897.

———. *The Principles of Ethics, vol. 2,* Indianapolis: LibertyClassics, 1897.

———. *An Autobiography.* London: Williams and Norgate, 1904.

———. "The Man Versus The State." In *Political Writings.* Cambridge: Cambridge University Press, 1994.

———. "The Morals of Trade." In *Essays: Scientific, Political and Speculative.* Vol. 11. Abingdon: Routledge, 1996.

———. *Social Statics.* Abingdon: Routledge, 1996.

Spieker, Jorg. "F. A. Hayek and the Reinvention of Liberal Internationalism." *International History Review* 36, no. 5 (2014): 919–942.

Spitz, Jean-Fabien. "From Civism to Civility: D'Holbach's Critique of Republican Virtue." In *The Values of Republicanism in Early Modern Europe,* edited by Martin van Gelderen and Quentin Skinner, 107–125. Vol. 2 of *Republicanism: A Shared Heritage.* Cambridge: Cambridge University Press, 2002.

Stack, David. "Charles Darwin's Liberalism in 'Natural Selection as Affecting Civilised Nations.'" *History of Political Thought* 33, no. 3 (2012): 525–554.

Stanton, Elizabeth Cady. Declaration of Sentiments and Resolutions—Seneca Falls (1848).

Stanton, Timothy. "John Locke and the Fable of Liberalism." *The Historical Journal* 61, no. 3 (September 2018): 597–622.

Steel, Ronald. *Walter Lippmann and the American Century*. Boston: Little, Brown, 1980.

Stoetzler, Marcel. *The State, the Nation, & the Jews: Liberalism and the Antisemitism Dispute in Bismarck's Germany*. Lincoln: University of Nebraska Press, 2008.

Sullivan, Robert E. *Macaulay: The Tragedy of Power*. Cambridge, MA: Belknap Press of Harvard University Press, 2010.

Sullivan, Vickie B. *Machiavelli, Hobbes, and the Formation of a Liberal Republicanism in England*. Cambridge: Cambridge University Press, 2004.

Tamir, Yael. *Liberal Nationalism*. Princeton, NJ: Princeton University Press, 1995.

Taylor, Barbara. "Mary Wollstonecraft and the Wild Wish of Early Feminism." *History Workshop* no. 33 (1992): 197–219.

Thoisnier-Desplaces, A., and Ulysse Tencé, eds. *Annuaire historique universel*. Paris, 1834.

Thompson, Alastair P. *Left Liberals, the State, and Popular Politics in Wilhelmine Germany*. Oxford: Oxford University Press, 2000.

Thompson, James. "Modern Liberty Redefined." In *The Cambridge History of Nineteenth-Century Political Thought*, edited by Gareth Stedman Jones and Gregory Claeys, 720–747. Cambridge: Cambridge University Press, 2013.

Thorsen, Dag Einar and Amund Lie. "What Is Neoliberalism." Department of Political Science, University of Oslo, Working Paper, October 10, 2009.

Tillery, Alvin B., Jr. "Tocqueville as Critical Race Theorist: Whiteness as Property, Interest Convergence, and the Limits of Jacksonian Democracy." *Political Research Quarterly* 62, no. 4 (December 2009): 639–652.

Tocqueville, Alexis de. *The Old Regime and the Revolution*. Edited by François Furet and Françoise Mélonio. Translated by Alan S. Kahan. Chicago: University of Chicago Press, 1995.

———. *Democracy in America: English Edition*. Edited by Eduardo Nolla. Translated by James T. Schleifer. Indianapolis, IN: Liberty Fund, 2010.

———. *Memoirs on Pauperism and Other Writings: Poverty, Public Welfare, and Inequality*, edited and translated by Christine Dunn Henderson. Notre Dame, IN: University of Notre Dame Press, 2021.

———. "Voyages en Angleterre." In *Oeuvres Complètes*, Vol. 5. Paris: Gallimard, 1951–2022.

Todd, David. *A Velvet Empire: French Informal Imperialism in the Nineteenth Century*. Princeton, NJ: Princeton University Press, 2021.

Todorov, Tzvetan. "Religion According to Constant." In *The Cambridge Companion to Constant*, edited by Helena Rosenblatt, 275–286. Cambridge: Cambridge University Press, 2009.

Treitschke. Heinrich von. "Our Prospects." *Preussische Jahrbücher*, November 1879.

Tribe, Keith. "Adam Smith: Critical Theorist?" *Journal of Economic Literature* 37, no. 2 (June 1999): 609–632.

———. "Liberalism and Neoliberalism in Britain, 1930–1980." In *The Road from Mont Pelerin: The Making of the Neoliberal Thought Collective*. Edited by Philip Mirowski and Dieter Plehwe. Cambridge, MA: Harvard University Press, 2009.

Tunick, Mark. "Tolerant Imperialism: John Stuart Mill's Defense of British Rule in India." *The Review of Politics* 68, no. 4 (2006): 586–611.

Vanberg, Viktor J. *The Freiburg School: Walter Eucken and Ordoliberalism*. Freiburg Discussion Papers on Constitutional Economics 04/2011, Walter Eucken Institut e.V.

Varouxakis, Georgios. "Guizot's Historical Works and J. S. Mill's Reception of Tocqueville." *History of Political Thought* 20, no. 2 (Summer 1999): 292–312.

———. " 'Patriotism,' 'Cosmopolitanism' and 'Humanity' in Victorian Political Thought." *European Journal of Political Theory* 5, no. 1 (2006): 100–118.

———. "Cosmopolitan Patriotism in J. S. Mill's Political Thought and Activism." *Revue d'Etudes Benthamiennes* 4 (2008): 24–25.

———. *Mill on Nationality*. London: Routledge, 2013.

Verhoeven, Timothy. Review of Pasquier, Michael. *Transatlantic Anti-Catholicism: France and the United States in the Nineteenth Century*, Church History 80, no. 4 (2011): 948–949.

Verjus, Anne. "Entre principes et pragmatisme. Députés et sénateurs dans les premiers débats sur le suffrage des femmes en France (1919–1922)." *Politix. Revue des sciences sociales du politique* 51 (2000) : 55–80.

Vick, Brian E. *Defining Germany: The 1848 Frankfurt Parliamentarians and National Identity*. Cambridge, MA: Harvard University Press, 2002.

———. "Of Basques, Greeks, and Germans: Liberalism, Nationalism, and the Ancient Republican Tradition in the Thought of Wilhelm Von Humboldt." *Central European History* 40, no. 4 (2007): 653–681.

Vincent, K. Steven. "Character, 'Sensibilité', Sociability and Politics in Benjamin Constant's 'Adolphe.' " *Historical Reflections/Réflexions Historiques* 28, no. 3 (Fall 2002): 361–383.

Voegelin, Eric. "Liberalism and Its History." Translated by Mary Algozin and Keith Algozin. *The Review of Politics* 36, no. 4 (1974): 504–520.

Voice, Paul. "Comprehensive Doctrine." In *The Cambridge Rawls Lexicon*, edited by Jon Mandle and David A. Reidy. Cambridge: Cambridge University Press, 2015.

Volkov, Shulamit. "Antisemitism as a Cultural Code: Reflections on the History and Historiography of Antisemitism in Imperial Germany." *The Leo Baeck Institute Yearbook* 23 (1978): 25–46.

Waldron, Jeremy. "Theoretical Foundations of Liberalism." *Philosophical Quarterly* 37, no. 147 (April 1987): 127–150.

Walker, Gina Luria. "Review of Wendy Gunther-Canada, *Rebel Writer: Mary Wollstonecraft and Enlightenment Politics*." *American Political Science Review*, 96, no. 2 (June 2002): 405–406.

Waxman, Chaim I. *The End of Ideology Debate*. New York: Funk & Wagnalls, 1969.

Weill, Rivka. "Dicey Was Not Diceyan." *Cambridge Law Journal* 62, no. 2 (2003): 474–494.

Weinstein, David. *Utilitarianism and the New Liberalism*. Cambridge: Cambridge University Press, 2007.

Welch, Cheryl. " 'Anti-Benthamism': Utilitarianism and the French Liberal Tradition," in *French Liberalism from Montesquieu to the Present Day*, edited by Raf Geenens and Helena Rosenblatt (Cambridge: Cambridge University Press, 2015), 134–151.

Williams, Bernard. *Truth & Truthfulness: An Essay in Genealogy*. Princeton, NJ: Princeton University Press, 2004.

———. *In the Beginning Was the Deed: Realism and Moralism in Political Argument*, edited by Geoffrey Hawthorn. Princeton, NJ: Princeton University Press, 2005.

Williamson, John. *Latin American Adjustment: How Much Has Happened?* Washington, DC: Institute for International Economics, 1990.

Winch, Donald. *Adam Smith's Politics: An Essay in Historiographic Revision*. Cambridge: Cambridge University Press, 1978.

Winch, Donald. "Commercial Realities, Republican Principles." In *The Values of Republicanism in Early Modern Europe*, edited by Martin van Gelderen and Quentin Skinner, 293–311. Vol. 2 of *Republicanism: A Shared Heritage*. Cambridge: Cambridge University Press, 2002.

———. "Scottish Political Economy." In *The Cambridge History of Eighteenth-Century Political Thought*, edited by Mark Goldie and Robert Wokler, 443–465. Cambridge: Cambridge University Press, 2006.

———. *Wealth and Life: Essays on the Intellectual History of Political Economy in Britain, 1848–1914*. Cambridge: Cambridge University Press, 2009.

Wolffe, John. "North Atlantic Anti-Catholicism in the Nineteenth Century: A Comparative Overview." In *European Anti-Catholicism in a Comparative and Transnational Perspective*, edited by Yvonne Maria Werner and Jonas Harvard. Leiden: Brill, 2013.

Wolin, Sheldon S. *Politics and Vision*. Princeton, NJ: Princeton University Press, 2004.

Wollstonecraft, Mary. *Maria, or the Wrongs of Woman*. Kindle Edition, 1798.

Wrong, Dennis H. "Reflections on the End of Ideology." In Chaim Waxman, ed., *The End of Ideology Debate*. New York: Funk & Wagnalls, 1969.

Yack, Bernard. "The Problem with Kantian Liberalism." In *Kant and Political Philosophy: The Contemporary Legacy*, edited by Ronald Beiner and William James Booth, 224–245. New Haven, CT: Yale University Press, 1993.

———. "The Myth of the Civic Nation." *Critical Review* 10 (1996): 193–211.

———. *Nationalism and the Moral Psychology of Community*. Chicago: University of Chicago Press, 2012.

Young, Michael Dunlop. *The Rise of the Meritocracy, 1870–2033: An Essay on Education and Equality*. London: Thames and Hudson, 1958.

Zimmermann, Moshe. "A Road Not Taken—Friedrich Naumann's Attempt at a Modern German Nationalism." *Journal of Contemporary History* 17, no. 4 (1982): 689–708.

INDEX

abuse of power, 38, 63, 89, 135

Act of Union, 171

Adams, Charles Francis, 189

Adams, John, 70

Addams, Jane: African Americans and, 256–57; altruism and, 258; Bourgeois and, 263–64; Catholicism and, 259; *Democracy and Social Ethics*, 257; diversity and, 252–58, 265; economics and, 255–58; fin de siècle and, 254–60; French Revolution and, 258; Hobhouse and, 270; hope and, 257; Hull House Settlement and, 257, 293; immigrants and, 256–58; impact of, 253–54; imperialism and, 258; individualism and, 258–59; industry and, 253–59; labor and, 255; laissez-faire approach and, 253, 255, 259; Lippmann and, 331; middle classes and, 257; morals and, 253–60; perfectionism and, 259; pluralism and, 254; politics and, 253, 258; poverty and, 254–55, 257, 259; Progressivism and, 31, 252–60; Protestants and, 256, 259; reform and, 253–59; religion and, 259; rights and, 253–56; social ethics and, 252, 254, 257–58; Solidarism and, 259; Spencer and, 255, 258; Stanton and, 220, 254n21, 313; "Survivals of Militarism in City Government", 254; United States and, 253–60; welfare state and, 262–63; "Why the Ward Boss Rules", 257

African Americans, 4; Addams and, 256–57; Berlin and, 356; Biden and, 429; Black Lives Matter and, 422; Catholicism and,

189, 198; civil rights and, 373–74, 381; colonialism and, 297; discourse of capacity and, 154n2; Dred Scott Decision and, 291; feminism and, 312; Jim Crow and, 136, 373; police and, 12; populism and, 422, 429; racism and, 12, 134, 136, 154n2, 256, 282, 291, 312–13, 356, 429; suffrage and, 154n2, 245, 307, 320; Tocqueville and, 134–36; voting and, 154n2

After Utopia: The Decline of Political Faith (Shklar), 407n85

Algeria, 218, 296, 300, 378n9, 425–26

altruism: Addams and, 258; evolution and, 229–35; Hayek and, 346–47; Lippmann and, 331; morals and, 229–35, 251, 258, 331, 346–47

American Civil Rights movement, 20, 379

American Civil War, 24n47, 35, 136, 154n2, 172, 313, 324

American Federation of Labor (AFL), 374

American People's Party, 421

American Revolution: Catholicism and, 188; four fears of liberalism and, 451; Kant and, 78–80; Locke and, 24; Madison and, 88, 92; proto-liberalism and, 69

anarchy: Bastiat and, 217; Constant and, 98; despotism and, 79, 98, 171, 247, 309, 429; Kant and, 79; Lippmann and, 333; Nozick and, 394–98; political upheaval and, 79, 98, 171, 217, 247, 309–10, 333, 394–98, 429

Anarchy, State, and Utopia (Nozick), 395–98

Anglican Church, 52, 122

433–37, 448; Protestants and, 171–72; Prussia and, 173; public opinion and, 168; Reform Act of 1832 and, 114, 157–58, 172–74; reform and, 172–75; religion and, 169, 171–72, 175; Renan and, 167, 177; ressentiment and, 169–70; rights and, 176–80; rise of, 165–81; Russia and, 171, 173, 426n18; slavery and, 172–73; Smith and, 166; suffrage and, 167, 170; Tocqueville and, 165–81; tyranny and, 169, 175; United States and, 171, 176; Whigs and, 172; World War I era and, 165

"Nationalism: Past Neglect and Present Power" (Berlin), 356

National Liberal party, 283–84, 302

National Movement, 172

natural rights, 5

Naumann, Friedrich, 31, 302–7

Navigation Acts, 117

Nazis: Dicey and, 278; end of ideology movement and, 377–78; fin de siècle and, 324; four fears of liberalism and, 11; Hayek and, 342; Hitler and, 326, 329, 337, 375–76; Jews and, 285, 452; ordoliberalism and, 362, 365; populism and, 421; Shklar and, 410; Williams and, 410

neoliberalism, 451; conspiracy theory and, 401–2; egalitarian liberalism and, 11, 19, 400–6; end of ideology movement and, 384; Friedman and, 33, 370, 374, 376, 380, 399–406; Lippmann and, 334; Nozick and, 395, 399; ordoliberalism and, 362; populism and, 416, 436; Rawls and, 385, 393; Shklar and, 406–7; totalitarianism and, 399–400, 403; Williams and, 406–7

Netherlands, 429, 434

New Deal, 326, 349, 365, 373–74

New Era, 161

New Labor Party, 402, 411

New Liberalism, 31, 89, 250n17, 252, 265, 349

New Republic, The (journal), 373–74

Nietzsche, 137, 170

Nixon, Richard, 426

North Shore WASP Progressives, 257

Norway, 181, 187, 193, 424n15

Nozick, Robert, 31; Anarchy, State, and Utopia, 395–98; background of, 395; Britain and, 395; conflict and, 396, 405; democracy and, 395; diversity and, 398; economics and, 396–99; egalitarian liberalism and, 395–99; equality and, 394, 396, 398; fin de siècle and, 394–95; impact of, 395–96; individualism and, 395–96; laissez-faire approach and, 295–96, 398; libertarianism and, 33, 370, 374–76, 380, 393–99; markets and, 395–99; morals and, 376, 394–409; neoliberalism and, 395, 399; ordoliberalism and, 370, 374–75; perfectionism and, 399; politics and, 399; Rawls and, 385–86, 396; Shklar and, 407; slavery and, 397–98; socialism and, 397–98; three pillars of liberalism and, 394; totalitarianism and, 375–76, 394–97; United States and, 395; utilitarianism and, 397n58; utopianism and, 398; Williams and, 407, 411–15

Oakeshott, Michael, 25, 448–49

Occupy Wall Street, 422

On Liberty (Mill), 136, 138–39, 142–45, 314, 345

On the Subjection of Women (Mill), 195, 314–18

Opium of the Intellectuals, The (Aron), 381

oppression, 200; Bastiat and, 215; Berlin and, 353, 357; Dicey and, 276, 279; discourse of capacity and, 165; feminism and, 308–10, 314–15; fin de siècle and, 12, 170, 256, 324; four fears of liberalism and, 12; Kant and, 79; Lippmann and, 331; Locke and, 28; Macaulay and, 115; Madison and, 6, 90–91; Mill and, 127, 143, 145, 147; nationalism and, 170; populism and, 427–28, 446; Smith and, 62

Orban, Viktor, 418

ordoliberalism, 32; aristocracy and, 363; autonomy and, 364; Britain and, 295, 299–306; communism and, 370; Constant and, 367; democracy and, 363; economics and, 361–70; egalitarian liberalism and, 370; end of ideology movement and, 370, 384;

A NOTE ON THE TYPE

This book has been composed in Arno, an Old-style serif typeface in the
classic Venetian tradition, designed by Robert Slimbach at Adobe.